Islanders
and
Water-Dwellers

Proceedings

of

The Celtic-Nordic-Baltic Folklore Symposium

held at

University College Dublin

16-19 June 1996

Editors

Patricia Lysaght   Séamas Ó Catháin   Dáithí Ó hÓgáin

Islanders and Water-Dwellers

Published in Ireland by
DBA Publications Ltd.
56 Carysfort Avenue
Blackrock
Co. Dublin

for the Department of Irish Folklore,
University College Dublin

ISBN 0 9519692 7 7 (hardback)
ISBN 0 9519692 8 5 (softback)

Design and layout by Barry O'Connor
Cover photograph by Ríonach uí Ógáin

Printed by the Leinster Leader

This Publication has received support from the Heritage Council under the
1999 Publications Grant Scheme.

Contents

Contents

iv

Contents

Introduction

A decade ago, the Department of Irish Folklore at University College Dublin and the School of Scottish Studies at the University of Edinburgh jointly organised a weekend symposium of which the topic was *The Supernatural in Irish and Scottish Migratory Legends*. The meeting was held at University College Dublin from 7-8 October 1988 and was adjudged a success by all concerned, including the many members of the general public who were in attendance. The proceedings of this symposium were published in *Béaloideas* 59 (1991) under the title *The Fairy Hill is on Fire!* They proved as popular as the Symposium itself and went speedily out of print.

This attempt to create new interest in the migratory legends – a genre that had been somewhat neglected, especially in the Irish context – was successful in providing the impetus towards the holding of a much larger and more comprehensive gathering, the *Nordic-Celtic Legend Symposium* which was held at University College Galway from 17-22 March 1991. On that occasion, with the help of the Nordic Council, the European Cultural Foundation (Amsterdam), the Finnish Ministry of Education and the British Council, the Department of Irish Folklore and the Department of Modern Irish (Galway) joined with the School of Scottish Studies (Edinburgh) and the Finnish Literature Society (Helsinki) in bringing together legend scholars from many of the countries of north western Europe. Most of the papers delivered on that occasion have also appeared in print, in *Arv, the Nordic Yearbook of Folklore* (1991, 1993), *Béaloideas* 60-1 (1992-3) and *Béaloideas* 62-3 (1994-5).

The *Nordic-Celtic-Baltic Folklore Symposium: Non-Narrative Folk Poetry* (organized by the Department of Folklore at the University of Copenhagen in collaboration with the Nordic Institute of Folklore) which was held in Copenhagen from 20-25 May 1993, saw a further widening of scholarly co-operation in this field to include, for the first time in the context, countries of the Baltic seaboard – Estonia, Latvia and Lithuania. A selection of these papers was subsequently published in *Arv* and elsewhere.

The latest in this series – the *Celtic-Nordic-Baltic Folklore Symposium* was held at University College Dublin from 16-19 May 1996. With the generous assistance of the European Cultural Foundation, the Finnish Ministry of Education and the British Council, the Department of Irish Folklore joined with the School of Scottish Studies, Universitas Færoensis (Tórshavn) and the Swedish Literature Society (Helsinki) in assembling a panel of contributors from the Nordic countries, Estonia and Latvia, England, Scotland and Ireland. Mindful of the waters which physically divide but in so many ways culturally connect our different countries and cultures, the Symposium adopted the theme *Islanders and Water-dwellers*. This was the keynote and guideline for the speakers and other participants in the Symposium. It was intended to encapsulate certain categories of belief about supernatural beings of sea, river and lake and to embrace legends, tales, songs and minor folklore genres with an aquatic setting or which reflected the influence of such ecological surroundings.

The thirty-one papers delivered at the Symposium addressed this theme in diverse ways and were not only the subject of much lively discussion but also a source of enjoyment. Twenty-seven of them have been made available to us and are edited here. The ready response by all concerned, speakers and audience alike, validated the choice of theme, and the various treatments given it convincingly illustrated the degree of popular fascination with water and the creatures which live in it, down the ages. The papers published here show how modern scholars, by collating such beliefs and legends, and by minutely investigating them by both synchronic and diachronic methods, can give insights into the workings of creative culture at its most enduring, and probably also at its most humanising, level.

Water is ideally suited as a substance with which human thought can play. On the one hand it is an undifferentiated and ever-present mass, and on the other hand it varies in its divisions and temperaments; its complexions provide a never- ending series of colour, shade, and imagery. Most of all, water highlights the manner in which environmental peril and environmental necessity are intertwined to constitute a hugely productive dichotomy in the lore concerning seas, lakes and rivers.

Humankind's connection with water is elemental, and it is no surprise that the idea of it as a primordial substance is widespread in human thought. *Amach as an uisce a bheirtear an duine* ('out of the water the person is born') is an old Irish saying, the meaning of which can be extended from the biological sphere into many others, including the evolutionary one itself. This essential and enduring, yet dangerous, substance touches upon human life in so many ways, and its expanses are so impressive and mystifying, that it calls forth all kinds of emotion. It is probably the symbol most suited for the disintegration and reintegration which is experienced as an essential part of life.

Small wonder, then, that culture places strong emphasis on water, and that so basic and general a part of culture as folklore is rich in speculation concerning the aquatic realms. Things necessary, frightening, and awe-inspiring must be explained on some level. Water-bodies and waterways impact so frequently and so generally on human life that these explanations take care to connect with physical reality; yet, especially in a marine context, the 'multitudinous sea' and the 'imponderable deep' allow for plenty of imaginative scope. Water, and particularly the great expanses of it, is a rich and changing canvas on which folklore can extend its brush, a vista which popular ways of thinking can probe in search of analogous readings into its own geographical and social forms. In it are found all kinds of expressions of the paradox – the delight and the dread – that hedges around us all as individuals and as social beings.

But what are the actual motifs which circulate traditionally in popular lore, how developed are they, and what are the circumstances which guarantee their continued currency? Furthermore, how does the aquatic folklore differ between various population groups, and how does it vary from area to area? The papers edited here attempt to answer these questions from the traditional culture of northern and western Europe. A wide range of scholars debates the various issues, each choosing his or her own geographical area, focus of research, and method of interpretation. In this way, the papers not only illustrate the diversity in water-lore, but also the variety in scholarly techniques, in collecting methods, in sources both ancient and modern, and in the individual flair of the authors.

The study of oral legends in the Celtic, Scandinavian, Baltic, and Finno-Ugric, areas is a process which promises to yield valuable results within international folkloristics. Such a study involves detailed research concerning provenance and historical development so that the growth and spread of particular motifs can be ascertained. It also entails interpretation of the legends, informed attempts to decipher their import in the psychology of tellers and hearers, and the ways in which they act as useful metaphors for social phenomena. Finally, and by no means of least importance, the legends function as tableaux which are illuminated by the aesthetic sense of the folk. Sensitive scholarship can help to delineate this by tracing developments in narrative taste and structure.

A knowledge of traditional culture is essential to an understanding of the full record of human experience. Folklore articulates unique insights into the surrounding circumstances as perceived by people, their preferences and hopes, their anxieties and fears, and this is particularly apparent in the case of aquatic legends. Seas, lakes, and rivers can be peopled with beings who alternate between this world and what lies beyond, with objects of allurement and destiny, with potential and danger. The obscurity of a world beyond the mist, of which real and apparent glimpses can sometimes be caught, provides a fertile breeding-ground for the imagination; the fruits of that process subsequently take concrete shape in terms of the known and familiar world around us.

All of these tendencies of the human mind are exemplified in the culture of the sea and of other bodies of water, and, thus, the analysis of aquatic legends and beliefs is of value to folklore studies and to related areas of research. The many examples of such material in these papers testify to the imagination of the communities who developed it, and, in a more indirect way, to the realism and logic of these communities.

We wish to thank the contributors to this volume. We hope that their efforts and ours will have served to demonstrate the importance of northern and western Europe as a *Kulturgebiet* rich in folklore and ancient literary traditions. We are happy to have been able to focus attention on a part of a tradition which is worthy of more intensive study in its totality.

Patricia Lysaght, Séamas Ó Catháin, Dáithí Ó hÓgáin

The Dead from the Sea in Old Icelandic Tradition

BO ALMQVIST

I

The life of an Icelandic sailor in the first half of this century has been summed up by Örn Arnarson in a masterly stanza in the poem 'Stjáni Blái':

Hann var alinn upp við sjó,
ungan dreymdi um skip og sjó,
stundaði alla ævi sjó,
aldurhniginn fórst í sjó.[1]

'He was fostered by the sea,
Dreamed in youth of ships and sea,
All his life he sailed the sea,
Agèd, got his grave in sea.'

The situation in Iceland a thousand years earlier is likely to have been very much the same. To take just a random example, we may recall the life story of Flosi Þórðarson, one of the central characters in *Njáls saga*, the greatest of the classical family sagas. He spent much of his life sailing – to the Orkneys, to the Hebrides, to France and Norway – and the last we hear of him is his setting out on a voyage in spite of his friends' warnings that the ship was not seaworthy. These warnings he brushes away, saying that it was 'good enough for old men, destined to die' (*ærit gott gömlum ok feigum*).[2] The statement turned out to be prophetic. The ship never reached its destination and nothing was ever heard of it again.

II

Stories and beliefs concerning ghosts and revenants can be expected to reflect closely the life conditions, fears and values of the society in which they are current. One might therefore imagine that there would be an abundance of traditions in Iceland – in classical as well as in modern lore – about the return of the sea-dead.

The latter-day traditions of this kind in Iceland have not been closely investigated. My impression, however, is that such beliefs and stories are rather rare in Icelandic folklore collections from the nineteenth and twentieth

---

1 Arnarson (1949), 93.
2 *Njáls saga*, chapter 159, *ÍF* 12, 463

centuries. This is in accordance with the opinion of Ólafur Davíðsson, the only scholar, to my knowledge, to have touched on these matters.[3]

In view of the fact that stories of ghosts and revenants in general are prominent in Old Icelandic literature – in particular in the sagas – the relative scarcity in these sources of such traditions in a maritime setting may also at first glance seem remarkable.[4] Perhaps, however, the explanation is partly to be sought in the fact that the sagas – though they make use of genuine folklore motifs so frequently – are sophisticated literary compositions. Drownings may be convenient vehicles for disposing of redundant characters once and for all, and in such instances the authors would not wish to bring them back as ghosts! Such considerations hardly explain the whole story, however. We will, I think, be better equipped to come to grips with the problem if we enlist help from scholars of the Finnish school of folk belief and folk religion, such as Lauri Honko and Juha Pentikäinen.[5]

One of the central questions we must ask ourselves in connection with ghosts and revenants is: who are these people who cannot find rest, but are forced, or feel an urge to return from the dead and interfere in one way or another with the living?

One quality shared by many of these revenants is that they have not died in a usual or natural way. They are, as the term goes, anomalous dead. This group includes murdered people, suicides, people killed in peculiar and gruesome accidents, or people swept away by unusual and incomprehensible diseases – in other words all those who have not been allowed to live out the span of life normally allotted to man. Another reason why the dead reappear as ghosts is that they have not been granted a proper burial or, in cases where the corpses have not

---

3 'Íslenzkar kynjaverur í sjó og vötnum', originally in *Tímarit hins íslenzka Bókmenntafélags* 1900, 159-88; 1901, 127-76; 1902, 29-47; reprinted in Gils Guðmundsson (1949), 263- 366. For ghost of the drowned (*sjódraugar*) see especially pp. 291-5.

4 To my knowledge no previous attempt has been made to survey the traditions of the sea-dead in Old Icelandic literature. The relevant sources have frequently been touched upon, however, in general surveys of Icelandic ghost lore, e.g. Mogk (1919), 103-7; Neuberg (1926), 23-6; Dehmer (1927), 26-77; Klare (1933-34), 1-56. In her thesis Sluitjer (1936) also comments on some Old Icelandic ghost stories and death beliefs and compares them to later Icelandic legends and beliefs. More specialised is Chadwick (1947), 50-65, 106-27, which deals mainly with the *haugbúi* or *draugr* in a burial mound. The chapter on the dead (pp. 91-122) in Briem (1945) also contains several good observations. A succinct modern survey, containing further references to scholarly treatments on the theme, is Ström (1956-78); see also the entry 'Gengångare', by the same author, and 'Draug', by Solheim, in the same encyclopaedia. Chapters 2-4 (pp. 13-7) of Ottósson (1983), also provide a good summary of the scholarship on Old Icelandic ghost appearances. A recent attempt to classify Old Icelandic ghosts has been made by Pálsson (1992), 1-8.

5 See e.g. Honko, *Geisterglaube in Ingermanland* (1962), especially the introduction, 86-158; Pentikäinen (1968), in particular the introduction, pp. 100-27, and Pentikäinen (1969), 92-102. Cf. also Solveig Almquist (1984), especially pp. 24-63.

been found, any burial at all. Such people, are described as being 'dead without status', dissatisfied with their condition which they sometimes try to rectify by their reappearance.

Deaths by drowning often fall within one or both of the above-mentioned categories. In spite of this, a drowning – and in particular a drowning at sea – might have appeared less anomalous to Icelanders, in saga time as well as in later centuries, than it does to us. Since such deaths were quite common, there might even have been a case for considering them as natural. The idea that death by drowning at sea – as opposed to drowning in fresh water – is not a bad means of departure is also reflected in an Icelandic proverb: *Sætur er sjódauði, vesall vatnsdauði*, that is to say 'Sweet is death at sea, wretched death in fresh water'.[6]

The Icelanders, in common with other people, hold the belief that drowned people whose corpses have not been found are suffering from lack of status and reappear in order to indicate where they can be retrieved.[7] This notion, however, co-exists in Icelandic tradition with another idea – that the sea is consecrated, in other words that to rest there is just as good as to be buried in an ordinary churchyard. A variant form of the Icelandic proverb just quoted, *Sæll er sjódauður*, 'Blessed is he who finds his death at sea', can be interpreted as containing this idea. It is also expressed in several folk legends, in which the drowned person appears in order to assure his relations that he is at rest in the sea, e. g. the dead sailor who, in a story, appears at his fiancée's window, reciting the stanza:

> *Við höfum fengið sæng í sjó*
> *sviftir öllu grandi.*
> *Erum nú á himni í ró,*
> *hæstan guð prísandi.*[8]

> We have found our bed at sea.
> free from all harm.
> Now we are at peace in heaven,
> praising most exalted God.

The concept of the sanctity of the sea could also be supported by references to the Bible, especially *The Book of Revelations* (20:13), where it is stated that the sea will return its dead on Judgement Day.[9]

---

6 For the proverb in this and similar forms see Vilhjálmsson & Halldórsson (1979), 286. The oldest example of the proverb quoted there is from c. 1780, but it is for various reasons, e.g. variations in phrasing, likely to be much older.
7 See e.g. Einar Guðmundsson (1932), 67 and Jóh. Örn Jónsson (1956), 269-70. In both these instances a drowned man appears in a dream, giving detailed instructions as to where to look for his corpse.
8 Kristjánsson (1945), 120.
9 Such beliefs are also met with in parts of Sweden. Cf. Hagberg (1937), 596.

Folklore sources from recent times, consequently, seem to indicate that the idea of the sea being on a par with a Christian burial ground was stronger in Iceland than elsewhere. This belief might well be old; quite possibly it existed already at the time the sagas were written. If so, it would help to explain why stories relating to ghosts of the drowned are relatively scarce in the saga literature.

Christianity was introduced to Iceland in the year 1000 and, though the sagas were written two or three centuries later, they mostly deal with the period 970 - 1030. Therefore the saga-writers frequently aim at depicting customs and beliefs in heathen times. Though such material might sometimes be a product of artistic imagination, it may well in other instances reflect factual circumstances and genuine pre-Christian ideas and attitudes. Viking-age people were, perhaps, not so much concerned with finding and burying the corpses of the sea-dead as with knowing for certain that those lost at sea were actually dead. This would mean that funerals could be celebrated in the appropriate manner with an *erfiöl*, a feast at which ale was copiously drunk in honour of the deceased. After all, what mattered was not the bodily remnants of the departed but the survival of that which never dies, *dómr um dauðan hvern*, – the perpetuation of the good name which the dead had won for himself in life. Such an attitude, however, is likely to have provided a less favourable breeding-ground for the belief in sea-revenants, than the Christian insistence on burial in accordance with the rites of the Church in consecrated ground.

Whatever the reason, it is a fact that stories of sea-dead revenants are rare in the classical Icelandic texts. They suffice, however, to illustrate variations in the belief and to provide a basis for the study of their chronological development.

III

We may begin by taking a look at *Eyrbyggja saga*, one of the classical family sagas, dating perhaps from the middle of the thirteenth century. This saga contains two stories of relevance to us.

The first occurs in the story about the drowning of the chieftain Þorsteinn Þorskabítr, which is set before the introduction of Christianity. This scene is included in chapter 11 of the saga:

> Þorsteinn rowed out to Hoskuldsey to fish. One evening that autumn Þorsteinn's shepherd went over to the north side of Helgafell to attend to the sheep. He saw the mountain open on the north side, and inside it he could see blazing fires and hear mirthful voices and drinking revelry. And when he

listened, trying to make out what was said, he heard that Þorsteins Þorskabítr and his shipmates were greeted, and that Þorsteinn was told to sit in the high-seat opposite his father. That same evening the shepherd told Þóra, Þorsteinn's wife about the strange sight . . .

The next morning men came ashore from Hoskuldsey and brought the news that Þorsteinn Þorskabítr had drowned while he was out fishing . . .[10]

The saga uses the word 'foreboding' (*fyrirburðr*) about the scene witnessed by the shepherd. This word normally entails a supernatural message which is conveyed, or hinted at, concerning something that is about to happen. From the point of view of an experiencer, however, it matters little whether the supranormal phenomenon observed refers to something that has already happened, something that happens at the very same moment, or something that is about to happen, as long as he himself has no previous knowledge of the occurrence to which it refers. Neither does it make any difference to the function of the supranormal occurrence. When, as here, related to death, the function remains the same: to prepare the living for the tragic confirmation of what has happened, which they will soon receive through normal means. That being the case, we understand why ominous ghostly appearances connected with tragic deaths, such as drownings, appear to near relatives of the deceased. This, as we note, is not the case in our episode, but since the shepherd reports his vision to Þorsteinn's wife before she has confirmation of the accident, the function of preparing for the tragic news remains unchanged.

The introduction of an intermediary in this case is not without good cause. It is connected with another unusual deviation in the saga from the traditional pattern of stories of this kind. In folk legends concerned with supernatural death messages, one would expect the foreboding to consist of one of the following: either some kind of sinister symbol; a vision of the accident as it takes place; a sighting of the dead man coming to his home (usually in such a condition or equipped with some attribute which indicates that he is dead and how he died). The passage in *Eyrbyggja saga* chapter 11 does not fit into any of these categories. True enough, the shepherd would draw the conclusion from his vision that Þorsteinn and his men have died, but there is nothing in what he sees that gives away the manner of death.[11] Neither is the shepherd in a mystical way able to see a catastrophe far out of his own sight; on the contrary Helgafell – the mountain that Þorsteinn and his companions enter – is right before his eyes. It is natural for him to be there because that is where he herds his sheep. This, then, is the reason why he – rather than Þorsteinn's wife – experiences the vision.

---

10 This and the following translations from Old Icelandic texts are mine. For the original texts see *ÍF* 4, 19.
11 Neither is there anything to indicate that Þorsteinn knows what the reader has been told, namely that Þorsteinn has rowed out to fish.

The most aberrant trait in the vision from the point of view of latter-day folk tradition, however, is that – in spite of being a foreboding of death – it conveys nothing of the coldness, fear and sadness one normally associates with such matters. Much to the contrary, the atmosphere is one of warmth, well-being, merriment and festivity. This must be seen in relation to information provided earlier in the saga, namely that Helgafell was the ancestral mountain of the Þórsnes family. Þorsteinn's father, the settler Þórólfr Mostrarskegg, we are told, 'believed that he and all his relations on the peninsula would go to live in the mountain after their death'.[12] When Þorsteinn is seen entering the mountain, that means that he has been received by his forefathers, and the statement that he takes the high seat opposite his father is a way of saying that he has been granted the highest honours. Rather than suffering loss of status, therefore, Þorsteinn has in fact gained high status. The welcoming in the mountain is as good as the best funeral feast, and it is perhaps no coincidence that there is no mention in the saga of a funeral feast given by Þorsteinn's widow. Neither is anything said about the burial of Þorsteinn and his crew. It is perhaps understood that the corpses never were found;[13] if so that would indicate that it was not considered important to retrieve them – which it certainly would have been, if the story had been set in Christian times.

Though the apparitions in our story are several, Þorsteinn and his shipmates – as one would expect in a story involving the drowning of a whole crew – the whole point of the story is to prove how honoured and satisfied Þorsteinn is in the afterlife. It is for this sole purpose that he is observed after death on one occasion only. It is totally out of the question that such a man should become a threatening, dangerous revenant appearing to many people on repeated occasions and having to be disposed of by violent means.

IV

The second story in *Eyrbyggja saga* relating to ghosts of drowned men – found in chapters 54 and 55 – forms part of one of the most complex and magnificent ghost stories in the saga literature, the so-called *Fróðárundr* or marvels at Fróðá.[14] This is set in the beginning of the Christian era. The farm Fróðá has been plagued by ghosts of people who have died on land and by other mystical appearances, of which the most recent, a supernatural seal, has foreboded drownings. Þóroddr, the farmer at Fróðá, and his men all drowned shortly before Christmas as they went out in a boat to fetch a supply of dried fish. The saga specifically mentions that their corpses were not found and then goes on:

---

12 *Eyrbyggja saga*, chapter 4, cf. *ÍF* 4, 9. Such a belief in an afterlife in mountains and hills is documented in several other Old Icelandic sources; see e.g. Briem (1945), 110-4 and Hartmann (1937), 201-17.

13 The report on the drowning by the men coming in from Höskuldsey does not clarify this matter.

14 For a full treatment of this remarkable chain of events see Ottósson (1983), 30 and works quoted there.

And when this news had reached Fróðá, Kjartan and Þuríðr invited their neighbours to a funeral feast there. Their Christmas ale was taken and used for the funeral. But the first evening at the funeral feast, when the people had sat down at the table, Þóroddr, the master of the house, and his shipmates walked into the hall, all of them dripping wet. People gave Þóroddr a great welcome, for they thought his arrival to be a good sign. In those days it was held for certain that those who had died at sea had been well received by the sea-goddess Rán if they appeared at their own funeral feast. For then the old beliefs had hardly at all been abandoned, even though all the people had been baptised and were Christians in name. Þóroddr and his men walked along the length of the sitting room and sleeping room, which had two doors, and out into the kitchen. They did not return anybody's greeting, but sat down at the fire. The people of the house fled from the room, but Þóroddr and his men stayed on sitting there until the fires had burned down to white ashes. Then they left. This happened every evening as long as the funeral feast lasted. There was a great deal of talk about this while the feast lasted. Some thought that the visits would come to an end once the funeral feast was over.[15]

So far the story shows a certain amount of similarity to that of Þorsteinn Þorskabítr. In both instances we are dealing with drownings close to land of a chieftain and his crew who have set out to sea for a specific purpose, and in both instances the dead appear in a group at a feast held in their honour (though here in the world of the living). Neither is the arrival of the revenants resented at first; on the contrary they are cordially welcomed and their presence at their own funeral feast is taken by some to indicate that they have reached high status in the otherworld and have been well received by the ruler of the sea, the goddess Rán.[16] In view of that, one would expect that there would be no reason to fear these revenants. It would also be quite natural to believe that they would appear on one occasion only, like that of Þorsteinn Þorskabítr and his men – or at least that they would disappear for good as soon as the funeral feast was over.

It is made quite clear, however, that those who thought in that way were the ones who held with the old heathen beliefs, and that now after the introduction of Christianity it was essential that they be proved wrong. Indeed, it is indicated from the very beginning that something unpleasant is going to happen, and the hints get stronger as the story goes on. Thus it seems unlikely that the statement concerning

---

15 Cf. *ÍF* 4, 148.

16 This particular piece of information is not found elsewhere in Old Icelandic literature and some scholars consider it to be an invention of the saga-writer rather than a piece of genuine tradition – see the discussion in Ottósson (1983), 96-8. In an attempt to reach a solution of this problem one must take into account the fondness for antiquarian details that the writer of *Eyrbyggja saga* shows elsewhere, as well as the degree of likelihood that such a specific detail should be invented. In our particular context it matters little, however, whether the Icelanders entertained the belief exclusively in regard to the sea dead, or whether they believed that the dead in general were present at their funeral feast.

the corpses not being found is intended merely as a piece of matter-of-fact information. Rather does this now, in Christian times, indicate the lack of status which such drowned people suffer through the deprivation of burial rites. The appearance of the revenants is also such as to strengthen our suspicions that all is not going to go well. The revenants are wet and cold – as ghosts of drowned people are often said to be in traditional stories.[17] Neither do their moroseness, sulkiness and taciturnity bode well, since these are traits encountered with some regularity in the descriptions of dangerous revenants in the saga literature.[18] The persistent way in which the revenants turn up every evening while the funeral feast is in progress also prepares the saga audience for the worst – that these ghosts will not go away and that they are of a permanent and malignant kind. Accordingly, on the evening of the day when the guests had left, Þóroddr and his men appeared again. This time, however, they were not alone, they have been joined by other ghosts who have died on land – a certain Þórir viðleggr and his six followers, who have haunted Fróðá before and who are men of the most evil and dangerous kind.

> Þóroddr came in with his crowd, all of them wet. They sat down by the fires and started to wring out their clothes. And as soon as they had sat down, Þórir viðlegrr and his six followers came in, all of them covered with soil. They shook their clothes and scattered the earth on Þóroddr and his men.[19]

The saga literature contains nothing comparable to this scene with its effective contrast between the dead from the land and the dead from the sea. It does not seem out of the question, however, for the scene to have been inspired by a folk legend, *Ghosts from the Land Fight Ghosts from the Sea*, Type 4065 in Reidar Th. Christiansen's *The Migratory Legends*.[20] If this is the case, *Eyrbyggja saga* offers the oldest known indication of the existence of this legend.[21]

The continuation of this ghost story in *Eyrbyggja saga* can be dealt with briefly, since it contains few new traits with any special bearing on the beliefs in ghosts from the sea. Following a new omen, six women pass away and appear after death. Three groups – the dead from the land, the dead from the sea and the dead women – now annoy the survivors to such an extent that many leave the farm because of the ghosts and apparitions (*fyrir reimleikum ok aptrgöngum*). It is now obvious that something drastic needs to be done. The composite methods include a formal court proceeding in which the ghosts are accused of unlawful intrusion and

---

17 But often as a proof that they have died through drowning, which is unnecessary in our cases, since the deaths have already been reported.
18 Cf. below, section VI.
19 Cf. *ÍF* 4, 149.
20 Christiansen (1958).
21 In its fuller form, in which the dead from the land take the part of a human who is pursued by the dead from the sea, this legend is, according to Christiansen, principally known in Northern Norway; there are variants, however, e.g. from Trøndelag, which refer to constant animosity between ghosts from the land and ghosts from the sea without the involvement of a pursued human.

of causing bodily harm and death to the humans.[22] They are found guilty and sentenced to banishment. They accept the sentence without protest and disappear for ever, once the leader of each of the three groups has uttered a short pithy alliterated phrase. In the case of Þóroddr – who was the last to leave – the phrase is *Fátt hygg ek hér friða, enda flyum nú allir.*[23] 'There is little peace here so let us all depart.' Finally a priest is brought in, holy water sprinkled around the place, relics carried around and a *messa solemnis* sung.[24]

Two typical traits relating to revenants, of the kind we are dealing with here, are illustrated in this final scene. When speaking at all, they talk in a way different from the living, tersely and to the point, in formulas or even in verse, and they are impossible to get rid of, unless some kind of violent measures, or magical or religious ceremonies are resorted to. It is also evident that our story is a complex literary composition by a highly skilled author, though many of the ingredients are derived from beliefs and legends current in folk tradition. As is often the case in such circumstances, however, this also leads to certain duplications, which are unnecessary from the point of view of folk tradition, e.g. getting rid of the ghosts *both* through religious means *and* through legal proceedings. It can also cause complicated and contradictory actions and feelings to be attributed to the characters involved – revenants visiting their funeral feast *should* be happy and benevolent, but are not. As suggested above, such deviations from the 'norm' may be due to the author's wish to contrast heathen and Christian attitudes towards death and the dead.

V

Strangely composite in form also is the story of appearances in connection with a drowning in *Laxdœla saga*, another of the classical thirteenth-century family sagas. The scene, which occurs in chapter 76, deals with the drowning of Þorkell Eyjólfsson, the fourth and last husband of Guðrun Ósvífsdóttir. It is to her that the apparitions appear, close to the church at their farm Helgafell, at the foot of the mountain into which Þorsteinn Þorskabítr entered according to *Eyrbyggja saga*. The action is set about twenty-five years after the introduction of Christianity to Iceland.

---

22 This scene is unparalleled in Old Icelandic literature, but as Klare (1933-34), 53, so neatly puts it: *So eigenartig auch das Türgericht ist, so fügt es sich doch in das Gesamtbild des heidnischen Totenglaubens gut ein durch die Gleichstellung des Toten mit dem Lebenden.* Because of this I see no major objection to accepting the court proceeding against the dead as an old and genuine trait in the tradition about the wonders at Fróðá. Cf. Ottóson (1983), 110, and see furthermore Jacoby (1913), 184-7; Schreuer (1915), 333-423 & (1916),1-208; Wallén (1958) 445-8.

23 *ÍF* 4, 152.

24 For examples of such means of exorcism elsewhere in Old Icelandic literature see Klare (1933-34), 52-3 and Ottósson (1983), 36-7.

There is a resemblance between the description of Þóroddr's drowning in that saga and the scene in *Laxdœla saga* in that both accidents were foreboded. In *Laxdœla saga*, however, the accident is foreboded no less than five times[25] – which is extraordinary even in the Icelandic sagas, notwithstanding their predeliction for this literary device. As in *Eyrbyggja saga*, the drowning also occurs close to land and involves a whole crew. Þorkell has gone out in Breiðafjörðr on a ferry together with ten (or, according to another manuscript, twelve) men, in order to bring home timber for a church but, just as they are about to reach an island called Bjarney, a strong wind blows up and the ferry is overturned and the whole crew drowned. The accident is witnessed both from the island and the mainland. Concern is expressed in the saga that only a small part of the church timber was saved, but no mention is made of the corpses being found or of any attempt to find them.

On the evening of the day of the drowning, *Guðrún*, has the following experience:

> Guðrún went to the church at Helgafell, when all the others at the farm had gone to bed. And as she came up to the churchyard gate she saw a ghost standing in front of her. The ghost leaned down over her and said, 'Grave news, Guðrún!'
> Guðrún answered: 'Keep your mouth shut, then, you wretch!'

> Guðrún went on towards the church, as she had intended, and when she came up to the church she thought she saw that Þorkell and his men had returned home and were standing in front of the church. She saw sea-water running from their clothes. Guðrún did not speak to them, but went into the church and stayed there as long as she thought it right and proper. Then she returned to the house, for she thought that Þorkell and his men would have gone there. But when she came in there was nobody there. And now Guðrún was greatly disturbed by everything that had happened.[26]

Then, on Good Friday, she sends out a search party and on Easter Saturday she learns about the drowning. 'Guðrún was much affected by Þorkell's death, but bore it with great bravery' – the saga concludes.

Looking more closely at this passage we observe that we are not dealing with one supernatural experience but two. First Guðrún meets with a being, referred to

---

25 First in chapter 33, where Guðrún's dream of a helmet falling into the water in Hvammsfjörðr is interpreted to mean that her fourth husband is going to drown there; then in chapter 73, first in another dream Þorkell himself has about his beard stretching out over the whole of Breiðafjörðr and again in a prophecy uttered by King Ólafr the Holy; furthermore, in chapter 75, in a curse uttered by one of Þorkell's enemies; and, finally, in chapter 76, through a sudden inexplicable loud gust of wind going through the house of his friend Þorsteinn Kuggason. This last phenomenon, however, is perhaps best interpreted as having taken place at the very moment of the drowning.

26 Cf. *ÍF* 5, 222-3.

in the saga as *draugr*. His behaviour is threatening, and he apparently tries to prevent her from entering the church ground. Since he also addresses her in the terse and laconic manner typical of ghosts, Guðrún is not left in any doubt as to what he is. She answers with an abusive term, calling him 'wretch' (*armi*) and telling him to keep his mouth shut – which should no doubt be seen against the background of the widespread believe that ghosts are repelled by abusive language.[27]

In the next vision, which Guðrún sees when she has arrived in the church ground and come up to the church, the situation is very different. She sees men standing outside the church, and she immediately recognises them as her husband and his crew, but she does not at first realise that they are dead. This she does not begin to suspect until she notices the water dripping from their clothes. Later on when it transpires that nobody has actually arrived, these suspicions come close to certainty, until they are finally confirmed by those who have observed the drowning.

In summary, then, the first unrecognized *draugr* belongs more or less to the same type as the *sjødraug* in Norwegian tradition (which will be discussed in greater detail below in section VIII). The appearance of such a *draugr* testifies to a drowning that is about to occur, or has just occurred, and which as a rule concerns the experiencers or those close to them; but apparently the same *draugr* is imagined to continue its existence and appear to others on other occasions. Such a *draugr* is totally repugnant and frightening, but it is exceptional to find more than one of the species cropping up at the same time. In visions of the second type, the person – or persons, since the number is dependent on the number of those drowned – can be recognised and, as a rule, is a close relation of the experiencer. Furthermore, some specific detail (as here, in the case of a drowning, the dripping water) reveals that he is not alive. The main function is, therefore, to confirm that the catastrophe has taken place and to prepare the living for the confirmation which they are about to receive. Consequently, in folk tradition such scenes would not be repeated.[28] Though such a once-off vision may of course also be frightening, it is not on a par with meeting a *draugr* of the evil kind who, so to say, rejoices in delivering the death message. This, I think, is indicated by the fact that the *draugr* is observed standing in the gateway leading into the churchyard,[29] apparently unable to follow Guðrún onto

---

27 As Einar Ólafur Sveinsson, the editor of *Laxdæla saga*, in the series *Íslenzk fornrit*, notes, the reason why Guðrún wants to prevent the ghost from speaking is likely to be that she fears that the verbalisation of a tragic message will render it true.

28 When this happens in the story in *Eyrbyggja saga* chapter 11 (see above, section IV) I take this to be another example of literary 'manipulation'.

29 One will of course also in this connection have to take into account the liminal significance of gates and doors. For examples of Old Icelandic ghosts blocking doors, preventing people from seeking shelter in houses, see *Eyrbyggja saga*, chapter 52 (*ÍF* 4, 146), *Eiríks saga rauða*, chapter 6 (*ÍF* 4, 215, 418) and *Flóamanna saga*, chapter 13 (*ÍF* 13, 255). For a Manx ghost legend containing the gate motif see Gill (1929), 468.

consecrated ground,[30] while the latter apparitions – being less demonical – are actually seen in front of the church. Be that as it may, it is clear that the saga-writer found his material in folk belief and legend, but the combination of the two concepts – which as far as I can see has no parallel in oral tradition – is likely to be his own.

VI

Færeyinga saga – which, though it deals with Faroese matters was written by an Icelander, probably around 1200 – contains two stories relevant to the belief in the sea-dead. Both of them are set in the first decades after the introduction of Christianity, which on the Faroe Islands took place at the same time as in Iceland. Both of them also, in different ways, are connected with people who have been hostile to the new belief and who led a far from Christian life – the crafty Þrándr, who had a reputation for being skilled in magic, and his brutal, violent, almostpsychopathic nephews.

The former of the two stories is told in chapter 40 of the saga, the latter in chapter 49. For certain reasons it is convenient to investigate the latter episode first.

The situation here is that Þrándr's three nephews, after having been outlawed from the Faroes because of an assassination in which they were involved, set out to sea, and headed for Iceland, it was rumoured. Great storms arose, however, and wreckage from their ship floated ashore at Eysturoy, where Þrándr's farm was. From this it was concluded that the nephews had drowned. Then, the saga goes on to say:

> When winter came powerful ghosts appeared at Gata and many other places in Eysturoy. They were often seen in the shape of Þrándr's nephews. People suffered much evil from this. Some got their legs broken or were maimed in other ways. They assaulted Þrándr so badly that he did not dare to go anywhere unaccompanied during the whole winter.[31]

In this instance we are not so much dealing with ghosts returning from the dead because of lack of 'status' as with people who are predisposed to appear as revenants because of their evil disposition and their ungodly deeds.

---

30 According to folk tradition meeting with a malignant *draugr* could often have dire consequences for the experiencer, such as temporary insanity, various diseases or deformations. That Guðrún got off so well might be due to her intention to go to church in order to pray and her quick escape into consecrated ground. It is hardly accidental that we are told that Guðrún became most devout (*gerðisk trúkona mikil*) a few lines after the description of the ghost experience. Those who are so inclined may also wish to see something symbolical in the specification that Guðrún sent out men to search for her drowned husband on a Good Friday.

31 Cf. Halldórsson (1987), 126.

The ghosts of Þrándr's nephews are, in other words, of the same character as some of the most powerful ghosts in the saga literature, such as Þórólfr bægifótr in *Eyrbyggja saga* or Glámr in *Grettis saga*. Such ghosts, or living corpses, as they are sometimes termed, appear very much as they were in life, except that they may be even stronger and more malicious than in life.[32] Breaking people's legs or mutilating them in other ways was quite in line with the general behaviour of such ghosts. Because the stress in such narratives is put on the actions of the ghosts, it does not really matter whether they have died on land, as Þórólfr bægifótr and Glámr, or by drowning, as the case is here in *Færeyinga saga*. It is sufficient for us to be told that they have left this life in one manner or another, which may furthermore be stated to have been violent or eerie. There is no need, however, to equip the revenants with any attributes or give other details to indicate the exact manner in which they died.

So far, then, there is nothing unusual or untraditional in this scene in *Færeyinga saga*. But we are in for a big surprise – the 'ghosts' are not real at all. The shipwreck has been staged, the nephews are alive and hiding at their uncle's farm the whole winter, only making occasional nightly appearances pretending to be ghosts, in the course of the acting even playing pranks (or pretending to play pranks?) on their uncle to render the act entirely credible. Finally they appear fully armed in bright sunlight at a gathering of the Law Thing. Thus they reveal themselves to be alive and force their own and their uncle's enemies to yield to their conditions and allow them to dwell freely on the Faroes, giving them the opportunity to commit further outrages. Even though these are fake ghosts, the scene nevertheless indicates how ghosts of this kind were believed to act. Neither is it necessary to suppose that the saga-writer is inclined not to believe in ghosts in other instances though this particular one was a fraud.[33] Many Icelanders – in later centuries also – had a firm belief in ghosts, though they knew, of course, that pranks and even criminal acts were sometimes carried out under cover of staged ghost appearances.

VII

In the other scene in *Færeyinga saga* (which occurs in chapter 40), dealing with the appearance of dead drowned men, we are – unlike the example in chapter 49 but like some of the other texts we have examined – concerned with ghosts that appear on one single occasion. These do not, however, announce that deaths have taken place. This is taken for granted both by the readers and by the saga characters, since the three men involved – Sigmundr Brestisson, his cousin Þórir Beinisson and their companion Einarr – were seen swimming away from Skuvoy years before the apparition in an attempt to escape their enemies and they had not been seen since.

---

32 See Ottósson (1983), 31-2.
33 Thus he expresses no doubt of the reality of the dream appearance in which the dead Sigmundr Brestisson shows himself to his wife to advise her, 'with God's special permission', as he puts it in chapter 54 of the saga.

Neither do the apparitions appear of their own volition. They are forced to materialise through a necromantic act undertaken by Þrándr, in order to ascertain who in fact is responsible for the deaths in question, so that the guilty party can be punished. This act Þrándr is especially willing to undertake in order to put an end to a persistent rumour that he himself killed Sigmundr Brestisson while swimming or when he had been lying helpless on the shore. The description of the magic act performed by Þrándr contains many obscure details and is largely without parallel.[34] Though it is of great interest from a general folkloristic point of view, it need not detain us in this connection,[35] since it only marginally concerns the apparitions. Suffice it to say that the act took place at the home of Þórgrímr illi on Suðroy, in a hall in which Þrándr had ordered a great fire to be built. It is here that the ghosts of Einarr, Þórir and Sigmundr appear in the following manner:

> After a short time a man came walking into the hall. He was wet to the very bones. He was recognised as Einarr the Hebridean. He went up to the fire, stretched out his hands to it, stayed for a short while and then went away. And after a little while another man came into the hall. He went up to the fire, stretched out his hands, and then went out. He was recognised as Þórir. Shortly after that a third man went into the hall. He was tall, covered in blood and carried his head in his hand. They all knew that he was Sigmundr Brestisson. He remained standing there on the floor for a while and then went out.

Þrándr then goes on to interpret the scene that has been witnessed by all:

> 'Now you may see, how those men met their death. Einarr died first, he froze to death or was drowned, for he was the weakest. Then Þorir must have died next. Sigmundr must had tried to drag him along and that must have exhausted him more than anything else. But Sigmundr must have got ashore, worn out, and these men [Þorgrímr illi and his sons] must have killed him, for we saw him bloody all over and without his head.'[36]

A search is carried out of the house of Þorgrímr and a golden arm-ring belonging to Sigmundr is found in a chest. Þorgrímr's guilt is thus taken to have been proved and he is forced to confess and show the place where the bodies of Sigmundr and Þórir had been buried. A while after, Þorgrimr and his sons are sentenced at the Thing Assembly in Tórshavn and executed.

---

34 It shows certain marked affinities, however, to a description of a magic act in which the devil is called up in a story about a certain Count Romaldus (Unger [1868], 147-8).

35 The scene has been treated in depth by Foote (1964), 84-98. It should now be consulted in Foote (1984), 209-21, since a postscript has been appended to this reprint. Apart from its importance in connection with the *Færeyinga saga*, this study contains a richness of ideas and numerous references to other works relevant to the study of Icelandic ghost belief.

36 Halldórsson (1987), 88.

It is interesting to note the minute and subtle correspondences between the way in which the apparitions appear during the séance and the information we receive afterwards of the manners of their deaths. Not only do we learn the order in which the three men died and that Einarr and Þórir drowned while Sigmundr was murdered and decapitated,[37] we also understand that Þórir's corpse must have floated ashore, since it was hidden and buried in the same place as Sigmundr's. Sigmundr's ghost is thus not that of a drowned man, and when he comes into the hall, he does not have so much need of heat as the other two, who both stretch out their hands in front of the fire. There is also a distinction between Einarr and Þórir. The former was not only cold, he was also – as the saga rather quaintly puts it – *allur alvotur*, 'very wet all over', indicating the extreme degree of wetness that is characteristic of him, whose corpse presumably is still floating around in the sea, as opposed to that of Þórir who, though drowned, has been buried on land. The idea that ghosts of drowned people seek to be close to the fire we have already met in the description of Þóroddr and his companions in *Eyrbyggja saga* chapters 54 to 55.[38] Obviously the manifestations of Einarr, Þórir and Sigmundr would not need to appear more than once, nor would they, considering the saga-writer's attitude to them when they were alive, be of a malignant nature. But they were not mere spectres or wraiths either. They must have been imagined as having corporeal substance, again like the ghosts of Þóroddr and his men in *Eyrbyggja saga* who went around sprinkling water on the living.[39]

We know Þrándr's slyness and preferences for acting, which is referred to in several places in the saga, and it was apparently on his instigation that his nephews went around acting as ghosts. It could, therefore, be argued that the whole séance scene here in *Færeyinga saga* chapter 41 is also a staged fraud and that the apparitions representing Einarr, Þórir and Sigmundr are nothing but human actors, perhaps Þrándr's three nephews. I have elsewhere discussed this possibility in somewhat greater detail.[40] If this is the way the scene ought to be understood, however, it provides further confirmation of how slight the difference between a ghost and a living person was imagined to be both in saga time and in the time of the saga-writer.

---

37 It has been pointed out that ghosts of drowned people also sometimes are imagined to be without heads, a trait that has been associated with the fact that corpses found in water are often found in that state (because the neck has rotted away or the head has been severed by sharks). This, however, has nothing to do with Sigmund's headlessness (cf. Foote [1984], 210, note 3). For other examples of headless ghosts in Old Icelandic literature see Klare (1993-94), 50.

38 The purpose of the great fire Þrándr had ordered to be made has been much discussed, some scholar going for an apotropaic, others for a helastic interpretation. In agreement with Foote (1984), 211 who also adduces the passage in *Eyrbyggja saga* chapters 54-55, I feel it reasonable to assume that the function is here helastic.

39 Here again I find myself in full agreement with Foote (1984), 211)

40 In the introduction to Almqvist (1992a), 51-3.

VIII

Whatever about the scene in *Færeyinga saga*, chapter 41, it is quite clear that the ghost appearance involved in the next and last text I will touch upon – the *þáttr* or short story about the poet and trickster Sneglu-Halli – is a faked one.[41] This is now preserved in two collections of so-called kings' sagas, *Morkinskinna and Flateyjarbók*, but, in all likelihood, it originally existed as an independent story, probably no later than in the first half of the thirteenth century. The action is set in the middle of the eleventh century. This is the gist of the episode that concerns us here: Sneglu-Halli is in England and is anxious to get away from there to Norway, since he has played a trick on the English king and fears his vengeance. It is not easy to get away, however - all the ships destined for Norway for that year have already left except for one, and the skipper on that ship refuses to take Halli on board on the grounds that the ship is already overloaded. But Halli is up to his reputation as a full-fledged trickster. He tells some of those who were to go on board that he himself no longer wishes to go, since he has dreamt that a terrifying man came up to him and recited a poem, indicating that the ship would be wrecked and everybody on it drowned. Those to whom he related the dream are then more than willing to stay in England, so Halli can take their place and escape to Norway.

We will focus our attention on the supernatural being, apparently the ghost of a drowned man, who is said to have delivered the message in Halli's pretended dream. This is in autobiographical fashion enshrined in the verse he recites. It is not easy to give even an approximate translation of verses of this kind. In this particular case we are dealing not only with the intricate construction of the *dróttkvætt* – as the metre is called – but also with a deliberate attempt to create an impression of a mystic and frightening message from the otherworld. The text also varies somewhat in the two manuscripts.[42] I will here follow the *Morkinskinna* text:

> *Hrang es, þars hávan þöngul*
> *heldk of, síz fjör seldak.*
> *sýnt es, at ek sitk at Ránar,*
> *sumir ró í búð með humrum.*
> *Ljóst es lýsu at gista,*
> *lönd ák út fyr ströndu,*
> *því sitk bleikr í brúki,*
> *blakir mér þari um hnakka,*
> *blakir mér þari um hnakka.*[43]

---

41 *Sneglu-Halla þáttr* is found in ÍF 9, 261-95.
42 In an earlier paper in Swedish on the ghost scene in *Sneglu-Halla þáttr*, (Almqvist [1992b], 17-20), I have tried to show how the folklore evidence makes certain readings in *Morkinskinna* preferable to those in *Flateyjarbók*.
43 ÍF 9, 292.

In a more or less literal prose translation this would be: 'Loud splashing is heard where I hold on to a long stalk of seaweed ever since I lost my life. I can be seen sitting here with Rán. There are those who have to live with the lobsters. It is light here in the homestead of the whiting. My living quarters are here along the shore. That is why I sit here pallid in a heap of seaweed on the shore. Seaweed is blowing back and forth along the nape of my neck. Seaweed is blowing back and forth along the nape of my neck.'

As we have seen, the story of Sneglu-Halli deals with a pretended rather than a real experience. Unlike the other manifestations of the sea-dead we have discussed, the encounter takes place in a dream, not while the experiencer is awake. Dream experiences of various kinds are very prominent in Icelandic tradition, old and new. Typically Icelandic also is the way in which the supernatural being speaks in verse. The ghostly echo-effect created by the repetition of the last line, as in our verse *Blakir mér þari um hnakka / blakir mér þari um hnakka* is typical of such verses; and it even has a technical name: *galdralag*.[44]

Apart from this, however, the passage in *Sneglu-Halla þáttr* contains traits, which are almost without parallel in other Icelandic sources,[45] but connect the supernatural being with Norwegian traditions about the *sjødraug* or, simply, *draug*.

This is perhaps the most prominent supernatural type of manifestation of people who have drowned at sea in latter-day Norwegian and west-Swedish coastal traditions. The salient traits in the *sjødraug* complex were outlined by the Norwegian scholar Svale Solheim – whose work is very important in the Nordic-Celtic context but far too little known outside his own country.[46] From Solheim's treatments it appears that the following five traits are particularly prominent in the *sjødraug* traditions and distinguish them from other supernatural manifestations of people drowned at sea:

1. Unlike the revenants of drowned people whom we encounter for instance in *Eyrbyggja saga* or *Færeyinga saga*, the *sjødraug* is not to be identified as a ghost of a particular person known to those who encounter him.

2. The abode and sphere of power of a *sjødraug* is almost exclusively limited to the sea and the shore. A *sjødraug* seems to lose his power if he comes up on dry land, or even to be be unable to set foot there. This again is in stark contrast to the revenants we have encountered in *Eyrbyggja saga*, who without the slightest hesitation enter houses and warm themselves by the fire.

---

44 Cf. Klare (1933-34), 33-5.
45 Cf. however the ghost Guðrún meets in the gate to the churchyard, above section, a passage that had not come to my notice when I wrote my earlier paper on the ghost scene in *Sneglu-Halla þáttr*.
46 Solheim (1941) and (1972), 44-57.

3. The bearers of the *sjødraug* traditions are almost exclusively fishermen and sailors. These traditions are intensely focused on the drowned fisherman or sailor who is floating around somewhere between the skerries.

4. Many of the manifestations of the *sjødraug* are also ominous. They forebode a drowning, which may involve the person who encounters the *sjødraug* or some person or persons close to him. This is again in contrast to sightings of sea-dead revenants, which as a rule announce that a drowning has already taken place.

5. Finally, the description of *sjødraugar* is scanty and sketchy. They are represented in an almost emblematic manner. They may, for instance, be said to carry a stalk of seaweed in their hand, or they are depicted as overgrown by sea-weed or covered in slime.

The description and behaviour of the mysterious being in Sneglu-Halli's verse thus correspond in the minutest details to Solheim's five points: the revenant appearing to Sneglu-Halli is anonymous, not identifiable with any particular person; he is clearly stated to have his abode along the shore, the setting of the tradition is clearly maritime: harbour, ship and crew are key words in the story; the manifestation of the supernatural serves the purpose of foreboding a shipwreck, in other words it is ominous; and, finally, the being is in an emblematical way depicted as holding a stalk of seaweed in his hand and having seaweed at the nape of his neck. Even the very phrasing here – *blakir mér þari um hnakka* – brings to mind the Norwegian expression *få eit tareblad under hovudet*, literally 'to get a leaf of seaweed under one's head', but used metaphorically in the meaning 'to die by drowning'.[47]

IX

In the restricted space available, it has only been possible to give a hasty sketch of the Old Icelandic texts referring to the ghosts of those drowned at sea. It is clear, however, that these beliefs vary greatly and that in more than one way they provide us with a historical perspective of importance for the understanding of later traditions in Iceland and elsewhere. Perhaps some indication has also been given of the extent to which folklore and philology can serve each other and of the importance of folklore for the analysis of old literary texts. These are approaches and methods which I would very much wish to see employed in future Celtic-Nordic-Baltic co-operation in the field of folk literature and folk beliefs.

---

47 Interestingly a similar phrase (*muntu spenna um þöngulshöfuð*) is used in *Laxdæla saga*, chapter 75 (cf. above, note 25). This curse directed towards Þorkell may not only indicate a wish that he should drown, but also that his corpse should not be found.

Economic Necessity and Escapist Fantasy in Éamon A Búrc's Sea-Stories

Angela Bourke

I

This paper is offered as a tribute to the memory of the Galway folklore collector Liam Mac Coisdeala, who died on 10 April, 1996. Without his work, little or no record of the storytelling genius whose artistry I discuss below would be accessible to us today. Liam Mac Coisdeala first met the storyteller Éamon Liam a Búrc in 1928, and worked with him at intervals until Éamon Liam's death in November, 1942. Over a period of eight years he transcribed stories longhand into notebooks, direct from Éamon Liam's narration; but from 1936, when he was appointed a full-time collector with the Irish Folklore Commission, he had the use of an Ediphone recording machine.[1]

II

In 1966, Seán O'Sullivan described Éamon a Búrc (1866-1942), as 'possibly the most accomplished narrator of folktales who has lived into our own time'.[2] Known locally as Éamon Liam, Éamon a Búrc was also acknowledged by his neighbours and contemporaries as the best storyteller in an area luxuriously rich in oral traditions. This reputation has been borne out and amplified in the two generations since his death as his stories have reached wider audiences at home and abroad, mostly through translations and editions by Seán O'Sullivan, Caoimhín Ó Nualláin and Peadar Ó Ceannabháin.[3] The two legends discussed here are a response to the issues of his own time, not a fossilised relic of an older way of life. They contemplate, among other issues, the restrictions placed on young people by a system of patrilocal marriage which had become increasingly rigid in the west of Ireland by the end of the nineteenth century.[4]

Éamon Liam was born in An Aird Mhóir, Carna, county Galway, in April 1866, and died just a few miles away from there, in Aill na Brón, Cill Chiaráin, in 1942. Most of his life was spent in Conamara, but when he was fourteen he and his family were among a group of three hundred and ninety Irish-speakers from Counties Galway and Mayo who migrated across the Atlantic to the tiny settlement

---

1 Mac Coisdeala (1942 & 1946).
2 O'Sullivan (1966), 262.
3 O'Sullivan, *op.cit.* Nos 13, 26, 29, 32, 34 & 35; (1977), Nos 35, 46, 64 & 71B; Ó Nualláin /O'Nolan (1982) – (includes a six-page essay on the storyteller by Liam Mac Coisdeala, 'Fear Inste an Scéil,' with editor's translation); Ó Ceannabháin (1983).
4 Breen (1984), 280-96.

of Graceville, Minnesota, at the invitation of the entrepreneur Archbishop John
Ireland. The project was a disaster, as documented on film by Bob Quinn and
Seosamh Ó Cuaig in 1996: the skills of fishing, seaweed-gathering, potato-growing
and turf-cutting, finely developed in the subsistence economy of Ireland's Atlantic
coast, were totally unsuited to farming on the American prairie, and nothing could
have prepared the people for the winter weather they encountered there in 1880.
Many of the migrants eventually settled in St Paul, Minnesota, but Éamon Liam's
family returned to Ireland after only three years: jumping on and off railway trains,
the seventeen-year old had lost a leg.[5]

Back in Ireland, Éamon trained as a tailor, a traditional occupation for lame
men, and kept a small shop selling basic groceries for many years; but he also became
a highly-skilled sailor and fisherman, in spite of his disability. A complex character
by all accounts, he married a second time after being widowed, but had no children.
When Liam Mac Coisdeala met him in 1928, he was sixty - two, and living in Aill
na Brón. Mac Coisdeala was twenty-one. From then until the storyteller's death in
1942, Mac Coisdeala visited him regularly, first as a free-lance collector of folklore,
later on behalf of the Irish Folklore Commission, taking down with pen and paper
or on Ediphone cylinders a total of some two hundred stories.[6]

Éamon a Búrc's reputation as a storyteller rests largely on his ability to tell the
long episodic hero-tales, or *scéalta gaisce*, with their 'runs', or rhetorical flourishes,[7]
but he was also a superb narrator of fairy-belief legends. Legends of the supernatural
typically appeal to the interest and credulity of listeners by their initial realism,
describing details of their protagonists' lives and environment before telling of
disruptions to those lives. This technique, invaluable to the performer in getting and
holding the attention of an audience, also allows the stories to encode a great deal of
incidental information in easily-retrievable form without the aid of writing, as facts
and ideas are tucked into the seams and pockets of narratives attractive enough to be
remembered.[8] Éamon Liam's accounts of meetings between human protagonists and
their fairy neighbours are set in the land- and seascape where he and his listeners
lived: the rocky, indented coast of Conamara, with its islands, bogs, lakes and hills.
His expertise as a narrator is rivalled only by his intimate knowledge of the real world
he describes; the legends he tells are filled with details of local history, topography,
and the tools and techniques of various types of work.

---

5 Ó Ceannabháin (1983), 11, follows Mac Coisdeala *op.cit.* (1942, 211), in giving Éamon's age at
   the time of migration as four or five; however Seosamh Ó Cuaig has established that the migration
   took place in 1880 and that Éamon Liam was one of those who sailed on the S.S. Austrian. I am
   grateful to Seosamh Ó Cuaig for generously sharing with me the results of his research for the film
   Graceville (Telegael, 1996), and to Peadar Ó Ceannabháin for valuable discussions. See also Moran
   (1996).
6 For a full list of this material see Ó Ceannabháin, *op. cit.*, 7-8, 317-21.
7 For 'runs' see Bruford (1969), Chapter 16.
8 For oral narrative as a repository of knowledge, and the use of colourful or 'heavy' characters in
   ordering thought in memorable form, see Ong (1982), 31-77, Chapter 3, 'Some Psychodynamics
   of Orality.'

Considerably longer than average, his legends of the supernatural often begin as though they were folktales, with the formulaic *Bhí anseo fadó agus fadó a bhí, dá mbeinnse an uair sin ann ní bheinn anois ann, dá mbeinn anois agus an uair sin ann bheadh scéal úr nó seanscéal agam, nó bheinn gan scéal ar bith,* ('Long ago, and long ago it was: if I'd been there then, I wouldn't be here now; if I were here now as well as then, I might have a new story, or an old story, or no story at all')[9]. The leisurely, authoritative opening hints at what is to come: not an offhand or perfunctory account of an odd encounter or inexplicable event, but a thoughtful weighing of human reactions to crisis, a meditation on obligations and desires which may sometimes be in conflict with each other. In these sophisticated fictions, which like all oral storytelling performances are transactions with the listeners, a master storyteller blends the narrative ingredients of traditional legend with description of his local environment, both physical and social, to express thoughts about human relations and the life of the individual.[10]

Two of Éamon a Búrc's legends tell of human fishermen, tempted by the love of women from beneath the sea, who weigh what is being offered against the responsibilities that bind them to their homes. He told the two-part legend called *An Dochtúir Ó Laoi agus Beag-Árainn*, published in translation by Seán O'Sullivan as 'Doctor Lee and Little Aran', for Liam Mac Coisdeala in January 1938.[11] During a later visit to Cill Chiaráin by Mac Coisdeala in September and October of the same year, he recorded *An tIascaire agus an Bád Sí*, given in translation below as 'The Fisherman and the Fairy Boat'.[12] Performed before audiences largely comprised of young men,[13] both stories twist together information about proper fishing practice with reflections on marriage and family, offering at the same time a richly-elaborated fantasy about escape from responsibility. Both dramatically illustrate the social paradigm which presents marriage as an aspect of responsibility to the stem family. Sex is forbidden outside marriage, but young men may marry only when by doing so they can enhance, rather than undermine, the status and security of their parents and dependent sisters; young women may marry only if financially provided for. These are very much the same terms as were sketched for county Clare in 1936 by the Harvard anthropologist Conrad Arensberg, who described the arranged 'match', involving parental negotiations and the payment of

9 Ó Ceannabháin (1983), 239, and Cf. 259, 288. Compare the much shorter legends, without formulaic opening, edited in Ó hEochaidh, Ní Néill & Ó Catháin (1977), and Ó Catháin (1983).
10 For discussions of other legends by Éamon a Búrc, see Bourke (1993), 25-38, and (1996), 7-25.
11 Ó Ceannabháin (1983), 288-92; translation, O'Sullivan (1966), 184-8. O'Sullivan gives the date of recording as 9 February, but this was probably the date of transcription. *IFC* 732:29, Mac Coisdeala's diary for 15 January, 1938, refers to ' .. *an cuntas is fearr dá bhfuaireas fós ar 'An Dochtúir Ó Laoi agus Beag-Árainn.*' ('the best account I've got of Doctor Lee and Little Aran'). *IFC* = Irish Folklore Collection, being the Main Manuscripts Collection of the Department of Irish Folklore, University College Dublin; the numbers on either side of the colon represent the volume and page number(s) respectively.
12 Ó Ceannabháin, *op. cit.*, 239-47.
13 Mac Coisdeala, *op. cit.* (1948); Ó Nualláin, *op. cit.*, 32-5.

dowry as 'the crucial point of rural social organization' in Ireland (p. 77), noting that
the apparent absence of romance did not necessarily mean people lacked strong
feelings about the proceedings (p. 80).[14] More recent research has shown that this
system was not old, only becoming common in the west of Ireland towards the end
of the nineteenth century.[15]

Strong feelings hum beneath the surface of both of Éamon Liam's sea-woman
legends: fear, fascination, grief and regret. With their meticulous descriptions of the
lives of ordinary fishermen who receive sexual overtures from beautiful, powerful,
mysterious women in the sea, they encapsulate what the American scholar William
Bascom in 1954 called the 'basic paradox of folklore':

> ... that while it plays a vital role in transmitting and maintaining the
> institutions of a culture and in forcing the individual to conform to them, at
> the same time it provides socially approved outlets for the repressions which
> these same institutions impose upon him.[16]

The story of 'Doctor Lee and Little Aran' occupies four-and-a-half pages of
print. *Beag-Árainn*, 'Little Aran,' is an island said to lie off the coast of county
Galway, but usually invisible, like Cill Stuifín, off county Clare, and Cathair Tonn
Tóime in Dingle Bay.[17] This story combines a narrative known in the Carna area at
least since the late seventeenth century, about a book of medicine obtained on a
magic island by a man called Ó Laoi (Lee), with one of 150 recorded Irish versions
of the story usually called 'The Knife against the Wave.'[18] Lee, a fisherman, escapes
drowning by throwing his knife against an enormous wave which threatens to
swamp his boat. Later he is brought to a place beyond or beneath the sea, identified
as Little Aran, to a house where a beautiful young woman lies, ill and in pain, his

---

14 Arensberg (1950), (1937), (lectures given at Harvard University in 1936). See Chapter 3: "The
Family and the Land," and Cf. Arensberg & Kimball (1940).
15 Breen (1984), 285-6.
16 Bascom (1954), 333-49. Reprinted in Dundes (1965), 298.
17 Compare Dáithí Ó hÓgáin's contribution in the present volume.
18 O'Flaherty (1684), 70-2, gives 1668 as the date when Muircheartach Ó Laoi obtained his book
of medical knowledge, and Iorras Aithneach – the Carna/Cill Chiaráin peninsula – as the place
from where he was carried off. For a version which gives the doctor's name as 'Murchadh Ó
Laidhe,' and like Éamon a Búrc's, specifies the place where he came back to land after his adventure as the bottom of Cnoc an Choillín (Coillín Hill), in Carna, see *Béaloideas* 10 (1940), 21-3.
The book in question has been identified as a fifteenth-century ms. translation into Irish of a
Latin medical text (*RIA* MS 23 P 10 ii). See Ó hÓgáin (1982), 191-3. For 'The Knife against the
Wave,' and 'Doctor Lee' as separate legends, collected by Máirtín Ó Cadhain from his uncle,
Máirtín Beag Ó Cadhain, in Cois Fhairrge, some thirty miles east of Carna, see *Béaloideas* 4
(1934), 62-3, 78. For other versions of 'The Knife against the Wave,' see *Béaloideas* 11 (1941),
86; O'Sullivan (1966), 184-8; notes, 274-5; Ó Duilearga (1948), 259-62; notes 430 (English
translation, *Sean Ó Conaill's Book: Stories and Traditions from Iveragh*, Dublin 1981, 223-5; notes,
393; Ó hEochaidh etc., (1977), No. 92, 218-23; notes, 384; Ó Cuinn (1990), 85; notes 117. See
also the discussion of this legend in Ross (1994).

knife stuck in her breast. A man who is apparently her relative asks that he remove the knife; he pulls it out and immediately she is healed. She confesses that she was attempting to abduct him for herself by drowning him, and asks him to remain, but he will have none of it and returns home safely.

In Éamon Liam's telling of this legend, the one chosen by Seán O'Sullivan for inclusion in *Folktales of Ireland*, Lee is unmarried. The man he meets in Little Aran is the young woman's father, and it is he who proposes that Lee stay, marrying his daughter and succeeding to ownership of Little Aran like any *cliamhain isteach*, or son-in-law marrying in. But Lee is an only son, with several unmarried sisters at home, so his excuse for resisting the woman's advances and her father's offer of an advantageous match is that he must see them settled before he can think of his own marriage. Unlike many other tellers of this legend, therefore, who present the woman beneath the sea as an enemy to be outwitted, often by a married man, Éamon Liam allows the story to dwell on the tempting possibilities she offers. He also presents a fully-furnished alternative social system, in which the young woman's advances are not delinquent, but are fully supported by her father.[19] As with matchmaking in the real world, Lee's reasonable explanation for refusing the offer of marriage is graciously accepted. Man to man, the sea-woman's father acknowledges that he had no alternative but to save himself from drowning, and presents him with a magic book which contains all the medical knowledge in the world. Later in the story, Lee uses the book to practise medicine over a wide area of Ireland, first discharging his family responsibilities by curing a cousin who has fallen ill. Eventually he fails to return from one of his journeys, and the storyteller suggests that he may have gone to live with the beautiful young woman under the sea, and may be there yet.

The phallic connotations of the knife stuck in the sea-woman's breast are obvious, as is the metaphorical significance of a narrative in which the strange woman's male relative demands that the man redress the injury done to her. Generally in the story of the 'Knife against the Wave', the fisherman manages to mitigate the harm he has inadvertently done, and to retrieve his weapon, while repudiating and escaping from the further demand that he remain among these strangers. In Éamon Liam's telling, however, while the sea-woman is clearly not a suitable bride, the suggestion that Lee stay with her is not a cruel or unfair attempt to trap him into marriage; rather it is an attractive and seductive prospect, honourably presented, and the story ends with the beguiling suggestion that he may finally have accepted it.

---

19 Compare a version of this story told by Éamonn Ó Conghaile (Eddie Bheairtle), from An Aird Thiar, Carna, at 'Scéalta Shamhna', in Bewley's Café, Dublin, on 21 November, 1996, in which both the fisherman and the sea-woman are already married. The strange man turns out to be the sea-woman's husband, embarrassed by her undisciplined sexuality.

III

'The Fisherman and the Fairy Boat' is another legend of seduction by a sea woman. The ingredients are similar, but the story is almost twice as long as that of 'Doctor Lee', and considerably more disturbing. Beneath the colourful mystery of its fairy-abduction narrative, the shape of a true story can be discerned: of bereavement, grief and illness, probably tuberculosis. The lessons it teaches are both moral and technical; not a word is wasted as it demonstrates how to live ethically and efficiently, alert to the possibilities presented by the new, while remaining respectful of traditional values. Like 'Doctor Lee', though, Éamon a Búrc ends it with a flight away from the constraints of the practical and social: the fisherman, who appears to have died, has really gone back to the sea-woman.

Éamon Liam told the story of 'The Fisherman and the Fairy Boat' on 10 October 1938, on the last night of a spectacularly productive six-week visit to Cill Chiaráin by the collector, Liam Mac Coisdeala. That same evening he had narrated the last of three episodes of the hero-tale, *Eochair, Mac Rí in Éirinn* / 'Eochair, a king's son in Ireland' the longest folktale ever recorded in Ireland. It filled a total of twenty-two Ediphone cylinders and ran to some thirty thousand words.[20] Mac Coisdeala has suggested that this may have been the first time the storyteller had ever told the tale in its entirety; the stimulation of an appreciative and discerning audience over a sustained and concentrated period seems to have encouraged him to produce some of his finest performances.[21]

Night after night from 2 September that year, while Europe teetered on the brink of war, and newspapers were full of the last-minute negotiations between Neville Chamberlain, Edouard Daladier and Adolf Hitler (which led to the signing of the Munich pact on 29 September), Liam Mac Coisdeala visited Éamon Liam's small, modest house in Aill na Brón, built on bare rock above the bay of Cill Chiaráin. Every evening, when he arrived about 8.30, he answered the storyteller's questions about the latest war news from radio and newspapers, and then stayed until about midnight, recording stories.[22] Éamon Liam was then aged seventy - two; Mac Coisdeala, who had by this time known him for ten years, was in his early thirties, and a large crowd of other young men gathered every night to listen, and to observe the modern recording technology at work. Pádraig Ó Cualáin (26) and Val Ó Donnchadha (36) were the two most regular visitors. They also would tell stories from time to time, to give the master storyteller a chance to rest, and at the end of the evening's work usually helped Mac Coisdeala to carry the Ediphone and its heavy box of wax cylinders back down the rough and rocky path to where his car was parked on the road, so that he could spend the following day transcribing. In fact,

20 Ed. and trans. Ó Nualláin (1982); Cf. Delargy (1945), 177-221; (1969), 16.
21 Ó Nualláin, *op. cit.*, 36-7.
22 *IFC* 732: 133-152 is Mac Coisdeala's field diary for this period.

so rich was the material he collected in Cill Chiaráin that autumn, that its transcription kept him occupied well into the following year.[23]

All three storytellers told large numbers of fairy-belief legends during this six-week feast of storytelling, but Éamon Liam's far exceeded those of the younger men in length, complexity and subtlety.[24] One of them, *Mícheál Mac Muiris agus na Daoine Maithe*, 'Michael Morris and the Good People,' told on 4 October, filled nine Ediphone cylinders and reads like a charter of fairy traditions.[25]

The 'Fairy Boat' legend concerns a young fisherman, lured to a land beneath or beyond the sea by a mysterious young woman. Éamon Liam may have been reminded of it by the final part of his long hero-tale, told the same evening. *Eochair, Mac Rí in Éirinn*, full of giants and magic, also features a sea-monster (Irish *ollphéist*, [f.]), which carries the hero on her back to the Land-under-Sea, *Tír-fó-Thoinn*.

Unlike the swashbuckling and fantastic story of *Eochair*, the 'Fairy Boat' is a legend, realistically presented. Like several other fairy-belief narratives told by Éamon Liam, it offers a subtle and penetrating analysis of a human predicament, dramatically presented through the storyteller's awareness of his physical and social environment and his keen appreciation of work in all its complexity.[26]

The 'Fairy Boat' story runs to eight-and-a-quarter pages in the printed transcription, representing some twenty minutes of oral narration, and links several episodes together, skilfully moving from place to place and also through time. The narrative is marked at every point by danger signs, but whereas Doctor Lee was presented as behaving impeccably at every stage of his adventure, here the protagonist is an innocent transgressor, whose first departure from the expected codes of behaviour – contracting an engagement without his family's knowledge – marks the beginning of what is, in human terms, his tragedy.

The story opens with the sudden illness and death of a brother and sister, grown-up children of a fisherman. Their surviving brother feels obliged to put off the marriage he has secretly planned with a young neighbour woman, but gives her his solemn promise that they will marry in two years, if he lives.

---

23 See, for instance, *IFC* 589:385, where a story recorded on 4 October, 1938, was not transcribed until 19 January, 1939. Some of the recording dates given by O'Sullivan and by Ó Ceannabháin, *op. cit.*, appear to be incorrect for this reason. According to his diary, Mac Coisdeala's autumn visit to Conamara was from 2 September until 11 October, 1938.

24 Returning to his lodgings after the second night of recording the long story, Mac Coisdeala wrote of Éamon Liam in his diary: ...*ní hé amháin gur fear mór sean-sgéalta gaisge é ach tá an domhan seanchais cho maith aige - seanchas den uile chineál.* (IFC 732: 151), ('... he's not only a great teller of old hero-tales; he has any amount of *seanchas* as well - of every kind').

25 IFC 589:385-427. Cf. Ó Nualláin (1982), 36-7.

26 Cf. Bourke (1993 & 1996).

The sudden death of young people in narratives of this sort is always open to interpretation as fairy abduction, but Éamon Liam moves quickly on to tell how the young man decides to go fishing for a living, alone. Many details illustrate his inexperience. When he goes to dig bait without remembering to take a container, he ends up removing the bailing can from his boat to use it. Carrying it on dry land, he first encounters the strange young man and woman who guide him to an unnaturally rich fishing-ground, and who will eventually abduct him. His father, an experienced fisherman, has never heard of this amazingly rich fishing-place so near to home, and nobody knows his two new friends. However, even after two days of unprecedented luck and two nights sitting up late salting huge quantities of fish, the young fisherman suspects nothing and insists on going out a third day.

This time he is surprised to find the young woman fishing alone, and is reluctant to accept her invitation to share her food at midday, although he has brought none of his own. Eventually, for fear of offending her, he leaves his own boat riding at anchor, and joins her in hers, in one of the story's major *tableau scenes*.[27] By this time he has offended not only against community ethics, by continuing to fish after he has caught more than enough and ought to rest,[28] but also against specific taboos. A woman ought not to be in a fishing boat, and ought certainly to be avoided if she happens to fish alone; food ought never to be accepted from strangers.[29]

As soon as he tastes the food the woman gives him, the young man forgets his own boat and all his obligations, and at the end of the day sails home with her to a delightful land where he is made welcome by her family. Like Doctor Lee, he is offered a liaison with the woman from the sea that is sanctioned by her family. He lives with her for two years, and has two children, but she then reminds him of his earlier life, and of his promise to marry his mortal sweetheart, confessing that she has abducted him by magic and must now return him. The story thus insists on the importance and validity of human promises, even when made without witnesses. A solemn promise is clearly proof against the magic of the fairies: many versions of the 'Knife against the Wave' include the detail that the fisherman, asked by the sea-woman's brother, father or husband to accompany him, extracts a promise that he will be left back home safely. Similar promises are given to midwives asked to accompany strange men into fairy dwellings in the well-known 'Midwife to the Fairies' legend.[30]

The dénouement of 'The Fisherman and the Fairy Boat' is a story within the story, as the sea-woman tells the young man all that has been going on unknown to him. By this device, Éamon a Búrc contrives to shift the focus from the young man's

---

27 Olrik (1965), 138.
28 For another story in which Éamon a Búrc cautions against greed and working too hard, see Ó Ceannabháin (1983), 259-66.
29 Thompson (1955-8), C211.1. : *Tabu: eating in fairyland.*
30 Mac Cárthaigh (1991), 133-43.

gripping adventure to its wider social implications and possible real-life background, while observing Axel Olrik's epic laws of *two to a scene* and *single-stranded narrative*.[31] We learn that during the two years of the fisherman's absence, a changeling has lived and worked in his place, so that his parents and sweetheart suspect nothing, although the young woman is somewhat aggrieved that he has become taciturn and withdrawn: – *thar beannú di ní dhearna sé* – 'he has done no more than greet her'. The force of this detail appears to be that whereas the young man has been quite comprehensively unfaithful to his fiancée, her fidelity is not in question. The child she later bears, who will eventually inherit the man's family name and goods, is, therefore, clearly his. If stories like this one are at some level meditations on emigration and separation, as well as fantasies of freedom, this motif, called 'the chaste friend' must reassure male readers that what is sauce for the gander is not needed for the goose.[32]

Stripped of its supernatural elements, 'The Fisherman and the Fairy Boat' is a story about a young man who throws himself into work after the deaths of his siblings, accumulating wealth while withdrawing steadily from social contact. After two years he surprises his fiancée by remembering his promise to marry her, but shortly after the wedding becomes ill: 'delicate' is the expression used – *deiliceáilte tinn*. He lives long enough to see his son born, and his parents secure in the companionship of their daughter-in-law, then dies. It could be a narrative of depression following bereavement, or of tuberculosis, a highly infectious and stigmatising disease, often referred to obliquely ('delicate' was a favourite euphemism), and probably underlying many stories of apparent fairy abduction; or of course it could be both.

The fisherman's story ends in sickness and death, but in spite of youthful ineptitudes, he has discharged his social responsibilities. A son has been born to carry on the family – 'to keep the name on the land' as Arensberg and Kimball were told – and his parents have their widowed (and exemplary) daughter-in-law to take care of them in old age. Meanwhile however, the private, or fantasy, narrative – the entertainment component of this highly didactic story, and what makes it memorable – is one of adventure and fulfilment.

The 'Fisherman and the Fairy Boat' presents the possibility that a man might respond to the overtures of a strange woman without disastrous social consequences – at least in the short term, or in fantasy. At the end of the story, after recounting the hero's peaceful death in the bosom of his family, Éamon Liam suggests that in fact he did not die, but that 'the first woman, who took him away in the beginning, took him the second time' (*an chéad bhean a bhí aige, thug sí léi ar dtús é, is í a thug léi an dara huair é*). Notwithstanding a certain amount of play with the fantasy though,

---

31 Olrik (1965), 135, 137.
32 A similar episode occurs in the medieval Welsh tale of Pwyll, Prince of Dyfed: see Jackson (1961), 81-4. Cf. Thompson (1955-58), K1311.1 and T351.1.

both this story and 'Doctor Lee' come to the conclusion that social contracts and family ties are absolutely binding. Both stories meditate in some detail on questions of illness, accident and premature death, and gently dissuade listeners from the pursuit of exceptional wealth. Like other stories of fantastic happenings at sea, they also carry a reward of prestige for those who make their livelihood by fishing, together with an acknowledgment, which is also a warning to the uninitiated, of the dangers they encounter.

Conclusion

Fairy-belief legend, with its race of beings present, but invisible, its focus on boundaries in time, in landscape and in human life, and its sliding scale of credibility, is a major container of paradox and ambiguity in Irish oral tradition, and an important discourse on change, nowhere more richly than in the stories of Éamon Liam a Búrc.[33] In 'Doctor Lee and Little Aran' and 'The Fisherman and the Fairy Boat,' amphibiousness works as a metaphor for ambivalence, allowing the men who fish the sea to have their cake and eat it too. The protagonists are young unmarried men who encounter adventure as they begin to take on the responsibilities of adult life, giving the stories a special appeal for young male listeners experiencing transition and decision-making in their own lives. Fictions like these are lenses which offer an alternative view of social custom: like wooden oars seen through the water's surface, the rigid conventions of sexual morality and marriage custom wobble and bend when scrutinised through legend, yet the storyteller's audience is well aware that once lifted back into normal view, their shape will be unchanged.

The marine environment in these two stories contains all that is abnormal on land, as the storyteller acknowledges those things that may be imagined or desired but that have no place among the hard practicalities of life. Instead of marriage contracts made between neighbours therefore, initiated by men, and requiring the assent of two families, these stories present sexual unions initiated by women, which initially appear to offer the possibility of escape from responsibility and from poverty. Like Yeats's 'The Stolen Child' however, and 'The Man who Dreamt of Faery,' as well as many other protagonists of popular legend, those who fantasise about escaping know that there is a price to be paid; they waver between the security of the known and the appeal of the exotic. In this they may well be rehearsing thoughts about emigration, for like other fairy narratives, these two sea legends told by Éamon Liam a Búrc are part of an ongoing discourse of negotiations with elsewhere.

---

33 For fairy belief as a discourse on time and change, see Rieti (1991), Chapter 7, 181-211.

The Fisherman and the Fairy Boat[34]

Long ago, and long ago it was: if I'd been there then, I wouldn't be here now; if I were here now as well as then, I might have a new story, or an old story, or no story at all. In any case, whatever way I tell the story tonight, may none of you tell it half as well tomorrow night. For there was a fisherman here in Ireland long ago, who had two sons and a daughter: a fine family. No woman was finer than the daughter, and the sons were just as good-looking. The older son was interested in a young woman who lived near them. She was as well-off as he was, and very good-looking besides, and young. And he and she were very close. They were even arranging – secretly, between themselves – to marry, when a sickness hit his brother and his brother died. When the brother died, he was buried. Then a few days afterwards, a sickness hit the sister, and she died too, a week later. When she died, there was nobody who pined more after the two of them – and no wonder – than the brother, except the father and mother. And the young woman he intended to marry pined for them nearly as much as the rest did. He told her he'd have to put off marrying.

'But if I live,' he said, 'for two years from today, I promise you my hand and my word I'll never have any wife but you, if you're willing.'

'All right,' she said, 'as long as you promise.'

'I do promise.'

'Well, never a husband will I have while water runs or grass grows, but you,' said the young woman.

The bargain was made.

Fishing was what the father did to support the family. He had a boat, and he used it a lot of the time, fishing all on his own. And then, a while after the two died – the brother and sister – the son said he'd go fishing. And of course the father said that if he wanted to, he could.

'And I'll go with you,' said the father.

'Well, you know,' he said, 'there's no need for you to come. You stay with my mother. She's in a bad way, and something might happen to her if she was left alone.'

'All right,' said the father.

The young man took his spade, the way they used to do then, and still do, and went to a small beach near where the boat was, but then he had nothing to put bait into. He walked over to the boat, climbed into it, took up the bailing can, and carried it back with him to hold his fishing-bait. So he came back, but as he got near the same spot, he saw a young man and a young woman, digging bait as hard as they could. He came up to them and said hello, and they said hello to him, but he didn't recognise either of them. From the day he was born until that day, he'd never seen them before. He kept looking at them, and they began to talk, but no matter how long he looked, he couldn't recognise them. At that time, people didn't travel much. People didn't go half as far from home in those days as they do now, from one

---

34 Éamon a Búrc, 'An tIascaire agus an Bád Sí' (Ó Ceannabháin [1983], 239-47). Translation, Angela Bourke.

village to another, so there could be a man living within two or three villages of you, or a woman, that you wouldn't know at all. In any case, he didn't recognise them. They went on talking about fishing, wondering whether the day would be fine, and the young man who was with the young woman said it would – that he thought it would.

'Do you get many fish?' he asked.

'Some days,' said the fisherman's son, 'but other days I don't get any – I just don't find any.'

'Well, there's no day that we go out,' said the young man, 'that we don't get all we can carry.'

'Well,' said the fisherman's son, 'that's something that doesn't happen to me.'

'Do you know what you'll do now,' said the other man: 'when you go out this time, when you see us sailing out, follow us. It's not far. We'll stay at anchor, fishing, and you come to the same place. It's a great fishing ground: not dangerous. There's no day we go there that we don't get a boatload.'

He was making his preparations. The tide was coming in, so as soon as the boat floated, he got himself ready, took his fishing line, and out he went. And as he headed straight out, he saw a little boat, not far from him, sailing out – after those people had left him. When he saw that, he sailed out to sea, but before he was very far out at all, he saw this other boat striking her sails and starting to fish.

'As sure as I'm alive,' he said, 'those are the crowd who told me to follow them. I may as well keep on going till I get to where they are, although I've never seen a boat fishing before in that spot, and I've often gone in and out past it' – in his own mind, talking to himself.

He sailed on until he reached them, and who was it but the same young man and the same woman. They told him to throw out his anchor right there. So he threw out an anchor-stone and stayed anchored there with them. And as soon as his line hit the bottom, he had a fish. They started hauling – all of them – as hard as they could, until it was late in the day and all his bait was used up. No man could carry the amount of fish he had. And when he was getting ready to go home, the man in the other boat, whom he didn't know, said he thought it would soon be time to sail home. He said it would. Both boats hoisted their sails and this man who was with the young woman said, 'Any time you want to come fishing, do. We'll be here again tomorrow. You can anchor here again. The name of the place is the Fishing Swell.'

'Well,' said the fisherman's son, 'I never heard tell of the Fishing Swell until today, and I've often sailed in and out past it. I never heard my father speak of it, or any man in this place ever, before today.'

'Well, this Swell has been here, and I've known about it as far back as I can remember. And if you come tomorrow, we'll be here, and you can come back to the same place. Tomorrow may be as good as today was, or even better.'

'By dad, I will,' said the fisherman's son, 'if I live.'

The two boats sailed on their way, staying close together until they were very near land. The fisherman's son watched to see where the other boat would put in, and it seemed to him that it wasn't more than one or two villages away. It landed at a harbour very near him.[35]

'That can't be anyone,' he said, 'but some one of the young people that I don't know, although by dad, it's odd that I don't!'

He came home and found the young woman waiting – his girlfriend – the one he used to talk to and had made a promise of marriage with.

And of course no woman was happier to see him when he came in from the sea, and they filled up two creels with fish. She carried one of them to the house with him. When he came in, his father asked him where he'd been.

'Well, I was in a place today,' he said, 'where I never fished before, or did you ever hear tell of it – the Fish Swell ?'

'I've never heard any talk of it,' said the old fisherman, 'until tonight.'

'Well now, it's often enough you have gone in and out past the Fishing Swell, the place where this boat was fishing. It came to land very near here – the place it landed is not far from us at all, only a village or two away. But I can't say who the people were.'

'I've never heard any talk of it,' said the father, 'but such a thing could exist unknown to us.'

They had to work hard to clean and split the fish. It must have taken a good part of the night, but then they were delighted with the quantity of fish they had, and he told his father and mother he'd go fishing again the next day.

He took his line and his creel, and went to the landing-place. As soon as he got there, he climbed into the boat and hoisted his sails. As soon as they were hoisted, he sailed. And when he had got a little way out to sea, he spotted the boat at anchor. And as soon as he spotted it he made no delay or hesitation until he arrived at the same place where he'd been yesterday. He asked if the fish were running, and they told him he had only to cast. He let out his own line, and of course as fast as he was able to let the line out, there they were – fish – until every single one of his baits was used up, and probably the other boat's as well – if they had them. But the man who had spoken to him yesterday said it was time, he thought, to head for home; that it was getting late in the day – in the evening. And he said he believed it was. So they all sailed for home.

And so the fisherman's son came home. And when he did, the young woman was waiting for him again. They each had a load as heavy as they could carry, and still he had to go back to the boat a second time to collect all the fish and bring it home, he had caught so much in that day's work. Of course when the father saw this, he said that never, ever since the day he was born had he seen such a catch before,

---

35 The heavily-indented coast around Carna has a stone pier or landing-place every half-mile or so. See Robinson (1990).

and that it must be a wonderful fishing-ground that they'd found, although none of them had ever known anything about it. They spent the whole night, until morning, I may as well say, cleaning and splitting fish and salting it, until it was all done. When they were finished in the morning, he said he'd go fishing. And he got himself ready. He dug his baits, climbed into the boat and sailed off. And sailing just the way he'd sailed before, he saw the boat at anchor in the same place. And bless me, when he came within sight – close enough to see in – there was only one person in it. Every other day until this day there had been two.

'By dad,' he said, 'you're as bad as myself – only one person in the boat today, I think,' he said. 'Unless he's lying down asleep, or resting; but I don't see anyone.'

And he was quite amazed. As he came closer to the boat, there was a woman alone in it and he said then surely that the man must be sitting down, or lying in the bottom of the boat, or doing something else. And he came up alongside and she spoke to him, asking him to come nearer. So he did. And then he let down an anchor-stone, and anchored there, with the two boats very close together. She spoke to him, and they were catching fish at a great rate, chatting to each other and talking. And still he couldn't see anybody else. 'I see,' he said, 'that you're all alone today – or are you?'

'Well, yes,' she said, 'my brother went to a fair,' she said, 'and he couldn't come with me. So I took the boat out myself, with my line, and I came fishing.'

Well and good. It came towards dinner-time, and when dinner-time came, she spread out a towel that had food wrapped in it and asked him whether he'd like some of it, or whether he'd brought food with him. He said he hadn't.

'Come on over here, then,' she said, 'and eat with me. There's plenty of food here.'

'Oh, well, thank you, and long life to you,' he said, 'but I'm a person who's not often hungry, so I won't.'

'Oh, come on,' she said, 'food never did any harm.'

And so the two boats came alongside each other and she told him to come into hers and eat something. And so, rather than offend her, he climbed into the boat and began to eat, and he ate until the food was all gone. And when he had eaten it, not a thing did he remember about ever having had a boat of his own. Not a thing. And a while after they had eaten their dinner they were chatting and talking like any two people. He had no memory whatever of his own boat; none whatsoever; and she set sail, with him in the boat, and off they went together. And he had no idea in the whole of God's creation that he had ever been in charge of a boat of his own. She landed then, and when she did, he found himself in the finest kingdom he had ever seen. He saw big houses, as well as small houses like he had always seen: it was a very fine kingdom, but he had no memory of his own life or of his home.

They walked into a house. An old man – not very old – stood up, and came over to him, shaking his hand and greeting him by his name and surname, making him a hundred thousand million times welcome. And a woman came up to him, herself neither young nor old, and did the same. And the young man who had been fishing every day came up as well and shook both his hands and made him a hundred thousand million times welcome.

Life went on, and he didn't remember father, mother or home, or the boat that he had left. But on Saturday evening, he remembered the boat, and his home, and 'Oh,' he said immediately, 'where's my boat?'

'Don't worry about the boat. The boat's all right,' said the woman.

And instantly he forgot about it again. But every week after that, for the rest of the time he spent there, he remembered the boat every Saturday and spoke those words. And every time the woman would tell him that the boat was all right, and that sort of thing, and that he needn't worry.

Well and good. Everything happened as before, until he'd been away two years. And by the time he'd been away two years, he had two sons with this woman. Then she said:

'Well, now. You made a promise of marriage a long time ago, and we have to take you back.'

'You see,' she said, 'I used magic on you, and brought you with me. I fell in love with you. But you'd made a promise and a pact with another woman at home, or do you remember her? You gave her your hand and your word, and you swore on the Book that you'd marry her in two years.'

'Oh!' he said, and that was when he remembered everything.

'Don't worry,' she said. 'Your father and mother are well, as well as they were when you left home. And at the time you left the boat, I put another man into it who looks like you and acts like you, to do your work at home as well as you'd do it yourself. And your father and mother don't know that he's not you all along. And the way he's spent his time since then is this: from the time he comes in, he doesn't say much at all, and if there's company in the house, he goes out.

Now when he went home the other day, he had a big fish dead in the boat, and it was full of diamonds. And the woman you have yet to marry – she was the one who was cutting the fish open. When she cut it open, she ran into the house – thinking he was you – delighted with what she'd found in the belly of the fish. He's been buying and selling and building houses in your name from the time you left home until today. Still, neither your father nor your mother has had any pleasure from his company, nor this woman you're to marry – he hasn't said more than 'hello' to her: going out when it gets dark, and staying out till bedtime, and getting up before day, on my instructions. And still your father and mother don't know he's not you. But now I'm going to let you go home' – and she gave him a stocking filled with gold.

'Take this home with you now,' she said, 'and be as nice as you can to your father and mother. And you may marry that woman when you get home. And indeed, you couldn't marry a better woman, for she wouldn't have married till the end of the world unless you married her, and on account of the promise you had made, we couldn't play false or deceive her.'

He remembered everything then, and soon afterwards she set sail in her boat, and he went with her. And she told him:

'In five or six weeks' time,' she said, 'you'll become sickly and delicate, but you'll live for a year,' she said, 'after you marry that woman, and you'll have a son with her. But then when he's not very old you'll die, and the woman and her son will stay living with your father and mother until they die.'

He got home, and straightaway of course everything was the same as it had been before. And the other man left. When he'd gone, the first man was as talkative and cheerful as he'd ever been. It wasn't long before the young woman arrived at the house.

'Well,' she said, 'I've had no satisfaction,' she said, 'trying to talk to you,' she said, 'for the last two years,' she said. 'You've been behaving strangely.'

'Oh well,' he said, 'I had a lot on my mind; a lot to think about. But anyway,' he said, 'since I've promised to marry you, and the pact is made, shouldn't we go ahead and get married?'

'Oh now,' she said, 'don't make fun of me. You're a big rich man now, and I'm poor, and it's many a day I haven't expected to marry you, or to get you in marriage.'

'There was a time,' he said, 'when I'd have been glad to get you, and I'm glad to get you today.'

'In that case,' she said, 'I may say that if you didn't marry me, never a man would I marry, while water runs or grass grows.'

They made an agreement, and named the day, and in the morning he went to fetch her, and indeed she was waiting impatiently. And they walked together as far as the priest, and they married. And when they were married, there was no woman who had ever come inside his father's or mother's door whom they liked better or preferred to her; she'd been so kind to them all along, since their own daughter died. Her people were delighted too, to have a man like him, who had succeeded in getting so rich.

But life went on, let's say for three months, and he began to get delicate,[36] although he was filthy rich, building houses and places at a great rate, until there was no wonder in the world like the place he had made. But he was getting sicker from day to day. Still, he had only been married nine months when his wife had a young son. His father and mother were pleased and delighted when the son was born – not surprisingly – except that he himself wasn't well, and his father and mother and his wife were all very worried about him. And the way it happened was that when he drew near to death, his father and mother and his wife never left his bedside, night or day, but watched him, and talked to him, and tried to make him comfortable. But

---

36 Irish *deilicéailte* Compare the Galway-born Gretta Conroy's use of 'delicate' to describe her dead sweetheart, Michael Furey, in James Joyce's short story "The Dead," where it is probably a euphemism for tuberculosis.

I may as well shorten the story. At the end of a year exactly, he said goodbye to them, with seven hundred blessings, and said he was going to the other world. He closed his two eyes and died, as far as they knew.

That's how I heard that story. I can't say whether it's true or false, but I often heard it. The dear blessing of God and of the church on the souls of the dead, and may we and the company be seven thousand times better a year from tonight!

But I don't think he really died. I think the first woman, who took him away in the beginning, took him the second time. And I don't know that he's not alive yet; or if he isn't, his children are, probably, or his descendants.

The Three Laughs:
A Celtic-Norse Tale in Oral Tradition
and Medieval Literature

MICHAEL CHESNUTT

I

In the classification of international folktales by Antti Aarne and Stith Thompson, Type Number 670 is assigned to a story with the conventionalized title of *The Animal Languages*. In its predominant (or, to use geographic-historical terminology, 'normal') form as abstracted from the mass of variants underlying the classification, this story is a little exemplum of how relations between husband and wife may be appropriately regulated. A husband who acquires knowledge of the languages of animals in reward for merciful behaviour toward one of their kind is cautioned that he must never reveal his secret knowledge to others. One day he betrays that knowledge by laughing at something he has overheard in animal conversation. His wife, demanding that he should share his secret with her, threatens him with violence should he refuse. Again overhearing animal speech, the husband decides to put up resolute resistance to the wife's threats; she is taught a lesson once and for all, and they live happily ever after.[1]

This is an immensely widespread international tale, and more than eighty years ago Antti Aarne devoted a whole monograph to it entitled *Der tiersprachenkundige Mann und seine neugierige Frau: eine vergleichende Märchenstudie*.[2] Aarne's main conclusion here, confirming the opinion arrived at long before by Theodor Benfey on a much more limited empirical basis, was that the tale, like many other misogynist statements of its kind, originated in India. The theoretically constructed normal form as displayed in the catalogue of tale types should not, however, be assumed to occur uniformly all over the world, for characteristically divergent versions are found in at least some tradition areas including Ireland. In his anthology of Irish folktales in translation published in 1966, Seán Ó Súilleabháin – long-serving archivist of the Irish Folklore Commission (IFC), and the possessor of unsurpassed knowledge of the material collected from Irish oral tradition under the direction of the Commission's founder, Professor Séamus Ó Duilearga – illustrated the occurrence of Type 670 with a tale narrated in 1937 by the 84-year-old Seán Ó Conaola of Doire Gimleach, Ballyconneely, county Galway. Though this variant is just one of seventy-eight indexed at the time in the IFC archives, there is no reason to doubt that Ó Súilleabháin thought of it as representative of the tale type as told in Gaelic-speaking parts of the West of Ireland.

---

1 Aarne & Thompson (1961), 233.
2 Aarne (1914).

Yet it is not in any sense an exemplum of a hen-pecked husband; rather it is a story straddling the generic boundary between folktale and belief legend, in which a farmer catches and imprisons a *leipreachán* who laughs enigmatically on three occasions. Unlike the shrewish wife in the normal form of AT 670, the farmer succeeds in getting the one who laughs to reveal what he knows; it turns out that the causes of laughter were three situations in which the captor or another mortal unwittingly had acted against his own interests. The *leipreachán*, well known as a familiar spirit of Irish folk belief and usually represented as a skilled shoemaker and guardian of treasure,[3] appears here instead of a mermaid caught by the main human character and kept as his wife, which Ó Súilleabháin tells us is the frame story in the great majority of Irish variants.[4] The Department of Irish Folklore has kindly provided me with an unpublished example of this more widespread mermaid redaction in the form of a text collected at almost exactly the same time as Seán Ó Conaola's *leipreachán* tale;[5] I have made use of it in the discussion below. The English translation of this story goes as follows:

A Man of the O'Sheas and the Mermaid

Here's another story I used to hear from old people and from many tramps, namely, that long ago one of the O'Sheas in An Ráth, in the parish of Caherdaniel, was fishing and that he was a noted fisherman – it was his livelihood. Well, he had a bit of land, though it was not very extensive. One day he caught a mermaid unawares while she was combing her hair and he thought her the finest woman he had ever seen; and she tried to escape him and he tried to grab her, but he caught her cloak (*brat*) instead and took it with him. And if he did she uttered a thousand cries and pleaded with him to give it to her. 'I won't,' he said, 'but just come along with me and we'll live quite comfortably.'

He kept a hold of the cloak and would not allow her a bit of it and she said that she could not return to her own people without the cloak, and she followed him back to the house, asking him for the cloak, but he did not give it to her, and he hid it up on the loft – a back-loft somewhere – where she could not get at it. That was that, and they lived comfortably and well there and got on well enough together, well enough to have children. She was a terrific servant and she never stopped working from the time she got up in the morning until bedtime, doing everything a woman does and doing it well in every way.

---

3 Cf. Ó Giolláin (1984), 75-150.
4 O'Sullivan (1966), no. 30 and notes. For the frame story – generally known to folklorists as M(igratory) L(egend) 4080 'The Seal Woman' – in Gaelic and Norse tradition see most recently Almqvist (1990b) 1-74, and Brimnes (1993), 99-119.
5 *IFC* 308:63-70. This was collected in March 1936 by Tadhg Ó Murchadha from Pádraig Mac Gearailt (77) of Cill a' Ghoirtín, Dromad, county Kerry. The Irish text is given in the Appendix below; the translation is by Séamas Ó Catháin. *IFC* = Irish Folklore Collection being the Main Manuscripts Collection of the Department of Irish Folklore, University College Dublin. The numbers on either side of the colon represent the volume number and the page number(s) respectively.

Then it happened that this man came in one Monday morning, and the man of the house – Mr O'Shea – asked the stranger to sit down and eat a bite for he hadn't eaten any breakfast. 'I won't', said he, and there was no use forcing him for he wouldn't. And she laughed. And after he had gone out Mr O'Shea asked her what was the reason she was laughing at the man just now. 'Why wouldn't I laugh,' says she, 'didn't he miss his opportunity when he refused food on a Monday morning; I think he is a fool.' Yes! That's the way they were. Another day he struck his big toe against a lump of stone and he fell and he hurt himself fairly badly. He wasn't thankful to the stone that tripped him and hurt him so much, and she gave a big laugh. Well, he did not question her at all that day – he was so badly confused – but just carried on doing whatever he was doing.

The following day he was killing a sheep and she laughed again and it really surprised him that she should laugh while he was killing the sheep, and he asked her what was behind the laughs or how she could explain it all. 'Why wouldn't I laugh at you,' said she, 'killing the animal,' said she, 'which would give food and clothing to you. I think you must have lost your mind to do that.'

Well and good, they carried on like that doing very nicely. And one day he had some business up on the back-loft, and he got the idea that the place needed to be tidied and cleaned up. There was a lot of old worn-out clothes there which were of no use to him or anybody else taking up space and gathering dust, and he started clearing them away and cleaning up the place. And he was throwing down all the old things that he thought were of no use until he got as far as the cloak, and he never thought what he was doing but threw it down and, goodness, didn't she see it and catch hold of it and put it on her; and she gave a great laugh and said to Seán O'Shea that she would now bid him farewell, and that she was very thankful that he had released her even though it had taken him some time to do so. 'Oh! my,' said he – he realised immediately that he had thrown down the cloak – 'upon my soul! You would not think,' said he, 'of leaving me.' 'I have to leave you now,' said she. 'I have spent a good while with you and I now bid you farewell. But you never asked me,' said she, 'about the day you struck your big toe against the stone and I laughed so loudly.' 'I didn't,' said he, 'for I was too confused and I hope you will tell me now.' 'I will, indeed,' said she. 'The reason for that,' said she, 'was that there is a pot of gold hidden under that stump of a rock, and if you had exposed it you would have found riches galore.'

She left him there and off she went – he begged her to stay but it was no good, for she said she had stayed with him a good while and that she wanted to return to her own people and that she was thankful to him and that he should be thankful to her and that that was the end of their life as a couple.

Off she went and she wasn't long gone when he started rooting up the stump of a stone, and he lifted it up and what did he find below but a pot of gold. He raised up the stone and the pot below it was in good shape. And, I think he put the gold in a safe place and the pot was used in the house for boiling potatoes and anything else that needed boiling, and he never paid much heed to the writing or 'brand' on the side of it for a good while until a poor scholar came the way looking for lodgings for the night. He gave him shelter for the night and he saw this pot which was boiling potatoes, or whatever it was boiling, on the fire, and he spotted this writing on it, and he asked the man of the house where he got this pot. 'I have no idea,' said the man, said he, 'that old pot is there a lifetime and I don't know where it came from,' said he. 'The reason I'm asking you,' said he, 'is to see if you noticed the writing on the side of it,' said he, 'or those letters saying there's another pot just like it full of gold in the same place.' 'Oh, by crile, indeed!' said he, 'if that's what's on it,' said he, 'I will tell you where it was found. It was found,' said he, 'in this part of this kitchen, nor was it empty.' 'Well, now,' said he, 'there's another one in the same place full of gold!'

They got their pickaxes, crowbars, and shovels and they started to make a hole, and they went on a good bit, further than the first time and what did they find down below but another pot full of gold. And he gave half of the gold to the poor scholar and the other half to himself, leaving himself and the family comfortably off from that on.

And it's often I heard that from old people as a true story, and, ever since, the O'Sheas that are around that place, they say that they are the breed of the mermaid, and they say that when they go near the sea the waves of the sea are very much given to hitting them.

Seán Ó Súilleabháin was a loyal adherent of the Finnish school of folkloristics founded by Kaarle Krohn and Aarne, and like all archivists he appreciated the practical convenience of the Aarne-Thompson typology in organizing the vast quantities of material brought in from the field by collectors. It should under no circumstances be interpreted as a criticism of decades of selfless labour if I suggest here that Ó Súilleabháin was in one respect too strongly influenced by a dogma of the early Finnish school according to which every significant narrative motif occurring in folk tradition was held originally to have belonged to one and only one tale type.[6] That is why he and his associate Reidar Th. Christiansen could take a body of material in which the constitutive story element of the shrewish wife is not present, and catalogue it without undue reservation under AT 670. Their reasoning must have been that the motif of enigmatic laughter revealing secret knowledge[7] was original to the story of *The Animal Languages*, and that any narrative containing it – irrespective of whether the secret knowledge belonged to a mermaid, a *leipreachán*,

---

6 Cf. Aarne (1913), 16.
7 Thompson (1957), motif N456.

or a browbeaten husband – must therefore be considered a variant of that tale type. A more appropriate view seems to be that the Irish material represents a distinct subtype or even an independent story.[8]

This story, which I shall refer to for brevity's sake as *The Three Laughs*, goes back to the Middle Ages and has its roots in the Judaeo-Greek culture of the early Christian era. It has long been known that it is attached to the figure of the wild soothsayer, Lailoken or Merlin, in Arthurian tradition and that the ancestry of the Arthurian tale is to be sought in Talmudic legendry.[9] There it is told about the captive demon Asmodeus that he laughed enigmatically at certain sights in the market-place. One of these sights was a man ordering shoes fit to last seven years, unaware that he was actually fated to die within seven days; another was a conjurer trying to perform magic, unaware that a great treasure was buried under his feet. The same tale is told in an old Romanian source about the angel Gabriel serving an abbot whose soul he was to collect after the space of thirty years: the angel laughed at the abbot when he sent for new shoes shortly before his death, and at a beggar sitting on top of a treasure hoard.[10] In Arthurian legend as represented by Geoffrey of Monmouth's poem *Vita Merlini* from the middle of the twelfth century, these features of the old legend recur almost unchanged: Merlin laughs in the market-place at a begging doorman who is actually standing on top of a coin hoard, and at a young man buying shoe-leather who is fated to die immediately.[11]

In the Near Eastern material so far brought to light by students of this tale the number of enigmatic laughs is not fixed at three, but such a development is implicit in the *Vita Merlini*, which makes the prophet laugh on just one more occasion than the two already quoted. This is when Merlin sees King Rodarch cheerfully removing a leaf that had caught in his queen's hair while she lay in the undergrowth with her lover.[12] An analogue to this episode has been adduced from the Sanskrit *Sukasaptáti*, which tells of a soothsayer laughing at an adulterous queen;[13] this does not mean that the whole Merlin story is of Indian provenance, but possibly – and in fact probably – that the threefold cause of the prophet's laughter had been established before the story set out on its long journey to Western Europe. How it reached Geoffrey of Monmouth's ears is an unanswered question. His dates, and that of the so-called *Lailoken B* fragment in which the episode of the adulterous queen is also present,[14] are surely too early for the exemplum books of the church to

---

8 There is some reason to think that they inclined to this view themselves (though without taking its systematic consequences), for in Christiansen & Ó Súilleabháin (1963), 137, they subjoin the specification 'Including The Three Laughs of the Mermaid' to the Aarne-Thompson title.
9 See Moe (1906), reprint, with minor alterations in Liestøl (1926), 152 ff; also Wesselski (1909), no. 153 and notes.
10 Gaster (1905), 407-27.
11 Clarke (1973), ed., lines 481 ff.
12 *Ibid.*, lines 246 ff.
13 *Ibid.*, 12-13, with reference *inter alia* to Paton (1903).
14 Ward (1893), 504-26; Clarke (1973), 231-4.

have played a part. On the other hand, we can see that *The Three Laughs* obtained a new lease of life in the West Norse and Gaelic culture areas, where the story pattern has remained productive right down to modern times. We owe this realization to the combinatory skills and unusual erudition of Norwegian folklorists Moltke Moe and Reidar Th. Christiansen.

II

The fundamental change that *The Three Laughs* underwent in passing into Norse-Celtic tradition was that the figure of the prophet was identified with a supernatural being of the ocean. The earliest evidence of this identification comes from Iceland, perhaps as early as the thirteenth century. In Sturla Þorðarson's redaction of *Landnámabók* there is a cryptic legend about the settler Sel-Þórir Grímsson, whose father fishes a merman (*marmennill*) out of the water and asks him for advice as to where he should make his home. 'I need make no prophecy about you', the creature curtly replies, but goes on to stipulate where little Selþórir should claim his future territory. No more is said by the *marmennill*, but the father drowns shortly afterwards.[15] This might be construed as a rudimentary form of the shoe episode in *The Three Laughs*, for in both cases the prophetic creature foresees an imminent death. Much more explicit is the correspondence between the Merlin story and a chapter about the legendary King Hjörleifr in the late medieval fornaldarsaga *Hálfs saga ok Hálfsrekka*. Here a merman is fished up and kept in captivity at the king's court, but not a word will he say until he witnesses a foolish incident: Hjörleifr, who has two wives, strikes the one who loves him and his faithful dog, and the merman laughs because the king has maltreated those who will later save his life.[16] The implicit disloyalty of the second wife constitutes a subtextual parallel to the adultery of King Rodarch's queen. In due course the king releases the merman, and on parting he prophesies in verse about future wars.[17] Finally, a retainer asks him as he goes overboard to tell them what is best for a man, and he answers (again in verse): 'Cold water for the eyes, whalemeat for the teeth, and linen for the body'.[18] This is the earliest evidence of a contamination with a different legend of the merman or mermaid to which I shall return at the end of this paper.

Leroy Andrews, who edited *Hálfs saga* at the beginning of this century, agreed with Moe in stating that the sagaman was indebted here to a pre-existing oral tradition.[19] Their proof depended on a much fuller version of *The Three Laughs* published by Jón Árnason in his pioneering collection of Icelandic folklore. The text in question actually derives from the *Tíðfordríf* (a kind of florilegium) by Jón lærði

---

15 Benediktsson (1968), 94-7 *(Sturlubók, chapter 68, cf. Hauksbók, chapter 56).*
16 Andrews (1909), chapter 7:1-2.
17 *Ibid.,* chapter 7:3-4.
18 *Ibid.,* chapter 7:5.
19 Andrews (1909), 13; cf. Moe (as note 9, 1926), 164-6.

Guðmundsson, an Icelander of eccentric genius who lived from 1574 to 1658. It may therefore not be a primary folklore witness, but even if excerpted from an otherwise lost written source it testifies to the presence in Iceland of a form of the story so close to the *Vita Merlini* that only two explanations are possible: either the poem of Geoffrey was known in Iceland, which in the light of its very limited circulation in the poet's lifetime seems quite incredible,[20] or there existed an oral tradition derived from (or more likely utilized by) the Welsh author that reached Iceland sometime during the High Middle Ages. It should be noted that the Old Norse-Icelandic *Breta sögur*, which is a translation of Geoffrey's *Historia regum Britanniae*, cannot have had anything to do with the transmission of *The Three Laughs* though it might, as Moe indeed surmised, have inspired the prophecies of war in *Hálfs saga*.[21]

Jón Guðmundsson's version of *The Three Laughs*[22] runs like this in English summary:

A man out fishing caught a merman and forced him to come ashore with him. His pretty wife came down to meet them and greeted him with kisses, and the man was delighted with her but kicked his dog when it tried to join in the welcome. Then the merman laughed for the first time. On his way home the man stumbled over a sod of earth and cursed it. Then the merman laughed for the second time. Merchants came to the farm and offered the man a hundred pairs of shoes to choose from, but he was satisfied with none of them. Then the merman laughed for the third time. After three days the man released the merman and asked him to recommend the best fishing tackle. He did so, and also explained why he had laughed three times: the wife was a treacherous whore, the sod was the man's féþúfa (treasure sod) where riches lay buried, and there was no need for him to worry about shoes because he would be dead within three days.

Another variant printed by Jón Árnason is associated with the farmstead at Kvíguvogar in the south of the country; it tells the same story with the omission of the shoe incident, and adds a sequel in which the grateful merman sends sea cattle ashore as a present to his former captor. This sequel is presented as an aetiological explanation of the first element in the place-name Kvíguvogar (*kvíga* f. = heifer). The suspicion that this variant might be dependent in some way on the manuscript of Jón Guðmundsson is allayed when we observe that the captor, before releasing the merman, verifies the truth of his statements by digging up the treasure sod. It has, I believe, escaped the notice of previous commentators that this closely parallels the market-place incidents in *Vita Merlini*, where Merlin challenges King Rodarch to see for himself that his words about the beggar and the young man are true.

In the supplement to Jón Árnason's folklore collection published after World War II we find yet another Icelandic variant of *The Three Laughs*, this time from the

20 Cf. Clarke (1973), vii.
21 Moe (as note 9, 1926), 163.
22 Böðvarsson & Vilhjálmsson (1954), Vol. 1, 126-7.

hand of Séra Páll Jónsson í Hvammi (Laxárdal), written down in November 1861 from the narration of a local farmer's wife, Guðrun Guðmundsdóttir, who had 'obtained the story in her youth from her foster-mother Ingiríður Bjarnadóttir, an intelligent woman with a good memory who ... is long since dead'.[23] This relatively concise text is closer to the Kvíguvogar variant than to Jón Guðmundsson, though it lacks the aetiological sequel. Here too the shoe motif has been left out, for the story is now one of good rather than bad luck and the human protagonist must survive to enjoy his good fortune. The transition from pessimism to optimism is in fact an important aspect of the historical development of the story, pessimism being the atmosphere of the older layer of tradition as received in Iceland during the Middle Ages. It is therefore interesting to see that this older stratum is still reflected in the Irish *leipreachán* tale from 1937, though not in the Irish mermaid tale from 1936. We may now compare these Irish oral texts with the Welsh and Icelandic material.

In the *leipreachán* tale the little man is not said to maintain obstinate silence (as Merlin and the Icelandic mermen were wont to do), but he laughs only three times in the course of his captivity. The first time is when the farmer sells a balk of driftwood that had in fact been full of money, the second when a pauper refuses hospitality and subsequently breaks his leg, and the third when the farmer unwittingly shows thieves the spot where he has buried his hard-earned savings in the field. The first incident has to be understood as a doublet of the last, and both as weakened reflections of the treasure sod motif in Welsh and Icelandic. Similarly, the pauper breaking his leg is said explicitly to have 'turned down his luck' when he turned down food, which can be interpreted as a weakened form of the shoe motif – the character in the story is unaware of his own imminent fate. Finally, the farmer on learning the causes of the three laughs becomes insane.

This denouement is not at all the happy ending of the nineteenth-century Icelandic variants, nor was it universal in Irish tradition. The mermaid redaction as represented by the Kerry variant collected from Pádraig Mac Gearailt in 1936 makes the protagonist, when eventually deserted by his supernatural wife, dig up the stone against which he had once struck his foot. He finds not only one pot of gold but two, the second with assistance from a poor scholar in what looks like an *ad hoc* addition to the story. This realization of the treasure sod motif appears as the second of the mermaid's three causes of laughter; the first is a more feebly expressed form of the second cause in the *leipreachán* tale, with a guest who refuses hospitality but without any consequent mishap; the third concerns the killing of an animal that could have given the protagonist food and clothing, and is an obvious allomotif of the dog in Icelandic tradition. As far as the causes of laughter are concerned, the mermaid tale thus displays more affinity than that of the *leipreachán* with the Icelandic tradition stretching back into the Middle Ages, while the prosperous

---

23. *Ibid.*, Vol. 3: Nýtt safn, Reykjavík 1955, 202-3 and note at 634.

outcome links it, as already mentioned, with Jón Árnason's nineteenth-century witnesses.

III

I shall offer no opinion as to how *The Three Laughs* became integrated into the Irish tale-complex of the man who married the mermaid, but it would seem clear that the *leipreachán* in Ó Súilleabháin's text from county Galway is not just a casual substitution for the mermaid. On the contrary, it is a reflex of a male creature that was more original in Gaelic ecotypes of the story of *The Three Laughs*. That this creature came from the sea is not just likely on the grounds that the mermaid usually assumes its role in the Irish tradition of the story, but well-nigh certain when we consider some Scottish Gaelic variants collected in the 1880s (or earlier) on the islands of Barra and Tiree. This Hebridean material was published after the death of the collector, the Rev. John Gregorson Campbell, minister of Tiree. The credit for introducing it into the comparative discussion is due to Reidar Th. Christiansen, who adduced it in an otherwise somewhat diffuse study of sea creatures in Norwegian folk belief.[24]

On Barra it was told that a fisherman caught a merman and kept him for seven years (the conventional folk expression for an indeterminate length of time, and the length of the *leipreachán's* captivity in the Irish story), but in all those years he said never a word and only laughed at three sights: a servant complaining of poor shoes though he was fated shortly to die, a husband brushing some barley beards off his unfaithful wife, and a young woman weeping bitterly for her laughter of the year before. 'Others say one of the occasions of the laughter was hearing people rating the two dogs belonging to the house, in ignorance that the animals were barking at robbers coming to plunder the house'. Exactly the same story was told on Tiree, where even the merman's name was known: he was called MacCeallaich and was some kind of judge in his underwater country, where the people addressed him as *am Britheir Bán*, 'the fair-haired prior'.[25] Here the treasure sod is gone but the shoes, the telltale evidence of alfresco love-making, and the dogs remain to forge a link between the medieval Welsh, the modern Gaelic, and the Icelandic variants. Warning of impending robbery is precisely the service rendered in *Hálfs saga* by the dog Flóki, whose distinctive characteristic was that he only barked when his master was in danger[26] but who was rewarded, as we have seen, with maltreatment by King Hjörleifr.

Unless the Hebridean reports are forgeries by Campbell or retellings by his informants of the *Vita Merlini* – both of which explanations are in my opinion out of

---

24 Christiansen (1935), 12.
25 Campbell (1908), 194-5.
26 Andrews (1909), chapter 8:2.

the question – they must surely be accepted as proof that *The Three Laughs* is one of those Celtic-Norse hybrids that scholars such as Einar Ól. Sveinsson, Nora K. Chadwick, Bo Almqvist, and myself – all following in the footsteps of Sophus Bugge, Moltke Moe, and Christiansen – have tried to introduce into the historical discussion of early Irish and Icelandic tradition.[27] It is notable that this hybrid character is reflected even at the surface level of vocabulary: the Icelandic word *féþúfa* for the human protagonist's treasure sod is an obviously analogous formation to Old Norse *banaþúfa* and Swedish dialect *döatuva* 'predestined place of death', which as Maura Carney pointed out many years ago offers an exact semantic parallel to the Irish locution *fót báis*.[28] A complete adaptation of the concept of the treasure sod to a maritime setting is found in a legend from the North of Norway referred to by Moltke Moe,[29] where a *marmæle* that has been fished up off Øksnes is put back in the water during a terrible storm. Out in the bay the creature laughs because they are passing over an excellent fishing place that none of the local people know; the man who receives this knowledge is afterwards successful in his fishing when his comrades catch nothing.

There is every reason to suppose that this last-mentioned legend is a rudimentary Norwegian variant of the younger Icelandic and Irish forms of *The Three Laughs* in which the merman's or mermaid's captor lives to enjoy the benefits of his encounter with the creature from the sea. On the other hand, it is not likely as proposed by Christiansen that the shoe-leather motif of the *Vita Merlini* should have been the point of departure for various Norwegian legends in which a merman or mermaid, when asked by its captor what is good for this or that purpose, laughs unkindly at the naivety of the enquirer.[30] Such legends belong rather to an independent branch of tradition with its roots in classical antiquity, the earliest example being the story of how King Midas captures a Silenus or satyr and asks him what is best for mankind. To this the Silenus offers the precociously post-modernist answer that it would be best not to have been born, but here we have an obvious intellectual conceit in the Greek text: more authentic are concrete answers like that offered in the Swiss legend quoted by Moe from Mannhardt's *Wald- und Feldkulte*, where a wild man is tricked into revealing an effective remedy against the plague.[31] Transferred to the Norse Atlantic maritime context this ancient belief legend becomes the vehicle of conventional wisdom about beneficial things as in *Hálfs saga*, or about good fishing tackle as in Jón Guðmundsson's version of *The Three Laughs*; but these Icelandic texts must be viewed as the result of a contamination process whereby the wise counsels of the supernatural creature were drawn, so to speak, into the magnetic field of a specifically Celtic-Norse narrative construction derived from Arthurian legend.

Moltke Moe wished to believe that Merlin had in fact originally answered the existential question addressed to the Silenus in the Greek tale and to the merman in

---

27 See *inter alia* Almqvist (1978-9), 80-105; Chesnutt (1989), 35-63, and references to earlier literature in both articles.
28 Carney (1957), 173-9.
29 Moe (as note 9), ed. 1926, 165-6 quoting O. Nicolaissen.
30 Christiansen (1935), 10-2.
31 Moe (as note 9, ed. 1926), 150-2.

Hálfs saga,[32] and Christiansen, probably influenced by this speculation, unfortunately clouded the issue by quoting a Gaelic legend from the Isle of Skye in which a captive mermaid is asked about the qualities of egg-water.[33] The latter would supposedly explain why some Norwegian mermaid legends have the sea creature mocking her mortal captor because he missed his opportunity to ask her about the best water for brewing.[34] But if there is any connection at all between the egg-water reference from Skye and these Norwegian mermaid legends, the route of diffusion must be from East to West rather than vice versa, whereas the distinctive epic configuration of *The Three Laughs* must undoubtedly take its place among those items of Gaelic tradition that have wandered from the Irish Sea area to Scandinavia by way of the Hebrides.

Appendix

Fear de Mhuintir Shé agus an Mhurúch

Seo scéal a chloisinn ag seandaoine agus ag mórán de lucht siúil, go raibh fear de Mhuntir Shé ar an Ráth fadó i bParóiste Chathair Dónall, ag iascach; agus an-iascaire ab ea é agus ar iascaireacht a bhí sé ag maireachtaint ... bhuel, bhí fáltas talún aige, ach níor mhór é ar fad. Agus, lá 'o sna laethanna, do tháinig sé gan fhios ar an murúch agus í ag cíoradh a cinn, agus do cheap sé gurbh í bean ba bhréatha í do chonaic sé riamh. Agus d'éalaigh sé ina diaidh aniar, agus do thug sé fé bhreith uirthi agus ar an mbrat. Do bheir sé, agus do sciob sé an brat leis, agus má sciob do chuir sí míle béic aisti agus do ghlaoigh sí air é sin a thabhairt di. 'Ní thabharfad,' a dúirt sé, 'agus siúlaigh ort in aonacht liom agus mairfimid go tábhachtach!'

Do chimeád sé greim ar an mbrat, agus ní thabharfadh sé aon ruainne dhe dhi. Agus dúirt sí ná raibh aon ghnó aici ar iompáilt ar a buín féin gan an brat, agus do lean sí é go dtí an tigh, d'iarraidh go bhfaigheadh sí an brat. Agus, más ea, níor thug seisean an brat di, agus do chuir sé in airde ar an lochta é – cúl-lochta a bhí ann - i bpoll éigin ná raibh aon dul aici sin ar é a fháil. Agus mar sin do bhí. Agus bhíodar ag maireachtaint ansin go tábhachtach agus go maith agus iad ag tuiscint a chéile, ar slí go raibh feaimlí eatarthu. Agus ana-sheirbhíseach go léir ab ea í - ní stadadh sí ó éiríodh sí ar maidin go dtí go dtéadh sí a chodladh ach ag obair agus ag gnó agus ag déanamh gach aon ní dár dhein bean riamh, agus í ana-mhaith ar gach aon tslí.

Agus, mar seo, do bhuail an fear isteach ar maidin Dé Luain. Agus dúirt fear an tí – Mac Uí Shé - leis an stróinséar suí aníos agus greim d'ithe ... nár ith sé a bhricfeast fós. 'Ní dhéanfad,' a dúirt sé, agus níorbh aon mhaitheas bheith ag tathaint air - ní dhéanfadh. Agus chuir sise gáire aisti, agus thar éis é a ghabháil

32 *Ibid.*, 167-8.
33 Cf. Campbell (1900), 201.
34 Christiansen (1935), 10-1, 13.

amach d'fhiafraigh a fear – Mac Uí Shé – dhi cad é an bhrí a bhí aici le bheith ag gáirí fén bhfear ó chianaibh. 'Canathaobh ná gáireoinn,' arsa sí, 'nár chuir sé a sheans as a láimh nuair a chuir sé suas den bhia ar maidin Dé Luain, agus ceapaim gur fear gan chiall é!' Sea, bhíodar mar sin, agus bhí sé lá eile ag cuir de agus do bhuail sé a ordóg i gcoinne turtóg cloiche agus do leagadh é agus do gortaíodh go maith é. Agus ní raibh sé baoch den chloich a leag é agus do ghortaigh go mór é, agus chuir sí ana-gháire aisti. Más ea, níor cheistigh sé í in aon chor an lá san agus ... bhí sé chomh mór san thrína chéile. Agus d'imigh sé air i mbun a ghnótha, pé ní a bhí ar siúl aige.

Mar seo, amáireach, do bhí sé ag marú caorach agus chuir sí gáire aisti arís, agus do chuir san an-ionadh air - cad é an tslí go raibh sí ag gáirí nuair a bhí sé ag marú na caorach. Agus d'fhiafraigh sé dhi cad é an bhrí a bhí leis na gáirí nó cad é an bun a bhí aici leis. 'Canathaobh ná beadh,' a dúirt sí, 'tú ag marú an ainmhí,' arsa sí, 'a thabharfadh bia agus éadach duit, agus ní cheapaim go bhfuil aon mheabhair agat agus é a dhéanamh!'

Bhí san go maith. Bhíodar ag cuir díobh mar sin, agus ag cuir díobh go hálainn, agus lá mar seo do thug gnó éigineach in airde ar an gcúl-lochta é. Agus do cheap sé leis féin gur theastaigh ón áit é a réiteach agus do ghlanadh. Bhí mórán de shean-éadaí críonna caite ná raibh aon mhaith iontu dhó féin ná d'aoinne eile ach ag teacht sa tslí air agus ag bailiú salachair, agus dhírigh sé ar bheith ag stobháil na háite agus á glanadh. Agus do bhí sé ag caitheamh anuas gach aon tseana-rud do cheap sé ná raibh aon mhaith ann, go dtí gur bhuail an brat leis. Agus níor chuimhnigh sé riamh air féin, agus do chaith sé anuas é. Agus, i ndomhnach, más ea, do chonaic sí é, agus do bheir sí air agus do bhuail sí uirthi é, agus chuir sí ana-gháire aisti. Agus dúirt sí le Seán Ó Sé go bhfágfadh sí slán agus beannacht aige anois, agus go raibh sí an-bhaoch de í a scaoileadh chun siúil anois féin. 'Dherú, faire, i mbasa,' a dúirt sé, 'ní chuimhneofá ...' D'aithin sé láithreach go raibh an brat caite anuas aige. 'I mbasa ní chuimhneofá,' a dúirt sé, 'ar imeacht uaim!' 'Ó, caithfead imeacht anois,' a dúirt sí, 'tá tréimhse mhaith caite agam in aonacht leat, agus fágaim slán agus beannacht agat! Agus níor cheistís riamh mé,' a dúirt sí, 'i dtaobh an lá úd gur bhuailis t'ordóg i gcoinnibh na cloiche gur chuireas an scairteadh gáire asam!' 'Níor cheistíos,' a dúirt sé, 'mar bhíos ró-mhór thrína chéile, agus tá súil agam go neosfair dom anois é!' 'Neosfad go maith,' a dúirt sí. 'Is é an bhrí a bhí agam leis sin,' a dúirt sí, 'tá corcán óir clúdaithe fén stocán cloiche sin, agus dá nochtfá air bheadh do dhóthain den tsaol agat ann!'

Do bhailibh sí léi, agus d'fhág sí ansan é, agus níorbh aon mhaitheas dó – chuaigh sé chun achaingeachais uirthi fanúint agus más ea níorbh aon mhaitheas é. Agus dúirt sí go raibh sí fanta tamall maith aige agus gur theastaigh uaithi dul ar a buín féin anois, agus a bheith ana-bhaoch di, agus go raibh sise baoch d'eisean agus go mbeadh deireadh acu lena chéile anois.

D'imigh sí. Agus is dócha ná raibh sí imithe i bhfad nuair a dhírigh sé ar an stocán cloiche seo a chuardach, agus do thóg sé aníos í agus do nocht sé síos, agus cad a bhuail leis thíos ach corcán óir. Thóg sé aníos é, agus bhí an corcán a bhí fé slán folláin. Agus do chuir sé an t-ór, is dócha, i gcimeád. Agus bhí an corcán i seirbhís timpeall an tí ag beiriú phrátaí agus ag beiriú gach aon ní a theastaíodh uaidh. Agus níor thóg sé aon *weight* riamh de scríbhneoireacht nó de *bh*rand a bhí ar a chliathán, go ceann tamaill mhaith go dtí gur bhuail scoláire bocht an tslí. Agus do loirg sé óstaíocht na hoíche air, agus do thug sé óstaíocht na hoíche dhó. Agus chonaic sé an corcán so ar an dtine agus é ag beiriú phrátaí, nó pé ní a bhí aige á bheiriú, agus chonaic sé an scríbhneoireacht so air. Agus d'fhiafraigh sé d'fhear an tí cá bhfuair sé é sin mar chorcán. 'Dherú, n'fheadar,' a dúirt an fear, a dúirt sé, 'tá sé sin mar chorcán ansan le fada 'e shaol, agus n'fheadarsa cé a thug ann é,' a dúirt sé. 'Is é réasún domhsa a fhiafraí díot,' a dúirt sé, 'an dtugann tú fé ndeara an scríbhneoireacht san ar a chliathán,' a dúirt sé, 'nó na litreacha san go bhfuil corcán eile mar é san áit go bhfuarthas é seo agus é lán d'ór. 'Ó, *by crile*, a mhaise,' a dúirt sé, 'má tá san amhlaidh – más é sin atá air,' a dúirt sé, 'neosfadsa dhuit cá bhfuarthas é. Do fuarthas é sin,' a dúirt sé, 'sa pháirt seo den chistin, agus ní folamh a bhí sé!' 'Bhuel, anois, tá ceann eile san áit go raibh sé sin,' a dúirt sé, 'agus é lán d'ór.'

Fuaireadar a bpiocóid agus a ringear agus a sluasad, agus dhíríodar ar pholladh arís agus do chuadar tamall maith síos – níosa shia ná a chuadar cheana. Agus cad a bhuail leo thíos ach corcán eile agus é lán d'ór. Agus thug sé leath an óir don scoláire bhocht, agus chinnibh sé féin an leath eile - ar shlí go raibh sé féin agus a fheaimlí go tábhachtach as san amach.

Agus is minic a chuala é sin ag daoine críonna - gur scéal fíor ab ea é sin. Agus an mhuintir Shé atá timpeall an bhaill sin riamh ó shin, deir siad gur de *bh*reed na burúiche [sic] iad agus nuair a raghaidís ar chóngar na farraige go mbeadh tonntacha na farraige ana-thugtha ar bhualadh orthu.

Gefjon, Goddess of the Northern Seas

HILDA ELLIS DAVIDSON

At first sight, it seems surprising that the Scandinavians of the Viking Age, those superb seafarers, had no major deity of the ocean resembling the Greek Poseidon, a powerful member of the inner circle of ruling gods and one who plays a major part in the mythology of the Odyssey. The Vikings might rely on Thor, the sky god, who like Poseidon caused earthquakes and split rocks as well as ruling storms at sea. Alternatively Njord, father of the fertility pair Freyr and Freyja, was a god of seas and lakes; he lived at Nóatún, 'enclosure of ships', and was ill at ease in the mountains, since this caused the break-up of his marriage with the mountain goddess Skadi. Yet he plays little part in the surviving myths, and it is mainly from the evidence of placenames that we assume that he was worshipped by lakes and fiords and on islands in Norway. We know, however, that ships were clearly associated with fertility from early times, occasionally left in bogs as sacrifices, and used at both inhumation and cremation funerals as a resting-place for the dead. The sea was not only a convenient route for merchants, raiders and pirates, but also a rich and essential source of food, and Njord could give aid to fishermen as well as seafarers.

It seems possible that the link between ships and the Otherworld was often by way of a goddess rather than a god. The goddess Cybele came to Rome by ship in a celebrated voyage to bring prosperity to its people. The Germanic goddess Nehalennia, possessing many of the characteristics of the Mother goddesses, had her shrine on the island of Walcheren at a point where travellers leaving for Britain appealed to her for a safe crossing, and she stands beside the prow of a ship on many of the stones raised in her honour. Njord's name corresponds to that of a Danish goddess Nerthus, whose cult, including the washing of her wagon in a sacred lake, was described by Tacitus in the first century AD, and there has been much discussion as to the nature of the link between them.

There is moreover one impressive myth concerned with a deity who possessed power over islands and the sea as well as the fruitful earth, and this is the tale of the ploughing of the goddess Gefjon. Her story is told twice by Snorri Sturluson, the brilliant historian of the early thirteenth century, who was an authority on pre-Christian mythological poetry. He tells it first in the introductory chapter of his Prose *Edda*, and again in *Ynglinga Saga* (5). The two accounts do not completely agree, presumably because Snorri was using them with different purposes in mind.[1]

---

1 Ross (1978), 151ff.

In *Gylfaginning*, the first section of the Prose *Edda*, he is concerned with the coming of the Æsir from Troy, and the story of how Gefjon obtained land for them from a Swedish king, Gylfi, can be compared with the founding of Rome by Aeneas; it brings out the deceptive nature of the old gods, whom he represents as ancient heroes skilled in magic. This serves as a ingenious introduction to Snorri's account of the early myths, since he turns Gylfi into a naive questioner seeking information about the new gods entering the north. In *Ynglinga Saga*, on the other hand, his concern is with the origins of the kings of Norway, and here Gefjon is linked with the royal house of Denmark because of her creation of Sjælland and marriage to Skjold, founder of the Skjoldung dynasty. In both cases Snorri acknowledges his debt to the ninth century poet Bragi Boddason, the Old, stated in Icelandic sources to have been at the court of a Swedish king, but more likely to have been the skald of a chieftain or minor king in Norway.[2] Snorri quotes a stanza not found elsewhere, which has been assumed by Holtsmark,[3] Frank[4] and others to come from *Ragnarsdrápa*, a poem describing several episodes from myth and legend decorating a shield given to the poet by the Danish king Ragnar Lodbrok. Sections of this poem have survived elsewhere, but there is no clear proof that the Gefjon stanza belonged to it. A recent suggestion is that it was an answer to a riddling question, a type of verse known as *grepparminni*, which poets used as a help in remembering myths[5]

The main lines of the tale emerge clearly from Snorri's two versions, in spite of many problems over sources and details. Gefjon visits Gylfi, a king ruling in Sweden, in order to obtain land. In one version she was sent by Odin; in the other she appeared as a vagrant woman, seeking land in order to establish herself in Denmark. The word used in *Gylfaginning* for what she provided in return for the gift is *skemtan* ('entertainment'), a word with a range of meanings, and Kiil[6] suggested that she behaved like Freyja in similar situations and took him as her lover. Indeed in one of the rare references to Gefjon in the poem *Lokasenna*, Loki accuses her of doing just this when she wanted to obtain a jewel from a youth. In the story told in the Prose *Edda*, there were conditions attached to the gift: she was granted as much land as she could plough up with four oxen in a night and a day.

A familiar theme in legend and folktale is a challenge to a man or woman (often the latter) to obtain as much land as can be travelled over in a limited space of time. Axel Olrik in his study of Gefjon published in 1910 (to my mind still unsurpassed), gives examples of this motif from Herodotus and Livy as well as in a number of popular tales from northern Europe. In six tales from Jutland and one from Germany, a plough is used, as in Livy's account, but the conditions are usually fulfilled by walking or riding. There is one interesting example from Iceland

---

2 Turville-Petre (1976), xxiiiff.
3 Holtsmark (1944), 170.
4 Frank (1978), 109.
5 Ross (1978), 157.
6 Kiil (1965).

of a woman settler whose husband had died on the voyage out, establishing her claim to a piece of land by driving a young heifer round it.[7] This is said in *Landnámabók* (H276; II, 321) to be a recognized method by which a woman could claim land; she might not possess more than she could encircle in this way between sunrise and sunset on a spring day. This sounds like a ritual taking over of land rather than a legal requirement, like the custom of men lighting fires when taking new land, and it is possible that the women's custom was linked with the fertility goddess. Ross suggests that Snorri may have had in mind the story of Dido and her trick with an oxhide, which she cut into strips to enclose sufficient land to build Carthage, as told by Geoffrey of Monmouth,[8] but this would not prevent him from also using a native tradition.

The trick employed by Gefjon was the obtaining of supernatural beasts of enormous strength to carry out the ploughing. She is said to have visited a giant by whom she had four sons, something which in *Gylfaginning* seems to have taken place in the past, and these she now transformed into oxen. With these powerful beasts and a great wheeled plough which could cut deeply into the earth she ploughed out a tract of land in eastern Sweden, leaving behind an extensive lake, now Lake Mälar, west of Stockholm. The oxen pulled this land away, and journeyed, presumably through the Baltic Sea, to Denmark, where they left it to form the island of Selund, modern Sjælland (Zealand), Denmark's most fertile region. Here Gefjon dwelt at Leire, and became the wife of Skjold, the founder of the Skjoldung dynasty. It was argued by Boer[9] that Gylfi must have lived in southern Sweden, not as far north as Lake Mälar, and indeed as Olrik originally pointed out, there is no obvious resemblance between the shape of that lake and the Danish island, though both have a complex outline, with many inlets. The water level of Lake Mälar has changed considerably since the early Viking Age. Olrik,[10] however, thought that this might be a rethinking of an early tradition, and that the narrow Oresund between Sjælland and Sweden could have suggested to storytellers a furrow cut by a giant plough, while there were resemblances between the approach through the fiord to Roskilde and that to Sigtuna by way of Lake Mälar. He thought the choice of these two points as the beginning and end of Gefjon's journey was based on the familiar merchant route up and down the Baltic between Roskilde and Sigtuna in early medieval times. The legend is told from the Danish viewpoint and not the Swedish.

Snorri has the admirable habit of often mentioning his sources, although he may give his own ingenious interpretation of an obscure poem or add details of his own to make a satisfactory tale. In this case he quotes the ninth-century strophe from Bragi the Old, concerning the exact meaning of which there has been ample discussion since Olrik's time; readings in various manuscripts differ, and there are some obscure

---

7 Olrik (1910), 7
8 Ross (1978), 163.
9 Boer (1924), 21.
10 Olrik (1910), 10ff.

words, although the language of the stanza is simpler than in other fragments of Bragi's verse. A possible translation of this runs as follows:

> Gefjon, rejoicing, dragged a deep circle of land, Denmark's increase, away from Gylfi, so that steam (spray?) rose from the swift-pulling beasts. The oxen with their four heads and eight brow-ornaments (? horns) went forward hauling the plundered island of meadows.[11]

There are several possible alternatives to the expression 'circle' or 'deep-ring' of land at the beginning: Holtsmark takes the words to refer to the deep-cut plough furrow, while Olrik makes it refer to the goddess as 'deep in wisdom' or 'rejoicing in the treasure of the deep' (i.e. gold). The translation 'ornaments of the brow', depends on use of a word meaning the ornamented beak of a ship (*tingl*), though most translators have kept tungl ('moon'), and taken it as 'moons of the brow', referring to the eyes. Eyes however are not on the forehead, while *tingl* supplies the correct internal rhyme (as pointed out in Vigfusson's Dictionary), and 'beaks of the forehead' seems likely to refer to the oxen's horns. Kiil[12] suggests that one obscure word (*œðal*) usually taken as *óðal*, referring to the land, might instead be from *œðl*, 'incitement to lust', and allude to Gefjon's seducing of Gylfi. While Olrik, Chadwick and Holtsmark emphasize the importance of the plough in the stanza quoted, Kiil and Ross think this element in the tale might be due to Snorri rather than to the original poem, which refers to the dragging of the land rather than the ploughing.

In any case, further possibilities are suggested by this myth of a goddess with power over land and sea. Olrik thought it might indicate rivalry in Sjælland between the merchant seamen and the farmers, and perhaps also between Denmark and Sweden as the centre of worship of the gods. There may also be a link with the tradition of the goddess as the supernatural bride of a king, suggested by her approach to Gylfi and later marriage to the Danish king Skjold.[13] In *Ynglinga Saga*, Gefjon is obeying the commands of Odin, but it seems likely that the earlier tradition on which the poem was based was that of the goddess who created for the Danes their most fertile island. Olrik[14] and Chadwick[15] emphasized the fact that memories of a plough ritual continued there, as in eastern England, well into Christian times. The concept of a powerful goddess with dominion over earth and water in the early myths could have deteriorated in the course of the Viking Age into that of a minor goddess, a follower of Odin and wife of the founder of the dynasty.

---

11 The original stanza, in the form given by Ross (1978:155), is as follows: *Gefjun dró frá Gylfa glöð, djúpröðul, öðla – svát af rennirauknum rauk – Danmarkar auka. Bóru øxn ok átta ennitingl, þars, gingu fir vineyiar viðri valrauf, fiogur haufuð.*
12 Kiil (1965), 65ff.
13 Ross (1978), 159-60.
14 Olrik (1910), 14ff.
15 Chadwick (1924), 245.

It can certainly be claimed for Gefjon that she has strong links both with the sea and with islands in northern tradition. Those who have written about her in recent years have been chiefly interested in the nature of the source material, the interpretation of the stanza attributed to Bragi and the relationship of the two versions given by Snorri, but I would like to return to the approach of two earlier scholars, Olrik and Chadwick, who saw Gefjon as a goddess whose influence may be traced far beyond Denmark. We may begin with her oxen, those cryptic giant beasts with horned heads.

It is difficult to see why the poet enumerated the heads of the oxen in this way; I remain unconvinced by Holtsmark's suggestion that he was describing a picture in which their heads were a dominant feature. She makes a valuable point, however, in reminding us that wheeled ploughs drawn by four oxen rather than two were in use in Denmark by Bragi's time, but probably little known in Norway or Iceland, where the simpler ploughshare, the ard, was still in use.[16] The plough proper was fitted with an asymmetrical share and a mouldboard which turned the earth over instead of merely cutting a shallow furrow, and had a wheeled carriage which meant it could be turned round without tipping over. This meant that more powerful animals were needed to draw it, and four oxen or even more might be used, although a skilled ploughman would then be needed to train and control them.

Emphasis on the number of oxen in the stanza may be due to the poet's unfamiliarity with so large a team; alternatively if this is an answer to a riddle poem,[17] we might expect something unusual about the numbers, as in a riddle about the one-eyed Odin and his eight-legged horse Sleipnir: 'Who are those two who have ten feet, three eyes and one tail?' (*Heiðreks Saga* 11). It was suggested by Cederschiold that there was only one pair of oxen here, but that each was two-headed, due to Gefjon's skill in enchantment;[18] there is however nothing to support this theory, and the heavy plough would need four beasts to draw it. The emphasis on the horned heads (if my suggestion is correct) and mention of the steam (or perhaps sea-spray) rising from their swift movement, may be intended to bring out their supernatural nature and the tremendous power of their swift passage through the ocean, while mention of horns might serve as a reminder that here we have giants transformed into beasts.

It is perhaps worth noting that in ritual ploughing there may be an unusual choice of beasts to draw the plough, and that men or women may be substituted for animals. In Roman tradition, according to Plutarch's *Life of Romulus*, the hero yoked a bull and a cow together when he marked out the course of the walls of Rome, lifting the plough the gap where the gates were to be. A little bronze figure of a ploughman with just such a male and female pair (not used in normal practice) was

---

16 Holtsmark (1944), 177.
17 Ross (1978), 156-7.
18 Holtsmark (1944), 177.

found in a third-century Roman fort at Piercebridge, and is in the British Museum. This was a ritual to mark and hallow the boundaries of newly established territory, as in the case of Gefjon. Another form of ploughing ritual was to create a defensive barrier keeping away harmful influences, and in such cases the ploughing seems often to have been done by women. There are some striking examples from the nineteenth century in Russia, recorded by Ralston,[20] where women in white shifts with loosened hair came together and the oldest was yoked to a plough which was dragged three times round the village. This was a desperate measure resorted to in times of serious epidemics. We have also the yearly plough ceremonies in both England and Denmark when preparations began for the spring sowing, held on Plough Monday, after the Christmas break in eastern England. The gangs of young men who dragged round the plough had various names such as 'plough stots' or 'plough bullocks'.[21] Gefjon with her giant sons transformed into oxen seems a fitting patroness of ceremonies of this kind.

Moreover, there are other powerful supernatural women who behave in a way resembling Gefjon. There is an Irish legend of the Hag of Dingle, in county Kerry, putting a rope of straw around an island and dragging it south to present to her sister Hag of Beare. But the rope broke, and the land split in two to form the islands of Scariff and Deenish.[22] Here no plough is involved, as the island did not have to be cut away from the land. The goddess Brigid according to the *Lebor Gabála* possessed two oxen, which could give her warning of any acts of pillage – presumably of cattle – happening in Ireland, and two plains in Carlow and Tipperary were said to be called after them.[23] It may be assumed that she used these for ploughing. St Brigid also was connected with the harvest, since seed grain was hung up beside her cross on her festival on 1st February, and kept there until it was time for sowing.[24]

Again, from Wales, we have the tradition of the Lady of the Lake, recorded in Carmarthenshire in the nineteenth century.[25] She brought a herd of wondrous cattle out of the water when she consented to marry a local farmer, and when years later he unwittingly broke the conditions she had laid down, she returned to her home under the lake, and called her cattle to accompany her, summoning them by name. In a version quoted by Sir John Rhys[26] she also called her four grey oxen, ploughing in a field six miles away. They came dragging the plough with them, and it was said that the furrow cut in the land could once be seen clearly. A woman in 1881 claimed to remember how people gathered at the lake on the first Sunday in

19 Manning (1971).
20 Ralston (1872), 396ff.
21 Hole (1978), 238.
22 Ó hÓgáin (1990), 67.
23 Ó hÓgáin (1990), 60.
24 Danaher (1972), 35.
25 Wood (1992).
26 Rhys (1901), I, 15.

August, hoping to see the water boil up as a sign that the Lady and her oxen would appear. Here again a supernatural woman is linked both with water and the ploughing of the land.

From Germanic areas there are also traditions of supernatural women who travel through the countryside with a plough, such as Holde and Holle from western and central Germany and Berchte or Perchte from upper Germany, Switzerland and Austria. In 1913 Waschnitius published a remarkable collection of legends and beliefs about such figures, showing how rich is the material available. The women were both benevolent and threatening; they helped young wives, girls and children, encouraging them in spinning and housekeeping and at time of childbirth, but punished those who were lazy, slovenly or disobedient. They were frequently said to travel with a plough around the countryside, in a way reminiscent of the journey of the fertility goddess to bless the land in pre-Christian times, and on these occasions they might be accompanied by a host of tiny children; it was suggested that these were children who had died unbaptized, or human offspring replaced by changelings, but another possibility is that they were the souls of the unborn. There are local tales of the plough breaking down and of the supernatural woman who guided it rewarding a helper by giving him chips of wood which later turned into gold.[27] The idea behind the taking of the plough round the countryside seems to be that it brought good fortune and prosperity, gifts of a benevolent goddess. Gefjon and her plough thus fit into a larger framework of the cult of a goddess associated with the fertility of both land and water.

But what of her connection with the sea? Grimm[28] called attention to the OE word *geofon* (also *geofen, gifen, gyfen*), a poetic name for the sea. This is used several times in *Beowulf,* and Battaglia has suggested that here we have memories of the same goddess, now personifying the sea but still recognizable to those familiar with Danish traditions about the goddess. In one passage (47ff.) where it is usually part of the verb *gifan* (to give), he thinks it refers to Gefjon bearing away the dead Scyld, who was her husband in Danish tradition.[29] In line 362, Beowulf is said to come with his followers far over Gefjon's realm when he crosses the Baltic to visit the Danish king on Sjælland. In line 515, the word appears in Breca's account of Beowulf's swimming contest, describing how Gefjon was stirred up into waves, and the young hero behaved as if in enemy territory, swimming with a naked sword in his hand. In line 1394, there is a reference to Gefjon's *grund* (earth or bottom of lake or sea) as a place to which Grendel might escape. Finally, in line 1690, there is a reference to the 'flood of Gefjon' destroying the race of giants, in the inscription on the hilt of the wonderful sword from the lake.

Battaglia suggests that these references are based on a background of hostility

---

27 Grimm (1883), I, 275ff.
28 Grimm (1883), I, 239.
29 Battaglia (1991), 47ff.

between the worshippers of the warrior gods, represented by Beowulf, and the earlier earth goddess with her powers over land and water alike. In Grendel's mother we may perhaps see an ancient goddess figure who has been demoted into a monstrous hag with a ogre-like son. I have elsewhere pointed out that she possesses characteristics of the Mistress of the Animals, the early hunting goddess who protected the creatures of the forest, permitting hunters to kill them as long as they strictly observed her behests.[30]

There is also the possible connection with the sea-giants, a mysterious race of beings to which Gylfi may have originally belonged. The chief of these was Ægir, whose wife Ran was said to welcome drowned seamen; in a late saga it is said to be prudent to carry a little gold when going to sea, in case it was needed for an offering to Ran (*Fridþjofs Saga* 6). Ægir held feasts for the gods and goddesses, like that into which Loki forced his way in the poem 'Lokasenna'. Just as Snorri begins the first section of the Prose *Edda* with Gylfi, so he introduces the second, *Skáldskaparmál*, with Ægir, who like Gylfi, asks leading questions about gods and heroes. Ægir is also called Hler or Gymir, according to Snorri, and more names of sea kings are given in his word lists in the Prose *Edda*. They may have been supernatural figures, among whom Gefjon moved in her character of goddess of the ocean. It was said that Ægir and Ran had nine daughters, the waves of the sea, and Dumézil[31] went in search of a similar Welsh tradition in which every ninth wave was more powerful than the rest, and they were known as white sheep while the ninth was a ram, from the flocks of Gwenhidwy. The concept of cattle and sheep from under the water is widespread in northern Europe, the property of underwater rulers whose daughters might marry mortals.

There seems ample indication that Gefjon represents one aspect of a once powerful goddess in the north, the figure represented in Scandinavian myths as either Frigg, the wife of Odin, or Freyja, sister of the fertility god Freyr. Freyja, desired by gods, giants and dwarves alike, acted as dispenser of bounty and inspirer of sexual love between men and women like the Greek Aphrodite. In her recent study of Freyja as 'Great Goddess of the North', Britt-Mari Näsström takes Gefjon to be a by-name of Freyja, emphasising her powers of giving,[32] and sees it as one of the various 'giving' names associated with fertility goddesses.[33] In *Lokasenna* (21), Gefjon is said to have knowledge of the future, like that attributed to Frigg, and it would seem that she was no minor goddess. Christian writers identify her with Athena and Vesta, two major 'virgin' goddesses, and again with Diana, the Roman equivalent of Artemis.[34] 'Virgin' goddesses could be independent deities not married to gods, although they might take lovers.[35] Snorri states that Gefjon welcomed

---

30 This is discussed in Davidson (1998), Chapter 1 ('The Mistress of the Animals').
31 Dumézil (1973), 143ff.
32 Näsström (1995), 51.
33 de Vries (1957), II, 329.
34 Ross (1978), 155.
35 Guthrie (1950), 102-3.

unmarried girls after death, and this is in keeping with the function of Artemis as guardian and instructress of young girls.[36]

It would seem that in Bragi's surviving verse and Snorri's tale we have traces of what is likely to be an early myth of the leading northern goddess, ruling over both land and sea. Like the sea, she offered adventure, food, and prosperity to northern peoples, but might also feature as deceiver and destroyer. Early huntsmen and fishermen might well have turned to such a deity for help and protection, but in the Viking Age seafaring warriors preferred Odin and Thor, and we are left with little more than a poetic personification of the sea as a vague feminine figure, like Ran in the work of the Icelandic poets. But some of the power in the old tale of Gefjon, creator of islands, has been superbly expressed in the great fountain at the water's edge in Copenhagen, depicting her ploughing through the sea in a cloud of rising spray with her giant beasts.

36 Kahil (1977).

Ormur, Marmennill, Nykur:
Three Creatures of the Watery World

Davíð Erlingsson

I

These ruminations on Icelandic medieval and later traditions concerning three particular water-world inhabitants – *ormur*, the great, snake-like water-monster, the *marmennill*, or merman, and the *nykur*, or water-horse – might be regarded as prolegomena to a thoroughly desirable but rather more ambitious project, namely, an examination and survey of the whole corpus of Icelandic stories of supernatural beings living in or under water. Nevertheless, it is my hope that these remarks may be of interest and, perhaps, succeed in stimulating further work in the area.

The classification proposed by the German scholar Konrad Maurer and followed by Jón Árnason, covering the entire corpus of Icelandic water-beings (both as regards the folklore contained in a variety of literary sources dating from the middle ages onwards, and the folklore collected in recent centuries, most especially during the last century) will serve admirably as a starting point. In this classification, the *marmennill* represents the anthropomorphous and the *nykur* the zoomorphous group. The third group – namely monsters, or skrímsli of various kinds – includes beings which do not fit into either of the previous categories, because they are not readily paralleled in nature; it is here represented by the ormur, or water-dragon.

II

Lagarfljótsormurinn

It is characteristic of the snake-like dragon living in water to have begun life, in some way or other, on dry land and, likewise, at a certain stage of its development, to have abandoned the land for the subaquaean realms. Such was the fate of the most famous of freshwater monsters in Iceland, *Lagarfljótsormurinn*. There is every reason to suppose that this beast was believed to have existed already in the Middle Ages, although I am not aware of any sources from that period. Reports of it begin around the year 1600, and these aver that it had been in existence since at least the early thirteenth century, when Bishop Guðmundr Arason the Good (*inn góði*), a legendary tamer of the forces of wild nature, is said to have greatly diminished by exorcism the monster's power for evil. Prior to this, two Finns (or Lapps), had managed to tie the beast down at both ends. Thus bound, the monster will remain alive until the end of time, with only limited potential for destruction. It has often been noted, of course, that the notions about *Lagarfljótsormurinn* resemble those of the famous *Miðgarðsormur*.

In various parts of Iceland, one finds quite a number of other snake-like river and lake monsters, although none of them is quite as well-known or credited with being quite as powerful. At the turn of the century, Ólafur Davíðsson surveyed supernatural beings, both freshwater and marine[1] and accounted for four others (those found in the rivers Hvítá and Skaftá, and in the lakes Skorradalsvatn and Kleifarvatn). All share the same origin legend, namely that sustained by the belief that, when brought together, a little worm and a piece of gold will both grow large. In the Icelandic legends, this 'worm' is most often the little snail called *brekkusnigill*, sometimes called *lyngormur*. In Icelandic *ormur* means both 'worm' and 'snake'. After a while, the worm will become dangerous, but it loves the gold so much, that it would rather be killed than separated from it. If such 'worms' are not killed (as, for example, in the case of the ancient 'worm' of princess Þóra which was killed by Ragnarr loðbrók [the well-known 'hairy-breeks'], according to his *fornaldarsaga*) they are usually cast into water, clutching on to their precious golden 'bed'. There, a fantastic transition occurs, and they grow to the immense proportions reported in Lagarfljót, in other places such as Loch Ness (Scotland), and at Liavåg [Hjörungavágr] in Sunnmöre (Norway). The legendary medieval beast of Hjörungavágr I would wish to treat as a special parallel to the worm in Lagarfljót. The legendary saga's account of the origin of the Lagarfljót 'worm' is possibly the earliest Nordic literary version of this motif.

Ólafur Davíðsson considers the belief that if 'worm' and gold are brought into close physical association this will result in the growth of both and be the core around which origin legends are formed. In a manner of speaking, this ancient idea survives in the language up to the present day, but this can hardly be accounted a matter of belief in any concrete sense. At an abstract level, the tradition is alive and, somehow, still meaningful, in other words it is credited with a metaphorical dimension. While we might not wish to define its content too closely in this context, we may sometimes feel that it has much to do with the consequences of professing the wrong values. In my view, the story of the dragon of Liavåg, or Hjörungavágr, as reflected in a variety of sources, constitutes an adequate parallel to the *Lagarfljótsormur*, and here the sources are medieval.

---

1 Davíðsson in Guðmundsson (1949), 265-366 (originally published in *Tímarit* [1900], 159-88, [1901], 127-76, and [1902], 29-47). This good and at all times useful survey article by one of the best connoiseurs, collectors, and editors of Icelandic folktales and poetry (who died in 1903 at the age of 41) was written with the not unknown, but still rather surprising dual zealous object, of saving these traditions and beliefs from oblivion, and at the same time and by the very same means – because they were seen as being so detrimental to social progress – eliminating them from the scene. Guðmundsson remarks on this, admitting that such beliefs have indeed lost much ground, but doubting that they could be regarded as entirely extinct by the middle of this century, as, doubtless, many people liked to think.

In this instance, we are greatly assisted by Dag Strömbäck's sensitive interpretation of the assembled source material.[2]

The story of how this dragon or water-monster came into being is connected with a famous Nordic naval battle which is supposed to have taken place at Hjörungavágr, in all likelihood some time towards the end of the tenth century (probably c. 990). This battle became the focal point of a great deal of highly imaginative storytelling which centred around a heroic legend climaxing in the tragic death of the champions of the Viking brotherhood from Jóm, the *Jómsvíkingar*. The members of this brotherhood carried out a foolish and ill-fated expedition to Norway and were defeated by Earl Hákon Sigurðarson, presumably at the place which is now called Liavåg in Sunnmöre. What interests us particularly, is the fate which befell one of the leaders of this band, one Búi Vésetason, a man of noble birth from Bornholm [Borgundarhólmr]. He had earlier robbed two chests of gold from the Danish king, Haraldr Gormsson. These chests had previously played a remarkable part in *Jómsvíkingasaga's* account of murderous intrigues within the royal family in Denmark, and the saga depicts the Norwegian, Hákon Sigurðarson, as having a central role in these atrocities. In the end, it is the same Hákon Sigurðarson who defeats the Danish-instigated expedition of the *Jómsvíkingar*. The gold, here as elsewhere symbolizing evil, is thus a thematic thread, one of the threads by which the whole of *Jómsvíkingasaga* hangs together. Búi Vésetason had the chests with him and, when the end was nigh, all versions of the saga confirm that he seized them, crying out: 'Over board, all Búi's men' (*Fyrir borð, allir Búa liðar*) or the like – and jumped overboard into the sea, carrying the chests, and Búi became a water-worm'. Here, at the point of transition to the water-world, the alliterative phrasing of the cry may, perhaps, have formed the core of an oral story about Búi's death. One version of the saga, preserved only in Arngrímur Jónsson's Latin translation dating from the end of the sixteenth century, may be worth recalling at this point:

A certain Þorkell miðlangr, one of Earl Hákon's men, boarded Búi's ship and attacked him, cutting off part of his nose, his front teeth and chin, with his sword. Búi retorted that surely the maidens in Denmark would be less desirous of kissing him after this, following which he hewed his attacker in twain, and jumped into the sea with the two chests of gold that he had once robbed from Strút-Haraldr. This was the parting of that man who, according to common opinion, turned into an enormous serpent and occupies the bay, lying upon the gold. The serpent is said to have been seen on many occasions.[3]

This origin legend obviously has nothing in common with the *Lagarfljótsormur* legend, apart from the basic element of 'brooding' on gold, or exhibiting some symbiosis with it. It is similar in part to the gold story which holds together the heroic poems in the

2 Strömbäck (1955), 383-9.
3 Cf. Arngrimi Jonae, *Opera omnia latine conscripta* in Benediktsson (1950), 136.

Codex Regius of the *Edda*, giving unity to that collection though the relevant parts of the story lack the sub-aquatic setting. However, a summary of the varying prose and verse accounts about the monster of Hjörungavágr reveals an impressive resemblance to the legends about the monster of Lagarfljót:

- it is dangerous to maritime traffic in the bay;
- it is immensely long;
- it manifests itself by rising clear of the water in a number of arcs or curves;
- when these are seen, it usually forebodes bad news.

According to a fourteenth-century version of the legend or saga of the aforementioned Bishop Guðmundur góði (ob.1237), originally composed in Latin and intended for international reading in the church, the bishop came sailing to the bay where the battle had taken place. The sailors on the ship wanted to enter the harbour there, but this was impossible since the 'worm' was lying on the surface of the water, stretching right across the bay and blocking the passage. The bishop then went up on the prow of the ship, said some prayers and sprinkled holy water on the beast. The monster then moved away, and the boat was able to make harbour. The following morning the company was graced by the sight of one of the miracles of the Lord. The dead beast, in twelve separate pieces, had now landed on the shore. Before that, it had sometimes been seen in the form of twelve humps arching out of the water. This is mentioned in Arngrímur Jónsson's *Guðmundarsaga*. The same miracle is also commemorated in a poem about Guðmundur by Abbot Árni Jónsson.[4] There it is the making of the sign of the cross which concisely severs the beast.

Dag Strömbäck points to important differences between the sources. It is in the texts of the so-called separate *Jómsvíkinga saga* that we find the most developed chests-and-serpent theme. According to Ólafur Halldórsson this text is not later than c.1220-30.[5] On the other hand, Búi is also mentioned in some old poems but the monster is not referred to explicitly in any source earlier than in the version(s) incorporated in the kings' saga compilations of *Fagrskinna* and later *Heimskringla*, though the chests of gold and Búi's final fate together with his cry to his men are mentioned. Although there also is some poetry preserved, in which Búi is mentioned, the monster is not found explicitly in place until the Orkney bishop Bjarni Kolbeinsson's poem, *Jómsvíkingadrápa*, which is probably not much earlier than 1200. Bjarni Kolbeinsson refers to Búi as 'Gull-Búi', which is altogether fitting since the earliest named owner of this particular treasure had been the Danish prince Gull-Haraldr (according to *Jómsvíkinga saga*). This calls to mind the story of Gull-Þórir, protagonist of the Þorskfirðinga saga who also ends his life by taking a chest of gold into or underneath a waterfall, which, of course, has been called 'Gullfoss' from then on. This treasure Þórir had acquired from a magnificent flying dragon which kept it underneath a waterfall

---

4 For the texts here cited, see Strömbäck (1955).
5 Halldórsson (1969), 7 ff. (introduction to his edition of the separate Ms AM 291, 4to-version)

at a certain place in the north-east, sometimes called Finnmörk, famed as the home of magical sorcery. Þórir is worthy of mention here because – although 'worms' and dragons are common enough in literature and folktales – he is the only Icelander from the saga time to which this motif has been attached, and the only person to have carried out such an action in Iceland.

This also affords us the opportunity of deliberating upon the name Gullfoss, taken to mean 'the golden waterfall', a name applied to several places in Iceland. Doubtless, the interplay of light on falling or running water can easily evoke the idea of gold. There is reason to be reminded also of the common poetic type of kenning where the precious metal is called 'the fire in the water' or 'that which burns in the water', or the like. The human predeliction for sometimes making notions concrete and for personifying ideas might have arisen in connection with just such a play of light, when things may seem other than what they are.

I will conclude this section by quoting the end of the *Flateyjarbók* version of the fall of the Jomsvikings, evidently composed by a critical mind. It goes as follows:

There is a saying later that Búi became a 'worm' and lay down on his chests, but we think the reason for that to have been, that the 'worm' must have been seen in Hjörunga bay, and it is possible that some evil wight did lie down upon the treasure and was seen there afterwards, but we can not tell which is true. It may also be that neither is true because things may appear in many ways.

Clearly, the writer does not deny the existence of evil beings resting upon treasure, but he does not think people can turn into such monsters.

III

The (more-or-less human) *marmennill*

We now address the issue of water-creatures which resemble humans, and here it is natural to begin by turning to the major printed folktale collections, from Jón Árnason onwards.[6] Our attention is soon caught by the increasing drive to systematize and classify their materials by collectors and editors. Much of these efforts at classification are now perhaps inevitably considered to be of little value. On the one hand, in the light of the far from uniform nature of the tradition, there may not have been a very good basis for them. On the other hand, it cannot be maintained that, in a living and developing culture, no attempt should be made to establish some sort of basic classification, expressing differences between, and

---

6 The main printed collections which I have in mind here are: Árnason (1961); Davíðsson (1935-9); Sigfússon (1982-93). The latter publication is the largest and most varied printed source of material on water-creatures; see volume IV, pp. 1-164 and pp. 165-202 for more fantastic, and less fantastic or more natural creatures respectively.

varying attitudes to, the different types of the man-like, the animal-like and the in-between (not to speak of the completely monstrous water-beings, for example in the not so traditionally divergent parts of nineteenth-century Iceland). Nevertheless, the overall picture was not clear, nor fixed, except in the broadest outline, thus probably rendering it difficult to work out a system of classification with any measure of certainty or degree of exactitude. What we have to hand are large collections of memorates and legends detailing various dealings with unfriendly or neutral water-creatures taking a wide variety of physical shapes. To mention a specific example, in my opinion, the corpus of material in Sigfús Sigfússon's collections from the early years of this century does not provide sufficient justification for the pigeonhole system of classification he promulgates and presses into service.

Writers on Icelandic water-beings prior to the nineteenth century do not appear to have had a great deal of popular material at their immediate disposal. Bishop Gísli Oddsson, writing in the early seventeenth century[7] speaks of *hafmenn*, 'men of the sea', and immediately arouses my suspicion with his declaration that it is the male of this species which is called *marbendill*, and that the female is called *margýgur*. This pronouncement sounds perilously like a construct based on etymological thinking. The good bishop's description of both these creatures does not seem to match more recently recorded notions of them, where the *marmennill* or *marbendill* is usually described as being almost perfectly human, and the *margýgur* markedly less so. The *margýgur* is a very dangerous beast, female of course (since *gýgur* is a troll-wife), and in certain legends she is also depicted as a siren, complete with treacherous song. These two creatures can hardly be regarded as being of the same species.

Gísli Oddsson also speaks of another evil beast called *hafstrambur*. It stands upright, partly rising out of the water, pale or pink in colour, and resembles a human corpse wrapped for burial. This beast is usually glimpsed going about its ghastly business of picking fishermen one by one out of their boats, tearing them to pieces and devouring them under the water. Those who manage to escape such scenes of horror subsequently tell their story. Gísli here mentions also a smaller beast, similar in shape, which, by contrast, is not harmful to people. It is called *mjaldur*, and whenever it is sighted, this is taken as an indication that a good catch of fish will be made in that very place. In later tradition, however, the *mjaldur* is usually accorded a sinister role.

It is reasonable to suppose – as the variety of memorates, descriptions and tales in Sigfús Sigfússon's collection would seem to confirm – that the dividing lines between degrees of anthropomorphism and various degrees and kinds of theriomorphism cannot be drawn with full certainty. Sigfús Sigfússon has difficulties in slotting the

---

7 His *De mirabilibus Islandiæ* – consulted here in Rafnar (1942) – and published together with a translation of another of Gísli's works, *Annalium in Islandia farrago*; see especially chapters 6 and 7 and, for the *hafstrambur*, 71.

material into his elaborate system of categories. Still, in a general way, among Sigfús Sigfússon's four main classes of underwater beings, the *marbendlar* are plainly the human ones, and his other three classes – namely *hafmenn, hafstrambar* and margýgjar, are not really human at all.

The merman or the little merman, *marmennill, marbendill* etc. in the vernacular, is, of course, a most fitting designation for characterizing otherworld people as human, at least in terms of those essential human-like qualities which form a central part of most of the stories about him. Collectors and scholars frequently remark upon this, often comparing the similarities observed between the *marmennlar* and human kind with those noted between humans and the supernatural people who live on land in close proximity to us, namely the elves or the so-called 'hidden-folk' (*álfar* or *huldufólk*). In a way, both of these realms – that of the *marmennill* below water and that of the 'hidden-folk' (usually beneath the ground) – are mirrors of our world, of human reality. This relatively close mirroring is obviously a function which the more distant, the semi-monstrous or animal-like beings, are not capable of sustaining. Their role is a different one. One is tempted to say that the *álfar* and the *marmennlar* both represent an Other of the Self, whereas other mythical creatures display demonic features in ways more distant from man's ideas about himself. In this connection I also feel tempted to quote the poet, W. H. Auden, who declared that:

> Present in every human being are two desires, a desire to know the truth about the primary world, the given world outside ourselves in which we are born, live, love, hate and die, and the desire to make new secondary worlds of our own, or if we cannot make them ourselves, to share in the secondary worlds of those who can.[8]

Auden was referring to the human need for access to the worlds of imagination of saga and of poetry. In a context like the present, there is no doubt in my mind that we are right to understand Auden's words as defining not merely a desire for, but also a general human requirement to imagine, other or secondary worlds, the better to know our own. In some cases we also seek to extend our primary world to encompass the secondary worlds of the present investigation. This is part and parcel of our endeavour to know our place and ourselves and to achieve a feeling of safety at home in an otherwise complicated and dangerous universe.

This is not idle talk when dealing with the *marmennill*. Endowed as he is with both a similarity to man and yet some difference, he is believed to have knowledge not possessed by ordinary mortals, and it is man's attempts to gain this knowledge from him and benefit by it that lies at the very heart of the *marmennill* traditions. In fact, the acquisition of this knowledge is what the *marmennill* tales are really about.

---

8 These are the opening words of his lecture entitled 'The World of Sagas', in Auden (1968), 46.

This mysterious knowledge is also the necessary premise of the motif which is the core of the international story – told of the merman in Iceland but elsewhere mostly of other wise beings – namely, the motif of the three laughs at man's stupid behaviour because of his ignorance of what really lies at the bottom of things. Thus, in a direct way, the *marmennill* stories may be said to give thematic resonance to man's search for knowledge.

The *marmennill* does not usually come out of the water of his own volition, but gets dragged up on a fisherman's hook. He is captured, and people ask him questions. But he is silent and refuses to share his knowledge until, at the very point of being released into the sea at the place where he was captured, he speaks and delivers some answers.

We meet with two occurrences of the wise *marmenill* in medieval Icelandic texts. One of these stories is set in Iceland, where the merman is pulled out, gives a prediction about the future of his captor and his family, and is then released right away. I will deal with this story later in another connection. The other occurrence is the version in *Hálfs saga ok Hálfsrekka.*[9] This adaptation has occasioned some changes from the international pattern familiar to us, which have not been adopted in Icelandic tradition. Hálfs saga deals with legendary kings in Norway. The merman tale has beem included in the episode about King *Hjörleifr kvensami* ('Hjörleifr, the womanizer').

First, two poor fishermen catch the merman and bring him as a gift to their king. He is silent, but his laughs show that he is mentally alert. He is promised release, and then predicts impending misfortunes in Hjörleifur's land, arising from his affairs. As an afterthought, when he is being released, a man on the boat asks him a question which I have not seen in other versions, but which very well illustrates my point. The question is: *Hvat er manni bezt?* ('What is best for people?') I think this question can be fairly perceived as one possible summation of the human, as well as the humanist and scientific, quest for knowledge, in this case, as so often in medieval and folk legendry, by its being extracted from a wise member of another world.

To this question, the *marmennill* replies in a stanza including a triad:

> Cold water for the eyes,
> lean whalemeat for the teeth,
> linen for the body -
> let me back in the sea!
> Never of a day
> shall a man pull me up into a boat
> from the bottom of the sea.[10]

---

9 The latest and best scholarly edition of this important text is that by Seelow (1981); for the *marmennill* story, see chapter 3.
10 Seelow (1981), 175.

I believe we may be justified in identifying this as part of the Otherworld view-point; it may be said, at least, that the point of view is not solely that of his captors, although, perhaps, there may not be much to differentiate between these two worlds as to what are to be considered the best things in life. The *marmennill* relates the question to himself as a human being, enunciates his reply, and descends to his cherished home.

The *fornaldarsaga* tells us that King Hjörleifur rewarded the two poor fishermen who had brought him this potential source of knowledge, with some land, and also gave them a male and a female slave to work it for them. If this was not a royal endowment establishing something tantamount to an academic institution, I hardly know what might qualify as such. It certainly is indicative of the saga writer's appreciation of scholarship that he permits its king to do this. This may then also be taken as an indication of the prestige and esteem appropriate to the *marmennill* as a source of knowledge.

In the most important *marmennill* legend type, usually nothing of importance happens in the interval between the merman's capture and his release, other than that which is directly concerned with efforts to acquire knowledge from him. The laughs, three in number, at the tragic folly of people's ignorance, and their later explanation, are, internationally, the most frequent and widespread motifs. Elsewhere, though, this motif is often attached to other kinds of supernatural beings. On occasion, other incidents occur in which the merman's wisdom, and especially his prescience, is revealed.

The literary version in *Hálfs saga* only contains one laugh, although at first sight there seem to be two reasons for the *marmennill* to give vent to laughter. However, considering the connection perceivable between the causes of laughter, on closer inspection, there may be only one reason after all. We are dealing here with the unfaithful wife vs. the faithful dog motif: the man who beats his dog when by rights he should be chastizing his wife. It is interesting to note that, outside of Icelandic tradition, it may well be that the dog does not have any role to play in the matter, although I cannot claim to have pursued this issue widely and diligently. There can be little doubt that the laughing-matters, as one might say, must have been three in number in the source-version for *Hálfs saga*. This three-fold laugh motif also occurs widely attached to other figures and in other contexts, although some of that material could perhaps still be classified as belonging to the same legend type: it is told of the prophet Merlin, by Geoffrey of Monmouth (writing c. 1130-40); such laughter also grips the Greek satyr Silenos, a demon in a tale of King Solomon in the *Talmud*, and various remarkable fishes in some oriental tales, usually revealing the unfaithfulness of queens. We do not find much mention of a human of the sea in the same laughing role outside of Norway and Iceland, but this motif is often connected also with some water-beings in a way that seems likely to be significant, though I am not in a position to investigate the matter further at this point. If A.H. Krappe was right concerning Hebrew or Indian origins of the Prophet's Laugh[11] – and, furthermore, if we can establish this motif as the backbone of the legend – then, perhaps, we may regard the Norwegian-Icelandic *marmennill* legend as an oikotype of a much older clever fish story. Perhaps, Einar Ólafur Sveinsson is right in tending to regard the *marmennill* as a Nordic innovation in this story, whose function is to enter the proceedings in the role of an appropriate native stand-in.[12]

Within this general ambit, and with many problems remaining unsolved, it is of particular interest – and not merely of Irish-Icelandic interest – to draw attention to a comparison between, on the one hand, the *fornaldarsaga*-narrative which forms the frame and context of the *marmennill* story in *Hálfs saga*, and, on the other, the story of the dealings of the legendary Irish king, Fergus Mac Léite with a king from another world, in a situation where the three laughs' motif occurs. Its occurrence in both these sources invites comparison, then, between the episode in *Hálfs saga* concerning the legendary king *Hjörleifr inn kvensami* and an episode concerning Fergus in *Imthechta Tuaithe Luchra ocus oided Fergusa* (a text from the thirteenth or fourteenth century).[13]

Both stories tell of a captive wizard who laughs at the ignorance of men; in the Irish story, he laughs three times. The prophet in *Imthechta Tuaithe Luchra* is king of the elves or a dwarf-like people, exceedingly small like himself, whose other-world home is rather mysteriously located across the sea. The 'laughing-matters' motif is present in both sagas, but, apart from the unfaithfulness of a wife, the details are not the same and, therefore, do not lend themselves easily to comparison. Included, in the Irish story, is the motif of the man who complains of the thinness of the soles of the shoes which he is buying, not realising how short a time he himself has left to wear them.

When, to this basic point of agreement, we add the fact that in these two literary works – despite their many substantial differences – the life and circumstances of their hero kings also have several other important traits in common, it seems impossible not to conclude that the two works must be connected in some way as to their origins. The common traits to which I refer may be summarized as follows:

- The heroes of both stories are exceedingly uxorious kings; we are regaled with stories about this aspect of their character and behaviour.

---

11 See Krappe (1929), 340-61; cf. also the article by Michael Chesnutt in this volume.
12 See his summary treatment of this matter, mentioning various parallels in Sveinsson (1929), Einleitung, p. xliv.
13 O'Grady (1892), 238-52. I have attempted to identify the salient points for comparison in Erlingsson (1980), 198-205 – the volume dedicated to Einar Ólafur Sveinsson, for his 80th birthday in 1979.

- They both have dealings with people of other worlds; in this respect both works share at least two special points which must be counted rare and important markers

  a) for both of these earthly kings, a being or beings from the otherworld pollute(s) the drinking water with urine (the *brunnmigi* ['well-pisser']) in *Hálfssaga*, or with fæces (in the Irish story, the elves pollute all the running water in Fergus' land);

  b) the captured wizard story.

- Both these kings have inimical encounters with other strange creatures or monsters of the sea or with lake monsters, though the beasts in question are not really similar.

The monster of Loch Rudraige is the cause of Fergus's death after his fight with it. This is the climax of his story, his heroic, violent and tragic death (*oided*), to which the preceding narrative forms the preamble.

As to the Norse king, when Hjörleifr was sailing home with one of his new wives, a 'mountain in the shape of a man' rose out of the sea and spoke a verse predicting the death *inter alia* of that new wife, and Hjörleifr's future capture.

Undoubtedly, the last word has not been said about these matters; much work remains to be done in reassessing and achieving a fuller understanding of them. In this context, Einar Ólafur Sveinsson's idea that the *marmennill* in the prophetic laughter legend is a west Nordic innovation should perhaps be taken to mean that the degree of innovation involved here merely consisted in finding on home ground a familiar personality to take the central role of the deliverer of the three laughs, the central character in this migratory legend. This might have meant little more than simply adding the three laughs to the role of an actor already known for his prophetic powers in the tradition. The *marmennill* episode in the story of Sel-Þórir in *Landnámabók* – which I will mention shortly in connection with the water-horse stories – would then fit our notion of the existence of a Norse-Icelandic merman tale prior to the advent of the three laughs motif.

The *marmennill* stories which have been preserved for us in modern folktale collections are not greatly varied in nature. In some ways they illustrate the kind of sameness which I have already mentioned. The *marmennlar* seem to lead a perfectly normal and happy life in the water, and they can also go ashore though they do so only rarely and never remain on land. Typically, the merman – seldom a woman of that breed – gets accidentally hooked by the fisherman while adjusting the chimney on the roof. The *marmennlar* dress in linen, as the triadic stanza in *Hálfs saga* attests. This triad reflects their similarities with humans and, at the same time, differences. Other motifs and characteristics show similarities to the alternative world of the elves or 'hidden-folk'. We may also consider in this context the many stories of a merman expressing gratitude for his release by sending cows ashore, the sea-cows which were always better than the home-bred variety. Occasionally this sea-cow motif is incorporated into stories sporting the three laughs motif, but, sometimes, it is treated in its own right. If the fisherman-farmer is lucky enough to burst the bubble on the nose of these cattle, they cannot return to their sea habitat. These stories were often told to explain placenames, and they always emphasize that these 'sea-grey' animals are a superior breed to ordinary cows.

Some *marmennill* legends are about luck in fishing: in gratitude for releasing the marmennill, the fisherman meets with success and his good fortune is noted by the fishing community. For this reason, the *marmennlar* are seldom taken ashore as captives, but rather released by their captors in the hope that they will gain a reward. On most occasions, an attempt is made by some temptation to force the *marmennill* to speak and share his wisdom, or some indication of a temptation to do so is given.

A particularly instructive version of a marbendill story was written down by Jón Guðmundsson the Learned in the seventeenth century.[14] It has an ending which, in a way, may be compared to the one in *Hálfs saga*. The marmennill, sitting out on the shaft of an oar an instant before plunging into the deep, is asked by his captor for information about the best kind of fishing tackle. He answers with a short discourse in language containing a lot of alliteration, which may indicate that the passage was originally in verse form. It goes as follows:

> Chewed and trodden iron one should use for hooks, and place the smithy for hook-making within hearing of both river and sea; and harden the hook in horse piss (probably, *jóra mæði*), use a line of grey bull's skin and a lead of raw horse hide, for bait have a bird's gizzard and a piece of halibut, but human flesh in the middle of the bend, and then you are fated to die if you do not fish. Side-twisted a fisherman's hook ought to be.[15]

Who, we might ask, would be more knowledgeable about these matters than one who lives in the water? It seems to me that I have seen or heard somewhere that the original twisting of the fishing hook has been ascribed to some important

---

14 In his work *Tíðfordríf*. This is the version printed in Árnason, I, 126-7.
15 *Tuggið járn og troðið skal til öngla hafa og setja önglasmiðju þar sem heyra má til ár og til lár (sjóar og vatns nið) og herða öngul í jóra mæði, hafa gráan griðungsvað og hráan hrosskinnstaum, til beitu hafa fugls fúarn og flyðrubeitu, en mannskjöt í miðjan bug, – og muntu feigur ef þú ekki fiskar. Fráleitur skal fiskimanns öngull.*

inventor other than our merman, but perhaps it would be as well for us to credit him with the advantage provided by his own particular vantage-point. It is in matters such as this that we can see – quite logically also – the use of creating other worlds.

IV

The nykur

Finally, I want to look at the Icelandic *nykur*, as a representative of the zoomorphous water-wights. Appropriately, it is termed 'water-horse', as equine shape appears to be its main form and identity. Icelandic tradition appears not to know of the possibility of supernatural beings with generic names that begin with n-, such as *nykur*, while Swedish *näcken*, or German *Nix*, can be naturally at home in human shape. This summary description, translated from Ólafur Davíðsson's survey article on Icelandic water-wights, serves as an excellent introduction:[16]

The nykur lives both in rivers and lakes and even in the sea. It most of all resembles a horse as to the shape of body, usually grey or stone-grey in colour, yet sometimes it is brown. Its ears are turned backwards, and so are all the hoofs, so that the hoof-tufts of hair turn the opposite way to other horses. Yet the animal is not confined to these characteristics, for it can alter itself in various ways, and some say that it can turn itself into almost anything.

In *Landnámabók* (The Book of Settlement), in addition to the water-horse-as-work-horse legend (there connected with a settler by the name of *Auðunn stoti*),[17] at least one or two other, perhaps more enigmatic items concerning water-horses, are found. To begin with, we may focus on the account of the settler Sel-Þórir, since this actually opens with a *marmennill* story:

A certain Grímr from Haddingjadalr (Hallingdal) in Norway moved to Iceland with his wife Bergdís and the young son Þórir. They first came to the northern part of the country and spent their first winter in the small island of Grímsey in Steingrímsfjörður. In the autumn Grímr went fishing with his workmen, and the boy Þórir was kept in the prow of the boat in a sealskin bag, laced together at the neck for warmth. Grímr caught a *marmennill*, and when he came to the surface Grímr asked him: 'What have you to tell me concerning that which is to come; where is it that we are to make our settlement in Iceland?' The *marmennill* answered: 'For yourself there is no need to predict, but the boy in the sealskin will take land and settle where Skálm, your mare, lies down with her burden on.' This was all that they could make him say.

16 Davíðsson (1935-9), 296.
17 Discussed by Almqvist (1990a), 15-42 and (1991a) 117–8.

It goes without saying that they released him. There are, to be sure, some small differences between different versions of the *Landnámabók* in what follows. As we know from other *marmennill* stories, a person of whom the *marmennill* finds it unnecessary to prophesy anything is fated to die soon, and so Grímr passed away in the course of that winter. In the spring, his widow and Þórir left Grímsey in pursuit of what was to be, and the texts make it clear that Skálm, the mare, led the way and never once lay down with the luggage packs on her back. They spent the next winter at Skálmarnes on the northern side of Breiðafjörður. When summer came again, they continued in the same manner with the mare in the lead, and they headed southwards until they came off the mountains down into Borgarfjörðr (the western part, i.e. in Mýrar), to a place with two red sandhills. There Skálm lay down with the packs on, below the western-most of these two hills. This is where Þórir made his settlement and he lived at Rauðamelr inn ytri.[18]

The account of the *marmennill* legend at the beginning of this episode is clear enough, although he is only briefly held captive on the boat. It is also common enough for fishermen in the later legends to let the *marmennill* go almost at once, and to expect his gratitude for his release to be expressed in plentiful catches of fish. The central issue in *Landnámabók* is the attempt to learn about the future from the mythical being. We note also the motif that the man who is asking for information stands in no need of predictions about the future, since his life is about to end. The *marmennil's* reticence makes it seem pointless to detain him further. But the story as told here is just an introduction to the interesting account of the settler Sel-Þórir, who was destined to become an important person. Later, when he was old and blind, he went outside one evening, and saw a giant rowing in an iron *nökkvi*, a mythical kind of boat. The giant came ashore, went up to a certain farmstead and dug a hole in a gateway there. That same night, a volcanic eruption started in that spot. Nor should we ignore any of the mystical or demonic sea- or water-wights or the various phenomena connected therewith, least of all those with an n- name that might seem to be etymologically related to *nykur*. The boats of some supernatural beings are regularly given this generic name, *nökkvi*, and they are sometimes made of stone, sometimes of metal.

To sum up, we find in a cluster here the *marmennill*, the connection with the seal, the n-named mystical boat, and, finally, the suspicion that the mare Skálm also has some aquatic connections. As to Þórir himself and his heathen offspring, they are said to have perished in a mountain, Þórisbjörg – not a watery afterworld. But at the very end, it is meticulously reported that Skálm, practically a member of the family, perished in Skálmarkelda, a pond which afterwards bore her name. I think the likelihood is – though there is no proof of this – that she may have entered this pond of her own volition, after the fashion of such supernatural animals as water-horses. The status and the role accorded Skálm in the story is unmistakable. She is invested with the fulfilment of the prophecy on

18 Benediktsson (1986), 96-9.

which the entire future depends. She is no ordinary animal: her demise, after the death of her owners, is formally noted by the texts. Doubtless, the legend of Skálm has partial counterparts in other stories of buildings raised where an animal halts.[19] That is what makes it necessary for the mare to lead the way to that spot. What clinches my belief that she shows kinship with the underwater breed is the motif of her lying down with the packs on. This is quite a prominent motif in a lot of Icelandic *nykur* stories. The *nykur*, in the world of ideas manifested in many *nykur* stories, shows a propensity for lying down, and, whenever there is water or some wetness around, of getting into it. This is quite well known as a traditional fault and characteristic of horses bred from a *nykur*. In conjunction with the other indications, the motif of lying down confirms one in the belief that the mare Skálm had a touch of *nykur* blood in her veins.

Regarding provenance, we stand to benefit from Almqvist's reassessment of earlier treatments of the topic of the water-horse of Auðunn stoti,[20] in the *Landnámabók*, and similarly his 'type II' work-horse and the features it shares with similar beasts in Scottish and Irish traditions. This has long seemed to be a strong case of Gaelic borrowing, and Almqvist succeeds in adding to the evidence in favour of this conclusion. I am tempted here to discuss some other horses which – as seems likely to be the case with Auðunn stoti's horse – may also be ultimately connected with the Irish *Liath Macha* and other fabulous racing horses of supernatural origin. I refer to the mare *Fluga* and her male offspring, the murderous stallion *Eiðfaxi.*[21]

Once, in the time of settlement in the north of Iceland, a ship brought a cargo of farm animals to Skagafjörður. The sailors lost a young mare, which managed to run away, but the settler Þórir dúfunef 'bought the hope' (*keypti vánina*), as the texts have it, of finding it, and he did. It was the fastest of horses and was named *Fluga*. Once when Þórir was travelling south across the uninhabited central highlands of Iceland, he was approached there by a certain Örn – a dubious fellow and a magician to boot – who, having heard of *Fluga* and thinking he had a very good horse himself, wanted to run his horse against Þórir's. The difference between these two race horses was such that órir on his way back met Örn only half-way down the course. Örn was so affected by the loss of his stake that he went up to the mountain Arnarfell and took his own life there. *Fluga* was exhausted, and Þórir left her there to rest and recover. When he came by on his way back, he found a grey stallion with a bright mane in the mare's company. She was in foal by him, and their offspring was the stallion *Eiðfaxi,*[22] who was taken to Norway where he killed seven men in one day beside the then lake Mjörs, and was killed there himself. *Fluga* died, as may be expected, in a bog at *Flugumýri, 'Fluga's* moor'.

This looks suspiciously like a condensed reference to a fuller account which

---

19 Benediktsson (1986), 96 in a footnote cites works by Dag Strömbäck and Ólafur Lárusson as to such parallels.
20 Almqvist (1990a).
21 Benediktsson (1986), 235-6.
22 See Halldórsson(1991 [1992]), 53-7.

was expected to be familiar to the audience. Ólafur Halldórsson has pointed out that the last sentence of this report in *Landnámabók* must be corrupt, and that this passage is likely to have made reference to the death of Þórir dúfunef himself, since otherwise the story misses its point, namely the revenge by the long dead Örn for his defeat in the race, a revenge carried out by his own animal embodiment, his 'son', *Eiðfaxi*. As the story is built up in the *Landnámabók* text, it is true to say that it has been geared towards just such a revenge ending; possibly even an ending which accounted for the death of, or the end of human knowledge of, the stallion by his entering the lake. This story, then, would form a parallel to the account of Þórólfur bægifótur in *Eyrbyggja saga*,[23] describing how, after his own death, he was reborn as a bull calf which became the bull Glæsir; Glæsir, in turn – following what may be conceived of as the culmination of Þórólfur bægifótur's evil-doings, namely the killing of his owner – descended into a lake or pond never to be seen again. There are also some other stories which ultimately may have to be considered in connection with water-horse stories, although they are not in isolation immediately recognizable as such. For example, *Fluga's* foal by a stallion corresponding to normal water-horse descriptions and serving a mare, may also be regarded as a kind of nykur and, similarly, in the phenomenon of reincarnation of a human, one may see certain interesting parallels to just such a duality of being.

V

I want to conclude these musings by examining an issue which, from one point of view, certainly may be a side issue, but which, in another way, may actually supply the key to the whole question, and provide a tool for investigators of tradition contending with our own and earlier generations' understanding of the water-horse in belief and legend. I refer to the role of the notion of water-horse in the context of its name, *nykur*, being used as the base of the term, *nykrað*, in describing a feature of poetic diction. The term *nykrað* (past participle) is the technical term for 'mixed metaphor(s)' in poetry. This arises when the picture or image inherent in the base-word of a kenning is not maintained all the way to the end of the immediate context (the exact confines of which are a matter of some doubt and disagreement – a matter which may be ignored here), but is exchanged for another image or images, and sometimes mixed up with other images by the use of verbs which do not fit the base word image, etc.[24]

This practice was rather frowned upon by the Icelandic medieval scholars in

---

23 Sveinsson & Þorðarson (1935). See esp. chapter 63.
24 This matter is very briefly but still satisfactorily mentioned and defined – with perfectly valid reference to the basic source texts – in Strömbäck (1967), cols. 432-38. See esp. col. 433 and the sources mentioned. The basic sources are Snorri Sturluson in his Edda and his nephew Ólafur Þórðarson in the text known as the *Third Grammatical Treatise*.

the field of poetics and viewed as a fault or defect. In a commentary on the term we read that this *nykrað*-figure works in the same way as the *nykur* itself, shifting its shape in many ways. It is indeed a feature of the Icelandic tradition that the water-horse can appear in almost any shape it chooses, although the horse-shape is its normal or legitimate native form, so to speak. It should also be mentioned that one of the masters of poetics at one point appends to the poetic term the alternative form *finngálknað*. The *finngálkn* was an imaginary monster composed of parts of different animals. It is acknowledged that in some ancient works on poetics such a beast is used as a descriptive metaphor for the putting together of things in poetry in a way that is contrary to nature. The Icelanders Snorri Sturluson and Ólafr Þórðarson were doubtless familiar with this. We cannot know for certain if this ancient wisdom has given rise to or influenced the use of the term *nykrað*. But it might also have found its origin on native ground, as the word itself indicates, and only later have been brought into contact with the classical parallel just mentioned. We should bear in mind that in the poetics of Snorri and Ólafur hvítaskáld *nykrað* is seen as the opposite of (as well as an aberration from) the ideal of *nýgjörving*, a term which means keeping the imagery within the confines of meaning determined by the base word of the first kenning, right until the end of the stanza, or relevant context. *Nýgjörving* is seen as the pinnacle of the art of court poetry, whereas *nykrað* is reckoned to be an imperfection, perhaps even a transgression beyond what is right and proper.

This attitude is probably to be expected ever and always of scholars in the field of poetics. What is aimed at is mastery of the *craft* of poetry, and, consequently, in the teaching of it there will not be much tolerance of the accidental, the spontaneous and the risky in composition. There is little room for recognition of what we may think we know for certain: that verbal art includes extending the borders of language as part of the attempt to extend our knowledge so as to come to grips with reality. This must involve both transgression and change. And it it is part of our experience in this respect that the most perfect and unassailable craftsmanship, which always keeps within the confines of the habitual grammar, can interest us only fleetingly, because within it everything soon becomes utterly predictable. In this sense, it may be said that in any age, the development of living poetry is bound to be associated with both a very general notion of *nykrað* and also of *nykrað* in the particular context outlined above, because *nykrað*, with its powers of discovery and surprise, alone in the end will be able to add new realms to our experience, to up-date our knowledge, to change our view of the world.

Seen in this way, I think the opposition between *nykrað* and *nýgjörving* assumes its proper significance, a significance which is much more far-reaching than the medieval text-books, with their craftsmanship outlook, would permit one to think. This contradistinction and oppositional pair – *nykrað-nýgjörving* – now in a sense comes to be perceived on a par with, and, therefore, partly synonymous with the basic distinction in literature at large between, on the one hand, real and earnest investigations of the world - which always have the potential for changing man's view of both the world and himself - and, on the other hand, the importance of literature as a significant and constantly repeated assertion of the received basic truths (which carries within it the tacit promise of not altering those truths, not interfering with the basic reality).

This distinction assumes an almost infinite importance in the eyes of one who tends to conceive of the humanities at large, and to look at folk culture and its phenomena especially, in the light of a social-constructivist approach. In such an approach – thinking in terms of a world of essentially three parts, namely, society or culture, the subject or I, and nature, – living folklore obviously has as its most important function or functions the role of investigating and marking the boundaries between the sphere of cultured society and wild nature. Man strives to create and maintain security and safety of life for himself in his society. He tries to keep nature at bay, and to extend his area of knowledge and culture. In this activity of knowledge, fear of the unknown is possibly man's most important endowment, since he must alleviate this fear by knowing his world well, and not allow the unknown wild to encroach upon his home sphere.

Against this elementary background, there is absolutely no difficulty in assigning a role and a meaning in a general sort of way to the beliefs and legends that cluster around the water-horse. The water-horse is a fearsome representative of the wild. In the same way, we are bound to feel more sharply than before that the teaching of the medieval scholastics regarding the meaning and role of the oppositional pair *nykrað* vs. *nýgjörving* in poetry should be extended to take its part in and, in a sense, to encompass, this general contradistinction between trivial and serious literature, with due regard to human experience in the everlasting struggle between culture and nature.

The poetic device of *kenningar* is also an important part of the field of investigation. Suffice it to say here that the kennings, in the narrower sense of that word, were the main feature of the poetic language of court poetry. It is clear from what I have said about *nykrað* that I would propose to extend this to also embrace the idea of that which sometimes takes even the poet himself by surprise in the exercise of his art, and which might change himself and his idea of truth, as well as the conception of the world view of the audience at large. Both parties have to take in the new image of truth, or leave it at their own risk – in a changing world which after all is created by language, in the sense here discussed. In short, I am proposing that the poetical term *nykrað* should be taken to describe that which does to people what the water-horse does to his rider in the legends - 'The Water-horse as a Riding Animal', in particular, though hardly exclusively.

Like the availability of powerful literature to a reader, the *nykur* is at first innocent enough and companionable enough until you find yourself astraddle. Then the beast takes you where you had no notion of going, as potent literature also has the capacity to do, heading right out of this world and into another, unless you know the controlling word, or else have such luck with words, that you release the magic hold the beast has on you and alight in time – in which case you can carry on with your existence in human society. If you are fortunate enough to survive, you are privileged to live your life with a sharpened awareness of dangers of the kind you have experienced on the border between culture and nature. It is easy to conceive of the water-horse legends, and 'The Water-horse as a Riding Animal'-type, especially, as a general metaphor for what we might call 'the human close call experience' and to regard it as a matter of life and death. If my proposal for understanding the overall ramifications of the poetical term *nykrað* is acceptable, then that same legend type may be understood as a metaphor for the understanding of literature as well. A poem may amount to an experience which takes you where you had never thought of going, perhaps out of the small world of your own home culture.

I wish to emphasize that I do not take my interpretation of the poetical term as conflicting with the view of the medievals, Snorri and Ólafur; indeed, far from it. In my view, this wide understanding in terms of aesthetics and human development may be said to encompass the medieval definition, and in either case the term *nykrað* relates to a frightening human experience. It is frightening to meet a monster composed of incompatible parts, but 'The Water-horse as a Riding Animal' injects more meaning into the metaphor because it only has two possible endings – to get off or to perish. It goes without saying that a lesson drawn from medieval poetics may hold the promise to be at least as valuable for the science of folklore. We cannot but agree with what Matthew Arnold and, doubtless, others have said, namely, that poetry is criticism of life. Obviously this holds equally true of matters pertaining to oral education, in other words folklore.

The limerick represents a contemporary poetic genre which has as its main characteristic a comparable turning upside-down of things. In that sense, it has made itself a carrier of this kind of experience. There is one particular limerick – possibly one of the best-known of all limericks – which has been preying on my mind while pondering the question of *nykrað*:

There was a young lady of Niger,

Who smiled as she rode on a tiger.
They came back from the ride,
With the lady inside,
And the smile on the face of the tiger.[25]

Perhaps, practically everybody has always considered this limerick to be a water-horse story in reality. If so, I for one did not realise this before and, therefore, can now indulge in the pleasure of allowing myself to make this association. Perhaps, one should not insist on absolute identification here, but only suggest that the verse contains the basic memorable notion contained in 'The Water-horse as Riding Animal', i.e. riding the otherworld animal, taking it to be a natural one, in this case with fatal results.

According to Ólafur Davíðsson, the *nykur* was the mythical animal most strongly believed in in Icelandic tradition in his time, more particularly in the south of the country than anywhere else. Mythical representations do have a way of turning into absolute fact. To this end, real natural phenomena are often called upon for support. In many places in Iceland, the *nykur* was cited as the reason for noises and cracking in the winter ice on lakes and rivers. Let me conclude these remarks by saying that such natural phenomena will seldom or never constitute the entire 'raison d'être' of any supernatural being. In this context, however, it is of enormous value that we possess medieval proof of the metaphorical functioning of the notion of *nykur*. This means that the beast had an existence and a means of capturing and expressing human experience. Translation and metaphor is the name of its game. It seems to me that understanding the ways and workings of such metaphors must be our game too.

---

25 I quote here from the first page of Rimmon-Kenan (1983), where the verse's narrativity is taken as the point of departure.

'And it was Such a Strange Bird . . .'
Two Men's Experiences and Narratives of the Water-Sprite

ANN-MARI HÄGGMAN

I first came in contact with the Endtbacka family in Esse, a parish in the Swedish-speaking area of Ostrobothnia, on the west coast of Finland, in August 1971. In the northernmost part of Esse there are several little woodland villages, and when you start out from one of them, called Lappfors, and travel some ten km through the woods in a south-westerly direction, you reach a wide glade and come in view of two dark woodland ponds separated by a tongue of land. On this narrow tongue of land, there is a farmhouse (red with white corners), a row of outhouses – a cow-shed, a drying barn, a grey sauna of undressed wood – and some fields and meadows. The place is called Hepovattnet ('The Horse Water'), after the name of one of the ponds.

The farm, which has belonged to the same family since the land was reclaimed in 1784, today comprises some eight hectares of farmland and forest. When I made recordings there in the 1970s, five grown-up siblings lived on the farm. The eldest of these was Albert Endtbacka (b. 1900), then there were Ellen (b. 1901), Alfred (b. 1908), Ingvald (b. 1913) and Ture (b. 1916). None of them is alive today.

Even before I got to know her, Ellen Endtbacka – the only woman in the family – had won a reputation as a good narrator. Lars Huldén, a dialectologist, had used her as an informant when researching his doctoral thesis on the local dialect, and as early as 1952 her narratives had been tape-recorded. Some of these narratives were about water-dwellers, both quite widely known stories, and other kinds of stories more original and more intimately connected with Ellen's own surroundings.

Here are two of the stories Ellen Endtbacka used to tell. The first one is about the water-nymph's clothes, the other concerns a man who tried to shoot a bird, which later turned out to be the sea-sprite. What I find interesting about these particular stories is that the very individuals who are mentioned in the stories could be identified and interviewed, for it turned out that those men were Ellen's own brothers, who were by no means unwilling to talk about their experiences. Over the next few years I visited the Endtbacka family regularly and was thus able to check details, ask questions and compare the versions of the narratives during this time. I tried to find an explanation as to why these people had this kind of experience, and why, when and how they talked about it. The two stories which I have chosen are both connected with a lake, Finnsjön ('The Finn Lake'), not far from Hepovattnet. This is how Ellen told the story about the water-nymph's clothes in 1952:

There's something very weird about Finnsjön. They say they've seen all sorts of things there. They've seen clothes. You see, there's an islet there in the middle of the lake. It's a beautiful lake, and a beautiful islet too. There's no road there of course, and of course nobody lives there. But several times they've seen those clothes. All sorts of women's clothes hung up to dry there on that islet, clothes that had been washed. And there are many people who have seen those clothes.[1]

Ellen did not mention that the people who saw the clothes were her brothers: she just told the story in the same way as she told other stories she had heard. Nineteen years later when I was interviewing Ellen, the whole family was present. The atmosphere was very relaxed and everybody made comments and wanted to take part. Often we were speaking all at once, so that when transcribing the tapes later, I had to concentrate really hard in order to be able to pick out each voice and reconstruct the conversation. Then, when Ellen started to tell this story, her brother Ture said he wanted to relate it himself. This is how it went:

Once we went fishing to Finnsjön. We didn't get any fish. But when we came to the other end of the lake, then I said to my pals – 'Just take a look now! What's the meaning of that?' The whole islet on this side of the lake was full of clothes. A lot of clothes fluttering there, women's clothes, just black female undergarments. All of them black. They say that other people have seen the same clothes too. And you have to believe what you see with your own eyes.[2]

The following year, in 1972, I recorded the same story twice, and in 1974 I made a documentary film in which Ture related the same episode.[3] Looking at that film one can easily see that Ture had developed his technique as a storyteller. This is how he told it on that occasion:

It must be over forty years since this happened one summer, round about the time of the summer solstice. The sun was shining and it was magnificent weather. We made an excursion to Finnsjön to fish. There were three of us, all men, and we walked all round the lake. Then I said to my pals – 'Just take a look now. What's the meaning of that?' There were a lot of women's clothes fluttering on the islet. And all were black. There were skirts and scarves and shawls. There wasn't one striped garment. Just black ones. And I said – 'If only we could only get out there.' I thought it would have been interesting. If we could have gone there just to touch them. But there was no boat. And I said to the others – 'Well, there you are. Now the water-nymph has washed her clothes.'[4]

---

1 *FKA* 1952:5.
2 *FKA* 1971:130.
3 *YLE.* Recordings in the archives of Oy Yleisradio Ab (The Finnish Broadcasting Company); *Med rådaren, tomten och bjäran* (Film). Producer Per: Uno Björklund, 1972.
4 *FKA* 1972:136.

As we can see, this version is much better structured than Ture's first attempt at telling the story. He begins by saying that it was a long time ago that it happened. He describes the weather and the place in greater detail, and he is the one who bravely maintains – 'If only we could get out there.' He even wanted to touch the clothes. And he maintained that he had even on that very occasion declared to his companions that it was the water-nymph who had washed her clothes.

Ellen also used to tell a story about a man who went one Sunday morning to Finnsjön to hunt and there met a strange bird. But, again, in 1971 her brother Albert wanted to tell this story himself – 'How would it be,' said he, 'if I told you how it really happened.' And so he began:

I was out hunting and had my gun. I had good shooting gear and I thought I'd shoot some proper animal. Well, then I got down to the lake – you know there's an islet there – and then I took aim with my gun and thought I fired a shot there. But nothing came of it. The gun didn't go off, there was no bang. And at the same time there was a splash. And a bird jumped from that islet into the water. And there was still no shot. And I had six, so it was only a matter of pulling the trigger. Well, then – it seemed as if that bird could do a lot of tricks. Then he jumped up and did all sorts of funny things in all kinds of ways. I just wondered why on earth I couldn't shoot. Whatever it was, I don't know. But there wasn't anything wrong. The gun was perfectly all right. It was just a matter of pulling the trigger. But there was no bang.[5]

Two years later, when Albert had the opportunity of telling the same story on a television programme, he gave a detailed description of how he went to Finnsjön, how good his gun was, and how he aimed and aimed. And the bird behaved as if it had been wound up – 'I haven't seen anything like it. That bird you know could sometimes behave as if he'd been able to perform all sorts of tricks like in the cinema. It could grow to be so big, so cruel looking that it was like nothing on earth. A while after it was only like a little sea bird. And I thought: I'd better leave. I won't stand here watching such foolish things. Not that I was afraid, no I wasn't. But I thought it was weird in some way.'[6] And Albert added that there was somebody in the village who had also seen that bird. When I asked him what all this could mean, he explained – 'Well, you see, it was that sprite they talk about. Or water-nymph or whatever. And it's just like that then, you see. It's just like that then, when that kind of thing happens.'[7]

How then are we to understand these experiences ? One can of course begin by noting that these, like most experiences of the kind, reflect society and people's world view. The *milieu* in which Albert and Ture lived bore in many respects the

---

5 *FKA* 1971:136.
6 *FKA* 1972:136.
7 *Ibid.*

stamp of the old peasant community. They had lived all their life on their parents' farm – apart from Ture's eight-month absence on military service. They grew up in the company of their father and mother, grandfather and grandmother, who taught them things and gave them good advice. They cultivated the land in the traditional manner and eked out their earnings by hunting and fishing. The bread, for instance, was always baked at home, and as late as the 1970s, when I visited them, the butter was still churned at home. On the whole they managed to live on what the farm produced, which of course did not mean that they had to dispense with radio and television and such things. When Albert for instance went shopping he went by moped. They took two daily papers in the house – the local paper and *Hufvudstadsbladet* [the biggest Swedish-language national newspaper in Finland]. When on one occasion I appeared slightly sceptical concerning Albert's stories about the wood-nymph, he took offence and said that there was nothing wrong with his eyes: 'I still read *the paper* without glasses,' said he.

When we discussed the existence of the water-sprite, Albert referred to the Scriptures: 'It says in the Scriptures that there are both wood-sprites, water-sprites and goblins and other such fellows. You can read about them in the Scriptures.' The clergyman in his confirmation class had impressed this upon him and Albert affirmed that the clergyman had added – 'I'll tell you this, dear children. If you know something and can do something, you must not do anything wrong. But if you know you can do something good, then you should do it.'[8] The Scriptures he referred to were Olof Svebilius' catechism of 1689, which for a long time – long after it ought to have been replaced by a more up-to-date catechism – was used in country parishes by elderly clergymen. In the parish of Esse there was an old, very orthodox clergyman named Olav Forsman, who, although it was forbidden, used this book till 1920, for he wanted to teach the children the one and only true faith. In this catechism you could read that you should beware of idolatry. It is, according to the catechism, idolatry if one 'seeks assistance from the devil and his agents, such as witches, sooth-sayers, wood-sprites, water-sprites, goblins and such like.'[9]

At Hepovattnet it was well known that the water-sprite as well as the wood-sprite could assume any shape. On the whole, supernatural creatures lived in the same way as human beings, had a dwelling, kept animals, cleaned, washed, etc. At Hepovattnet and its neigbourhood quite a few had seen the water-nymph's cows grazing and some had heard the water-nymph calling the cows too.

In his excellent analysis of the narratives which P.A. Säve recorded in Gotland, Ulf Palmenfelt has pointed out that the legends often deal indirectly with people's mutual relations; it might, for example, be tempting to keep a cow that had joined the domestic herd. But the legends often deal with the situation from the

8 *FKA* 1971:130.
9 Landtona (1919), 37.

point of view of the unfairly treated party. This is also the case in the stories of the Esse farmer who took an unknown cow and placed it in his own cow-shed. The water-nymph appeared in the shape of a dark-haired woman and sat down on the threshold of the cow-house, complaining that her children were dying of hunger. When the earthly powers cannot see to it that people comply with the norms and laws that obtain in relations between man and man or between man and nature, the supernatural powers who guard the right to hunt and fish will intervene[10]

When Albert Endtbacka went out hunting on a Sunday morning during the hour of public worship, he knew that he was breaking the Sabbath. He knew that strange things might happen if one went hunting during church hours. The legend about the enchanted bird which cannot be shot is widespread, and, perhaps, Albert had already heard something about this kind of bird. Probably he also felt a little worried about being on the territory of the neighbouring parish. Possibly he was a little tense at the thought of meeting somebody and was therefore exceptionally vigilant – especially as he was a little deaf and, therefore, had to be particularly on his guard. The fact that he rehearsed the episode when he came home also shows that Albert felt ill at ease. Together with his brothers and his sister he could then sort out this conflict situation: he had defied a prohibition and gone hunting, he had been scared and he came home without bagging anything.

When his brother Ture Endtbacka with two other brothers, Edvin and Ingvald, went out to fish it was at the time of the summer solstice. They all knew that this was an important time in nature. They had gone to Finnsjön as well and were thus also on forbidden ground. They were a bit scared that they might meet someone and kept a close eye on everything that moved – in fact Ture once before had seen an angler who suddenly disappeard. And this time they did see something odd too – clothes hung out to dry in a place where nobody lived. And only black clothes. Finnsjön was attractive because it abounded in fish and birds. At the same time they knew that Finnsjön was a dangerous place – their grandparents and parents had come across weird things there too.

Esse, the community where the Endtbacka family lived, is one of the most religion-conscious areas in the Swedish-speaking part of Finland, a place where a lot of people have experienced different kinds of religious revelations. Albert and Ture were grateful and happy because they were able to have this kind of experience too. They were of the opinion that people today have too little faith and that that is why they don't see or hear these things. The manner in which these stories were related is, of course, closely connected with the situation and the intensity of communication between the teller and the listener. There is no doubt whatever that the Endtbackas were happy about the attention their stories attracted from researchers. At the

---

10 Palmenfelt (1993b), 19.

beginning of our acquaintance they were more reserved, but in time we became good friends. I visited them often and I could not avoid noticing that the men of the house were especially pleased at my visits – twenty years ago I was a relatively young lady who paid these men great attention. Albert had an enlargement made of a photo of him and me which he hung up on the wall and jokingly pointed out his girlfriend to visitors. I felt grateful for the confidence they had in me. But at the same time I noticed how they tested my understanding, solidarity and friendship. Through these stories we were able to communicate. I had a reason to go and see them. They had something to offer. We knew the rules. The Endtbacka brothers showed their gratitude by sending me letters, presents, offering a piece of ground for a summer cottage etc. They were grateful because they felt they belonged to the select few. They were the ones I and my colleagues had chosen to interview, not their neighbours. Through us they came to the fore in the newspapers, on radio and television. They soon came to realise that there was a niche for them; they knew something others did not. They availed themselves of the opportunity. And they wanted to show what they were worth. For instance when I asked them to tell me more about the water-sprite, they would become downright embarrassed if they could not oblige.

The stories told by the Endtbacka family reflect the world view of the family members and their relations to recent history, to nature and to the supernatural. Although they showed a profound distrust of today's secularized society, they knew how to adapt themselves to its values and make the most of the interest the people of today took in their history and in their unusual experiences. Here, my colleagues and I became the catalysts: we opened the floodgates, drew their attention to the resources they represented and gave them a chance to create a distinctive image for themselves as popular storytellers in our time.

Tradition and Changes in the Concepts of Water-Beings in Faroese Folklore

Jóan Pauli Joensen

The natural surroundings with their phenomena, also here in these islands, have stirred the Nordic spirit of the people so that imagination has lent life to the dead surroundings; peopled them locally in mounds, stones, lakes and so on, with the now disappearing, and in the more material eyes of the present, dying creations of superstition of a particularly Faroese conception, such as we find in the stories about the ingenious dwarfs in the mounds, *huldrefolk*,[1] or elves that wander unseen amongst human beings on land and at sea, but who can also appear as wicked, tempting creatures offering a draft of nepenthe to charm a human being away from this world it has been placed in. There are, too, the lovable pixies in the home, water-sprites in streams and lakes, mermen, *niðagrisur*.[2] All of these are described in the folk tales. These beings are disappearing and with them the poetry that created them, which in turn influenced the cultural life.[3]

These are some of V. U. Hammershaimb's reflections on superstition in the introduction to his 'Faroese Anthology'. The purpose of this paper is to provide a survey of the supernatural beings whose territory was water – the sea and bordering areas. The material on which I have based my work is divided into two parts, namely, material collected before 1900 and material collected after 1960. The material concerning Faroese tradition which is to be found in the works of early writers is both unsystematic and sporadic. Tarnovius' account from 1669 deals particularly with trolls and *huldufólk* ('hidden people') and people who have disappeared – taken away temporarily or permanently by the *huldufólk*.[4]

The supranormal incidents which are described in greater detail by Lucas Debes (1673) in the chapter on 'Ghosts and The Devil's Temptations in the Faroe Islands'[5] are of the same nature. The two clergymen, Thomas Tarnovius and especially Lucas Debes, do not reject these supranormal phenomena and, indeed, believe in them themselves. The scholar, natural scientist and linguist Jens Christian Svabo, held a different view. He had little sympathy with superstition, but confirmed that superstition existed in the Faroes, where 'one sees water-sprites, *niðagrísar*,[6] pixies, gnomes that live underground, apparitions, ghosts, yes, maybe even the Devil himself along with his great grandmother.'[7]

---

1 The Faroese form is *huldufólk*. In Danish it is *huldrefolk*. Hammershaimb's text is in Danish.
2 The clumsy creature with a big head and small body that lies curled up like a ball of wool and rolls about in front of people's feet. The *niðagrísur* is also a dead-child being. Cf. Almqvist (1971).
3 Hammershaimb (1891), XLIV.
4 Tarnovius (1950), 82.
5 Debes (1673), 319.
6 See note 2.
7 . . .*seer man Nikar (Nøk) Niägrísar (Nisser), Vajttrar, Underjordiske Folk, Gjenfærd (Hamfeer) Spøgelser, ja maaskee Fanden selv tillige med hans Oldemor* – Svabo (1959), 163.

The clergyman, Jørgen Landt, in his book published in 1800 gives sparse information about supernatural beings, but he does, nevertheless, talk about *nykur*, nixes or water-sprites, 'that live in fresh water or lakes into which they drag people and drown them.'[8] It is not until the second half of the last century, that V. U. Hammershaimb and Jakob Jakobsen – pioneers in the collection of material about tradition in the Faroe Islands – give us more detailed descriptions of supernatural beings. These two men were both products of their time. In 1843 Hammershaimb was, for example, in contact both with the Danish folklorist Svend Grundtvig and the Swedish folklorist G.O. Hyltén-Cavallius, who was at that time, very interested in *Die niedere Mythologie* and visited Hammershaimb on the 18th of July 1843.[9] Hammershaimb told him about supernatural beings, dwarfs, *huldufolk*, trolls, giants and other phenomena of popular belief.[10] The substance of the notes which Hyltén-Cavallius made is the same as that of the narratives which Hammershaimb later had published in the *Færøsk Anthologi* ('Faroese Anthology') in 1891. This classic work of Faroese literature was supplemented by another classic a few years later, namely, Jakob Jakobsen's *Færøske Folkesagn og Æventyr* ('Faroese Legends and Folktales'). Jakobsen says in the introduction to his work that it only contains 'such stories as are not found in the Anthology'.[11]

The material concerning tradition which we find in Hammershaimb and Jakobsen was collected in the latter half of the last century. For more than fifty years no systematic collecting of any significance was done. This activity did not start again until the 1960s. The collection and documentation of Faroese folk culture was regarded as one of the important tasks to be carried out by the Faroese University after its establishment in 1965.[12] The inspiration for renewed collecting was mainly due to the visit paid to the Faroes in 1967 by Professor Séamus Ó Duilearga from Dublin.[13] The folklorist Mortan Nolsøe also made a very significant contribution to the collection of material, particularly with regard to folklore.[14] This new material, which consists mainly of tape recordings, is filed in the archives of the Faroese Language Department of *Fróðskaparsetur Føroya*.[15]

---

8 Landt (1800,1965), 254.
9 My thanks to Professor Nils-Arvid Bringéus, Lund, for sending me a copy of the Gunnar Olof Hyltén-Cavallius records. The original material is in Kungliga Biblioteket, Stockholm, and is part of Vs 6, fol. 295 - 296. The complete records were published by Joensen (1985).
10 The complete notes of G.O. Hyltén-Cavallius are published in Joensen (1985).
11 . . . *sådanne sagn, som ikke findes trykte i anthologien,* Jakobsen (1898-1902). Here quoted from the 1961-64 edition: Indledning, vii.
12 The work of Andreas Weihe in 1933 should, however, be mentioned in this connection.
13 Joensen (1990), 36.
14 He was appointed to Fróðskaparsetur Føroya in 1973. Prior to that he worked in the Institute of Folklore at Oslo University. He was appointed professor in 1986. Sadly, he died in the following year, which was a great loss to the study of Faroese folklore.
15 The custodian of the archives, Rannveig Winther, has been of invaluable assistance to me in finding records of traditions that are scattered throughout this collection, of which she has such great knowledge.

The supernatural beings which are most closely akin to human beings are the hidden people, *huldufólk*, in Danish *huldrefolk*, and the traditions concerning them are many and varied. The *huldufólk* live in a parallel supernatural world, where the borders between their world and that of human beings can at times be crossed. Human beings and *huldufólk* could be mutually attracted to each other and sometimes even have children together.[16] The essence of the *huldufólk* legends is indeed just this crossing of the boundaries. There was a combination of co-operation and competition between the *huldufólk* and human beings in many aspects of life, and their field of activity was just as wide as that of human beings, both on land and on water. There are legends telling of men who fished alongside *huldumenn*,[17] and that they competed for landing places[18] and boathouses with them.[19] The *huldufólk* commanded respect, and Tarnovius (1669) says that, 'nobody should curse such *huldufólk*, but bless them'.[20] By a variety of supranormal means of communication, the *huldufólk* could give warning of good or evil to come.[21] It is not, however, my intention to talk about *huldufólk* in this paper.[22] I shall confine myself to supernatural beings and creatures with a more limited field of activity. These are the nix or water-sprite, merman, sea monster, mermaid, seal woman, and sea cattle. And, in addition to these, some indefinable supranormal experiences are dealt with. The accounts are based on the material contained in Hammershaimb's Anthology.

Nykur. The Nix or Water-Sprite
Hyltén-Cavallius made the following note during his conversation with Hammershaimb in 1843:

> The nix looks like a horse. Lives in a lake and goes ashore to graze. He draws people to him in the lake. A man tamed him, got him to pull tremendous stones down from the mountain. Then built a churchyard. Is dangerous to approach, because he has the power to draw people into the lake.[23]

The nix is a fresh-water being that lives on the bed of a lake. It can appear in rivers, lakes, or on land near a lake, in a variety of shapes – such as a beautiful horse or young man – to attract human beings, especially girls. Although it looks like a horse, it is the size of a dog. It could change itself into any four-footed animal – 'the

---

16 Hammershaimb (1891), 367, legend no. II. Cf. also Tarnovius (1950), 80: 'Yes, they appear in the form of women in front of the farmhands and men in the fields, all dressed up, wanting them to fornicate with them, so that these men had a lot of bother with them, so that they could not go anywhere in the field, they were all around them, there was an example of this in my childhood...'
17 Hammershaimb (1891), 339.
18 Jakobsen (1898-1902), legend no. 31.
19 Jakobsen (1899-1902), legend no. 78.
20 Tarnovius (1950), 80.
21 Nolsøe (1964), 20.
22 The folklorist Anna Brimnes made a detailed study of *huldrefolk* for her thesis on folklore in 1992 entitled 'An account of the significance of *huldrefolk* in the ideology of the Faroese'.
23 Joensen (1985), 100.

only thing it could not assume was the tip of a ram's horn.'[24] If you touch a nix you stick fast to it and are drawn into the lake. The nix loses its magic power if you say its name. It is fantastically strong, but a human being can gain control over it by making the sign of the cross on its back. There are several examples of stone dykes and walls of churchyards made from stones which people forced nixes to pull. It pulled with its strong tail.

There is only one legend of the nix in the Anthology,[25] but Jakobsen has two such legends: no. 68, 'The Nix in Leitisvatn', and no. 85, 'The Nix at Eiði'. There are several motifs in the legend about the nix in Leitisvatn. The first is about some children who mount a nix thinking that it is a horse and the nix dashes towards the lake with them. One of the youngest gets afraid and shouts *Nika baggi* ('Nicholas, brother!'), to his brother who is also on the horse. The child could not say Nicholas; the nearest he could get to it was '*Nika*', which is almost the Faroese name for a nix – *nykur*. The nix thought that the child said its name and therefore it lost its power over the children.[26] The same legend tells that many people who walked by the lake disappeared, 'but their lungs came up again and floated on the water'. This was a sign that it was the nix that had taken them. Two motifs in the legend are connected with the clergyman Rasmus Ganting. One is about the disappearance of a nix in the shape of a horse when the clergyman wanted it to carry him over a river, and the other concerns the clergyman seeing someone combing his hair with a golden comb in a sheepfold close to the lake. He knew at once that it was a nix. The clergyman, who was skilled in the magic arts, turned a small stone into a big one, which has since borne the name *Leiðasteinur*, and into this he enticed the nix, which was never seen again.

The main theme in the legend about 'The Nix at Eiði' is about the power of human beings. The nix was made to pull stones around for the churchyard. When the work was finished the nix was about to run away when two small children came and jumped up on its back, thinking that it was a horse. More and more joined them, and all the time there was room for one more 'until all the people of Eiði were mounted'. The nix dashed off with them towards the lake. Some had food with them and, when a little child was handed a bit of whale blubber, the child pulled back and said, *"ikki "nika" meg!"*. The child had not yet learned to talk and said '*nika*' instead of '*snika*'[27] meaning that he did not want to be made greasy, but to the nix it sounded as if someone had said its name and it lost its power over the children, who fell off before the nix disappeared into lake Eiíisvatn.

There is a lake called Toftavatn on Eysturoy. Neither Hammershaimb nor Jakob Jakobsen mention any nix in Toftavatn, but in the third edition of Sofia Petersen's rhymes, fairytales and legends from 1988, there is the following legend about 'The Nix in Toftavatn':

---

24 Winther (1875), 367. Winther's work is based on Hammershaimb's earlier work.
25 Hammershaimb (1891), 334.
26 Jakobsen notes that he has heard the same version in the village of Gásadalur about the nix in the lake 'Vatnið lítla'.
27 'snika' can be translated as being made greasy as from oil.

It was midsummer and in the middle of the day. The mistress of the house in Leigustova at Toftir was busy in the kitchen and her child was playing on the floor. All of a sudden the door opened and a big dog came in, black as coal except for the tip of the tail, which glittered like gold. It circled the room a couple of times and then came close to the child. Suddenly the child grabs the tail with both its hands, but sticks to it and starts to cry. The mother hurries to free the child but is herself caught fast. The dog goes out of the door dragging both of them behind it. Their cries for help were heard all over the village, and everyone who could walk came to help, but as soon as they touched the tail, or those who were already stuck to the tail, they themselves stuck fast. When the beast went over the fence around the fields it was dragging most of the villagers behind it.

That same day the farmer in Leigustova and his comrades were at the fishing at Rituvík, in the north. The farmer, who was usually a cheery man, was unusually quiet that day, but suddenly he burst out: 'I feel that there is something far wrong in Toftir today; I want you to put me ashore'.

The others thought that this was strange, but of course they did as the farmer asked, and put him ashore at Kráargil, and he went round by Rituvíksháls. When he gets to the top he hears terrible cries for help and sees this horrible creature dragging all the people down in the middle of the outfields on the other side of the lake. He realized at once what the trouble was: it was the nix on its way down to the lake with his villagers. He started to run as fast as he could, but by the time he got to Sandin Lítla, the nix had reached the shore of the lake about forty metres away from him. It was impossible to reach the nix, but in his distress a good idea struck him; he tore up a piece of turf, scratched a cross on it, threw it at the nix and hit it on the tail – that set them all free. The nix disappeared out in the lake and the Toftir folk went home, having got off with a fright.[28]

The legend also appears together with fictive material in a religious short story by the Faroese writer Christian Høj which was published earlier,[29] a summary of which goes as follows:

But over in the lake there lived a nix who was very ill-natured. And the story goes that one day he had made up his mind to destroy the whole village. He was going to drag all the villagers down into the lake where he lived. So he starts to change his appearance. First of all he changes himself into a young man, elegant and handsome. The sort of person he thought the girls would fall for. But when he saw his reflection in the lake he did not like it. So he changed himself into a horse that all the fine young men would want to have; but alas, when he had looked at his reflection for a while, he sees that there is

---

28 Petersen (1988).
29 Høj (1979), 4.

something missing. He sits thinking for a while down at the bottom of the lake... At last he has an idea. This time he changes himself into a nice little dog with a burning stump of candle on its tail... Then he goes to the village. At the first house he comes to, he sees a child playing on the floor. The child goes to him full of confidence and wants to have the bright shining light, but as soon as it touches the tail the child sticks to it; no matter how hard it pulls and tugs the child cannot get its hand free again. Then the child starts to cry bitterly. 'My dear child, what is the matter with you?' says the mother and makes to take the child in her arms ... then the mother was stuck too... The story goes on to tell how the nix goes from house to house and everyone sticks to it, and then it rushes down to the lake with the tail of people behind it. The story's main character, Eyðun, had been at the fishing that day and finds that nobody is down at the shore to meet him. He discovers that the nix is on its way to the lake with all the villagers. Then he suddenly remembered what his grandmother had said to him years ago, that all evil must yield to the holy sign of the cross. He pulls his knife out of its sheath and cuts a cross in the turf, cuts loose the piece of turf with the cross on it and casts it down towards the lake after the nix. When the turf with the sign of the cross on it hit the nix's tail, the nix lost all its strength. Everyone was freed, and the nix had to go alone and disappointed down into the lake, where he went into the darkest corner to sulk.

Although neither Hammershaimb or Jakobsen collected material about the nix in Toftavatn, it appears that the tradition is still known there, both amongst older people (those between sixty-five and eighty years of age), and younger people (those of forty years of age). The fish-filleting factory in the village is called *Nykur* ('Nix'). In a recent telephone interview an informant told that 'The nix lived at Bøllunesi and he had a light in his tail. If you touched him, you stuck to him. He would come and take us if we misbehaved.'[30] Another informant told that the nix came in the dark. 'He tried to look in a way that made people feel sorry for him and to touch him, and when they tried to let go of him they were stuck. He had a light on his tail. I remember several old people who believed firmly in the nix'.[31] Younger people tell that their parents, usually the mother, frightened them with the nix to keep them away from the lake when it was dark. "Mind the nix", I remember my mother often shouting after us when we went up to the lake.'[32] An informant can also remember the story of a man who was in the outfield to fetch peat and who fell into Toftavatn and was drowned when he went over a stone bridge. It was said that the nix was the cause of this.[33] The special characteristic of the nix from Toftavatn was that it had a light on its tail, or had a luminous tail.

---

30 H.O., Toftir. Telephone interview 3 October 1996.
31 J.I.O., Toftir. Telephone interview 3 October 1996.
32 L.L. born at Toftir 1954, verbal information 1 October 1996.
33 J.H. born and bred at Toftir, telephone interview 3 October 1996. The legend can be verified by another informant, who does not, however, associate the nix with misfortune. P.L. 4 October 1996.

In the legend about *Húsfrúgvin í Húsavík* ('The Lady of Húsavík') the story goes that all the big stones that she used in her buildings 'she had got the nix to pull down to her from the mountains; but at length it came to grief: when it came from Takkmyri with a big stone, the nix's tail broke off, and the mark from it can still be seen in the stone that lies there, but the nix disappeared into "lítla vatn" and lives there still'.[34]

In 1971 the reminiscences about nixes were further enriched by the addition of two new recordings about a woman in Øravík. 'There was a woman in Øravík, Marin Laðansdóttir. She was supposed to have got hold of a water-sprite and she got it to pull stones for a house in Øravík. Well, the stones were so big that he did not know how they could have got there, but there is an old tale that when an animal gets terribly skinny, it was Marin Laðansdóttir's nix. She had been so cruel to it that its bones came through its skin.'[35]

In another version the story goes that 'She was so good at casting spells that she called forth the nix that was supposed to live in the lakes up there.' She used it to 'pull all the stones for the farm at Øravík, the dairy in Øravík and a farm there. The nix was exhausted from pulling stones. It was so worn out that all that was left of it was the ribs and the rump.'[36] The same recording tells that in Fámjin they had a special nix rhyme that contained the name of the nix. This was recited aloud so that the nix would lose its power.[37] A recording from Sumba in 1980 confirms that a nix was said to 'live in the lake, but now the lake is filled up, but it was said to have taken a child at one time, the nix, from somebody in Liða'.[38]

The nix (*näcken* or *vattenhästen*) is well-known in Scandinavian tradition and is the subject of several studies,[39] but it is not intended in the present context to make a comparison between the nix of Faroese tradition and that of the rest of Scandinavia.

Marmennil. The Merman
According to the legend, 'The merman and Anfinnur, the farmer from Elduvík', a merman resembles a human being, but has very long fingers. It lives on the sea-bed and teases fishermen by eating the bait from their hooks, or by fixing the hooks into the sea-bed so that the fishing lines break. If it gets caught in the hook itself, it is so good with its hands that it can quickly loosen the knot on the snell. Nevertheless, the farmer Anfinnur was able to catch a merman and take it on board his boat. The

---

34 Hammershaimb (1891), 374 legend XXIX. In the recording *FMD* BS 1256, H.B. b.. 1901, MN 1983 the informant says that he remembers 'that as little boys, we used to look for this bit of tail'.
35 *FMD* Tape 7/1971 arch. 3 E.E. b 1893, MN 1971, Fámjin.
36 *FMD* BS 400 6, N.J.N. b. 1893, MN 1970, Fámjin.
37 *FMD* BS 360 N.J.N b 1893, MN 1970, Fámjin.
38 *FMD* 1030 M.T. b. 1906, MN 1980, Sumba.
39 See Egardt (1944), Stattin (1984): and Almqvist (1990a).

farmer got the merman in his power by making the sign of the cross over it. This had to be done continuously every day and in certain situations. The farmer took the merman fishing several times. It was very good at finding fish: 'If they rowed over a shoal of fish, it started to laugh and play in the boat; if they then cast, they did not get fish, especially when it put its fingers down in the sea.'[40] One day when the farmer forgot to make the sign of the cross over the merman, it disappeared.[41] The Faroese word for a merman is *marmennil*, which is defined as being the same as the Danish *havmand*.[42] Hyltén-Cavallius did not record the word *marmennil* in his interview with Hammershaimb in 1843. *Marmennil* is the oldest known Nordic name for merman and actually means 'the little *havmand*',[43] but Hyltén-Cavallius only recorded the later form, the Faroese word *havmaður*. 'Little is said about the *havmand*. His head is completely bald. Naked. Above a human being, below fish.'[44] The *havmand* is also mentioned in the legend about the *haffrú* (mermaid), and then as her male counterpart: 'But if the *havmand* comes up to her, the weather will be good'.[45] To what extent the *marmennil* and *havmand* are identical supernatural phenomena in Faroese tradition is not quite clear, but as the merman usually appears alone, it is most likely that they are two closely-related phenomena. Stories of the merman were used to frighten children so that they would not go down to the sea at places where it was steep and the water deep. This is brought out in a recording from 1976.[46] In a recording from 1968, an informant tells that a couple of years earlier he had talked to a man who believed in mermen. This man 'had once been out fishing with an older man. They had been at the sound on the south of Svínoy fjord. When they got to the fishing ground and were lying still, suddenly it (the boat) touched something and one of the moorings was cut off, and it drifted to the shore. There was no doubt that it was a merman: 'They were in no doubt that it was a merman that had bitten, that had cut their mooring'.[47]

Sjódregil. The Sea Monster

The earliest instance of the supranormal creature, the sea monster, is found in the following extract from Tarnovius in 1669: 'There is another kind of phantom that they call Siodril. And this sits in the evening and at night on the cliffs at the edge of the sea, and glitters all over and gives off sparks, and shouts to the boats that row past saying: "Row boat, Row boat." That is "Row the boat here." But they do not answer him and row on.'[48]

---

40 Hammershaimb (1891), 335.
41 Hammershaimb (1891), 335.
42 Jacobsen & Matras (1961).
43 Holbek Piø (1967), 83.
44 Joensen (1985), 100.
45 Hammershaimb (1891), 337, legend X 'Haffrú'.
46 *FMD* BS 891 1976 MN, N.J.N. b. 1893, MN 1976 Fámjin.
47 *FMD* BS 338 17 E.W. MN 1968.
48 Tarnovius (1950), 82.

Hyltén-Cavallius does not refer to the sea monster, but it is described in the legend *Sjódreygil* ('Sea Monster') in Hammershaimb's 'Færoese Anthology'.[49] It has only one foot or a fish-tail, but it can make long hops on it; it has left its traces in the snow. Its natural habitat is the shore, where it stands on the rocks and shouts to the fishermen to take it on board. The legend tells that sometimes it has been taken on board. The sea monster is very strong and can row for several men, and it is good at finding fish. But it could only function in the twilight and darkness. As soon as it begins to be light, and the sun rises, it gets smaller and at last disappears. Attempts have been made to keep it on board by 'making the sign of the cross over it'.[50] It, nevertheless, disappeared, but the pelvis was left behind because that is said to be of human origin. The sea monster is also able to change its appearance. It can resemble a man or dog and can emit loud sounds that can be heard a long way off, and it gives off sparks when it is ashore. It can talk, but more like a child than a grown-up person, as was mentioned in the foregoing description by Tarnovius. Another of the sea monster's characteristics is that if it meets a man on land, it tries to push the man into the sea. Niels Winther, who also wrote about superstition says, 'When it meets people on land, it tries to force them out into the lake, but if you have a dog with you there is no danger.'[51] This particular characteristic is documented in a recording from 1968 from Dalur, Sandoy, in the following combination of legend and reminiscence:

> The sea monster was said to be a harmful beast that came up on the land and kept close to the shore - most likely it did not go far from the shore. And they used to say that if the sea monster got past a man, between the sea and himself, then the man would be the one that would suffer. But it was a struggle not to let the sea monster get past. I have heard of a man, I remember the man well, he was a cousin of mine, and it is a long time since he died. He was a good deal older. Once he had to run away from a sea monster, but how it happened I don't know, but there was something. There was something supernatural, or there was a sea monster, he didn't really know. But he thought it was a sea monster. And the sea monster, he ran alongside him, and they were running even. But when they were running they came to a boathouse, and the sea monster was to the north side of the boathouse and he was to the south of the boathouse. But when he came north of the boathouse he saw nothing, but he thought he heard something behind him so he kept on running. But the thing with the sea monster is that when you are right in front of it, the story goes that it lost its power. The sea monster was said to be high in the hind quarters and have short forelegs. And cried, I think, something like a seal. It was like an animal with a long tail and black... I heard the man himself say that this one was coal-black and had rather long hind legs, but short forelegs and a long tail.. It could change its appearance so that it could be nearly unrecognizable, so as to be able to sneak in front, because, if it could get ahead of a person then it would be the victor.[52]

---

49 Hammershaimb (1891), 336, legend IX.
50 *rista kross fyri hann.*
51 Winther (1875), 266.
52 *FMD* BS 337 3, O.G.J. MN 1968, Dalur.

A reminiscence was recorded from Skúvoy in 1972, in which it is stated that 'Jóannes í Geil had gone north to catch cormorants. They caught sleeping cormorants in the dark and he takes hold. He reaches out for it and when he touches it, it was as if it flared up and roared as well, and then disappeared in a phosphorescent light. It was supposed to be a sea monster....But it was most likely a seal that had been lying on the land'.[53]

In Sumba, the most southerly village in the Faroes, the sea monster was called *Símun á Tanga*. The following is related in an account from 1968:

Símun á Tanga... that was a sea monster. He went howling amongst the seaweed in the evening, in the twilight. At night he came ashore. At a place that we call Pollurin ... there was a lot of sand down there... He walked on the sand and splashed about. He had three legs, one like a human being and two that were like hooves. He was black. All the children were terrified of him ... It was probably just that they were afraid of him when he howled. And especially when he came ashore and created a fuss.[54]

Another account from the same collection in 1968 provides a detailed description of the supernatural experience[55] in which the whole frame of reference of the supranormal becomes reality:

It was said to stand in the twilight on a strip of land that jutted out into the sea and shout at boats. It was supposed to be able to talk, but very little – just single words – simple and not really like a human being. Here for several generations they called a beast that came up on to the little island *Símun á Tanga*... It was something like a sea monster. When the wind was in the north... he sat roaring and howling. And if the north wind brought dry weather, he howled very loudly, so it was like a barometer. My grandmother, she remembered him well... She was about to be married the last time they heard it, but that is several generations ago. My great grandfather, Sámal í Geilini, once came upon him in a midden heap of seaweed. He had gone out to catch cormorants, there used to be a lot of cormorants around here. He had just come in the evening, there was a northerly wind, and it was unusually calm. He goes down to the heap of seaweed to see if there were any cormorants. Well, down he goes. He saw that there was something there, that ought not to be. He crept up to this creature and grabbed at it. And there was a terrible howling in his face when this thing wakened up – he nearly fainted with fright

---

53 *FMD* BS 125 155 J.T. b. 1896 JHWP 1972. The same informant also tells that when they are in the bird mountains at night 'catching the young fat Manx shearwaters at the cliffs, they often hear the seals below them, how they lie and cry up to the land. And that was the same.' Question: 'It could have been a sea monster?' Answer: 'Yes, it has been a sea monster. But it is weird to listen to when they lie and cry down there.'
54 *FMD* BS 441 13/1968 arch. 8 track 1. MN J.P. and I.D b. 1893 1895 MN 1968 Sumba.
55 *FMD* BS 340 12/1968 MN D. í H. b. 1903 MN 1966, Sumba.

– it went away out along the fjord to the holm. The night was clear, so there was a lot of phosphorescent light on the fjord. He said it looked as if there was fire in its jaws ... it was almost like a dog with four legs. Just what its head was like, I don't know, but I suppose like a dog's or something like that... it was blue in colour. I heard that from Janus í Skemmuni, because he was with them once when they went to catch cormorants at Hellu Longu. There were his father and himself and Dímunar Tummas and Jóhan Pauli and the grandfather of Hørg and Tummas, the son of Bartali, as they called him. They went to the east, it was often difficult in spring and winter, because there could be such a long time without calm weather – three months or so it could be. But now they went to the east. Sørin went up on the rocks to hold the boat and Tummas tied it up, and the others all went up. There is such a big cave in the tuff – tuff that has been eaten away – that several men could be in it, it was always full of cormorants. Now they are getting near it, and now a great flash of lightning comes out, and it is *Símun á Tanga*... it was terrifying, the noise in their ears, the noise of howling from it... and went down Hellu Longa, and by this time I think the two old men were scared and begging the others to hurry and save them. But he didn't go down to the boat, but ran west of the rock – it is a long way down. And he ran so far as they could see out in Røstina, splashing about on the way down. It was not a good swimmer. It didn't go under when it played around on the sea, and there was phosphorescence, said Jenis. He sat down and watched. It looked like fire the way it stirred up the sea. Some believed that this came out of the jaws of the sea monster. But it didn't... And then it was in on the sand, indeed up to my time, I remember that a beast had walked on the sand, and there were four legs, and it looked like hooves – completely round – the holes. It went all round the sand... the strip under the cliff... it had always dug big holes in the sand there to sleep in ... I never saw it, no, nobody was there who really did... see it... It was the traces, yes, when the weather was fine the beach was bigger, it could be covered with traces.... as if it had just wandered backwards and forwards. But it was plain to see that it had four legs – not webbed feet, but completely round holes... normal animals could go into them. If it was sheep, you know, and bigger animals didn't come – the holes were about the size of an ordinary horseshoe.[56]

Símun á Tanga was also used as a cautionary tale (1968):

The story was that a sea monster lived here. And in earlier times he could often be seen dressed in sealskin out on the island, on the rocks. And there he sat and howled. The old people called him *Símun á Tanga* to frighten the children; *Símun á Tanga* would come when they were out too late in the

---

56 For frame of reference see Honko (1973), 22, or Honko (1962).

evening and it was time for them to go home. And the old story was, I remember, an old man told me, a girl disappeared once in the river going to the sheep fold. It was said that she had slipped into a hole that was called Gudrunargentuhylur ('Gudrun girl hole'). And the young people who were with her hurried home to tell what had happened. People went to help, but when they got there, there was no girl to be found. And they said that it was *Símun á Tanga* that had taken this girl because they had been misbehaving – they had been swearing and so on, so he had taken her away.[57]

Havfrúgv. The Mermaid

According to the description in Hammershaimb's 'Faroese Anthology', a mermaid is human above the waist and fish below, and it has long fair hair that it spreads out on the water. The mermaid acts as a presager, so that if it turns towards a boat that means bad weather, and one must row home quickly. If, on the other hand, the mermaid is accompanied by a merman that augurs good weather. It is particularly the song of the mermaid that captivates 'and, therefore, they ought to plug their ears with wool or else they will jump in madness and distraction from the boat out in the sea to her'.[58] In his notes from 1843 Hyltén-Cavallius noted the word *Sævarkvinna* as being synonymous with *havfrú* or *havfrúgv* ('the mermaid'):[59] 'The mermaid resembles a human being above the waist, a fish below. Has long loose hair, golden. Appears before the storm. When she is seen on the water, people try to throw something at her and stop her from singing. If she sings there will be a terrible storm. She sings very beautifully. She is quite harmless. Only her song causes harm.'[60]

Kópakona. The Seal Woman

Hammershaimb's legend 'The Seal Woman' is one of the best known in the 'Faroese Anthology'[61] and has been treated in a modern drama. Hammershaimb told the story to Hyltén-Cavallius, who made the following note in 1843: 'Seals become human beings once a year. Then they dance, are very beautiful. Takes its skin off, dances and is happy. Goes ashore. A man took the skin of a female seal. Took her as a wife. Begot several children. One day the man left his key in the chest. The woman found the skin and disappeared.'[62]

It is amongst the longest of the legends in the 'Faroese Anthology'. The main action takes place in the village of Mikladalur in the Faroe Islands, where a young man has heard that the seals come ashore on Twelfth Night (corresponding to the18th of January in the new calendar). Then they take off their skins and dance

---

57 *FMD* BS 149 11 N.J.P. MN 1963, Sumba.
58 Hammershaimb (1891), 337.
59 It is unlikely that the word *sævarkvinna* was in common use, but in the ballad *Sjúrðarkvæði sævarkvinna* and *sævarmaður* occur in the meanings 'mermaid' and 'merman' (Hammershaimb [1881-55], 40).
60 Joensen (1985), 100.
61 Hammershaimb (1891), 345, XVIII.
62 Joensen (1985), 100.

and enjoy themselves in the form of human beings. He hides and watches the dancing. He falls in love with a seal woman and prevents her from returning to the sea when the sun rises. He takes her seal skin home, and she goes with him. He marries her and they have children. But she always wants to return to the sea. One day the man is at the fishing and has forgotten the key for the chest where he keeps the seal skin. She puts it on and disappears into the sea, but leaves everything in order for the children that she left behind. As a seal she sometimes comes back from the sea to look at her children on the land. The legend goes on to tell how one night in a dream she begs her husband not to kill a big male seal and some young seals, because they are the young of her mate and herself. The husband pays no attention and kills both the male and the young. Later in the evening, when seal meat is being prepared in the crofter's house, the seal woman comes into the kitchen looking like the most hideous troll and swears to take revenge on the whole village. In revenge, so many of the people will die in accidents on the cliffs and at sea that in the end they will be able to hold hands in a ring round the whole of Kallsoy. The account tells that there were similar tales from Sandoy, but without the dramatic epilogue. It is said that there are families on Sandoy that are descended from a seal woman.[63]

The legend of the seal woman, both as folklore and booklore, is very common in the Faroe Islands. Hammershaimb's legend is well known, but new elements have been added to it in the course of time. An account from Mykines in 1974 tells that the seal woman was pregnant when she left the crofter. 'She was pregnant when she jumped back into the sea, with twins. And it was them that he had killed, and he was told that revenge would be taken and that the revenge would last until they could join hands all round Kallsoy. So many would be lost in accidents at sea or on the cliffs. And there was hardly a man that was buried there in the North, my grandmother used to say, for so many, many years. Grandma came from Mykines, she grew up in Sørvagur. She was a very knowledgeable woman, I can tell you.'[64]

According to an interview recorded in 1971 in Skálavík on Sandoy, the crofter in Mikladalur killed his own children. His seal wife 'was with child and gave birth to twins. And then they went to the seal-breeding ground, and they killed the pups that she had warned him about the night before they went, that he should not kill the pups that were furthest in on the shelf because they were their own children. But he went and killed them all, and that is why revenge was taken on Mikladalur, and that revenge was to last for twenty generations, but in Skálavík he only lost his wife.'[65] In 1971, Mortan Nolsøe made a tape recording which gives a very detailed account of the tale of the seal woman at Skálavík on Sandoy. Here, too, it appears that short fingers and a lot of skin between the fingers is a sign that certain families are related to seals:[66]

---

63 Cf. the last part of the legend (Hammershaimb [1891], 348).
64 *FMD* Bs 860 KJ. b. 1889, A.N 1974, Mykines.
65 *FMD* BS 387 band 10/1971 arch. 18 W.T. MN 1971, Skálavík.
66 The author has himself often heard that people who have short fingers and a relatively large amount of skin between the fingers say that they are kinsfolk of the seals.

This is what the man said – I won't leave anything out on purpose, nor add anything on purpose, but I shall try to tell it as my grandmother told it to us.

This was a man from Hamar whose name was Demmus. And it was an old story that the seals came up on Twelfth Night to dance on Borgarfløtu in the most northerly hills. There is a meadow above Borgarsandi, under the cliffs at Borgarhamri. A lovely meadow. It is between Borgin and Borgarhamar. Borgin is a hill below Borgarhamar – a very beautiful hill. And there is a lovely flat meadow between them, and this was where the seals amused themselves.

Well, well, so he left the house. He left the house late in the evening. Then the seals came swarming from all directions up to Borgarfløtu and took off their skins and started dancing together. And there is a girl who is pretty and attractive, and he takes a fancy to her. And he looks where she lays her skin – or covering. And he goes after it, and at the foot of the cliff he hides himself with it behind a stone there.

Well, and they dance and amuse themselves, but now the sun is coming up. They put on their skins again. But now there is none for her. Now there is none for her, and she searches and searches, and all the seals go away and she is left behind. Then he goes to her and tells her where her skin is. And she begs him and pleads with him in tears to let her have it back. But he puts her off and says not to bother about it and rather come home with him. She is not keen about this, but it ends with them going. They go home, but I can't honestly remember whether my grandmother said that they got married. But they lived together and had children.

So now they are at the fishing. And he was the leader in the boat, she said. And when they are far out at sea, then – he is tugging on a fish, and he feels under his belt, or on the cord for his knife – the key is gone. And he smacks his hand on his thigh and says to them 'I am without a wife today. Haul on the boat, everyone, and row with me as hard as you can.' Well, they do this and when they come into the bay she was on the skerry under the water. There is a seal on the skerry under the water, and it has been there, I can't say to this day, but it was there up to the time of my brother's wife's son. My brother was twice married and the second wife had two sons. And the elder son shot that seal. And I remember that my father was so angry about him shooting the seal. Maybe he didn't really believe that it was the seal woman, but it was a bit of history that it was always there. And the reason that it was there must have been, as the story says, that there is a seal breeding-ground just north of that corner, where the cliff begins. We call it out 'at the corner'. But we haven't seen it since. It was huge.

Well ! They go ashore and he hurries to his house. And when he gets there, everything is cold. There is no wife. She has put out the fire. She has put out the fire and everything sharp that was in the house – knives and axe and such things – she had locked away in the chest that her skin was in. And the story goes that the chest was in the house up until the First World War. It was very clumsily made, but the design was not so bad – it was broader around the bottom than at the lid. And each part was one whole piece, so it was sawn out of big trees. The bottom was one piece and the sides and the ends and the lid were each a single piece. It was dovetailed and nailed with wooden nails. But then during the war there was no wood to be had. The old man, the father, had a lot of land and used a horse and cart, and he had a horse that was so bad at breaking things, and it had broken the cart. And so he took the chest. Grandma was very upset. Not for that reason; possibly the chest that the seal woman's skin was in had already gone, but it was a historic item – if nothing else – in the house. Indeed ! She was not pleased about that.[67]

As can be seen from this mixture of legend and reminiscence there is no motive of vengeance in the Sandoy version, rather an inherited respect for the seals as relatives. In a tape recording of another version the informant compares the local legend and that from Mikladalur, which appears in the Anthology:

I have heard two tales about men who got seal wives. And they sound similar from both places. The one is in the north in Mikladalur and the other in Skálavík. In Skálavík it was a Hamar man. He went out, it was said to be on the old Twelfth Night (18th January), because then the seals would take off their skins and dance. So he went to the place they call 'under Skútanum' on Twelfth Night. And then the seals came and took off their skins. And he took one of the skins and sat beside it, or he laid it down where he was sitting. And then when the seals were finished dancing, they came back to get their skins and put them on again. But this Hamar man had one of the skins. So she went to him and asked him to let her have the skin again. But he said no, that she would not get the skin back again, but that she should go home with him because he wanted her for his wife. And she went home with him willingly. And he locked the skin in the chest and he always had the key with him – whether he was up in the hills or at the fishing, it didn't matter. If he was out of the house he had the keys on him. And they lived together, they lived happily together and had children. I think that they were supposed to have – I don't think I am wrong in thinking I was told that they had three children. And then one day when they were at the fishing, when they were out at the fishing ground, he put his hand on his thigh and said that the keys had been left at home and now he would have no wife tonight. And he asked them to row to the shore at once.

And when they came to the slipway, she was at the landing stage, there

---

67 *FMD* BS 387 band 10/1971 arch. 16 MN, W. T. b. 1965.

looking at him. He went home and found that everything, the fire and everything was tidied up and the children were playing happily on the floor. And there was no more to the story than that he had lost his wife.

But up north in Mikladalur, it was in a different way, because there that woman was with child and gave birth to twins. And when they went to the seal breeding-ground they killed the pups that she had warned him about the night before they went, telling him that he must not kill the pups that were innermost on the shelf because they were their own children. But he killed everything and, therefore, vengeance was wreaked on Mikladalur, and that was to last to the twentieth generation, but in Skálavík he only lost his wife.[68]

Sæneyt. Sea Cattle

The legend *Sæneyt og Hulduneyt* tells that sea cattle (or sea cows) look like other cows, but give much more milk; people are, therefore, very keen to have these cows. Sometimes on Twelfth Night they have been found in byres along with the other cows. If the sign of the cross is made on their backs, these sea cows stand quietly amongst the others.[69] Here too the old material can be supplemented with new accounts, e.g. the following from a reminiscence recorded in 1970, but which, according to the context, must be earlier than 1880:

Father had a storehouse to the west of our house, to the west of the hay barn. One evening he had gone to the storehouse. The dog had followed him, the dog was in the storehouse with him. And it was dark, it was late in the evening. And while he is in the storehouse, he hears a strange noise outside. And the dog began to growl. There was something moving ... it was like snoring, a bit like sniffing ... it was walking round the storehouse. He had a knife on him, a big knife. He wondered if he should go out, but then he thought it was better not to. And the dog started to growl. And when it ... came towards the door and went past the door, he opened the door enough to let the dog out. And this thing, it must surely have been something that had come up from the sea, something or other ... a sea animal or some such thing. Because the dog followed after, it followed downwards, and the phosphorescence flared out of it, and the dog followed it right down to the beach, and it turned out to be something like a big cow ... it was so dark that he didn't exactly see what it looked like.[70]

The same informant tells also about a sea bull:

The old folk in the smithy had a cow once, a cow that they kept at home, that they had standing down under Sondum ... And the cow had never been to the bull, but

---

68 *FMD* BS 337 O.G.J. b. 1888, MN 1968, Dalur.
69 Hammershaimb (1891), 337, legend XI 'Sæneyt og hulduneyt'.
70 *FMD* BS 357 7 J.L., b. 1882, MN 1970, Fámjin.

the cow was nevertheless with calf, and they didn't know anything about a bull. So then she had a calf and the calf had horse hair down its back. And it was a heifer calf, a lovely calf, except for the horse hair on its back. And the minister at that time lodged with the old folk in the smithy. He asked to get the calf. He got it, they gave him the calf. The calf thrived in every way, but when it was a year old it became ill and died.

When asked by the collector about where the bull could have come from, the informant answered: 'it must have been one that came up from the sea ... a sea bull.'[71]

According to the following account from Nólsoy in 1980, whole flocks of cattle could come up from the sea to graze on land:

It was part of the ideology of the old people. There were bovine animals in the sea that looked like the animals on the land, and, of course, cattle too. There were cows in the same form as our cows. One Sunday, fairly far on in the summer, they see that there are seven cows up at the place we call 'Lundi', on the hill to the east above Grønadalur, and they were exactly like the cows from Kongstovu, and seven [in number]. That was the number that could graze there, the herd in Kongstovu then, because all the land was there. And they thought it best to hurry and milk them, because the cattle were roaming all over the place. They knew that from the morning, and so they hurried out ... and didn't stop before Gjógvarágarð, that was where they were going, and when they got up here to the pasture, the cows were gone. And they hadn't gone out from the pasture , because people had been watching them. There was nothing that could be done about it. The thing is that they were sea cows that had come up to the land and had gone back to the sea. And this story was told as far back as I can remember and as long as the people were alive who had taken part in this incident...[72]

Fjørutrøll. The Shore Troll

In legend no. 57 in Jakob Jakobsen's 'Faroese Legends and Folktales' there is a supernatural being, a fjørðutrøll, a 'shore troll' – an ugly troll that lived down at the beach. In the story, this shore troll creates havoc in the village of Hattervík on Fugloy, especially in the dusk and in the evening. 'It was monstrous to see, a lot of seaweed grew on it, and it brought a lot of stones up with it ... When the troll came it sounded as if it was pulling two millstones with it, and it was as if the whole of the cobbled yard was loose and being ground down under its feet. This troll was so big that it was higher than the ridge of the roof down at the house. Nevertheless Sakaris, who was a wise and learned man, was able to get rid of the shore troll.' Weihe has also an account of this creature, which he calls Sjódýrið ('sea animal'),[73] and which the merchant and farmer Hans Dávur Matras had seen in the latter part of the last century:

---

71 *FMD* BS 357 J.L., b. 1882, MN 1970, Fámjin.
72 *FMD* BS 949 8, S.D. b. 1905, MN 1980, Nólsoy.
73 Weihe (1933), 40.

As they are standing there, someone catches sight of something in the stone dyke that was about the length of three fishing lines further south; everyone looks in the same direction and sees a sea animal getting up on dry land. Then it makes its way south along the fjord, straight towards them.

They were afraid and the farmer asked them all to come into his house, which they did, and he locked the door.

Hans Dávur said that this was the absolute truth. He too saw the sea animal. It was overgrown with seaweed, so he couldn't really see what it was like, even though it came close to them before they fled into the farmer's house ... He had heard that there were animals in the sea that looked like the animals on the land. He thought that this animal that we have been talking about had the shape of a horse or cow, but it was as if there was something hanging down on both sides at the middle of the back. If it had really been a horse they might have been panniers or sacks. The animal had from time to time let out frightening cries that were like loud snuffling.

While the others, half afraid, are thinking about this huge animal, the farmer is walking to and fro. At last he reaches for his whale knife that was hanging in its sheath from a beam, straps it round his waist, lifts the latch and goes out.

The animal that was now a short distance from the door starts snuffling when he sees the farmer. He turned round and went in again and locked the door once more. He said that nobody was to go out again that evening.

The next day there was no animal to be seen.

Two accounts from Hattarvík (dating from 1974[74] and 1977,[75] respectively), make it clear that the story was still told in Hattarvík, but it is not clear whether this was booklore or a continuation of the local tradition: 'it always went between the houses, and the handles of the pots clattered ... it went amongst the children and played.'

Other Supernatural Animals

There is also an account from Suðuroy of a strange whale – a mixture of seal and whale that they called kettuhvalur – cat whale:

There is a story about an animal, a seal or whale that was seen about 1913 from a boat far out at sea. The animal put its flippers on the railing of the boat and let out a sound: 'the sound was a bit like a cat, when a cat spits ... and it laid its flippers on the gunwale, its flippers and snapped, but before anything happened, he put the mouth of his gun between its jaws and shot. And it fell backwards from the gunwale. It looked to them as if it sank, but they couldn't say whether it was dead. But they had never in their lives seen such

---

74 *FMD* BS 631 A.M.H and A.P., E.J. 1974, Hattarvík.
75 *FMD* BS 795 H.H, b. 1900 and J.M.H. b. 1909 (Gjógv). MN 1977, Hattarvík.

an animal... It looked like a man with a white beard. It was paler under the chin, but terribly hairy, and the hair stuck straight out. That could have been from anger or something like that. And it had rather long ears... It had horrible skin – woolly... Then they came ashore and told this story. Jenis í Andrasgarði said that it must have been a cat fish, cat whale, not a seal, or whale. He called it a cat whale. That was its right name, he said.

From the same informant there is an account of a *tröllahvalur* – a 'troll whale' - which was said to have drifted ashore:

...it was shaggy. It was a bit like a seal. I don't know whether it's true, but I heard it from some old folk. They said that that whale was always in the north. It was from Jensi í Skemmuni that I heard about the troll whale....and he was the one I listened to most when I was young. Later I hadn't time to listen to such tales.[76]

There are also accounts of another whale, *tjørnubøka*, meaning 'the blue whale', which either had a small pond on its back, or made a pond by curling itself up and biting its own tail. If it rose suddenly to the surface, a boat could find itself lying on this little pond:

All that I can say about the blue whale is that some thought that there was a pond in it, some thought that it could be a whale that curled itself round. Jens Vestergaard did not think that he had seen one, but from what the old people had told him, he thought that it was a whale that was curled round ... The last person I know who had any experience of a blue whale was Jákup í Toftum, the farmer in Vág. He was out in the west, that is west of Fámjin, and while they were at the fishing ground, one of them came to the surface... It didn't surface for more than six hours – one tide ... You mustn't touch it, except to keep the boat free of it so that it wouldn't be overturned. That could happen, if the pond was very small ... But one thing they did say was that something like that, which happens seldom, was seldom a good sign ... [77]

Finally, there is also an account of a *flundra*, a supernatural halibut, that was said to be black on both sides:

But they say that this halibut was not an ordinary halibut because it was black on both sides ... and besides it was said to be so extraordinarily big and broad that they thought that bad luck must follow something that was so different from the other halibut.[78]

---

76 *FMD* BS 340 D.J.J.b. 1903, MN 1968, Sumba.
77 *FMD* BS 340 D.J.J. b. 1903, MN 1968.
78 *FMD* BS 355 A.D. b. 1912, MN 1970, Sumba.

The Man on Board

The traditions which have been discussed up to now belong to the traditional Faroese peasant farmer society, and to the cosmos of the village. By the end of the nineteenth century many changes had taken place in Faroese society, on many different levels. The world had opened up both ideologically and economically.[79] The most important source of income was the production of dried cod. This brought about an intensification of inshore fishing and later sea-fishing. Fishing with sea-going vessels started seriously from 1872, so that as time went by the fishermen were away from home from March to September. This created new environments. In this connection certain forms of beliefs in connection with the fishing became clearly manifested. This is something which I have discussed in earlier studies. These beliefs were particularly connected with fishing luck (success in catching fish). According to the pay system on board the Faroese smacks, each man was paid according to the number of fish that he personally caught on his hand line. This led to a great deal of competition. If you had 'fishing luck', it meant that you earned a lot. This competition, which was new to Faroese culture, resulted in a boom in various forms of superstition on board these fishing boats.[80]

A new supernatural being, that is otherwise better known by the name *klabautermanden*[81] and can be defined as a ghost,[82] made its appearance in the complex of Faroese beliefs. The *klabautermand* tradition was completely unknown in the Faroe Islands until the advent of sea-fishing with smacks. The material concerning this was collected by the author in 1971. Prior to that it had only been dealt with in a literary form in two short stories.[83] If we apply the concepts popular belief, reminiscence and legend,[84] an analysis of the whole body of collected material shows that, in the main, it can be classified as reminiscence and popular belief. The legends which exist are connected mostly with the oldest boats, especially 'Suðringur', the boat that ran aground off Iceland in 1912, but with the whole crew being rescued.[85] It is evident from the analysis of the whole body of material that the fishermen could see, and at times also hear, the man on board. They could

---

79 Joensen (1987).

80 This matter is dealt with in detail in the chapter on supernatural communication in the book *Færøske sluppfiskere* (Joensen 1975:116) and in the article 'Tradition och miljø i faroiskt fiske', (Joensen 1981).

81 Cf. Buss (1973) and (Gerndt) 1971. See the article by Mare Kõiva in this volume.

82 The subject of *Klabautermanden* has been dealt with in a special study 'Lemperen eller Manden ombord' ('The Trimmer or the Man on Board') (Joensen [1975a]).

83 In the collection of stories *Útrák* 1947 the writer Martin Joensen wrote about the phenomenon in "*Maðurin umbord*" (The Man on Board). In *Ítróttartíðindi* 12, Tórshavn, Sigurd Joensen published 'Tjúgundi maður umbord' ('The Twentieth Man on Board').

84 Honko (1962), 132. A *legend (sagn)* has a definite form with an epic backbone, which is stereotyped and follows a fixed scheme of development. A *reminiscence (memorate)* is an account of an authentic supernatural experience. It often gives an insight into the situation surrounding the experience, which is individual, but usually influenced by the collective tradition. *Popular belief (folketros udsagn)* is a wider concept and covers material, which does not lend itself to being included in the other categories. There are no certain criteria for the form in which it is presented, and it is usually very brief.

85 Joensen (1975b), 92.

usually hear him trimming the salt in the hold at night, from which he got the name, the 'trimmer'. They could also hear him fishing from the deck at night. They could see him working with the sails. If the boat went down or ran aground, he disappeared into the sea, to which the many accounts about the boat 'Suðringur', bear witness.

The man on board was believed to have come with the boat. These Faroese smacks were all bought second-hand from England, and, therefore, had a history which was not properly known. The reason for his being on board might be a murder, an accident, or just chance. In the material, there are also accounts of women being on board, but their role is very unclear. Usually the woman was only seen on board. The explanation for their presence on board is that they died on board the boat for some reason or other. The 'man on board' had a supranormal communication function, in that he acted as a *presager*, and furnished the crew with important information such as warning of danger, of stormy weather, of running aground, of ships coming towards them, of lanterns going out, as well as letting them know that good fishing was in the offing. In short he provided the crew with some of the information for the acquisition of which more advanced electronic equipment is used today.[86]

Conclusion

Practically no systematic documentation of the type of tradition described in this paper was carried out for sixty to seventy years. We have been able to demonstrate, however, that there were still bearers of the nineteenth century tradition alive a hundred years later. Furthermore, new forms of tradition could be adapted to the new working environment on board the Faroese fishing boats in the twentieth century.[*]

---

86 Cf. also Andreassen (1976) who deals with various forms for warnings in Faroese tradition.
* Translation by Mrs Sheila Arnskov.

Narrators and their Notions of the *Klabautermann*: The Ship-Spirit of Estonian Folk Belief

Mare Kõiva

I

At first sight, stories of the ship-spirit – the *klabautermann* – appear to be not nearly as old and venerable as other types of supernatural lore. This figure is not mentioned in the older sources such as those in which the witch trial of Holy Michel of Tattra in 1699 is recorded. Under interrogation, 'Tattra Michel', as he was called, related that a water-spirit by the name of '*Neck*' had helped him with his sorcery. *Neck*, he said, looked like a man but wore a white shirt. In order to summon this spirit, Tattra Michel had used the formula: 'Water-spirit, come and deliver this man from his malady' (*wee algias, tulle awwita sedda meest ommast tõbbist*). In the course of cross-examination, apart from *Neck* (a river-dweller), the accused also named other spirits, one of which was called Judas (*Juda*).

The use of this and other invocations officially recorded in witch trials to secure the assistance of spirits implies that they commanded some importance in the religious climate of the time and could be invoked in the hope of gaining help. In this context, seeking the help of spirits was as common as turning for assistance to God or the devil. Rather than being thought of as accidental utterances and admissions extracted in pain and panic on the rack, such incantations should be regarded as authentic formulae which bear true witness to the living faith and spiritual experience of the time, as represented in healing practices.

Drawing on materials from the Estonian Folklore Archives and recordings and transcriptions from the Estonian National Museum (the majority of which predate the Second World War), I wish to focus here on certain problems relating to the *klabautermann* tradition involving variations in classical narratives about the *klabautermann*, their connections to personal experience narratives and the use of dialogue in religious narratives in general. In addition, some impression of the character and atmosphere of Estonian maritime lore will be given.

II

Compared to other mythological beings, the *klabautermann* appears to be of relatively recent vintage. According to Loorits, *klabautermann* lore was transmitted to Estonia in the course of the nineteenth century by North German or Dutch seafarers.[1] Buss is of the opinion that belief in the *klabautermann* stretched far beyond the German cultural and linguistic sphere of influence and was widespread among northern seafarers.[2] Both Loorits and Buss also connect the *klabautermann* with older mythological beings and instances of religious imagination, primarily the ship-spirits.[3]

In his treatment of water-spirits in Livonian folklore, Loorits maintains that the earlier notion of a good or evil spirit associated with a ship has been supplanted by the notion of the *klabautermann* and its derivatives, a body of folk tradition which spread from cities and urban centres. Folk belief retained the characteristics and functions of both the benevolent/malevolent spirit and of the sea-spirit whose principal business was the protection of the ship and its crew from danger and whose departure from the ship was considered to be a sure sign of impending disaster.[4] In his catalogue of Livonian folktales, Loorits has classified the *klabautermann* lore as a separate type of narrative;[5] Simonsuuri has allocated two separate type numbers to the Finnish material.[6] On the other hand, mention of the *klabautermann* is missing from Aarne's catalogue of Estonian folktales.[7] In the most comprehensive treatment of Estonian folk beliefs available – Loorits (1951) – the author restates his earlier view that the *klabautermann* is a being of Germanic origin, the 'west-of Tallinn' counterpart of the ship-fairy, and he characterises it as a deficient adaptation to Estonian marine mythology. He enumerates most of the *klabautermann*'s designations, gives descriptions of its appearance and lists its functions. To the older motifs attaching to it, he assigns the dispute concerning priority of the various supernatural beings on the ship in terms of the order of their arrival on board.[8]

Otherwise, the prevailing tendency is to play down or overlook the *klabautermann*. Eisen grants it and the ship-spirit only thirteen lines in his 'Estonian Mythology', picturing the ship-spirit as a close cognate of the house-spirit and mentioning its anthropomorphic appearance, its role as a weather prognosticator (frequently portending disaster) and its frequenting of ships, either singly or in pairs. In brief, Eisen sees the *klabautermann* as a local variety of ship-spirit (which, in fact, is the

---

1 Loorits (1951).
2 Buss (1973), 109 ff.
3 Loorits (1931),76, examines the Estonian material in greater detail and traces parallels in the other countries. Loorits (1932) confirms these findings.
4 Loorits (1926), 202 ff.
5 Loorits (1929).
6 Simonsuuri (1961), (G1001, G1002).
7 Aarne (1918)
8 Loorits (1951), 272-3.

way it is understood in the tradition of the island of Saaremaa) and he describes how one should go about acquiring one (for example, by the captain of the ship carrying in his pocket the first splinters of the timber that went into the making of it).[9] Paulson[10] makes no mention of the *klabautermann* at all; while Masing includes a couple of sentences about it, referring in the main to connections between it and the Finnish ship-spirit and house-spirit, and mentioning, *inter alia*, that the spirit entered the ship when the keel was being laid.[11]

We may suppose that, on the one hand, researchers of the older mythological lore may have been put off by the relatively wide international spread of the *klabautermann* tradition and its partial attachment to what we might call vocational lore and, on the other, by its tendency to incorporate material associated with paranormal experiences of a general kind as well as material drawing on various less reliable oral sources.

III

In religious lore, spirits and ghosts often speak in rather unusual tongues. In classical older folklore, they frequently employ a language partly or even fully unintelligible to humans; should the wording not be entirely of foreign origin, it may contain words or phrases obviously adopted from other languages. Thus, Oinas (1979) has, in this context, identified some war-time looters' expressions as stemming from the Tatar language and linked these to specific Tatar horde units. He has found data in the historical annals concerning parts of the Tatar horde which ravaged Estonia, and these expressions which subsequently became part of our folklore might be matched with such data. Peegel's approach on the other hand has been to interpret the appearance of *peninukid* (beings with pointed snouts), not as quasi-mythical, half-dog, half-human creatures, but as ordinary warriors whose outstanding feature was their uniform, most particularly their helmets complete with protruding beavers.[12]

A feature of the speech of ghosts, spirits and revenants is that it may also resemble child-like babble. This is quite appropriate, since the language of children may be regarded as having had a magical significance insofar as children's visions and speech may be considered oracular. Yet, ghosts, spirits and revenants also make use of a quaint language not to be met with in everyday life and thus not easily identified. Frequently the words are disconnected, adapted words, recognisable as borrowings from the tongues of close neigbours. Thus, a revenant, irked at the traveller mistaking it for an ordinary house cat, exclaims – 'It is yourself who is the *ko ka* [the adapted form of a Russian loan word]. Me, I am ...[naming the late head of the relevant household].'

---

9 Eisen (1995), 49.
10 Paulson (1964).
11 Masing (1995), 139.
12 Peegel (1968), 480 ff.

Word-switching and adaptation of this sort is also a feature of certain varieties of folk poetry. Hence, in songs (especially those in the more recent fashion), the comic part is based on an alternation between two languages which implies an understanding of both. As I have tried to illustrate elsewhere, the same may be said to hold true for Russian-language incantations in Estonian tradition, the meaning of which can often be strikingly at variance with the language of origin.[13] Most probably, this variation arises from the lack of competence of the learner and user of the incantations in the other language. It is only fair to note, however, that even in the case of incantations learnt by rote in other languages, quite often the usage is normative and relatively correct. Occasionally, free standing couplets and individual sentences have been joined together, but generally this is not a matter which generates any great difficulty in interpretation or in determining the language of origin.

The fact that the language of origin, even when it is directly adverted to by the individual using the invocation, may not be known to the recipient of such services and might be judged by him/her to be nonsensical, reveals yet another interesting dimension of this process. A fascinating example of this kind in Estonian folk poetry is the so-called 'Romany Lord's Prayer' which turns out in reality to be an altered form of the Latvian version of the Lord's Prayer.[14] The language of origin of children's couplets can usually be guessed at fairly easily. If, however, the text has been mythologised, it may be that an intelligible function and meaning for it in the human tongue may be claimed. It is as if meaninglessness or glossolalia sanctifies what has been said, an issue which is important in the case of texts considered magical in folk belief. Such arguments are well buttressed by the existence of religious attitudes which hold that the so-called foreign-language incantations are effective in healing and that foreigners are better healers etc etc. Words known to be devoid of meaning may be deliberately added to one's speech out of religious considerations, much as is the fashion currently pertaining to praying in some religious sects where speaking in tongues is regarded as lending additional power to such utterances.

The speech of the *klabautermann* is fairly normal insofar as the language of communication is the sailor's mother tongue, and language – just as in the case of modern paranormal beings – does not play an especially important role. Indeed, language does not appear to be a problem, folkloristically or otherwise, in either case, for there is no mention in Estonian folklore of communication occuring in a foreign or unknown tongue in this particular context. We may conclude therefore that the message of the mythological being is rendered comprehensible from the context even when it may not be properly Estonian in form.

---

13 Kõiva (1990), 143.
14 Ernits (1987), 13-29.

A further difference of note is the alternate use of monologue or dialogue format in communications between human and supernatural beings. The protagonist's monologue may give expression to some emotion or arise from an event of one kind or another, and forms only a rather brief interlude in the story. The message uttered by the supernatural being is, for the most part, also of short duration, generally consisting of a sentence or just a couple of words. Longer passages of direct speech would in any case be quite out of place in a folklore context, where – more often than not – a text consists of short dialogues seldom amounting to more than a straightforward exchange of remarks between the human and supernatural beings. The following account of a quarrel between two *klabautermann* figures yields three sentences in direct speech :

> The captain asked – 'Which of you was the first ?' One replied –'I came when the keel was laid.' The other said – 'I came when they fixed the foremast.' The captain then gave pride of place to the one that came when the ship's keel was laid. The other one walked off with the foremast.[15]

Analysis of folklore texts shows that, in one and the same story, some of the characters may use direct speech while others avoid it as much as possible. In certain situations, direct speech may occur in dialogue between the characters – for example, when someone gains oracular knowledge by eavesdropping on a conversation between supernatural beings, enabling, as a consequence, a wise course of action to be pursued and disaster to be avoided. A case in point with regard to the *klabautermann* tradition would involve a faulty mast mentioned in a conversation which is overheard by a human being.

We also have the example of a dialogue which takes place between a human and a supernatural being. In several types of myth, or narratives arising from a religious experience, the human realises respectively that his collocutor is a mythological being, a non-human – the structure and composition of the narrative being such that this is stated at the conclusion of the narrative, only after the encounter between the two is over and done. Very occasionally this constitutes the whole point of the story. Among the narratives of this type in the *klabautermann* lore, we may count stories about a nocturnal aide ordering a change of course or different visions of impending death where a captain, mate or sailor is pictured in tragic circumstances – in a state of helplessness or about to meet his end, something which subsequently comes to pass.

The human speaker may sense a foreign or supernatural element in the collocutor, in which case the difficulty may be resolved in one of two ways: the dialogue may incorporate deliberately uttered repulsion formulae, including

---

15 *Kapten küsind: 'Kumb teitest ennen oli ?' Teine ütlend: 'Ma tuli siis, kui looskiil pandi.' Teine ütlend: 'Ma tuli siis, kui võõrmast pandi.' Kapten andis seliele õiguse, kes siis tuli, kui looskiil pandi. Teini läind tükkis mastiga minema.(ERA 11 1, 673/4 (6), Reigi - P. Ariste [1928])*

invocations of scripture (specifically the Lord's Prayer), or an indication may be given that religious songs were chanted, the latter course of action being the more common of the two.[16] Such myths are closely related to narratives in which the human actor unwittingly utters a repulsion formula or uses some expression linked to and functioning within the sphere of nominative magic. It is only subsequent events that lead him to the realisation in hindsight that he has been dealing with a supernatural being.

We have no evidence of repulsion formulae being used against the *klabautermann*, whose ill-natured, rambunctious behaviour and pranks are tolerated and borne with equanimity. Insofar as it may not be opposed, it may be said to belong to the same genus as spirits on whose loyalty to a dwelling the future luck of that dwelling and the luck and very existence of its inhabitants depends.

The oral format does not favour longer characterisation and the exchanges tend to be brief. Dialogue in *klabautermann* lore is also curtailed, consisting mostly of single sentences containing no extensive passages of direct speech. Most often the message is relayed in a simple telegram-style. Even in the case of a narrative where it is indicated that a human overhears a conversation between supernatural beings, only a short dialogue is reproduced consisting of two or three sentences in which the gist of the message is communicated.[17] The formulae present in these narratives have been classified under the headings 'initial', 'medial' and 'final'. In *klabautermann* tradition, there is a great deal of 'medial' dialogue; while in religious lore it is mostly 'final' formulae which occur – constituting the climax of the narrative and completely altering its course. Elsewhere, formulae appear to serve as the framework of the narrative.

In *klabautermann* lore, myths containing visual experience and auditive dialogue predominate over other types of narrative. The 'supporting of the ship's mast' is undoubtedly a story which belongs to this category. Here the spirit repeatedly asks a sailor if it can let go of the mast. The sailor tells it to wait a while, but, worn down by this constant repetition of the question, eventually relents and grants the supplicant permission to let go the mast if he so wishes, whereupon the mast collapses. This myth is analogous to narratives of buried treasure where a voice offers to deposit the treasure at someone's feet and eventually does just that when the person in question gives it permission to so do.[18]

Myths with a tactile dialogue – as exemplified in the following account – are fewer in number: A sailor dozing on watch suddenly receives a punch between the eyes and is warned – 'The mast is so bad I can't hold it any longer.' The mast does,

---

16 Kõiva (1990), 136.
17 The question of the relative importance of formulae and dialogue in accounts of such encounters has been investigated by Viidalepp (1938).
18 Loorits (1929), S214.

indeed, prove to be bad. Among other narratives founded on tactile contact or dialogue are legends in which the *klabautermann* demands that the ship sets a new course, often guiding the vessel to the location of a shipwreck where the shipwrecked are rescued, or causing the ship itself to steer clear of disaster.[19] Commonest of all are the accounts which describe sightings of the *klabautermann* and the overhearing of conversations in which *klabautermann* figures are involved.

In both cases – those including dialogue and those which lack it – the primary role is played by the narrator. The relater (or experiencer) may avoid dialogue and communicate the whole event in a thoroughly captivating manner, yet excluding direct speech. However, direct speech might also form an inseparable part of the narrative which could not be discarded without spoiling the whole account. Let us here revert to an example of the supposed speech of the *klabautermann* in a situation where it is represented, yet with no actual dialogue with the human taking place:

> In Greensmouth there was once an Estonian and a Finnish ship. Both captains went ashore. One of the crew heard two men talking on the cabin roof telling about their travels. One of the men said the foremast was bad and that it had to be supported. The crewman went to look but not a soul was to be seen. The next day they checked the mast and it was shot through with dry rot and had already sunk two inches.[20]

Another version goes like this:

> Once two spirits had a row. One spirit said – 'You must get out!' The captain overheard them. Our Jürg was first mate – it was a foreign ship, from Denmark or somewhere. The captain replied – 'Whichever came last must go!' One of the spirits said – 'I was here when the foremast was put in place.' The other said – 'I was here when the keel was laid !' Then the captain said – 'Whichever came last must go.' That spirit then left of its own free will, snapping the foremast as it went, which fell down. It left, and the mast with it. Those must have been the ship-spirits. Jürg was also on that ship.[21]

---

19 Cf. Loorits (1926), 207 for an analagous description in Livonian lore.
20 *Inglismaal Grensmutis oln üks esti ning üks suõmõ laev. Kaptenid löin mõlõmad mualõ. Üks mies kuln, et kaiutilae piäl aan kak miest juttu. Riäkn oma reisest. Üks üteln, vokkmast ollõ mädä. Sedä piäde oidma. Madrus läin vällä uatama - mitte enge põlõ kusagil oln. Teese päävä mindud uatama: mast oln pulbõr mädäd. Oln juba kaks tolli all vaibun* [ERÄ II 79, 441 (2) < Kihnu - T. Saar (1934)].
21 *Ükskord oln riius kaks aldijast. Teine oli öeld: sina pead välja minema! Kapten oli kuuld. Meie Jürg oli tüürman, see oli vieras laev, Taanist vai kust see oli. Kapten öeld selle ääle pääle: Kes viimaks tuli, see peab välja minema! Teine oli öeld: Mina olin siin, kui pandi võörmasti. Teine oli öeld: Mina olin siin, kui pandi põhja alusteti! Siis kapten öeld: See peab minema, kes viimaks tuli. Siis mend iia meelega välja, ahga oli ottand võörmasti ka robinal kaasa, kukkus maha, läks ise ära, oli masti ka. Need pidand laevahaldijad olema. Jürg oli seal laeva peal.* [ERA II 114, 547/8 (55) < Kuusalu – R.Põldmäe (1935)]. For Livonian parallels, cf. Loorits 1926:206-207, (Loorits S29).

IV

When I was a folklore student in the mid 1970s, I used to spend time in the company of my father-in-law and other fishermen on the island of Saaremaa who were waiting onshore for favourable weather. On Saaremaa, men did not participate in farmwork or take care of the cattle, such work customarily being done by women. The men would gather on the seashore or assemble in a house near the shore and while away the time sipping home-made beer and telling jokes, narrating legends, and discusssing old customs and beliefs while they waited for a good wind.

There were several good storytellers in that company at Ruhve harbour, one of whom was from the Sõrve peninsula, a place where, according to popular belief, several well-known witches lived. This individual usually told stories about witches and witchcraft, and his companions believed him capable of changing the wind and of being able to ensure good luck with the catch. Another man in that company was a highly appreciated jester, while a third specialized in stories about the everyday life of the local people and was especially adept at adding a humorous touch to stories of the supernatural. In these gatherings, through an amalgam of gossip and actuality peppered with humour, politics were also discussed, the government criticised and the life of the village generally reviewed.

Folklore and para-folklore made up a large part of all this. The older men belonged to the generation born in the early decades of this century, but even the repertoire of those born in the 1950s and 1960s (thus having no direct high-sea or 'big-ship' experience of their own) also had an old-time flavour. Beliefs connected with boat-building and fishing were relatively well-known and, although some of the supernatural stories were recounted half in jest, the admonitions of others were strictly followed. Stories of the *klabautermann* were known but not believed, the only exception being stories describing an encounter with the *klabautermann* which foreboded someone's death. It was thought that in the old days every boat had its own *klabautermann*.

Otherworld beings were often discussed in my father-in-law's home, generally as a result of questions put by visitors from town such as myself and my husband. My husband had been raised in a family rich in tradition and consequently was himself able to recall a number of unique stories. This helped considerably in counteracting any tensions that might have arisen in direct interview situations, and sometimes also resulted in no notice being taken of someone like me noting down or recording items of conversation. Such activity would be accepted in the following spirit: 'Oh, she's writing again, she must have heard something of interest.'

Any attempt to characterise the atmosphere of these sessions must take account of a very important circumstance which influenced the whole folklore repertoire, both narrative and song, particularly that connected with the sea – namely, that, following the Second World War, these coastal dwellers were denied the right to use their boats and so were like birds whose wings had been clipped. The islands, together with the whole of the Estonian coastline, were declared part of the border zone which was guarded meticulously. Entry to these areas was by special permit only and even these permits were invalid in the vicinity of large army and air-force bases. Only on one small stretch of the coast could one walk without special permission and out of sight of armed guards.

Local seamen no longer had access to the sea, and fishing was conducted from collective farm-owned boats in inshore waters. People tried to obtain nets and traps to catch sufficient fish for themselves and their neighbours secretly. There was little point in large-scale fishing undercover, as it were, since no outlet for marketing the catch existed. In addition, there was precious little that could be done with the income derived from collective-farm fishing: the land belonged to the state and the maximum size of dwellings and outhouses as well as numbers of ownable cattle was determined by law. The more active youth attended 'sea school' and sailed the oceans of the world on Soviet ships. However, this was not, as in pre-Soviet times, a case of sailors making a choice of ship and working as free men, but rather a matter of signing up for duty as a loyal citizen who had no intention of jumping ship and defecting to a foreign country. Ship-building and boat-building, a source of income for centuries, ground to a halt,[22] as did net-making and fish-peddling. Ties of barter between the islands and the mainland were severed and communication between fisher-folk and farmers slackened.[23]

The main changes in the repertoire of maritime narration might be summed up as follows: Following the last war, to begin with, high-sea lore continued to be retold as long as it was remembered, but it gradually faded into oblivion together with the old sailing vessels and steam-ships. There was no addition of new material, with the result that overall the corpus grew more and more attenuated. Attention began to focus upon inshore fishing-boats (rather than ships) and coastal life in general. Life on the periphery in relative isolation helped to preserve old-fashioned customs and beliefs. Side by side with this, however, the arrival of new folklore material including accounts of the supernatural was rendered difficult if not entirely impossible, and so too this genre became incapable of renewing itself and began to show its age. In common with otherworld lore, new maritime tales, jokes etc, the vitality and spread of the *klabautermann* lore was similarly dampened and curtailed.

---

22 Naber (1995), 334-5.
23 In earlier times, when coastal dwellers went fish-mongering inland, their activities acted as a vehicle for mediating folk poetry.

Another noteworthy characteristic of the *klabautermann* tradition is that it belonged to so-called 'men's lore'. Stories of this kind were told by sailors and to sailors, and even ashore such stories were told mostly by men to men in farm-house gatherings along the coast (and especially in Saaremaa), from which gathering women and children were often excluded or in which context they are at best to be considered marginal. Furthermore, it was not just any one who told stories of the sea, but rather experienced individuals with a reputation for storytelling and often visiting from a distance.

V

The lore of the *klabautermann* is international in character and, while it is considered to be of relatively recent origin and a borrowing into Estonian tradition to boot, nevertheless, it has proved to be a rewarding subject of investigation. We have observed the *klabautermann*'s function as a protective spirit on whose presence the welfare of a vessel may be entirely dependent, noted the common ground between its role in this respect and that of other widely differing beings such house-spirits, and seen how the folk may have combined these figures on occasion.

No defensive action was taken against the *klabautermann* even when its appearance was attended by the kind of ill-tempered racket or otherwise unpleasant manner typical of evil-minded house fairies. Also worthy of note is the fact that the *klabautermann* has attached to it both older and more recent features and behavioural traits, for example, appearing as a person's double (out-of-body experiences), as a ghost and other such beings, and as a *mardus* (in the context of auguring someone's death) all of which which demonstrates the fact that it was sufficiently well established as a part of the folk tradition to incorporate different kinds of supernatural experiences. Accounts of visions of a beautiful girl aboard ship – sometimes found haunting a sailor – indicate that the *klabautermann* complex is also capable of incorporating haunting motifs, including the ghosts of birds, and of cats and dogs and other animals. While the *klabautermann* could appear in a variety of guises, it seldom appeared as a woman. Ships were mostly crewed by men, of course, which probably accounts for the predominance of male *klabautermann* figures, particularly as a portent of someone's death. I do not believe that the *klabautermann* can be explained away as a manifestation of the sexual fantasies of lonely sailors far from home, on the one hand, or as a phenomenon deriving from 'pub talk', on the other.

On the contrary, two main attitudes can be clearly identified in the folklore accounts and in the usual legends – the serious respect in which the appearance of a an otherworld being portending tragic events was held and the fun to be had from good-natured jesting and humourous banter. In particular, the role of the latter cannot be underestimated – as can be judged from the existence of several sets of directions for dealing with a *klabautermann*, accounts of such actions, a number of nonsense guidelines for dealing with a *klabautermann*, and also details of how 'rooky' sailors were inaugurated using *klabautermann* figures manufactured in this fashion.

Estonian *klabautermann* lore contains both usual legend forms and accounts drawn from ordinary conversation and entertainment. We witness side by side with accounts dealing with topics such as portending disaster, foretelling fate – death, suicide, and the shipwreck of particular vessels – the spread of fantastic stories detailing altercations between ship-spirits. By and large, it is well-nigh impossible to determine from the manuscript sources in which they are contained the likely attitude of the narrators to these stories, whether they viewed them with deadly seriousness, entertained doubts as to their authenticity, or treated them as a joke. In other circumstances – for example, when working with sound-recorded material (available only since the 1950s) – one is often able to make up one's mind about these matters on the basis of contextual remarks and prosodic features such as the tone, stress, pitch and tone of voice. Though maritime folklore of this sort has disappeared in Estonia and is unlikely to return to the scene, the manifestation of the *klabautermann* and the function and spread of the traditions pertaining to it serve a useful function in enabling us to make comparisons with other supernatural beings and their associated lore. Similarly, this provides a valuable vantage point from which to observe how changing social and economic conditions and the contribution of the narrator can dictate the nature of the concerns of otherworld beings.

The Magic Mill:
AT 565 in Irish Folk Tradition

GERALDINE LYNCH

I

It would appear to have been widely believed that when the world began the sea-water was as free from salt as was the water of the rivers and springs.[1] In an effort to explain the ensuing saltiness of the sea there are many folk beliefs, legends and folktales from around the world. The tale-type 565 – *The magic mill: Why the sea is salt* – has been collected in Ireland as well as in the Nordic and Baltic areas and further afield. The Irish versions of this aetiological folktale – one of a series of tales which explain the origins of natural phenomena – form the subject matter of this paper. In addition to being of interest to adults, this tale would have had particular importance for parents of young children, as a way of stemming, momentarily at least, the perpetual question 'Why?' Some versions of the story have, in fact, been adapted for telling to children.

This paper is a preliminary investigation of the Irish versions of tale-type 565 listed in *The Types of the Irish Folktale*.[2] The following short, concise example of the tale was collected by a Galway schoolgirl named Mary Burke, from her father in 1937:

> There was once a man and he was very poor. He went to his brother's house for something to eat and he gave him a ham. He told him to keep walking until he would sell it. So the poor man walked until he came to a house. He walked in. He met an old man at the door and he said: 'They will try to buy the ham but do not give it till you get the handmill that is behind the door. I will tell you how to start it and stop it.'

---

1 Salt plays an important role in Irish folk belief. It was placed in the mouth or on the clothes of a child being brought to church for baptism (*Béaloideas* 6 [1936], 258; *IFC* 96:331), or at Samhain or Hallowe'en (Andrews [1913], 15, 96) to prevent abduction by fairies. In some districts salt was placed on the lid of the churn during churning to prevent the 'profit of the milk' (*sochar an bhainne*) being stolen by an envious neighbour (*IFC* 117:93; *IFC* 96:343; *IFC* 109:256; *Béaloideas* 6 (1936), 261-2; *Béaloideas* 7 [1937], 110). It was also put on meat to ward off fairies (*IFC* 256:333-5). Salt also appears to have been used to avert bad luck and to guard against evil (*IFC* 65:196a-7; *IFC* 70:54; *IFC* 305:54-5; *Béaloideas* 4 [1934], 142; *An Stoc* 4 [1928], 1, vol. 2). Salt was also used in folk medicine (*IFC* 65:203; *IFC* 107:326-7; *IFC* 265:591-3, 595, 597; *Béaloideas* 9 [1939], 182). Sea-water was thought to possess special properties – sea-water or salt water was placed in an infant's mouth during the baptismal ceremony to prevent sea-sickness in later life (*IFC* 65: 195). *IFC* = Irish Folklore Collection being the Main Manuscripts Collection of the Department of Irish Folklore at University College Dublin; the numerals on either side of the colon represent the volume number and page number(s) respectively. *IFC* S (below) = the Schools' Manuscripts Collection.

2 Ó Súilleabháin & Christiansen (1967).

121

Sure enough they asked how much for the ham. The poor man said the handmill if you please, and he got it then. The old man told him how to work it. He came home to his wife and children and left it on the table, turned the handle, and out came all kinds of food.

One day the rich brother heard the story and he came and brought it with him and gave three hundred pounds for it. But he never told him how to stop it. He took home the mill and set it to work, and off it went turning out food till he was almost smothered.

He ran to the poor brother and told him to take it away. When the poor brother had it again the wife said it might make money. 'Mill grind money', he said and it started out all kinds of coins till at last he had enough.

One night a sea captain came in and stole the mill and brought it to his boat. When he was out in the water he set it to grind salt. It kept tumbling out salt until the boat sank to the bottom of the sea, and the mill is there yet grinding salt. So that is why the sea is salty.[3]

II

Distribution Pattern

Of the fifty-eight versions of AT 565 collected from Irish oral tradition listed in *The Types of the Irish Folktale*, thirty stem from the Main Manuscripts Collection and twenty-eight from the Schools' Collection. The Main Manuscripts Collection consists of material assembled by both full-time and part-time adult collectors and questionnaire correspondents for the Irish Folklore Commission (1935-1971) and the Department of Irish Folklore (1971-). All the Main Manuscripts versions of the tale were collected in maritime or coastal counties, mostly on the west coast – eleven versions stem from county. Galway and two from county. Mayo in the west, ten from county. Kerry in the southwest and four from county. Donegal in the northwest. One version was recorded in county. Waterford and another in county. Wexford on the south coast, while one stemmed from county Louth on the east coast (See Appendix A). Since these latter versions must be considered somewhat dubious for a variety of reasons,[4] the heartland of the tale appears to be in the western

---

3 *IFC* S77:468-9 (= Galway S 11).

4 Further examination of the listed versions shows that the Leinster or east-coast examples of the tale in the Main Manuscripts Collection do not fit the general pattern of the tale as found in the western parts of Ireland. The provenance of the Louth version is questionable – it was submitted as an entry for an *Oireachtas* competition from a person in county Louth who does not say where he originally heard the story. In addition we are informed that the writer originally heard the story in English from an Irish speaker and then translated it into Irish (The following note appears in the manuscript: 'This story I got from an Irish speaker in English and is translated by myself. *Réaltóg na Mara*.'). It would appear that the writer has embellished and adorned the tale so that it has been transformed into a quasi-literary version of the folktale. The Wexford version bears little resemblance to the accepted form of tale-type 565 – the only recognizable elements are the existence of a magic mill which is set to grind salt on board ship. The ship sinks and the mill continues to grind salt at the bottom of the sea.

seaboard counties and in the *Gaeltacht* or Irish-language areas. It is not surprising, therefore, that (apart from two versions – Kerry 2 and Wexford 1), the examples are in the Irish language, and this linguistic pattern is borne out by the versions of the tale found in the Schools' Manuscripts Collection.

The Schools' Manuscript Collection is the result of a scheme organized by the Irish Folklore Commission with the co-operation of the Department of Education and the Irish National Teachers' Organization.[5] During the school-year 1937-38 children in senior classes in primary schools in the Irish Free State (now the Republic of Ireland), instead of writing their weekly essays, collected folklore from the older members of their local communities. Teachers and pupils were given guidelines by the Irish Folklore Commission on the topics which might be covered and on the type of questions which might be asked.[6] The year's work resulted in 1128 bound manuscript volumes and numerous small copy-books. The story of 'Why the Sea is Salt' is not mentioned specifically in the guidelines, so it is unlikely that the children were advised to collect it. Nevertheless, twenty-eight versions were recorded by them.

All but three of these[7] stem from the maritime counties of the west and southwest of Ireland,[8] and, in addition, more than half (57%) of them are in the Irish language.[9] Thus, the distribution and linguistic patterns evident in the Main Manuscripts are borne out by the versions of the tale in the Schools' Manuscripts Collection.

Despite the contrasting collection methods used by the full-time collectors and those methods employed in the course of the Schools' Scheme, a clear picture emerges of a story found almost exclusively on the west coast of Ireland, although one would have expected this kind of tale to be of interest to children all around the coast of the island.

---

5 Ó Catháin (1988).

6 An Roinn Oideachais (1937).

7 One each from counties Tipperary, Westmeath and Kildare. All schools versions are designated by S in this article – for concise references to these see appendix A.

8 Twelve versions from county Galway, five from county Sligo, three from county Mayo, three from county Donegal, one from county Leitrim, and one from county Cork in the south west.

9 Irish-language versions: Galway S1, S2, S3, S4, S5, S7, S8, S9, S10, S12; Mayo S1, S3; Sligo S2, S3; Donegal S2, S3. English-language versions: Galway S6, S11; Mayo S2; Sligo S1, S4, S5; Leitrim S1; Cork S1; Tipperary S1; Westmeath S1; Kildare S1; Donegal S1.

III

Analysis

Reidar Th. Christiansen in his *Studies in Irish and Scandinavian Folktales* identifies four episodes which he considers to be essential to the story:

A. The poor man who asks his rich brother (neighbour) for food, which is given with a curse: 'Go to Hell!'
B. The journey to Hell, where he obtains the mill and learns how to use it.
C. The disastrous consequences when his brother tries to use the mill.
D. A sea-captain buys the mill, and sets it going to grind out salt; his ship, being filled, founders, and the mill goes on grinding in the sea, hence the reason why the sea is salt.[10]

All four episodes as outlined by Christiansen are found in only four of the Main Manuscripts versions and in two of the Schools' versions.[11] One of these, from county Galway, would appear to be a direct retelling of the Norwegian version in the collection of Asbjørnsen and Moe from the mid-nineteenth century.[12] This version would have been accessible in English translation and it is likely that the storyteller, Micheál Breathnach, heard a version based on this translation.

Of the thirty Main Manuscripts Collection versions listed in *The Types of the Irish Folktale*, three[13] consist of very brief accounts containing only the last aetiological motif – A1115.2. *Why the sea is salt: magic salt mill.*[14] A fourth short version from county Donegal introduces the mill by saying that a man about to travel by ship was given a present of the mill by a girl who tells him that the crew often forget to bring salt on board and that he would be able to sell salt.[15] The story as told by Micheál Ó Gaoithín (*An File*), son of the well-known Blasket-Island storyteller, Peig Sayers, to the full-time collector Seosamh Ó Dálaigh from Dún Chaoin, mentions only a poor man.[16] The poor man sets out to earn his fortune and on the way meets a fairy woman who feels sorry for him and gives him the magic mill.

Apart from these four brief stories, the introductory episode where the poor brother is sent to hell is found in nine of the remaining twenty-six Main Manuscripts versions.[17] In another he is said to have died and gone to hell.[18] In four of the

---

10 Christiansen (1959), 154.
11 Galway 2, 4; Mayo 1; Donegal 1. Galway S2, S12.
12 Compare IFC 163:25-32 with Asbjørnsen & Moe (1960), 108-1.
13 Mayo 2: Kerry 6, 8.
14 Thompson (1955-58).
15 Donegal 2.
16 Kerry 7.
17 Introductory episode: Galway 2, 4, 5, 6; Mayo 1; Waterford 1; Donegal 1, 3, 4.
18 Poor brother dies and goes to hell: Galway 9.

twenty eight Schools' Manuscripts versions the poor brother is sent to hell,[19] while in a fifth the poor man goes there to try to earn some money.[20] In those versions in which the poor brother is given a piece of meat – bacon or ham – by his rich brother before being banished to hell, he is able to negotiate the exchange of the meat for the small mill. In seven Connacht versions the poor brother goes to Hell with nothing to exchange, and in these a vivid description of the fires of Hell is given.[21] The following account is by Seán Breathnach, a labourer from Leitir Móir na Coille, Conamara, then living in Na Forbacha, Conamara, Co Galway. This version of the story was collected in 1938 by Proinnsias de Búrca:

> He set off this day. He was going down, down, down, down, until he came to the place below. It was a strange place. There was every single kind of fire there, yellow fires, red, purple, and every other kind of colour. Well, the poor brother was afraid, and when he stood inside the door the attendants caught him and put him over the hottest fire that was there. But the head man came by in the end and he asked him how he was. 'I am well', said the poor brother, 'no thanks to you'. The devil didn't like this at all and he told the attendants to make the fire hotter than ever. Some time after that he came by again, and he asked the poor brother how he was. The poor brother said he was much better. The devil was amazed, he started shaking his tail. Back with him and he asked the attendants to put more coal on the fire and to make it hotter than they did before. After another while he came over and asked him how he was. Well, he said, he was better than ever, no thanks to him.[22]

In these seven Connacht versions the devil gets tired of trying to torture the poor brother with fire – the poor brother is enjoying the heat as he never had enough money to buy fuel at home – and he does not want to leave Hell. Eventually, the devil bribes him to leave by giving him the magic mill. In two versions from county Donegal the poor man is given directions to Hell by the local priest.[23]

Christiansen reports that 'Going to Hell might seem too impressive to a storyteller who would explain that he went to a homestead called Hell, such grim names being not infrequently applied to uncongenial homesteads in Norway; or substitute some other uncongenial place.'[24] Irish storytellers who opted for a less impressive opening, neither sending the hero to Hell nor to a fairy fort, said that the poor brother was sent to the end of the earth, or, as in the version written by the Galway schoolgirl, Mary Burke, told to keep on walking until he sold the meat. This introduction was particularly popular in the Schools' Manuscripts Collection – perhaps in an effort, by the storytellers to make the story suitable for the young

---

19 Galway S2, S4, S7, S8.
20 S12.
21 Galway 4, 5, 6; Galway S4, S7, S8; Mayo 1.
22 Galway 5; IFC 525:168-9. My translation. See Appendix B, Item 1 for the original Irish text.
23 Donegal 3, 4.
24 Christiansen (1959), 155.

collectors. In these versions the poor brother walks for a very long time until he comes to a house – indeed, some storytellers say that he walked until the soles of his boots were 'as thin as a butterfly's wings'.[25] He meets an old man who advises him that the people of the house will want his ham but that he should only exchange it for the mill.

Christiansen's Episode B – the journey to Hell, where he obtains the mill and learns how to use it – is found in all but one[26] of those versions (which contain the introductory episode of the poor brother being sent to Hell). In those versions in which the poor brother is sent to the end of the earth, the second episode consists of a long journey to a distinctive-looking house, and the exchange of the meat for the mill.

Versions of tale-type 565 from county Kerry attribute original ownership of the mill to the fairies – this is also either stated or implied in some Connacht versions. Two versions of 'Why the Sea is Salt' were collected from Seán Ó Mainín, a small farmer from Corca Dhuibhne, county Kerry in the 1930s – one by Seán Ó Dubhda, a primary-school teacher from Baile na nGall and the other by the full-time collector Seosamh Ó Dálaigh.[27] The latter version, recorded on the Ediphone and subsequently transcribed by him, is a fuller example of the tale than that collected by Seán Ó Dubhda, which appears to have been written down directly from the oral telling of the tale. It is in the version recorded by Ó Dálaigh that the most detailed account of the circumstances in which the poor brother obtained the mill from the fairies, is given: the poor brother, returning from his brother's house with a piece of meat on the bone which his sister-in-law has given him, decides to take a short cut by the side of a *lios* or fairy fort. The queen of the *lios* who is pregnant has a craving for meat, and, smelling the meat as the poor man passes by, sends a man out to ask him if he would give it to her. He readily agrees, and the fairy man advises him not to accept fairy gold in exchange for the meat as its form is unstable, but to ask for a small machine which will mill grain and flour and whatever he wants.

Christiansen's Episode C – which outlines the disastrous consequences when his brother tries to use the mill – is found in almost one third of all the Irish versions.[28] It is most frequently, although not exclusively, found in those versions in which the rich brother sends the poor brother to Hell and conforms closely to the Scandinavian versions analysed by Christiansen.[29] The following example was collected in county Galway:

By this time the rich brother was getting jealous of the small poor brother and

---

25 'D'imigh an pleidhce leis, agus lean sé ag siúl go dtí go raibh a bhróga chomh tanaí le sciathán feileacáin.' (Galway S2:360).
26 Waterford 1.
27 Kerry 4, 5.
28 In 11 of the 30 Main Manuscripts versions, and in 8 of the 28 Schools' Manuscripts versions, that is, in 33% of the total number of Irish versions.
29 It is found in 71% of these versions.

he didn't waste much time until he went to ask him how he had got all the wealth. 'It all comes from that small mill', he said. 'You only have to tell the mill what you want and say "Grind that for me, little mill, and grind it quickly" and it will start grinding at once.' The rich man didn't wait to hear any more, but said: 'Will you give me a loan of the little mill?' 'I will and welcome', said the other man, 'but ...' The other brother didn't listen to any more out of him, but off he went with the mill under his arm. When he was approaching the house he saw his workmen also making for the house for their dinner. The rich man ... thought that it was a great waste of time for the men to be walking to the house like that. He called them to him and told them to bring their bowls to the place where he himself was, and he put the little mill on the ground and said to it:

'Grind oatmeal porridge for me, little mill, and grind it quickly.' The little mill started grinding and the porridge came down out of it in a fine stream. Each man put his bowl under the neck and it filled up. When that was done the rich man told it to stop, but alas it was wasted work for him as it wouldn't stop even if yesterday came back. In the end he had to bring the poor brother in a boat across the big lake of porridge which the mill had produced. The brother came and said the magic word in a whisper and the little mill stopped, but it was a long time before the porridge soaked into the ground and for ever after that nothing but oatmeal would grow in that place.[30]

Christiansen describes Episode D as follows: 'A sea-captain buys the mill, and sets it going to grind out salt; his ship, being filled, founders, and the mill goes on grinding in the sea, hence the reason why the sea is salt.' In the Irish versions, the mill may be either bought or stolen by the captain. This episode is found in forty-one of the fifty-eight versions (71%), in nine more, episodes C and D are combined – the rich brother having obtained the mill (sometimes in exchange for his house and land) sets sail and is unable to stop the mill which is grinding out salt.[31]

From the versions listed in *The Types of the Irish Folktale* four redactions can be identified:

Redaction A: The tale which consists of Christiansen's four episodes and in which the mill is given to the poor man by the Devil. This corresponds to the version found in the Norwegian collection of Asbjørnsen and Moe. One of the Galway versions would appear to be directly taken from a translation of this tale while other Irish versions are also very close to it in structure and detail.

---

30 Galway 4, 107-11. My translation. See Appendix B, Item 2 for original Irish text.
31 **Episode D:** Galway 2, 3, 4, 6, 7, 8, 10, 11; Mayo 1, 2; Kerry 1, 2, 4, 5, 6, 7, 8, 9, 10; Waterford 1, Donegal 1, 3, 4; Galway S2, S6, S7, S11, S12; Mayo S1, S2, S3; Sligo S1, S3, S5; Leitrim S1; Cork S1; Tipperary S1; Westmeath S1; Kildare S1; Donegal S1, S3.
Episodes C and D combined: Galway 1; Kerry 3; Galway S1, S3, S5, S9, S10; Sligo S4; Donegal S2.

Redaction B: In the majority of Kerry versions the mill was originally the property of the fairies. The fairy origin is also alluded to occasionally in Connacht versions. In this redaction the humorous episode C is not usually present.

Redaction C: This consists of either three or four episodes. The poor man goes to his rich brother to look for food, he is given a piece of meat and told to find the end of the world. On his journey to the end of the world he comes to a house and exchanges the meat for a small handmill. The humorous episode is present in half the versions. Episode D is also present. This form of the tale is most popular in the Schools' Manuscripts Collection, and would appear to be a version of Redaction A 'censored' by parents.

Redaction D: This is a single episodic version of the tale explaining why the sea is salt.

IV

In the Finnish Sampo poems the Sampo provides great wealth. Although there has been much debate about the precise meaning of the word Sampo, Clive Tolley in a recent article on 'The Mill in Norse and Finnish Mythology' points out that 'poets have made full use of connexions of the word sampa with parts of the mill, so that the sampo was conceived as a mill ... grinding out salt, wealth, and so forth ....', and indicated, for example, in the lines:

> Get a sampo ready,
> A grain mill on one side,
> A salt mill on another side,
> And a money mill on a third.[32]

Many of the references to the mills in the Irish versions of AT 565 are vague – in some the mill is only referred to as an 'article' or a 'machine'. In a version from county Kerry, however, the mill has three functions – it can grind flour, grain, and salt.[33] The fairy man, demonstrating the use of the mill in this story, is very careful to point out the three separate ways of setting up the mill, and starting and stopping it in order to obtain the three products. The Sampo, too, is credited with causing salt in the sea-water. The Sampo is stolen, smashed, and the pieces lost at sea. The pieces bring fertility, well-being, salts and minerals to the sea-water and to the sea-shore.

In Norse tradition, the mill Grotti has also been associated with the saltiness of the sea-water. Mysingr takes Grotti, Fenja and Menja. He bids them grind salt.

---

32 Tolley (1995), 63-82.
33 Kerry 4.

They grind until the excess of salt sinks the ship. This causes the sea's saltiness. Although the motif of the magic mill causing the saltiness of the sea is found in these accounts, they lack the introductory episodes which are an integral part of most versions of AT 565.

V

AT 565 is an aetiological tale, its function being to explain the origin of the salt in the sea-water. It is also a didactic tale – the greedy rich brother and the greedy sea captain, who only wanted to know how to set the mill to grind, but did not wait to hear the magic words needed to stop the mill, have to live with – or in the case of the captain, die because of – the consequences of their greed. The lesson of the story, in certain versions, may be to listen carefully to the instructions given – in these versions the new owners of the mill have been told the correct words needed to stop the mill but have not been attentive. This story also demonstrates the classic triumph of good over evil and of the poor or downtrodden over the rich, mean and greedy. The story of 'Why the Sea is Salt', particularly those versions of the story which contain Episode C, is also a humorous tale.

Just as tales from the cycle about Fionn mac Cumhaill and the Fianna have always been an integral part of the Irish primary school history curriculum, certain legends and folktales have been popular among writers of structured English-language reading programmes for children in Irish primary schools. Tale-type 565 is one of the tales which appear again and again in such programmes from the early *Young Ireland Reader* version listed in *The Types of the Irish Folktale*,[34] up to the most recent versions in the reading programmes of the early 1990s. No doubt the story is popular among compilers of such programmes because of its aetiological, didactic, and humorous elements. However, in these versions the mill does not originate in Hell. It may, as in the version given in the *Wide Range* series of readers first published in Scotland in 1949 but in use in many Irish schools up to the present day, be simply given in exchange for the piece of meat which the poor brother is carrying:

> Once upon a time there were two brothers, one poor and the other rich. The poor brother was walking home from his work one evening, carrying a piece of bacon, when suddenly he met an old woodcutter. He thought it strange that he had not noticed him until that moment, and he thought it strange that he had heard no footsteps.
> 'Good evening,' said the poor brother.
> 'Good evening,' replied the old woodcutter.

---

34 Ó Súilleabháin & Christiansen (1967), 119.

He looked hopefully at the piece of bacon and said,
'Please give me that bacon. I am very hungry.'
'I am sorry,' said the poor brother. 'I cannot give it away. If I do my wife and I will have nothing to eat for our supper.'
'Please give me that bacon,' said the woodcutter again, 'and I will give you this little mill for grinding flour.'[35]

Although this type of aetiological tale is popular with children who are always asking 'Why?', it does not appear to have re-entered children's folk repertoire from such printed sources. A survey of more recent collections from or by children[36] failed to uncover any versions of this kind. The restricted vocabulary and structure in versions of tale-type 565 published in school reading programmes – in accordance with Department of Education guidelines – means that the story is not very memorable in comparison with the rich oral versions collected in both English and Irish in the 1930s and 1940s. Even when, as in many of the versions presented by schoolchildren in 1937-38, the text of the story is concise, reduced to its main elements and unadorned, we can imagine that the child struggling to produce an acceptable essay for the teacher, in legible neat handwriting, with no spelling mistakes, at a time when children were not encouraged to draft and redraft their stories or essays, produced a mere summary of the exciting tale told to them by a parent or grandparent.

Appendix A

Main Manuscripts Collection:

Connacht: Galway (1) *IFC* 157:593-7, (2) *IFC* 163:25-32, (3) *IFC* 165:246-56, (4) *IFC* 209:99-117, (5) *IFC* 525:167-73, (6) *IFC* 525:341-7, (7) *IFC* 739:526-9, (8) *IFC* 784:251-2, (9) *IFC* 868:97-8, (10) *IFC* 931:88-91, (11) *IFC* 969:471; Mayo (1) *IFC* 693: 562-71, (2) *IFC* 804:147.
Munster: Kerry (1) *IFC* 2:36-9, (2) *IFC* 21:244-8, (3) *IFC* 97:89-97, (4) *IFC* 272:292-303, (5)*IFC* 293:57-61, (6) *IFC* 667:65, (7) *IFC* 847:489-93, (8) *IFC* 995:28, (9)*IFC* 1166:417-30, (10) *IFC* 1278:501-8; Waterford (1) *IFC* 978:139-49.
Ulster: Donegal (1) *IFC* 171:98-101, (2) *IFC* 187:19-20, (3) *IFC* 270:109-13, (4) *IFC* 342:34-6.
Leinster: Louth (1) *IFC* 650:559-73; Wexford (1) *IFC* 545:535-55.

---

35 Schonell and Flowerdew (1976), 33-44.
36 For example, the Irish Life Assurance Company Schools' Folklore Competitions 1976, 1978; Urban Folklore Project 1979-1980; *Irish Times*, 'Newspaper in the Classroom Project', 1985.

Schools' Manuscripts Collection:

Connacht: Galway (S1) *IFC S* 9:270-2, (S2) *IFC S* 11:360-1, (S3) *IFC S* 32:305-12, (S4) *IFC S* 32:348-50, (S5)*IFC S* 40:338-42, (S6) *IFC S* 58:262-4, (S7) *IFC S* 69:111-3, (S8) *IFC S* 69:256-61,(S9) *IFC S* 71:374-8, (S10) *IFC S* 71:408-11, (S11) *IFC S* 77:468-9, (S12) *IFC S* 82:326-7; Mayo (S1) *IFC S* 109:191-2, (S2) I *IFC S* 110:25-7, (S3) *IFC S* 131:396-9; Sligo (S1) *IFC S* 155:363-4, (S2) *IFC S* 170:512, (S3) *IFC S* 170:599-600, (S4) *IFC S* 172:90-1, (S5) *IFC S* 181:74-5; Leitrim (S1) *IFC S* 209:442-5.
Munster: Cork (S1) *IFC S* 284:121-2; Tipperary (S1) *IFC S* 583:187-8.
Leinster: Kildare (S1) *IFC S* 780:219; Westmeath (S1) *IFC S* 748:125-6.
Ulster: Donegal (S1) *IFC S* 1037:165-9, (S2) *IFC S* 1056:135-43, (S3) 1064:367-71.

Appendix B

1. Ach d'imigh leis an lá seo. Bhí sé ag gabhail síos, síos, síos nó go dtáinig sé go dtí an áit thíos. B'aisteach an áit a bhí ann. Bhí 'chuile chineál saghas tine ann - tinte buí, dearga, corcra, 'chuile chineál 'e dhath. Bhuel, bhí an-fhaitíos ar an driotháir bocht, agus nuair a sheas sé taobh istigh dhon doras rug na fir freastail air agus chuireadar os cionn na tine ba teocha dá raibh ann é. Ach tháinig an fear ceannais anall sa deireadh agus d'fhiafraigh sé dhó cé mar a bhí sé.
    'Tá mé go maith,' arsa an driotháir bocht, 'ná raibh maith agatsa!'
    Níor thaithnigh sé sin leis an deabhal ar chor ar bith, agus dúirt sé leis na fir freastail an tine a dhéanamh níos teocha ná ariamh. I gceann tamaill ina dhiaidh sin tháinig sé anall aríst agus d'fhiafraigh sé dhon driotháir bocht cén chaoi a raibh sé. Dúirt an driotháir bocht go raibh sé i bhfad níos fearr. Bhí ionadh an domhain ar an deabhal. Thosaigh sé ag creathadh a dhriobaill. Ar ais leis, agus d'iarr sé ar na fir freastail tuilleadh guail a chur ar an tine agus í a dhéanamh níos teocha ná a rinneadar cheana. I gceann tamaill aríst tháinig sé anall agus d'fhiafraigh sé dhó cé mar a bhí sé. Bhuel, dúirt seisean go raibh sé níos fearr ná ariamh, ná raibh maith aige-san.

2. Fán am seo bhí an driotháir saibhir ag glacadh éad leis an driotháir beag bocht, agus níor bhain sé cos as rith nó gur fhiafraigh sé dhó cén chaoi a bhfuair sé an saibhreas ar fad.

    'Teagann sé go léir ón muileann beag sin,' ar seisean. 'Níl le déanamh agat ach a inseacht don mhuileann céard atá uait agus a rá "Meil é sin dom, a mhuilinn bhig, agus meil go mear é!" agus tosóidh sé dhá mheilt ar an bpointe.'

Níor fhan an fear saibhir lena thuilleadh a chloisteáil ach dúirt:
'An dtiubharfaidh tú an muileann beag ar iasacht dom?'

'Déanfad agus fáilte,' arsa an fear eile. Ach níor éist an driotháir eile lena thuilleadh uaidh, ach as go brách leis agus an muileann fána ascaill aige. Nuair a bhí sé ag tarraingt ar an teach chonaic sé a chuid fear oibre ag déanamh ar an teach freisin i gcomhair a ndinnéir - cheap sé gur mhór an chailliúint aimsire na fir a bheith ag siúl go dtí an teach mar sin. Do ghlaoigh sé orthu chuige, agus dúirt leo a gcuid báisíní a thiubhairt leo go dtí an áit a raibh sé féin. Tháinigeadar, agus chuir seisean an muileann beag ar an talamh agus dúirt leis:

'Meil leite dhom, a mhuilinn bhig, agus meil go mear í!'

Thosaigh an muileann beag ag meilt, agus tháinig an leite mhin choirce anuas as ina sruthán breá. Chuir gach fear a bháisín fán scrogall agus líonadh suas é. Nuair a bhí sin déanta d'fhuagair an fear saibhir air stopadh ach, mo léan agus mo ghéar, obair in aisce a bhí aige ann, óir ní stopfadh sé dá dteagadh an lá inné ar ais. I ndeireadh thiar thall bhí air an driotháir bocht a thiubhairt i mbád treasna an loch mór leitean a bhí meilte ag an muileann. Tháinig an driotháir agus dúirt sé an focal draíochta i gcogar, agus do stad an muileann beag. Ach b'fhada go raibh an leite súite ag an talamh, agus as go brách ina dhiaidh sin níor fhás rud ar bith san áit ach coirce.

The Hunt that Came over the Sea:
Narratives of a Maritime 'Wild Hunt'
in Irish Oral Tradition*

PATRICIA LYSAGHT

In the Dingle and Iveragh peninsulas, Irish-speaking areas in the southwest of Ireland, narratives of a hunt coming over the sea were collected between the 1920s and the 1950s. In this paper, these sea-coast narratives are discussed in the light of the well-documented Wild Hunt belief of northern Europe in an attempt to establish, firstly, whether they might be regarded as an Irish reflex of that belief, and secondly, whether they might also be considered to reflect ancient ideas about the dead and the location of the Otherworld in Irish tradition. As a prelude, therefore, to discussing the provenance and meaning of these maritime-hunt narratives from the southwest of Ireland, the main characteristics of the Wild Hunt belief in northern Europe are outlined. My comments are concerned mainly with Germanic tradition, and in this context I refer in particular to Hans Plischke's work entitled *Die Sage Vom Wilden Heere Im Deutschen Volke* (Leipzig 1914), which outlines the principal traits of the belief and also contains an extensive bibliography for the German-speaking areas.

The Wild-Hunt Belief in Northern Europe

Belief in a Wild Hunt, that is in a group of ghostly hunters (horsemen) riding through the sky at night or along lonely roads relentlessly pursuing a quarry, is widespread in northern Europe. The belief is found in varying forms in Norway, Sweden, Denmark, France, The Netherlands, Germany, Austria and Switzerland, as well as in Britain; the situation in Ireland is under discussion in this paper. As Dr Hilda Davidson has recently shown, there is an early twelfth-century record of the belief in England – that found in the Peterborough version of the Anglo-Saxon Chronicle for the year 1127 – and she also notes that it still remained an active element of the oral tradition in parts of England in the 1940s and 1950s.[1]

---

* An earlier version of this paper will appear in a volume on Supernatural Enemies, edited by H. E. Davidson and Anna Chaudhri, published by Carolina Academic Press.
1 I wish to thank Dr Davidson for a copy of her as yet unpublished paper entitled 'The Wild Hunt' (henceforth referred to as Davidson 1995), presented at a conference on 'Supernatural Enemies', London, 1995, and forthcoming in the conference proceedings.

The Hunt that Came over the Sea:
Narratives of a Maritime 'Wild Hunt'
in Irish Oral Tradition

Known by a variety of names such as *Die wilde Jagd, Das wütende Heer, Wildes Heer, Odinsjäger, Chasse Fantastique*,[2] this phantom host is said to be led by different leaders, both male and female, in the different regions where it is known. Some of the leaders mentioned are mythological or legendary figures while others are historic or romantic personages. Jakob Grimm, for example, was of the opinion that Wodan, the Germanic god of battle, was the original leader of *Die wilde Jagd* or *Das wütende Heer* before becoming a demonic and devilish figure under the influence of Christianity.[3] In Thompson's *Motif-Index of Folk Literature* (Motifs E501. *The Wild Hunt*, and E501.1. *Leader of the Wild Hunt*),[4] reference is made, for example, to such characters as King Herla, Theodoric, and wild Edric, as leaders of the Wild Hunt. Charlemagne and King Arthur also figure in this connection, as do other regional personages in the Germanic area such as Hans von Hackelberg and Dietrich von Bern who also figure in the so-called 'Barbarossa Legend'.[5]

---

2 Thompson (1955-8): E501. *The Wild Hunt*; Plischke (1914), 10-20. In Act II of Carl Maria von Weber's (1786-1826) most famous opera *Der Freischütz*, set in the Bohemian forest shortly after the end of the Thirty Years War, there is a brief dramatic description of the Wild Hunt. Kaspar, described as one of Prince Ottokar's rangers, is depicted as being in the fearsome Wolf's Glen forging seven bullets, the last of which will belong to the devil. Each casting is accompanied by an echo as he calls out the number, and by apparitions. The elemental reaction to the forging of the fifth bullet is described as follows:
Echo
Fünf!
(Hundegebell und Wiehern in der Luft; Nebelgestaltungen von Jägern zu Fuss und zu Ross, Hirschen und Hunden ziehen auf der Höhe vorüber. [*Echo* Five. Barking of dogs and neighing in the air; misty images of hunters, on foot and on horseback, stags and dogs fly past overhead.])
Chor
(Unsichtbar)
Durch Berg und Tal, durch Schlund und Schlacht,
Durch Tau und Wolken, Sturm und Nacht!
Durch Höhle, Sumpf und Erdenkluft,
Durch Feuer, Erde, See und Luft,
Jaho! Wauwau! ho! ho! ho!
Kaspar
Weh, das wilde Heer! ...
Chorus
[Invisible]
Over hill, over dale, through abyss and pit,
Over dew and clouds, tempest and night,
Over chasm, bog and abyss,
Through fire, earth, sea and air,
Yahoo, bow-bow, ho, ho, ho!).
Kaspar
Alas, the wild army...)
(Cf. Warrack [1973], 24-5, 118-9).
3 Plischke (1914), 4.
4 Thompson (1955-8).
5 Thompson, D1960.2. *Kyffhäuser*. King asleep in mountain (Barbarossa, King Marko, Holger danske, etc.) will awake one day to succor his people. For studies of the Barbarossa Legend in Ireland see Ó hÓgáin (1974-76; 1991).

Among the women leaders of the Wild Hunt are numbered Artemis and Diana, the Greek and Roman goddesses of hunting, respectively, as well as Hecate, identified in later times with Diana. Herodias, *domina Herodiana*, also linked to Diana and later perceived as the leader of a nigh-time band of demons, is mentioned, too, as a leader of the wild hunt.[6] Dame Bertha, named from Bertha, the mother of Charlemagne, and also Frau Holle were supposed to travel over the country at night with a troop, sometimes of unbaptised children (*Züg der Kinderseelen*).[7] Gudrun as well as Sigurd might lead the Wild Hunt in Norway.[8] Persons unbeloved in the community because of injustice or misdeeds often connected with hunting, or those who profaned the Sabbath by incessant hunting, are also said to lead the Wild Hunt. Mention of the devil in this connection points to the stamp of Christianity on the Wild Hunt belief.[9]

The riders of the Wild Hunt are usually said to be mounted on dark horses, sometimes brown, sometimes black, but occasionally also white, and they are often said to have fiery eyes and flaming nostrils; two-legged and headless horses also make their appearance in the Wild Hunt, and despite their shortcomings, as it were, they manage to storm wildly by. The riders may be dressed in black or red or white, they may be headless or carry their skulls under their arms. They may have animal heads or their heads may be on back to front, and like their horses and dogs, they may exhale fire and have fiery eyes. Baying and yapping dogs, black in colour, also with fiery eyes and tongues, sometimes crowding together, but usually springing forward furiously in the chase, (even though they are sometimes stated to be three-legged), are an integral part of the Wild Hunt. Sows, sometimes with only one eye, or a raging, blind, wild boar, are also imagined to appear in the Hunt. The presence of the phantom host is signified by the sounds of the hunt – the noise made by the galloping horses and especially by the baying hounds.[10]

As with other ghostly manifestations, the Wild Hunt is most often perceived at night. It is said to ride out on long, dark, winter nights, at times particularly associated with the dead and the ghost world – such as during the twelve days of Christmas, the so-called *der Zwölften* or *die Zwischennächte* in the middle of winter,[11] and the *Oskereia*, or *Julereia* ('Yule Riders') said to visit farms in west Norway, are, as their name suggests, Yuletide riders.[12] The Wild Hunt is also associated with certain Holy Days and festivals of the Catholic-church calendar during which Christian practices are particularly pronounced, such as Good Friday or Easter, but it is also said to be heard at carnival time, when such Christian practices are also often parodied or threatened. Manifestations of the Wild Hunt are also linked to special junctures or

---

6 Plischke (1914), 47-9; HDA, 3, 1790-1.
7 Plischke (1914), 30, 49-51; Thompson (1955-8), F475.1. *Dame Berchta.*
8 Davidson (1995).
9 Plischke (1914), 39-40.
10 Plischke, 28-37; Thompson, E501.4. *Animals follow wild huntsman.*
11 Plischke, 54-5.
12 Davidson (1995).

The Hunt that Came over the Sea:
Narratives of a Maritime 'Wild Hunt'
in Irish Oral Tradition

transition periods of the year, such as midsummer[13] or, especially, during the spring and autumn seasons with their changeable weather.

Riding high in the sky the Wild Hunt is associated particularly with stormy weather, and is then experienced in wild nature – in moors, forest and mountain regions.[14] Riding closer to earth, the Wild Hunt is also associated with ancient roads and pathways, with places particularly connected with the dead and the ghost world in popular imagination, such as ancient battle fields, and also with cross-roads, the assembly place of ghosts and witches.[15]

A hunt must have a quarry, and the Wild Hunt was no exception in popular imagination. Indeed, such a fast and furious hunt seemed to be hell-bent on tracking down its quarry. Woodwives (*Holzweiber, Holzfräulein, Moosfräulein, Buschfrauen*) seem to have been a favourite quarry of the Wild Hunt. In narratives of the Wild Hunt reflecting Christian influence, it is the souls of those who died a bad death or who died unbaptised that are commonly said to be followed, and foremost among these is the soul of the so-called sinful woman - the prostitute or witch[16] or, of particular relevance in view of the Irish narratives discussed below, the priest's concubine. In this connection it is the devil, or others among the wicked or restless dead, who ride forth accompanied by the hounds of hell to pursue the woman, as in the twelfth-century German work *Dialogus miraculorum* which tells of a priest's concubine asking to be buried in a pair of shoes with strong soles. It also tells that she was subsequently hunted down and seized by a devilish huntsman accompanied by baying hounds.[17] Objects of the chase such as hares, does and stags[18] – the so-called soul animals (*die Seelentiere*) – are said to be hunted.[19] The various hunt victims mentioned here – the hare, doe and the sinful woman also feature in the Irish maritime-hunt narratives.[20]

Various attempts to trace the origin of the belief have been made, especially by scholars in Scandinavia and Germany in the nineteenth and twentieth centuries.[21] In this endeavour special attention was paid to the dogs or otherworld hounds (called *conairt gadhar* in some of the Irish material). These are a central feature of the Wild Hunt in popular imagination, and it is the baying of these animals which

---

13 Reported from England – see Brown (1979), 36.
14 In parts of Germany where the night riders are known as *Das wütende Heer* ('the Furious Army'), this phantom host is said to burst forth from the mountains – the dwelling place of the dead and the resting place of the sleeping army ready to come forth to protect the fatherland in the hour of need (Thompson [1955-8], E502. *The Sleeping Army*).
15 Plischke (1914), 56-62.
16 *Ibid.*, 64-7.
17 Book XII, Ch. XX – Scott & Swinton Bland (1929), vol. 2, 306-7. Cf. Meisen (1935), 58.
18 Thompson (1955-8), E501.5.5. *Animals pursued in Wild Hunt*; Plischke (1914), 66.
19 Plischke (1914), 31.
20 See references in Appendix D: The *hare* appears as hunt quarry in narratives no. 1-4, 6, 7; the *doe/deer* in nos. 5, 11, 14; and the *sinful woman* in narratives no. 8, 9, 12, 13.
21 This is indicated by the relatively long list of publications concerning the wild hunt in Thompson (1955-8), E501. *The Wild Hunt.*

is said to be the particular signal of the manifestation of the phantom aerial host. This has led some scholars to explain the belief in the Wild Hunt in terms of natural phenomena – as the Danish folklorist Feilberg, for example, did in the last century. He asserted that the sound of the wings of migrating wild geese in flight on autumn nights, which suggested the baying of hounds drawing close to their quarry, was the basis of the wild hunt belief. Other scholars suggested that the sound of winter storms gave rise to the belief in a phantom host riding through the sky. Such blanket explanations for the Wild Hunt were criticised by Axel Olrik[22] and by Carl W. von Sydow,[23] for example, who acknowledged, however, that such phenomena must have helped to keep the concept of the Wild Hunt alive, and Plischke also leans towards this conclusion.

Wild geese and storm winds have also been discounted as a basis for belief in the Wild Hunt by the the German writer Otto Höffler, who contended that the explanation of the tradition lay not in natural phenomena, but rather in the riualistic behaviour of wild companies of young men in masks – representing the dead and keeping up an earlier cult of the ancestors, who periodically visited houses and who were remembered in popular imagination as demons.[24] This interpretation has been criticised – by the Swedish scholar Celander (1943), for example – but it found favour with other scholars such as the Norwegians Lily Weiser (1927), and more recently Christine Eike in her detailed study of the *Oskoreia* (1980).[25] But the Wild Hunt belief is a complex one, with, therefore, no one explanation of its origin necessarily sufficing. It would seem that there are many and diverse strands of tradition underpinning this belief in an ominous host of night riders, and that they are linked, *inter alia*, in the northern European tradition of the Wild Hunt, to ancient beliefs about the hostile and restless dead. As appears below, this kind of connection would also seem to be borne out by the Irish material.

Supernatural Hosts in Irish Tradition

Various types of earthbound supernatural hosts or groupings of otherworld denizens are described in Irish oral tradition. Legends tell of supernatural night-time hunts with huntsmen blowing horns and riding with hounds in areas where the local hunt rode out, or along lonely roads or countryside. Individual huntsmen similarly engaged are also encountered. These appear to be earthbound hunts and it is not always clear if the hunters are perceived by tradition bearers as representing the dead or the fairy folk.[26]

---

22 Olrik (1901), 139-73, cited in Davidson (1995).
23 von Sydow (1935), 117ff.
24 Höffler (1934, 1936, 1973).
25 Davidson (1995).
26 *IFC* 36:96-8; Ó Súilleabháin (1942), 460.

The Hunt that Came over the Sea:
Narratives of a Maritime 'Wild Hunt'
in Irish Oral Tradition

Fairy cavalcades or sinister companies of riders, but not necessarily in pursuit of a quarry, are also reported, as is the *slua sí* ('trooping fairies'), a malevolent company of the fairy folk said to travel along lonely roads by night or raise whirlwinds by their movement during the day. Known also as *an slua aerach* (the 'airy' host), *an dream aerach* (the 'airy' group') and *an slua le doineann* ('the inclement/stormy weather host'), they are, because of circumstances of their origin according to Irish oral tradition (which regards them as the fallen angels cast out of heaven by God and the Archangel Michael),[27] linked (though not exclusively so) to the upper regions of the sky or considered to be the cause of gusty or stormy weather.[28] They are associated *inter alia* with the abduction of humans, animals and even crops, and are thus considered sinister and dangerous, but baying hounds and the idea of a relentless pursuit of a quarry – aspects central to the Wild Hunt theme – are not, as far as I know, normally associated with them. It appears necessary, then, to look to other tradition complexes for such a company of riders and such a hunt, and it is in that context that the maritime-hunt narratives already mentioned deserve close examination.

The Irish Maritime-Hunt Narratives

A hunt which is neither in the sky nor on land but rather comes over, or through the surface of the sea, is one of the wonders included in a number of the narratives listed in tale-type 2412A, entitled 'Who Has Seen The Greatest Wonder' – one of the 'Unclassified Tales' in *The Types of the Irish Folktale*[29] (though the narrative is more akin to a *fabulat* or migratory legend than a folktale). Two main varieties are indicated. In one a very old woman (*Cailleach an Daingin* 'The Hag of Dingle') tells of strange things she has seen or experienced. In the other – which is of relevance here – two men vie in telling of the greatest wonder each has seen, and in roughly one third of the (forty-four) narratives listed in tale-type 2412A, a hunt which comes over the sea is one of these wonders. However, two of these narratives must be discounted as they have clearly been copied from a printed source.[30] Three further relevant published variants, collected in the first two decades of the twentieth century, giving a corpus of fourteen versions, are also included in this discussion.[31]

On the basis of the variants known to date, the narratives appear to have a particular linguistic and geographical provenance, that is, they are in the Irish

---

27 See O'Sullivan (1977), 44-7, for examples of common legends about the origin and final fate of the fairies according to Irish oral tradition. See also Christiansen (1971-73), 97-8.
28 Ó Súilleabháin (1942), 463-4 and (1967), 85.
29 Ó Súilleabháin & Christiansen (1963).
30 See Appendix D below. These two narratives (*IFC S* 170: 55-6, 640-1) were written by school-children in county Sligo in 1937-8 but it is clearly evident that both are very closely based on a variant from the Dingle peninsula, county Kerry, collected in 1927 and published in *Béaloideas, The Journal of the Folklore of Ireland Society* in 1930 (*Béaloideas* 2 [1930], 146-7 – see Appendix D: 8). They need not, therefore, be considered separately here.
31 See Appendix D: 6, 7, 14.

language and, as already pointed out, they have been collected in the Gaeltacht or Irish-speaking areas of the southwest of Ireland – in the Dingle and Iveragh peninsulas of county Kerry, from male tradition bearers, who were, by and large, elderly men at the time. That the narratives were far more common in these areas of the southwest of Ireland than the available variants indicate, is evident from comments made to that effect by some of the collectors and narrators.[32]

The following two examples of the narratives – one from each area – show, that while both involve a hunt (indeed, core elements of the Wild Hunt, namely, the horsemen, dogs, and a quarry which is usually a woman, are present in both), it is still possible to draw a distinction between the two sets of narratives on the basis of the *identification* of the hunt victim.

The following example is from the Dingle Peninsula:

·The Captain and The Farmer
A ship's captain and a farmer met each other in a port town in Ireland and that town is called Dingle. The captain came into Seán Ó Longaigh's public house on Sráid na Trá.

There was drinking going on and there was a poor man there and he asked the sea captain 'Did you ever see a wonder?' He said he did. The poor man said he would lay a bet then that he saw a greater wonder even though he never left his own townland. The captain asked him how much would he bet and the poor man said he would wager his farm.
'How much will you bet me?', said the poor man to the captain.
'Tomorrow I will put down thousands of pounds worth.'
Then they put the bets firmly in place and brought with them two referees from each side so that there would be no complaint from any side.
'Now, then,' said the poor man to the ship's captain, 'tell about the wonder you saw'. And he set about telling the story.

He said that he was at sea one day with his ship and he saw the pack of hunting dogs coming after him over the surface of the sea. He and the sailors were very surprised when they saw them coming, and there were horses and riders after them. When the hare and the hounds reached the ship, the hare bounded on to the ship. Then, when the riders reached the ship one of them asked the captain if he had anyone else other than the crew on board.

---

32 See comments to that effect in, for example, Appendix D : 6, p. 147 and 14, p. 104.

The Hunt that Came over the Sea:
Narratives of a Maritime 'Wild Hunt'
in Irish Oral Tradition

The captain said that he hadn't, that he hadn't seen anyone.

' I say that you have,' said he [the rider], 'and if you don't put out that person to me in three minutes I will bring the ocean over you and your crew' (i. e. I will sink the ship).

The captain spoke to one of the sailors and told him to search the ship to see if there was anything odd or unusual in it. He went and searched and he saw a young woman out in the prow of the ship sitting on the ropes. He got very frightened when he saw her and he came back to the captain.
'Did you see anything,' said the captain to him.
'I did,' said he, 'a woman out in the prow of the ship and I got afraid of her.'

The captain then sent three other sailors to accompany him and told them to throw her out of the vessel. When they went to approach her they caught her by the hands and feet and threw her out of the ship. While she was being thrown out she transformed herself again into a hare and took to the sea *westwards again from him.* [author's italics]

'That is my wonder now,' said the captain to the poor man.[33]

Since the maritime-hunt narratives are normally told as part of a competition – indeed there is competition and comparison not just in relation to storytelling, but on a number of other levels in these narratives – there is always a thematically-linked parallel narrative, which I have titled 'The Devil Comes for a Dead Woman and Gets the Body but not the Soul'. The narrative sequence in relation to the above and the other variants, is usually as follows: The sailor first of all tells of the greatest wonder he has seen and then the poor man/farmer tells his story. This is usually set in a wakehouse, and concerns a tall dark horseman [the devil] who has come for a dead person who was wont to say in life 'my body to the devil,' and the devil, it appears, has taken him at his word. The sinister visitor, however, is overcome by the priest who says to him: *Bíodh an corp agatsa, agus beidh a anam agamsa;* 'You can have the body and I will have the soul.'[34] The poor man's story is judged to be the better one – possibly because the devil is defeated and the soul is saved – and the poor man wins the bet and is, therefore, poor no longer! Of course, the poor man/farmer has also made the point for his local audience that it is not necessary to sail the seven seas in order to find adventure; life can also be exciting and fulfilling in one's own locality, even by one's own fireside. Contrasting attitudes of farmer and sailor, particularly in relation to money, are also alluded to, and in a number of versions the farmer chides the sailor for recklessly wagering his life's savings (though in this instance the farmer seems happy enough to accept them!).

---

33 Appendix D: 1. An Com, Dún Chaoin, 1932. My translation. For original Irish-language text see Appendix A.
34 Cf. tale-type 810 in Aarne & Thompson (1961).

The example from Iveragh is as follows:

The Two Wonders - Which was the Greatest?
There was a boy in Ballinskelligs long ago and he became a sailor in his youth. He spent twenty years as a sailor and had travelled the whole world. He came home to Ballinskelligs and one night he visited one of his old neighbours. They welcomed each other.

'Well!', said the man of the house to the sailor, 'I suppose you have seen many wonders by now?'

'Oh!, I saw a lot of wonders', said he.

'I never left the ashes (hearth, i.e. his own local area), and I'm thinking that I have seen as much in this house as you did who have travelled the world.'

'That could happen,' said the sailor; 'what is the greatest wonder you saw,' said he?

'Since it is you who has travelled most you must tell first about the greatest wonders you saw,' said the man of the house.

'The greatest wonder I ever saw – It was in the East Indies, at sunrise. The vessel was creaking with the heat of the sun and the sea was [calm and unruffled] like a well. We heard the most wonderful hunt coming through the ocean, and soon a hare jumped on board ship and three hounds after it. As soon as they came on board the hare became the most beautiful woman ever seen and the hounds became three priests. The captain ordered the woman to his room and ordered the three priests out of it.

'She won't leave,' said the captain, 'until she tells me who she is and why you are hunting her.'

[The Priest's answer:] 'She is a priest's concubine, and it is our purgatory to hunt her through the ocean as long as God is in the City of Glory'.[35]

In the above, and in a further two narratives from the Iveragh peninsula, county Kerry,[36] the victim of the hunt is a priest's concubine. This is probably implied in two other variants from the same region, one involving three priest-huntsmen and a woman victim said by them to be damned,[37] and the other in which the 'priests as huntsmen' motif occurs, but the female quarry is not identified.[38] In yet another variant (without the 'priests as huntsmen' motif), the woman/quarry is

---

35 Appendix D: 12. An Rinn Ruadh, Uibh Ráthach, county Kerry, c. 1949. My translation. For original Irish-language text see Appendix B.
36 Appendix D: 8, 9 collected by different collectors from the same informant 1931-3.
37 Appendix D: 11.

141

The Hunt that Came over the Sea:
Narratives of a Maritime 'Wild Hunt'
in Irish Oral Tradition

said to have been an adultress.[39] This batch of narratives is important in that the identity and status of the dead are declared or implied. It is evident that they involve discourse about the damned, and, therefore, the hunt – as indicated by the narratives – is a perpetual one destined to continue for all eternity. A commonplace in Irish tradition is that the priest's concubine (céile sagairt), is one of a triad of beings for whom salvation is not in store – céile sagairt, leanbh gan baiste agus na daoine maithe ('a priest's concubine, an unbaptised child and the good people' [the fairy folk]). Actually, one of the versions of the legend makes it quite clear that both the pursuers and the pursued are damned. In this the leader of the pursuing priestly group informs the captain of the ship that the woman is damned, and that they are three student priests who died unprepared, and their punishment (purgatory) is to hunt the woman through the sea – forever.[40] In this narrative the hunt is represented by the hounds – the dogs of the otherworld (the Cwn Annwn of the Mabinogi), the dogs of death.

Like the Iveragh narratives, those from the Dingle peninsula also involve a hunt and a hare; indeed the hunt motif is even more specific in these variants since horses, as well as hounds, also take part. That these narratives also involve a discourse about the restless and hostile dead can be shown in a number of ways.

This can be done, first of all, on a symbolic level. The ship-symbol has been related to the holy island and the true sense of sailing is transition, salvation or safe arrival at the haven.[41] Neither the huntsmen nor their quarry may be said to have any right to dwell on the holy island; thus the huntsmen stay by the side of the ship, or in the case of the three priests they must leave the ship, and the evil woman is forcibly removed from the ship/island – in some instances she is said to be whipped off the ship by the captain. There is no salvation or safe haven in store for either, so they must set out again, the hunters and the hunted, endlessly travelling over the sea. There are also further clues in the narratives that we are dealing with the dead and probably also the realm of the dead.

It is, perhaps, not accidental that the core area of the maritime-hunt narratives is in the southwest, or that a number of the narratives state that the hunt went or returned towards the west or southwest.[42] There is a persistent tradition of mystic islands along the west coast, not least from Iveragh to the Dingle peninsula, but, perhaps, of more significance is the identification of Bull Island, a small rocky island at the mouth of Kenmare Bay, with Donn, the Irish god of the dead. This dolmen-like structure with its natural arch or bridge and chasm, was known as Teach Duinn, and in sources from the eighth to the tenth centuries it is referred to as the

---

38 Appendix D: 13.
39 Appendix D: 14.
40 Appendix D: 11.
41 Cirlot (1984), 295.
42 For example, Appendix D: 1, 2, 10.

assembly place of the dead before they began their journey to the otherworld.[43] It is tempting, and perhaps not incorrect to view the maritime hunt as emanating from and returning to the kingdom of Donn in the southwest. Thus a hunt involving the restless dead, could be perceived, in the Irish context, as a maritime hunt coming over or through the sea.

Tradition bearers are at pains to emphasise that it was a maritime hunt that was involved, that it could not possibly be a land hunt, and that weather conditions were such that it was possible to hear the sound of the approaching hunt – that is to say, that the weather was very calm. A maritime hunt, is, of course, most likely to be experienced by those sailing the seas. A ship, or at least a large vessel to ward off the hunters and to give the quarry momentary sanctuary, is necessary for the action of the narrative. The following extract shows how precisely tradition bearers set the scene for the actualisation of the hunt:

> We went for a season to the Indies – nine vessels – to collect a cargo – of ... silk and such things – and from six o'clock in the morning to six in the evening no white man could go on board because the sun would burn him, the heat was so great. We raised the sails but it was of little help to us as there wasn't a puff of wind. We had to stay there for nine days and nine nights, and one morning we heard the finest hunt that ever was heard in a mountain glen with a pack of dogs. There was neither hill nor land to be seen in any direction but the hunt coming towards us through the ocean ...[44]

Of course it was not necessary that the hunt be actualised; it could have been imagined or experienced when the storm winds howled on a winter's night – as was recorded in narratives in northern Europe. But its actualisation in the Irish versions contributes powerfully to the dramatic energy of the narratives. First of all, it enables the hostile confrontation and the dramatic momentary respite for the female hunt victim to be presented. Secondly, the dialogue between the (male) ghostly hunters and the human being – the ship's captain – which seals her fate, can be highlighted.

There are, of course, differences in relation to the time, place and manner of manifestation between the maritime hunt in Irish narratives and the Wild Hunt theme in Northern Europe. But it seemed possible to resolve or accommodate these differences within the context of the maritime setting of the narratives. The question remains to be answered, however, whether the hunt which comes over the sea can be regarded as a reflex of the northern European Wild Hunt ? In this context it should be mentioned that in the 1950s and 1960s, two scholars – Seán Ó Súilleabháin and Séamus Ó Duilearga – both of whom had a wide knowledge of Irish and European traditions, identified narratives of such a hunt in Irish tradition as belonging to the

---

43 Mac Cana (1973), 42-4.
44 Appendix D: 11, 57. My translation. For original Irish-language text see Appendix C.

The Hunt that Came over the Sea:
Narratives of a Maritime 'Wild Hunt'
in Irish Oral Tradition

international Wild Hunt theme, In 1952 Ó Súilleabháin – former archivist and compiler of the *Handbook of Irish Folklore* – linked a version of the maritime hunt from the Dingle area, county Kerry, to *Odinsjäger* of Scandinavian tradition in his notes to the version of the narrative he included in his collection in *Scéalta Cráibhtheacha* ['Religious Tales'].[45] Furthermore, in a 1961 publication, Ó Duilearga also identified a version of the maritime hunt which he had collected in Iveragh in the 1920s, as a variant of the European Wild Hunt theme.[46] On the basis of the further versions of the narrative included in AT 2412 A and those found in printed sources which have been dealt with here, it seems possible, therefore, to support the view that the maritime-hunt of the southwest of Ireland is a reflex of the Wild Hunt theme of northern European tradition, and that the narratives which give expression to it reflect beliefs and ideas about the dead and the otherworld in Irish tradition.

Appendix A

An Captaen agus an Feirmeoir

Do casadh captaen árthaigh agus feirmeoir ar a chéile i mbaile cuain in Éirinn, agus is an t-ainm atá ar an mbaile sin ná Daingean Uí Chúise. Tháinig an captaen isteach go tigh tabhairne Sheáin Uí Longaigh a bhí i Sráid na Trá.

Do bhí an t-ól ar siúl ann, agus do bhí duine bocht istigh ann, agus d'fhiafraigh an duine bocht den gcaptaen farraige: 'An bhfeacaís aon iontas riamh ?' Dúirt sé go bhfaca. Dúirt an duine bocht go gcuirfeadh sé geall síos leis ansan gur mó an t-iontas a chonaic sé féin ná é, ar a shon nár fhág sé a bhaile féin amach riamh. D'fhiafraigh an captaen farraige de cad é an geall a chuirfeadh sé síos, agus dúirt an duine bocht go gcuirfeadh sé a fheirm síos leis.

'Cad é an geall a chuirfirse síos liomsa?' arsa an duine bocht leis an gcaptaen.
'Cuirfidh mé amárach síos leat luach na mílte punt.'

Ansan do dhaingníodar síos na geallta, agus do thugadar leo dhá mholtóir ón dtaobh acu sa tslí agus ná beadh aon achasán le cur le aon duine acu ó aon taobh.

'Sea, anois,' arsa an duine bocht leis an gcaptaen, 'eachtraigh ar an iontas do chonacaís féin!' Do chrom an captaen ansan ar é a insint dóibh.

Dúirt sé go raibh sé féinig lá ar an bhfarraige lena loing, agus go bhfaca sé ag teacht ina dhiaidh an chonairt ghadhar amach ar dhrom na farraige móire, agus go raibh ionadh mór air féin agus ar na mairnéalaigh nuair a chonaic sé ag teacht iad; agus do bhí capaill agus marcaigh ina dhiaidh. Agus nuair a tháinig an giorria agus an chonairt suas leis an árthach do léim an giorria as a chorp le lúth, agus do tháinig sé isteach sa loing. Ansan nuair a tháinig na marcaigh suas leis an loing do

---

45 Ó Súilleabháin (1952), No. 56 – see Appendix D: 3.
46 *Béaloideas* 29 (1961 [1963]), 140; Appendix D: 14.

dh'fhiafraigh duine de sna marcaigh den gcaptaen an raibh aon duine bun os cionn lena chriú féin ar bord aige.

Dúirt an captaen leis ná raibh, agus ná faca sé é.

'Deirimse go bhfuil,' ar seisean, 'agus mura mbeidh sé curtha amach chughamsa as an loing i gcionn trí nóimeataí cuirfidh mé an fharraige mhór lastuas díot féin agus ded chriú!'

Sea, do labhair an captaen ansan le duine dá mhairnéalaigh, agus dúirt sé leis an long do chuardach féachaint an raibh aon rud bun os cionn istigh inti. Do dh'imigh sé sin ag cuardach, agus do chonaic sé bean óg amuigh i dtosach na loinge suite anuas ar na téada. Do tháinig crith cos agus lámh air nuair a chonaic sé í, agus do tháinig sé thar n-ais go dtí an captaen.

'An bhfeacaís faic?' arsa an captaen leis.

'Do chonac,' arsa é sin, 'bean amuigh i dtosach na loinge, agus do tháinig eagla orm roimpi.'

Do chuir an captaen ansan beirt eile des na mairnéalaigh in aonacht leis. Dúirt sé leo í do chur amach as an árthach. Nuair a chuadar ag triall uirthi, do bheireadar ar dhá láimh agus ar dhá chois uirthi, agus do chaitheadar amach as an loing í. Le linn í a chaitheamh amach do dhein sí giorria aríst di féin, agus do dh'imigh sí fén bhfarraige siar aríst uaidh ...

Appendix B

An Dá Ionadh na Beirte [Cé acu ba mhó]

Do bhí buachaill i mBaile an Sgeilg fadó agus dheaghaigh sé sna mairnéalaigh as a óige. Sheirbheáil sé bliain is fiche iontu. Bhí an domhan go léir siúlta aige. Tháinig sé abhaile go Baile an Sgeilg.

Agus bhuail sé isteach oíche do dhuine dá sheana-chomharsain. D'fháiltíodar féin dá chéile.

'Bhuel!' a dúirt fear an tí leis an mairnéalach, 'is dócha go bhfuil a lán ionaí feicthe agat anois?

'Ó, chonac mórchuid ionaí.'

'Níor fhágas an luaith riamh,' a dúirt fear an tí leis, 'agus táim á cheapadh go bhfaca istigh anso mar thigh comh mór is a chonacaís a shiúlaigh an domhan.'

'Thitfeadh san amach,' a dúirt an mairnéalach. 'Cad é an t-ionadh é sin a chonacaís?' a dúirt an mairnéalach.

'Ós tusa is mó a shiúlaigh is ort a théann an scéal d'insint ar dtúis ar na hionaí is mó a chonacaís,' a dúirt fear an tí.

The Hunt that Came over the Sea:
Narratives of a Maritime 'Wild Hunt'
in Irish Oral Tradition

'An t-ionadh is mó a chonac riamh, sna hIndiacha Thoir ar éirí gréine, bhí an t-árthach ag cnágarnaí le teas na gréine agus bhí an fharraige ar nós an tobair. Do chualamar an fiach ba bhreátha ag teacht tríd an bhfarraige mhóir, agus ba ghearr dúinn gur léim giorria ar bhord árthaigh chugainn agus trí chú ina diaidh. Comh luath is a thángadar ar bhord do dhein an bhean ba bhreátha, dár luigh súil peacaigh uirthi, den ghiorria, agus do dhein trí sagairt do sna trí chú. D'ordaigh an captaen isteach ina sheomra an bhean agus d'ordaigh an trí sagairt amach as an seomra. Ní raghaidh sí amach go neosfaidh sí dom cé hí féinig agus cad fáth go bhfuileann sibh ag fiach ina diaidh. Céile sagairt is ea í agus is í an phurgadóireacht atá orainn a bheith ag fiach tríd an bhfarraige mhóir, faid a bheidh Dia i gCathair na Glóire.

Do scaoil an captaen amach í. Is chomh luath is a dheaghaidh sí ar an bhfarraige do dhein giorria di. Agus nuair a dheaghadar siúd ar an bhfarraige do dhein trí chú díobh agus as go brách leo tríd an bhfarraige mhóir arís ag fiach ina diaidh.

Sin é an t-ionadh is mó a chonacsa riamh!'

Appendix C

Chuamair ar bhiaiste sna hIndiacha – naoi n-árthaí dhinn – chun *cargo* a thabhairt linn – dath ime[47], síoda agus rudaí mar sin – agus óna sé a chlog ar maidin go sé tráthnóna n'fhéadfadh fear bán dul ar bord, mar dhóifeadh an ghrian é bhí an teas chomh mór san. Thógamair na seolta ach ba bheag an chabhair dúinn é, mar ná raibh leoithne gaoithe ann. Bhí orainn fuireach ansan ar feadh naoi lá agus naoi n-oíche. Agus maidin amháin chualamair an fiach ba bhreátha a chualaís riamh i ngleann cnoic aige paca gadhar. Ní raibh cnoc ná talamh ar radharc in aon bhall ach é ag teacht orainn tríd an bhfarraige mhóir...

Appendix D

Abbreviations

IFC: Irish Folklore Collection, Main Manuscript Collection, Department of Irish Folklore, University College Dublin.

IFC S: Irish Folklore Collection, Schools' Manuscripts Collection (1937-38), Department of Irish Folklore, University College Dublin

Variants from Corca Dhuibhne, county Kerry, listed in AT 2412A

---

47 See *dath-iomdha* 'multi-coloured' in Dinneen (1927). Perhaps [*éadach*] *dath-iomaí*, 'multi-coloured cloth', was intended (or even spoken) by the narrator.

1. *IFC* 99:277-284 (1932); published in *Béaloideas* 15, 1945 [1946], 288-9. Collected by Máire Ní Éigeartaigh, Baile Átha Cliath, from Mícheál Mac Gearailt, An Com, Dún Chaoin, county Kerry.
2. *IFC* 218:308-9 (1936). Collected by Peadar Ó Niallagáin, Baile an Bhuanaigh, Daingean Uí Chúise, county Kerry, from Domhnall Ó Murchadha, of the same area.
3. *IFC* 241:165-7 (1936); published in : Seán Ó Súilleabháin (eag.), *Scéalta Cráibhtheacha*, 1952 (= *Béaloideas* 21 [1951-52]), no. 56, 153-4; English summary, 322, notes, 293. Collected by Seosamh Ó Dálaigh (Full-time collector for the Irish Folklore Commission) from Seán Criomhthain, Comineoil, county Kerry.
4. *IFC* 571:470-72 (1938): Another version collected by Seosamh Dálaigh (Full-time collector for the Irish Folklore Commission), from Seán Criomhthain, Cumineoil, county Kerry.
5 *IFC* 386:313-18 (1937). Collected by Seosamh Ó Dálaigh (Full-time collector for the Irish Folklore Commission) from Micheál Mac Gearailt of the same area.

Variants of the narrative in printed sources:

6. *Béaloideas* 2 (1930), 146-7 (1927). Collected by 'An Seabhac' (Pádraig Ó Siochfhradha) from Tomás Ó Murchadha, Baile Loiscithe, Daingean Uí Chúise, county Kerry.
7. Seosamh Laoide, *Tonn Tóime*, Dublin 1915, 15-17. Collected by Laoide from Tadhg Ó Ciabháin, Ceanntrágha, county Kerry 'before 1915' - see An Seabhac' (Pádraig Ó Siochfhradha), *Béaloideas* 2 (1930), 147.

Variants from Uibh Ráthach, county Kerry listed in AT 2412A:

8. *IFC* 25:464-466 (c. 1931-2). Collected by Pádraig Ó Connroigh (garsún scoile, Coláiste Caoimhín, Glas Naoidhean, Baile Átha Cliath), from Domhnall Ó Murchadha, Imleach Mór, Baile An Sceilig, county Kerry.
9. *IFC* 602:19-21 (c. 1932-3). Another version from Domhnall Ó Murchadha, Imleach Mór, Baile An Sceilig, county Kerry, was collected by M. Ó Cróinín, DúnGéagáin, Baile an Sceilig, county Kerry.
10. *IFC* 997:98-101 (1947). Collected by Tadhg Ó Murchadha (Full-time collector for the Irish Folklore Commission), from Séamas Chrócháin Shéafra Uí Chonaill, Lóthar, Uibh Ráthach, county Kerry.
11. *IFC* 498:54-58 (1934). Collected by Máire Nic Cárthaigh, Imleach na Muc, parish of Prior, county Kerry, from Seán Mhártain Ó Súilleabháin, Imleach Mór, Baile An Sceilig, county Kerry.
12. *IFC* 1278:4-7 (c. 1949). Collected by An Bráthair P. T. Ó Riain, Luimneach, from Dónal Ó Murchú, An Rinn Ruadh, Uibh Ráthach, county Kerry.

The Hunt that Came over the Sea:
Narratives of a Maritime 'Wild Hunt'
in Irish Oral Tradition

13. *IFC* 1315:347-9 (1953). Collected by Tadhg Ó Murchadha from Tadhg Ó Foghladha, Cúm an Bhóthair, Paróiste na Dromad, county Kerry.

Variant in a printed source

14. *Béaloideas* 20 (1961[1963]),102-3; notes, 140. Collected by Séamus Ó Duilearga in the 1920s from Seán Chormaic Ó Sé (1853-1934), Currach na nDamh, paróiste na Priaireachta, Uibh Ráthach, county Kerry.

The Irish Analogues of Mélusine

Proinsias Mac Cana

The Mélusine legend is not of course the earliest instance of the type of tale to which it commonly lends its name. I assume that what has ensured this particular legend and title their special prestige and currency is the fact that they were linked to the dynastic history of the ruling family of Poitou and that they became widely known in literary versions from a relatively early period. Other stories of the Otherworld Bride, of whatever date and provenance, are often named after the legend of the lady Mélusine provided they correspond more or less closely to its thematic structure. The essential element of this structure is that a woman of the otherworld proposes or accepts a liaison with a mortal man on condition that he submits to a certain interdiction which, through fate or the weakness of human nature, he is destined to violate after a period of great happiness and prosperity. The inevitable consequence of this transgression is that the union is broken and the woman departs. That is the basis of the legend which had become attached to the family of Lusignan in Poitou already before 1350, for it is at this date that we find it so mentioned by the then prior of the abbey of St-Éloi, who was himself born not far from Lusignan.[1] The woman is not named there, which may indicate that she had not yet acquired the designation which was to enjoy a measure of lasting fame. Even the provenance of the name is uncertain: was it taken from the château of Lusignan or was it Mélusine who lent her name to the château? M. Claude Lecoutuex is inclined to favour an explanation proposed in the last century and which would derive the lady's name from the expression 'mère des Lusignan' (pp. 39-43).

The first written version of the legend is that put together by Jean d'Arras in 1392 under the title *Roman de Mélusine*. It is a story that is quite well known and it will be sufficient here to sketch briefly some of its principle elements:

> At centre stage is Raymondin, son of the count of Forez and nephew of the count of Poitier. He has just accidentally killed his uncle while hunting and wanders distraught in the forest on horseback before coming finally to the Fontaine de Soif, where three young women, one of whom was Mélusine, are enjoying themselves. As the rider, preoccupied, passes on without even noticing their presence, Mélusine seizes the bridle of his horse and reproaches him for passing by without greeting them. Raymondin is struck by her beauty and falls in love with her, and she promises to make him rich and powerful on condition that he agrees to marry her. But first she makes him swear never to try to see her on Saturday. After their marriage Mélusine sees to the

---

1 Lecouteux (1982), 42.

construction of the château which will henceforth be the seat of the Lusignans and busies herself in improving the family domain by clearing forests and building towns and castles. She gives birth to ten sons, several of whom become kings by marriage and all of whom are marked by some physical blemish. After some time the count of Forez, Raymondin's brother, tells him that as rumour has it she engages in debauchery every Saturday or else she is an enchanted spirit. Raymondin makes a hole in the door of his wife's chamber, spies upon her while she is having her bath and discovers that from the navel down she has the tail of a serpent. However, instead of departing forthwith, Mélusine forgives him because he has not divulged her secret to anyone. But this is but a respite. Soon after, when their son Geoffroy burns the abbey of Maillezais and its monks, among them his brother Fromont, Raymondin in a fit of rage berates his wife as a loathsome serpent who is the origin of the blemishes and misdeeds of his children. Mélusine can no longer remain. She flies off through the window, transforming herself into a serpent, and utters a piercing cry before disappearing. She returns at times to care for her two youngest children without anyone seeing her, and she appears three days before the château of Lusignan is taken in charge by each new master or before the death of one of her descendants.

As we have seen, the legend of Mélusine as such makes its appearance relatively late in medieval literature, but, as other scholars have noted, it comprises already at that time elements that are well attested between 1140 and 1200, for example in the Breton lays, and which point towards the Celtic world and the *matière de Bretagne*. One of the most important of the sources thus indicated is Walter Map's *De nugis curialium* which he wrote between 1181 and 1193 and in which he relates the adventure of a certain Wastin Wastiniauc from Brycheiniog, in south Wales:

Another, not miracle but prodigy, the Welsh relate to us. Wastin Wastiniauc, they say, lived by the lake of Brycheiniog [identified with Llyn Syfaddon (or Llangorse Lake)], which is two miles broad, and saw on three clear moonlight nights bands of women dancing in his fields of oats, and followed them till they plunged into the water of the lake; but on the fourth night he caught one of them. Her captor also said that each night after they had plunged in he heard them murmuring beneath the water and saying: 'If he had done so and so he would have caught one of us.' So he learnt from themselves the way in which he caught this one. She yielded to him and married him, and her first words to her husband were these: 'I will gladly serve you and obey you with all devotion till the day when you are about to rush out at the shouting beyond the Llyfni, and strike me with your bridle.' Now Llyfni is a river near

150

the lake. This actually happened: after many children were born to him of her, she was struck with a bridle by him, and when he got back he found her fleeing with the children, followed them, and barely succeeded in catching one of his sons, named Triunein Vagelauc ['bent', 'carrying a crutch'].[2]

The sequence to this episode concerns the fortunes of Triunein. He moved to north Wales where he lived a long time until in a foolish moment he angered the king by boasting of the superior power and valour of his own lord, Brychan of Brycheiniog, and was compelled to lead the northern host to invade and ravage his home territory.[3] In the event Brychan routed his attackers and all but exterminated them. Triunein disappeared and according to the tradition 'was rescued by his mother and still lives with her in the lake', presumably Llyn Syfaddon. This close association of the appearance and provenance of the fairy woman with water, whether lake, river or source, is common to most of the insular variants of the Mélusine legend.

The next stage in the history of the legend in Britain brings us to the modern period, to a group of tales which were recorded for the most part during the last century. The best-known of them if not necessarily the most authentic, at least in its extant form, is that which purports to explain how a family living at Myddfai in Carmarthenshire in south Wales acquired the hereditary gift of medicine. This is the substance of the tale:

One day a widow's son who lived near the little lake called Llyn y Fan Fach sees on its surface a beautiful woman combing her long hair. He offers her bread and cheese, but she disappears saying: 'Hard is your bread; it is not easy to catch me'. The next day, following his mother's advice, he offers the woman unbaked bread, but she rejects that also. On the third day, however, when he brings her lightly baked bread, she willingly accepts it and agrees to become his wife on condition that he shall never strike her three times without cause. The marriage takes place, the couple live happy and prosperous for many years, and three sons are born to them. Unfortunately it comes about on three occasions that the husband unintentionally violates the injunction, and on the third occasion she immediately summons all the cattle and other animals she had brought as her dowry and disappears with them into the lake. She only returns to see her sons and to transmit to them the knowledge of medical treatments and healing herbs for which they and their descendants were to be famous.[4]

---

2 For the Latin text and the translation see James (ed.) 148-55. Cf. Wood (1992), (57-8) and, more recently, Roberts (1999), 287-302; also Rhys (1901), 70-3.

3 Actually the text says that Triunein went to Deheubarth, which is south Wales, though an emending gloss *id est Noruuallie* has been added.

4 For the narratives see Rhys (1901), 1-23; also Williams (1861), xxi-xxx. For recent commentary see Wood (1992) 56-72; Gwyndaf (1992-1993), 241-66.

The threefold offering of bread which figures so prominently here invites interpretation in symbolic or mythological terms. For example, Alwyn and Brinley Rees suggest that the lightly baked bread which the woman finally accepted, being neither cooked nor uncooked, represents the coincidence of opposites which creates a common terrain for the meeting of the mortal with a supernatural being.[5] The fact that the motif occurs in such a well known tale has perhaps tended to give the impression that it is more widely attested than it really is, whereas there does not appear to be any very certain evidence of it apart from the Llyn y Fan Fach story. Sir John Rhys, in his lengthy commentary on the Welsh legend, cites only one other version containing the motif, but it is possible that the tale in question, which was associated with another lake, Llyn Elferch (*Celtic Folklore* 70-3) is merely a somewhat altered or corrupted version of the Llyn y Fan Fach narrative. It is all the more interesting therefore that the motif is also recorded in Ireland, in an Irish version of the fairy bride legend which was collected from an elderly woman in county Waterford in 1931. I give it as summarized from the original Irish by Máire MacNeill:

> One of the caves [the Mitchelstown Caves in Co. Cork] is called 'the cave of the gray sheep'. One morning a young farmer saw a beautiful woman who ran away from him into the cave, saying as she went in: 'Son of the little hag of the hard bread, you couldn't catch me!' He told his mother to give the bread only a turn and a half-turn on the griddle, but next morning the woman got away from him again saying the same thing. On the third morning he had told his mother just to put the bread on the griddle and lift it off: this time he caught the woman as she reached the hole and brought her home. She put him under bonds not to touch her until she had eaten three meals of the new food. When he was reaping the harvest she came out to him and said: 'It is a fine day to be eating the first meal of the new food and lying with another man's wife!' and she ate a grain of the wheat. The second day she did the same, and on the third day as she ate the third grain she taunted him for being a laggard and said he would never see her again but that she would send him something to keep. She ran as swift as the wind into the cave. Next morning he found a gray sheep and kept it until it had nine lambs. Then he decided to kill it but the ewe and the nine sheep ran away and were never seen again. People told him that he should have kept the ewe and sold the lambs, and that if he had taken the woman before she had eaten the three meals she would have stayed with him.[6]

This is a fascinating little tale, even if its credentials may call for some further scrutiny. It has been noted by Brian Earls that variants of the story of the grey sheep are recorded in association with the Mitchelstown Caves from the mid-nineteenth

---

5 Rees (1961), 344.
6 MacNeill (1962 [1982]), 569-70.

century onwards and that, occurring as they do in contexts related to tourism, they probably reflect the growing publicity for these caves which had been discovered only in 1833.[7] He concludes that the story of the grey sheep cannot have been connected with the Mitchelstown Caves before their discovery in 1833, but accepts that it was probably already in existence and merely adapted to a new location in the neighbourhood.[8] For our immediate purposes it is also important to note that, so far as I have been able to ascertain, the variants to which Brian Earls refers are variants of the story of the grey sheep and do not contain the tale of the fairy bride and the triple offering of bread as it is found in Máire MacNeill's text. It seems very likely therefore that this latter text represents a conflation of the two tales, in which case the authenticity of the 'Mélusine' component is not affected by the very useful discussion by Earls of the grey sheep segment.

In the version told by the Waterford storyteller this tale is essentially the same as that of Llyn y Fan Fach, though there are some discrepancies which are interesting in themselves. The woman is of the otherworld, of course, but the route by which she comes and goes shows, if that were necessary, that the legend need not always be associated with a lake, or even with water. In its recorded form the tale does not explicitly mention the first offer of bread, but this is implicit in what follows: as she flees from the young man at their first encounter she dismisses the hard bread baked by his mother, and it is because of this that he asks his mother to give the bread only 'a turn and a half-turn on the griddle'. And while the two other variants are not described in precisely the same terms as in the Welsh tale, the fact remains that the bread which portends success is neither cooked nor raw. It is precisely at this point, however, that our narrative departs most obviously from its Welsh analogue. Instead of behaving as we have every right to expect her to do by accepting the young man's offering and staying with him dutifully thereafter, she takes off as before and it is only as she enters the cave that he catches her. It would appear very much as if the Llyn y Fan Fach theme has been combined with a motif that is familiar both in medieval Irish literature and in the popular tradition of the modern period and according to which the hero seizes a supernatural being at the very instant that the latter crosses the threshold of the otherworld, or, in other words, as he stands momentarily in the liminal space between the natural and the supernatural worlds. Thus, on the functional level, to win the fairy woman through the choice of the ambiguous bread is essentially the same as to capture her within the ambiguous space. If, as seems likely, this duplication is the result of textual or thematic conflation, it is hardly unreasonable to assume that it came from an awareness on the part of a storyteller redactor that the two narrative mechanisms were mythological equivalents.

---

7 Earls (1992-3), 105-6.
8 It might be helpful to have a more precise definition of what was actually discovered in 1833. For example, one of the sources cited by Brian Earls is Mr and Mrs S. C. Hall, II, 80, and it should perhaps be noted that the Halls there speak of the Mitchelstown neighbourhood as already being famous for its caves for centuries and that they distinguish between the 'old cave' where the grey sheep disappeared and the 'new' one which was discovered in May, 1833.

In this regard it may be noted that this is not the only doublet in our tale, for, subsequent to the experiment of the tripartite foodstuff which enables the mortal to win the fairy woman, there is another tripartite foodstuff which allows her to make her escape from him – a deft balancing of positive and negative which looks almost too subtle to be accidental. The ambivalence it conveys manifests itself also in the attitude of the fairy woman towards her human partner: in the manner of traditional and popular storytelling she imposes upon him a condition or an interdiction which has the effect of postponing or avoiding a marriage which she does not desire, whereas in the end she appears to reproach him for his lack of virility in observing the terms of her condition. This ineptness on his part, this lack of *savoir-faire*, appears again even after the departure of the woman (and in that part of the tale which may be a secondary addition to the original fairy bride legend). Here she leaves a prolific ewe with the farmer, and he, for the second time, loses what he prizes most through his lack of good sense. One obvious disparity with other versions of the legend is that in this instance the woman has not had time to give birth to children during her cohabitation with the mortal and therefore she cannot bring them with her when she leaves. There may also have been other changes in the final episode of the tale and in the precise circumstances of the woman's departure. These may have been affected by the content of the gray sheep episode if this was joined on secondarily to the preceding narrative; in that case one might suppose that in an earlier version of the Waterford tale, as elsewhere, she carried off with her both animals and prosperity.

Even this does not exhaust the complexity of a little tale which in some ways gives the impression of leaving unsaid as much as it actually reveals. 'It is a fine day,' the woman says, 'to be eating the first meal of the new food and lying with another man's wife!', which suggests that she already had a husband in the otherworld. It is all the more curious then that in one of the versions of the legend of Llyn y Fan Fach the woman, when summoning her cattle to follow her to the otherworld, declares a little laconically that the woman 'from the house on the hill' will never milk her cows.[9] Does this mean, as John Rhys believed, that the farmer had already taken a new wife, a mortal woman, in her place by the time she 'came to call her live stock into the lake'? If so, there may be a certain broad parallel to this in two of the Irish versions (the stories of 'the man from Inbhear' and Maolmhuire 'of the purse') to be discussed later.

Given the setting and the circumstances of the narrative it is hardly surprising that the husband in the Waterford tale is a young farmer. It is rather more noteworthy, however, that his counterpart in the earliest Irish cognate of the Mélusine legend should also be a farmer, considering this tale is set within the framework of the Ulster Cycle, where the mortal who joins with an otherworld woman is more typically a prince or a hero than a farmer, however well endowed. The tale in question, *Noínden*

9 Rhys (1901), 26-7 .

Ulad ('The Debility of the Ulstermen'), dates from about the ninth century. Its similarities to the thematic constituents of *Lanval, Graelant* and other medieval variants of the fairy bride type are striking, and French and other scholars have long recognized its central importance for the historical development of the theme. It may, for example, be recalled that in Marie de France's *Lai de Lanval* the knight of that name encounters by a river two young girls who lead him to their mistress. She tells him that she has left her own country for love of him, and he falls in love with her. She promises him wealth without limit, but on condition that he will never speak of her if he is not to lose her. She will come to visit him whenever he desires her presence, but only he will see her; for all others she will remain invisible. Following his return to the court of King Arthur, Lanval rejects the queen's advances, and when she through spite lodges a complaint against him he can only defend himself by declaring in public that he already has a lover even more beautiful than the queen. This he must then prove or be banished, and it is at that point that the otherworld woman comes to his rescue. Lanval goes off with her, and it is said that she brought him with her to the marvellous land of Avalon. Virtually all the constituent elements of this tale are familiar to readers of medieval Irish literature, and one can readily see how close are several of its essential features to those of *Noínden Ulad.* This is the substance of the Irish narrative:

> There was a wealthy farmer of the Ulstermen, Crunnchu mac Agnomain, who lived on the deserted upland territories. His wife and the mother of his many sons died, and he was for a long time without a wife. One day while he was alone on his couch, he saw a beautiful young woman enter and come towards him. She sat by the fireplace and kindled the fire. They both remained there until the end of the day without speaking. Then she fetched a kneading trough and a sieve and set about preparing food, and after that she went to milk the cows. When she came in again, she turned righthandwise (*for deisiul*) and went to the kitchen to do the chores. When everyone else went to bed, she remained behind, smoored the fire, made a righthand turn, joined Crunnchu under his covering and put her hand on his body. They were together until she became pregnant by him, and in consequence of their union he became ever more rich.
>
> In time the great assembly of the Ulstermen approached and Crunnchu was preparing to go there. The woman tried to dissuade him, 'for', she said, 'our union will be at an end if you make mention of me in the assembly'. He promised not to speak of her. However, when he saw the two horses of the king had won the victory in the great race and that the eulogists praised them saying that they were without equal, he could not refrain from declaring that his wife was swifter than they. The king had him seized and his

wife sent for. They threatened to kill her husband if she did not run against the king's horses, and in vain she explained that she was already with the pangs of childbirth and sought a delay until she be delivered. The king refused and she was obliged to take part in the race. On reaching the end of the course ahead of the horses she uttered a cry and gave birth to a boy and a girl. Then she predicted that the shame she had suffered would be inflicted also on the men of Ulster, and that from that time forth when things were most difficult for those who guard the province they would have no more strength than a woman in childbirth, and that that affliction would endure until the ninth generation.[10]

For those familiar with medieval Irish literature and tradition this little tale is rich in mythic resonance. In its actual form it is an etiological story which purports to reveal the origin of the name of the sanctuary and seat of the king of Ulster, Emain Macha, by the birth of twins to the goddess Macha, and which, in addition, accounts for the strange weakness which leaves the Ulstermen *hors de combat* during the incursions of the armies led by Ailill and Medb of Connacht. It goes without saying that the redactor was aware of all this, as no doubt were his readers/listeners, yet, following the common usage in many such tales by which the fairy woman is not named until the narrative is well advanced, in this instance Crunnchu's wife also remains anonymous, not merely for part of the tale but throughout. With the exception of a phrase in one of the manuscript copies of what is considered to be the earliest version (a phrase which the most recent editor, Vernam Hull, treats as a secondary gloss)[11] the name Macha does not appear. It is a type of counterpoint reticence much favoured by medieval Irish storytellers. In reality it matters little that the woman goes unnamed or that her future husband does not seek to know her provenance: there are some facts, or truths, which create all the more profound impression for not being put into words, and in this instance it is by her actions that the wife of Crunnchu reveals whence she comes and who she is.

As in many other fairy bride tales, including the Mélusine legend itself but not those of the Llyn y Fan Fach type, it is the otherworld woman who takes the initiative. When she enters Crunnchu's house without invitation or explanation – an interesting contrast this to the story of 'The Inver man and the fairy woman' (p. 158 – 9 below) – the significant thing is that she immediately takes the housework in hand without a 'by your leave'. We know that in Macha's two other personifications as attested in other medieval texts she sometimes appears in the guise of queen and spouse of the king and sometimes as warrior-defender of the sovereignty. Here she assumes another of the principal aspects of the Irish and Celtic goddess: that of source and guarantor of the prosperity of land and people, in as much as she is represented carrying the cornucopia or other symbols of fertility in gallo-roman

10 *Celtica* 8 (1968) 1-42.
11 *Op. cit.*, 30.

iconography. Once within Crunnchu's dwelling everything that she does has reference to this role. She goes straight to the fireplace and rekindles the fire,[12] just as, at the day's end, she smoors or covers the fire before proceeding to enter into union with Crunnchu. The multiple function of fire is well known, in the Celtic world as elsewhere: a ritual taking possession (of land etc.), a means of fertilization, and, finally, the hearth-place itself as centre of familial and social unity. It may be recalled that it was a custom until fairly recently in some parts of Ireland that the mother-in-law handed the tongs to her daughter-in-law and invited her to adjust the fire on the open hearth.[13]

Indeed one of the most striking features of *Noínden Ulad* is the quasi-ritual atmosphere that the redactor has succeeded in creating and conveying through a style and treatment which are succinct, restrained and impressionistic. Twice we are told that Macha made a right-hand turn (*for deisiul*): before going into the kitchen and before entering Crunnchu's bed. Going right-handed was of course a procedure commonly resorted to for bringing good fortune and avoiding misfortune, and as such it figured generally in ceremonies and in serious enterprises, very much as did the *pradaksná*, the Indian ritual of circumambulation. Until recent times it was the custom during the ceremonies which took place within the family to mark the feast of St Brighid for a young girl bearing the saint's name to go outside and to walk around the house three times before being welcomed inside with a formal salutation. In this regard it is perhaps worth remarking that Macha and Brighid, goddess and saint, have many similarities as deities of fertility and abundance. The main disparity between them is that Macha exists only in medieval literature while the legends of Brighid have survived copiously in popular tradition, by virtue of the fact that she made a seemingly effortless transition from goddess to saint, from paganism to Christianity. But both, Macha and Brighid, form part of the same mythological network of the goddess who exists and functions under several different aspects. This is why, for example, Crunnchu can boast that his wife is faster than the king's horses (though there is nothing to support his assertion in what has transpired in the story so far), for the indications are, to judge from various Irish and Celtic sources, that Macha has certain attributes in common with the British and continental Epona and the Welsh Rhiannon as equine manifestations of the great goddess.[14]

---

12 The verb *ataid*, used here in the Old Irish expression *ataid tenid*, means 'to light' in the broadest sense (cf. Vendryes (1981), A-102 s.v. *atúd*), which explains Dumézil's translation (1968, 608) 'alluma le feu' and Vernam Hull's 'kindled a fire', but in this particular context it probably refers rather to the act of rekindling the fire, just as one has continued to do down to our own day in those areas where turf remains the normal domestic fuel. Similarly, where the text has *tálgedar in tenid*, which Dumézil translates as 'éteignit le feu', the verb *tálgedar*, literally 'to calm, soothe, pacify', has doubtless the meaning 'cover, smoor', in other words to cover the embers with the ashes (*coigil* in Modern Irish), so that the fire can easily he rekindled the following morning. Vernam Hull translates the two phrases as 'kindled a fire' and 'slacked down ('?) the fire', which seems to reflect quite accurately the sense of the Old Irish. It is a detail which has considerable importance since it gives expression to the sense of continuity which pervades the whole narrative.

13 Ó Danachair (1974-6), 151.

14 Cf. Sterckx (1986), esp. 9-48.

157

The story of Macha as it has been preserved belongs to the Ulster cycle, and, appropriately, the closest analogue to it in modern oral tradition comes also from the north of Ireland. This story, *Fear Inbheara agus an bhean sí* ('The Inver man and the fairy woman'), is an exceedingly well crafted tale, which, incidentally, names neither the young man or his wife. It can be summarised as follows:

The man's father and mother are dead, and, as in the Old Irish tale, it is the woman who comes to the man's dwelling. She approaches his door three days in succession, but does not enter until he invites her in on the third day. Then she offers to stay with him as his wife on condition that he does not reveal her presence to anyone. In a year's time she gives birth to a son, and everything is fine until the neighbours notice how the household has improved and until a passing woman hears a child cry. When the husband meets his brother the latter reproaches him for having a wife of whom no one knows where she comes from, and he advises him to put a knife with a black handle between them in the bed; she will know why he has done so and will depart. [One might perhaps compare this negative intervention with that of the brother of Raymondin, count of Poitou.] However, when the husband returns home he decides not to betray the wife who is so good and kindly, and he throws the knife into the middle of a field of oats. He says nothing to her about it, but she nonetheless divines all that has happened and out of loyalty to her husband she decides to go off with her son. She bears no ill-will towards her husband nor is he guilty of revealing his wife's presence. Before leaving him she tells him that he will soon remarry and she asks him for three things: never to leave the hearth without a fire, never to leave the house without water, and never to leave the table without food during the night, for she and her son could come at night from time to time. But, she said, if he happened to see her there, he was not to speak of it to his new wife.

He was broken-hearted, but in the course of time he married another woman and they got on very well together. She however noticed what he did with regard to the fire, the water and the food, and she kept asking what was the reason for it. When finally he explained it to her she asked him to let her know on the next occasion he saw his first wife. And so, when sometime later he saw her during the night sitting with the child by the fire, he awoke his wife. When she saw the fairy woman she gave three bursts of mocking laughter, whereupon the woman went off promising that she would pay dearly for her laughter. From then on their situation deteriorated and their animals died day by day until there only remained a single foal a week old. Having themselves almost died of hunger they kept the foal for a year, at which time the husband brought it to the fair of Letterkenny. There he met a handsome boy with whom he struck a bargain for the foal. He accompanied the boy home and found himself in a castle face to face with his first wife. He lowered his head in embarrassment, but she told him not to be ashamed to look at her. She told the boy to give his father three times the price agreed upon for the foal, and told the father to buy cattle with the money his son had given him and that his affairs would then prosper. She finished by associating their own story with the traditional theme of a national saviour: 'You will not see us again, neither me or your son, until such day as the great war between the Irish and the English shall take place, and it will be then, when my son shall cross the host mounted on this black foal, that the Irish will win the day.[15]

This little tale poses many problems. Even at first glance it is clear that it is related to the story of Macha, but it is less easy to define precisely the nature of this relationship. Is it that they have a common traditional source, or are we to suppose that the modern tale derives in one way or another from the Old Irish text as it has survived in manuscript? While awaiting a more confident answer to this question one may nonetheless note several interesting features of the modern tale. *Mutatis mutandis* it resembles the story of Macha in its situation and the fact that it opens with the woman's initiative. On the other hand, while Macha enters the house without bidding; here the woman, though she comes three days in succession, cannot or will not enter the house until she is invited to do so. And when things go wrong it is not the husband who breaks the contract, and when his wife leaves him it is not to abandon him but rather to protect him. Indeed the story is rather remarkable for the way in which it represents the woman's attitude towards her husband as one of considerable flexibility and tenderness, even to the extent that she restores to him and his human wife the prosperity he had lost with her departure. Fire and hearth figure interestingly in both tales. In the earlier one Macha assumes the housewife's role by smooring the fire before retiring to bed, while in the later the husband leaves the fire unsmoored at his fairy wife's request so that she may warm herself and her child when she visits during the night. Subtle resonance or inverted coincidence? And how are we to assess the significant role of the foal which in the end appears to belong to the otherworld? Is this simply a reflection of Macha's contest with the king's horses in *Noínden Ulad*, in which case why is it so very different from that episode and why is there no association with horse-racing as there is in several other modern Irish versions of the fairy bride tale ?

Another Donegal version of the tale has been recorded which is much simpler in structure and which ends with the violation of the injunction (in this instance not to bring anyone to the couple's home) and the disappearance of the wife with her two children, a boy and a girl.[16] A connection with the Macha tale is suggested by the fact that there are two children and that the husband betrays his wife's existence

---

15 Ó hEochaidh, Ní Néill, Ó Catháin, (1977), 292-303. Cf. Murphy (1956-7), 276-7.
16 It occurs in two written versions in Ó Domhnaill (1940),149-54, and Ó Dónaill (1948), 69-72.

while at the horse-races. In the context of the present conference it may be noted that the fairy wife makes her exit from the otherworld through a well and that the fairy wife theme is combined with a local application of the inundation motif in which the overflowing well creates a lake. The similar prohibition, the two children and the association with horse-racing occur in others of the small number of variants of the Mélusine theme attested in Ireland and indicate a connection with the early Macha tale. There is for example a legend from county Clare which tells of one of the Ó Cuinn family who, walking by the lake of Inchiquin, saw a beautiful woman combing her hair by the lake shore. She vanished as he approached. This happened three times, until at last, seeing her remove a dark hood, he stole up and seized it so that she could not escape. She consented to marry him on condition that the marriage be kept secret and that he was never to invite anyone to the house to see her. They lived happily for several years and had two children, but eventually he attended horse races organized by the head of the Ó Briain family and, forgetting his promise, afterwards invited him and his friends home to meet her. Thus betrayed, she took her hood, returned to the lake and was never again seen. T. J. Westropp refers to several versions of this tale recorded in the nineteenth century, and notes that in some of them the event is connected with Tadhg an Chomhaid Í Bhriain, lord of Thomond in the middle of the fifteenth century.[17] Undoubtedly there is room for further enquiry into the dynastic associations of this particular local variant of the Mélusine legend.

As we have seen, the connection of the husband's indiscretion with horse-racing would seem to derive from the Old Irish tale told of Macha and the farmer Crunnchu, and indeed modernized texts of that tale are found in a number of eighteenth- and nineteenth-century manuscripts. In Conamara an abbreviated version of the oral tale is used as an introduction to a modern telling of the birthtale of the Ulster hero Cú Chulainn: here we have the rash boast at the races, the pregnant woman racing against the horses to save her husband's life, and the birth of the son whose future heroic career forms the main body of the tale. The late Alan Bruford suggested that this ecotype may have derived from the Old Irish tale by way of Geoffrey Keating's retelling of it in his seventeenth-century history of Ireland,[18] perhaps on the grounds that both Keating's brief version and the Conamara tale omit the woman's injunction or explicit reference to its violation.[19] This in itself is quite plausible. On the other hand, for the very reason adduced by Bruford, Keating's version cannot, on its own, account for the other modern variants of the 'Mélusine' legend.

---

17 Westropp (1913), 378-80.
18 Keating (1908), 154-5.
19 Bruford (1969), 94. Bruford rather curiously refers to the 'Debility of the Ulstermen' (*Ces Ulad* or *Noínden Ulad*) under the title *Echtra Macha*, which normally belongs to a quite different Macha tale. For a synopsis of the Conamara tale cf. Ó Súilleabháin, (1973) 25-6, and for a recorded telling of the tale in Irish cf. Mac Giollarnáth (1936), 37-46, esp. 37-8.

From this review of the Irish analogues to the Mélusine legend it will be clear that one of the problems in tracing its origins and evolution is the dearth of closely relevant material to help bridge the gap between the Old Irish *Noínden Ulad* and the various versions that have turned up in modern popular tradition. It is this which confers a special significance on an episode from an account of Clann Suibhne (the Sweeneys) written in the sixteenth century. It concerns the ancestor of Clann Suibhne and son of the Suibhne from whom they took their name. I quote from the translation by the text's editor, Fr. Paul Walsh:

> A son of that Suibhne was *Maolmhuire an Spáráin* ('Maolmhuire of the Purse'), and that Maolmhuire is the ancestor of the three Clanna Suibhne. He had a fairy lover, that is, a fairy woman was his wife, and it was she who bestowed on him the famous purse above mentioned. Of that purse this was a property: every time it would be opened a small penny and a shilling would be found within it. And for a long time Maolmhuire lived thus: but at length his kinsfolk wished to give him another wife, and the one they chose was Beanmidhe, daughter of Toirrdhealbhach Mór Ó Conchubhair. And a great fleet set out for Ireland, and they who brought it rested not until they reached Sligo. They spent two nights in the town, and they carried away the lady with them.
>
> One night, after that, Maolmhuire was in Castle Sween [Caislen Suibne, in Scotland], and the fairy woman afore-mentioned had promised to bring him her child, and had told him to remain awake to receive her; but when she came, there was no one awake in the house except the daughter of Ó Conchubhair. And she seated herself by the fire, and asked if Mac Suibhne was awake. Ó Conchubhair's daughter said he was not, and she offered clothes to her to put about the child. And she would not accept them, but said that that sleep would bring destruction on Mac Suibhne, and on his children after him. And she departed in anger then, and has never since been seen. Neither has anyone ever seen her son, that is, Fearfeadha, except whenever he came to render help to Clann Suibhne in battle or necessity...[20]

This tale is interesting in that, like the story of Mélusine of Poitou, it is set in a dynastic context, even if its dynastic relevance is not made explicit. It lacks the interdiction which is central to the Mélusine legend, but this is most likely due to the constraints of the historical context to which it has been accommodated. The editors of the tale of 'The Inver man and the fairy woman' have remarked on the similarity in outline between it and the Clann Suibhne legend,[21] but there are also one or two points which are tantalizingly suggestive of a more complex relationship. There is, for example, the uncomfortable encounter between the mortal wife and the

---

20 Walsh (1920), 4-9.
21 Ó hEochaidh *et al.* (1977), 387-8 (see n. 16 above).

fairy woman. The earlier tale omits to recount the circumstances in which the fairy woman and her husband separated: she was with him 'for a long time' and bore his child, and one might surmise that her departure was occasioned by the arrival of the new wife, as in the modern tale. There is also the curious correspondence, despite the obvious discrepancies, between the circumstances in which the displaced wife revisits her old home and comes face to face with her rival. She comes at night, carrying her child, and sits by the fire; the offer of clothing for the child could be an apt allusion to her request in the modern tale that a fire be left at night to warm her and the child. There is the equally curious fact that the otherworld woman threatens that dire consequences will follow her unfortunate meeting with her successor, yet, notwithstanding the ensuing tribulations experienced by husband and wife in the later tale – at a point where the earlier text is terse to the point of silence – the final outcome in both cases is that the fairy woman brings succour to her husband and his family through the mediation of her son. And finally there is the convergence of the two tales in the transcendent role of the son as the promised one, the prophesied saviour of his, that is of his father's, people. In both instances he remains with his mother in the otherworld; in the earlier text he was never again seen 'except when he came to render help to Clann Suibhne in battle or necessity', in the later he would lead the Irish to final victory in their crucial contest with the English. At this point one is tempted to refer back to the conclusion of the medieval Welsh story of Triunein as reported by Walter Map. Walter mentions briefly and dismissively the tradition that Triunein continued to live in the otherworld under the lake with his mother, but, given the the tenor of the whole episode, it might not be unreasonable to speculate that in the oral tradition referred to by the Latin author Triunein, son of the fairy bride, also stood ready and waiting to come to the aid of his people.

As if this close interweave of surface discrepancy with underlying identity were not daunting enough, there is also the minor problem posed by Maolmhuire an Sparáin's epithet which, we are told, he acquired because of the 'famous purse' (*an sparán orrderc*) given him by his fairy lover. If his story, of which we appear to have a mere outline in the Clann Suibhne text, derives from the same source, or one closely related, as the 'Man from Inver' tale, then what is the provenance of the purse motif? We have had occasion to mention the French *Lai de Lanval* as one of the key versions of the Mélusine legend. In it Lanval's fairy lover confers on him the faculty of obtaining anything he desires, but in the English verse translation by Thomas Chestre this gift is commuted – perhaps, Claude Lecouteux suggests, because it was not sufficiently definite – and instead Sir Launfall receives a purse in which he finds a golden coin each time he inserts his hand.[22] This is the magic purse of folklore whose contents do not diminish however much is taken from it.[23] That this particular form of the otherworld gift occurs in these two analogous tales may or may not be significant (Thomas Chestre's translation belongs to the late fourteenth century, the

---

22 Cf. Lecouteux (1982), 42-3.
23 Cf. O'Rahilly (1927), 20.29, and note on p. 76. This passing allusion to *sparán na sgillinne* 'the purse of the shilling' shows that the motif was a familiar one.

text containing the Maolmhuire anecdote was written in the sixteenth), but it illustrates how difficult it can be to differentiate between thematic congruity and textual filiation.

This uncertainty is in a sense inherent in the whole broader context of our topic. For one thing, those tales, which for convenience, I have referred to as analogues of the Mélusine legend, are obviously not distinguished as such within the wider reaches of the literary tradition. Throughout the centuries they have been part of a continuing process of transmission, interacting with numerous other narratives, especially those dealing with visitants to and from the otherworld. Since many of these *comparanda* have not survived and some were never written down, there will always be many instances where we must parse and present the evidence as clearly as possibly, set out the alternative interpretations, and leave firm conclusions aside pending the advent of new evidence or more convincing arguments. In the all too rapid *tour d'horizon* undertaken in the present essay I have sought merely to outline the nature of the relevant evidence and to indicate some of the more interesting questions it raises, in the firm belief that often the elements that go to make up the question are more interesting and perhaps even in some instances more significant than a clear answer might be, even if there were one. Walter Map's anecdote shows that fairy bride legends of the Mélusine type already existed in British oral narrative by the twelfth century and, more specifically, that this particular one may have been part of the traditional lore associated with the kings of the south Wales kingdom of Brycheiniog.[24] In Ireland it is clear from the ninth-century Macha text that this type of legend had already by then been assimilated to the native mythological corpus. Its distribution in Wales is such as to suggest a widespread currency at an earlier period, and the relative thinness of the dossier for modern times has been variously attributed to an inadequate and unrepresentative record and – not unrelated to this – to religious prejudice directed against the vanities and superstitions of popular belief, particularly in the eighteenth and nineteenth centuries. In Ireland versions recorded more or less directly from oral tradition are small in number and this makes it all the easier to suggest, or to assume, borrowing in order to explain similarities.[25] Thus, the Macha tale is plausibly invoked to explain several features in some modern versions, and in the case of 'The Inver man' story it is difficult not to discern the earlier tale in the background. But even if that is so, can we be wholly certain that in all these cases this is necessarily the Macha tale in the precise form in which it has survived to us in manuscript, and must we exclude the possibility that one or more versions of the tale also circulated in oral transmission and may have contributed to the making of our rich and fascinating web of allusions and ambiguities.

In some ways even more tantalizing than this extended diachronic problem is the roughly synchronic one of how to account for the striking parallel between the

---

24 Cf. Wood (1992), 56-72 (57-8); Roberts, (1999).
25 On the distribution of the versions see Kavanagh (1995), 71-82.

Llyn y Fan Fach and Mitchelstown legends, in particular the threefold offering of bread to the woman from beyond. If one has certain misgivings as to the traditional character of the Mitchelstown story complete with this motif, it is mainly because it chimes almost too neatly with the Welsh Llyn y Fan Fach tale – apart of course from the fact that it has a cave in lieu of the lake – and because, so far as I am aware, the motif of the threefold bread is not attested elsewhere in Irish. And yet when the Irish tale deviates from the Welsh one observes that the differences seem meaningful and fully integrated within their actual context as well as in the broader context of Irish tradition, so that they are not easy to reconcile with a simple process of literary borrowing. Furthermore, as we have seen (p.152), the motif seems to be rare also in the Welsh variants and only somewhat doubtfully attested apart from the Llyn y Fan Fach tale itself. For my own part, I confess I have no ready explanation for this curious Cambro-Irish parallel, though when an explanation comes it may be a very simple one; and after all this is only one of a number of intriguing questions raised by the extant Irish analogues of the Mélusine theme.

An Bád Sí: Phantom Boat Legends in Irish Folk Tradition

Críostóir Mac Cárthaigh

Few published collections of folk legends originating along the south and west coasts of Ireland lack a story of a phantom boat manifestation.[1] Stories of this kind are a significant component of the legend repertoires of fishermen, but are also recorded from coastal dwellers whose occupations are entirely land-based.

A small percentage of stories concern 'ghost' ships – generally large sailing vessels – which periodically haunt certain places. In the majority of cases, however, the phantom boat may be identified with various types of small craft in general use among inshore fishermen until recent years. It is also noteworthy that the manifestation generally occurs in an occupational context and that the ensuing events follow certain well-defined patterns. The craft in question are, typically, wooden rowing boats, a minority of which was also fitted with sails. Alongside these, but even more numerous, are craft of the skin-boat tradition: light lath- or wicker-built craft – *curaigh* or *naomhóga* – covered with tarred canvas (or, in earlier times, with animal hides). Few of these craft are above thirty feet in length and their small size restricts their range of activity to little more than ten miles offshore. Their small size was determined to a large degree by the difficult topography of this maritime zone, but also by the size and economic circumstances of the small island and coastal settlements. In heavy seas these boats are vulnerable to capsizing and require sure and skilled handling. Nevertheless, for the purposes of local transport and inshore fishing – generally part-time and seasonal – they have proved adequate. Indeed, many of these craft are still in everyday use.

Since a great many accounts are told first-hand, or at most one or two steps removed from the participants, the story has greatest meaning in the first instance for the participants themselves. There is meaning also for fellow fishermen, and friends and relatives in the wider fishing community who may be affected by a loss or who may wish to comment on the ability or the behaviour of others at sea. The stories exhibit all the characteristics typical of the folk legend: the plot is uncomplicated, and they are exclusively short, unadorned narratives, impressively realistic and authentic in tone. Place is specific, and belief in the supernatural is a central feature of all of the stories considered. The familiar shape of the phantom boat and the occupational context of many narratives combine to produce a realistic setting for the story. The crew of a certain boat, engaged in line-fishing or net-fishing (or other activity) at night, are interrupted by the sudden appearance of a mysterious boat which travels

---

1 The bulk of these derive from the Irish Folklore Commission's collecting efforts between the years 1935-1971, and since 1971, by the Department of Irish Folklore, University College Dublin.

at great speed through the water or otherwise behaves in an erratic manner. Certain motifs recur – the phantom boat forewarns of a storm, for instance, or a drowning.

The traditional concerns and preoccupations of fishermen – success in fishing, the vagaries of the weather, and the vulnerability of their craft – form the substance of most phantom boat stories. The supernatural manifestation may serve to explain why a certain fisherman lost his nerve and ceased to fish, or why a reckless and unsuitable fisherman is later drowned. In the following story, breaking a religious edict against fishing on a Saturday night is the ostensible reason for the supernatural manifestation:

There were three men from my home village of An Sruthán, in Aran (i.e. Inis Mór). These were fishermen who went fishing one Saturday night. People were reluctant to go out fishing on a Saturday night but in any event these men did so. They were mid-way between Aran and Conamara [the mainland] and the night was neither dark nor bright. Late in the night they observed a curragh heading towards them.
'Whose curragh is that?' asked one of the men.
'I don't know,' said another. 'Perhaps it is Beairtle Neid coming from Conamara.'
'Good heavens, this is no time of night to make the crossing from Conamara!' said the other.
Before little more could be said the approaching boat turned out to be a very large vessel. In fact she proved to be a large sailing vessel, with great billowing sails. They became very frightened at this point, and began to haul their nets. Two of the men set to rowing, leaving the third to haul in the net rope, and when this was done he too commenced to row. They rowed for a time and then one man said they were drawing away from the other vessel. But no sooner had he said this than the vessel appeared to be closer still to their stern. They each blessed themselves and the strange vessel halted. And soon afterwards one of the three exlaimed: 'Well, now we've shaken it!'
'I believe you are right,' replied the other.
They continued rowing but as soon as the first had spoken the vessel appeared once more at the curragh's stern. But they kept rowing and finally reached the shore. Surprisingly, the vessel followed them into shallow waters where a sea-shell could hardly float. The first man to emerge from the curragh – I'm not sure if he was the most ill-tempered of the three – grasped a sea-rod and, bending it with his hands declared: 'The devil take me, but if I lay my hands on the man steering that vessel I'll bend every one of his ribs.'
The three then got under the curragh and carried it to the stands on which it rested. They secured it there; and when they emerged from

underneath and looked about no boat or vessel, ship or curragh could be seen anywhere.[2]

This story may be interpreted in a narrow moral sense – that unpleasant consequences attend the breaking of a taboo. However, the questionable wisdom of venturing far from home at night in a small open rowing boat is at the heart of the account. The men's initial amazement at seeing (as they thought) Beairtle Neid's curragh making the crossing from Conamara merely emphasises their own recklessness. The motif of the phantom boat failing to make landfall is the single most common feature of stories of phantom boats recorded in Ireland and elsewhere.[3] The motif is a simple narrative device which gives a convenient climax to the story: the threat recedes once the fishermen reach the safety of land. But, in the context of the present story, it also serves to contrast land and sea, the former encompassing the natural world and the latter the world of the supernatural.

In the legends under discussion here it is usual to attribute the origin of the phantom boat to the fairies. Thus, at the conclusion of a narrative – when the identity and purpose of the phantom boat is revealed – the terms *bád / curach / soitheach sí* ('fairy boat / curragh / vessel'), etc., are used. This is not surprising since a great many supernatural phenomena in Irish folk tradition are ascribed to the fairies. And, like their land-based counterparts, the sea-fairies engage in activities comparable to those undertaken by humans. They fish the same stretches of water fished by mortals, in identical small craft, using the same methods of fishing:

> They (the fairies) are in the sea as well as on the land. That is well known by those that are out fishing by the coast. When the weather is calm, they can look down sometimes and see cattle and pigs and all such things as we have ourselves. And at night their boats come out and they can be seen fishing, but they never last out after one o'clock.[4]

Glimpses of fairy fishing boats may be tantalisingly brief, or confined to only one member of a boat's crew:

---

2 My translation from the Irish of Seán Tom Ó Dioráin, An Sruthán, Inis Mór, Árainn, county Galway. The story was recorded in London in 1934 on the occasion of the filming of a short film *Oidhche Sheanchais,* set in Inis Mór, in which the narrator played a principal part. The story was published by Parlophone Records (record E4075) in that year, to my knowledge the first such commercial recording of Irish storytelling, an initiative of Séamus Ó Duilearga, then Director of the Irish Foklore Institute – see note in *Béaloideas* 4 (1934), 455. A copy of the record is preserved on Tape 2311, Sound Archive, Department of Irish Folklore, University College Dublin. My thanks to Micheál Ó Curraoin MPhil for his assistance in transcribing the story, the full Irish text of which can be found in the Appendix, Item 1, below.

3 See for example *HDA* under 'Geisterschiff'; *FW* under 'Phantom Ships'; see also Childs (1949), 146-65.

4 Gregory (1920), 17. Of the fifty or so phantom boat legends so far identified in the manuscript collections of the Department of Irish Folklore, the 'fairy' association is explicit in the majority.

Myself and Muiris Cuainí set off one day for the cliff in the boat with the sail raised. I saw a three-man curragh coming towards us. I felt it should be easy to make out who they were if I looked carefully. The other man was tending to the sail at the time and I said nothing to him. She was heading directly towards us, and when she got very close she swung away to our starboard. As she did so her bow passed out of sight behind our sail and then her stern, and I expected to see her bow emerge on the other side of the sail, but it didn't. We lowered the sail immediately, but there was no trace of it. At no stage did Muiris Cuainí ever see her.[5]

The same informant, a fisherman from the Great Blasket Island, county Kerry, told of another, similar, incident involving several curraghs that make the journey from the island to Dingle (a distance of about ten miles). They are accompanied part of the way by an otherworld curragh:

Seven boats with fish from the island left for Dingle one day and were followed by another. The seventh boat noticed its presence after they passed Slea Head. All of the boats were under sail.[6] When they reached the quay in Dingle a man approached them and offered to buy their cargo of fish. When he had completed his purchases with the seventh boat he asked its crew was there any other one due. They said that there was, but if they waited forever the boat would not arrive. They thought that it was an otherworld boat.[7]

A clear statement of belief regarding the presence of fairy fishers is contained in a story originating in the salmon fishery based around the Cashen River, near the mouth of the Shannon:

I heard from the fishermen down in Ballyhorgan that a fairy boat used (to) be seen some nights from Ballyhorgan Quay to the Cashen, and when they'd see that boat they'd all go away home for they'd catch no more fish that night. That was handed down to them. I don't think there was any other danger in the boat.[8]

---

5 *IFC* 701:299-300, recorded by Seosamh Ó Dálaigh from Pádraig (Peats Tom) Ó Cearnaigh, a fisherman aged 60 years, of An Blascaod Mór, Dún Chaoin, county Kerry, on 22/6/1940. My translation from the Irish. See Appendix, Item 2, for the full Irish text. *IFC* = Irish Folklore Collection, being the Main Manuscripts Collection of the Department of Irish Folklore at University College Dublin; the numbers on either side of the colon represent the volume number and page number(s) respectively.

6 Until comparatively recently, craft in the Aran Islands and in Kerry were fitted with a removable mast and simple lug sail.

7 *IFC* 701:300, recorded by Seosamh Ó Dálaigh from Pádraig (Peats Tom) Ó Cearnaigh, a fisherman aged 60 years, of An Blascaod Mór, Dún Chaoin, county Kerry, on 22/6/1940. My translation from the Irish. See Appendix, Item 3, for the full Irish text.

8 *IFC* 1177:34-5, recorded by Seosamh Ó Dálaigh from Davey Nolan, a labourer aged about 69 years, from Carrigcannon, Kilfeighny, county Kerry, in March 1950.

Accounts of fairy boats patrolling inshore waters and competing with mortal fishermen for precious fish stocks are recorded from other parts of the south, west and north coasts.[9] The predatory image of fairy fishermen is spelled out very clearly in a story from the Ballinskelligs area of south Kerry:

In the old days they used to be on the look-out for day-fishing as well as the night fishing. One of the days a seine-boat crew saw fish from the land. They gathered the seine-net quickly and put it aboard, and set out then for the fish and made a turn around it. It stayed inside the seine while they surrounded it and covered it. They were working away at the seine without a thought that anything could take it from them. They spent the day so, setting and pulling, until they were tired and worn out with it, and they had to give up in the end. They came into shore and went home.

When they came ashore, people on the land told them they had made no turn during the day that a third boat had not passed through their corks. They hadn't seen a sight of her, but the people on land had been watching her during the day. It was the strange boat which had upset their fishing.[10]

An extension of the belief in the existence of fairy fishers is that the fairy boat warns fishermen of approaching danger, actively discouraging them from straying too far from home and forewarning them of storms. A story from Inis Meáin (set in the same stretch of water between the Aran Islands and the Conamara coast as the first story quoted above, and of a similar type) reflects this idea. It was recorded in 1975 from the grandson of one of the story's participants. The fairy boat – in this instance a large sailing vessel – alerts the fishermen to the danger of straying beyond traditional fishing limits:

My grandfather told me that they were out in a curragh fishing for bream at Lag an Oileáin, between Aran and Conamara. And they decided to move in closer to the mainland in the hope of finding larger bream. But no sooner had they hauled the anchor into the curragh than they observed a large sailing vessel bearing down on them. They rowed as hard as they could to get clear of it but the vessel continued to bear down on them. They were frightened by

---

9 See, for example: *Béaloideas* 3 (1932), 323 (Brandon, county Kerry); *Béaloideas* 29 (1961 [1963]), 122-3 (Prior, county Kerry); *Béaloideas* 8 (1938), 481-2 (Carna, county Galway); Ó Catháin (1983), told by John Henry (Cill Ghallagáin, county Mayo); and *Béaloideas* 8 (1938), 155-6 (Teileann, county Donegal).

10 Ó Duilearga (1981), 279. The story was recorded in 1927. As recently as 1950 seine fishing was the preferred method of fishing in these inshore waters of the south west. The fish were surrounded with a large wall of netting the head-rope of which was fitted with corks. When the fish were fully surrounded the net was 'pursed' and the fish trapped within. The operation could be observed with ease from adjacent high ground – indeed the fishing was at times directed from land by means of hand signals and shouts – and it is therefore quite realistic to include land-based witnesses in the story. There was great urgency attached to this type of fishing, as it was only occasionally that large shoals of mackerel and herring (and, in the past, pilchards) came so close to the coast.

now and thought no more of fishing or dropping anchor. The vessel followed them until they reached land at Port Chorruach.

The instant they came ashore the vessel was no longer visible. A storm arose then, although the night was calm until that moment. If they had stayed out fishing they would have drowned – they could not have withstood the storm.

My grandfather said the vessel appeared in order to drive them home; it was to protect them, you understand. It is well known that this happened.[11]

In this story, the appearance of the phantom boat is interpreted as a positive manifestation of the supernatural world, which acts to forewarn the men of the coming storm. This type of manifestation is the most common motif in all of the accounts of phantom boat sightings in Ireland of which I am aware. The men's decision to move closer to the mainland and further from home is the decisive point in the narrative. Until then the men had noted no signs of a turn in the weather, and their fate then rests with the phantom boat whose timely appearance drives them homeward. The next example illustrates how the instinct and experience of some fishermen are rewarded while the foolhardiness of others is punished. The story was recorded in 1940 from Seán Ó hAodha, a retired fisherman from Glandore, west Cork:

A boat was engaged once in lifting pots, and a southerly gale began to blow. One of the crew, an old man – both of them, in fact – happened to look towards the shore and saw a yellow boat rowed by two men going in. The boat went in to the spot where men were loading their nets – hake nets.

The men (in the boat) returned to shore and asked had anyone seen the (yellow) boat come in, but they said they had not. They insisted that the boat came in but the others said they had seen nothing.
'We saw it plainly, with two men on board.'
'No man or boat has come in here,' the others replied.
'Well,' the old man said, 'take your trammels out and beach your boats, or you will have no trammels to put out tomorrow.'

He was right. Some boats from other districts put out their trammels and lost them. The following morning the storm had made the sea's surface white and the waves were as high as the hills. Those people on the shore who heeded the advice were relieved to have saved their trammels. And those who had put out their trammels found no trace of them, and never will.[12]

---

11 *IFC* 1833:354-5, recorded by Ciarán Bairéad from Josey Costello, a labourer aged 72 years from Inis Meáin, Árainn, county Galway, on 16/7/1975. My translation from the Irish. See Appendix, Item 4, for the full Irish text.
12 Ó Cróinín (1985), 231-2.

Supernatural legends connected with the sea are strongly represented in the comprehensive collection *Síscéalta ó Thír Chonaill / Fairy Legends from Donegal*. In one particular legend from the collection the narrator prefaces his story with the belief statement that the appearance of a phantom boat may herald not just a storm but also a drowning:

> In the old days it often happened that herring-fishers saw ghost-boats before a drowning or a storm. It was the tradition that these apparitions often saved crews from being lost.
>
> There was a boat-crew out from Teelin one night looking for herring. At that time there was great fishing being done out west by Malinbeg and when this crew left home they intended to go to Béal na hÚige. As they passed the back of Slieve League they came on signs of a big shoal and decided to go no further but to put out the net where they were.
>
> They did so and when they examined the net there was a fine haul of herring in it. They lifted the net and when it was all in, suddenly another boat came up outside them.
>
> 'Your souls from the devil,' cried one of the crew, 'that is so-and-so's boat. Get at the oars and we will race them to Gob na Leice!'
>
> The rowing began and at times they were within an oar's length of the other boat but no word was spoken from it. They kept hard at it and when they were turning in at Cúl an Dúin the strange boat had passed Inneoir na Leice. They pulled after it stroke by stroke until they came to Gobán Phaddy Dhónaill. The boat ahead went past the Gobán. Immediately they got to the shore two of the crew jumped out and searched to see if any of the boats of the place was out. None was, and wherever the other boat went, no sight of it was seen from that day to this.
>
> A great gale rose soon after the Teelin crew had pulled up their boat, and if they had been at the mouth of the harbour then not a man of them would have been seen again.[13]

The race between a mortal boat and fairy boat – like the inability of phantom boats to reach land – is a recurring element in phantom boat stories. Often the fairy oarsmen are stripped to their shirts – just as oarsmen in curragh-races might be dressed. In the context of fishing, race episodes of this kind are entirely plausible and realistic; sporting challenges between rowing boats have always been very much a part of life among inshore fishermen, as illustrated by the many rowing regattas still held each year around the coast. The race episode thus emphasises further the occupational context in which most accounts of phantom boats are set.

---

13 Ó hEochaidh/ Ní Néill/ Ó Catháin (1977), 211-3. Recorded by Seán Ó hEochaidh from Seán Mac Seáin, a fisherman from Leirg an Dachtáin, Teelin. Ó hEochaidh does not note when the recording was made but it is likely to have been about the year 1945, when Mac Seáin was 75 years old.

Perhaps the most significant function of phantom boat manifestations is to forewarn of drownings. In this connection the phrase 'the sea must have her own' comes to mind, a phrase which, though well-worn, is an accurate reflection of the mindset of fishermen. The phrase implies a resigned, almost fatalistic, attitude to the sea. This is hardly surprising, since fishing is one of the most dangerous professions, one likely to generate a potent mixture of fear and respect for the sea. In a traditional context these feelings find expression in a variety of beliefs, customs and narratives too numerous to discuss here. Where there is a death at sea, a heightened collective sense of grief follows in its wake, and the narratives generated by such events typically possess a very vivid supernatural content. The appearance of a phantom boat matching the kind rowed by the narrator of the following story, recorded from a Tory Island fisherman in 1964, signals the imminent drowning of his companion:

Myself and another man were fishing for pollock one evening at Port an Dúin. At the time my two brothers were to the east of us in another curragh. We remained there till about 10 o'clock. It was a bright moonlit night and the sea was dead calm. The pollock were not biting so we decided to return home. We went to where my two brothers were and informed them of our intentions. They said they would stay another hour, beach the boat at Port an Dúin and then make their way home by land. They asked us had we seen a strange curragh amongst the other boats during the night, but we answered that we had seen nothing of the kind.

We left then and headed west for Port Mór. Not long after setting out, a curragh began to follow us. I said to the man who was with me that it must be my brothers' curragh – that they wanted to race us and that we should not give them the satisfaction of reaching home before us, especially as they could say they had given us an hour's head start. We rowed with all our might, but they still gained on us. Eventually they were within ten yards of us. We did not greet them nor did we make any effort to speak with them. Myself and my companion took a wider approach into Port Mór, while the other boat kept closer to land. We lost them then for a little, but by the light of the moon caught sight of them again between us and land. Both boats made for the quay, but when we reached it the other boat was nowhere to be seen. It was as though the ground had swallowed the curragh whole.

Not long after this my companion was drowned and the curragh which he was in was lost.[14]

The narrator, a participant in the story, presents a very detailed and compelling picture of the events surrounding the phantom-boat sighting. Note that he is careful to add to the story the corroborative evidence of his two brothers who, he states, had observed an unidentified curragh earlier that night. The confusion of

---

14 *Béaloideas* 33 (1965), 32-3, recorded from Jimí Dixon, a fisherman aged 76 years, by Seán Ó hEochaidh in December 1964. My translation from the Irish.

his brothers' curragh with the phantom boat gives a realistic edge to the story. Indeed, it is only the disappearance of the boat before reaching land that betrays its supernatural origin. The concluding statement – as is usual in belief legends – is brief and emphatic: the appearance of the phantom boat and the subsequent drowning of the narrator's companion are linked.

In a group of legends from the Iveragh and Beara peninsulas in the south west of Ireland, the precise number of men seen aboard the phantom boat is equal to the number of drownings that occur:

> We were seine-netting next to Ceann an Dúna. There was another boat too – eight in each boat. It wasn't long before we heard the splash of oars coming towards us; she passed us, and she was very low in the water. She was unlit but we could see the men in her – eight of them. About two nights later one of our two boats was lost. Every single man aboard her was lost. She was sent to warn us.[15]

Since seine-fishing boats operated in pairs, with eight men or more in each boat, this particular manifestation symbolises the loss of one half of the members of the seine. A legend from the same district makes a connection between the loss of a single fisherman and the number of oars seen to be in use aboard the phantom seine-boat:

> A relative of mine – a young boy from Beare – told me this story. He was fishing from the rocks for wrasse one day in the company of other men when they noticed a boat approach them. It passed them by, propelled by five oars only, the sixth oar out of the water. The boat was steered by a captain and it moved off in an easterly direction. There were some other men fishing to the east of them. She returned soon afterwards, on this occasion with all six oars in the water. Before too long they heard the news that a fine young man from the east was drowned.[16]

Six was the usual complement of oars propelling the seine-boat, so the image of the idle sixth oar is therefore an effective way of prefiguring a drowning. The phantom boat is also the vehicle which actually carries away the dead and, as other Irish phantom boat legends suggest, it is generally the fairies who are thought to be responsible for these phenomena. A legend from the same district of south Kerry recalls how all but one of the crew and passengers of a seine-boat lost their lives, and explicitly connects the event with the fairy world. The boat was transporting men

---

15 *Béaloideas* 3 (1932), 412, recorded from Pádraig Ó Súilleabháin, a fisherman aged 73 years, of Láithreach, Tuath Siosta, county Kerry, by Domhnall Ó Dubhda, *c.*1932.
16 *Béaloideas* 1 (1927), 106, recorded from Seán Ó Sé, a fisherman aged 74, of Imleach Mór, Ballinskelligs, county Kerry, by Séamus Ó Duilearga, 29 August 1927. My translation from the Irish.

and women to a certain spot between Coonanna and Cooncrome harbour where 'dilisk' (sea lettuce) grows in abundance when the boat struck a reef and capsized, all but one man drowning. At the time of the tragedy a woman who was tending cattle in the vicinity witnessed an otherworld boat which was rowed vigorously by five men, one of whom shouted to the others 'Hurry, or we will not get them !'[17] In another phantom boat legend from the same district, however, a fairy man appears one night to the father of a young fisherman and informs him: 'We have been after Seán Ó Murchú's seine (boat) for four years and tonight we succeeded in sinking her.'[18] This dark vision of the fairies is not unique. Similar examples can be quoted from other parts of the south and west coasts.[19]

In the early years of this century an old man in Culdaff, county Donegal, described to the folklore collector Elizabeth Andrews how 'a fishing-boat was nearly overwhelmed, when a fairy boat was seen riding on the top of a great wave, and a voice from it cried: "Do not harm that boat; an old friend of mine is in it."'[20] Besides drowning fishermen, therefore, the fairies are also wont to abduct them, an idea which may well underpin many of the legends I have discussed here. As the Donegal folklore collector Seán Ó hEochaidh (who started out in life as a fisherman) observes in relation to the concept that the sea must get its own: 'The old people in Teelin believed of anyone who was drowned that it was the wee folk who had taken him away and because of that he could not be saved.'[21] In Irish fairy belief the dead are routinely encountered in the fairy world, the suggestion being that they have not actually passed away but have been abducted.

In summary, then, legends of the kind discussed here should be understood firstly in the context of fishing as an occupation. Since they are primarily the invention of fishermen, they therefore hold particular meaning for that occupational group. Regardless of form or content, it is the motivation behind the narrative that is of central importance – did a certain fisherman lose his nerve, did he behave foolishly, rashly, or whatever. The point of crisis is marked by a supernatural phenomenon – the appearance of the phantom boat. Secondly, the legends may be viewed as bearing witness to otherworld or fairy manifestations at sea, where fairies were believed to actively fish, frequently in competition with mortal fishermen. One development of this tradition is that the fairies, because of their special position, are able to alert their mortal counterparts to the approach of storms, and that they do this in a variety of ways without communicating directly with the fishermen. Lastly, there is the association

---

17   *IFC* 146:568, recorded by Tadhg Ó Murchadha from Cáit Bean Uí Mhurchadha, a farmer's wife aged 96 years from Waterville, on 13/10/1935. My translation from the Irish.
18   *IFC* 28:228, recorded by Tadhg Ó Murchadha from Seán Mhártain Ó Súilleabháin, An t-Imleach Mór, county Kerry, in June 1934. My translation from the Irish.
19   See for example *IFC* 107:216, recorded by Tomás Ó Ciardha from William Cox, Duncormick, county Wexford, in May 1935. The survey of supernatural legends of the sea in Gregory (1920) has several examples, *op. cit.*, pp. 9, 17 and 19.
20   Andrews (1913), 53.
21   Ó hEochaidh/ Ní Néill/ Ó Catháin (1977), 187.

of 'fairy' boats with death. The fairy boat is the boat which carries off the living to the twilight world of the dead, an overwhelming supernatural force governing the fate of the fisherman.

Appendix

1.   Bhí triúr fear ar an mbaile a rugadh is a tóigeadh mise...insa Sruthán, istigh in Oileán Árann. Bhíodar ina dtrí n-iascaire, agus chuadar ag iascach aon oíche amháin Shathairn. Agus níor mhaith le muintir na tíre gabháil amach oíche Shathairn ar bith, ach ar chaoi ar bith chuadar seo amach. Bhíodar leath bealaigh idir Árainn agus Conamara, agus ní raibh an oíche dubh agus ní raibh sí geal. Agus chonaiceadar curach i gcionn píosa maith fada don oíche idir iad agus Conamara, agus í ag déanamh orthub.
'Cén curach í sin ?' a deir fear acub leis an bhfear eile.
'Níl a fhios agamsa,' adeir an fear eile, 'marab é Beairtle Neid atá ag tíocht as Conamara é.'
'Ó, go sábhála Dia sinn,' a deir an fear eile, 'cén tráth d'oíche dóibh ag tíocht as Conamara anois !'
   Ní...ach ní neart ach...(ní) mórán eile a bhí ráite acub nuair a d'iompaigh sí amach gur bád mór millteach í. Ní go leor cainte eile a bhí déanta acub nuair a d'iompaigh sí ina soitheach mór, seolta móra geala, pochóideacha, pacóideacha. Tháinig scáth agus faitíos ansin orthub, agus thosaíodar ag tarraingt suas. Chuaigh beirt fhear ag iomramh agus chuaigh an fear eile acub ag tarraingt na téide, agus nuair a bhí an téad istigh aige chuaigh sé féin ag iomramh. Agus bhíodar ag iomramh, agus dúirt fear acub leis an bhfear eile go rabhadar ag tabhairt dhóibh – go rabhadar ag imeacht uathub. Níl ann ach go raibh sé sin ráite aige nuair a bhí an soitheach ag deireadh na curaí thíos acub. Ghearradar comhartha na croise orthub féin, agus sheas an soitheach. Agus dúirt siad le chéile, faoi cheann scaithimh, 'Bhuel, táimid ag tabhairt anois uathub !' 'Bhuel, tá !' a deir an fear eile.
   Bhíodar ag imeacht agus ag obair, agus níl ann ach go raibh sin ráite acub nuair a bhí an soitheach ag deireadh na curaí arís acub. Bhíodar ag obair agus ag imeacht go dtáinigeadar i dtír sa gcladach agus gur lean an soitheach isteach iad ins an áit ná raibh ann ach go snámhfadh sliogán de bhairneach ann. An chéad fhear acu a chuaigh amach as an gcurach – níor éirigh liom déanamh amach go mba fear fiáin taghdach a bhí ann – casadh slat mhara faoina chosa ar an taisriú. Rug sé ar an tslat mhara agus bhain sé glionda as. Agus...'M'anam don diabhal,' ar seisean, 'dá bhfaighinnse greim ar an bhfear seo atá ag gabháil an tsoithigh sin do lúbfainnse féin na heasnacha aige !'

Chuadar isteach faoin gcurach agus chuireadar suas í, agus chuireadar ar na prapaí í. Agus nuair a bhíodar amuigh ón gcurach agus í socraithe acub, ní fhacadar bád, ná soitheach, ná long, ná curach.

2.　　　Bhíos féin is Muiris Cuainí ag dul 'on bhfaill lá agus bhí seol ar an naomhóg againn agus chonac féin naomhóg triúir im choinne agus í ag déanamh orainn. Agus ní bheadh a bhac orm iad a dh'aithniúint dar liom dá dtógfainn aon cheann mór dóibh. Bhí an fear eile i mbun an tseoil, agus ní raibh aon radharc aige ortha agus ní dúirt aon ní leis. Bhí sí ag déanamh orainn cruinn díreach agus nuair a bhí sí ana-gheairid dúinn ghaibh sí lastuaidh dúinn. Agus chuaigh a tosach ar scáth an tseoil orm ar dtúis agus bhí a deireadh le feiscint agam, agus nuair a chuaigh a deireadh ar scáth an tseoil bhí súil agam go bhfeicfinn a tosach ach ní raibh sé le feiscint agam. Leagadh an seol láithreach ansan, agus ní raibh aon phioc ann di. N'fheacaigh Muiris Cuainí ó thúis deireadh í.

3.　　　Bhí seacht gcinn do naomhóga ón Oileán ag dul 'on Daingean lá le hiasc, agus bhí an naomhóg so ina ndiaidh ón Oileán. B'in í an seachtú ceann, agus thugadar fé ndeara an naomhóg eile ina ndiaidh ó Cheann Sléibhe. Bhíodar go léir fé sheol. Nuair a chuadar ar ché an Daingin tháinig fear chúchu a cheannaigh an t-iasc uathu. Cheannaigh sé ón seachtú naomhóg é, agus d'fhiafraigh sé dhóibh an raibh aon naomhóg eile ag teacht. Dúradar go raibh, ach dá mbeidís ann ó shoin ní thiocfadh an naomhóg. Dheineadar amach nárbh aon naomhóg saolta í.

4.　　　Bhí mo shean-athair ag inseacht dom, bhíodar amuigh ag iascach bréams sa gcurach agus suas leis an meán oíche ansin, bhídís an t-am sin amuigh ar Lag an Oileáin, sin idir Conamara is Árainn, agus dúradar ansin go ngabhaidís isteach píosa níos goire don talamh agus go mb'fhéidir go mbeadh bréams níos fearr ann. Ach ní raibh ann ach go raibh an chloch chaillí tarraingthí isteach acub sa gcurach, an dtuigeann tú, nuair a chonaiceadar soitheach mór seoil ag déanamh orthub, ag tíocht anuas díreach orthub. Agus bhíodar ag iomradh ar a ndícheall go ngabhfaidís glan uathub, agus bhí sí ag déanamh orthub i gcónaí. Agus bhí an-aistíl orthub, agus ní dheachadar aríst ag iascach. Níor chaitheadar síos an chloch ancaire aríst, agus choinnigh an soitheach ina ndiaidh ariamh nó go ndeacha siad i dtír sa gcaladh Phort Chorruach.

　　　Agus ar an bpointe is a bhíodar i dtír, ní raibh aon amharc ar an soitheach. Ach tháinig stoirm, agus bhí an oíche chomh ciúin an chéad uair. Ach 'á mbeidís amuigh san áit a rabhadar bheidís báite. Ní sheasfaidís in aghaidh na stoirme. Agus séard a dúirt m'athair mór gurb é chaoi a tháinig an soitheach le iad a chuir abhaile, bhí sí ar mhaithe leob, an dtuigeann tú. Ach tá a fhios gur éirigh an méid sin suas.

Hvítramannaland Revisited[1]

SÉAMUS MAC MATHÚNA

Medieval Irish voyage tales, called *immrama*, owe much of their inspiration to the eremitical tradition, the practice by monks and clerics of seeking out a solitary place – a *terra secreta* or *terra deserta* – in order to live an ascetic life of prayer, contemplation and mortification.[2] In the sixth century, and in the centuries following, the Irish Church combined this tradition with a remarkable missionary activity which was to spread throughout Europe. One of the first areas outside Ireland to witness the impact of Irish eremitical and missionary zeal was Scotland and the northern islands of Britain. The route along the west coast of Scotland to the Orkney and Shetland Islands, and further north to the Faroe Islands and Iceland, must have been quite well known to Irish monks by the eighth century. As early as the late seventh century in Adomnán's Life of Columba, the *Vita Columbae*, we have evidence of the existence of a flourishing practice of clerical sea voyages. Adomnán refers to three attempts made by a certain Cormac ua Lethain to find a desert in the ocean (*qui tribus non minus vicibus hermimum in oceano laboriose quesivit*).[3] According to the account of the second voyage, Columba interceded with Brude, the king of the Picts, on behalf of Cormac. He informed Brude that some people from his community had recently left to find a desert in the ocean and he asked him not to cause them any harm if they should reach the Orkney Islands. On account of Columba's intervention, Cormac was saved from almost certain death there.[4] In his *Liber de Mensura Orbis Terrae*, written in or around 825 AD, the Irish monk and geographer Dicuil states that there are many small islands in the ocean to the north of Britain. These islands may be reached from Britain's northern islands in the space of two days and nights. A certain religious told him that he had reached one of these islands. They are small and were for nearly a hundred years frequented by hermits from Ireland (*ex nostra Scottia*). But just as they were deserted at the beginning of the world, so now is the case also. They have been vacated by the Irish anchorites on account of Norse

---

1 A version of this paper appeared in Josephson (1997), 211-24. The present paper modifies and extends my earlier conclusions. It gives more prominence to the views expressed by Pálsson (1960), which I had not read in detail before the publication of the earlier version. See also Pálsson (1997) and Guðmundsson (1997) which works were not available when this article was penned.
2 See Mac Mathúna (1994), 313-57; Hughes (1960), 143-51.
3 See Anderson & Anderson (1961), I, 6.
4 *Alio in tempore Cormacus Christi miles de quo in secunda vice conatus est erimum in oceano quaerere. Qui postquam a terris per infinitum oceanum plenis enavigavit velis, iisdem diebus sanctus Columba, cum ultra Dorsum moraretur Britanniae, Brudeo regi, praesente Orcadum regulo, commendavit, dicens; 'Aliqui ex nostri nuper emigraverunt desertum in pelago intransmeabili invenire optantes; qui si forte post longos circuitus Orcadas devenerint insulas, huic regulo cujus obsides in manu tua sunt, diligenter commenda ne aliquid adversi intra terminos ejus contra fiat'. Hoc vero sanctus ita dicebat quia in spiritu praecognovit idem Cormacus esset ad Orcadas venturas; quod ita postea evenit, et propter supradictum sancti viri commendationem de morte in Orcadibus liberatus est vicina. Ibid. II., 42.*

sea-pirates. These islands are full of sheep and many diverse kinds of marine birds.[5] The islands he refers to are almost certainly the Faroes. He also says that he spoke to Irish clerics who had lived on the island of Thule – most probably Iceland – thirty years previously, that is about 795.

Íslendingabók ('The Book of the Icelanders'), written by Ari Þorgilsson about 1130, confirms the presence of Irish clerics in Iceland around the middle of the ninth century. Ari states that there were Christians in Iceland when the first Norsemen arrived (about 870), that they called them *papar*, and that it may be inferred from the Irish books, bells and croziers which they left behind that they were Irishmen. They left because they did not want to live alongside heathen men.[6]

By this time, arising from the Norse settlements in Ireland and Scotland, close contacts between the Gaelic and Norse cultures had been established. The settlement of Iceland, moreover, entailed an Irish element. Although its extent and influence are disputed and difficult to determine with precision, it is not in doubt.[7] One can readily agree with the general observation that some of the Icelandic and Faroese settlers 'came via Ireland and Scotland and had sometimes lived there and absorbed Gaelic culture',[8] that some of them had married Irish women, and that they took with them a considerable number of Irish and Scottish slaves. There also developed over the years a Gaelic-Norse north-west commercial and cultural corridor, through which goods and ideas were exchanged, the Orkney Earldom being a particularly important channel of communication and translation between the cultures.[9] It is not surprising, therefore, to find some Gaelic influence on Icelandic culture.[10] This influence is much easier to prove in respect of placenames, personal names and word-borrowing than it is in the matter of literature. Where literary similarities are of a specific nature – for example, verbal correspondences, motifs and themes of a predominantly Gaelic or Celtic character – cases for borrowing have been successfully argued.[11] Where they are of a more general nature, it is much more difficult to

---

5 *Sunt aliae insulae multae in septentrionali Britanniae oceano quae a septrionalibus Britanniae insulis duorum dierum ac notium, recta navigatione, plenis velis, assiduo feliciter vento adire queunt. Aliquis probus religosus mihi retulit quod in duobus aestivis diebus et una intercedente nocte, navigans in duorum navicula transtrorum, in unam illarum introivit. Illae insulae sunt aliae parvulae. Fere cunctae simul angustis distantes fretis in quibus, in centum ferme annis, eremitae ex nostra Scottia navigantes habitaverunt. Sed, sicut a principio mundi desertae semper fuerunt, ita nunc, causa l atronum Nortmannorum, vacuae anachoretis, plene innumerabilibus ovibus ac diversis generibus multis nimis marinarum avium. Nunquam eas insulas in libris auctorum memoratas invenimus.* See Tierney (1967), VII.3.

6 *þá váru hér menn kristnir, þeir es Norðmenn kalla papa, en þeir fóru síðan á braut, af því at þeir vildu eigi vesa hér við heiðna menn, ok létu eptir bækur írskar ok bjollur og bagla; af því mátti skilja, at þeir váru menn írskir.* – Benediktsson (1986), 5. See also a similar passage in *Landnámabók*, 31-2, probably based on *Íslendingabók*.

7 See Sigurðsson (1988), 24 ff.

8 See Almqvist (1978-81), 89.

9 *Ibid.*, 80-105; Chesnutt (1968), 122-37.

10 See, for example, Sveinsson (1959), 3-24; also, the numerous contributions by Bo Almqvist and others, some of which are listed in Sigurðsson (1988) 131-55. See also Almqvist (1997).

11 See Almqvist (1997) for further discussion.

accurately determine the form and the extent of possible influence. Voyage literature is such a case in point. In this paper, attention will be drawn to some well-known Irish-Norse parallels in this field. These have been discussed previously by others, including T. J. Westropp and Jean Young.[12]

Westropp concluded that there were few features in common between the Irish *immrama* and the Norse sagas. In his view, the main ones are 'the vines in Vinland, the wooded grassy shores, and the attack of the dark-skinned natives, the "wonder-strands", the sea full of maggots which attack Bjarne's hide-boats, and the adventures with whales.'[13] Not a particularly impressive list, and certainly not one which inspires confidence in the hypothesis that Icelandic has borrowed significantly from Irish voyage literature. Westropp thinks there was mutual influence, but seems loathe to attribute specific borrowings from one tradition to the other. The critical factor in establishing possible influence here is not so much the presence of such features in both traditions but rather the fact that some of them occur in similar contextual clusters. Most of the Icelandic items referred to above are from the so-called Vínland Sagas, particularly from *Eiríks saga rauða*. The fact that these stories do not distort the historical record in attributing the discovery and colonisation of Greenland to the Icelanders suggests that the information which they contain in regard to other reputed discoveries should be closely examined for possible historical accuracy. And they have, of course, come in for a great deal of critical scrutiny over the years. According to Magnus Magnusson and Hermann Pálsson, although 'no scholar doubts the authenticity of the central facts of exploration and colonisation of the New World ... there has been endless argument about their relative merits as historical evidence'; the picture they paint is 'tantalizingly hazy'; and it has been impossible 'to make irrefutable identifications of any of the particular bays and havens visited by the Norsemen, or of the exact location of their main settlement in Vinland'.[14] This, then, is a notoriously difficult and controversial subject on which opinions vary widely. Are the references to a bountiful land full of vines and corn, for example, based on authentic historical discoveries or are they the literary embellishments of the authors, possibly derived from the Classical or ecclesiastical traditions – perhaps having a biblical origin as was suggested by Westropp, or, nearer to home in the case of the vines, drawing on the Brendan tradition, as exemplified by the *Navigatio Brendani* 'The Voyage of St Brendan'?[15] The latter was an immensely popular and influential text in the Middle Ages, which was translated into most of the vernacular languages of Europe, including Norwegian-Icelandic.[16] On the basis of this text and other references, there are those who hold that Irish seafarers – probably clerics – reached America before the Norse.

---

12 Westropp (1912), 223-60; Young (1937), 118-26. See also Nansen (1911), II, 42-56.
13 Westropp (1912), 235-6.
14 Magnusson & Pálsson (1965), 8. See also Halldórsson (1978), and Almqvist (1997).
15 See Selmer (1959).
16 Unger (1877), 272-5.See also Selmer (1956), 147: 'Brendan's *Navigatio* must have appealed particularly to the descendants of Leif and his Vikings who centuries after St. Brendan are believed to have crossed the ocean.'

Like the Vínland Sagas, the *Navigatio* and the Irish *immrama* also contain material which has clearly been inspired by actual voyages and seafarers' accounts of features such as icebergs, volcanoes, islands full of sheep and birds etc.[17] The description of the iceberg, for example, in the *Navigatio Brendani* ('The Voyage of St Brendan') and in *Immram Curaig Máele Dúin* ('The Voyage of Máel Dúin') is so vividly realistic as to be almost certainly based on information concerning this natural phenomenon.[18] And the same applies to the description of volcanoes in these texts.[19] Sheep Island in the *Navigatio* may owe its inspiration in part to knowledge handed down concerning the Faroe Islands (whose name actually means Sheep Islands),[20] and the predilection for birds and bird motifs in the Irish sources, while frequently highly developed in terms of Christian symbolism and drawing partly on ecclesiatical sources, is probably linked with the fact that there was a particularly rich and diverse bird population on the rocky islands off the coasts of Ireland and Scotland which were inhabited by seafaring hermits.[21] The Irish vernacular and related narratives, however, are essentially works of imaginative fiction, written by Christians and greatly inspired by ecclesiastical literature; they also draw on the world of classical learning, they are imbued with traditional native elements from Irish myth and legend, and they rejoice in romantic inventiveness. While the Icelandic narratives are more realistic than the Irish *immrama*, they are indeed 'tantalizingly hazy' in many respects. Despite the tone of reason and realism, they too are works of literature and are subject to the same laws of tradition, creation and invention as all other literary artifacts of this kind.

Although the lack of verbal correspondence between the two sets of narratives makes it difficult to prove direct influence of specific Irish voyage texts on the Icelandic material, both traditions share a cluster of features which occur in similar contexts. An examination of the features, the clustering and the contexts suggests that the Icelandic authors were probably influenced in their development of the concept of a mysterious island situated in the western ocean by stories relating to the tradition of Irish monks seeking out and inhabiting solitary islands off the coasts of Ireland and Scotland and in the north Atlantic. It is also likely that they were influenced in particular by the Brendan tradition.[22] They called this country *Hvítramannaland* ('White Men's Land') or *Írland it mikla* ('Greater Ireland'),[23] and they developed the concept in their own way to suit their own purposes, drawing on translations and adaptations of medieval texts which described primitive countries and their inhabitants. The remainder of the paper will be concerned with a reassessment of the evidence relating to this matter.

---

17 See, for example, Marcus (1952-54), 312-27.
18 See Selmer, (1956), § 22; Stokes (1888), §26; see also Stokes(1893), §51.
19 Selmer (1956) §§23, 24; Stokes (1888), § 21.
20 Selmer (1956), §9; see also Stokes (1888), §12.
21 See, for example, Selmer (1956), §11; Stokes (1888), §§ 3, 18.
22 See Mac Mathúna (1994), and Mac Mathúna (1996), 247-62.
23 The translation of *Írland it mikla* in Mac Mathúna (1997), 214, should also read 'Greater Ireland'.

Landnámabók ('The Book of Settlement'), originally compiled in the twelfth century, relates that a man called Ari Mársson from Reykhólum was driven off course and came to *Hvítramannaland,* which some call *Írland it mikla.* It lies in the ocean to the west close to *Vínland* the Good; it is said to be six days' sail west of Ireland. Ari was held captive and baptized there. Hrafn Limerickstraveller, who had spent a long time in Limerick in Ireland, was the first to tell this story. Þorkell Gellison said that Icelanders, who had heard it from Þorfinnr, the Earl of Orkney, related that Ari had been recognized in *Hvítramannaland,* but that he could not leave there, although he was held in high regard.[24] *Hvítramannaland* appears again by name in chapter 12 of *Eiríks saga rauða.* Þorfinnr Karlsefni and his men captured two native boys (*skrælingar*) in Markland – which some scholars would identify with the coast of Labrador – took them with them, taught them their language, and baptized them. The boys told them that there was a country opposite their own land where people went about in white clothing uttering loud cries, and carrying poles with patches of cloth attached. It is thought that this was *Hvítramannaland* or, adds the text of *Hauksbók, Írland it mikla.*[25]

There is a close similarity between the two accounts. In both, *Hvítramannaland* is close to *Vínland;* both refer to the baptizing of people either in *Hvítramannaland* itself or in its immediate vicinity. The role of the Icelanders, however, is reversed, the two narratives referring to different periods of time: Ari is a pagan who is baptized by the people of *Hvítramannaland;* Þorfinnr belongs to the Christian period and it is the Icelanders who baptize the heathen native boys. In both accounts, the country is also called *Írland it mikla,* and in both there is a further Irish context: *Landnámabók's* account infers that Hrafn, who had resided in Limerick in Ireland for a long time, first heard the story of Ari in Ireland, and in the Hauksbók version of *Eiríks saga rauða,* the episode concerning *Hvítramannaland* is followed by that of the maggots which infest Bjarni's ship, the ship's-boat eventually reaching Ireland.[26]

According to Jean Young, *Landnáma's* story of Ari is a composite account, originally consisting of two distinct parts. The first part, related by Hrafn, deals with

---

24 *Hann varð sæhafi til Hvítramannalands. þat kalla sumir Írland et mikla. þat liggr vestr í haf nær Vinlandi enu góða; þat er kallat sex dægra sigling vestr frá Írlandi. Þaðan náði Ari eigi á brutt at fara ok var þar skírðr. Þessa sögu sagði fyrst Hrafn Hlymreksfari, er lengi hafði verit í Hlymreki á Írlandi. Svá kvað Þorkell Gellisson segja íslenzka menn, þá er heyrt höfðu frá segja Þorfinn jarl í Orkneyjum, at Ari hefði kenndr verit á Hvítramannalandi ok náði eigi brutt at fara, ok var þar vel virðr* – Benediktsson, (1986), 126.

25 *Þeir sögðu þar liggja öðrum megin, gagnvart sínu landi, er þeir menn byggðu, er váru í hvítum klæðum ok báru stangir fyrir sér, ok váru festar við flíkr ok æpðu hátt, ok ætla menn, at þat hafi verit Hvítramannaland eða Írland it mikla.* Sveinsson & Þorðarson (1935), 234; cf. Halldórsson (1985), 432.

26 In the account of Cormac ua Lethain's third voyage in the *Vita Columbae,* loathsome and dangerous sea-creatures, the size of frogs, infest the oar blades and threaten to pierce the hide-covering. See Anderson & Anderson (1961), II.42. Also in the Voyage of the Uí Chorra, worms from the sea pierced through one of the lower hides of the boat. See Stokes (1888), §66. For discussion, see Oskamp (1970), 70-1. According to *Eiríks saga rauða,* Þorfinnr Karlsefni's great grandmother was the daughter of King Kjarval of Ireland.

Ari being driven off course and coming to a strange country to the west of Ireland, from which he could not escape and where he was baptized. The second part, based on the word of Þorfinnr, the Earl of Orkney, depicts him as being seen and recognized there, as being held in high honour, but unable to get away. This part came into being later 'and was simply tacked on to Hrafn's story'.[27] As regards the first part, she argues that the disappearance of Icelandic traders and rovers would have been a common occurrence on trips from Iceland to Ireland and would have led to all manner of strange stories concerning their fate. Icelanders would have heard of Irish stories in the Norse colonies of Ireland, such as Limerick, about voyagers coming to strange and exotic islands in the western ocean from which they could not escape; moreover, 'the allusions in an Irish tale to "clothes as white as snow" would immediately conjure up a picture of baptismal robes and so Hrafn would assert that Ari had been baptised in White Men's Land'.[28] Young conjectures that the Þorfinnr story also arose from the speculation of Icelanders concerning the loss of a comrade on a sea voyage between Iceland and Ireland. In this scenario, Ari sailed off course and eventually landed on a part of the Irish coast far from any Norse settlement and was made prisoner there. In due course he rose to a position of prominence in the community, and voluntarily remained there. Many years later, he was recognized in a remote part of the west of Ireland by one of Þorfinnr's men. The tale was then relayed to Iceland by Icelanders who heard it from Þorfinnr and it was added to Hrafn's account of *Hvítramannaland*, the identification of the latter with Ireland being made all the easier since it was also known as *Írland it mikla*.

Young's analysis is not without merit, but it is too complicated to stand up successfully to close examination. In the first place, it requires two different locations for *Hvítramannaland* – one off the coast of Ireland, the other on the west coast of Ireland itself. As she correctly points out in her critique of Havdan Koht's identification of *Hvítramannaland* with the west of Ireland, 'it seems absurd to imagine that the Icelanders, when they spoke of a country far to the west of Ireland, really only meant the extreme west of that land, the more so when we reflect that the first man to spin the yarn came from the extreme west of Ireland himself'.[29] Secondly, as far as I know, there is no linguistic or literary justification in the text for assuming that the Hrafn story was written earlier than that of Þorfinnr. Thirdly, given that this is an Icelandic story which partly glorifies the settlers and their descendants, the fact that Ari Mársson is held in high honour is quite natural.

In the case of *Landnáma*, it is possible that floating traditions concerning *Hvítramannaland* were compiled by the cleric and scholar Ingimundr Einarsson, a descendant of Ari Mársson who flourished towards the end of the twelfth century. Hermann Pálsson has argued that the name *Hvítramannaland* was coined by Ingimundr as a secret name for Scotland, which was called Alba ('white', 'the white

---

27 Young (1937), 123-4.
28 *Ibid.*, 125.
29 *Ibid.*, 123.

one') in Irish and Scottish Gaelic both in his time and earlier still in the time of Ari Mársson towards the end of the tenth century.[30] It is still the name for Scotland in these two languages to the present day. Both Ireland and Scotland were also called *Scotia* by medieval scholars, and their Gaelic-speaking inhabitants were known as *Scotti*. By glossing *Hvítramannaland* as *Írland it mikla*, Ingimundr gives further information on how the riddle of the name is to be solved. Scotland (*Alba*) is inhabited by Gaels. It is an extension of Ireland and is known by the same name, Scottia. It is possible that Ingimundr had heard Ari's story from Þorkell Gellisson, Ari fróði's uncle. However, Ingimundr did not wish people to think that his ancestor Ari Mársson had been enslaved on an island off the coast of Scotland. Hence the name and the riddle. This explanation would also account for Ingimundr locating the island at a distance of six days sailing to the west of Ireland near *Vínland*.

As for the description of *Hvítramannaland* in *Eiríks saga rauða*, Young took the view that it referred to a tract of land inhabited by a tribe of Red Indians who wore a ceremonial dress of white skin. She emphasises the point that the text does not say that the country was *Hvítramannaland*, merely that this was thought to be the case. In other words, it is a later deduction based on the description of the explorers. Their description recalled the accounts of *Hvítramannaland* and the tradition which located it far away to the west of Ireland. Hence it was identified with *Hvítramannaland*.[31]

It is very probable that the description has nothing to do with Red Indians. The author of *Eiríks saga* almost certainly knew the *Landnáma* account, and the reference to the baptizing of native heathens in a faraway country to the west of Ireland which lies in the neighbourhood of *Vínland* and opposite *Hvítramannaland* is no doubt partly based on it. It would seem that the author embroidered the description of *Hvítramannaland* from various sources, including translations of medieval texts into Icelandic concerning primitive lands in Asia. There is an account in *Hauksbók* of a country called *Albaníaland* (from Latin *albus* 'white'). This country could quite easily have been identified by the author of *Eiríks saga* with *Hvítramannaland*. It is described as follows: *Til norðurættar frá Indíalandi er næst Bactríaland, og þar er Kvenland; á ví landi eru engir karlar. Þar í hjá er Albaníaland; þar eru menn bornir hvítir sem snjór, en þeir sortna svo sem þeir eldast. Þar er kaldast þess, er byggt er í heiminum. Þar eru hundar svo stórir og sterkir, að eir bana yxnum og óarga dyrum.*[32] *Hauksbók* also describes the natives of primitive lands as having feet as big as the earth and as running about carrying poles: *Einfætingar hafa svo mikinn fót viðjörð, að þeir skyggja sér í svefni við sólu. Þeir eru svo skjótir sem dýr og hlaupa við stöng.*[33] This description is reminiscent of the natives of *Hvítramannaland* in *Eiríks saga* and Hermann Pálsson is probably correct in his view that it has influenced the account in that saga.

---

30 Pálsson (1960), 48-54.
31 Young (1937), 122, 126.
32 Pálsson (1960), 51.
33 *Ibid.*, 53.

Eyrbyggja saga, probably written in the middle of the thirteenth century but containing much older material dating to the twelfth century and earlier, has an account of an unnamed country, located somewhere in the western ocean, which has close similarities with the previous accounts of *Hvítramannaland*.[34] Commentators have quite justifiably equated it with *Hvítramannaland*.[35] In chapter 47, it is related that Björn Breiðvikingakappi had to leave Iceland because he was in conflict with the chieftain Snorri goði (died 1031), with whose married sister, Þuríðr from Fróðá, he had an affair. He set sail late in summer with a north-easterly wind which blew steadily throughout that summer; and nothing was heard about the boat for a long time. The next chapter refers to Snorri Þorbrandsson's voyages to Greenland and Vínland,[36] the saga then continuing with other matters but returns again in chapter 64 to a further important reference to Björn. It is related there that in the last year of Saint Olaf, Guðleifr Gunnlaugsson of Iceland, a great sea-travelling merchant, went on a commercial trip to Dublin. On his return to Iceland, he and his crew sailed west of Ireland and encountered an easterly and north-easterly wind which drove them off course into the western ocean so that they did not know in what direction they should sail. They promised to make many offerings if they were delivered safely from the ocean (*ok hétu þeir mörgu, at þá bæri ór hafinu*). And it happened then that they sighted land; it was a large country, but no-one knew what country it was. They decided to land, and they found a good harbour there. They had been on land but a short time when some men came upon them: they did not know any of these men, but thought it most likely that they spoke Irish (*en helzt þótti þeim, sem þeir mælti írsku*). Soon after there came a great band of men, amounting to hundreds. These men attacked them, tied them up, and took them further up on land, where a process of judgement took place. Guðleifr and his companions thought that while some of the men wanted to kill them, others wanted to enslave them. Then a band of men came riding in. They carried a banner, under which rode a great warrior-like man, who was advanced in years and had white hair (*sá þeir, at undir merkinu reið mikill maðr ok garpligr ok var þá mjök á efra aldr ok hvítr fyrir hærum*). The men who were already there bowed before him and treated him as their lord. He called Guðleifr and his men to him and spoke to them in Icelandic, enquiring after various people in Borgarfjörður and Breiðafjörður, especially about Snorri and Þuríðr and her son Kjartan. He then went aside from them, taking twelve of his men with him, and they spoke together for a long time. The men's fate is left in his hands. He frees them, advising them to be on their way as there are dishonourable (or, heathen), ill-disposed and lawless people in this country (*því at hér er fólk ótrútt ok illt viðreignar; en þeim þykkja áðr brotin lög á sér.*). When they ask who it is that has given them their freedom, he says that he cannot tell them because of the danger to his kinsmen and foster brothers who might make a similar journey as they have made: he is old, and the country has more powerful men than him who are unfriendly to strangers. He gives them gifts to take back to Þríðr and Kjartan. Guðleifr asks what he shall say when asked from whom the gifts have come. He is told to say that they are from one who was a greater friend to the lady of Fróðá (that is, Þuríðr) than to the chieftain of Helgafell, her

---

34 See Sveinsson & Þorðarsson (1935), xliii-lvii.
35 Young (1937), 121.
36 Snorri goes to Greenland and Vínland with Þorfinnr karlsefni in *Eiríks saga*, chapter 8.

brother (namely, Snorri). He also forbids anyone from seeking him out again, saying that this is an impassible and expansive land with few good harbours in which strangers can only expect conflict. Guðleifr and his men take their leave then and come to Ireland in the autumn, remaining there through the winter. In the summer they set sail for Iceland and pass over the gifts. All were certain that the man was Björn Breiðvikingakappi, but no-one has any further information concerning him other than that which is related here.

Here again a number of the same features occur as in the two accounts discussed above. In this case, however, there is more detail and there are significant new turns and developments in the narrative. As in the *Landnámabók* account, both Ari and Björn disappear and are later recognized in the mysterious country far out in the western ocean; there is a close connection with Ireland in that Guðleifr sets out on a journey to Dublin, and probably spends some time there before embarking on his return journey home when he is blown off course and comes to the mysterious country far out in the western ocean. Moreover, the connection with Ireland is greatly strengthened here by the reference to the opinion of the voyagers that the inhabitants of the country spoke a language which they thought most likely to be Irish. As in *Eiríks saga*, the events of the narrative take place when Iceland has been Christianized, the voyagers promising to make what almost certainly are votive offerings if they are delivered from their plight. The motif of placing oneself in the hands of God when lost on the open sea is quite a commonplace hagiographical *topos*. It occurs frequently in Irish voyage literature, generally taking the form of shipping the oars and permitting God to steer the boat where He will: God is the steersman, the ship's pilot. The Christian influence is further underlined by the civilized behaviour of the leader, who later emerges to have been Björn. The manner in which Björn arrives on the scene appears in many respects to be a fairly stock description of a chieftain and his men and his taking aside a number of his men to discuss the fate of the travellers is probably intended to reflect the Icelandic judicial system. However, his Christian demeanour and the reference to his twelve companions may also have religious associations. The manner of his arrival on the scene could possibly be interpreted as a kind of religious procession, with a banner at its head under which comes the principal celebrant – an old man with white hair. It is reminiscent of the description of *Hvítramannaland* in *Eiríks saga* in which the inhabitants go about in white clothing carrying poles with patches of cloth attached. Young compares this with a religious procession.[37] The number twelve recalls the twelve apostles and is frequently employed in accounts of the founding of churches and missions. One must be cautious, however, of attributing the use of this number to the influence of any particular cultural tradition other than that of Christianity in general. It does, however, appear frequently in reference to Irish clerical sea voyages.[38]

---

37 Young (1937), 122.
38 In the Litany of Irish Pilgrim Saints', the following references occur: The twelve pilgrims of whom Brendan found one alive in the Cats' island (Invocation no. 15) The twelve pilgrims who went with Maedoc of Ferns across the sea (Invocation no. 12) Twelve men who went with Ailbe to death (Invocation no. 43) Twelve men with Morioc across the sea (Invocation no. 45). See Hughes (1959), 305-31; Sanderlin (1975), 251-62.

If we are to sanction the possibility of Irish or Irish-related influence, the most likely place to look for it would be in the *Navigatio Brendani* in which vines and religious processions figure prominently. The ·*Navigatio* contains a number of episodes which appear to contribute to a greater understanding of the various Icelandic accounts. One of these episodes combines the elements of procession, the old man with white hair, and the number twelve. When the voyagers come to the island of St Ailbe for the first time, they are conducted to the monastery by a very old cleric, whose hair was as white as snow. They are met by a procession of eleven monks, in their habits and crosses, who chant a hymn of welcome to them. The ancient cleric appears to be the abbot, so that we have the abbot plus the eleven processors.[39] In chapter 17, we have the processional motif again, combined on this occasion with the wearing of white garments. The voyagers come to an island – the Island of the Strong Men – in which there are three groups of clerics, consisting of boys, young men, and elders respectively. The first group are dressed in snow-white garments and all groups chant psalms unceasingly. Moreover, a cloud of marvellous brightness comes over the land, and after the Holy Sacrifice the voyagers are presented with a basketful of purple grapes and asked to deliver their chosen brother who is to remain on the island with the holy community.[40] On the Island of Paul the Hermit, the voyagers are welcomed by the ancient cleric with the kiss of peace, and he calls each of them by his own name. He is covered from head to foot with the hair of his own body, which was as white as snow, and this was his only clothing.[41] This is followed by the wonderful final lyrical description of the earthly paradise – the *terra reprommisionis sanctorum* – which is the ultimate goal of the voyagers: it is a land teeming with ripe fruits without any blight or shadow in which there is no night, but a light always shining, like the light of the sun.[42] In *Eiríks saga*, the capture of the *skrælingar*, their baptism by the Icelanders and the description of *Hvítramannaland* are preceded by the account of Vínland.

The manner in which places are named in the texts contributes not only to an understanding of the name *Hvítramannaland* but also to the socio-cultural content of the material. The naming of a place involves an act of possessing and of knowing, the name conferred being often a representation of its distinctive or natural characteristics. Confining our attention to the Icelandic material, we can say that this naming process involves different kinds of knowing. In the Vínland Sagas, for example, names are conferred on places and countries which have been recently discovered by the explorers themselves; hence, Eirik named *Greenland*, 'for he said that people would be much more tempted to go there if it had an attractive name' [*Eiríks saga*, (2), and in *Grænlendinga saga* (chapter 3)], Leif named various places: *Helluland* (lit.

---

39 Selmer (1956), §12.
40 *Ibid.*, §17.
41 *Ibid.*, §26. See also the Hermit of Tory who was clothed with the white hair of his own body, W. Stokes (ed.), (1888), §33; and the hermit in the Life of Brendan who has no clothing but white feathers like dove or gull feathers, see Mac Mathúna, (1994), 330 and *passim* for details and references.
42 *Ibid.*, §28.

Slab-land, possibly Baffin Island), *Markland*, named after its natural resources (lit. 'Forest-land', possibly Labrador), and, of course, *Vínland*, named after its natural qualities (lit. 'Vine- or Wine-land', reputedly New England). *Hvítramannaland*, however, has already been named. In *Landnáma* and *Eiríks saga*, it is understood that the Icelanders do not conquer, possess and colonise it. It is inhabited by other people, not by Icelanders; and its name, whether given to it by Icelanders or by others, belongs to an earlier period. *Eiríks saga* does not say why it is thought to be *Hvítramannaland*, but the logic of the naming process in the story suggests that it is so called because the people go about in white clothing. In the context, this is a perfectly reasonable interpretation of the name. Given the Irish context of the various accounts, it is quite possible that it is partly based on knowledge of the Irish medieval voyage tradition which describes the sacred island as being exceedingly bright and depicts hermits and clerics dressed in white ceremonial clothing or covered in the white hair of their own bodies. While this appears to rule out the suggestion of the name being a translation of an Irish name for a Norse district in Ireland,[43] Hermann Pálsson's theory that it is originally a secret name for *Alba* (Scotland) is more convincing than I had thought at first.[44] The influence of anecdotes concerning a country called *Albaníaland* is also reasonably certain.

In *Eyrbyggja saga*, the island or country is also a site of cultural conflict, and language is one of the vehicles which signifies and defines the cultural participants. The voyagers do not understand the inhabitants, who appear to be speaking Irish, and they are confused and fearful. When Björn arrives, on the other hand, he speaks Icelandic, and significantly, he is the leader of the people, clearly held in the highest respect. This reminds of Ari Mársson in *Landnámabók*, who was also reputed to be held in high regard. Matters are taken a step further here in the *Eyrbyggja* account in that there appears to be at least two groups. On one side, the unfriendlies, who are represented as being dishonourable heathens (*folk otrútt*); and, on the other, Björn and his group. Björn and some of his people behave in a Christian and friendly manner (like Paul the Hermit or the Procurator in the Land of Promise), but others are distinctly hostile. The role of the Irish speakers is somewhat ambiguous: they appear to belong to the hostile element although they are not explicitly identified as being heathen and they recognize Björn as their leader. The Christian voyagers identify culturally, linguistically and religiously with Björn. The meeting which takes place is akin to an Icelandic 'thing', and the case of the voyagers serves to highlight in microcosm the cultural conflict between paganism and Christianity. This land still has a dark side, just as does the Land of Promise in the *Navigatio*. The island has been integrated in the Icelandic cultural and political tradition, and its original significance and essence as a land inhabited by Irish monks and clerics is but dimly perceived, the role of the Icelanders and the Irish having been reversed.

---

43 See Young (1937), 123.
44 See Pálsson (1960).

Ívarr the Boneless and the Amphibious Cow

Rory McTurk

In this paper I shall make use of a Faroese folktale in trying to explain the curious nickname (inn) beinlaus(i) ('the Boneless') that is applied in Scandinavian tradition to Ívarr, son of the legendary Viking hero, *Ragnarr loðbrók*. This Ívarr, for whom the ninth-century Viking king of Dublin, Ímhar, is thought to be a historical prototype,[1] appears most prominently in the Icelandic *Ragnars saga loðbrókar* ('the saga of Ragnarr Hairy-breeks'), which survives in two redactions, one fragmentary and the other complete, and known respectively as X and Y, the former dating from the middle and the latter from the second half of the thirteenth century.[2] Although not actually nicknamed 'Boneless' in Ragnars saga, Ívarr is described there as boneless in the sense that he had only a kind of gristle where his bones should have been.[3] Ívarr also figures prominently in the Icelandic *Ragnarssona þáttr* ('story of Ragnarr's sons'), dating from the early fourteenth century. This appears to have had, among its sources, a now lost redaction of *Ragnars saga* older than either X or Y, and dating, in all probability, from before 1230.[4] In *Ragnarssona þáttr*, where Ívarr is given the nickname *beinlausi* ('the Boneless'), mention is made of his childlessness, and it is implied in that context that he was impotent, and that this was the reason for the nickname.[5]

Unless otherwise indicated, references here to *Ragnars saga* will be to the Y redaction, preserved in Ny kgl. saml. 1824b 4to, dating from c.1400. This redaction, the youngest and only complete one, has formed the basis for all modern editions and translations of the saga.[6] It may be regarded as an expanded version of the X redaction, which in turn may be regarded as an expanded version of the older *Ragnars saga* reflected in *Ragnarssona þáttr*. X is preserved in AM 147 4to, dating from the second half of the fifteenth century, and *Ragnarssona þáttr* is preserved in the codex known as *Hauksbók*, mainly dating from the early fourteenth century.[7]

In *Ragnars saga*, an account is given of how the hero, Ragnarr, invaded England from Denmark with only two ships, was captured by King Ella of England, and thrown into a snake-pit, where he eventually died, though first he made the enigmatic statement

---

1 See McTurk (1991a), 39-50. In the present article, the name Ívarr is spelt variously with and without the double r according to whether it is the Icelandic or the Faroese tradition that is being referred to.
2 *Ibid.*, 54-6.
3 See Olsen (1906-8), 129, ll. 14-6.
4 See McTurk (1991a), 56, 178-9.
5 See Jónsson & Jónsson (1892-96), 465, ll, 10-3. Cf. Smyth (1975-79), I, 28, with references.
6 Lists of these may be found in Hermannsson (1912), 34-5; and in Hermannsson (1937), 60-1. Particular mention may be made of the English translation of *Ragnars saga* in Schlauch (1930), xxxi-xxxviii, 183-256, and of the recent edition by Thorsson (1985), 99-153, 167-9.
7 McTurk (1991a), 56, and the article on *Hauksbók* by Harðarson and Karlsson in Pulsiano, et al. (1993), 271-2.

189

that 'the porkers would grunt if they knew the fate of the boar'.[8] Ella, suspecting and anxious to confirm that it was indeed Ragnarr who had been his victim, sent messengers to Denmark with the news of his death. The messengers were received by Ragnarr's sons Björn, Hvítserkr, Sigurðr and Ívarr. When they heard the news of Ragnarr's death and of his words about the porkers, Björn, who had been smoothing a spear-shaft, held onto it so hard that the print of his hand could be seen on it afterwards; Hvítserkr, who had been playing a board-game, squeezed one of the pieces so hard that it drew blood; Sigurðr, who had been paring his nails with a knife, let the knife cut him to the bone; and Ívarr changed colour, going sometimes red, sometimes blue, sometimes pale. He also became swollen as a result of the cruelty in his breast. When the messengers told King Ella of the sons' reaction, Ella said that Ívarr was the one he and his followers had most cause to fear. Back in Denmark, however, Ívarr angered his brothers by telling them that he would take no part in any attempt to avenge Ragnarr, who in his view had only himself to blame for his death, but that he would accept wergild for Ragnarr if it were forthcoming. The other brothers, who were intent on immediate revenge, sailed with Ívarr to England and joined battle with Ella, but were defeated because Ívarr did not give them sufficient support and was not himself present at the battle. Ívarr then stayed in England while his brothers returned to Denmark, and persuaded Ella to grant him, in return for a promise never to fight against him, as much land as might be covered by the largest ox-hide he, Ívarr, could find. Ívarr then obtained the skin of an old bull, had it stretched and cut into strips, and had the strips made long enough to encircle a vast tract of land, on which he founded London. He gradually became so popular that he won over most of Ella's followers. He then sent for his brothers, who came to England and defeated Ella in battle. Ella was taken prisoner, and at Ívarr's command a blood-eagle was cut on his back.[9]

Some of the other information given in *Ragnars saga* needs to be outlined before the Faroese folktale can be discussed. In contrast to *Ragnarssona þáttr*, which makes no mention of cows, *Ragnars saga* makes much of the fact that Ragnarr's sons, and Ívarr in particular, more than once had occasion to fight against magical cows; in the saga, these events are presented as taking place well before Ragnarr's death. Ívarr's earliest exploit, according to the saga, was to assist his brothers in their conquest of Hvítabær – a town at which sacrifices took place and which had proved invincible to all its previous attackers – by killing the two sacred cows which until then had protected the town;[10] and later in the saga it is described how Ívarr killed the cow Síbylja, to which sacrifices were made at Uppsala by King Eysteinn of Sweden, and which had the magical gift of protecting that country from invaders by driving them insane with its lowing noise, and thus causing them to fight among themselves. Ívarr, who, because he was boneless, could not walk and consequently had to be carried everywhere, instructed his bearers to bring him as close to the cow as possible, and

---

8 See Olsen (1906-8), 159, ll. 1-2; cf. 158, ll. 15-6.
9 *Ibid.*, 167, l. 2 and 168, l. 7. On the supposed sacrifice of the blood eagle, see most recently McTurk (1994), ll. 539-41, with references.
10 *Ibid.*, 131-2.

to make him a bow and arrows. He fired an arrow into each of the cow's eyes, whereupon its bellowing grew worse than ever; but then, at his instructions, his bearers threw him onto the cow's back, where he became as heavy as a rock after being as light as a child to throw, and every bone in the cow's body was broken. In thus defeating King Eysteinn, who was slain in the battle that ensued, Ívarr was avenging his two half-brothers Eirekr and Agnarr, the sons of Ragnarr's first wife Þóra, who had both died at Eysteinn's hands.[11]

The impression given in the saga is that Ívarr's bonelessness resulted from a curse. His mother Áslaug, Ragnarr's second wife, the daughter of Sigurðr and Brynhildr, had been brought up under the name of Kráka by a farmer and his wife living at Spangereid in southern Norway, who had treated her harshly. When he married Áslaug, Ragnarr insisted on consummating the marriage forthwith, claiming that the farmer and his wife had no gift of prophecy, though Áslaug implied that unless they remained chaste for three nights, their first child would be born without bones.[12] The saga's implication is, thus, that it was as a result of a curse placed on Áslaug by the farming couple who had brought her up, that Ívarr was born boneless.

Ragnarssona þáttr, on the other hand, appears to explain Ívarr's nickname 'the Boneless' in terms of his childlessness and possible impotence, as indicated above. This idea has been taken up in modern times by Jan de Vries, in an article in which he also quoted in full the Faroese folktale that will form the main subject of this paper; it was this article, indeed, that first brought the folktale in question to my attention. Here de Vries argued that the original form of the nickname was not *inn beinlausi*, meaning 'the boneless one' (or 'the legless one'), but *inn barnlausi*, meaning 'the childless one'.[13] In a later article, however, de Vries abandoned this idea in favour of the view that the nickname arose as a result of the Latin adjective *exosus*, meaning 'hating' or 'hateful', being misread or misheard as *exos*, meaning 'boneless'.[14] Ívarr's hatred and hatefulness are certainly well attested in Scandinavian tradition, not least in the account, referred to above, of his having the blood-eagle cut on Ella's back.

Without losing sight of the connection of the nickname with impotence, which does seem to have, in *Ragnarssona þáttr*, the support of a medieval source,[15] I should like to argue in this paper that Ívarr's nickname refers to the wind, and may have signified his skill as a navigator, specifically his capacity for battling successfully with the winds at sea. Here I have in mind the fact, noted by Svale Solheim, that the terms *beinlaus, Eivind beinlaus and Ivar beinlaus* have been used in modern times by Norwegian fishermen as noa terms for the wind, that is, as roundabout, euphemistic

---

11 *Ibid.*, 132-50.
12 *Ibid.*, 128-9.
13 de Vries (1922), 27-8.
14 de Vries (1928a), 259-60.
15 Further medieval evidence in support of the connection from one of the Old English Riddles will be offered at the end of this paper.

names chosen in preference to those that are tabooed, as the Norwegian word for 'wind' seems to have been in this case, among sailors, at least.[16] Strangely enough, Solheim makes no reference in this context to the Scandinavian traditions of Ragnarr loðbrók and his sons. It is true that the Icelandic traditions make no explicit connection of Ívarr with the wind; but the Danish historian Saxo Grammaticus, who devotes most of the ninth book of his *Gesta Danorum*, completed by 1216, to the legendary king of Denmark Regnerus Lothbrog (i.e., Ragnarr loðbrók), applies the nickname 'Ventosi Pillei' ('Wind-hat') to Ívarr's half-brother Ericus, the son of Regnerus by his wife Svanlogha i.e. Svanlaug (cf. Eirekr, the son of Ragnarr by Þóra, mentioned above).[17] Dag Strömbäck has linked this nickname with that of the Swedish king Erik Wäderhatt ('Weather-hat'), about whom there was a tradition that he could control the weather, in that the wind was believed to blow from whatever direction in which he turned his hat.[18] In Modern Faroese, moreover, the expression *Ívar beinleysi* may be used to refer to the wind, or to a draught.[19]

Further support for my argument can, I believe, be found in the Faroese folktale referred to above, which I now quote, with a facing translation.[20]

Ívar hin beinleysi

Mær er sagt um Ívar hin bein-leysa, at hann átti tríggjar brøður: Björn jarnsíðu, Hvíting, Kváða og Sjúrð ormeyga. Teir fingu boðini, at faðir var deyður; ein helt á spjótinum og hann kroysti hann so fast, at tað stóð brúnt í hondini; men Ívar hin beinleysi gjordi einki uttan sat og star-di í eldin og talaði einki, men fekk ymsar litir, so hann var bæði grønur og gulur, reyður og bláur [allir søgdu nakað, sum eg ikki minnist uttan tað, at alt var um at hevna faðir]. Boðini fóru aftur við tí svari, teir fingu. Nú spurdi Kongur Ella teir eftir, hvat hinir

Ívar the Boneless

They tell me about Ívar the Boneless that he had three brothers: Björn Ironside, Hvítingur, Kváði and Sjúrður Snake-eye. They got the news that their father was dead; one of them was holding onto his spear and he pressed so hard that it left a brown mark in his hand; but Ívar the Boneless did nothing, but sat and stared into the fire and spoke not a word, but took on various colours, so that he was both green and yellow, red and blue [they all said something which I don't remember, except that it was all about avenging their father].

---

16 Solheim (1940), 104-6.
17 McTurk (1991a), 40-1, 53-4, 77-8.
18 Strömbäck (1935), 135-44
19 McTurk (1991b), 357, note 34, with references
20 I am grateful to Professors Bo Almqvist and Michael Barnes, of the University Colleges of Dublin and London, respectively, for help with this translation, and to Professor Barnes for confirming to me, in a letter dated 26 January, 1997, that de Vries's text of the folktale (here copied verba-tim from de Vries [1922], 24-5) does not conform entirely to contemporary Faroese usage. Needless to say, any remaining errors of translation are entirely my responsibility.

segja; so søgdu teir, hvat ið hvør
svaraði, men Ívarin hann talaði ikki,
uttan stardi í eldin og fekk ymsar litir.
"Já", segði Kongur Ella, at tað var tað
einasta hann ræddist fyri: honum
óttaðist hann fyri, men ikki teim
hinum. Brøðurnir foru nú at gera seg
til. Nú teir voru lidnir, segði Ívar hin
beinleysi við teir, at hann vildi sleppa
við teim: teir søgdu hann kundi einki
gera: hann segði: jú, hann skuldi við
teimum fara kortini.

Tvey hendilsir møttu teimum,
sum eg ikki minnist, men tó av sjógv
og ovegri, sum alt var útsendingar, so
teir hildu sær ikki til nakað lív: men
Ívarin segði tá, at teir doyðu ikki enn: at
teir fingu verra at møta enn so; bað teir
hyggja væl eftir, tá ið land kom í
eygsjón. Teir hugdu. Nú søgdu teir, teir
sógu landið, men tað kom av landinum,
søgdu teir, eftir sjógnum kom tað, so
tað sást hvorki himmal ella jörð Já,
segði Ívar hin beinleysi, og nú máttu
teir væl óttast, og tað var blótkúgvin,
ið nú kom: har í voru bein síni, og tá
ið hon legði at skipunum, áðrenn hon
nærti við tað, skuldu teir taka seg og
blaka seg millum hornana á henni og
síggja til, at teir blakaðu beint, tí
blakaðu teir ikki beint, var teirra lív
burtur. So nærkaðist hon til teirra, so
teir hildu seg blaka tá til hennara; so
tóku teir Ívarin beinleysa og teir
blakaðu hann millum hornana á henni;
tar drógust tey bæði á sjónum; tá var
hann so tungur á henni, at hövdið
snaraðist av hálsvølini, og tá fekk hann
øll síni bein aftur, sum hann skuldi
hava; so fóru teir til lands, og so fløttu
teir blótkunna; so fór Ívarin hin

The messengers returned with the
answer they received. King Ella now
asked them what the brothers said:
then they told him what each of them
answered—'but Ívar, he didn't speak,
he just stared into the fire and took on
various colours.' 'Yes', said King Ella,
that was the one thing he was afraid
of; he feared him, but not the others.
The brothers now started to prepare
themselves, and when they were ready,
Ívar the Boneless told them that he
wanted to go with them; they said he
could do nothing; but he said yes, he
would go with them, even so.

Two things happened to them,
which I don't remember, except that
they arose from the sea and bad weather,
and which were all due to witchcraft, so
that they hardly thought they would
survive; but then Ívar said they wouldn't
die yet: that they would have worse
things to deal with than that. He asked
them to pay careful heed when land
came in sight. They looked. Now they
said they could see the land, but
something was coming from the land,
they said, across the sea it was coming,
so that neither heaven nor earth could
be seen. Yes, said Ívar the Boneless,
now might they well be afraid; that
was the sacrificial cow that was coming:
inside the cow were his bones, and
when she attacked the ships, before
she touched the ship, they were to take
him and throw him between her horns
and see to it that they threw straight,
for if they didn't throw straight, their
lives were lost. Then she approached
them, and then they felt able to throw
him at her; then they took Ívar the

beinleysi til kongin, og hann segði, hann vildi ongar bøtur hava fyri faðir, tar-sum hann vildi geva sær so mikið af landørum, sum ein neytshúð kundi rökka út yvir; tað lovaði kongurin, at hann skuldi fáa og so risti hann húðina sundur í halar, so klenar, sum hann kundi fáa teir, og tað rak um alla Lundina í Onglandi; Lundina fekk hann ikki, men bleiv við eitt annað petti, sum húðin rak um, og har bygði hann: men eftir tað drupu teir kong Ella kortini og hevndu so pápan.

Boneless and they threw him between her horns; they both struggled there on the sea; then he was so heavy on her that her head was wrenched from her neck, and then he got back all his bones, which he was supposed to have. Then they went ashore, and then they skinned the sacrificial cow. Then Ívar the Boneless went to the king, and he said he wanted no compensation for his father, provided he would give him as much land as a bull's hide could extend over. The king promised that he would have that, and so he cut the hide up into strips as fine as he could make them, and it extended across the whole of London in England. He did not get London, but settled for another small area, which the hide extended over, and there he settled. But after that they killed King Ella even so, and thus avenged their father.

This account, as de Vries indicates, was recorded by Johan Henrik Schröter (1771-1851) from a woman on the island of Suðuroy, and was included by Svend Grundtvig and Jörgen Bloch in the second volume of their sixteen-volume manuscript collection *Corpus carminum Færoensium*, compiled between 1872 and 1905. It shows many close resemblances to *Ragnars saga*, from which, according to de Vries, it derives almost exclusively. He maintains that *Ragnars saga* became known in the Faroe Islands after the publication of its first edition in Erik Julius Biörner's Nordiska kämpadater (vol. XII), in 1737, that its story was subsequently told there orally, and that such differences as are apparent between the saga and the folktale are due to the stylising tendency of oral narrative, rather than to the influence of any independent tradition. The only feature of the folktale that de Vries admits might be derived from a source other than *Ragnars saga* is its statement that Ívar did not in the end acquire London by his ruse with the hide. This may show the influence of Ragnarssona þáttr, where it is York, rather than London, that Ívarr acquires by this means.[21] It might have

---

21 See de Vries (1922), 23-4, 25, 29; and cf. *Hauksbók*, 463, ll. 18-27 (Harðarson & Karlsson 1993). For bibliographical information on the Grundtvig-Bloch manuscript collection and related matters, see Chesnutt (1970), 109-37, esp. 125.

suited de Vries's argument to mention, though he does not do so, that the first edition of *Ragnarssona þáttr* appeared in 1773, in Jacobus Langebek's Scriptores rerum Danicarum medii ævi, vol. II, not so very long after the first edition of *Ragnars saga*, and could presumably have influenced this folktale before it came to be recorded by Schrøter.[22]

I should however like to raise here the question of whether the mention in the folktale of Ívar's failure to acquire London, and, more importantly, the idea that he had difficulties at sea while sailing to England to avenge his father, could have derived ultimately from medieval traditions other than *Ragnars saga* and *Ragnarssona þáttr*, and independent of them. Even so, there is no doubt that de Vries is right in much of what he has to say about the indebtedness of the folktale to *Ragnars saga*, and I wish to be as fair as possible to his argument. He is certainly right to emphasise that it is the folktale's concentration on the idea of Ívar's bonelessness that explains the major differences between *Ragnars saga* and the folktale.[23] In the saga, for instance, Ívarr resists the brothers' attempts to involve him in their initial revenge mission to England, ostensibly because he is unsympathetic to their cause, but, in fact, because he has secret plans of his own for taking revenge, which he later puts into practice by the blood-eagle method, as indicated above. In the folktale, by contrast, he insists on accompanying his brothers, who are reluctant to have him with them, presumably because they believe that in his boneless condition he can be of no help to them. This idea is indeed reinforced in the folktale by the absence of any prior demonstration of Ívar's effectiveness in battle. The folktale lacks, for example, any mention of his successful defeat of the cows at Hvítabær, and presents his victory over the cow Síbylja as an event following, rather than preceeding, the departure of Ragnar's sons as their revenge mission. The folktale does, it is true, reproduce the saga's description of Ívarr's initial reaction to the news of his father's death, in only slightly altered form; but the alterations are sufficient to give the reaction an almost comic effect in the folktale, very different from the mainly heroic impression that it makes in the saga; and the reference to Ella's particular fear of Ívarr, which the folktale also retains, provides, in the latter, an increased effect of suspense, raising, even more than in the saga, the question of how the boneless Ívar is going to make his contribution to the revenge. In the folktale, it appears, an effect of contrast is intended in the portrayal of Ívar's condition before and after the confrontation with the cow, which it presents as something of a turning-point in his fortunes, and to which it gives a central position.

It is in discussing this confrontation that I find myself least in agreement with de Vries, whose arguments here seem to me in the one case too simple, and in the other too complicated. The argument that I consider to be too simple is his view that the reason why Ívarr's fight with the cow is removed from its setting on land in the saga, to one at sea in the folktale, is that the home of this particular folktale, the

---

22 Hermannsson (1912), 39.
23 de Vries (1922), 25-9.

Faroes, is a group of islands in the North Atlantic.[24] Iceland, where I am assuming *Ragnars saga* was written,[25] is of course also in the North Atlantic, and the Icelanders are hardly less of a seafaring people than the Faroese; an Icelander would presumably have almost as much general interest as a Faroe islander in providing a sea setting for Ívarr's fight if he had a specific reason for doing so. I shall suggest below that the setting at sea in the folktale is due to an awareness, inherited by the folktale independently of either *Ragnars saga* or *Ragnarssona þáttr*, of an ancient tradition according to which Ívarr encountered adverse winds on the North Sea when sailing to England to avenge his father.

The argument of de Vries that seems to me too complicated, on the other hand, is his contention that the folktale has made a closer connection than the saga does between the circumstances of Ívarr's procreation and birth, as the saga describes them, and the fight with the cow. He is led to this view by a consideration of certain differences between the saga and the folktale in their accounts of the fight. In the saga, as indicated above, Ívarr is as light as a child when thrown at Síbylja by his bearers, but suddenly becomes as heavy as a rock when he lands on her back, so that every bone in her body is broken. The folktale develops this account in relating that Ívar, when thrown between the cow's horns (as the folktale has it, rather than onto her back), not only becomes so heavy that her head is wrenched off, but also recovers all his bones, which were contained in the cow's body. According to de Vries, the Faroese oral tradition in which the folktale developed, with *Ragnars saga* as its ultimate source, has linked the supernatural cow with the supernatural forces which, according to the saga, caused Ívarr's bonelessness in the first place, so that, in recovering his bones after slaying the cow, as happens in the folktale, Ívar is to be understood as freeing himself from the curse which the saga implies was placed on his mother, Áslaug, by the farmers who had brought her up as a child under the name of Kráka.[26] While this is an ingenious argument which it is tempting to accept, it must be emphasised that the folktale itself, in its preserved form, makes no mention of a curse, or of Ívar's mother, or of the circumstances of his birth; it seems to me that a relatively simple view, if one can be found, is here called for. I would suggest, then, as a view of this kind, that the folktale has inherited, again independently of *Ragnars saga* and *Ragnarssona þáttr*, a memory of Ívar as a legendary battler with the wind at sea, who achieved his success in that capacity by partaking of the nature of the wind itself, a process represented in the folktale by its account of the same set of bones being shared, as it were, by Ívar and the cow; it is as if Ívar, in defeating a cow which represents an adverse wind, comes to personify an even more powerful wind than the one he and his brothers were up against. In its present form, the Faroese account no doubt shows the influence of *Ragnars saga*, and particularly of the statement in the saga that every bone in the cow's body was broken; but it may also reflect an ancient association of Ívarr with the wind that was unknown to either the saga or *Ragnarssona þáttr*.

---

24 *Ibid.* (1922), 26.
25 Cf. McTurk (1991b), vi.
26 de Vries (1922), 26-8.

One other difference between the saga and the folktale that needs to be mentioned briefly, is the fact that in the saga it is a bull's hide that Ívarr uses to trick King Ella into granting him a large tract of land, whereas in the folktale it is apparently the hide of the cow Ívar has slain that he uses for this purpose. This surely is a clear example of the Faroese oral tradition making a connection between different events of the saga that the saga itself does not make: in the folktale, as we have seen, the cow is left boneless by the slaying, and this motif presumably leads on naturally to an equation of the bull's hide with the cow's hide, and so to the idea, found in the folktale, of skinning the cow; and the fact that the cow is a supernatural one, in the folktale no less than in the saga, helps to explain the fact that the strips cut from its hide are able to stretch as far as they do. Jan de Vries is surely right to view this difference between the saga and the folktale in the way I have just outlined, and to see the folktale's version of the events in question as an example of the unifying, consolidating tendency of oral narrative.[27]

Before producing my evidence for an independent tradition of Ívarr having encountered adverse winds while sailing to England to avenge his father, I should like to raise the question of whether the idea of such an encounter – which I assume is what lies behind the folktale's account of Ívar's fight with the cow – could have been supplied to the folktale by *Ragnars saga* itself, or by *Ragnarssona þáttr*, rather than by an independent source. The answer is that it could have been, but if it was, it must have been borrowed from the saga's account of Ragnarr's earlier, ill-fated voyage to England, and applied in the folktale to Ívar's ultimately successful one. Such a transference is certainly not impossible, and could be seen as another result of the folktale developing links and similarities between different events of the saga. *Ragnarssona þáttr* is a relatively unlikely source here, since although it reports, as the saga does, that Ragnarr's two ships were wrecked on the English coast, it does not mention the wind but rather the current and the shallow water (*straums ok útgrynnis*) in this connection.[28] The saga, on the other hand, clearly attributes the wrecking of Ragnarr's ships to 'sharp winds' (*byri hvassa*).[29] Winds are mentioned not infrequently in *Ragnars saga*, which here contrasts with *Ragnarssona þáttr*, where as far as I can discover they are not mentioned at all. In the saga, however, the references to winds are mostly conventional, occurring in contexts of people setting sail when the winds are favourable; the *andviðri* or head-wind in chapter 5 of the saga, which temporarily prevents Ragnarr's messengers from summoning Kráka-Áslaug for the first time into his presence, is hardly relevant here.[30]

---

27 *Ibid.* (1922), 28.
28 See *Hauksbók*, 462, l. 22 (Harðarson & Karlsson 1993).
29 Olsen (1906-8), 156, l. 23.
30 *Ibid.*, 124, l. 4.

Winds and storms are, however, also a feature of the account by the monk of St Albans, Roger of Wendover, in his *Flores historiarum* (written most probably between 1219 and 1235),[31] of the death of one Lothbrocus, and of the vengeance taken by his sons Hinguar and Hubba; the names of these three figures seem to correspond respectively to those of Ragnarr loðbrók and his sons Ívarr and Ubbo in Scandinavian tradition.[32] This account has long been recognised as an important analogue to *Ragnars saga*, and is thought to be quite independent of Scandinavian traditions of the avenging of Ragnarr loðbrók by his sons.[33] It forms a prelude to Roger's account of the martyrdom of Edmund, King of the East Angles, and represents a considerable elaboration on Abbo of Fleury's account of that same martyrdom in his late tenth-century Passio Sancti Eadmundi, to which, even so, Roger seems largely indebted in his treatment of this subject.[34]

According to Roger of Wendover, then, Lothbrocus, a member of the Danish royal family, was driven out to sea by a sudden storm while hunting waterfowl in a small boat off the Danish coast, and landed in East Anglia, where he became an honoured guest at the court of King Edmund. His skill as a huntsman soon aroused the jealousy of the king's huntsman, Bernus, who consequently murdered him one day when they were hunting, and hid his body in a wood. A greyhound that was with Lothbrocus at the time led to the discovery of the body and of the murderer's identity, and Edmund and his court decided that Bernus should be punished by being set adrift in Lothbrocus's boat without any means of navigation, to see if God wished to preserve him from danger. This was done, and Bernus came to land in Denmark, where the boat was recognised as belonging to Lothbrocus, and Bernus was taken to Hinguar and Hubba, who proceeded to question him about their father. He lied to them that it was at Edmund's instructions that Lothbrocus had been slain. The brothers then swore vengeance on the innocent Edmund, and, taking Bernus with them as a guide, set sail for East Anglia, where they eventually arrived after being driven off course near Berwick-on-Tweed. They killed everyone they found in East Anglia, and Hinguar sent a message to King Edmund, who was then at Hellesdon, challenging him to battle. After consulting with a bishop who advised flight, Edmund met the Danes in battle, but the English suffered such severe losses that the king decided to surrender his own person to avoid further bloodshed. Roger then reproduces Abbo of Fleury's account of Edmund's martyrdom.[35]

---

31 Galbraith (1944), 15-21.
32 Ubbo does not feature by name in the Icelandic accounts of Ragnarr loðbrók and his sons, but appears as a son of Regnerus Lothbrog in Book IX of Saxo's *Gesta Danorum*. See McTurk (1991b), 40, 78.
33 de Vries (1928b), 160-1.
34 Loomis (1932), 84-94.
35 Cf. *ibid.*, 92-4.

Roger and Abbo are also in agreement in stating that the Vikings responsible for the slaying of King Edmund landed first in Northern Britain before proceeding to East Anglia. Their accounts are here at variance with the Anglo-Saxon Chronicle, Asser's *Life of King Alfred,* Æthelweard's *Chronicle* and other writings, which report that the Vikings came first to East Anglia, then proceeded northwards, and later returned to East Anglia,[36] and which, in this respect (among others), represent a relatively reliable historical tradition. Roger of Wendover was in fact aware of this other tradition, as is clear from some statements with which he precedes the story just summarised.[37] His account seems to reflect an uncertainty as to what precisely were the movements of the Viking invaders of Britain in the eight-sixties and -seventies. This uncertainty, I suggest, has origins in common with the Faroese folktale's vagueness as to the area eventually won by Ívar in England – a feature of the folktale that need not, therefore, be explained by reference to *Ragnarssona þáttr,* which, as we have seen, specifically mentions York. More importantly, though, I would suggest that Roger's apparently unique statement about the winds driving Hinguar's fleet off course as it sailed to Britain on a mission of vengeance derives from a tradition that has also influenced the Faroese folktale, mainly in stimulating the latter's adaptation of its principal source, *Ragnars saga,* whereby Ívar's encounter with the cow – which in the folktale, at least, seems to represent a wind or storm at sea – takes place after, rather than before, his father's death, and at sea rather than on land. In this context, it may be noted that Roger of Wendover's account, which involves three sea-voyages in each of which the wind plays a significant part, and in the third of which Hinguar features as a battler with the winds at sea, illustrates the so-called 'law of three' characteristic of oral narrative; and that the same seems to have been true of the folktale before it came to be told in the form recorded above, to judge from the fact that the storyteller, before describing Ívar's encounter with the cow, says: 'two things happened ... which I don't remember, except that they arose from the sea and bad weather.'[38]

Jan de Vries has argued convincingly that Roger of Wendover's account, with its attempts to present in as favourable a light as possible the ninth-century actions of the Danes as well as the English, has its origins in stories told in the Danelaw in the eleventh century.[39] Jan de Vries and others have also shown that the content of *Ragnars saga* derives largely from oral traditions that proliferated in Norway from the twelfth to the thirteenth century. These traditions included material of English origin which appears to have reached Norway by way of the Orkneys on the one hand and Denmark on the other.[40] As was indicated above, *Ragnarssona þáttr,* though it does mention, as *Ragnars saga* also does, the motif of the use of a bull's hide to win land, nevertheless differs from *Ragnars saga* in making no mention of the cow Síbylja, or

---

36 Hervey 1907, 1-5, 82-3, etc.
37 *Ibid.,* 168-71.
38 Olrik (1992), 52.
39 de Vries (1928b), 161-3.
40 See de Vries (1927a), 145-6; de Vries (1927b), 81-4; and McTurk (1991b), 103-14; 211-35.

of the cows at Hvítabær. This makes it reasonable to assume that the motif of Ívarr's fight with a cow or cows did not form part of the older *Ragnars saga* from which the *þáttr* largely derives, and which is believed to have been composed before the year 1230, as also indicated above. The first appearance of the motif in the written tradition of Ragnarr loðbrók would thus have been in the X version of *Ragnars saga*, composed near the middle of the thirteenth century.[41] It has been suggested that the original form of the cow's name *Síbylja* was the Sanskrit word *savala*, meaning 'piebald', which in Hindu mythology is applied as a proper name to a cow of plenty, one of whose capacities is to produce hordes of warriors from different parts of her body, lowing as she does so; and that when this word came into contact with Scandinavian traditions of Ragnarr loðbrók and his sons, it was very close in form to the forms in which *Ragnars saga* has preserved it.[42] The text of the saga preserved in AM 147 4to, representing the X redaction, has a y in the second syllable of the name; while the text preserved in Ny kgl. saml. 1824b 4to, representing the Y version, has an i. Because of these spellings Lidén has argued that the original form of the name was not, as some have thought, *Síbelja*, meaning 'constantly lowing or bellowing', but *Síbylja*, meaning 'constantly booming, roaring, echoing'; the second element in the word, in Lidén's view, is thus related to the verb *bylja*, meaning 'to boom, roar, echo',[43] an expression which could apparently be used of the noise of the wind, and which is indeed cognate with the masculine noun *bylr*, meaning 'a squall or gust of wind'.[44] Progressing as they do from the two relatively manageable cows at Hvítabær to the much more problematic cow *Síbylja*, Ívarr's fights with cows as described in *Ragnars saga* show the so-called 'law of progressive ascent' characteristic of oral narrative, as well as the law of three, of which examples have been given above from Roger of Wendover's account of the vengeance taken by the sons of Lothbrocus, and from the Faroese folktale.[45] With the foregoing considerations in mind, we may imagine that the X redactor of *Ragnars saga* developed the stories of the Hvítabær cows and of *Síbylja* from a tale orally current in mainland Scandinavia about a hero who overcomes a number of supernatural beings, one of them a cow called Síbylja, in a series of increasingly difficult encounters. Lidén's arguments are helpful in showing that, if the manuscript forms of the name *Síbylja* do indeed reflect accurately the form in which it first came into contact with traditions of Ragnarr loðbrók and his sons, the name, when it did so, whatever its ultimate origins, would have carried associations of ideas connected with the wind. It is easy to see how the story of *Síbylja* could become attached most readily to Ívarr if the latter's association with the wind were already established. I would suggest that this association, of which Roger of Wendover provides a uniquely explicit instance and which must be of English origin, travelled from England to mainland Scandinavia – most probably to Norway, which, as indicated above, was a seed-bed for traditions that eventually

---

41 Cf. McTurk (1991b), 54.
42 Hüsing (1903-06), 143-4; cf. McTurk (1991b), 115-6.
43 Lidén (1928), 361-4.
44 It is also cognate, in fact, with the Icelandic verb *belja*, meaning 'to low', or 'to bellow'; see Magnússon (1989), 49, 97, 809.
45 See Olrik (1992), 44-5.

took written form in *Ragnars saga* – where it helped to attract the story of *Síbylja* into the developing oral traditions of Ragnarr loíbrók and his sons, and subsequently influenced the Icelandic and Faroese traditions in different ways. Since the Faroese tradition differs from the Icelandic in making a relatively obvious connection between the hostile cow and the wind, however, the possibility must also be considered that information relevant to Ívar's encounter with the wind reached the Faroes from England by a more direct route than that just suggested. Ívarr's and *Síbylja's* associations with the wind appear to have been lost on the X and Y redactors of *Ragnars saga*, neither of whom makes any explicit connection between either of these figures and the wind. On the other hand, both *Ragnarssona þáttr* and *Ragnars saga* have recorded the wrecking of Ragnarr's ships on the English coast (the former without mentioning the wind, however, see above);[46] this information is comparable to Roger of Wendover's statement that Lothbrocus's boat was driven to England by a storm, and must presumably also have reached Scandinavia from an English source. If one were looking for a specific means by which some, at least, of the relevant information was conveyed to Scandinavia, one might fasten on the visit of Matthew Paris to the Norwegian island of Nidarholm (now known as Munkholmen) in 1248;[47] Matthew, like Roger of Wendover, was a monk of St Albans, and a copier and continuator of Roger's work who, in two of his extant writings, reproduces word for word the story of Lothbrocus by Roger summarised above;[48] his visit was perhaps not too late for his information to have been taken into account – albeit incompletely and without being fully understood – in the X version of *Ragnars saga*, which I have said above was 'composed near the middle of the thirteenth century', and which, though it includes the stories of Ívar's cow-slayings, makes no obvious connection between them and the wind.

Returning now to the Faroese folktale, I would argue that the two features of Roger of Wendover's information to which I drew attention above – the uncertainty with regard to the movements of the Vikings in England and the tradition of Ívarr encountering adverse winds on his way there – became known in the Faroes by one or other of the routes just discussed, and eventually made their own contribution, in the ways I have indicated, to this folktale, which, however, clearly had *Ragnars saga* as its main source, whether in written or printed form. I suspect that it would be rash to assume that the association of the name *Síbylja* with the wind was made or known in the Faroes, and would repeat the suggestion made above that the folktale's presentation of Ívar and the cow as opponents sharing the same nature, at least as far as their bones were concerned, was stimulated by the saga's statement that, when Ívarr slew Síbylja, every bone in her body was broken. I do suggest, however, that, taken together with Roger of Wendover's account, the Faroese folktale provides

---

46 Cf. note 28, above, and Olsen (1906-8), 156, ll. 21-4, and 186-7.
47 See Vaughan (1958 [Reprint 1979]), 4-7, and McTurk (1997), 445-52.
48 The writings in question are Matthew Paris's *Chronica majora* and *Flores historiarum*, the latter not to be confused with Roger of Wendover's work of that name. For further information and references, see McTurk (1991b), 231-2.

evidence of an association of Ívarr with the wind going back at least as far as the thirteenth century.

It was at the end of the last paragraph that I concluded the version of this paper that I delivered at the Symposium of which this volume forms the Proceedings. The main argument of the paper, as will (I trust) be evident, is that Ívarr's nickname 'the Boneless' derives from a noa-expression for the wind.[49] In the present version of the paper I have avoided saying, however, that this was the sole or original derivation of the nickname, because of two points that have come to my attention since I delivered the paper at the Symposium. I should like now to add a couple of extra paragraphs in order to take these into account.

Both points relate to the possible connection of the nickname with impotence, mentioned at the beginning of this paper. The first of them was made by Séamas Ó Catháin in the discussion following the paper's delivery at the Symposium. Professor Ó Catháin raised the question of whether the Faroese evidence that the expression *Ívar beinleysi* refers to a draught, i.e., to a relatively weak wind, could be related in some way to the idea of Ívarr's impotence, hinted at in Ragnarssona *þáttr*. In the course of the discussion, mention was made of Alfred Smyth's dismissal of the *þáttr's* evidence for this being the explanation of the nickname on the grounds that, in Smyth's view at least, Ívarr, who was identical with Imhar of Dublin, had descendants, and must, therefore, have been capable of begetting children.[50] As I pointed out at the time, this seems to me a fallacious argument; the fact that someone is nicknamed 'the impotent' need not mean that he was totally unable to perform sexual intercourse, but might rather arise from a reputation for impotence in attempted sexual relations with women other than the mother (or mothers) of his children. Although the circumstances are not exactly parallel, one might compare Hrútr Herjólfsson's relations with his wife Unnr Marðardóttir as described in the Icelandic *Njáls saga*; his problem – if the evidence of *Njáls saga* may be taken together with that of *Laxdæla saga* – appears to be that, far from being impotent, he is too virile for Unnr to accommodate him physically when they make love, though with other women he does not encounter this difficulty, to judge from the fact that, according to *Laxdæla saga*, he has sixteen sons and ten daughters by his second and third marriages, after Unnr has divorced him.[51] Although *Njáls saga* explains this in terms of a supernatural curse placed on Hrútr by Gunnhildr Özurardóttir, Queen of Norway, with whom he had been intimate before his first marriage,[52] it is a situation which it is surely easy enough to imagine arising in real life; it does not necessarily require a supernatural explanation. It also becomes common knowledge, as Njáls saga describes it; after Unnr has divorced

---

49 This is also the main argument of McTurk (1997), in which, however, the emphasis is more on Matthew Paris's visit to Norway than in the present paper, and which was completed before the arguments of John Frankis, to be discussed below, came to my attention.
50 Smyth (1975-79), I, 28.
51 Sveinsson (1954), 24, and Sveinsson (1934), 48.
52 Sveinsson (1954), 13-5, 20-1.

him, Hrútr is teased in public about the reasons for the divorce.[53] In much the same way, it is not difficult to imagine, *mutatis mutandis*, a man acquiring a reputation for impotence as a result of unsuccessful sexual relations with women other than those, or the one, to whom he is particularly attached. Without wishing to enter here into the question of whether Ívarr's historical prototype did or did not have offspring, I would simply submit that the application of a nickname meaning 'impotent' to a man need not preclude his having, or having had, children.

The second relevant point was brought to my notice by John Frankis, of the University of Newcastle-upon-Tyne, in a helpful letter of 7 April, 1997. Here Mr Frankis drew my attention to the fact that, in one of the Old English *Riddles* preserved in the Exeter Book, dating most probably from the late tenth century,[54] the Old English adjective *banleas*, meaning 'boneless' and cognate with the Icelandic and Faroese expressions, is used in a clear context of sexual potency. The riddle in question – no. 43 as edited by Craig Williamson in his edition of the Old English *Riddles* of the Exeter Book[55] – may be quoted here from Michael Alexander's translation of a selection of these riddles, where it is numbered 45:

> I have heard of something hatched in a corner:
> It thrusts, rustles, raises its hat.
> A bride grabbed at that boneless thing,
> Handled it proudly: a prince's daughter
> Covered that swelling creature with her robe.[56]

The accepted correct answer to this riddle is 'dough', but it is obvious that the riddle is making joking use of ambiguity, comparing the need for kneading in the making of bread to the need for a helping hand in bringing about a state of full male potency.[57] Since an expression meaning 'boneless' thus occurs in a context of sexual potency in an English source dating from the late tenth century, and since the name and nickname of Ívarr are linked with impotence in an Icelandic source (*Ragnarssona þáttr*) dating from the early fourteenth,[58] it now seems to me that one should hesitate before using the thirteenth-century evidence of Roger of Wendover on the one hand, and that of modern Norwegian and Faroese folk tradition on the other, in support of the view that the association with the wind was the original connotation of the nickname, at least until evidence for this association can be found from as early as, or earlier than, the Exeter Book, which does, after all date from within roughly a hundred years of the lifetime of Ívarr's likely historical

---

53 *Ibid.*, 28-9.
54 Williamson (1977), 3-4.
55 *Ibid.*, 96-7.
56 Alexander (1980), 40.
57 Cf. Williamson (1977), 282-3.
58 See the first reference given under note 5, above. It may be significant in this context that, as has recently been pointed out by Haldane (1996), 43, 'boner' is a frequent word for an erection in some dialects of English.

prototype.[59] Until such evidence is found, I would follow John Frankis in suggesting that this historical figure was originally nicknamed 'Boneless' either for a reason connected in some way with sexual potency (or, perhaps, because of a severed leg or legs, remembering the evidence of *Ragnars saga* that he had to be carried everywhere, and bearing in mind the fact that *bein* could also mean 'leg' in Old Norse, as it does in Modern German; and that the association with the wind was a secondary development, made when expressions meaning 'boneless' or 'legless' had come to be applied to the wind, very likely (in the light of the arguments of this paper) by the early- to mid- thirteenth century.[60]

---

59 On this prototype, who most probably died in 873, see McTurk (1991b), 39-49.
60 The fact that John Frankis's observations have made it necessary for me to modify my main argument in this way does not, of course, make me any the less grateful to him for them.

Come All Ye Dry-Land Sailors!
Comic Voyages in Irish Song Tradition

Tom Munnelly

Introduction

The attitude of any maritime nation towards the sea is always a combination of affection and gratitude for its bounty and respect for, and fear of, its strength and unpredictability. Although a sustainer of life, this facilitator of travel could cause any journey to end in death, and leave the dependants of the fisherman or traveller, not only without sustenance, but even without a provider. Indeed, even entire families and complete ships' crews could perish in sea tragedies brought about by nautical incompetence, inadequate vessels, or by the inexorable cruelty of the sea as an unyielding and predatory primeval force. In such circumstances, when man feels powerless before forces over which he has no control, a common protective technique has been to adopt an attitude of nonchalence – 'whistling past the graveyard', so to speak – though, perhaps, this is an inappropriate analogy, as, among many seafaring communities whistling, it was believed, could call up a storm. While laughing at danger may not necessarily lessen a feeling of jeopardy, it may, nevertheless, instil a sense of confidence which – even if it is false – may assist one in facing forces which might otherwise be considered unnerving. It is not my contention that all the songs I am about to discuss were motivated by such reasoning, for many were, no doubt, composed with probably nothing more than entertainment in mind. However, I am suggesting that even these songs may owe something of their popularity to the uneasy relationship which exists between the Irish as an island people and the sea which surrounds us.

This relationship has been explored in ancient sources such as those in which the adventures of the famous St Brendan the Voyager are documented. In this context we may recall the episode in which he and his monks prepared a fire on an island only to discover that they had disembarked onto the back of the whale, Jasconius.[1] Oddly, having made good their escape with divine aid, they later proceeded to repeat the exercise, this time in the full knowledge that what they clambered upon was a whale and not an island. Once aboard, –

> they proceeded to sing the praises of the Lord all night, and to say their Masses in the morning. When the Masses had concluded, Jasconius moved away, all of them being still on its back; and the brethren cried aloud to the Lord: 'Hear us, O Lord, the God of our salvation.' But St. Brendan encouraged them:

---

1 O'Donoghue (1994), 127-8.

'Why are you so alarmed? Fear not, for no evil shall befall us, as we have here only a helper on our journey.' The great whale swam in a direct course towards the shore of the Paradise of Birds, where it landed them all unharmed, and on this island they sojourned until the Octave of Pentecost.[2]

At a didactic level, we can appreciate that the writer is seeking to demonstrate the love of God and his omnipotence over even the greatest creatures of land and sea. At another level we can see that, on the face of it, the monks themselves do not appear to have been among the brightest of God's creatures. On another island, they come across a spring of limpid water and begin to drink. For no apparent reason, Brendan warns them –

Take heed, my brethren, that you use this water in moderation. But the brethren paid not equal heed to this caution, for some drank only one cup of the water, others drank two cups; so that upon some of them there felt a sudden stupor, which lasted for the space of three days and nights; when upon others it befell only for one day and night; but St. Brendan prayed without ceasing to God to help them, as they incurred this great danger through ignorance. When three days had passed, the father said to his companions: 'Let us, my children, hasten away from this fatal place, lest greater evil befall you; the Lord had given you refreshment, but you have turned it to your detriment.'[3]

So they leave, but every man made sure to bring a cup of the marvellous water with him.

Maol Dúin and his voyagers encounter a similar source of intoxication on the Island of the Miraculous Fountain. However, this spring exhibited more varied and abstemious qualities, yielding –

whey or water on Fridays and Wednesdays, milk on Sundays and feasts of martyrs, and ale and wine on the feasts of Mary, of John the Baptist, and on the high tides of the year.[4]

The juice of the fruit on the Isle of Intoxicating Wine-Fruits was so inebriating that when Maol Dúin drank it, it –

threw him into a sleep of intoxication so deep that he seemed to be in a trance rather than in a natural slumber, without breath or motion, and with red foam on his lips. And from that hour till the same hour the next day, no one could tell whether he was living or dead. When he awoke the next day, he bade his people to gather as much of the fruit as they could bring away with them; for the world, as he told them, never produced anything of such surpassing goodness.[5]

---

2 *Ibid.*, 172-3.
3 *Ibid.*, 142-3.
4 Rolleston (1949), 320-1.
5 Joyce (1879), 156-7.

We do not know what the tipple of the inhabitants of the Island of the Laughing Folk may have been, but so infectious was their gaiety that Maol Dúin's foster brother who went ashore was unable to return to his companions, just as one of Bran's crew, having gone ashore on the Island of Joy became as one with the permanently laughing local population and had to be abandoned there.

In later times, the ostensibly comic dimensions of voyaging in the older Irish tradition is complemented in the wider European context by accounts such as that contained in Sebastian Brandt's *Narrenschiff* (published in Swabian in 1492). Here we learn of the shipping of blockheads from many locations and classes to the Land of Fools where they were reprimanded for their fatuous ways. More moralising than humorous, Brandt's poem was translated and adapted to English conditions by Alexander Barclay who published his version – *The Ship of Fools* – in 1509. Another sixteenth-century satire in verse, *Cocke Lorrell's Bote* tells of a voyage through England by the rascally eponymous tinker who engages various trades-people to join the voyage and gives unflattering accounts of them. Similar catalogues of individuals make up a significant number of the songs concerning humorous voyages in Irish tradition.[6]

I believe the most abundant of this type to be the song form known as 'Skellig Lists'. There was a tradition that Easter was celebrated a week later on Sceilg Mhíchíl, the site of an ancient monastic settlement on a barren sea-stack off the coast of Kerry; and thus those unmarried men and women who had missed their chance on the mainland could still get married on the Skelligs during Lent when the rite of matrimony was prohibited elsewhere in Ireland.

> Local poets were encouraged to compose verses on the occasion, verses which told of a grand sea excursion to the Skelligs, praised the splendid vessel which would take the party there and gave a long list of the participants, *linking together the names of the bachelors and old maids as incongruously as possible*. (My italics).[7]

These verses enjoyed huge popularity in the nineteenth century. Crofton Croker estimated that in 1836 no less than 30,000 copies were printed and sold in a matter of days.[8] These verses, which were always published anonymously, could be very scurrilous indeed and were not always taken in good spirits by the parties described in them. The practice of making Skellig Lists continued, adapting itself to contemporary situations over the generations. For instance, in a List of 1941, the voyagers encounter a German submarine.[9] The custom of making this verse-form lampooning the unmarried continues sporadically to this day.

6 Although directly related, comic terrestrial journeys, from the quixotic *The Irish Hudibras* (attrib. James Farewell, 1689) to such ballads as *The Dingle Puck Goat* are beyond the scope of this essay.
7 Danaher (1972), 49.
8 Croker (1839), 126-8. In the Madden Collection held in Cambridge University are 179 Skellig Lists on large quarto sheets purchased from Croker's library in 1854. All are from Cork printers. (Madden 24, Irish Ballads, vol. 1. Microfilm 1805).
9 'The Longfellow's List', *IFC* 813:281-304. Kerry, 1941 (where *IFC* = the Main Manuscripts Collection of the Department of Irish Folklore at University College Dublin, and the numbers on either side of the colon indicate the volume number and page number[s] respectively).

Any attempt to evaluate the humour of previous generations, never mind that of previous centuries, is likely to be a perilous pursuit at the best of times. As contexts mutate and disappear over time, one generation's wonder can easily prove be the next generation's incongruity. With this *caveat* in mind I will now proceed to look at a selection of Irish songs in the English language about travel on water.

Comic Voyages : Sea Travel

A common motif used in Irish songs in English is the wonder (feigned or real) expressed by the simple countryman on encountering the sophistication of the city. So too, Poor Paddy from the bogs of Ireland is amazed on seeing his first ship:

> The next place they sent me was down to the sea,
> On board of a warship bound for the Crimea.
> Three sticks in the middle all rowled round with sheets,
> Faith, she walked thro' the water without any feet.
> ('The Kerry Recruit')[10]

Likewise, the press gang who capture Patrick O'Neal get no bargain:

> They scampered away, as they thought, with a prize,
> Taking me for a sailor, you see, in disguise,
> But a terrible blunder they made in their strife,
> For I ne'er saw a ship nor the sea in my life.
> Then straight to a tender they made me repair,
> But of tenderness divil a morsel was there!
> Och, I ramped and I cursed, but it did not avail,
> Till a great swimming castle met Patrick O'Neal.[11]
> ('Patrick O'Neal')[12]

---

10 Laws J 8. O'Lochlainn (1939), 2-3. In *'The Antelope'* Darby has never seen a ship before and describes her as having two trees growing in the middle of her, two wheels splashing water on each side, and a man pushing her with a bit of a stick. Collected in Fermanagh by Michael J. Murphy from Eddy Kieve, *IFC* 1803:97-9.

11 The colloquial pronunciation of O'Neill as 'O'Neal' (Irish: *Ó Néill*) recalls a confidence trick by which innocent emigrants were duped by unscrupulous shipping agents. They promised the emigrant passage on a *mail* boat which, being government controlled, would be swift and clean, but when the emigrant went to embark he found he had bought steerage on an old tub used for conveying corn or Indian meal (pronounced 'male'), (Hugill [1969], 47.) Conversely, a notorious boarding-house keeper, Paddy West, ran an 'Academy' and he gave certificates stating that his 'cadets' (who had only been with him a few days) had 'crossed The Line' four times and been around 'The Horn six times.' He conveniently forgot to mention that 'The Line' was not, as implied, the Equator, but a piece of string on his kitchen floor. And 'the Horn' was not Cape Horn but an old cow's horn in his parlour! (Hugill [1969], 47). See also Hugill (1961) and Hugill (1977), 80-1.

12 Huntington, Herrmann, Moulden (1990), eds., 102.

Once on board ship the actual voyage itself is seldom to Paddy's liking:

> For Amerikay, darlint, ye'll think it is quare -
> Is twenty times furder than Cork from Kildare;
> And the say is that broad, and the waves are that high,
> Ye're tossed like a fut-ball 'twixt wather and sky;
> And ye fale like a pratie just burstin' the skin,
> That all ye can do is to howld yerself in.
> ('Pat's Letter')[13]

> From there I got away, my spirits never failin'
> Landed on the quay just as the ship was sailin';
> Captain at me roared, said that no room had he,
> When I jumped on board, a cabin found for Paddy.
> Down among the pigs; I played some funny rigs,
> Danced some hearty jigs, the water round me bubblin'
> When off Hollyhead, I wished myself was dead,
> Or better far instead, on the rocky road to Dublin.
> ('The Rocky Road to Dublin')[14]

> Up wint the ship - oh, dear! sez I,
> Up wint my accounts that very minute,
> Then down to Hell or very nigh
> I thought, by gosh! I was half-way in it;
> The big waves broke out our mast of smoke.
> It was no joke, at dead of night, then,
> For sails and riggin both danced a jig in
> The gale beneath the moon's dim light, thin.
> ('Paddy's Trip to America')[15]

> Well, I was not very far out on the sea,
> When first there came thunder and then there came rain;
> I wish in me heart I was home again,
> The waves began rolling, the ship was a-holing,
> And every blow to the devil we'd go,
> There come in a big wave, knocked me out in the sea,
> I was there in despair, saying a prayer,
> When one come behind, more swift than the wind,
> And knocked me right in on top of some men;
> Says one: 'For your jumping I'll give you a thumping.'
> So he up with his stick and he gave me a lick

---

13 Wright (1975), 411.
14 O Lochlainn (1939), 103.
15 Wright (1975), 589.

And he knocked me down flat on the broad of me back,
A sailor come by, 'Arrah, master,' says I,
'Bring me home to me father, to me sisters and brothers,
And I swear on the Book that if I get home I'll never more roam
. On the boat that first brought me over.'
('The Boat That First Brought Me Over')[16]

The theme of storms and the hazard of shipwreck occur as the subjects of the songwriters' attention, both in the serious songs and in the humorous ballads. The dangers of the crossing constitute a large part of travel and emigration ballads, but in the songs under examination here they are merely windmills which will be successfully tilted by the guileless, but always victorious, Paddy. His method of emigration may itself be a subject for humour as in the song called 'Innocent Mike':

I didn't pay me passage, kase I was smuggled o'er
The great and wide Atlantic, to friends upon this shore,
They put me in a barrel, and fastened it down tight,
So that's the way they smuggled me, meself poor Innocent Mike.
('Innocent Mike')[17]

Unfortunately the barrel had two nails projecting inside it which caused Mike great distress when it is rolled about on the deck. Other adventures during the voyage include encounters with pirates as in 'Captain Coulston', but in this case the passengers had special protection:

The number of the passengers was three hundred and sixty two
And they were all teetotallers, excepting one or two.
The lemonade was passed around to nourish them at sea
And Father Matthew medals they wore unto Americay.
('Captain Coulston')[18]

---

16 Sung by Thomas Moran, county Leitrim. See *Topic Records* 12T194. Cf. Wright (1975), 594.
17 Wright (1975), 563.
18 Ranson (1948), 78-9. Mrs Brigid Tunney of Beleek, county Fermanagh, sang a fragment which included the verse:
From the eleventh to the twenty-eight we sailed upon the sea
All bound for New York City, it was our chief desire.
We shoved about the lemonade to nourish us on seal
And Father Matthew's medals we brought to Americay.
(BBC recording no. 18528).
Her son, Paddy Tunney, includes a similar version in his textually-complete version on the long-playing record *The Flowery Vale*. See Tunney 1976. Peter Donnelly of Castlecaulfield, county Tyrone, omits the verse in his rendition. See Donnelly (BBC 18531) and Sam Henry's informant, Alexander Horner of Mosside, county Derry, does not sing it either (Huntington, Herrmann, Moulden [1990], eds., 113). It is most likely that this verse was dropped from some singer's texts because they felt it reduced the gravitas of a serious song.

When I quoted that verse in an article in *Béaloideas* in 1980[19] it was intended by me as an example of satire on the Temperance Movement of Fr. Matthew.[20] On reflection, however, I am not at all sure that that was the intention of the verse. In fact, I would now be almost certain that this song, 'one of the most popular ballads on the Wexford coast' according to the collector Joseph Ranson[21] is totally serious in its praise of Father Matthew, 'the Apostle of Temperance' in the nineteenth century. Here we have an example of the dangers, mentioned earlier, of applying the modes of thought of our generation to earlier times.

'George's Quay' or 'The Forgetful Sailor' is a parody on the extremely popular song-type in which the fair damsel dons male attire and goes searching for her sailor lover. In this case Mary's quest is for Johnny Doyle, the father of her now grown child who had left her years before and sailed –

>... ....for foreign waters,
>To China where they're very wise,
>and drown at birth their surplus daughters.
>
>Now years and years have past and gone
>and Mary's child is self-supporting,
>And Mary's heart is fit to break
>when that young buck goes out a-courting;
>'And so,' says she, 'on one fine day
>he'll leave me lone and melancholy,
>I'll dress me up in sailor's clothes
>and scour the seven seas for Johnny.'
>
>She shipped aboard a pirate bold
>which raided on the hot equator,
>And with these hairy buccaneers
>there sailed this sweet and virtuous crathur;[22]
>The Captain thought her name was Bill,
>his character was most nefarious,
>Consorting with this heinous beast
>her situation was precarious.
>('George's Quay', or, 'The Forgetful Sailor')[23]

The orthodox broadsheet ballads which this song parodies almost invariably have the female as the searcher after the male lover. The majority of such quest ballads

---

19 Munnelly (1980-1981), 30-58.
20 This movement was founded at Cork on 10 April, 1838.
21 Munnelly (1980-1981), 79.
22 'Creature'.
23 Written by Jimmy Montgomery. Quoted from O Lochlainn (1965), 176-7. Under the misnomer 'Johnny Doyle' this song can be heard sung by the Dublin singer Frank Harte. See Harte (1973).

are wholly serious,[24] with only occasional texts such as 'The Handsome Cabin Boy' (Laws N 13) in which comic elements dominate the narrative. In this song the ship's crew are amazed when the 'cabin boy' gives birth to a child. If not overtly comic, 'Short Jacket and White Trousers' (Laws N 12) is at least whimsical. Here the captain is attracted to a pretty sailor among his crew and wishes the sailor was a maid. Unfortunately for the captain she is safely ashore before he discovers that she really *was* a female! Similarly the song known in Ireland as 'The Astrologer' (Laws N 6) tells of the disguised heroine who is actually a bunkmate of her lover who had been pressed to sea. He has no inkling of her sex or identity until she tells him! This song-type aside, in the burlesque ballads which concern us here, the protagonists are more usually male and constitute a motley crew in the full sense of that expression.

And here we come back to the catalogue of characters, a device favoured in the composition of 'Skellig Lists'[25] and utilised in other forms in Ireland, particularly in songs telling of the individuals assembled for house-dances and listing their attributes in very uncomplimentary detail. Stereotypes in the comic sea-related songs dictate that the crew are drunken, licentious and incompetent, and very often they wreck the ship for good measure. On the barque, the Campanayro:

> The skipper was a dandy-O, far too fond o' brandy-O.[26]

On the Ebenezer:

> The Old Man wuz a drunken geezer / Couldn't sail the Ebenezer [27]

The captain of the Mary Ann McHugh is uncouth:

> The Captain's name was Duff / His manners they were rough [28]

The master of the Calabar is not exactly heroic either:

> The Captain was a strapping youth
> His height being four foot two.

---

24 They constitute a significant percentage of the total of 'forebitters' (non-work songs sung by ships' crews in their leisure time). It is noteworthy that Stan Hugill, generally regarded as the most authoritative writer on songs of the sea, goes so far as to say that most forebitters were of Irish origin (Hugill [1969], 230). See also Munnelly (1980-81), 34-5.
25 Danaher (1972), 49; Croker (1839), 126-8.
26 Hugill (1969), 471. *IFC* 1151:344-5, 'The Barque Carabinero' is another version of the story found in a manuscript presented to the Irish Folklore Commission in 1948. This manuscript contains songs in English sung by Swedish sailors in the Skanör region, Skåne and was written c. 1900. The song is also sung by Bill Cameron of the Scilly Isles, see *Topic Records* 12T194.
27 Hugill (1969), 476-7.
28 De Burgh Daly (1980), 61. A recording of this song sung by Séamus Ennis of Dublin was made on 30 August 1947 by the BBC (Recording no. 16119).

His eyes were red, his ears were green
His nose was a Prussian blue.
('The Cruise of the Calabar')[29]

In the bawdy song, 'The Good Ship Venus':

The captain's name was slugger,
He was a dirty bugger
He wasn't fit to shovel ****
On any bugger's lugger.
('The Good Ship Venus ')[30]

And the catalogue of stereotypes goes on; the cook is always drunk, the mates are hard task-masters and life below decks is unmitigated hell for sailor and passenger alike.

As we already noted above, storm and shipwreck are the most frequently encountered trauma on the high seas, and, consequently, they are themes we will be returning to repeatedly. In 'Paddy's Trip to America' the poor emigrant finds himself terrified among the bedlam of a storm-tossed ship:

The captain cried - mate, I shouted - dhrink,
The ship has struck, she'll go assundher,
We reel upon the grave's thin brink,
That moment our cargo was boults of tundher,
The engines melted, the hailstones pelted,
And faith, I felt it, dear, mighty quarely;
The vessel parted, and so I started
For shore on my stick that morning airly.
('Paddy's Trip to America')[31]

A shipwreck can be the starting point for another series of adventures, for instance, Paddy may vanish Jonah-like down the throat of a whale to reside there for several weeks before emerging:

Now Pat he got scared and he made for the mast.
With his arms wrapped around it, 'twas there he held fast,
But the ship made a heave and poor Pat lost his grip

---

29 Healy (1967), 121.
30 See Green (1967), 68. 'The Good Ship Venus' is still 'afloat' in oral tradition outside of the locker room, in Ireland and elsewhere. The only version to be noted in *IFC* is incomplete and lacks the verse about the captain himself; see, 'The captain's wife was Mabel', in *IFC* 1970: 185-6 (Dublin, 1980).
31 Wright (1975), 590.

And 'tis down the whale's throat the poor lad he did slip.
With me fal de dal, al de dal, al de dal ee.
Now Pat he began for to roar, bawl and shout,
Or to look for a hole or some place to get out.
'Arra musha,' sez he, 'I've been into a row.
I was on a big ship, but sure where am I now?'
With me fal de dal, al de dal, al de dal ee.

For a month and five days in this whale he did stop
Till one fine summer's day in his throat he did pop.
'Let me out now,' sez Pat,'or your teeth out I'll screw.'
But the whale let a belch and on land Paddy flew.
With me fal de dal, al de dal, al de dal ee.
('Paddy and the Whale')[32]

Another 'man overboard', who was not exactly a fatality, is the merman who is discovered when a ship drops its anchor on his underwater house. He says he had once been a sailor, was washed overboard, married a mermaid and grew a tail.[33] It is worth mentioning that this is a burlesque inversion of the medieval account of the ship seen in the air over Clonmacnoise which dropped its anchor down among some praying monks. The anchor got snagged on the church and the sailors from the airborne ship swam down through the air to free the anchor and encountered the monks on the ground.[34]

Most of the craft in our songs have noteworthy bills of lading. The Ragamuffin is almost ordinary in that she is bringing to Calcutta a cargo of Irish butter, pig's cheek and bacon.[35] The Calabar carries a mere half-ton of coal, the Bugaboo is a turf-boat. On the other hand, the narrator in the Irish Rover says that, beside its main cargo of bricks:

We had one million bags of the best Sligo rags,
We had two million barrels of stone,
We had three million sides of ould blind horses' hides
We had four million barrels of bone,
We had five million hogs, we had six million dogs,
We had seven million barrels of porter,

32 'Paddy and the Whale' sung by Paddy Berry, *IFC* 1326d/1, Recorded by T. Munnelly, October 1995. See Berry (1987), 17, and Palmer (1980), 32. When the tipsy 'Ben Backstay, the Boatswain' is devoured by a shark his ghost returns to warn his shipmates: '... never mix your liquor, lads, but always drink it neat.' See Holloway & Black (1979), 176-7.
33 *IFC* 736:474-6 'The Merman' (Laws K 24) collected from Seán 'Hamit' Uí Aodha by Seán Ua Cróinín, Cork, 1940.
34 *Q.v.* 'A Ship seen in the Air', Bergin *et al.* (1910), eds., 8-9. Cf. Todd (1848), 210-2. I am indebted to Professor Dáithí Ó hÓgáin for these references.
35 *IFC* 1971:41-5, Dublin, 1979.

We had eight million bales of ould nanny goats' tails
On board the Irish Rover.
('The Irish Rover')[36]

The Donegal parody of 'The Irish Rover', entitled 'The Mulroy Rover' has a similarly diverse cargo:

We were filled fore and aft from the keel to the taft
With hard hats, donkey shoes and horses reins.
We'd a dozen clocking hens, a score of cock wrens
With their tails sticking out straight behind
We had fifty tom-cats and a pair of black rats
And a half a ton of clover,
We had a barrow full of holes and ten donkey foals
In the hold of the Mulroy Rover.
('The Mulroy Rover') [37]

The Mary Jane also carried an unusual cargo:

The Mary Jane was a one-mast ship,
She was built in the town of Taghmon,
She carried a crew of a hundred and two
With a cargo of farmer's dung.
('The Wreck of the Mary Jane')[38]

Not only were the cargoes somewhat exotic, but so too were the gifts brought back by these gallant voyagers to their faithful Penelopes at home. The navigator who goes to sail on the thirteenth lock tells his love to:

.... calm your woman's fears,
And I'll bring to thee a chimpanzee,
A parrot, a jabberwock,
A kangaroo and a cockatoo
From the wilds of the Thirteenth Lock, yo, ho!
('The Thirteenth Lock')[39]

Cockatoos were also in demand by the lover of the sailor on 'The Good Ship Kangaroo.'
Our vessel she was homeward bound from many a foreign shore,

---

36 Crofts (1966).
37 Written by Hugh Friel about 1948. Recorded by Ann Kerr, county Donegal in 1974; *IFC* 1854:57-60.
38 O Lochlainn (1939), 40.
39 O Lochlainn (1965), 3.

And many a foreign present unto my love I bore.
I brought tortoises from Tenerife and ties from Timbucktoo,
A China rat, a Bengal cat, and a Bombay cockatoo.
('The Good Ship Kangaroo')[40]

The Mary Jane was likewise bound for Timbuktu, and in another song, Nancy awaits the return of her bonny boy in blue, in anticipation of presents from that same port:

He's going to bring an elephant, a monkey and a bear
And a bunch of foreign feathers to match his Nancy's hair.
He's going to bring a hurley-stick that came from Timbuktu,
Just as a present to his Nan from her bonny boy in blue.
('My Bonny Boy in Blue')[41]

Comic Voyages : Inland Waterways-Canals

Up to the late 1950s canal barges were still commonplace throughout Ireland carrying various cargoes, but in particular Guinness's stout from the Dublin brewery at James' Gate and turf (peat) from the central bogs to the cities for fuel. Generations of city children used to stand on the canal bridges and shout to the bargemen to 'bring us back a parrot.' The extremely leisurely pace of these horse-drawn barges and their diesel-powered successors, with their continuous proximity to land, have always made them appear vaguely ridiculous in comparison to their ocean-going sisters. This incongruity has acted as a spur to humorous song-makers for more than a century and has resulted in a whole genre of mock heroic adventures on the inland waterways of Ireland.

Much of the humour in these songs is drawn from the fact that the action takes place within familiar, frequently urban, surroundings, though the deeds described would be more usually associated with epic tales of adventure on the high seas:

Come all ye dry-land sailors bold and listen to my song.
There are only forty verses, so I won't detain you long,
'Tis all about the history of a bold young Irish tar,
Who sailed as man before the mast on board of the Calabar.
('The Cruise of the Calabar')[42]
Come all ye lads who plough the seas and also seize the plough,

---

40 Hugill (1969) 476, contributed by Séamus Ennis from the singing of Mrs Elizabeth Cronin, Baile Mhúirne, County Cork. Written by the music-hall performer, Harry Clifton (1832-1872) and published in 1856. See Shuldham-Shaw, Lyle and Petrie (1995), 572.
41 Munnelly (1994), 137-9.
42 O Lochlainn (1965), 34.

> The cruise of a canal boat I am telling to ye now
> It was the Mary Ann McHugh that braved the angry surf
> And bore away from Mullingar with a terrible load of turf.
> (The Mary Ann McHugh)[43]

The vessel is usually described as having a draught of twenty inches or less, and her method of locomotion is another favourite target of the song-writers:

> The engine was of one-horse power,
> propelled wid a blackthorn stick,
> Wid the wind astarn, and filled with corn,
> the horse went a terrible lick.
> ('The Mary Ann McHugh')[44]

The Calabar's crew defend themselves with cutlasses and Gatling-guns when attacked by pirates in the Dublin suburban village of Clondalkin or, in another version, in central Belfast. And, *in extremis*:

> 'Put on more steam', the Captain cried,
> 'For we are sorely pressed',
> But the engineer from the bank replied
> 'The horse is doing his best.'
> ('The Cruise of the Calabar')[45]

> The morning that we left Taghmon
> Our ship ran short of wind,
> So the crew had to get right out in the wet
> And everyone shove behind.
> ('The Wreck of the Mary Jane')[46]

The Dublin Gas-works figures largely on the navigational charts covering these voyages; the lighter Avondale:

> Unto the Gasworks she was bound, with horse-power, sail and pole,
> When she became a total loss with thirteen tons of coal.
> ('The Wreck of the Avondale')[47]

---

43 By Percy French: see De Burgh Daly (1980), 61.
44 *Ibid.*, 61. Percy French also wrote 'The Cruise of the Pirate Bus' about two mechanics who steal a bus and ply the city of London picking up illegal fares and cargo. In its use of nautical terminology to add to the humour, this ballad is obviously a parody of the parody song-form under discussion here. *Ibid.*, 138-9.
45 Hammond (1978), 33.
46 O Lochlainn (1939), 40.
47 O Lochlainn (1965), 228.

On board the Fury:
>Little Mick gave a shudder
>When ordered to rudder
>And steer for the Gashouse Chimley.
>('Changing Berth')[48]

The Gwendoline is wrecked when:
>... the day grew dark, and our bounding bark
>Was struck by a sudden squall;
>The captain grew pale in the driving gale,
>As we swept by the Gashouse wall.
>('The Wreck of the Gwendoline')[49]

The 'Vanderdecken' or 'Flying Dutchman' theme is parodied in Arthur Griffith's ballad 'The Thirteenth Lock' in which the reckless skipper and his crew ignore the dire warnings of a grey-haired mariner and a distressed maiden and sail to the ill-fated canal lock. Unable to see landfall on the shore of Inchicore the lookout at the masthead recommends anchoring in the Bay of Dolphin's Barn. For his trouble he finds a grave 'neath the deep blue wave'. The captain warns the remainder of his crew:

>'Thus ever', quoth he, 'perish mutiny.'
>And he turned him with a smile
>About and round and lo! he found
>A shape behind the while
>With fiery eyes and horns of size
>And a tail that might Pether shock;
>At the skippers gape up spake the shape -
>'I'm bound for the Thirteenth Lock
>Ho-ho!
>I'm bound for the Thirteenth Lock'.

And, like the bootless ladies who await Sir Patrick Spens, the maiden awaits the return of her sailor:

>By the harbour a maiden stands
>With her gaze fixed out to sea;
>But she'll watch in vain, for never again
>Will he come with that chimpanzee.
>('The Thirteenth Lock')[50]

---

48 *Ibid.*, 233.
49 *Ibid.*, 257.
50 By Arthur Griffith (1871-1922), and included in his satiric play *The Conspirators*, of which only acts two and three seem to have survived; see Béaslaí (n.d.), 6-13. See also, O'Lochlainn (1965), 3. This ballad echoes 'James Harris or, The DÆMON Lover' (Child 243).

Yet another, this time anonymous, ballad on supernatural happenings at a canal lock in Cork tells us that:

> Every night of the year, about twelve of the clock
> The ghosts and the spooks of Draferteen flock
> Sit swinging their bodies all this and that way
> And mournfully singin' 'Right Toor-al-i-ay'.
> There once was a Captain both gallant and bold
> And he laughed at the warnings of young and of old
> 'D'ye think', he'd remark and most scornfully say
> 'That I'd fear a dead ghost singin' 'Toor-al-i-ay'?
> ('Toor-al-i-ay')[51]

Once again the captain disregards the warnings, with fatal consequences.

A tragedy shared by both the Mary Ann McHugh and the Calabar is the wreckage of the boat which happens when they strike an uncharted lump of coal in the canal. The Captain of the Bugaboo has the unfortunate habit of smoking his pipe in bed and so sets his ship alight, and, as a consequence –

> ... a thousand sods of Terf and eleven Million Fleas
> went to blazes in the Bug-a-boo.
> ('The Bug-a-boo')[52]

Although the narrators of the sea-going Irish Rover and the Mulroy Rover are, according to the ballad, sole survivors of the disaster which happened to them, crews of other wrecked vessels are not always so unfortunate. The luckless company of the canal boat the Calibar receive assistance from shore in a somewhat unlikely manner:

> So we all fell into the water
> And let out a terrible roar
> There was a farmer standing there
> He threw us the end of his galluses
> And he pulled us all ashore.
> ('The Cruise of the Calibar')[53]

The crew of the Gwendoline whom we last observed as being storm-bound resolve their plight by putting a plank on to the Tipperary shore:

---

51 Healy (1962), 47-8. Healy actually entitles this song 'The Ballad of The Thirteenth Lock' but says it was known to his family as 'Toor-al-i-ay'. He undoubtedly used the former title because of his familiarity with Griffith's ballad.
52 *Ibid.*, 46.
53 Hammond (1978), 33. It may be noted here that matters of scansion do not greatly concern the writers of these ballads, and lines could be contracted or extended casually by the use of *recitative*.

> Then we walked ashore, half dead or more,
> The dog, and myself, and the tar,
> And we shouted 'Ahoy' to a creamery boy,
> And went home in an ass an' car.
> ('The Wreck of the Gwendoline')[54]

> As the skipper's voice sank.
> They jumped out on the bank,
> And walked home by the Gashouse Chimley.
> ('Changing Berth')[55]

Undoubtedly, the most frequently recurring motif in these comic voyages is the resolve to try seafaring by some other means of transport:

> Now Pat was once more on his own native shore
> And he vowed he not go near those big ships no more.
> But whenever oul' England he wanted to see,
> It would be when the tramway went over the sea!
> ('Paddy and the Whale')[56]

Pat invites Mary to join him in America but warns her:

> Ochone! but, me jewel, the say may be grand,
> But when ye come over, dear, *travel by land!*
> ('Pat's Letter')[57]

And perhaps most tellingly of all:

> No more I'll be a sailor
> To sail the raging main
> And the next time I go to Portadown
> I'll go by the bloody train.
> ('The Cruise of the Calibar')[58]

The Irish Navy

Finally, it is worth noting that the Irish Navy itself has not escaped the satiric pen of the songwriter. From the foundation of the Irish Free State in 1921, until it encountered the responsibilities entailed in joining the Common Market in 1972,

54 *Ibid.*, 258.
55 O Lochlainn (1965), 234.
56 Berry, *IFC* 1326d/1.
57 Wright (1975), 411.
58 Hammond (1978), 33.

this maritime nation had fewer government naval vessels than Switzerland. In the 1940s the Muirchu was the backbone of the naval coast-guard. A rusting old ex-British gunboat, she was regarded with affectionate derision by the people of Ireland. In 1947 she set out on her final voyage from Haulbowline to the Hammond Lane scrapyard in Dublin, but she never made it:

> We joined the Muirchu me boys
> To fight thro' shot and shell-
> We got half-shot in Cobh, me boys
> To brave the ocean's swell.
>
> We started out for Dublin Town
> The Captain steered us straight
> But when we reached the ocean
> The poor oul' ship was bate
> She took one look at the rolling sea
> And knew she could not do
> So off the coast of Wexford
> We lost the Muirchu.
> ('The Sinking of the Muirchu')[59]

Even when the Navy was strengthened by the addition of the vessels Clíona, Maedhbh and Macha, the belief persisted that the sailors disembarked each evening and went home to their beds every night:

> Each year they go on manoeuvres,
> To prepare for defence they are keen.
> Sometimes it's the Lakes of Killarney;
> More often the pond in the Green.[60]
>
> We are a seafaring nation
> Defence of our land is a right;
> We'll fight like the divil all morning
> Provided we're home by the night.
>
> The Clíona, the Maedhbh and the Macha.
> The pride of the Irish Navy;
> When the Captain he blows on his whistle
> All the sailors go home for their tea.
> ('The Irish Navy')[61]

---

59 Healy (1962), 52-2. Written by Healy himself.
60 The pond in St Stephen's Green, Dublin!
61 Sung by The Dubliners; see The Dubliners (1968).

Conclusion

An abundance of similar kinds of songs exists apart from the examples chosen to illustrate this article. I hope that a sufficient sample has been quoted here to demonstrate the preoccupations of the writers who have used this genre as a vehicle for burlesque humour and satire. The use of selected verses from different ballads to illustrate the genre means that the integrity of the individual ballads has been unavoidably disrupted. As with any songs, only in their complete form can they be judged fairly, and I would, therefore, recommend to the reader to enjoy them in their entirety, and conclude by expressing my conviction that ballads of comic voyages represent some of the wittiest songs in the Irish song repertoire.

Tadhg, Donncha and Some of their Relations: Seals in Irish Oral Tradition

Bairbre Ní Fhloinn

I

The relationship between mankind and the environment is a subject of ongoing lively interest and debate. Different communities evolve different ways of viewing and of living with their natural surroundings, in accordance with their various needs and value-systems. Traditional societies have their own understanding of the order of things, and the beliefs and narratives of such societies offer us an insight into popular perceptions of the natural world, and of mankind's place within the greater scheme. In this context, we might also remember that the distinction between the natural world and the supernatural is often a subjective one, determined largely by culture.[1]

This article attempts to provide an outline of some of the beliefs and stories relating to one small part of the natural world, as recorded from Irish oral tradition. They concern a group of creatures commonly found around the coasts of Ireland – namely, *pinnipedia* or, to most of us, seals.

The coast-line of Ireland is a rugged and a rocky one, for the most part, full of inlets and indentations, with countless numbers of caves and coves. Such an environment provides an ideal habitat for the various kinds of seals which breed in their hundreds around the coasts. An Irish naturalist writes:

> Seals . . . are aquatically-adapted mammals with the limbs so highly modified for swimming that they are only able to move rather clumsily on land, where they come to calve. They are represented in Ireland by two species which commonly live on the coast – namely the Grey or Atlantic Seal (*Halichoerus grypus*), and the Common Seal (*Phoca vitulina*). The Grey Seal is common all around Ireland, and breeds in caves on Lambay Island, within fifteen miles of Dublin . . . The Grey Seal is a northern species which is not common in

---

1 As an illustration of this point in an Irish context, see, for example, Ó hEochaidh, Ní Néill & Ó Catháin, 34-5, where the following description of the fairies is given:
Nuair a bhí mise i mo ghasúr chluininn m'athair mór ag caint ar bhunadh na gcnoc. Ní rabh aon fhear scéalta sióg ins an taoibh seo den tír a ba mhó ná é. Chreid sé féin go láidir go rabh siad ann, agus ní rabh aon iarraidh dá dtéadh sé chun an phortaigh fá dhéin cliabh mónadh nach mbiodh sé ag feitheamh ar a bhfeiceáil!
(When I was a child I used to hear my grandfather talk about the hill-folk. No man in the countryside had more tales of the fairies than he had. He himself was a firm believer in them, and he never went to the bog for a creel of turf without expecting to see them.)
For the man in question here, the fairies, would seem to have been almost a part of the natural world.

English waters, although it is abundant in western and northern Scotland, particularly on the Islands.[2]

Given their widespread distribution, it is not surprising that seals had a part to play in the economic life of many Irish coastal communities. They were often hunted, and either clubbed to death or, in later years, shot. Several uses could be made of the dead seal. The skin could be sold, and we are told that a man's waistcoat made from sealskin was a particularly prized article. Seal-oil was in demand for a variety of human ailments, from pains in the bones to burns. The oil was used for other purposes also, as a tanning and waterproofing agent in treating the sails of boats, for example, and as fuel for oil-lamps.[3] The seal also served as food for coastal-dwellers in some areas, and there is evidence that seal-meat was eaten in Ireland as early as medieval times, and possibly earlier.[4] Seals have long been the enemy of fishermen, and were often hunted for this reason also.

Since they have been so much a part of the everyday life of coastal communities for so long, it is inevitable that a body of belief and tradition should have evolved over the centuries concerning seals and their habits. The supernatural aspects of that tradition, in particular, are very rich and varied, and it is these aspects of seal-lore which I would like to focus upon here.[5]

---

2 O'Rourke (1970), 127-8. According to a distribution map included in O'Rourke's book, the Common Seal also seems to occur all around our coasts. The exact species of seal which figures in Irish legends and beliefs may possibly be of some significance when viewed in the context of the distribution patterns of similar legends and beliefs in other parts of western Europe. The usual word for a seal in the Irish language is *rón*, and this word can refer to either of the two principal species of seal found in Ireland. The terms *rón liath* or *rón glas* are also found for the Grey Seal and the Common Seal, respectively, and the latter two are listed accordingly in the Department of Education's publication, *Ainmneacha Plandaí agus Ainmhithe*. In most accounts of seals from Irish oral tradition, however, in both the Irish and English languages, the species of seal is not specified. Still on the subject of naming, specific terms were apparently often used to differentiate between seals of different ages, and between male and female seals. See, for example, Ó Criomhthain (1929), 115.

3 For information on the hunting and killing of seals, and on the subsequent uses made of the various parts of the seal, the archives of the Department of Irish Folklore in University College Dublin contain material from various coastal areas. These include, for example, *IFC* 142: 1662-4 (Donegal); *IFC* 988:72-4 (Donegal); *IFC* 1191:270 (Mayo); *IFC* 1208:393-4 (Mayo); *IFC* 1548:229 (Mayo); *IFC* 159:423 (Galway); *IFC* 62:292-3 (Galway); *IFC* 27: 254-5 (Kerry), etc. *IFC* = Irish Folklore Collection, being the Main Manuscripts Collection of the Department of Irish Folklore at University College Dublin; the numerals on either side of the colon represent the volume number and page number(s) respectively. *IFC S* and *IFC Tape*, below, refer to the Schools' Manuscripts Collection and to the sound archive collections of the Department of Irish Folklore respectively). For the Blasket Islands in south Kerry, in particular, see especially Ó Criomhthain (1928) and Ó Criomhthain (1929). The unpublished work on the Blaskets by Atlantic European Research (1990), Part 1, 37-8, also contains a useful summary of information regarding seals and their uses, as found in the published and unpublished writings about the Blaskets.

4 See note 3. See also O'Rourke (1945), 115-8.

5 Most of the information published to date on this subject is to be found included in general collections or descriptions of one kind or another. There are at least two publications which deal specifically with seal-beliefs in Ireland and Scotland, however – these are Thomson (1965) and Ballard (1983).

There are a number of possible reasons for the abundance of otherworld beliefs about seals. In the first instance, seals are liminal creatures *par excellence.* They are beings of both land and water, belonging complete-ly to neither element. This places them in an ambiguous position, and such ambiguities and anomalies tend to attract supernatural beliefs and associa-tions in popular tradition generally. Secondly, the wealth of beliefs relating to other supernatural inhabitants of the sea must have provided a suitable matrix for the easy establishment of traditions about the supernatural nature of seals. Tales of enchanted seals could fit very comfortably into a maritime otherworld of submarine lands, well-populated with mermaids, sea-fairies, and the spirits of those lost at sea, and it is easy to see how such stories could quickly combine with, and flow into, stories about other supernatural denizens of the deep.

Belief in the supernatural nature of seals is not, of course, a uniquely Irish – or even a Celtic-Nordic-Baltic – phenomenon, which brings us to another probable reason for the richness of the belief in Ireland. Supernatural seals are essentially an international lot. Traditions of super-natural creatures of the sea, including seals, can be traced back to Greek and Latin literature and to classical mythology. They represent a body of belief of great antiquity and one which can be found over a vast geographical area. The fact that supernatural beliefs about seals are to be found in neighbour-ing parts of western Europe must have helped to bolster and encourage the existence and the spread of similar beliefs and narratives in Ireland.

Transformation beliefs about seals were probably sustained also by the occurrence of webbed fingers or toes in certain families and individuals, which feature was said to be the legacy of an aquatic ancestor. Here, we see the beliefs serving a straightforward aetiological function. In this connec-tion, it is worth noting that such beliefs were undoubtedly encouraged by the fact that seals often appear to act in a manner similar to human beings, and by their apparently sympathetic behaviour to humans, which is illus-trated in some of the accounts which follow.

Supernatural beliefs regarding seals could therefore be said to exist for a number of different reasons, operating at various levels and in different ways, with each acting as a reinforcement to the whole. These reasons range from the psychological to the geographical to the aetiological, and can each be seen as contributory factors to the richness of the overall body of belief.

II

In Irish oral tradition, information about the supernatural nature of seals is to be found primarily in descriptions of popular beliefs, and in their associated narratives and legend-types.[6] Almost all of these narratives have one fundamental feature in common – they hinge on the idea that seals are enchanted people and that they are somehow related to human kind. There is, in effect, an entire complex of traditions about seals, all of which pivots on this central belief. The material in question ranges across the narrative spectrum, from incidental snatches of stories and semi-anecdotal accounts of the human-like behaviour of seals, to belief-statements and thence to fully developed legends telling of unions between seals and mortal people. The implicit or explicit message in all cases is that seals are not 'ordinary' creatures, but that they possess a human dimension of some kind.

To start at the anecdotal end of the spectrum, the following account is typical of the many recorded from oral tradition which describe seals behaving like people. It was recorded in Ros Muc, in west Galway, in 1937:

> We were going back one day fishing, and over at Carraig Tíre there were two seals on a rock there. And a bit away from them, there was a big grey seal on another rock. But it wasn't long before the two seals started fighting. And the big seal came over, and he started hitting one of them until he separated them, and he waited a while until everything was over.
>
> It wasn't long before he went back onto his own rock again, and the seal went up on the rock he had been on, and it was no length before the two seals were fighting again. And over with the big seal for the second time and he started slapping the same seal again, until he put him off the rock, just like

---

6 Most of the information recorded in Ireland about seals is in the Irish language. In the early decades of the Irish Folklore Commission (1935-71), quite intensive collecting work was carried out in several of the Irish-speaking parts of Ireland, as opposed to the English-speaking areas (which included the east coast). The comparative paucity of English-language material about seals might therefore be seen as merely a reflection and a result of the history of collecting activities in general in Ireland. Even when we take into account the inherent linguistic imbalance of the collections, however, the Irish-language material on seals is not only more extensive but also much richer in content than the English.

The fact that parallels to the Irish language material are often to be found in the Scottish Gaelic tradition may also be significant, and may indicate that some of the beliefs belong essentially to the common Gaelic tradition of the two countries. As is the case in Ireland, however, seal-lore is also to be found in the English-language traditions of Scotland. In Scotland, as in Ireland, stories about enchanted seals abound, and seals were often said to be people who had been transformed. They were said to have the power of speech, and there was a belief in Scotland also that certain families were descended from seals. For a short summing-up of similarities in seal-traditions between various parts of Scotland and Ireland, with occasional references to the Faroe Islands, see Ó Murchadha & Ó Súilleabháin (1939), 135-8. See also Thomson (1965); Hull (1928), 153-6; Croker (1825-8), II, 3-20. A brief survey reveals that this Scottish-Irish material fits into the overall north-west Atlantic picture as we know it, and also indicates that a further examination of the comparative material outside of Ireland might well shed light on certain aspects of Irish seal-lore and its origins.

a mother with two children. And he stayed on the rock himself, and he put the young seal over onto the other rock. We were very much surprised at it.[7]

There are several other accounts recorded from oral tradition which describe seals behaving in a manner which could be taken to indicate sympathy with human beings. These include stories of seals helping people who have got into difficulties at sea, as well as at least one account of a seal nurturing a stray child.[8] The objective truth of such accounts is not, of course, particularly important for students of oral tradition; their primary interest lies not so much in what may *actually* have happened on a given occasion, but rather in what people *said* happened. As such, anecdotal material of this type is of considerable value as an indicator of popular perceptions.

The following narrative is also anecdotal in its style and content. Despite the individual character of the account, however, it articulates and illustrates the collective belief in question (according to the narrator, i.e. that the seal was a good omen), and provides a good example of a belief-statement embedded in a narrative. The account was recorded in Corbally, county Clare, in 1955:

When we used to go harvest fishing for mackerel, this big black seal used to appear behind a certain canoe. It had done so for over seven years, and this year in particular the big seal was seen following this same canoe. When this canoe would be about twenty yards from the beach, up would pop the seal, right at the stern of the canoe. It would dive and come up in the same position, when the canoe would be farther out.

He would keep diving and coming up at intervals of about ten to twenty minutes, and the seal always appeared right at the stern end of the canoe. One of the men made an attempt to strike the seal with an oar, and sure 'twas the worst thing that man ever did. That night when he was going home after fishing, didn't he slip on the road and burst five ribs, and he never got out of his sick bed for twelve years until the day he died. They said around here that the seal was a good omen, and the fact that this man struck it caused the good omen to turn into a curse, and sure 'twas true enough.[9]

---

7 *IFC* 442:486-7. The collector was Eibhlín Ní Standúin, and the storyteller was Mícheál Ó Fualáin. For the original text in Irish, see the Appendix. The translation given here is my own. On the subject of seals behaving like people, see also, for example, *IFC* 458:246-7 (Donegal); *IFC S* 316:195 (Cork), etc.
8 See, for example, material collected in north-west Mayo in *IFC* 1191:270-3 and *IFC* 1239:177-8, 179-80.
9 *IFC* 1393:319. The collector was Seán MacGrath, and the narrator was Pádraig Ó Briain.

III

Unlike anecdotes and incidental material, traditional legends are, by definition, relatively structured and formalised genres of narrative. In Irish tradition, a number of distinct legend-types about seals can be identified, notwithstanding a significant measure of intermixing and overlapping between the various types. The word 'theme' might better describe the content of these stories, in that it conveys more accurately the idea of a number of basic underlying narrative threads. Some of these narrative/legend-types are here described under various headings.

The Wounded Seal
The following story was recorded in Cloich Cheann Fhaolaidh, county Donegal, in 1941:

> I was reared at the far end of Ros Goill, and when I was a young fellow there was an old man living in the second house away from us and I used to spend all my time with him. I wouldn't ask for anything else from the time darkness fell until it was time to go to bed but to listen to the fine old stories he had, as well as traditions about all sorts of other things. He often told us so many stories about 'the little people' that he would have to bring us home himself, because we were so frightened that they would get us on the way. I have forgotten all of these now, but maybe when I'd hear a crowd chatting about old times and things like that, maybe some of them would come back to me.
>
> Mánus Jondy was this man's name, and he was surely a fine storyteller. I remember one night he told me a story, and I never forgot that story since, and I think that nobody who heard it could ever forget it. 'This is one of the stories', as he said himself, 'which I heard my father saying that he heard from his grandfather'. Well, long ago, it appears that there came a time when the fish were very plentiful off the Irish coast here. They were so plentiful that they were being washed up on the strand, and at the same time there were no fish at all to be caught off the coast of Scotland or England. This enraged the Scottish people so much that their wise women turned themselves into seals and came over to the Irish coast to drive away the fish.
>
> There were a couple of men in the district then who used to go around the place with forks, gathering sea-wrack in the spring-time. What should happen only that these seals were in among the submerged rocks at the water's edge, underneath the seaweed. One of these men stuck the fork down through the seaweed, as he thought himself, and what did he do only stick it into the eye of one of these seals. And away goes the seal with the fork stuck in him!
>
> A few years after that, these men were themselves fishing over off the

coast of Scotland. They had boats that time which were something like the curragh we see on the shore today, except that they were made of boards on the inside, and hare-skin on the outside. They used to rub fish-oil on it so that it would last and so that it wouldn't let the water in. Well, one of these boats was fishing off the coast of Scotland, like I said, and one evening, when they were lying in harbour, a couple of the men went off through the countryside, for a bit of a walk. When they were going past the door of this house, what did one of them see only (the) fork he had lost on the strand, a couple of years before that.

He was more than surprised, and he thought to himself that he would go inside and find out how his fork had got to this place. When he put his head in the door, there was an old woman sitting in the chimney-corner, with a piece of cloth wrapped around her eye. He took hold of the fork in his hand, and he said, 'Where did ye get this fork?' 'It doesn't make much difference,' said the old woman, 'and in any case, what do you know about it?' 'Well', he said, 'it's like one I lost long ago beyond in Ireland – one that I got stuck in a seal.'

'Oh, damnation!', she said, taking a pot of steaming water off the fire and making a go for him. 'It was you that stuck the fork in me, and left me sitting here since, with my eye nearly hanging out!'

The man took to his heels as fast as he could, and he was glad that he did get away. They fled away a couple of days after that, and I'm telling you he wasn't seen around the coasts of Scotland from that day to the day he died.

Mánus, the old man, often told me that there wasn't a word of a lie in that story, and he could name the place in Ros Goill where the man this happened to was living. He was definite, too, that all seals were people who were under a spell, and he wouldn't have anything to do with them for love or money.[10]

This story brings to mind two other relatively common Irish transformation legends. The first of these is the story of *The Knife Against the Wave*, which tells of a fisherman at sea who is threatened by an enormous wave.[11] The fisherman eventually overcomes the wave by throwing his black-handled knife into it. Subsequently, he is brought to a land beneath the sea, where he is asked to draw his knife from the body of a young woman, as only he has the power to save her. The similarity in plot to *The Wounded Seal* is obvious. Both legends seem to have a roughly similar distribution also, and have been recorded primarily in the northern and western coastal areas. Unlike *The Knife Against the Wave*, however, *The Wounded Seal* is not a particularly common story, and versions noted to date can be numbered in single figures.

The second transformation legend which *The Wounded Seal* brings to mind

---

10 *IFC* 799:238-42. Recorded by Seán Ó hEochaidh from Séamus Mac Aodha. For the original text in Irish, see the Appendix. The translation given here is my own.
11 See the article by Miceál Ross in the present volume.

is, by contrast, an entirely land-bound affair. It has been titled *The Old Woman as Hare*, and it tells the story of a milk-stealing hare who is seen sucking milk from cows, thus depriving their owners of both milk and butter-profit.[12] In the standard version of the story, a group of men hunt the hare with dogs, one of whom manages to bite the hare before she succeeds in escaping. Shortly after, the huntsmen encounter an old woman who is found to be bleeding heavily from an injured leg, thus revealing her true identity.

The many similarities and points of comparison between these three tranformation legends have yet to be investigated in full, but both *The Wounded Seal* and *The Knife Against the Wave* should probably be seen as maritime counterparts of the witch-hare story. The latter appears to be particularly common in the midlands of Ireland, especially in the north midlands, a fact which may be of significance in the context of its possible relationship to the two maritime stories. On the subject of the transformation element which is central to all three legends, this motif lends itself to a wide range of possible interpretations and readings which, however, lie outside the scope of the present article.

The Seal Who Speaks

Our second narrative-type concerns a seal who speaks, often just as it is about to be killed. Sometimes, the seal-hunter has his arm raised to strike, or has taken aim with his gun, when the seal begs for mercy. Single-episodic accounts of this kind have been recorded on many occasions along the south-west, west and northern coasts. The following version was collected on Rathlin Island, county Antrim, in the 1950s:

> The old men certainly didn't like you to meddle with the seal – although I shot two.
> I heard my grandfather tell a story about them certainly. He said that, like now, the seals were becoming very plentiful and going for all the fish; and they went out with a gun in the boat, and this old seal come up and when he lifted the gun, this man, the seal lifted his paw and he says: 'Donal, Donal, don't fire at me.' It was in Irish, but it meant that. They said that was true enough that time.[13]

Variations on this basic theme are not uncommon, and they include a number of stories in which the seal is about to give birth to her young, and asks her attacker to wait until she does so. The following version was recorded in 1952 on the Uíbh Ráthach peninsula in south Kerry:

> They used to say that they (i.e. seals) were old people that were under a spell.

---

12 For a brief survey of this story, see Ní Dhuibhne (1993), 77-85.
13 Murphy (1987), 58. The collector in this case was Michael J. Murphy, and the narrator was Paddy Anderson.

There aren't many of them around now, but there used to be plenty of them long ago. They have five fingers, like a person.

There's a cove at the bottom of my land back in Ródaibh – a big underground cove – and the seals used always be inside in it. They call the place Killurley Commons. At the bottom of that is the cove – The Cove of the Seal. A man came from Faill Móir to that place one day – a man who used to be always killing them – and they used call him Féilim Mhic Eoin. And there was a seal in the cove. She was in labour. She was having a young seal, and she spoke to him. 'Féilim Mhic Eoin,' she said, 'don't kill me until I have my young one.' 'I won't, or ever again!', he said, leaving her there. He cleared off, and he never again went killing seals.[14]

There are other legends also which feature speaking seals as part of the dramatic action. These include a number of stories about grateful or vengeful seals, which tell of favours rewarded or ill-treatment avenged. The following account is from the Erris area of county Mayo, where it was recorded in 1937:

There was a seal around these parts, and this man was walking along the shore. And he met this young seal between two rocks on the shore, and he took the young seal up and he carried him home. And he didn't do anything to him, but just brought him home.

When the old seal came to that place in the evening, looking for the young one, the young seal wasn't to be got. And herself and the other old seal, her mate, started crying. And you'd hear them wailing below in Erris – it happened up there in Mulranny – and you'd hear the two of them crying. Well, when this good man heard the pitiful crying at home, he said that surely the reason the two seals were crying was because of what he had done – that he had taken this young seal up from the beach with him.

And he takes the young seal, and he carries him back down again until he leaves him in the very same spot. And the tide was coming in. And he went away up the strand. And the two seals came in to where the young one was, and they kissed him and licked him and rubbed him and combed him, and the talk started then. 'Well, long life to yourself, Mártan Bhriain Rua. Long life and prosperity to you, Mártan Bhriain Rua. Long life and prosperity to you, Mártan Bhriain Rua.' He went off home, and the whole village was listening to the seals saying these words.

And Mártan Bhriain Rua did have a long and prosperous life. And he was a good man. And he's not dead seven years yet. From that day to this, he let no-one harm a seal, and he had luck. That man had luck. And no-one

---

14 *IFC* 1226:323. The collector was Tadhg Ó Murchú and the narrator was Seán Ó Bortacháin. For the original text in Irish, see the Appendix. The translation given here is my own.

from this village would touch them.[15]

Again, there are clearly identifiable counterparts on land to this type of legend, most obviously in the many stories about the fairies and the way in which they might help or reward people who are kind to them, while punishing people who offend or harm them or their property in any way. Indeed, this repeated mirroring of land- and sea-traditions is very much a feature of Irish folk belief and narrative in general, and is a predictable state of affairs in a society where most fishermen also worked the land to some extent, and where there was usually no very clear division between fishing and farming communities. Consequently, there is a constant overlapping and intermingling between the two types of environment, in oral tradition as in daily life.

The tale of Tadhg and Donncha also concerns seals who speak. This simple tale, describing how one seal sets out to search for the other, is not uncommon in the oral tradition of the west and south of Ireland, but seems to be rather more rare in the north. The following short version was recorded by school-children near Skibbereen in county Cork, in the late 1930s:

One time, a man caught a seal in the sea beside Trá Ligeach. He brought the seal home with him, and he was alive. He put the seal into the kitchen.

That night, there was a man going across the strand and he heard a voice speaking, 'A Dhonncha Dhonn! A Dhonncha Dhonn!' The man continued on his way, and he went into a house on the other side of the strand. It was in this house that the seal was, and the man told his story to the man of the house. As soon as the seal heard the words 'A Dhonncha Dhonn,' he spoke. 'That was Tadhg looking for me!' They let the seal go, and they didn't hear the voice from that on.[16]

Some years ago, I recorded the following variation of the story from Mrs Theresa McHale, of Moyne near Killala in county Mayo:

This man was down at the shore too gathering seaweed in a . . . creel, and he saw this seal, coming in on the strand. And he went and he took the seal and he put her into the creel, and he carried the creel up on his back. And he left the creel and the seal down in the end of the house. So, eh, they went to bed. The parents went to bed, but they couldn't sleep a wink during the night, but listening to the seal crying. And the seal used to say, 'Oh, Mícheál, if you knew where I was tonight, wouldn't you be in trouble!'.
So the wife told him in the morning when they got up, to take the seal

---

15 *IFC* 524:291-3. The narrator was Mícheál Mac Máistir, and the collector was Proinnsias de Búrca. For the original text in Irish, see the Appendix. The translation given here is my own.
16 *IFC* S 298:105-6. The narrator was Bean Uí Dhálaigh. For the original text in Irish, see the Appendix. The translation given here is my own.

and to bring it down and to leave it out on the water. So he did. He let the seal go.[17]

These stories illustrate a belief which must be seen as related to the tradition that seals have the power of human speech, namely, that they are possessed of Christian names. Underlying these and similar narratives is the idea of the importance of a name in defining the true nature of an entity. The perception of Christianity as a primary and defining characteristic is also evident in these accounts. One such account, from Kerry, states that seals are *Críostaithe* – Christians or people – who were put under a spell.[18] Similarly, a Galway account tells of fishermen who were fishing off the Aran Islands one Sunday when they met with a seal who had the power of speech and who, in the course of their ensuing conversation, remarked to the fishermen that his family was not at home, but gone to Mass.[19]

The names accorded to seals in different areas may be significant in helping to establish the distribution pattern of particular traditions. The seal's name is often said to be Tadhg, especially in the south, where narratives featuring named seals appear to be longer and generally more cohesive than their Connacht counterparts.[20] In this connection, however, it might also be mentioned that the name 'Tadhg' figures in traditions concerning a group of three rocks, known as the Stags, off the coast of Donegal. We are told that these rocks are in reality enchanted people, one of whose name is Tadhg.[21]

The story of Tadhg and Donncha, as it appears in the Cork version given above, contains echoes of another legend which is popular throughout most of Ireland. This is the story of *The King of the Cats* – the so-called Pan legend of classical literature.[22] The Irish versions of this legend have as their kernel an account of a man who is on his way home one night when he encounters a cat with the power of human speech. The cat tells the man that the king of the cats is dead. When the man reaches home, he recounts what has happened, upon which the household cat jumps up and runs out the door, sometimes with an exclamation or imprecation of some kind, or worse. While the story of Tadhg and Donncha is clearly a separate narrative, the two legends do have some features in common, and may have influenced each other.

---

17 *IFC Tape* BFT 32:2.
18 *IFC* 963:173.
19 *IFC* 1306:196-7. Note the use of the word 'Críostaí', meaning a person, in this account also.
20 Cf. the unpublished student essay by Ní Lochlainn (1993). In western accounts, various common Christian names, such as Diarmaid, Dónal, Seán, Mícheál, Anna etc., are attributed to the seal.
21 *An Claidheamh Soluis* VIII, 22.12.1906, 5-6.
22 See the study of this legend in Ó Néill (1991), 167-88.

233

ML 4080 The Seal Woman

This migratory legend tells the story of a union between a mortal man and a seal in human form. In Irish tradition, however, it is usually a mermaid, rather than a seal-woman, who plays the central role in the story.[23] In its mermaid form, the legend is very common in Ireland, with over 300 versions on record. In contrast, versions of the story which feature a seal-woman can be numbered in single figures. One such version was recorded on the Dingle peninsula in county Kerry, in 1948:

> There was a man in Machaire, and he was down at the sea one night, looking for seaweed to gather. And he saw a seal, and he caught the seal. And he took the seal home with him, alive. When he saw her, she was sitting on a rock, as a woman. She had a cloak beside her, and she was combing her hair. He crept up on her when she was combing her hair, and he snatched the cloak and took it with him. And she had to follow the cloak, so she came after him to his house. He came inside, and he threw the cloak into the back of the loft, as far as he could.
>
> She stayed there with him, and she spent some years there, and they had children. And the children's feet were webbed, like the foot of a goose or a duck. There were no spaces between the toes. The toes were stretched out, if what they say is true, and between them was all closed over, up to the very tops.
>
> She had a few children by him, and she spent several years there and was very hard-working. Anyway, there came one particular day when he had to put oats or something up on the loft. He went up on the loft, for the first time in so many years, and he was throwing down old things that were up there. And with all the throwing down, he threw down the cloak. She spotted the cloak, and she got up and grabbed it and put it under her on the chair. He went out then, to bring the oats in. When he was gone out, she took the cloak and hid it. And when it was coming on for evening, she brushed her children's hair and cleaned and tidied them. Then she threw the cloak on herself and made off down for the shore, and nobody ever saw her again.[24]

In oral tradition, certain families are believed to have their origins in such a union, the best-known example being Muintir Chonaola/Chonghaile, or the Conneely/Connolly families, who are well represented along the west coast.[25] As such, the story of the man who married the seal-woman could be described as a

---

23 For a description of research carried out on the legend of the man who married the mermaid, see Almqvist (1990b), 1-74. See also Lysaght (1996), 45-6, 159-63, 172, 180-1, etc.

24 *IFC* 1100:578-9. Recorded in 1948 by Seósamh Ó Dálaigh from a storyteller by the name of Seán Ó Muircheartaigh. For the original text in Irish, see the Appendix. The translation given here is my own.

25 Surnames variously written Mac Conghaile, Mac Conghaola, Ó Conghaile etc. are no longer distinguishable from each other, although they may have had varying origins. In anglicised form, variants such as 'Conneely, Connolly, Kenneally, MacCunneela' etc. are used. See Woulfe (1923). On the origin and etymology of these and other names, and on the connections between these names and seals, see also Mac Suibhne (1961), 15-9 etc.

family-origin legend. The following excerpt is taken from a version of *The Wounded Seal*, as described above, and it vividly illustrates this belief about the Conneelys, as well as again exemplifying the constant overlap which exists between the various types of seal narratives. The story was recorded in Conamara, west Galway, in 1939:

> When he was leaving, he said 'What family do you belong to yourself, ma'm, if you don't mind me asking?' 'I am one of the Conneelys,' she said, 'because we are under a spell. The Conneelys are under a spell.' It was a Conneely woman and her child who were on the rock when he fired at them.
>
> In this place [i.e., Leitir Mucadha], a person from the Conneely family is given the nickname 'The family with their head up'. Because the seal sticks his head up over the water, and because it is said that the Conneely family is descended from the seals, they are called 'The family with their head up.'[26]

The belief that certain families are related to seals or mermaids is almost certainly a very old one. Some such family-names (as well as several others, it should be said) are described by one authority as tracing a part of their origins back to medieval times to the Uí Fiachrach clan of Connacht.[27] These names include Ó Dubhda, Ó Catháin, Ó Conghaile, and Ó Sé. This would seem to suggest the possibility, at least, that the belief about aquatic origins may originally have attached to the afore-mentioned clan, and survived thus in modern oral tradition.[28]

The maritime links of the Ó Catháin family may have other roots also.[29] The origin of this family is, in a small number of modern oral tales, explained by the well-known mythical story of the vanquishing of Balar by his grandson, Lugh. The story is one which has its roots in early Irish literature, going back to at least the eleventh century.[30] In literary versions of the story, and in some of the modern oral versions

---

26 *IFC* 641:65. Collected by Brian Mac Lochlainn from Seán Mac Confhaola. For the original text in Irish, see the Appendix. The translation given here is my own. As mentioned earlier, it is sometimes said that the descendants of this type of union have webbed fingers and/or toes as a result of their aquatic ancestry.

27 Woulfe (1923).

28 This brings us into the whole area of totemism, about which so much has been written since the time of Frazer, and which has attracted so much controversy and debate. For the purposes of this artice, a short quote might not go amiss, especially as it is from one of the most famous writers on the subject. Lévi-Strauss (1987) tells us (p.32): 'The complex and various problems subsumed under the label of totemism, then, send us back to the modes of seeing and knowing that we need to recognise as essential to all cultures where relations with Nature are of primary importance'. Elsewhere in the same publication, and still on the subject of totemism, he writes (p.30):'. . . it is as metaphorical relations that we should interpret the analogies noted between certain animal or vegetable species and human beings.' I feel that this last point may be most useful in our attempts to arrive at an understanding of the nature and meaning of aspects of Irish seal-traditions. Also on the subject of the possible totemistic nature of aspects of Irish seal-beliefs, see Mac Suibhne (1961) and Ballard (1983).

29 'Ó Catháin' is very often 'translated' into English as 'Kane' ('Keane') – see Woulfe (1923). See also Mac Suibhne (1961), 18.

30 For an overview of the story in early Irish literature and folk tradition, see Ó hÓgáin (1990), 43-4, 272-6, etc. My sincere thanks are due to Professor Ó hÓgáin for his help with many of the sources referred to in this article in connection with the early literature, and for his advice on their signifi-

also, Lugh's father is called 'Cian', or its equivalent.[31] In a small number of these oral versions, we are told that, with the exception of the boy (the Lugh figure) who is destined to become the hero of the tale, the children of Cian are released into the sea, where they become seals, 'and it is said that the seals are Kanes ever since.'[32] The association of the Ó Catháin family with the Lugh story may be quite old, as the mid-Ulster branch of that family was of the Ciannachta, a sept whose designation meant 'those of Cian.'[33] The medieval literature claims that the Ciannachta were descended from one Tadhg Mac Céin, a fictional character who, interestingly, also had a special connection with a particular species of animal, namely badgers, according to an eighth-century text.[34]

It may also be noted that, in a handful of other versions of the Lugh/Balar myth from the oral tradition of county Donegal, the hero's father is called 'Mac Conaola' or the like, thus providing a link with the belief, described above, that the Conneelys are also related to seals.[35] It is possible that the occurrence of this name results from the topography of the north-west of the county, where the region Cloich Cheann Fhaolaidh (Cloghaneely) is situated on the mainland between Tory Island (Balar's residence) and Dún Lúiche (Dunlewy, popularly interpreted to mean 'the fort of Lugh').[36] If this name for Lugh's father became known to storytellers in more southern parts of Donegal and possibly also in north Connacht, it could very easily have coalesced with the (generally southern) Connacht tradition that the Conaola/Conneely families are descended from seals.

---

31 For the literary versions, see note 30. For the oral versions, see for example, *IFC* 83:55-8 (Mayo); *IFC* 58:289-324 (Galway); *IFC* 12:41-51 (Kerry); Larminie (1893), 1-9 (Mayo); Curtin (1911), 1-34 (Kerry); *idem.*, 296-311 (Galway); Thomson (1965), 194-7 (Mayo). Among other versions of the story which occur in oral tradition, Ballard (1983), 38-9, offers an interesting example from Rathlin Island which appears to be a corrupt version of part of the story of Balar and Lugh, and one in which seals figure prominently.

32 *IFC* 83:58 ('. . . agus tá sé ráite gur Cathánaigh na róntaí ó shoin.')

33 MacLysaght (1957), 191; O'Brien (1962), 453; Byrne (1973), 114, 126. It might also be argued that the association of the Ó Catháin family with the Lugh story could have come about in very recent times, due to the phonemic correspondence of 'Céin' (gen. of 'Cian') with Kane (an anglicised form of Ó Catháin). This, however, is a rather unlikely explanation, and is in any case unnecessary, in view of the above.

34 See Byrne (1973), 68-9; Ó hÓgáin (1990), 399-400. Curiously, the name Tadhg originally meant 'badger' – see Mac an Bhaird (1980), 150-5. It is tempting to connect this human-animal correspondence with the popularity of 'Tadhg' as a name ascribed to seals in Munster oral tradition, and it is possible that the tradition has here preserved an echo of the animal-meaning of the name. With regard to the fact that Tadhg Mac Céin is, like Lugh, a son of Cian, it is unlikely that the name 'Tadhg' is traditionally ascribed to seals because of any influence from oral versions of the Lugh/Balar story, as described above, as Tadhg Mac Céin does not feature to any extent in the oral tradition.

35 See, for example, O'Donovan (1835), typescript pp. 46-51 (ms. pp. 90-8); Curtin (1911), 283-95 (Donegal); Laoide (1913), 63-5 (Donegal).

36 Cf. Ó hÓgáin (1990), 43-5, 275. See also O'Donovan (1835), typescript pp. 47-8 (ms. pp. 91-3), where he writes that 'Mac Aneely was Lord of that district comprizing the Parishes of Ray-Fionain and Tullaghan-Begly . . . (he was) the chief of the tract opposite the (i.e., Tory) island . . .' See also Andrews (1913), 73, where she recounts the story of Lugh and Balar as she heard it on Tory Island. In her version, Balar's smith is said to live at Cloich Cheann Fhaolaidh.

There is obviously a considerable degree of overlap between the early literary versions of the Lugh/Balar story and the modern oral tales, and just one of the many points which requires elucidation concerns the motif of the children's transformation into seals.[37] It is not possible to say at what exact stage in the the development of the story this motif was introduced, but it would seem reasonable, partly in view of the arguments outlined above, to conclude that the seal-motif is probably a later addition to it, and one based on oral tradition.[38] This conclusion is obviously strengthened by the apparent absence of any evidence of the motif in early literary sources.

A few other medieval Irish sources do make mention of seals. More to the point in the present context, these sources mention seals specifically in terms of transformation and enchantment. Two such texts are found in the Book of Lismore, which dates to the fifteenth century. One of these describes how St Brendan, on his way to the high king at Tara, summons fifty seals from the sea and turns them into horses. He then gives the fifty horses to the king in exchange for the freedom of a nobleman whom the king is holding prisoner. The saint guarantees the horses for fifteen months. After that time, the riders of the horses use whips on their mounts one day, at which point both horses and riders are turned into seals.[39] This story, or one similar to it, is also told about a small number of other saints in the medieval literature, with or without the seals motif.[40] The story is of interest also for the connection which it establishes between horses and horse-racing on the one hand, and supernatural sea-beings (in this case, seals) on the other. It would seem that horses and water were among the major elements of otherworld imagery in early Irish thought.[41] This connection would appear to be reflected in the well-known story of Macha, the otherworld woman who dies after engaging in a race against horses, according to a ninth-century text, and whose story appears to be an early prototype for a small group of later folk legends which centre on supernatural women, often of aquatic origin, in which the motif of horse-racing is also often

---

37 Ewing (1995), 119-31, writes about the story of Balar and Lugh in its modern oral forms and in its older literary versions, and points to similarities between the story and other stories from the medieval literature of Welsh and Old Norse. He lists a number of correspondences between the Celtic Lugh/Lleu and the Norse Loki, among others, and notes that, while the Irish Lugh's step-siblings are turned into seals, the Norse Loki and Heimdall fight in the shape of seals. On the basis of other correspondences and points of comparison, Ewing argues that the tales in question probably derive from 'the common inheritance of Celtic and Germanic peoples alike'. His argument would seem to suggest the possibility, at least, of an origin of considerable antiquity for the appearance of seals in the story of Balar and Lugh, despite their non-appearance in the earlier sources examined so far. See also Mac Suibhne (1961), 18-9.

38 Among the early texts which I have examined to date, there are several descriptions of shape – shifting, but seals are not mentioned.

39 O'Grady (1892), II, 70-6. This text provides us with an early literary example of the motif of the water-horse returning to the sea when struck. For a study of water-horse legends in Ireland, see Almqvist (1991a), 107-20.

40 For a summary of the various sources in question, see Ó hÓgáin (1990), 53, 197-8, 252, 289-90, 377-8, etc.

41 See Ó hÓgáin (1990), 251-2.

found.[42] Interestingly also, the horse of Cú Chulainn in the Ulster Cycle, the Liath Mhacha, is a water-horse in origin.[43]

The other text from the Book of Lismore consists of a version of *Agallamh na Seanórach,* or the Colloquy of the Ancients, which was originally written in the twelfth century.[44] This tells of Fionn mac Cumhaill and other members of the Fianna, including Oisín and Caoilte, who have survived their contemporaries by some 150 years, and who encounter St Patrick and various other notables. The text in question contains an account given by Caoilte to the king of Ulster on the origin of two graves at a place called Rudhraighe's strand, which is situated near Rudhraighe's wave, a feature we find mentioned in other early sources also.[45] In explaining the origin of the graves, Caoilte's account includes a description of a dream which Fionn mac Cumhaill had wherein he sees two grey seals sucking his breasts.[46] His dream turns out to be a vision of the two sons of the king of Connacht in the form of two seals. They have been mortally wounded in combat in an effort to protect Fionn and the Fianna while they were sleeping. The two sons are buried on Rudhraighe's strand, having first of all been lifted over Rudhraighe's wave, for reasons which are not clear.

The main interest of this account, as far as we are concerned, lies in the fact that Muintir Mhic Ruairí, or the Rogers family, are one of the families who are believed to be descended from seals, according to a story recorded from modern oral tradition on Tory Island, Donegal. This belief may have become attached to the Rogers family due to a confusion in popular etymology between the names 'Rudhraighe' and 'Ruairí', but the twelfth-century text is itself evidence of some antiquity for the belief that human and seal forms can be interchangeable. The story, collected on Tory Island in 1945, is as follows:

> We are forever hearing that the Rogers family of this island is connected with the seals, and that they are related to them still. I can't say whether this is true or not, but I only have what I heard the old people saying.

---

42 For a recent study of this legend in Irish tradition, see Kavanagh (1995), 71-82. See also Ó hÓgáin (1990), 186-7, 283-5; and the article by Proinsias Mac Cana in the present volume. Still on the subject of horse-racing, the Norse god Óðinn is also identified with horses and horse-riding, and Hull (1928) – quoting MacDonald (1894) and various other sources – writes as follows (p.156): 'The MacCodrums, legend says, were metamorphosed into seals, but they retained the human soul and, at times, a human form . . . North Uist legend speaks of the family as the Clan MacCodrum of the Seals. The Rev. A. MacDonald connects them with a horse-race or horse-fight which he thinks was part of a festival to Odin, who was closely connected with the district'. It may also be of relevance that Ewing (1995) and others have commented on the points of similarity between the Norse god Óðinn and the Irish Balar, the latter of whom also has seal connections, as we have seen.
43 Ó hÓgáin (1990), 252, etc.
44 O'Grady (1892), 181-4, etc. See also Ó hÓgáin (1990), 219.
45 See, for example, Cross (1952), 27; Ó hÓgáin (1990), 177-8.
46 For the history and significance of the breast-sucking motif in early literary sources, see Bieler (1953), 26, 83, and Ó hÓgáin (1982), 210-1.

In the old days, there was great sale for seal-oil in this village. It was a cure for pains in the bones, and for many other ailments like that. There were men on the island and, after the season was right, the trade they had was killing these seals and making oil from their flesh. One nice summer's day, in the middle of summer, a big crowd of them went up here to the north side of the island, to a place they call Scoilt na Rón (The Cleft of the Seals). There was a big fissure there, with a shore at the top of it and, on a hot day with an ebb tide, the seals used go in here so that they could lie out along the shore. You'll see them doing the same thing today as well as that day.

Anyway, when this crowd was going down that day, there were seven or eight seals stretched out along the shore, and there was one big grey one in the middle, as big as a bullock. They thought to themselves that he would be a grand prize, if they could manage to finish him off. They had no big instrument to kill him - they had only short clubs. There was no gun on the island that time, nor until long enough afterwards. All the same, if a couple of men gave a seal a blow of this club, he'd be finished.

Well, as I've just said, they thought that this big grey seal would be a great catch, if they could give him the belt in the right place. They completely surrounded him, so that he had no route of escape. A Rogers man was nearest to him, and he had the club drawn over his head to strike, when the seal opened his mouth and spoke, as piteously as a person might.

'Oh Rogers, the generous,
Don't do the senseless thing.
I am of your flesh and blood, to the very marrow . . .'

The old people had a big long verse about what the seal said, but I don't think anyone in the village has it now.

As soon as the men heard the seal talking, they went off and left him, and they headed for home as quickly as they could. It was years and years after that before any fishermen on this island had the courage to kill a seal. And maybe there would have been none killed since either, only for the fact that guns came to the island, and the men back at the lighthouse used to be shooting them. The people weren't as afraid after that, and they killed hundreds of them. The fishermen wouldn't have a living at all now, if they were afraid, and there would be no use in their casting a salmon-net from the stern of a boat, unless they had a gun with them.[47]

At the very least, the two texts from the Book of Lismore serve to provide us with evidence that supernatural seals have been a part of Irish tradition for quite some time. As such, they also supply a literary/historical backdrop, however sketchy, for the later oral accounts about seals. Beyond this, it is difficult to assess their significance, if any, on the development of the oral tradition.

---

47 *IFC* 988:72-4. Recorded by Seán Ó hEochaidh from Jimí Ó Díocháin. For the original text in Irish, see the Appendix. The translation given here is my own.

IV

This brief overview of Irish seal-beliefs raises a number of interesting questions on a variety of different levels. Further investigation is undoubtedly required of the inter-relationship between seal-beliefs found in Ireland and those found abroad. Such investigation might well, for example, suggest reasons for the apparent displacement of the seal by the mermaid in Irish versions of the story of *The Seal Woman*, in contrast to the general situation in Scotland, Iceland and Scandinavia.[48] In Ireland, however, and with an apparent inconsistency, traditions about families descended from seals are not uncommon, as we have seen. Similarities in Irish tradition between the mermaid and the supernatural death messenger, or banshee, may be of significance in this connection, and also deserve further attention.[49]

The functional aspects of the beliefs and narratives also call for study. As has been pointed out elsewhere, there is an obvious didactic element to many of them – i.e., the danger and risk involved in having anything to do with otherworld beings.[50] Almqvist has also discussed some of the social and psychological functions of the legend of *The Seal Woman*, in his various studies of it.[51] Suffice it to say here that Irish traditions regarding seals undoubtedly touch on issues which have to do with control and with survival, with man's perceptions of the otherworld and of the after life, with appearance and reality, and with the true nature of things.[52] Here we find ourselves partly in the realm of metaphor and symbolism which, as we know, has its own importance.

Mention of metaphor and symbolism brings us conveniently back to the comments made at the beginning of this article, regarding the relationship between mankind and the environment. Briefly, it should be said that one of the most

---

48 See Almqvist (1990b). Further attention must also be directed towards the somewhat unexpected appearance of a seal, rather than a mermaid, in a small number of Irish versions of *The Seal Woman* which have been noted, contrary to what we might expect, in the south of Ireland.

49 Both are solitary, supernatural, female beings, often associated with water and often seen combing their hair. Both are perceived as harbingers of misfortune and both have associations with particular families. One of the most common stories about the banshee describes how her comb is stolen from her, and how she subsequently manages to retrieve it. This story, in its essence, is not unlike the story of the seal/mermaid who has her cloak/tail/,etc. stolen from her, and who subsequently retrieves it. It would be very possible that one tradition might have exerted an influence on the other. In this connection, see Lysaght (1996), 45-6, 66, 101, 159-63, 172, 180-1, etc., for her comments on some of these similarities and possible cross-influences.

50 Almqvist (1990b), 38-9, etc.; Kavanagh (1995), 81.

51 Almqvist (1990b), 8-9, 38-9, etc. Here, he has written of the importance of the story's human dimension, and of what the story has to tell us about nature versus nurture (culture), about marital relationships and love, and about conflict between double loyalties.

52 The complex question of gender enters the equation at this point also. In looking at the story of *The Seal Woman*, for example, we must consider matters such as the autonomy of women, and the dependence of women on men – whether that dependence be real or imagined – as well as the fraught question of women who leave their children, along with all of the related emotional bondage and baggage which that involves. This is, of course, by no means the only type of reading to which the story lends itself, but it is one which should not be ignored.

important things to realise about Irish seal-traditions is that they are ultimately true – or at least that they have a truth of their own, albeit not necessarily in a literal sense. In their own way, the beliefs and stories can be seen to reflect an infinitely more refined and sophisticated understanding of the delicate balance which exists between mankind and the natural environment – and of man's place in the overall scheme of nature – than we find in what would usually be regarded as more advanced systems of belief.[53] As such, the legends and beliefs still have much to offer us.

Appendix

IFC 442:486-7.

Bhí muid lá ag gabháil siar ag iascach, agus thiar ar Charraig Tíre bhí dhá rón ar charraig ann. Agus tamall uathu bhí rón mór liath ar charraig eile. Acht ní raibh sé i bhfad gur thosaigh an dá rón ag troid. Agus tháinig an rón mór anall agus thosaigh sé ag bualadh cheann acu gur chuir sé ó chéile iad, agus d'fhan sé tamall go raibh 'chuile shórt thart.

Ba ghearr gur imigh sé anonn ar a charraig féin aríst, agus chuaigh an rón suas ar an gcarraig a raibh sé cheana uirthi, agus dheamhan i bhfad go raibh an dá rón ag troid le chéile aríst. Agus anall leis an rón mór aríst agus thosaigh sé ag *slap*áil an róin chéanna aríst gur chuir sé den charraig é, mar a bheadh máthair le beirt pháistí. Agus d'fhan sé féin ar an gcarraig agus chuir sé an rón óg anonn ar an gcarraig eile. Rinne muid an-iontas dhe.

IFC 799:238-42.

Tógadh mise thíos in íochtar Ros Goill, agus nuair a bhí mé i mo ghasúr bheag bhí seanduine ins an darna doras domh, agus ba ghnáthach liom an t-am uilig a chaitheamh aige. Ní iarrfainn pléisiúr ach aige ó thuitim oíche go ham luí ag éisteacht le seanscéalta breátha a bhí aige, agus seanchasc fá achan seort eile chomh maith. Is minic a d'inis sé oiread scéalta dúinn fán 'mhuintir bheaga' (sic), agus go gcaithfeadh sé féin a dhul linn chun an bhaile le a mhéad agus a bhíodh muid scanraithe go dtiocfadh siad orainn ar an bhealach. Tá dearmad déanta agam daofa sin uilig anois, ach b'fhéidir nuair a chluinfinn scaifte ag seanchasc fá rudaí mar seo, b'fhéidir go dtiocfadh cuid acu ar ais in mo chuimhne.

Mánus Jondy a bheirimist ar an fhear seo, agus cinnte go leor seanchaí ar dóigh a bhí ann. Tá cuimhne agam ar oíche amháin a d'inis sé scéal domh agus cha dtearn mé dearmad den scéal seo ariamh ó shoin. Agus saoilim nach dtiocfadh le duine ar bith a chluinfeadh é dearmad a dhéanamh de. 'Seo scéal de na rudaí,' mar

---

53 Ballard (1983) also mentions this dimension of seal-lore. She writes (p. 40) of the seal 'as a symbol of the islander's relationship to the environment'. Thomson (1980) writes as follows (p.12): 'For all great story-telling, spoken or written, contains layer upon layer of meaning and the older you grow, the more you experience actual and imaginative life, the deeper you are drawn'.

a dúirt sé féin, 'a chuala mé m'athair ag rá gur chuala sé a athair mór ag rá.' Bhuel, fadó ó shoin, is cosúil go dtáinig am a rabh an t-iasc an-fharsaing ar chósta na hÉireann anseo. Bhí sé chomh farsaing sin agus go rabh sé ag teacht isteach tirim tráite ar na cladaigh, agus ins an am chéanna cha rabh aon bheathaíoch le fáil ar chósta na hAlbana nó na Sasan. Chuir sin oiread mire ar mhuintir na hAlbana agus go dtearn na cailleachaí pisreogacha a bhí acu rónta daofa féin, agus tháinig siad anall go cósta na hÉireann leis an iasc a dhíbirt.

Bhí cúpla fear ansin ins an chomharsain ansin a bhí ar shiúl le beangláin ag cruinniú leithigh ins an earrach. Goidé a bhí ach na rónta seo istigh fríd na boilgeacha ag imeall an uisce faoin leitheach. Sháigh fear acu seo an beanglán síos fríd an leitheach, mar a shaoil sé féin, agus goidé a rinne sé ach a shá isteach i súil ceann de na rónta seo, agus siúd ar shiúl as go bráthach leis an rón agus an beanglán i bhfastó ann.

Seal de bhlianta ina dhiaidh sin, bhí na fir seo iad féin ag iascaireacht thall ar chósta na hAlbana. Bádaí a bhí leofa ins an am sin atá rud inteacht cosúil leis an churach a tchí muid ar na cladaigh inniu, ach amháin go rabh siad déanta ar an taobh istigh le cláraí agus ar an taobh amuigh bhí craicne giorria. Ba gnáthach leofa úsc a chur ansin ins an chruth go mairfeadh sé agus nach bhfaigheadh an t-uisce fríd. Bhuel, bhí ceann de na bádaí seo ag iascaireacht ar chósta na hAlbana, mar a dúirt mé, agus tráthnóna amháin, nuair a bhí siad ina luí ins an phort, chuaigh cúpla duine de na fir amach fríd an tír fá choinne giota siúil. Nuair a bhí siad ag dhul thart ag doras an toighe seo, goidé a tchí fear acu ach beanglán a chaill sé ar an trá cúpla bliain roimhe sin.

Bhí iontas mór air, agus dar leis féin go rachadh sé isteach go bhfeicfeadh sé goidé mar a fuair an beanglán go dtí an áit sin. Nuair a chuir sé a cheann isteach, bhí seanbhean ina suí ins an chlúdaigh agus bratóg éadaigh casta thart ar a súil. Bheir seisean ar an bheanglán agus thóg sé ina láimh é, agus dúirt sé mar seo: 'Cén áit an bhfuair sibh an beanglán seo?' 'Ní dhéanann sé cuid mhór difir,' arsa an tseanbhean, 'agus i gcás ar bith, goidé atá a fhios agatsa fá dtaobh dhó sin?' 'Bhuel, tá,' a deir sé, 'tá sé cosúil le ceann a chaill mise i bhfad ó shoin thall in Éirinn, ceann a chuir mé i bhfastó i rón.'

'Ó, a dhiabhail!' arsa sise, ag tógáil pota uisce ghalaigh a bhí ar an teinidh, agus ag tabhairt iarraidh air. 'Tusa a chuir an beanglán i bhfastó ionamsa, agus tá mé i mo shuí anseo ó shoin, agus an tsúil crochta liom.'

Bhain an fear na bonnaí as chomh tiubh agus a thiocfadh leis, agus a sháith lúcháire a bhí air go bhfuair sé ar shiúl. Theith siad cúpla lá ina dhiaidh sin, agus níl mé ag rá go bhfacthas ar chóstaí na hAlbana é ón lá sin go dtí an lá a chuaigh sé chun na huaighe.

Bhí an seanduine, Mánus, ag inse dúinn go minic nach rabh smid bhréige ins an scéal sin, agus thiocfadh leis ainmniú dúinn an áit i Ros Goill a rabh an fear ina chónaí ar éirigh seo dó. Ba léar leis fosta gur daoine faoi gheasa a bhí ins na rónta uilig, agus ní bhainfeadh sé daofa ar ór nó ar airgead.

IFC 1226:323.
Deiridís gur seandaoine ab ea iad (i.e., rónta) a bhí faoi dhraíocht. Níl puinn acu anois ann ach do bhíodh mórán acu fadó ann. Tá cúig méireanta orthu ar nós an duine.

Tá cuas i mbun mo chuid talúnsa thiar ins Na Ródaibh – cuas mór fé thalamh ann – agus bhíodh na róinte i gcónaí istigh. *Killurley Commons* a thugann siad ar an áit. Ina bhun san atá an cuas – Cuas an Róin. Tháinig fear ón bhFaill Móir ann lá, fear a bhíodh ag marú i gcónaí, go dtugaidís Féilim Mhic Eoin (?) air. Agus bhí rón sa chuas – bhí sí i dtinneas, bhí sí ag cur cúram róin óig di agus do labhair sí leis. 'A Fhéilim Mhic Eoin,' a dúirt sí, 'ná mairbh mé go deo go gcuirfead cúram an oisín óig seo dhíom.' 'Ní mharódh, ná go deo!', a dúirt sé, ag fágaint ansin. Bhailibh sé leis, is níor chuaigh sé riamh ó shoin ag marú aon róin.

IFC 524:291-3.
Bhí rón insa tír seo agus bhí an fear seo ag siúl insa chladach. Agus casadh leis an rón óg seo idir dhá charraig insa chladach agus thóig sé suas an rón óg agus d'iompair sé abhaile é. Agus níor rinn sé tada air ach (é) a iompar abhaile.

Agus nuair a tháinig an seanrón go dtí an spot tráthnóna insa tóir ar an rón óg, ní rabh an rón óg le fáil. Agus thoisigh sí féin agus an seanrón eile, a comrádaí, ag caoineadh. Agus mhothófá iad thíos in Iorras ag caoineadh – agus thuas ansin ar an Mhala Raithní a tharla sé – agus mhothófá an péire acu ag caoineadh. Bhuel, nuair a mhothaigh an fear maith seo an caoineadh truamhéile insa bhaile, dúirt sé cinnte gurbé an fáth a rabh an caoineadh go rabh an dá rón ag caoineadh faoin rud a rinn sé féin, go dtug sé leis aníos ón chladach an rón óg seo.

Agus beireann sé ar an rón óg seo agus iomchraíonn sé síos ar ais aríst é gur lig sé insa spot cheanann chéanna é. Agus bhí an t-ionradh ag teacht isteach. Agus d'imigh leis suas an cladach. Agus tháinig an dá rón isteach san áit a rabh an cionn óg agus phóg siad é agus ligh siad é agus shlíoc siad é agus chíor siad é, agus thoisigh an chaint ansin.

'Muise, fad saoil agatsa, a Mhártain Bhriain Ruaidh. Fad saoil le séan agatsa, a Mhártain Bhriain Ruaidh. Fad saoil le séan agatsa, a Mhártain Bhriain Ruaidh.' D'imigh leis abhaile, agus bhí an baile uilig go léir ag éisteacht leis na rónta ag rá na focla sin.

Agus bhí saol fada le séan ag Mártan Bhriain Ruaidh. Agus ba mhaith an fear é. Agus níl sé marbh seacht mbliana go fóill. Ón lá sin go dtí an lá inniu níor lig sé sin aon lámh ar aon rón agus bhí an t-ádh air. Bhí an t-ádh ar an fhear sin. Agus ní leagfadh aon nduine ar an mbaile aon lámh orthu.

IFC S 298:105-6.
Uair amháin, do ghabh fear rón ins an bhfarraige in aice le Trá Ligeach. Thug sé an rón abhaile leis agus bhí sé beo. Do chuir sé an rón isteach san gcistin.

An oíche sin, bhí fear ag dul treasna na trá agus d'airigh sé glór cainte, 'A Dhonncha Dhonn! A Dhonncha Dhonn!' Do lean an fear ar a thuras, agus chuaigh sé isteach i dtigh ar an dtaobh eile den dtrá. Is istigh san dtigh seo a bhí an rón, agus d'inis an fear an scéal d'fhear an tí. Nuair a chlois an rón na focail 'A Dhonncha Dhonn', do labhair sé. 'Ó! Ba é sin Tadhg a bhí do mo lorgsa.' D'fhág siad an rón saor agus ní airíodar an glór ón uair sin amach.

IFC 1100:578-9.

Fear a bhí ins An Mhachaire, do bhí sé ag an bhfarraige istoíche ag faire ar fheamnaigh a bhailiú. Agus do chonaic sé rón agus do rug sé ar an rón, agus do thug sé leis an rón abhaile ina bheathaidh. Bhí sí ar chloich ar dtúis ina suí ina bean, agus cochall in aice léi, is í ag cíoradh a cinn. Agus do dh'éalaigh sé uirthi nuair a bhí sí ag cíoradh a cinn. Agus do sciob sé an cochall agus do thug sé leis an cochall. Agus do chaith sí an cochall a leanúint, is do tháinig sí ina dhiaidh go dtí an tigh. Do tháinig sé isteach agus do chaith sé an cochall faid a urchair siar ar an lochta.

D'fhan sí ansan ina theannta, is thug sí tamall blian ann. Agus bhí páistí acu agus bhíodh cosa na bpáistí ina *web*-anna, ar nós chos na gé nó na lachan. Ní raibh aon oscailt ar na méireanta. Bhí na méireanta tarraigthe amach ann, má b'fhíor, agus do bhíodar iata eatarthu amach go barra.

Bhí ábhar páistí aige léi agus thug sí tamall blianta ann, agus í an a-sheirbhíseach. Agus tháinig lá éigint áirithe air go raibh *pinch* air chun coirce a chur in airde ar an lochta nó rud eicínt. Agus chuaigh sé in airde ar an lochta i gcionn áirithe blianta, agus do bhí sé ag caitheamh anuas seana-rudaí a bhí in airde ar an lochta ann. Agus ins an chaitheamh anuas dó, do chaith sé anuas an cochall. Agus do chonaic sí an cochall, agus do dh'éirigh sí agus do rug sí air agus do bhuail sí féna tóin ar an gcathaoir é. Do dh'imigh sé amach ansan chun an choirce a chur isteach. Nuair a bhí sé imithe amach, do thóg sí an cochall agus do chuir sí i bhfolach é. Agus ag déanamh ar thráthnóna, do chíor sí agus do ghlan sí suas a leanaí go glan, agus do bhuail sí uirthi an cochall. Agus do bhuail sí síos chun na trá, is ní fheacaigh éinne as san amach í.

IFC 641:65.

Nuair a bhí sé ag imeacht, 'Cé dhár dhíobh thú, a bhean an tí,' a deir sé, 'le do thoil?' 'De Chlainn Mhic Conaola mé,' a deir sí. 'Mar tá muide faoi dhraíocht. Tá Clainn Mhic Conaola,' a deir sí, 'faoi dhraíocht.' Bean de Chlainn Mhic Conaola agus a páiste a bhí ar an gcarraig nuair a chaith sé leob.

(. . . Ins an áit seo [i.e., Leitir Mucadha], tugtar 'cineál chloiginn aníos' mar leasainm ar dhuine de Chlainn Mhic Conaola. Mar bíonn an rón ag cur a chloiginn aníos thar an uisce, agus ó deirtear gur uaidh na rónta a shíolraigh Clainn Mhic Conaola, tugtar 'cineál chloiginn aníos' orthu.)

IFC 988:72-4.

Tá muid ariamh ag éisteacht go bhfuil baint ag Clainn Mhic Ruairí an oileáin seo leis na rónta, agus go bhfuil siad muinteartha daofa fosta. Cha dtig liomsa a rá cé acu atá sin fíor nó nach bhfuil, ach níl agamsa ach an rud a chuala mé ag an tseanmhuintir.

Ins an tsean-am, bhí díol mór ar ola an róin ar an bhaile seo. Bhí sí ina leigheas ar phian cnámh, agus ar fhichid pian mar sin. Bhí fir ar an oileán agus bhí sé ina cheird acu, nuair a bheadh an séasúr ceart, ag marbhadh na rónta seo agus ag déanamh ola as a gcuid feola. Lá deas samhraidh a bhí ann (i lár an tsamhraidh) agus d'imigh scaifte mór suas anseo go dtí an taobh ó thuaidh den oileán, chuig áit a dtugtar Scoilt na Rón air. Bhí scoilt mhór ansin, agus cladach thuas ag a barr, agus nuair a bhíodh trá ann, agus an lá te, thigeadh na rónta isteach anseo go luíodh siad thuas ar bharr an chladaigh. Tchífidh tú iad á dhéanamh sin inniu chomh maith leis an lá sin.

Ach a dhul síos daofasan an lá seo, bhí seacht nó ocht de cheannaibh de rónta móra ina luighe ar bharr an chladaigh, agus bhí ceann mór liath ina measc a bhí chomh mór le bolóig. Dar leofa féin gur bhreá an éadáil é seo, dá dtéadh acu deireadh a chur leis. Cha rabh aon ghléas mór acu lena mharbhadh. Cha rabh acu ach smaichtíní maide. Cha rabh gunna ar bith ar an oileán an uair sin nó go cionn fada go leor ina dhiaidh. Mar sin féin, an rón a bhfaigheadh cúpla fear buille den smaichtín seo air, bhí deireadh leis.

Bhuel, mar tá mé i ndiaidh a rá, dar leofa gur bhreá an éadáil an rón mór liath seo, dá dtéadh acu an cnagán a thabhairt dó san áit cheart! Chuaigh siad fá dtaobh de ar achan taobh sa dóigh nach rabh bealach teichte aige. Fear de Mhuintir Ruairí a ba ndeise dó, agus bhí a smaichtín tógtha aige os cionn mhullach a chinn a dhul a thabhairt an bhuille dó, nuair a d'fhoscail sé a bhéal agus labhair sé chomh truacánta agus a dhéanfadh duine:

> 'A Mhic Ruairí na féile,
> Ná déan díth na céille,
> Do chuid fola agus feola go bhfuil ionam go smior!'

Bhí rann mór fada ag an tseanmhuintir fán rud a dúirt an rón uilig, ach ní shaoilim go bhfuil duine ar bith ar an bhaile anois a bhfuil sé acu.

Chomh luath agus a chuala na fir an rón ag caint, d'imigh siad agus d'fhág siad é, agus bhain siad an baile amach comh hachomair agus a tháinig leo. Bhí sé blianta agus blianta ina dhiaidh sin sula bhfuair iascaire ar bith de chuid an oileáin seo uchtach rón a mharbhadh, agus b'fhéidir nach marbhfadh ó shoin ach go b'é go dtáinig gunnaí chun an oileáin, agus go dteachaigh na fir atá thiar i dteach an tsolais á scaoileadh. Cha rabh oiread eagla ar na daoine ó shoin, agus mharbhaigh siad na céadta acu. Ní bheadh beo ar bith ar iascairí anois, dá mbeadh eagla orthu, nó ní bheadh maith daofa eangach bradán a chur amach as deireadh báid gan an gunna a bheith ar iompar leo.

The Mystical Island in Irish Folklore

DÁITHÍ Ó hÓGÁIN

The lore of otherworld islands off the western coast of Ireland is generally similar in nature to that concerning sunken towns or cities in other coastal areas of the country as well as in numerous inland lakes. In many respects also – as we shall have occasion to mention – the lore is related to beliefs and legends concerning otherworld dwellings situated within the ordinary landscape, such as fairy palaces within raths and tumuli.

We may begin with a general enumeration and description of these mystical islands off the coast. The best known of them in tradition is Uí Bhreasaíl, references to which name have been found in all the western coastal areas.[1] This is a very old designation. It occurs as the name of an island off the western Irish coast in maps from the fourteenth century onwards, and remained in some nautical charts as something of an anachronism even as late as the year 1865.[2] So influential was the name of this wished-for land, indeed, that on the discovery by the Portuguese of a vast and very real new colony in the western world in the year 1499 they decided to use this name, Brazil, for it.

There is some doubt as to the origin of the toponymic Breasaíl. Some authorities have claimed that both imaginary island and real country are named from a Spanish word meaning 'red wood', but it would appear more appropriate to look for its origin in Irish sources. A Venetian writer from the year 1459 seems to give a hint as to its origin, when he explains it as 'Berzel, anesto isola de hibernia, son dite fortunate'.[3] Here the island's name is taken to mean 'fortunate', and an Irish source for this explanation may be indicated by the semantic proximity to the word *bres*, which meant 'noble'. Breasal was a personal name in early Ireland, and there is no scarcity in our early literature of instances of the name, though these refer to population groups in inland areas. *Uí Bhreasail* (meaning 'descendants of Breasal') occurs in particular as the name of a sept who inhabited present-day county Armagh, on the southern shore of Lough Neagh.[4] One early mediaeval story told of this lake

---

1 *IFC* 561:185-6 (Donegal); *IFC* 1311:502-7 (Galway); from Kerry the following: *IFC* 12:118-9 ; *IFC* 215:867-9; *IFC* 446:249-51; *IFC* 587:279-83; *IFC* 966:533-6; *IFC* 979:453-4; *IFC* S 432:166. Further evidence for this general designation is in Westropp (1912), 254-7. In the Kerry instances the name takes the form 'an Bhreasaíl'. *IFC* = Irish Folklore collection being the Main Manuscripts Collection and *IFC S* = the Schools' Manuscripts Collection of the Department of Irish Folklore at University College Dublin; the numerals on either side of the colon represent the volume number and page number(s) respectively.
2 Westropp (1912), 241-7 and (1911-1915), 76-8.
3 Westropp (1912), 242, 255.
4 Hogan (1910), 662.
5 Gwynn (1913), 450-9, 560-1 and (1924), 62-9, 388-91. See also Ó hÓgáin (1990), 181.

springing up from dry land,[5] and another told of an Ulster king called Breasal Breac going on an adventure under the sea for fifty years.[6] It may be that the original association of Uí Bhreasail with a sunken city originated in such traditions.

Be that as it may, the mystical island of Breasaíl or Uí Bhreasaíl was well-established in Irish folklore by the late Middle Ages, and the other named islands of a similar nature probably owe much of their origin to it. When departing from that designation, oral tradition in Donegal is not very specific concerning the names of such islands. The usual alternative designation in that region is *oileán sídheanta*, which we can loosely translate as 'fairy island', and the most noted instance was such a mirage seen off Rossan Point. This mystical island contained trees, cattle-herds and all other features of an ordinary landscape, and could be seen to emerge above the water just before sunrise on May morning every seven years.[7] When it surfaced once, a number of men set out in a boat towards it, bringing a pot of red embers with them with which to disenchant it. Coming near to the island, they saw a girl sitting underneath a tree knitting. She threw the knitting-spool into the boat. It stuck there, tying the boat to the island with the thread. The boat began to shake violently. One of the men placed a red ember on the thread and, as it burned through, the island began to sink into the sea. If they had thrown the embers onto the island, it would have remained forever above sea level.[8]

Going southwards from there, the next clear instance of an alternative name was Mainistir Ladra, which was seen from the coasts of south Donegal, Sligo and north Mayo. This was a great enchanted land (*talamh atá faoi dhraíocht*), which was also sunken in the sea, and it appeared above water once in every seven years. Accounts describe it as a delightful green land, with hills and woods, and churches and monastery and a tower. Sheep were browsing on the slopes, cattle were grazing in green pastures, and clothes were drying on the hedges. It was believed that this great island could be disenchanted if a coal of fire were thrown onto it. One reference to the island, but without mentioning its name, dates as far back as the year 1636.[9] From another such island off the coast of Mayo, though unspecified as to name, it was said that fishermen once heard, through a fog, the bleating of sheep and lambs and saw leaves of oak and apple-trees.[10] The situation of Mainistir Ladra must be based on the fact that there is a breaker in that place, the *Tuile Ladrann* ('flood of Ladru') which was famed in the mediaeval literature as being one of the great waves of Ireland.[11]

---

6 Best//Bergin/O'Brien (1954-67), 3, 759. See also O'Grady (1892), 2, 471.
7 *IFC* 1228:572-3.
8 *IFC* 140:374-7; *IFC* 1034:79-81. Further north, it was said that an enchanted island lay off Inishowen, which could only be seen by a member of the O'Doherty family – *Dublin University Magazine* 18 (1861), 215-6. For reports of other such islands off the Donegal coast, see Westropp (1912), 254.
9 General discussion of Mainistir Ladra, with citations, in Westropp (1912), 252-4.
10 *Ibid*, 252. See also *Dublin University Magazine* 18 (1861), 301.
11 Best/Bergin/O'Brien (1954-67), 3, 749.

A celebrated island was said to lie off the Galway coast. It was sometimes referred to as Uí Bhreasaíl, but more usually was called Beag-Árainn or Árainn Bheag. It lay west of the Aran Islands, and used to surface very near to the three rocky eminences called Skerd. Tradition generally claims that it was sunk under the cod bank known as *Iomaire Buí* ('Yellow Ridge'). An account from the year 1684 describes it as a great city, with apparitions of people running to and fro, and of ships and great stacks of corn.[12] Many descriptions of this phantom isle have been collected from later lore. It used to surface once in every seven years on the Twelfth Night of Christmas. The specific choice of this time – the Feast of the Epiphany - must be based on the tradition of other mystical occurrences, such as the idea that at midnight on this feast water briefly becomes wine, rushes become silk, and gravel becomes gold.[13] It was said that Beag-Árainn could be disenchanted if a spark or a burning ember were thrown onto it,[14] and its existence is taken to be proven by branches of holly or heather or sticks found floating in the water far out at sea.[15] In appearance, we are told, it is just like any big town, with lamplights in the streets.[16]

Lore of Beag-Árainn has been greatly developed due to a claim made by a certain Muircheartach Ó Laoi, who practiced medicine in the seventeenth century. This is how the scholar Roderick O'Flaherty, writing in the year 1684, described that claim:

> There is now living, Morogh O'Ley, who immagins he was himself personally in O'Brazil for two days.... in the month of Aprill, Anno Domini 1668, going alone from one village to another, in a melancholy humour, upon some discontent of his wife, he was encountered by two or three strangers, and forcibly carried by boat into O'Brazil, as such as were within told him, and they could speak both English and Irish. He was ferried out hoodwink'd, in a boat, as he immagins, till he was left on the sea point by Galway; where he lay in a friend's house for some days after, being very desperately ill, and knowes not how he came to Galway then. But, by that means, about seven or eight years after, he began to practise both chirurgery and phisick, and so continues ever since to practise, tho' he never studied nor practised either all his life time before, as all we that knew him since he was a boy can averr.[17]

---

12 O'Flaherty [Hardiman] (1846), 68-9.
13 Ó Súilleabháin (1942), 324 and (1967), 61-2. Belief in such mystical events on the night of 6 January goes back to Christian tradition of the fourth century AD in the Middle East – see Cullmann (1956), 23-8.
14 *IFC* 627:122-3, 371-6; *IFC* 739:383; *IFC* 801:192; *IFC* 1025:132-4; *IFC* 1105:3; *IFC* 1239:99; *IFC* 1320:272-3; *IFC S* 61:276-84; *IFC S* 68:238-9; *Irisleabhar na Gaedhilge* 4 (1889-93), 47. In *IFC S* 61:164-6 the disenchanting object is a bullet from a golden gun.
15 *IFC* 627:372-3; *IFC* 1105:4.
16 *IFC* 1320:273.
17 O'Flaherty [Hardiman] (1845), 70-2. For comments on this claim by Ó Laoi, see Ó hÓgáin (1982), 193, 435.

Folk tradition invariably claims that Beag-Árainn was the island visited by Ó Laoi, and that he was presented with a special magical book there.[18] This book, which still exists, is in fact a rather fanciful medical treatise which was compiled in the fifteenth century and which came into his possession.[19] The claim by Ó Laoi is the basis of the later folk tellings, which usually describe him as fishing in a boat when he is accosted by three boatmen and brought to Beag-Árainn. According to these folk accounts, when he begins to light his pipe, or otherwise make use of a red ember, the inhabitants of that island beg him not to do so and, as a reward for complying with their request, they give him the wonderful book. They tell him not to open it for seven years, but either himself or his wife or his son breaks this prohibition within a shorter time. The amount of knowledge gained from the book is incomplete, being in direct ratio to the amount of time which has passed.

One other noted tradition attaches to Beag-Árainn. This is that it will one day be disenchanted, and simultaneously the real islands of Aran will subside and sink beneath the sea.[20] A variant of this is that the city of Galway itself will be subsumed,[21] and a traditional triad states that *Béal Átha an Rí a bhí, Gaillimh atá, agus Beag-Árainn a bheas* ('Athenry was, Galway is, and Beag-Árainn will be!').[22] Such comparisons between three places was to be found more generally in Irish folklore, the places mentioned being real towns or cities,[23] and so the instances of an otherworld island appearing in such triads can be seen as a late derivative.

The triad concerning Beag-Árainn was also known in north Clare,[24] but in that county the lore of a mystical island generally centred on a place called Cill Stuifín. This was said to have been a tract of land which had sunk long ago under the waves outside Liscannor bay, to the south-west of Lahinch. The usual explanation was that it had been an extension of that seaside town, and the belief was that when, at some future time, Cill Stuifín would resurface, then Lahinch would sink beneath the waves.[25] This comparison between the real place and the otherworld island was patterned on the Galway triad, in the form *an Leacht atá, agus Cill Stuifín a bheidh!* ('Lahinch is, and Cill Stuifín will be!').[26] It is clear, moreover, that this borrowing was facilitated by two local details. One of these details was a play on the placename 'Lahinch', which derives not from the ordinary Irish name of the town, *Leacht Uí Chonchúir*, but rather from another local toponymic *Leath Inse*. This latter really

18 *Irisleabhar na Gaedhilge* 4 (1889-93), 47; *An Stoc* 12/1923-1/1924, 3; Ó Direáin (1926), 24-6; *IFC* 64:102-7; *IFC* 76:1-7; *IFC* 157:526-9; *IFC* 627:373-5; *IFC* 786:92-9; *IFC* 801:192-3; *IFC* 1105:3; *IFC* 1311:502-7; *IFC S* 5:103-5; *IFC S* 11:457; *IFC S* 61:164-6; *IFC S* 68:238-9.
19 RIA 23 P 10, ii.
20 *IFC* 801:99.
21 *IFC S* 5:102.
22 *IFC* 109:180-2; *IFC* 627: 371-2.
23 e.g. the triad *Luimneach a bhí, Baile Átha Cliath atá, Gaillimh a bheidh!* ('Limerick was, Dublin is, Galway will be!').
24 Ó Duilearga & Ó hÓgáin (1981), 273 – see also *IFC* 1011:124-5.
25 *IFC S* 618:81-2; *IFC S* 621:317; *IFC S* 622:146.
26 A triad could be formed by the verse *Cill Stuithín a bhí, an Leacht atá, agus Sráid na Cathrach a bheidh!* ('Cill Stuifín was, Lahinch is, and Milltown will be!') *IFC S* 622:146; *IFC* 339: 340-1.

meant 'the side where the water-meadow is', but literally it could also be taken to mean 'half of the island'. That Lahinch was a half of the lost island was expressly claimed by some storytellers.[27]

The second local detail results from an account in the annals of an earthquake which took place in the year 803 AD. The annals describe this event in the following way: 'Great thunder, with wind and lightning, on the night before the festival of St Patrick, dispersing a great number of people – that is, a thousand and ten men, in the country of Corca Baiscinn; and the sea divided the island of Fiotha into three parts, and the same sea covered the land of Fiotha with sand, to the extent of the land of twelve cows.'[28] Fiotha has been identified with Mutton Island, some miles south along the coast from Lahinch.[29] All of this would indicate that the originator of this idea – that the mystical island was the other half of Lahinch – was some speculative scholar in recent centuries, who was interested in placenames and aware of the annalistic account.[30]

Accounts of Cill Stuifín are similar to those of the other mystical islands – it has gold-roofed towers and large buildings, a monastery, and luscious fields on which cattle and horses graze.[31] It surfaces once in every seven years, and there is a strong tradition that whoever sees it dies within the year.[32] Its position under the water is over a break-tide, and a solitary breaker can be seen there.[33] An elaboration of the tradition is that Cill Stuifín can only be disenchanted by a certain key, which has been lost in some nigh irretrievable place – such as in the sea itself, in some old ruins, or in a lake on the top of Slieve Callan.[34]

Variants of a particular legend are told of how Cill Stuifín first became enchanted. These usually focus on a druid of old, who resided beside Lahinch. Once, when going to war, he caused his residence to be surrounded or submerged by the sea-water so as to protect the household until his return. He was killed in the war, and since nobody else had his magical power the place remains in its mystical state.[35]

---

27 *IFC S* 618:177; *IFC S* 622:339, 340-1.
28 '*Tonitruum ualidum cumuento et igni in nocte precedenti feriam Patricii disipante plurimos hominum, id est mille et decem uiros i tir Corco Bascinn, et mare diuisit insolam Fitae in tres partes, et illudh mare cum harena terram Fitae abscondit, id est ined da boo deac di thir'* – Hennessy (1887), 288. This catastrophe is listed also – though variously for the years 800, 801, and 804 in other sources, for which see O'Donovan (1851), 410; Murphy (1896), 128-9; Hennessy (1866), 124; Todd (1848), 204-7.
29 Professor Patricia Lysaght, a native of the area, considers that the name Oileán Fiotha may be preserved in that of Wattle Island, one of the small islands off the coast in that place.
30 The earthquake is referred to – in the context of Cill Stuifín – by Frost (1893), 145-6, and by the collector of the version in *IFC S* 624:238.
31 Westropp (1912), 250-1; *IFC S* 622:547.
32 *IFC* 860:485, 491; *IFC* 1011:124; *IFC S* 624:241; *IFC S* 626:177-8; *IFC S* 622:541, 546-7; *IFC S* 622:340.
33 *IFC* 860:491; *IFC S* 621:204; *IFC S* 22:539, 544-7.
34 Ó Duilearga & Ó hOgáin (1981), 273; *IFC S* 621:317; *IFC S* 21:204; *IFC S* 625:119-20; *IFC S* 624:241; *IFC S* 618:81-2; *IFC S* 22:336-41, 539-41, 548-9.
35 *IFC S* 620:475-6; *IFC S* 622:146, 539-41; *IFC S* 626:177-8.

Variants do not mention that he was killed, but rather have him losing keys or an enemy deliberately throwing them away.[36] In some cases, he is described as a local chieftain called Stifín or Stiofán,[37] and he is even identified with St Stephen.[38] The existence of Cill Stuithín was taken as proved by the occasional drawing up by boat-anchors of buckets, pothooks, potatoes, meat, or masonry from the sea.[39]

The otherworld island in the folklore of south Clare and north Kerry is called Cill Stuithín, and in these areas it is said to be outside the mouth of the river Shannon.[40] It is clear, however, that the tradition of such an island as found all along the Clare coast is homogenuous, and so I take 'Cill Stuifín' and 'Cill Stuithín' to be dialectal variants of each other.[41] Accordingly, the north Kerry accounts are merely borrowings from county Clare. Narratives tell of a boatman in Limerick city who was approached by a stranger who hired him to bring some newly bought timber to his island home. That home turned out to be Cill Stuithín, and as they approached the island the stranger told him to set the timber afloat in the water. The boatman did this, and when he turned around again to speak he found that the stranger had disappeared.[42]

In one south Clare variant, the island is said to have surfaced as the boatman approached, and he was brought into a dwelling there by the stranger and entertained to tea.[43] A similar account was collected in Kerry concerning an enchanted island – apparently derived from Cill Stuithín but called *An Chathair idir Dhá Dhrol* ('City between Two Loops') – which was said to lie outside Ballyguinn Point in Brandon Bay.[44] This story of the visit accords with memorate-type accounts from the west Kerry area of the island of Breasaíl. In that area, certain named fishermen are said to have visited Breasaíl and to have walked the beautiful streets there and to have been treated to food and drink.[45]

The fact that something sinister was felt to be connected with Breasaíl in the west Kerry area, however, is illustrated by the motif of an old resident there who offers a handshake to the fisherman. The fisherman wisely declines, for the

---

36 *IFC S* 621:204, 317; *IFC S* 624:238-42; *IFC S* 25:119-20.
37 *IFC S* 621:204; *IFC S* 622:337-8, 539-41; *IFC S* 624:238.
38 Frost (1893), 145-6; *IFC S* 622:339; *IFC S* 24:238.
39 *IFC S* 622:340; *IFC S* 625:235.
40 For south Clare *IFC* 860:481-5, 490-1. For north Kerry *IFC* 353:632-4; *IFC* 658:470-3; *IFC S* 399:10-11, 16.
41 The phoneme 'f' is often changed to the phoneme 'h' in Munster Irish, especially in the palatal varieties. The reverse is sometimes found, as for instance the word *sruthán*, pronounced *srufán* in Limerick Irish – see Bruen & Ó hÓgáin (1996), 31. Thus 'Cill Stuithín' would be a natural development from 'Cill Stuifín', and vice versa. The name of St Scoithín was pronounced 'Scoifín' in county Kilkenny – see note 90 below.
42 *IFC S* 399:10-11; *IFC S* 622:306-7, 341; *IFC* 860:481-5.
43 *IFC S* 604:157-8.
44 *IFC* 272:91-3. For this see island, see also *IFC* 272:69-72; *IFC* 744:45.
45 *IFC* 12:118-9; *IFC* 215:867-9; *IFC* 240:199-214; *IFC* 834:428-38.

handshake would have crushed his hand.[46] This handshake-motif was also quite popular in ordinary lore concerning visits to otherworld raths and tumuli in that area.[47] In common with other areas, in west Kerry the island called Breasaíl was said to surface once in every seven years,[48] and if a fistful of clay were thrown at it it would be disenchanted.[49] A person who saw it could be left with a twisted mouth or some other deformity or illness.[50] This type of motif is also attested from the north Kerry lore of Cill Stuithín, where a man is reported to have lost his sight and to have had his speech affected after seeing the island.[51]

On the pensinsula of Iveragh in south Kerry, and spreading north from there to parts of the Dingle peninsula, there was a strong tradition regarding a sunken island-city under the wave of Tóim. This breaker is just outside Rossbeigh, and the city there is known as Cathair Tonn Tóime. The legend concerns how a fine cloak was to be seen drying on a wall in the island, and a daring young man called O'Shea determined to seize that cloak. When the island surfaced, he raced towards it on horseback and took the cloak. A resident of the island shouted out a warning, however, and the island began to sink. The wave of Tóim raced after O'Shea and cut away the hind-quarters of his horse as he escaped.[52] The young man is in Irish called Mac Uí Shé, which would be translated into English as 'Shea's Son'. Since this is a tolerable folk-equivalent of Jason, it is difficult to avoid the conclusion that this legend is derived from a version of the story of Jason's Fleece read out by some scholar in recent centuries. The tradition of the wave of Tóim is an old one,[53] its name probably being derived from the word *túaim*, meaning 'bank' or 'tumulus'.[54] The fact that a breaker is caused by such a geological feature on the sea-bed would mean that the bank could be imagined as a burial mound (*túaim*) of some mythical personage. Such lore was in existence in mediaeval Ireland, as instanced by the texts concerning the drowning of Clíodhna at the breaker which bore her name at Glandore in county Cork.[55] The reputed otherworld of the wave of Tóim would accordingly have been used by some eighteenth-century scholar – perhaps the poet Diarmaid na Bolgaí Ó Sé[56] – on which to hang his version of the Jason story.

---

46 *IFC* 587:281-2; *IFC* 979:308-10; *IFC S* 432:166.
47 Designated type ML (Migratory Legend Type) 5010 by Bo Almqvist in *Béaloideas* 51 (1991), 271.
48 *IFC* 8:386; *IFC* 12:119; *IFC* 215:869; *IFC* 241:179-84; *IFC* 587:280.
49 *IFC* 8:386; *IFC* 446:249.
50 *IFC* 12:119-20; *IFC* 215:869.
51 *IFC* 353:633.
52 Many versions of this legend have been collected – these are listed and compared by Ruth Langan in a student essay for the years 1992-1993 in the Department of Irish Folklore, entitled 'An Brat ar Oileán Inse'.
53 Hogan (1910), 642.
54 RIA Dictionary s.v. 'túaim'.
55 Gwynn (1913), 3, 206-15. The wave of Clíodhna was one of the three great waves of Ireland, according to the old literature. A mythical woman was also drowned at another of these, the wave of Tuagh – see O'Grady (1892), 2, 483.
56 See the witty reference by this poet – probably intended by him as word-play on his surname – in Ó Súilleabháin (1937), 48.

Much more could be said by way of detail concerning these mystical western islands, but it is better to pause here and to synopsise some of the material. First of all, it can be said that several motifs from ordinary otherworld lore have become attached to the narratives in the different areas. In Donegal, for instance, the person who sees the island uses an implement to mark the spot where he or she is standing. The person then goes to call the neighbours, but on returning finds the area filled with similar implements.[57] This means that a view of the island is dependent on one standing in a special place, as is expressed directly in one Kerry version.[58] In versions from Donegal, Clare, and Kerry, the attempt is foiled in another way – the viewer looks away, and when he looks again the island has disappeared.[59]

Another significant addition to the narrative is found occasionally in almost all areas. This involves an account of a fisherman who throws an object against a threatening wave, and is later conducted by a stranger to an aquatic dwelling where an otherworld person lies injured from the object which the fisherman had thrown. The fisherman cures the patient by removing the object, and is escorted back to land. This is in fact a separate legend,[60] and a related motif tells of an anchor getting stuck in a house on a sunken enchanted island, and how an inhabitant of that island surfaces to complain of this.[61] Yet another interesting addition, found in accounts of a mystical island in Galway and Kerry, and also in a version from the southern coast of Cork, concerns a beautiful woman who is encountered by the visitor to the mystical island. She waits for him to speak, or addresses a question to him, in expectation that he will ask for her hand, but he fails to take the initiative and so loses both her and the island.[62]

Mention should also be made of islands which were said to have once been enchanted and which were freed from that state. In Donegal hagiographical lore, for instance, the island of Tory was said to have been disenchanted from paganism by St Colm Cille with a throw of his crozier onto it.[63] The most dramatic case, however, is that of Inis Bó Finne off the coast where counties Mayo and Galway meet. Accounts of this say that, long ago when it had risen from the sea, some fishermen lit a fire on it, or threw some ashes from their pipes onto it. Although they did this with no special intent, by their action the island was restored to the real world.[64]

---

57 *IFC* 1034:79-80.
58 *IFC* 658:470-3.
59 Donegal version in *IFC* 140:374-7. Clare versions at note 40 above. Kerry versions in *IFC* 272:69-72; *IFC* 446:249, 251; *IFC* 966:535-6.
60 See Ó hÓgáin (1990), 340-1; and the paper published here by Dr Miceál Ross.
61 *An Stoc* 9-10/1927 and *IFC* 793:571-5 (Galway); *IFC* 860:491 (Clare).
62 *IFC* 106-8 801:99 (Galway); *IFC* 798:265-6 (Kerry); *IFC* 53:411-23 (Cork). Further types of otherworld legends have become confused with the enchanted island in a more haphazard way. These include 'Midwife to the Fairies' and 'The Sleeping Army' – designated types ML 5070, 8009 by Bo Almqvist in *Béaloideas* 59 (1991).
63 See Ó hÓgáin (1985), 28, 324.
64 Westropp (1911-1915), 58-9; *An Stoc* 12/1928, 6; *IFC* 641:1a-4; *IFC* 780:125-6; *IFC* 868:153-9; *IFC* 1264:571-3.

Something should be said regarding the antiquity of some motifs concerning these mystical islands. We may start with the Clare accounts of how a druid caused Cill Stuithín to be engulfed for its protection. This is curiously similar to a story in the mediaeval literature of how the supernatural Manannán by magic had surrounded the whole area of the Owels, in North Mayo, with a wall of brass.[65] In literature of the same period, Lough Corrib (called Loch nOirbsean) is claimed to have sprung up from the place where Manannán was buried.[66] Among several associations of the same Manannán with both sea and inland lakes in later folklore, there is an account from Galway of how he saved one of his daughters from drowning by causing an island (called Mana) to suddenly appear in the sea.[67]

It is clear that aquatic lore concerning Manannán survived in a mixture of literary and oral forms down through the centuries, and the Manannán-like druid of Cill Stuithín is probably a by-product of the eighteenth-century literary story *Cuireadh Mhaoil Uí Mhanannáin*.[68] This story connects Manannán with the Clare area and particularly with Slieve Callan,[69] where folklore claims the key to Cill Stuithín lies hidden in a lake. This interpretation would seem to be confirmed by the prominence in that literary story of the Fianna personage Conán Maol, who also occurs sporadically in versions of the Cill Stuithín lore.[70] A late eighteenth-century reformulation of the Cill Stuithín tradition is also indicated by some influence on the accounts from another text composed in county Clare in that same period, *Eachtra Thoroilbh Mhic Stairn*.[71] And the best-known text from Clare in that period, deals with the visit of the Fianna hero Oisín to the island of youth, Tír na hÓige.[72]

We have already alluded to the possibility of eighteenth-century development of the lore in Kerry in respect of the Tonn Tóime legend, and indeed the aura of many descriptions of the mystical island, with paraphernalia such as shops and street-lamps, shows a tendency towards modernisation of the lore, in its imagery at least. That is not to say, of course, that the general aspects are of recent vintage. In his discussion of such traditions, T. J. Westropp has illustrated that speculation concerning mystical islands off the west coast of Ireland has been a live issue for a long time. For example, he cites a legal claim made in the seventeenth century for possession of Uí Bhreasaíl, and also the claim made by a sea-captain in 1674. The captain's crew had left Killybegs in county Donegal and had come upon Uí Bhreasaíl in a fog. The ship's mate with some crew went ashore and found there cattle, sheep, horses and black rabbits. There was also a strong castle, on which they knocked in

---

65 Gwynn (1924), 274-5.
66 *Revue Celtique* 16 (1895), 276-7; *Irische Texte* 3 (1897), 356-7; Macalister (1941), 128-9.
67 *IFC* 202:105. See also the curious designation, 'Isle of Man', given to Cill Stuithín in a north Kerry source (IFC 658:472).
68 *Lia Fáil* 3 (1930), 91-113.
69 See note 34 above.
70 *IFC S* 617:364-5; *IFC S* 621:204; *IFC S* 624:241.
71 Ó Neachtain (1922). See also Bruford (1969), 260-1, 279.
72 O'Looney (1859); also in Ó Siochfhradha (1941), 213-26.

vain, but when they lit a fire the castle fell. Before they left, they were told by an inhabitant of the island that the place had been enchanted by 'a great necromancer'.[73]

The occurrence of Uí Bhreasaíl in maps stretching through many centuries can also be taken as evidence for the lively nature of the speculation, as also can the references to mystical isles in the Atlantic in mediaeval Norse sources. These Norse references were indebted, at least in part, to Irish sources – witness, for instance, the description in the Vinland Saga of 'the Land of the White Men', far out to the west of Ireland, 'which some call Great Ireland'.[74] Irish monks played a role in the development of the speculation, and perhaps also in reality, as would appear from the twelfth-century description in the *Landnámabók* of the books, bells and croziers left by Irish monks in Iceland.[75] The descriptions in the celebrated *Navigatio Brendani* and in other early Irish monastic sources are largely drawn from Christian metaphor regarding the quest for holiness symbolised as Tír Tairngire ('the Promised Land'), but the prominence of strange islands in that literature must in some degree be related to native ideas known to these monks. God's 'varied secrets in the great ocean'[76] could indeed call to mind, not only Christian metaphysics, but also a more primitive form of mysticism from ancient Irish belief.

Immram Brain is an early eighth-century text which describes a fantastic sea-voyage undertaken by one Bran mac Feabhail. He did this after receiving an invitation from an otherworld woman to go to Eamhain, where wondrous apples grew.[77] On his way there Bran met with Manannán, who described the sea as his estate, it being as solid earth and a flowery plain to him, and the fish being his calves and lambs. He travelled in a fine chariot, the waves being his horses, and he was described as 'the rider of the maned sea'. This Manannán gave directions to Bran as to how to reach the wondrous island before sundown.[78] When Bran reached it, he found that only women were there. The leader of the women welcomed him, and threw a spool of thread towards him. The thread stuck to his hand, and in this way his boat was drawn ashore. This was an island where time did not move, and they were entertained lavishly by the women there.[79]

The motif of the island of women and of the spool of thread is repeated in another sea-voyage text written a century later and entitled *Immram Maíle Dúin*.[80] Interestingly, in this latter text, the hero Maol Dúin is the son of a warrior of the Eoghanacht Ninussa, a sept which occupied the Aran Islands and the north Clare area.[81] The thread-motif is, as we have seen, also found in late Donegal folklore of a

---

73 Westropp (1912), 256.
74 Magnusson & Pálsson (1965), 103. Full discussion in Mac Mathúna (1997).
75 *Ibid.*, 13; Plummer (1910), 1, cxxii; Westropp (1912), 233-6.
76 O'Meara (1981), 68-9.
77 Mac Mathúna (1985), 33-8.
78 *Ibid.*, 38-43.
79 *Ibid.*, 44.
80 Oskamp (1970), 152-9.
81 *Ibid.*, 51, 100.

mystical island. This gives rise to an important question regarding the interplay of literary and oral traditions. Access to the otherworld by following a roll of thread is found in ordinary inland folklore also,[82] and the antiquity of such mystical thread-motifs is demonstrated by their occurrences in Greek and Hindi literature.[83] It may well be that the thread in the Donegal instances occurs as a natural element in such an otherworld context and is therefore independent of the old literary texts.

Manannán, 'the son of the sea', occurs in early Welsh literature in the form Manawydan and – as his name in both forms indicates – he represented a mythical or ritual lord of the Isle of Man.[84] When it is taken into consideration, indeed, that 'Monu' also referred to the isle of Anglesey and to an island off the Scottish coast (probably the Scottish Aran), it becomes all the more likely that Manannán was the personification of a ritual island off the west coast of Britain.[85] Curiously, in a Manx ballad from about the 15th century about Manannán, the Isle of Man is described as an 'ellan sheeant',[86] which is precisely the same term as 'oileán sídheanta' used in Ulster folklore for the otherworld island.

As is clear from what we have been saying, the cult of Manannán enjoyed considerable vogue in mediaeval Irish storytelling, and the word-play involved in sea- and water-metaphors was exploited to the full. Several examples of such word-play could be cited, but in this context one is of considerable importance. This concerns the allusions in *Immram Brain* to the sea of Manannán as being filled with *scotha* ('flowers').[87] Seizing on such an attractive image, the mediaeval hagiographers connected it with the name of a certain saint Scoithín (literally 'little flower'), and so we find in a source from about the eleventh century a description of this saint which owes much to the imagery of Manannán. According to this description, St Scoithín walks effortlessly on the sea, which to him is 'a plain full of clover-blossoms', and he plucks a flower from the water.[88] Once such imagery became attached to this saint, he would have been taken as a patron of the sea. We can speculate that – probably in recent centuries – some clergyman in the Clare area, by referring to St Scoithín in this role, gave rise to the identification of the otherworld island with a supposed maritime *cill* (monastic cell) of his.

This could easily have developed into a tradition of St Scoithín along the west Clare coast. The date of the saint's feast, 2 January, must be of importance. Since

---

82 See Danaher (1972), 223; Ó Duilearga & Ó hÓgáin (1981), 313.
83 See Thompson (1952-5), motifs A189.10, F152.1.7, R 121.5.
84 See Bromwich (1961), 428, 441-3; Ó hÓgáin (1990), 286-9.
85 For possible connections between these toponymics and the ancient Celtic tribal name, Menapii – see Moore (1890), 130-2; Kneen (1925), xxii-xxiv; Wagner (1981), 24; Rivet & Smith (1979), 410-1.
86 Thomson in *Études Celtiques* 9 (1961), 521-31.
87 Mac Mathúna (1985), 39-40.
88 Stokes (1905), 40.

this would be a time for rough seas, a priest may have referred to the saint as a protector for fishermen negotiating the dangerous breakers off the coast. There would have been good occasions for mentioning the saint in that role in church on Scoithín's own feast, and especially in years when 2 January would fall on a Sunday. In such years, the congregation would be attending obligatory Mass for the fourth time in the eight days since Christmas, and the priest would find it convenient to explain that this unusual circumstance resulted from the feast of St Stephen having fallen on the Sunday before. This would, of course, provide a special connection between Stephen and Scoithín.[89] Scoithín was rather an obscure saint, and so his name in the popular memory could easily become corrupted through the connection, leading to the forms 'Stuithín' and 'Stuifín'.[90] Hence the otherworld island in that area would become known as Cill Stuithín and Cill Stuifín.[91]

Speculative sightings of a mystical island can, of course, be explained by optical illusions and the curious shapes made by a sunburst far out at sea. The motif of a maritime tower, evident in several of the late folklore accounts, can be explained as just one of these chimerae. But it is notable that this tower-motif can be matched from the earlier literature, and that in settings which look entirely more primitive. A great silver pillar which rises from the sea in *Immram Maíle Dúin,*[92] for instance, would appear to entail more than a mere spontaneous fancy, and this is confirmed by some other early examples. In the mythical and quasi-mythical sections of the *Lebor Gabála Éirenn,* in the early Middle Ages, there are accounts of a golden or glass tower in the sea to the west of Ireland, at which a primaeval battle is fought.[93] This tower (*tuir*), sometimes identified with the pinnacled Tory Island off the Donegal coast, was obviously thought to have been a place where otherworld conflicts or paradoxes were acted out. Such an early narrative seems to lie behind the much more dramatic but inland battle between two otherworld armies, *Cath Muighe Tuiredh.*[94]

This battle of Maigh Tuireadh is regarded as a version of an Indo-European primordial myth of a great contention between two sets of deities.[95] In the Irish tale, these deities are the Tuatha Dé Danann, representing brightness, and the Fomhoire, representing the more shadowy and sinister realm. Yet both groups belong to the otherworld, and to trace this contrast between light and darkness is, we may suggest,

---

89 Some folklore accounts from county Clare refer to the spire or tower of a church on Cill Stuithín causing the breaker there, and claim that this church was built by St Stephen – see note 38 above.
90 Scoithín's cult was strongest in north county Kilkenny, where a church dedication to him was Tigh Scoithín, anglicised as Tiscoffin – O'Hanlon (1875), 1, 34-8. This bears witness to the 'f' pronunciation referred to at note 41 above.
91 It is noteworthy also, that Scoithín's feastday comes within the especially sacred and mystical time of the Twelve Days. The last of these days, 6 January, is the reputed time for the appearance of Beag-Árainn in Galway lore (see note 12).
92 Hamel (1941), 42; Oskamp (1970), 150.
93 Macalister (1939), 249 and (1940), 122-5, 128-31, 138-43. A similar maritime tower or pillar is mentioned also in Hamel (1932), 21-2 and in O'Meara (1981), 68-9.
94 Gray (1982). The title of this text means 'the battle of the plain of the pillars' – for this *tuir* connection see Ó hÓgáin (1990), 315.
95 Murphy (1953-5), 191-8; Mac Cana (1970), 60; Vries (1961), 148-56.

relevant to our quest. The most tantalising account of an otherworld island from ancient literature is that given by Plutarch in the first century AD. Using information which he had from a traveller, Plutarch describes how the Britons believed that an otherworld lord reigns over the dead on an island off the coast. Boatmen were awakened at night by a knock on their door, and were required to row the spirits of the dead to that island.[96]

The name which Plutarch gives to the lord of the island is Cronus, a borrowing from Greek myth, but the personage corresponds to Donn in early Irish tradition. *Donn* meant 'the dark one', and he was said to inhabit a rock which lies a good distance from the south-west coast of Ireland. The rock is a real one. It was called 'the house of Donn', and it has an unusual formation, being a natural archway under which the sea crashes with tremendous force.[97] A statement attributed to Donn in early Irish literature seems to be an echo of genuine paganism – 'to me,' he says, 'to my house, you shall all come after your deaths!'[98]

Donn obviously represents the underworld – in another text he is referred to as 'toothless Donn from the tumuli'.[99] In other words, whether on inland sepulchral sites or under his south-western rock, he was lord of the dead. In this, the early literary accounts of him are in accord with the lore of the otherworld, right down to the folklore of modern times. Just as one can reach the otherworld through sea-water, so can one also within or under an inland lake, and indeed within an old tumulus or rath on solid ground. Perhaps most significantly, in folk-belief the land of youth (*Tír na hÓige*) is an island on the western sea, but it is also a dwelling situated underneath the earth.[100] As such a dwelling, though dark to our eyes, it is splendidly bright in its own realm. One passage in the *Immram Maíle Dúin* describes an island surrounded by a revolving wall of fire, through which glimpses are caught of handsome beautifully-dressed people drinking ale from goblets while wondrous music is played.[101]

Many examples of such paradoxes could be cited, but it may suffice to say that they probably entailed a dialectic between darkness (personified as 'Donn') and brightness (personified as 'Find').[102] What was meant, we can gather, was the otherworld where the sun goes down, the otherworld into which the sun disappears each night to return again to the world of the living in the morning. We know that

---

96 Zwicker (1934), 65-6; Brown (1943), 339-41.
97 For this 'house of Donn', see Müller-Lisowski (1948), 147-53.
98 The phrase is from a poem by Máelmuru of Othan (+887) – Best & O'Brien (1957), 3, 520; see Müller-Lisowski (1948),152.
99 Knott (1936), 10.
100 *Irisleabhar na Gaedhilge* 11 (1900-1), 141; *IFC* 24:105-9; *IFC* 85:293; *IFC* 407:148; *IFC* 1099:58; *IFC* 1239:11-13; See also Ó Súilleabháin (1942), 275-6, 469-70.
101 Hamel (1941), 48-9; Oskamp (1970), 166.
102 This dialectic would appear to lie behind the continuous enmity in the heroic literature between the two bulls, called respectively *Donn Cuailgne and Findbheannach* – see the text edited by Roider (1979). See also Ó hÓgáin (1990), 167-8, 423 and especially (1999), 124-7.

the ancient Gauls on the Continent, in honouring their divine ancestor, insisted that the night has precedence over the day.[103] In Irish tradition, the night is also computed as preceding the day, which leaves *Oíche* ('night') with the ordinary meaning of 'Eve' when in conjunction with the name of a festival. Similarly, the dark half has precedence over the light half in the traditional Irish method of measuring the year – *ó Shamhain go Bealtaine, agus ó Bhealtaine go Samhain* ('from November to May, and from May to November'). It is not surprising, then, that November is the time of year *par excellence* for the otherworld and for the dead in Irish folk belief.[104]

The mystical island has undergone many developments through different cultural epochs – developments such as symbolism, fantasy, geographical speculation, and motif-attraction – and it is difficult to speculate on its ultimate origin. Considering Plutarch's account, it would appear that the concept had passed from Britain into Ireland in prehistory, and we may surmise that the notion had earlier passed to Britain from Gaul. The ancient peoples of the Middle East did, of course, have the idea of the otherworld situated on a strange island,[105] but its actual location in the west, making it coincide with sundown, appears most clearly from Greek literature. From Homer onwards, Elysion or Erytheia was thought to exist somewhere west of the Gates of Gibraltar. It was among other things a sepulchral island on which stood the pillars of Hercules or the pillars of the afore-mentioned Cronus.[106] It could be somewhere near Cadiz, a region rich in megalithic tombs, or more tantalisingly off the western coast of Gaul.[107]

One is struck by the visual imagery of such great gates – of pillars through which the sun sinks – and by the same sun disappearing into the sea through the dolmen-like structure of the rock of Donn.[108] One's imagination can equally be stirred into picturing the spread westwards of a poetic idea which probably always skirted the water-fronts of antiquity.

---

103 Zwicker (1934), 24.
104 See Danaher (1972), 200-29.
105 Sandars (1972), 39, 104-5, 125.
106 For early Greek references by Homer and Hesiod, see Rieu (1946), 26, 79; Evelyn-White (1959), 100-1, 116-39, 150-1.
107 Graves (1960) 2, 132-5, 140-1.
108 See Mac Cárthaigh (1966), 51, viz. 'The sunlight, shining on the surface of the water, may be plainly seen through the archway, from a point on the mainland eighteen miles distant.'

Seductive, Generous, and Dangerous like the Sea itself: Gotlandic Mermaid Legends as Moral Examples

ULF PALMENFELT

Characteristic of all folklore is its dual quality of being both collective and individual. Any corpus of folklore can be understood, at one level, as the collective expression of ideas and values existing within a certain group of people. From this communal stock the individuals of a society are free to compose their own repertoires of stories, jokes, songs, or proverbs, all in accordance with their respective personalities. The collective ownership of folklore permits the individual users to hide behind a screen of anonymity, liberating them from taking personal responsibility for the values expressed in it.

Viewed in this way, as a collective corpus, legends about supernatural beings can be understood as metaphorical expressions of human relations which have been narratologically elaborated to suit the characteristics of the legend genre. In such stories the human actors often experience situations of conflict with supernatural beings in which questions of ethics, morals, justice, economy, and other delicate matters are discussed. These legends give a survey in which human relations are regarded as awkward, emotionally charged, or even tabooed in the society in question.

When folklore is performed in a communicative situation, we must assume that each story, each legend, each proverb carries some kind of meaning for the person who chooses to use it, as well as being understood by the listener as a more or less meaningful part of the conversation. To be able to understand, on this performative level, what personal connotations a certain story might have had for the participants in the conversation, we have to know something about the teller and the collector, as well as something about the situation in which the collection was made. Elsewhere I have argued that even archive collections of legends can be discussed on this performative level by using such a contextual or communicative approach.[1]

In this paper I will apply this two-level model of analysis to nineteenth-century Gotlandic legends concerning the dominant maritime supernatural being which in the Gotlandic dialect is called 'havfrui'. The direct English translation is 'sea-wife' and I will use that expression here, since one of her roles in the legends actually was to be the wife of a human being. Let me first introduce the four thematic groups into which the legends can be divided on a collective level.

---

1 Palmenfelt (1993a, 1993b, 1993c). Cf. also Solheim (1952), and Tangherlini (1994).

The first one describes the sea-wife as an owner of natural resources and a controller of natural phenomena. This is one example:

The sea-wife moves her residence four times a year. She then brings all fish and all her children with her, sailing on pieces of bark and using their tails for sails. Before that they live on the shore in the guise of squirrels. When she moves, she also brings her cows and calves, which she often grazes on the shore; these can be distinguished from other cattle by their blue stripes. As soon as the sea-wife moves, all the fish move too, so that nothing can be caught along the coast when the sea-wife has left it.[2]

In these stories it is often pointed out directly that it is the sea-wife who decides whether a catch of fish will be big or small.[3] It was also said that the sea-wife can arrange storms, create big waves, or change the water level of the lakes.[4] To profit from her powers, one should speak about her in a respectful way and give her offerings in the form of useful tools, food, or clothing.[5] Apart from providing good catches, she could also give warnings of bad weather to those who behave properly.[6] On the other hand, she could be very touchy and would take revenge on anybody insulting her.[7]

One of the obvious messages in these legends is that man's exploitation of the natural resources is limited and subject to conditions beyond human control. This is a Scandinavian example of an idea well-known to anthropological research. Many hunting and fishing societies have developed different forms of taboo notions which make it culturally and socially impossible to over-exploit the natural resources on which they are economically dependent.

Another theme derives directly from the experience of a seafaring people, who notice that changes in weather and sea conditions can be so sudden and so fierce that they may be interpreted as acts of revenge from somebody who feels insulted.

Furthermore, when we look upon the interplay between men and supernatural beings in these legends we immediately recognize situations that must have been common in human relations. As I have already said, these relations are often unpleasant, annoying, or disgraceful. In one legend a person is illegally using fishing water belonging to somebody else;[8] in another a person enters a house belonging to somebody else without being invited;[9] in a third a farm-hand is spying on his

---

2 Gustavson/ Nyman (1959), Vol. 1, 185.
3 *Ibid.*, 173 f.
4 *Ibid.*, 175 f.
5 *Ibid.*, 173, 176 f.
6 *Ibid.*, 175 f, 178 f.
7 *Ibid.*, 168, 171, 177.
8 *Ibid.*, 167.
9 *Ibid.*, 171.

master's secret economic (or perhaps erotic) affairs;[10] in a fourth a person starts a quarrel with somebody on whom he is dependent;[11] in a fifth an upper-class individual in a foreign country must be obeyed;[12] in a sixth a child is obliged to talk to a stranger whom it fears.[13]

The stories in the second group describe the sea-wife as a beautiful seductive woman, who is as attractive to men as the glittering sea on a calm sunny summer day.[14] In some stories she sneaks into young boys' bunks as they lie sleeping in their shacks by the shore and seduces them.[15] Of course it must have happened that young men, sleeping away from home, had erotic dreams which might be so realistic that the only explanation they could give of why they woke up alone was that they had had a visit from a supernatural being. In other stories, like the following one, the sea-wife is an actual adulteress trying to separate a married couple:

> A young farmer from Kinnare in Lummelunda was out fishing at sea once. He did not return and nothing was heard from him, for the sea-wife had taken him as her own. He had a good time with her, they had children together, she loved him highly and did not want to lose him. But one day she told him: 'Today your wife is re-marrying!' The farmer asked the sea-wife's permission to go there and take a look at the festivities. When the farmer came home, he wanted to have his old wife back, but the sea-wife said that he had been with her for so many years that he ought to be hers for ever. The priest intervened, however, and made her change her mind, and the farmer promised to pay seven barrels of wheat every year to the sea-wife and his children. After that the farmer had good luck at fishing.[16]

You may have observed that the sea-wife in this story had no magical, supernatural, or evil reasons for carrying the man away. On the contrary, her reasons were very human: 'she loved him greatly and did not want to lose him.' To my mind stories like this illustrate some universal phenomena in the life of married people, phenomena experienced not only by fishermen and seafarers, namely, that it is possible to experience deep love for somebody other than one's own spouse, that it is possible to live for a while with somebody else besides one's spouse, that a threatened marriage can be repaired, and that one result of extra-marital adventures may be that one has to pay alimony.

---

10 *Ibid.*, 173.
11 *Ibid.*, 177.
12 *Ibid.*, 186.
13 *Ibid.*, 173.
14 *Ibid.*, 163, 169 ff.
15 *Ibid.*, 163, 167.
16 *Ibid.*, 164f.

In this example it was the man who made up his mind to go back to his wife; in other legends the adulterous man has an energetic and cunning wife who succeeds in recapturing her husband.[17] There is also a story about a woman who is seduced by a male sea spirit and has a child by him. She is forced back to the human world by her strong mother.[18]

I think that it will be agreed that these stories, too, in metaphorical form deal with delicate human relations that often cannot be discussed openly.

The third group of legends deals with young people's growing sexuality. The following story is typical:

> Once upon a time there was a young boy, who lived with his poor parents in a forest by the shore of a lake, where he often used to fish. He loved music, always carried his flute with him, and as soon as he had the time he played it.

> One day as he sat alone on the shore playing his flute, he saw a beautiful maiden on the waves. Her hair was set with pearls and jewels, she had pretty rings on her fingers, and she sang very beautifully when he played. As soon as he stopped, however, she stopped too. He decided to approach her, but she disappeared. Night and day he could not but think of the beautiful girl. Soon he was back on the shore again, and he blew his flute and the mermaid appeared again on the water. She sang even more beautifully, more touchingly and more temptingly than before. The young man was aroused and delighted and hurried down to the sea to catch the beauty. But when she turned around to flee, he discovered that her back was hollow. He was disgusted. All his love for her disappeared, and for a long time he did not play his beloved flute.[19]

This story was told by a schoolgirl, and beside the obvious description of tender young love it contains at least two themes familiar to adolescents. One is the experience that love makes you blind to the physical imperfections of the beloved, the other is the usefulness of playing and singing together as a way for young people to get into contact with each other. When the same legend is told by adults, there is often the addition that accepting the love of the sea-wife would mean drowning. Of course parents know that if their children fall in love, they will lose them as definitely as if they had drowned.

The fourth group of legends deals with a delicate but common situation in an agrarian society – what do you do with a runaway cow which you find grazing on your land?

It might seem a paradox for a sea-spirit to own cows. I do not think it seemed strange at all to a nineteenth-century Gotlander. In those days all farmers were more

---

17 *Ibid.*, 168.
18 *Ibid.*, 187 f.
19 *Ibid.*, 165 f.

or less fishermen too, spending at least some weeks every autumn to provide the household with enough fish to last through the winter. Some worked for certain periods of their life as seamen. In addition to that, the sea-wife was one of the dominant legend characters in nineteenth-century Gotlandic folklore and thus an obvious choice when you needed a protagonist in stories about everyday problems:

> One Christmas night the sea-wife let all the cows out of the cow-shed at Nårs on Fårö and put her own cattle in the cribs instead. The farmer went into the cow-shed, all the foreign cows fled wildly, but he managed to catch one of them. This became his best milking-cow. Several years later the farmer at Nårs was hunting seals far out on the ice. The ice broke and he saw no possibility of getting ashore. Then the sea-wife appeared and promised to save him if she got her cow back. He refused, and with the help of God he managed to get ashore all the same.[20]

This story places the moral right with the farmer who locks the trespassing cow up in his own cow-shed. Encroachment, and in other similar stories illegal grazing,[21] or outright hay-theft,[22] are regarded as worse crimes than stealing a cow, although this was hardly the case in real life. The legend should not be judged as a juridical document, but as a moral testimony, a proof that negligence in keeping your cattle well guarded or safely enclosed would arouse very strong feelings among the neighbours.

The legends I am using for this discussion were all collected by the same person, the Gotlandic school-teacher Per Arvid Säve. Typical of his time, the mid – ninteenth century, he was interested mainly in registering the story-line of the legends and took note of the individual differences between the storytellers only with regard to dialectal details, not narratological traits. Thanks to a study of Säve's informants by the Gotlandic folklorist Ragnar Bjersby,[23] we know so much about the storytellers that it is possible to apply a contextual or communicative perspective to the material collected by Säve.

Säve met the thirty-six-year-old farm-hand Lars Nordin when the latter had been married for less than a year. For most people marriage means a change in their sexual relations, either from chastity to sexual activity or from polygamy to monogamy. We do not know anything about Nordin's sexual experiences during the first thirty-five years of his life, but obviously sexuality was often on his mind when he talked to Säve, for he told several legends with erotic themes. His sea-wife legends belong to the second group that I mentioned earlier, the one where the sea-wife is depicted as a sexually attractive female being, and all of Nordin's stories are of the type where a married man is seduced by an unknown girl. Perhaps marriage did not mean monogamy to Nordin, or perhaps he wished that it would not.

---

20 *Ibid.*, 179.
21 *Ibid.*, 179 f.
22 *Ibid.*., 178, 181.
23 Bjersby (1964).

At the age of ten Elisabeth Bolin lost her father, and her mother died only eleven years later. Bolin worked during her short life-time (she died of 'nervous fever' at the age of thirty-eight) as a teacher at a school for poor girls. Her sea-wife legends belong to my group three, those dealing with adolescent sexuality. One recurring side-theme in these stories is the relationship between parents and children. It is quite logical that this would interest an orphaned school-teacher. I mentioned earlier that adults tell these legends in a manner different from adolescents. Elisabeth Bolin gave Säve examples of both versions. One of them had been told to her by one of her schoolgirls. The young teacher with the sad childhood had no problems in adopting a young person's perspective.

When Jacob Wallin was a young soldier some officers made him drink too much and, without knowing what he was doing, he agreed to sign his name as security for a loan taken by one of the officers. Many years later the debt fell due and Jacob Wallin had to sell his wife's parental farm, which he had acquired when they married. His legend repertory abounds in stories about people who lose their houses, farms and land. One of his sea-wife legends (#224) is about a farmer who gets hold of one of the sea-wife's fine fat cows. He takes good care of the cow, never slaughters any of her calves, and after a good many years all his live stock are her calves. One autumn day the farmer suddenly sees the sea-wife standing at the gate-post, and hears her call: 'Come back, my cow, and bring all your calves with you!' In a minute all the animals disappear into the sea and the farmer has lost all his cows. The parallelism between this story and Wallin's own life is easy to see.

Lars Olsson was Säve's foremost legend teller, contributing 140 stories to his collection. He worked as a hired farm-hand all his life; and almost all his legends are recognizable as migratory ones that Olsson has planted firmly in his own neighbourhood, with his friends and relatives as actors. All his stories are seen by an outdoor observer. His sea-wife legends belong to type four, where the sea-wife is a cattle owner among others. One of Olsson's stories tells of a farm-hand who early in the morning comes out to the stable to feed the cows and finds the sea-wife standing in the hay-loft, stealing hay. It is likely enough that this was an experience Olsson had had several times in real life. On the other hand, his own reputation was not the best, so at some time he may have been revealed as a thief.

In a given situation some stories are told because they comment upon current phenomena within a group or a society. This is the collective level I mentioned earlier. Other stories are told because they mean something to the teller. This is the performative level which is illustrated by my last examples. Some stories are told because the teller supposes that they will please the listener, whether the listener is a folklore collector or not.

Finally, I would like to give an example of how the conversational context can trigger the telling of certain stories. Conversations about legends and other folklore are governed by similar cultural conventions as other kinds of human interaction.[24]

Säve's field notes from four consecutive days of collection from Jens Jacobsson make it possible to follow how the two men's associations are allowed to govern the conversation. At a certain point they are discussing economic and juridical rules for seal hunting. This leads to two stories about hunting and fishing around Gotska Sandön, a small sand island to the north of Gotland. Jacobsson subsequently gives the Gotlandic word for the special leather apron used when slaughtering seals. After that come two stories about women who died and gave birth in their graves. The first of these women appears as a revenant, borrowing an apron which is later found in her grave. At that point, Jacobsson tells several short stories about other ghosts and revenants. The last of these concerns a female ghost with supernatural powers who appears on the shore. Next in the chain comes the first sea-wife legend of this session. It belongs to group one, the sea-wife as the owner of natural resources, and tells about a woman who is able to exercise magical control over her own and others' catches of fish, and it is soon revealed that she has a pact with the sea-wife.

A total understanding of all layers of meaning in folklore is impossible to acquire. Each story's place in the chain of conversation is, however, a factor which must be taken into consideration. The interplay between the teller and the collector, which I just mentioned, is another factor.

On a performative level each legend, each single piece of folklore, each utterance is meaningful to the individual user. By analyzing the narratological profile of an informant's total repertoire, we can get a fairly complete picture of some aspects of that teller's personality.

At the same time, on a collective level, the legends I have mentioned in this paper deal with social and economic situations well-known from historical studies of traditional Swedish society. The nineteenth-century Gotlandic mermaid legends dealt with delicate human relations, such as fishing and grazing rights, adultery, and love separating young people from their parents. But folklore adds personal feelings to history. The legends dramatize human conflicts and put a dressing of words onto people's feelings about them. By telling legends, listening to them, and reacting to them, people discuss and evaluate moral attitudes.

---

24 Palmenfelt (1994).

The Water Element in Arctic Finno-Ugric Mythologies[1]

Juha Pentikäinen

Water is a central element in many Northern world views. This paper is based on the folklore and oral mythologies of some small Finno-Ugric peoples living in the most extreme territories of Northern Eurasia. For these peoples (see map on following page), the Arctic Ocean represents the beginning and the end of their universe, functioning for them as the gate from the known world to the unknown. With the exception of the early (probably Proto-) Sámi settlements which seem to have appeared on the Northern Atlantic and Barents Sea coasts soon after the Ice Age (*c.* 10,000 BC), most of these sparsely distributed peoples have been nomadic, making an appearance on the coast mainly during their annual seasonal migrations. Accordingly, their world views and cultures have been structured on a land to sea axis. This is in sharp contrast to northern Scandinavian fishermen and islanders who have rather looked towards the land from the sea.

Because of their geographical location, the world view of the Finno-Ugric peoples has been more oriented towards the tundra, the forests or Siberian taiga and inland waterways than towards the open sea. Rivers and lakes have formed a familiar aquatic setting for the northern Finno-Ugrians. Concepts such as 'river', 'fish', and 'waterbird' belong to the most archaic layer of the vocabulary of the northern Finno-Ugric peoples. Typically, many of them are named and defined after the rivers along which they lived e.g. the 'Ob-Ugric' Khanty concept *Agan* means both 'river' and 'mother'. Dr Lennart Meri, the first post-Soviet President of Estonia, conducted extensive field work in the Siberian North and subsequently named his successful ethnographical film documentary 'The Peoples of a Waterbird'.

This paper introduces a selection of the Arctic beliefs about the supernatural, in relation to water. As is the case with blood in Oriental sacrificial cults, water in Northern world views is designated as a liquid element marking the most important symbolic transformations between natural borders in the ecological sense as well as in the context of the human body e.g. water/snow/ice, virginity/womanhood/ motherhood, life and death.

---

1 This paper was accompanied by three ethnographical video documentaries by the author – 'Silent as waters we live' (which deals with the Old Believers in Komi (1992), 'We still remember' (on Nanay death customs (1994) and 'Reindeer sacrifice' (concerning a Khanty shaman and made in 1991). These documentaries illustrate the current revival of Siberian shamanism as demonstrated in the rituals conducted by a Ugric shaman on the Ob, and a Nanay shamaness in the Lower Amur region; the Nanay (or Golds) belong to those Mandshu Tungus peoples whose language contains the native concept of 'saman' (Pentikäinen 1993).

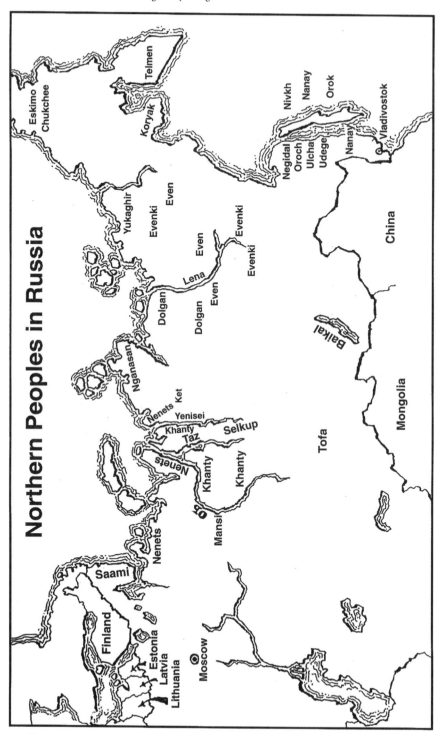

Northern Peoples in Russia

In contemporary Northern folklore, myths are not only narrated, but – as in the symbolic enactment of the religious rites of these peoples – sung, danced, painted or acted out. Mainly, I wish to examine water as a mythical element in the Finnish, Finno-Ugric and other Northern cultural contexts. This kind of survey has relevance for the interpretation of the meanings of such ritual codes and practices as are traditionally performed in the course of the human life cycle. Here, the symbolic use of water is an essential part of many rituals.

Pouring water over a new-born child at name-giving is an ancient Arctic ritual defining the first social status before the institution of Christian baptism. In shamanic mythologies, crucial emphasis is laid on the ability of the shamans to be victorious over death. On behalf of their societies, they are believed to be capable of travelling to their abodes, located either behind a river (the Finnish *Tuonela*) or under lakes or under the sea (as in the Sámi *Jábmiidáibmu*). Shamanic mythologies depict the shaman's last achievement as being a journey to the mythical clan river in order to bury his drum and die by the bank of the river.

The Creation of an Island – a Karelian Mythical Rune

Finnish creation drama (which has been thoroughly analyzed in my *Kalevala Mythology, pp.* 131-220) takes place in the Northern aquatic setting. A text of an orally transmitted epical song about the creation of an island is quoted below. I heard this song in 1960, during the first field work I conducted with Marina Takalo, an illiterate Karelian rune singer. It was one of the first songs with which she introduced a young student to her huge folklore repertoire, She was a competent singer of Karelian epics even though she had been a refugee living in Finland for many years. The delivery of this paper would probably not have been possible had she not proved to be such an eager and capable guide to the esoteric messages inherent in her Karelian world view, culture and life history. A study of the narratives transmitted between 1960 and 1970 by Marina Takalo (1890-1970) can be found in Pentikäinen (1978).

> The swallow is a day bird,
> the night bird is the bat,
> the swallow flew a summer day,
> a dark fall night as well,
> searched for land to lie on,
> a field to nest on,
> a thicket for its eggs,
> it found no land to lie on,
> nor a field to nest on,

nor a thicket for its eggs.
It flew to a high hill, to a high peak,
even saw a ship sailing,
a red-mast sailing.
It flew to the ship's gangway,
came down on the ship's bow,
cast its tiny copper nest,
laid its tiny golden egg.
God created a great wind,
sent it from the west,
tipped the ship's bow,
turned the ship on its side,
into the black mud of the sea,
into the dense sand of the sea.
From this there grew an island,
there grew a hillock,
there grew a maiden on the hillock.[2]

My field work with Marina continued throughout the 1960s and, gradually, I realized that she repeatedly sung this song for me without providing any mythical meaning or interpretation of it. It was clearly one of Marina's favourite songs: she recalled having learned it from her great aunt who was drowned when Marina was eight years old. For her, it was 'a beautiful song about a bird of God'; no reason was given for *riähka* or 'sin' in the strict ethical terms of the Karelian Old Believers. The 'Old Faith', as it was called, was the most common religious identity in Karelia and also in the other Northern Russian territories in the seventeenth-nineteenth centuries. Plenty of schismatic groups existed within it. Marina, for example, had been baptized in 1890 into the so-called *tuhkanes* a *bezpopovtsy pomorski* ('priestless coastal') branch of the Old Faith named after Tuhkala village in White Sea Karelia.

To my questions as to the origins and primordial phases of the Universe and of Mankind, Marina Takalo repeatedly answered: 'God, of course, created everything...'. In her mind, biblical narrative had displaced mythical interpretations without, however, hindering the survival of the ancient mythical runes. It was the ambition of the Karelian rune singers to transmit faithfully, word for word, mythical plots and epical contents even when these had lost their former pre-Christian religious meaning. A deeper analysis of the song quoted above has shown that it tells not only of the creation of the 'Island', i.e. the Cosmos, but of Man as well, woman being the first to be created. It was '...in the black mud of the sea, in the heavy clay of the sea where there grew an island, there grew a green grass, and there grew a virgin on the green grass.'[3]

---

2 Pentikäinen (1978), 296.
3 *Ibid.*

As the song continues, its plot becomes more problematical, however. The first human being suddenly becomes the target of a wooing competition between several suitors: 'bishops, priests, slim gentlemen who in-waiting went'.[4] The climax of the epical song comes when the maid refuses to accept any suitor candidate. Instead *Nurmi Tuomas* (Turf Thomas) comes, puts the maiden into his sledge, strikes the stallion with the reins, the horse runs, the road rings out...'[5]

A detailed folkloristic study of the poem shows that Mrs Takalo's variant is a combination of three mythologies and several songs as well, the last of these being *'Tuonelta kosinta'*, or 'The Suitors from Death'. The unique narrative sung by Marina Takalo concerns the Universe, Mankind and, last but not least, Death. While everything is created on an island in an aquatic milieu, the name 'Turf Thomas', as a personification of death, embodies at one and the same time, a reference to Earth. The personification of death occurs in other names found in the unique genre of Finnish, Karelian and Estonian lullabies related to the topic of death. One of the most popular appellations is *Surma*, Death as Destiny who comes at His time. Another Karelian rune singer of our era, Stepanie Kemova, who was Marina Takalo's daughter (born in 1912), having told how she was widowed three times, stated: 'next time I will be engaged to *Nurmi Miikkula* ("Turf Michael").'[6]

The third mythical meaning of the narrative sung by Marina Takalo is thus intended to offer a reply to one of the most crucial and fascinating problems in the religious quest of mankind: what is death and why is it as it is, and what might lie beyond? I will try to show that, in accordance with this myth, there is no deep threshold between life and death in Northern world views. Here, it is rather a case of a narrow border, one which may be expressed symbolically as a 'line drawn in water'.[7]

The Primordial Sea as the Mythical Base of Origins

Water plays a crucial role in the mythical epics of many world religions. Their cosmological narratives often start in a manner somewhat similar to Genesis. In the beginning there usually was Chaos, out of which the Cosmos is created. Chaos is a vague state of silence and emptiness consisting of nothing except for air, water and darkness. What is important here – on the basis of religio-phenomological comparison – is the notion of the Primordial Sea as the most common arena of Creation. The aquatic setting seems to have been needed, whatever way creation itself may have transpired in the mythologies or mythographies of various religions. This applies to narratives told both in religions which have a founder – as, for example, Buddism, Confucianism, Christianity, Islam etc. – and in 'ethnic' religions, where no founder

---

4 *Ibid.*
5 *Ibid.*
6 Pentikäinen (1989), 139-40.
7 Pentikäinen (1983), 123-36; (1989), 200-20.

is mentioned, such as Hinduism, Judaism, ancient Greek, Roman, Celtic, Germanic, Finnish, Estonian, Sámi, Inuit, and American Indian religions.

In the famous creation hymn of the *Rgveda* (dated c. 1200 BC), Chaos is symbolized by water. There the initial impetus for creation is presented as an abstract desire to create. From this power, the Original One is formed as the being and then is separated into masculine desire (above) and feminine energy (below).

> For in the beginning there was nothing, there was neither air nor heaven beyond. What was there then? Where? In whose charge? Was there measureless, deep water? There was no death then, nor deathlessness, no signs of day or night. That One breathed, of its own power, without wind. There was not yet anything but that One. In the beginning darkness was hidden in darkness, undifferentiated, all this was water. That which came into being was shrouded in emptiness, the One was born of the warmth of its own desire. The sages, searching their hearts with wisdom, then found the bond of being in non-being. Their bond was extended across, did there exist an 'above' or 'below'? Impregnators and powers existed, there was energy below and desire above. Who can say for sure? Who here can say, whence those were produced, whence this creation? Even the gods were born only after this creation. Who then can say whence it evolved? He, from whom this creation has evolved, whether he initiated it or did not – he who is the surveyor of this in highest heaven, he alone knows, or perhaps even he knows not.[8]

The Bible and Indian epics established a pattern followed by many later epical works. Their mythologies became particularly significant in the evolution of the creation rune of the *Kalevala*, as I have described elsewhere.[9] Having become acquainted with Vedic sources published by Max Müller and others, Elias Lönnrot became eager to adopt the Indian deity, Brahma, and change the plot of his works accordingly. Hence, the female figure of Ilmatar was created for his New Kalevala (1849), on the basis of the ancient Vedic mythology which had originated in India. The main hero of the Finnish epics was now born in the primordial sea from Ilmatar, the Maiden of the Air, thitherto a completely unknown goddess in Finnish epical poetry.

After this process, which took place in Lönnrot's mind between the *Old Kalevala* (1835) and the *New Kalevala* (1849), the *Kalevala* now began in accordance with *Genesis*, though featuring a creation drama with Vedic roots. A primordial goddess of India displaced the native hero, Väinämöinen, who had been cast in the main role of Creator god in the *Old Kalevala*, in accordance with the oral poetry recorded by Lönnrot from his singers of epics. In the original epical song sung by

---

8 Quoted in Pentikäinen (1989), 142.
9 Pentikäinen (1989), Chapter 7.

Ontrei Malinen and the other White-Sea Karelian singers whom Lönnrot met, the creation of the universe is depicted as follows:

A slant-eyed Lapp held a week-long grudge against old Väinämöinen....he shot three arrows; the first two missed, but the third one reached its destination, the blue elk....Väinämöinen fell into the water for seven years, and plowed the sea bottom....Where the land lies against the land, there he blessed the places for casting nets, dug the fish-filled lake-bottom. Where he stepped upon the sea, there he cast rocky islets, raised rock reefs. Ships were sunk upon them, merchants' heads were lost....The goose, bird of the air, flew in search of a place to nest. Väinämöinen raised his knee from the sea as a green hillock. The goose made a nest on Väinämöinen's knee, and laid six eggs, the seventh one of iron. As the bird brooded her eggs, Väinämöinen felt his knee grow warm and moved it. At this point the eggs rolled into the sea. Väinämöinen said:

What's in the bottom half of the egg, that's the bottom mother earth.
What's in the upper half of the egg, that's the upper sky.
What's brown in the egg, that's to shine as the sun.
What's white in the egg, that's to gleam as the moon.
What's bits of bone in the egg, that's to be stars in the sky.[10]

After Ilmatar had taken over the main role in the creation drama of the epics, in the arena of basic origins, only the water element remained the same. While floating in the Primordial Sea, Ilmatar raises her knee from the sea in the midst of her pains and finally gives birth to Väinämöinen. In the *New Kalevala*, Väinämöinen is given a peculiar by-role from the very beginning: He is born as an old man who was allotted the complicated task of serving as the vehicle for furthering the plot of the epics. His wooing competition against such younger heroes as Ilmarinen and Lemminkäinen, set in the North, Pohjola etc., is particularly problematical. Of particular interest here in the context of water is Lönnrot's hypothesis that the name of Väinämöinen is feminine, being, as he believed, derived from *Vein emoinen* ('the Mother of Waters').

Water birds such as the swan, the goose, and the loon play an important role in various episodes of Baltic-Finnish creation drama. Neolithic rock art testifies to the antiquity of this mythology. Water-bird motifs form central themes in the Karelian petroglyphs and Finnish pictographs from 4000 BC. The mythical gigantic swan appears in *c.* 70% of the pictographs found at Lake Onega, for example. The basic theme exemplified in these symbolic pictographs is ecological, and it is also descriptive of human rotation from Chaos to Cosmos, from Birth to Death.

---

10 Quoted in Pentikäinen (1989), 131-2.

The River as Mother – an Ob-Ugric Myth

The Finnish words for 'water' (*vesi*) and 'fish' (*kala*) – along with the names of different species of fish and various concepts related to food and to water transportation – belong to the the oldest layer of the common Finno-Ugric vocabulary. As we have seen, the Ob-Ugric word *Agan* means both 'mother' and 'river', and this is also one of the most ancient of Finno-Ugric concepts – compare, for example, *jugan* in Ugric and *joki* ('river') in Finnish.

The overview provided by the map of Northern Eurasia and Siberia offers self-evident reasons for the significance of river routes in these cultures. One characteristic of these waterways is that they form huge networks. In earlier times, they united rather than separated territories far distant from one another, for example, the waterways around the rivers Volga, Vjatka, Kemi, Mesen, Petchora, Sysula, Vyzegda, Ob, Irtysh and Yenisei (see map). The Finno-Ugric peoples, as long-standing inhabitants of these regions, were greatly experienced in exploiting and controlling the resources of the water element.

Another common feature of these waterways is that they usually run from south to north , finally reaching the Barents Sea and Arctic Ocean beyond the zone of permafrost. Since the melting process starts upstream in the south, the rivers of Northern Eurasia see springtime flooding in their northern reaches, and the huge flows downstream create great problems and instability for the Northern peoples. The problem has been so bad that the Soviet administration once had plans to reverse the flow of the rivers, forcing them to run north to south instead.

Accordingly, the river issue has been crucial in ethnic mythologies. The Khanty are an Ob-Ugric people (numbering *c.* 20,000) who are settled or who live along the tributaries of the huge river Ob, called *Agan* in their language. In Khanty mythology, the Ob is their mother. More sacred than any other of its many by-rivers is Trom-Agan, named after the Khanty chief god, Num-tarum. The reindeer sacrifice, filmed in 1990 by the present author, was held at Woki-reh-jugan winter village, at the tip of this tributary. The comprehensive mythical background of the system of waterways is incorporated in the legend of Agan-Imie, told as follows by the shaman in the course of the sacrificial dinner-feast:

> The Father sent his daughter to the Agan-river. He told her – 'It is high time for you to go downstream. There, a place is waiting for you; the river has to be watched.'
>   Not thinking twice, she made everything ready for the journey downstream, along the Surgut river. There is a high headland there where people used to pray. From there she decided to go down the Ob river, then

up the Trom-Agan and Agan. At the mouth of the Trom-Agan, she stayed the night. She heard a tree fall somewhere. A man skied down the mountain and said – 'Let's go together. One year we shall watch the Agan and, the next year, the Trom-Agan.' Agan-Imie answered – 'No, I shall go upstream, my Agan, as my father told me.' But the man persuaded her – 'Let's go together.' Then they decided to hold a competition to see who was the fastest. Agan-Imie lagged behind. She looked away and saw that he had hitched a frog to her skis. Angry then grew Agan-Imie and went up the Agan alone, and the man stayed to watch the Trom-Agan.

Walking upstream, Agan-Imie reached the place pointed out to her by her Father. There she had a hut prepared for her to live in and everything in it. As soon as she sat down to have a rest, a man suddenly skied down a mountain again. 'At least, you have come. We two are appointed by the Father to watch the Agan. We shall live together.' Agan-Imie first grew angry, but then she thought – 'Evidently, the Father decided so. It was he who sent me here.'

So, they began living together. Once, the wife told her husband – 'Look, the water in the river rises, the flood starts. You are the master, aren't you? Go and see what is going on on the Agan.' He took a bow and arrows and went out. He moved up the Agan and shot one arrow. He must have hit somebody because the water sank at once. In the upper reaches of the Agan, villains lived in former times. One of them made a brook and let the water out. When the master of the Agan hit him, his belly burst and a lake appeared in that place. And from that lake seven brooks flowed in different directions.

They lived on. Once, the master said – 'It seems that again the flood is rising. Now the river is closed downstream.' The mistress said – 'This time I shall go to watch.' She went out of the house, turned into a frog and went downstream to the place where the Khanty lived. She looked. There a fence had been built by the villains. She moved her hands apart, went like a frog to the fence, and it fell down. The villains scattered in two directions. Some of them cried – 'Long-long, we shall enter the water.' Where they spoke, a long-long lake appeared. Other villains cried – 'Yim, yim, yim...' In that place a very big lake appeared. Yim is its name.

The masters of the Agan lived on and a son was born to them. Now the Khanty go there to pray. The long lake is called Souslore.[11]

The epics concur with the fact that the Ob with its tributaries and great floods regulates, in a variety of ways, the economy and life style of the Khanty. Their religious centre used to be in the area of the Barzava Mountains by the Ob where, until recently, they would gather to worship. The recent archaeological excavations in the Barzava area indicate a continuity of culture from 3,000 BC onwards,

---

11 Pentikäinen (1994), 392-3.

making it in all probability one of the most ancient continuous Finno-Ugric settlements yet discovered.

On the one hand, the river Ob united the Khanty, while, on the other, it was also regarded as the element separating the territory of the living from the realm of the dead. In line with this, the sacred grove of the winter village is situated on the opposite side of the river from the settlement. Today, a couple of hundred skulls are found hanging in it. When the red Siberian sun casts its rays over the grove, it is possible to gain a sense of that ecological balance which is such an important element in Khanty mythology. The sacred grove is a symbol of peace, not yet overshadowed by the flames of the oil rigs.

Water as Sacrament

The importance of water, blood and milk in the symbolics of the sacred is an issue which has not been sufficiently emphasized in ritual studies thus far. What these elements have in common is that they are liquid. First, they symbolize unstructured Chaos when, according to the myths, the Universe, Mankind, Death, and everything else of significance, was created in the setting of the Primordial Sea. Secondly, in their representations of the flooding liquid state, they act as ritual markers, emphasizing vague unstructured positions which focus on the 'transitus' between the crucial moments and the boundaries of the human life cycles.

Arnold van Gennep's work on 'rites de passages' (first presented in 1909) was more structural than functional. In his opinion, every change in place, state, social position and age is made public through rites which follow a pattern. First comes the 'séparation', when the individual is removed from his former social position. This is followed by an interim period – 'marge' – during which the individual is posed on the borderline between the two positions. The third and last phase is the full entry into the next position 'agrégation' . Hence the 'rites de passage' are divided into rites of – 1. separation, 2. transition, and 3. incorporation.

Arnold van Gennep identified territorial and religious moves. He placed heavy emphasis on the door as representing the borderline between 'this world' and 'the other' –

Precisely: the door is the boundary between the foreign and domestic worlds in a case of a temple. Therefore to cross the threshold is to unite oneself with a new world. It is thus an important act in marriage, adoption, ordination and funeral ceremonies... Consequently, I propose to call the rites of separation from a previous world 'preliminal rites', those executed during the transitional

12 van Gennep (1960), 8 f, 20 f.

stage, 'liminal' (or 'threshold') rites, and the ceremonies of incorporation into the new world, 'postliminal' rites.[12]

This theory has been modified by such scholars of symbolism as Mary Douglas, Mircea Eliade, Victor W. Turner etc. Eliade shifted the emphasis to hierophanies in the sacred state of religions, Douglas to purity and taboo. Turner's concept of 'communitas' with its 'anti-structures' also seems valuable here:

> In liminality, communitas tends to characterize relationships between those jointly undergoing ritual tradition. The bonds of communitas are anti-structural in the sense that they are undifferentiated, equalitarian, direct, extant, nonrational, existential, I-Thou relationships. Communitas is spontaneous, immediate, concrete – it is not shaped by norms, it is not institutionalized, it is not abstract.[13]

Communitas is a typical manifestation of marginality. According to Turner, within initiation –

> ...the novices are outside society, and society has no power over them, since they are actually sacred and holy, and therefore untouchable and dangerous, just as gods would be ...They are dead to the social world, but alive to the asocial world ... The social order may seem to have been turned upside down but by way of compensation, cosmological systems (as objects of serious study) may become of central importance for the novices, who are confronted by the elders, in rite, myth, song, instruction in a secret language, and various non-verbal symbolic gestures, such as dancing, painting, clay-moulding, wood-carving, masking, etc., with symbolic patterns and structures which amount to teaching about the structure of the cosmos and their culture as a part and product of it, in so far as these are defined and comprehended, whether implicitly or explicitly. Liminality is a complex series of episodes in sacred space-time...[14]

Liquidity is symbolically marking the vague liminality of *marge*. In the sacred acts of various religions, some kind of symbolic treatment with water plays a central role. When a Hindu, Taoist, Moslem, Catholic or Orthodox Christian enters a temple or church, they cleanse or bless themselves with water. Water is not only used for cleansing but, what is far more important, being a liquid element, it marks the significant borderline between the sacred and the profane. The object of pilgrimages is often located beyond water. In *rites de passages*, water usually marks the 'abnormality' of liminality within communitas, in contrast to the 'normal' structured society with its statuses.

---

13 Turner (1974), 272 ff.
14 Turner (1974), 18 ff.; Pentikäinen (1978), 182 ff.

Accordingly, water is an essential part of Christian baptism, like blood in the context of the sacrament of Holy Communion. The latter carries symbolical mythical references both to the flight of the Israelites from their houses marked with blood in Egypt and to the 'red'-coloured wine in relation to the blood of Jesus. Another significant area with mythical and ritual connotations relates to the treatment of menstruation blood and associated taboos and behavioural patterns carefully analyzed by Mary Douglas in the complex of puberty and initiation ceremonies.

In Old Norse sagas and legal traditions naming is considered the most important criterion for the social acceptance of children into their kin. There, the ritual of water-pouring (*vatni ausinn*) preceded Christian baptism. It has been referred to in the Icelandic sagas as *skírn*, 'cleansing'. According to *Harðar saga* (a late thirteenth-century work, set in the tenth century) 'the killing of a child after it had been "poured with water" was called "murder".' Neither could a child which had been placed at its mother's breast be abandoned. The same held true in Frisia where, according to a pre-Christian legend associated with an eighth-century saint, it is stated that if a child was to be drowned, this had to be done before it was suckled. It is interesting that the bestowal of a name and the first feeding were considered to be criteria of equal importance for determining not only a child's right to survival, but its rights to inheritance according to Nordic laws. What is important here is the fact that liquid elements, viz. milk and water, again mark the initial status at the commencement of the social life of the individual.

'A Running Steam they dare na cross'; The Dead without Status
This quote comes from Robert Burns' poem 'Tom o' Shanter'. The Finnish folklorist, Martti Haavio (himself a famous poet who wrote under the pseudonym P. Mustapää), reminds us in his splendid essay on the quoted rhyme that the central character of the poem was just returning from his 'nocturnal adventures' to the public house when –

In the middle of the storm, Tom is riding by dreadful and haunted places on his grey horse Meg until he arrives at the church of Alloway. The dead are dancing on the graves while the devil is providing the music. The bones of the murderer and those of one who has died on the gallows bedeck the altar. Tom sees two unbaptized children and 'other horrid things'. He is keenly aware of a maiden who is dancing among the witches, clothed in a child's shirt, and he shouts at her: 'Good!' But then the infernal crew attacks him and he flees on his mare Meg, while the ghosts pursue them:

Now, do thy speedy utmost, Meg,
And win the key-stane of the brig;
There at them thou thy tail may loss,
A running stream they dare na cross.

But before Meg reaches the 'brig', the pursuers sever her tail.[15]

It would be exciting indeed to follow Martti Haavio on his survey of the phenomenology of narratives and beliefs relating to the dead and witches unable to follow a fugitive.[16]

Another interesting topic for future Celtic-Baltic-Nordic co-operation might be a comparative analysis of narrative folklore in relation to archaeology. Special cemeteries for dead children which I visited in the west of Ireland following the Symposium would be a worthy subject for inclusion in an interdisciplinary folkloristic and mythological survey of Nordic and Baltic tradition of this kind.

A comprehensive corpus of supernatural legends related to dead-child beings exists in these cultures. They tell how such beings haunt the living in order to wreak revenge on their parents and others responsible for neglecting the proper ritual treatments, thus resulting in their being assigned a status in the realm of the mythical interaction between the living and the dead. Name-giving or Christian baptismal formulas have been used accordingly as a means of getting rid of these 'dead without status'. Their position in the complex of Nordic beliefs and narratives is very much related to that of other supernatural beings manifesting themselves in an aquatic setting, beings such as the *draug* and other categories of the 'drowned' which are dealt with elsewhere in these proceedings.

Eahpáras is the Sámi name for the dead-child being. Such a being is often met with on the tundra or in the fells, in the form of a *ptarmigan* – the sacred bird whose colour is transformed from brown in summer to snow-white in winter. The bird may appear with a rope around its neck as a reminder of the way in which the child was done to death. On appearing by a fireside, for example, the bird may transform itself into the shape of a naked child. If the experiencer is daring enough to enquire, the child may name its mother. Sometimes the experiencer may be the mother herself, in which case the child may attack her, sucking her to death like a vampire. One way of ridding oneself of this kind of ghost was to say to it – 'Go to your mother and suck her breasts.' Another method was to baptise it by means of formula containing a male and a female name such as 'Adam' and 'Eve', since the experiencer had no way of knowing the gender of the *eahpáras*. Another charm of a Christian origin involves the recitation of the Lord's Prayer backwards. I have met

---

15 Haavio (1948), 28.
16 *Ibid.*

several Sámi who have it off by heart in this way to this very day. A River Sámi, Ola S. Rasmus, from Ohcejohka on the border between Finland and Norway, told me the following legend in 1967:

> I heard of a newly wed Fell Sámi from Norway. He was a rich man and so was the girl he married. They were travelling in a reindeer *raido* in the fells. An *eahpáras* started crying terribly. There was one elderly man in the group who was riding behind in the loose sledge pulled by a reindeer, along with the young wife. The old man said – 'How you cry! Go suck the breast of your mother !' Immediately it attacked that woman and tore her completely open with one sweep. I heard it happened just like that. The old reindeer people were certain that the child had been buried there by that girl. That's the way it appears – wherever it has been laid, on the earth or whatever – at the time the person who put it there is passing by. It only appears at that time and not any other time. This happened at the Gaisa fells in Norway when they still travelled by reindeer *raido*, at least a hundred years ago.

The Sámi word *ráibma* describes extreme fear caused by supernatural beings. A person in such a state is said to be *ráimmahallan*, a condition which is said to lead to death. Just K. Qvigstad recorded the following narrative about this in Finnmark:

> A man was going from Avdsje to the church place. He wanted to take a rest, to sit down and smoke his pipe. He thought the sunset was beautiful. As day turned to evening, a *ptarmigan* started to laugh nearby. It became an *eahpáras* and started to cry. The men stood up and went a bit further. The *eahpáras* started to run after him. Finally it circled around him, ran between his legs, climbed up his back and began choking him by the neck. The man asked who its parents were. It answered: 'Lars and Marit'. After this, it released the man but still ran after him until he came in sight of the houses of the village. The man fell ill for a year. The doctors could not say what was wrong with him. The man died, and it is believed that the *eahpáras* rendered him powerless (in Sámi: *ahte son lei ráimmahallan eahpárazzii*).[17]

The frightened man made use of the traditional method of getting rid of the ghost, finally escaping from it when he felt he was safely home. Catching sight of the houses of the village meant refuge. Another effective remedy was to jump over running water. According to Sámi beliefs 'the dead or the underground people cannot cross water'.[18] Sámi children are still advised in cases like this that they should try to get to running water as quickly as possible. Narratives such as the following also bear witness to this belief:

---

17 Qvigstad (1928), 338-9.
18 Qvigstad (1928), 332-3.

Once, Per Jonsen and Anne Samuelsdatter were going home on the road to Alta, this side of the Ravdo river. Suddenly they heard a strange voice from the nearby forest. At first they did not know what it was. After some time the voice began to sound like crying. Per Jonsen got very much afraid and started to walk like a dead man. As the voice followed them, he shouted – 'Go away from us! We owe you nothing!' But the crying voice continued to strike fear into them until they came to the Ravdo river. When they crossed the river, the voice remained on the other side. But Per Jonsen was still very much afraid when he got home. When the people asked – 'What happened to you, Per?' – he told them all that had happened on the journey. [19]

The River of Death in Arctic Shamanhood

Siberian shamanhood (*samanstvo* in Russian) – the concept I prefer instead of shamanism – is generally characterized by the shamans themselves as the 'painful gift'.[20] In shamanic cultures, induction into shamanhood involves acquiring an expertise in the native mythology and folklore of one's people. As the Nanay shamaness, Lindza Beldy told me in 1994 – 'I treat the pains of my people only.'[21] Painful dreams and experiences with symptoms of madness of a sort are part and parcel of the life of shamans, to such an extent that the vocation to shamanhood has the capacity to excite fears and even pose a threat to those involved, in particular the shaman himself and his family. Abnormal behaviour and marginal experiences are even expected at the shamanic initiation as a testimony to the fact that the spirits have accepted the shaman-to-be. After that, the shaman's life may continue more or less normally until old age when, again, many shamans may undergo moments of crisis.

The mythical target of the shamanic soul journey is the river of Death. Kristfried Ganander's *Mythologia Fennica* (1789), attempted to represent not only the mythology of the Finns but also that of the Sámi. According to Ganander, the Finnish concepts of *Manala* ('the underground place') and *Tuonela* ('the place beyond') mean the realm of the dead. Ganander compared them to *Glitnis*, the Goths' concept of that abode. He acknowledged the Sámi word *Jabmeaivo* (in Northern Sámi, *Jabmiidáibmu*) with special reference to the netherworld of the *jabmi* ('the dead').

Of particular interest from the point of view of the mythology of ancient Finnish shamanhood is his notion that expressions such as *Tuonella käydä* ('to visit *Tuoni*'), *Tuonelassa vaeltaa* ('to wander in *Tuonela*') and *loveen langeta* ('to fall into a "hole" [i.e. trance]'), mean falling into ecstasy or making a shaman's journey to Tuonela. According to Ganander, everything lacking on earth was found in

---

19 *Ibid.*
20 Pentikäinen 1993.
21 *Ibid.*

abundance in *Tuonela*. It was believed that the deceased kept their treasures there after death. The kingdom of the dead was ruled by a female figure known as *Tuonelan morsian* ('the Bride of Tuonela') or *Tuonen neito* ('The Maiden of Tuoni') who lived on *Kipumäki* ('Pain Hill') or *Kipuvuori* ('Pain Mountain').

In Finnish runic poetry, the shaman when he falls into ecstasy is said to *käy Tuonelassa* ('visit *Tuonela*'). There are several runes which tell about the adventures of the heroes of the *Kalevala* in *Tuonela* or *Pohjola* ('the North'), both of which signify 'the abode beyond'. 'Väinämöinen's Journey to *Tuonela*' is one such detailed description of a shaman's journey to the realm of the dead which can be read as a mythological map of the topography of *Tuonela*. Here, the main hero of the Finnish epic goes to *Tuonela* in search of the charm needed to build a boat. He comes to the river of *Tuonela* where he is received by *Tuonen tyttö, Manalan matala neiti* ('Girl of *Tuonela*, Manala's low maiden'). After making his return, Väinämöinen warns:

Many have gone there,
But few have returned,
From there in *Tuonela*'s halls,
From *Manala*'s eternal house.
No, good fellows,
Young men, do not,
Old men, do not,
Fetch a spike from *Tuonela*,
A crowbar from *Manala*,
For mending sleighs,
Building mounts !
Do not go there.[22]

Madness is said to be typical of the ageing shaman. A well-known Siberian myth tells how the aged shaman leaves his kin to 'go to bury his drum'.[23] The shamanic belief behind this mythology is focused on the consideration that the drum is identical with the soul of the shaman who made it and used it; when a shaman dies, nothing should be left behind to bring him or her back. Shamanic death is also said to be 'the departure of a lonely man.'[24] He or she should also die in the specially prescribed fashion – 'by the river of his/her clan without returning home any more.'[25] There is a drum in a Khanty local museum in Russkinskie on the river Ob which was found in a *tshum* ('cabin') by the body of a dead shaman. He had frozen to death on the all too long road to bury his drum. Modern society might deem this 'deliberate suicide', but from the point of view of shamanic society, it was rather a 'voluntary departure', a normal end to a life which had been normally abnormal.

---

22 Quoted in Pentikäinen (1989), 206.
23 Pentikäinen 1994.
24 Pentikäinen 1983.
25 Pentikäinen 1983, 1994.

Misty Islands and Rescues Forgone:
Unexpected Features of a Sea Legend – An Innovation or a Part of Tradition?

MICEÁL ROSS

I

The idea for this paper came from reading that fine collection, *Scottish Traditional Tales*,[1] published in 1994 only months before the tragically early demise of Alan Bruford, one of its editors. My attention was caught by the editors' note on a story, told by James Henderson from the Orkneys, called 'The Magic Island'. The editors' comment to the effect that 'the father's refusal to rescue his daughter is a nicely cynical touch which gives this story a character of its own',[2] struck a chord with me. In the course of my reading, I had come across similar observations about other stories that, at first sight, seemed to be what one might call 'maverick' in character.

An example of one such legend can be found in the study of fairy abductions by H. F. Feilberg, who remarked about a certain story from Sylt (Denmark) concerning the captain of a storm-tossed ship asked by a submarine man to assist his wife in giving birth: 'I know of no parallel to this tale.'[3] Seventy years on, Séamas Ó Catháin published a similar tale from county Mayo in western Ireland[4] and other Irish examples might also be quoted.

I will focus here upon some marine aspects of fairy abductions of young women. My initial examination concentrates on two stories which bear a remarkable resemblance to each other, even as to their title – The Magic Island – one stemming from the southern part of Ireland, the other belonging to northern Scotland. The evidence which they provide for the existence of a separate legend type (which I have here designated *The Forgone Rescue*) is buttressed by the presence of similar motifs in other Irish material. In particular, the apparently idiosyncratic ending of the Scottish version is scrutinised and, by reference to another legend type (relating to the foiled abduction of a young fisherman – namely the *Knife Against The Wave*), it is hoped that this ending and, indeed, other aspects of the legend here under discussion, may be seen not to be as unusual as might otherwise be imagined.

---

1 Bruford & MacDonald (1994), eds., 370-2.
2 *Ibid.*, 478.
3 Feilberg (1910), 69 ('Til denne fortælling kender jeg ingen sidestykker', quoting Müllenhoff [1892], 339).
4 Ó Catháin (1980), 95-7.

A recent American publication reports that 'one traditional teller may be noted for artistic individuality and verbal remodelling, another for humor, another for memory and historical information, and another for characterizations.... Differences are valued by a performer's peers and serve both to maintain and to revitalize folk tradition. But in a traditional culture certain conservative restraints on the storyteller's freedom are operative.....The so-called law of self-correction ensures that radical changes do not normally occur: audience-performance inter-action inhibits them.'[5] This paper lends support to this conclusion and argues that what at first looks like radical innovation may prove on closer scrutiny to be part of tradition.

II

The Irish version of the 'The Forgone Rescue'

The Irish version of *The Forgone Rescue* shares some motifs with the *Knife Against The Wave*. It comes from the south-east of Ireland and was written down in July 1936 by Labhrás Ó Cadhla.[6] He had heard it twenty years previously from his mother, Siobhán, wife of Risteárd Ó Cadhla of Scairt, Ballinamult, in the western part of county Waterford. It is not stated where Mrs Ó Cadhla grew up; Ballinamult itself is in the Knockmealdown Mountains, inland from the port of Dungarvan. The story goes as follows:

The Enchanted Island

Way, way beyond in the west of Ireland a beautiful young maiden rose very early on the morning of May Day and was taking the air by herself along one margin of the sea. She was a girl among girls for loveliness. Her tresses were as black as a beetle and they cascading down to the ground behind her, almost six feet long. Her face was finely moulded and her cheeks were so radiant that the thorn of a gooseberry could draw blood from them. She wore neither socks nor shoes and she walking on the edge of the strand, sweeping the dew with the hem of her cloak. She was not long so engaged when a magic mist enveloped her. When the mist dispersed once more no trace was found of the beautiful young maiden.

Her father and brothers searched land and sea for her for a full year and a day, but no trace or clue was to be found either on the heights or in the hollows. It was just as if the ground itself had swallowed her or as if she vanished as a vapour into the sky.

---

5 McCarthy (1994), ed.,165.
6 *IFC* 289:116-20. My translation from the Irish. *IFC* = Irish Folklore Collection being the Main Manuscripts Collection of the Department of Irish Folklore at University College Dublin; the numerals on either side of the colon represent the manuscript volume number and the page number(s) respectively. See also footnote 36.

That year passed and soon two years had gone by. Time moved on from year to year until seven years had elapsed from that day and still there was no word of her.

On the morning of May Day seven years later her father and brothers were out at sea drawing their nets when they were surrounded by a magic mist. They did not know where to steer the boat so they let her drift on, ever and always following her own way. Finally she went aground on a fine sandy beach they had never seen before; nor had they known that such a strand existed at all.

Out before them they saw a fine smiling house perched on an airy little hill inland on the island and they made for it. Who should open the door of the pleasant lime-white house for them only the girl who went from them seven years before that. How was she only married to the heir of this enchanted island and they had a little flock of children?

It was not long before the man of the house and his son came in to them from the sea, sailing in a small boat used for shell fishing. They extended them a thousand welcomes to the enchanted island and set the best of food and of drink before them.

Later on the mist cleared and the sky brightened. The father and the brothers were on for taking the girl home with them, but she would not go along with them. She gave them, however, a magic talisman – a black-handled knife which would enable them to come to visit her whenever they wished. They said their farewells to her then.

The father had the knife with him into the boat as it was moving out from the beach. They were looking at it and passing it among themselves when it slipped away from the youngest son into the sea. Once the knife was lost the enchanted island and everything sank once more into the sea. No one has ever seen the island or the girl again.

Since the legend in this form appears to be unique in Ireland, some comment may be in order. The abduction occurs on May morning when the girl is out walking in the dew. She may have been attracted outdoors because, on that morning, the dew is said to have the property of enhancing a maiden's beauty, while walking in it barefoot would give her pretty and healthy feet.[7] The dew was considered to be especially potent if taken and used before sunrise. However, being abroad so early at this liminal time between night and day, between summer and winter, carries certain risks. 'So powerful were the preternatural forces abroad in the night between sunset on May Eve and sun-rise on May Day,' notes Danaher,[8] 'that almost anything might be expected to happen.' 'There is a widely-held belief,' he adds, 'that this is the time of the year when abduction by the fairies was most feared. Infants of both sexes and

---

7 The virtues of May dew have been long known – Danaher (1972) quotes from a book by Dr Gerard Boate of 1652 (108).
8 Danaher (1972), 109.

marriageable young women were most in danger of being spirited away.'[9] B.N. Hedderman, a nurse who worked on the Aran Islands, agrees that the fairies were particularly active at that time and likely to 'sweep' along with them any children and young girls met by them as they changed residence.[10] Thomas Crofton Croker claimed that on May Eve 'youth and loveliness are thought to be especially exposed to peril. It is therefore a natural consequence that not one woman in a thousand appears abroad.'[11] While there are those who maintain that May-morning is a morning for staying late in bed until the smoke of someone else's chimney is visible, others are up early, or indeed up all night to ensure they be the first to draw water from the well and so protect the luck of the farm. Yet others might be out searching for herbs, believed to be especially potent at this time, or gathering May flowers.

Whatever may have caused her to be up and about so early, we find the young girl walking along the shore in the liminal area between land and sea. This is where *Rabharta Mór na nÉan* ('The Great Spring Tide of the Birds'), occurring in May, marks the highest point of the sea's summer advance on land, where it deposits the sea wrack on which the ringed plover may subsequently build its nest in safety. It is an area for trysts with lovers from the sea. In versions of the *Knife Against The Wave*, it is the place where both O'Sullivan and Cluasach Ó Fáilbhe kept their rendezvous with undersea maidens on May morn.[12] On that day, too, Maurice Connor, king of all the pipers in Munster, waded into the sea from Frasga Strand, having accepted a marriage proposal from a beautiful young sea maiden who wore a cocked hat on 'her long green hair'.[13] Maurice sent his mother an annual memento in the form of a half-burnt sod of turf (peat) washed ashore, a practice which Cluasach and others subsequently adopted. The half burnt sod is reminiscent of the embers of the May bonfire used to protect the fields. O'Sullivan's sea-wife was more practical, sending the orphaned old mother an annual gift of gold in a floating log.[14] All these gifts arrived on May morning. It was to a strand on May-morn that Caitlín Triail, the sea-woman, immortalised in the song of the same name, brought horses to collect her lover.[15] On this same morning, it was across lake waters that Gearóid Iarla and O'Donoghue of the Lakes urged their ethereal steeds.[16]

Among the many stories of fairies abducting women, three occur which feature kidnappings at the sea shore. A Mr Lucey[17] and his daughter, out strolling

---

9 *Ibid.*, 122.
10 Hedderman (1917), 106. Cf also IFC 42:149. Danaher (1972), 122 notes that there 'was a widely-held belief that this was the time of the year when abduction by the fairies was most to be feared.'
11 See Danaher (1972),124.
12 *IFC* 1715:256-63. See also Ó Duilearga (1981), 225.
13 Crofton Croker (1834), 201.
14 This is reminiscent of dollars from America. Once the child emigrated the parents were unlikely to see it again, at least in the early days of mass emigration.
15 See *Jack Mac na Baintrí* ('Jack the Widow's Son') – *IFC* 155:105-4.
16 Danaher (1972), 121.
17 *IFC* 8:274-6.

near Dingle, sit on a sea wall, where he falls asleep. He awakens to find his daughter, his hat and his walking stick gone. Later, when he is invited to stand as baptism sponsor for a baby, he meets his daughter again. He recovers his hat and stick, but she chooses to remain with her new family among the *Slua Sí* ['The Fairy Host'], subsequently becoming the banshee of the Luceys. Brother P. T. Ó Riain collected another version of this story in which three girls were said to be collecting limpets when one was swept away unexpectedly by a wave.[18] A similar fate was reported to have befallen another girl, her disappearance being brought about by 'a great assault out of the breast of the calm sea' [*as bhrollach na farraige socair ruathair mór*].[19] Sudden waves in a calm sea are to be met with in versions of the *Knife Against The Wave*, but none of these involve mist.

According to a saying from Iveragh in county Kerry, mist, music and sailing are three things under enchantment.[20] Ancient Irish manuscript sources contain numerous references to magic mists of concealment, two examples of this being the druidic mist which hindered the Milesians landing at Loch Garman[21] and, to mention one with religious associations, the mist which, as St Brendan was told by Barinthus, the holy man, came down when he set out with his son, Mernoc, the monk, to visit the island called the Land of Saints – 'so that we could hardly see the prow of our boat.'[22] The poet in the eighteenth-century *Aisling* or Vision poem, tells his audience of a *ceo draíochta* or 'magic mist' which takes him through unfamiliar terrain to meet the *spéir-bhean*, the sky or dream woman, who represents Ireland.

While there is plenty of evidence for their popularity, mists, magical or otherwise, do not seem to feature as prominently in modern Irish folklore as, perhaps, one might expect. In fact, apart from the few accounts in versions of the *Knife Against The Wave*, only three other instances are known to me. The first of these relates to a partial abduction:[23] a man is frightened to hear weeping coming from *Tobar na bPúicíní* ('The Fairies' Well'), near Dingle; a less timorous individual investigates and finds a human girl there. The storyteller comments: 'going up the hill-side she was after sheep when a mist came on her of a summer's afternoon. She was taken and left by the well. It was the *Slua* [*Sí*] that met her. She remembered riding pillion on a horse behind a man.' She had been swept there from Sliabh Luachra on the other side of the county. Generally, it is the *Sí Gaoithe* ('Fairy [Whirl-] Wind') which functions as the fairies' means of transport in such situations and not, as in this case, the mist.

---

18 *IFC* 10:141-2.
19 *IFC* 39:60-1
20 'Ceó nú céol nú séolhóireacht – trí nidh atá fé dhraoidheacht' – *IFC* 997:117-9 (published in *Béaloideas* XI (1941), (69).
21 Keating, 83.
22 'Life of Brendan of Clonfert' in Plummer (1922), 49.
23 *IFC* 4:111-2.

The second of these accounts stems from the same place as the Irish version of *The Forgone Rescue*, namely west Waterford. A man, lost in a hill mist, is saved from falling into a lake by a woman who crosses his path at the hitherto invisible edge of the water. He follows her to a wake house where he recognises the dead man as a neighbour. She gives him a herb and, later, when he applies it to the dead man, he revives.[24] The third account containing a mist comes from West Cork and is discussed below.

The *Knife Against The Wave* provides us with some more accounts of mists. In the story of O'Sullivan and the Woman from the Sea (referred to above in the context of May-morn),[25] a dense fog causes O'Sullivan from Ventry to cast anchor. Later, when he dives to release it from a snag, he meets the 'Woman from the Sea' who had used this device to bring him within her power. He promises to meet her on Ventry Strand on May morning. His mother, who accompanies him thither, is promised gold in a floating log every May morning of her life. In a Donegal version of The *Knife Against The Wave*,[26] a beautiful [*sic*] boy from Maghera agrees to travel by boat to the Otherworld to remove his knife from the cheek of a beautiful red-haired girl. She, in the guise of a drowning wave, had attempted to abduct him: 'Soon they were surrounded by a fog until they reached an island outside Sliabh an tSuaith, an island they had not observed before...' The man who came from Inishmeane, in the Donegal story of that name,[27] wounds the red-haired woman who is attempting to sink his currach and refuses to withdraw his knife from her hip: 'You will suffer for it some foggy morning !' is her enigmatic threat. In fact, he takes to his bed immediately he gets home, never to rise again.

The use of mist seems to be a more common device in Scottish fairy abductions. For example, in a Scottish folktale with the anglicised title of Koisha Kayn [*Cosa Chéin*?] or [the Leeching of] Cian's Legs, which was recorded in Oban in 1881-2, Machkan-an-ahar, son of the King of Lochlann, tells Geur-mac-ul-Uai that when his mother and sister entered a newly built church the doors closed 'and the church went away into the skies in the form of a tuft of mist.' When Machkan-an-ahar sets out to search for them, he declares – 'I was overtaken by a great mist and I came to an island.'[28]

---

24 *IFC* 85:194-6.
25 *IFC* 1715:256-63.
26 *IFC* 365:212-4
27 *IFC* 478: 517-20.
28 MacInnes (1890) quoted in Philip, 145.

III

The Scottish version of '*The Forgone Rescue* ('The Magic Island')

The main focus of this paper – the discussion of the father's action – is centred in the second part of the story, the relevant section of which is reproduced below. The first part resembles the Irish version closely, with only minor differences occurring – the girl goes missing while gathering limpets on the sea shore (a setting found, as was noticed earlier, in an Irish story of abduction). She is presumed drowned since her body was never found. The telling does not refer to a mist taking her away or mention that the kidnapping occurred on May-morn. Apart from these variations the story goes as before: Years later, her father and brothers are enveloped in a mist while fishing and row to where they can hear the sound of waves beating on a shore. When they reached the house on the mysterious island they realised that 'the woman of the house' was the missing girl:

> So when they saa that they thought there wis somethin kind o queer aboot it, an they didna like to ask ony questions. But ... she asked hoo they wis, an oh, they wis aal fine, an she said, oh, they would hev somthin tae aet, set doon a grand diet to them tae aet. An they wis taakin awey aboot different things, an the man said, did they hev ony beests that they would sell?
>
> 'Oh yes,' the old fella says, 'we hev a coo, a grand coo 'at A wis thinkin on sellin indeed.'
>
> 'Weel,' he says, 'A'll buy her. What dae ye want for her?'
>
> Oh, he named a good price for her, he would want that onywey
>
> 'Oh,' he says, 'A'll give ye that,' an he paid him in gold sovereigns.
>
> So he thought, 'Noo . . . A'll fin oot whar this place is,' so he says, 'Weel, ye'll hev to tell me noo what wey to com here, or A'll no be able to tak the coo tee ye.'
>
> 'Och,' he says, 'don't you worry aboot that. A'll com for the coo masel.'
>
> So ... wan o them said, 'I think 'at the fog's offerin to lift a little.' So the... lass says tae them, 'Weel, afore ye go, are they anything here in the... in the hoose 'at ye would fancy to tak wi ye?'
>
> An the man said, 'Oh, ye're welcome to onything 'at's here, jist pick onything ye would like an tak it wi ye!'
>
> So the lass, she gied them a kind o look, I suppose thinkin 'at they would say, 'Well A'll take - A'll tak you wi us!' Hooever, they lookit aroond an they saa a grand big gold dish, an they said, oh, they would like tae hev that. So she handed it to them: 'Well,' she says, 'tak it an go!'
>
> So they gaed doon to the boat, and the man gied them a hand to

laanch, an he said, 'Jist pull ower that way a bit.' So they pulled oot an the island disappeared in the fog an the fog lifted an they were no distance aff o their own land. So they pulled for home, an soon as they cam in, the. wife was meetin them at the shore very agitated. She says, 'An aafu thing's happened.' She says, 'Wir best coo's lyin in the byre deid!'

'Ach,' the man says, 'let her be gaan, she's ower weel paid for!'

So that wis the end o that.

Both the Scottish and Irish versions feature an encounter between a father and his abducted daughter in the otherworld. As we have noted above, this motif is not unknown in other Irish accounts of fairy abductions. Often such meetings involve negotiations about a cow and, in this regard, the Scottish version of *The Forgone Rescue* is close to many Irish accounts of this sort. Lurking in the background here is the notion that, if the 'Good People' do not get the woman, they will take a cow in her place. In one case, a woman on her way to buy a cow at a fair is asked to give suck to an otherworld child.[29] She is told that the *Slua* [*Sí*] are on a kidnapping raid and will snatch a cow if they fail to get a woman. As a reward for her kindness she is advised not to buy the best cow at the fair, just in case. She ignores this advice and the cow suffers an accident on the way home and has to be put down. Sometimes, substitution of a cow for the woman seems to be the arrangement agreed in connection with a rescue from the otherworld. In one account, the rescue so depletes the husband's herds that he has to ask his wife's family for help. Perhaps, we may conclude, the Scottish otherworld islander, in asking about cows, did so because he was expecting to lose his wife.

Other Irish and Scottish stories on a similar theme could be instanced, including ones where the woman and the cow 'die' simultaneously. One such occurrence led to the witticism recorded by Dean Ramsey:[30]

A countryman had lost his wife and his favourite cow on the same day. His friends consoled him for the loss of his wife; and being highly respectable, several hints and offers were made towards getting another for him. 'Ou ay,' he at length replied, 'you're a' keen eneuch to get me anither wife, but no yin o' ye offers to gie me anither coo.'

Another episode recalls the account of a man returning from Cork after selling two firkins of butter. He is approached by a stranger who asks him to stand as sponsor for a child to be christened. He follows the man very nervously, fearing a mugging, yet not wishing to give offence in case the request is genuine. The child's mother turns out to be his own daughter who had 'died' a year earlier. When asked about a christening gift, he promptly declares – 'The best cow in my byre!' The cow is dead

---

29 *IFC* 271:564-6.
30 Ramsay (1862), reproduced in Philip, 339.

when he gets home but he does not mind because the milk is for his grandchild. Thereafter, everything went well for him.[31]

Both the Irish and Scottish versions of *The Forgone Rescue* hint that the father may have been lured to the otherworld for a special reason. Similar stratagems employed by stolen girls are to be found in other Irish stories of fairy abduction. Thus, the Scottish version, in particular, resonates with the following Irish tale of a young couple about to be married: She is 'taken' on her way home from walking out with him. The young man goes astray on the way to her wake and finds himself in a fairy rath. He does not recognise his girl friend. She had lured him there, hoping to be rescued. This event is said to have given rise to the song *Mac Uí Bhrádaigh*.[32] In another version of this story, the dead girl takes him to find a priest so that they can marry. Her motto is *Is fearr bainis ná tórramh!* ('A wedding is better than a funeral') – a saying also found in other such stories. He does not realise what is happening but is prevented by a dead tailor from entering the place where the priest is said to be. As a result he escapes back to this world.[33]

Failure to rescue a person from the Otherworld is a frequent feature of stories of fairy abduction. However, the Scottish version of *The Forgone Rescue* depicts the father as actually being unwilling or unable to take the hint of the possibility of rescue, even though success seemed assured. Bruford and MacDonald attribute this failure to act to a cynical twist given to the story by the storyteller. I do not believe this necessarily to be the case, for it is my contention that this, or a similar motif, occurs in other legends relating to the sea.

One such legend is from Kerry and may be summarized as follows:

The hero, Diarmaid Ó Sé, while on his way to Mass, follows a bobbing barrel which lures him to a strange beach with a fine palace nearby. Within, he meets a fine young girl and a wizened old man who appear to know him. He is generous in giving the old man the fill of his pipe of 'the right kind of tobacco that you get at wakes' and is given a meal by the young woman. As a reward for his open-handedness, the old man offers him anything at all that he would like to have in the place. Like the Scottish father, he chooses 'a gold cup on the dresser.' With that, the atmosphere changes and he is ordered out of the girl's sight. The old man urges him to race for the curach which is about to become afloat as a result of a sudden incursion of the tide. He gives Diarmaid three dock leaves to ward off an impending attack by three pursuing waves. Diarmaid escapes this threat, not realising that the waves contained the spurned girl who has now opted fror a more direct method of abducting him. He is in time for Mass and afterwards gives the

---

31 *Irisleabhar na Gaedhilge* 4 (1889) 239-40.
32 Timony (1906), 14-6.
33 *IFC* 62:234-7.

priest the gold cup. 'The priest said: "You missed your chance. Herself was after you hoping you would marry her; hoping you would take her when you were offered anything you fancied in the house. That is the place they call Hy Brazil, the Island of Eternal Life. It appears above the sea once in seventy years. There was a woman back in *Baile 'n Ghleanna* saw it appear. It is like *Tír na nÓg*. You could have lived there and you would never have known a poor day."[34]

This is not an isolated account, as other versions of this story from Cape Clear Island and mainland West Cork show. The Cape Clear telling, a joyful caricature of Irish legends the islanders delighted to tell, was taken down by Fr Donncha Ó Floinn and may be summarised as follows:

A couple of islanders were supposed to be fishing, but in reality were on the look out for any food the wasteful transatlantic liners might jettison. They found a meat bone. When it was picked clean one of them said– 'To heck with you' – and threw it overboard. Shortly afterwards a horseman arrived and asked the thrower to come with him. The bone had lodged in the shoulder of the old man of the sea. The rider warned the fisherman not to shake hands with the old man after his cure would be affected but to offer him the bone instead. He followed the advice and the bone is duly reduced to powder: 'You [Cape Clear islanders] are as tough as ever,' says he, 'and now since you were so good as to come here and give me relief, look around the house and you may have anything that you lay your eye on.'

He looked around the house. There was a young girl sitting on a chair but he paid no attention to her. He saw a hank of rope hanging up, and he said that if he was at home that it would suit him because he had an old boat and it would do for mooring it.

'Bad cess to you,' says the girl, 'that you did not ask for me and a poor day would never come near you, because the last chance has been given me and I will be here for ever.'

He could not remedy the situation. He mounted the horse again and he returned free and safe, making for the boat. His comrade asked him what news he had from the lower lands.

'It is the grandest country I ever visited. They have cocks of hay made,' says he, 'fine rich level fields; horses grazing in some of them; cattle in some of them; sheep in some of them; and the harvest is almost ripe.'[35]

The forgone opportunity to rescue the girl in the Cape Clear account is explicit. It occurs in the context of a blanket offer to the hero to choose whatever he liked. Such offers also appear in other legends. For example, a Mr Nicholls, who

---

34 *IFC* 241:179-84
35 *Béaloideas* 11 (1941), 112.

lived at Finea near Lake Sheelin, in county Westmeath, was offered 'anything he liked to bring. He asked for a little copper skillet'[36]; and a Jack McGuinness, who lived by Lough Gowna, county Longford, refused to take anything for his services – nevertheless he was pressed to take a gold kettle filled with gold and, we are told, 'the gold kettle is still retained by the family and is only used on state occasions, or when there is a wedding or an increase in the family.'[37]

The Cape Clear story introduces the motif of the tough old man crushing the bone. This episode shows up again in two Galway stories where a man is summoned to cure a seal that he has injured. In both cases, he is warned against shaking hands with the wounded old man.[38] One of these accounts tells us that –

> They landed on the bed of the sea. They were walking a while when they came to a great fishbone. The man from under the sea took up the fishbone and gave it to the young man and said to him: 'When you come into the house the man there will welcome you. He will put out his hand to you and welcome you, and you stretch out the fishbone to him. Do not give him your hand.[39]

This motif is appropriate where the Otherworld person suffers an unprovoked attack from a mortal and is male. It would not be appropriate to versions of the *Knife Against The Wave* legend where the initiative is taken by an Otherworld girl seeking to abduct the handsome fisherman by feigning his drowning. The motif is well known in the context of ML 5010 'The Visit to the Old Troll'. In the collection of Scottish folktales edited by Neil Philip,[40] it occurs in *The Pechs*. Speaking of their king who survived all his people, 'baith bedrid and blind' it is said:

> Maist folk had forgotten there was sic a man in life; but ae night, some young men being in the house where he was, and making great boasts about their feats of strength, he leaned owre the bed and said he would like to feel ane o' their wrists, that he might compare it wi' the arms of men wha had lived in former times. And they, for sport, held out a thick gaud o' ern to him to feel. He just snappit it in tway wi' his fingers as you would a pipe stapple. 'It's a bit gey gristle,' he said; 'but naething to the shackle-banes o' my days.' That was the last o' the Pechs.

A West Cork version of this was recorded on two occasions over an interval of eighteen months by the same collector, from the same tradition bearer. It happens to contain the mist motif and is the third of the three such accounts referred to above. It may be summarized as follows:

---

36 *IFC S* 719:333-4 *IFC S* = Irish Folklore Collection, Schools' Manuscripts Collection See Note 6 above.
37 *IFC S* 76:178-82.
38 *IFC* 687:77-9; see also IFC 523:54-62 .
39 *IFC* 687:78.
40 Philip (1991), 228.

A fishing boat lost in a fog reaches an unfamiliar shore. A crewman ventures out to see if he can identity the place. Following a path in the woods, he reaches a house. A woman is within before him, combing her red hair. When he asks for an ember to redden his pipe, she asks whether he would prefer the ember to a woman. He chooses the ember and she exclaims – 'Aw, shame on you! Why did you not say a woman?' If he had, the storyteller explains, the enchantment would have left the island.[41]

This account contains a curious mixture of motifs. The fog and the visit to the house on the mysterious island resemble the Scottish and Irish versions of *The Forgone Rescue*, and it also overlap with many details in several versions of *The Knife Against The Wave*. Thus, it reminds us of the beautiful Donegal boy from Maghera, referred to above, who agreed to travel to the otherworld to remove his knife from the cheek of a beautiful red-haired girl – 'Soon they were surrounded by a fog until they reached an island outside Sliabh an tSuaith, an island they had not observed before...' Often the woman combing her beautiful red hair occurs in versions in which the hero is lured to the woman's home by the difficulty of freeing an anchor.[42] In such cases, it is the woman who takes the initiative, rather than waiting demurely for the hero to propose to her.

Such stories often make mention of a man entering a dwelling to seek an ember in order to redden his pipe, a normal enough practice in the days before the advent of safety matches or gas lighters. Sometimes when the house is located on his way to a fair, he unwittingly enters the otherworld. At other times, the dwelling he enters lies under the sea. In 'The Concur [sic] Eel Girl', for example, the girl from the sea, disguised as a conger eel, is wounded in the eye. The sea recedes creating dry land. A man enters a house to redden his pipe and is advised by the girl's mother to hasten back to the stranded boat before the returning sea overwhelms it. As in the story about Diarmaid Ó Sé, which it parallels to some extent, the man in this story manages to escape with his life. The otherworld in this case is called *Brachlainn*, and is said to be situated near the Aran Islands.[43] This is also the location of the otherworld of Little Aran which features in the 'Dr Lee' story where the hero is about to strike his flint and tinder to light his pipe in the otherworld house, but is offered an ember instead; had he struck a spark, Little Aran would have lost its otherworld status. He is compensated for his forbearance with a medical book which makes him the wisest doctor of his day.[44]

---

41 *IFC* 535:9 and *IFC* 660:348 This was collected on the 12 May 1938 and on the 17 November 1939 by Seán Ó Cróinín from Seán Ó hAodha, a 75-year old fisherman from the parish of Cill Fachtna Beag in West Carbury.
42 These legends are the subject of a separate study 'Anchors in a Three-Decker World', *Folklore* (1998), 63-76.
43 *IFC* 1133:267-8
44 For example, *IFC* 157:526-9. See article by Dáithí Ó hÓgáin in the present volume.

IV

A Legend Field

At the outset, I noted that this paper was inspired by Bruford and MacDonald's comment on James Henderson's telling of 'The Magic Island' viz. 'the father's refusal to rescue his daughter is a nicely cynical touch which gives this story a character of its own.' In challenging this suggestion of uniqueness I have instanced occasions in the oral tradition of Ireland where the man, given a wide-open choice, opts for something else in preference to the woman, thus indicating that that particular feature of the Scottish version of *The Forgone Rescue* may not be as unusual in oral tradition as seems to be suggested. The idea of exchanging a woman for a cow – hinted at in Scotland – is more explicitly stated in some Irish fairy abduction stories in which these and other motifs can be seen to re-occur and overlap. Éilís Ní Dhuibhne has noticed a similar phenomenon in her study of the 'Old Woman as Hare', where she states:

> Such floating traditional motifs can be expected to emerge in widely different legends, because many legends share the same mysterious atmosphere and same concern with supernatural belief, and, I suggest, they also share the similar structures and meanings. ..[A] very substantial corpus of them focus on some sort of conflict or encounter of two worlds: the normal and the abnormal, the natural and the supernatural.
>
> In fact in this complex there are not all that many such loosely floating images drawn from legendry in general. There is a definite concentration of images deriving from the butter- and milk-stealing syndrome, and it is very obvious that the narrators have considered this legend as a part of that gamut of beliefs and legends, and have to some extent used the images, beliefs and motifs of the entire corpus interchangeably. The term 'legend field', which is now increasingly used, is once again the most pertinent description of what we are dealing with.[45]

Whereas Ní Dhuibhne concentrated on the 'butter- and milk-stealing syndrome', this paper has been preoccupied with the field of marine fairy abduction. However, in both scenarios, as she says, it is clear that 'the concrete details which are in theory infinitely variable ... in practice vary only slightly.'[46]

'The folktale,' according to Neil Philip, 'being an oral form, is essentially a performance art. ..... The tale is made afresh each time it is told. Each telling is a new creation, an exchange of energies between storyteller and story, creativity and tradition. In the endless rehearsal and reappraisal of traditional themes, each telling is as valid

---

45 See *Folklore* 1993 (i) and (ii), 81.
46 *Ibid.*, 80.

as the last, or the next.'[47] This is even more true of legends. Philip expresses the opinion that 'while the contribution of the storyteller to the tale varies greatly, in general, folktale narrators intend to pass on a tale as they heard it rather than using it as a peg for their own creativity.'[48] In the case of legends, I am more attracted to Ní Dhuibhne's view that narrators use, to some extent, the images, beliefs and motifs of the entire corpus interchangeably. While this corpus tends to be defined conservatively within traditional limits, its very richness offers such scope in terms of narrative creativity as to surprise an observer.

47 *Ibid.*, xvi.
48 *Ibid.*, xxiv.

The Loathly Lady among the Féin*
and her North Atlantic Travels

JOHN SHAW

In the third volume of John Francis Campbell's major collection of Scottish Gaelic folktales from the nineteenth century, *Popular Tales of the West Highlands,* the motif of the Loathly Lady (D732 in Stith Thompson's motif classification system) appears in the story summarised below:[1]

> Fionn Mac Cumhaill and his band are passing a wild and snowy night on Beinn Eudainn in Ireland when they are approached around midnight by an uncouth female with hair down to her heels who knocks on Fionn's door, asking him 'to let her in under the border of his covering'. When Fionn comments on her hideous appearance and sends her away she gives a scream and approaches Oisean, asking the same favour, and he likewise remarks on her bizarre appearance with the same detail and sends her away, giving rise to a second scream. Diarmaid, however, after treating her to the same observations, invites her in. Once under the covering she relates her story, saying that she has spent seven years 'travelling over ocean and sea' and during that entire time has not spent one single night.[2] After warming herself beside the fire, much to the distaste of the Fenian band, they retire and she asks to come under Diarmaid's blanket. Diarmaid comments on her boldness but agrees, tucking a fold of it between them, and before long he glances over to find himself beside 'the finest drop of blood that ever was, from the beginning of the universe till the end of the world'. He immediately summons the Féinn and on viewing her they agree that she has become 'the most beauteous woman that man ever saw'. She awakens shortly thereafter, asking Diarmaid where he would like a castle to be built, and when he next awakens she shows him a fine castle on the spot he had specified above Beinn Eudainn. Diarmaid asks her to go there with him, and she agrees on the condition that he never say to her three times how he had found her.
>
> After three days in the castle, which is equipped down to the last detail including a herd for the geese, Diarmaid begins to miss his comrades and goes to find them, entrusting the woman with the care of his female greyhound and her three pups. The Féinn welcome Diarmaid, but in the meantime have begun to harbour ill-will toward him on account of their own lost opportunities and their envy of his good fortune. Consequently while Diarmaid is away Fionn approaches the woman, requesting one of the pups, which she hands over without question, giving Fionn his choice of them. Diarmaid returns and

---

* Féin/Fianna and Oisean/Oisín are used interchangeably.
1 (1892), 421-40.
2 Under shelter, presumably.

299

is met by the greyhound who gives a yelp, and when he finds one of the pups gone he reproaches the woman, saying, 'But if thou had'st mind of how I found thee, how thy hair was down to thy heels, thou had'st not let the pup go'. He immediately asks her forgiveness for his first breaking of the prohibition, which she grants him. Nevertheless over the following two days she allows Oisean and another member of the Féinn to take their pick of the remaining two pups. Diarmaid is met by the greyhound who gives two and then three hideous yelps. Despite the woman's warnings Diarmaid on each occasion violates the injunctions set for him and he finds himself on the final evening 'without wife or bed beside him, as he ever had been'.

On the following morning, upon awakening in a moss-hole with no trace of the castle remaining, he determines to find her. He carries the greyhound, which has since expired, over his shoulder and traces the woman to the strand where she was last seen by a herd. Eventually, still carrying the greyhound, he boards a boat rowed by one man which descends to a plain where he disembarks. After a short time walking he comes across three gulps of blood, which he carefully gathers into a napkin and transfers into his pouch, thinking they are the greyhound's. A short distance further on he encounters a woman busily gathering rushes, who tells him that he has arrived in *Rìoghachd fo Thuinn* ('Realm Underwaves') and that the rushes are to provide a wholesome bed for the king's daughter who has returned after seven years under spells and is ill with an ailment that the assembled leeches of Christendom cannot cure. Diarmaid asks to be taken to the princess, and the woman obligingly wraps him in a bundle of rushes and conveys him there on her back. They are joyfully reunited, and the princess tells him that although her ailment is partially cured she has lost a gulp of her heart's blood for every time she thought of him on her journey. When Diarmaid offers to administer to her the three gulps in a drink she replies that they will have no effect since she cannot have what she most needs, namely three draughts from the cup of *Rìgh Magh an Ioghnaidh* ('the King of the Plain of Wonder') and neither Diarmaid or any other man in the world is capable of obtaining the cup. Diarmaid resolves to try, however, and she directs him to *Rìgh Magh an Ioghnaidh,* a year and a day's journey removed and close to her own father's dwelling. Diarmaid departs on his quest and is aided in crossing a rivulet by a little russet man, who then accompanies him. When he reaches the king's house at the Plain of Wonders he demands the cup. In spite of the terrific odds he vanquishes the king's champions in three battles and the king, upon learning who he is (his arrival and victory over the kingdom having been foretold seven years before his birth), presents him with the cup which no man has ever obtained before. The king also offers a ship to return in, which he declines, and he is joined again by the little russet man.

On his return journey Diarmaid, on the little russet man's advice, fetches a bottle of water from a certain well to mix with the gulps of blood. His helper also advises him that he will take a dislike to the princess once she is cured, and that she will be 'the one for whom thou carest least that ever thou hast seen before thee'. Her father King Underwave will then come and offer him much silver and gold for healing her, along with her hand in marriage. He will not accept the offer, but instead will request a ship to take him back to Ireland. The events unfold as described. Diarmaid fetches the water from the well and arrives back at the palace with the cup, and is welcomed by the princess who says that she had not expected him to succeed, since no one had ever accomplished such a feat before. He administers the three gulps of blood with the water in the cup and the princess is instantly and completely cured. At that very moment Diarmaid finds that he can barely bring himself to look at her, which he admits to when confronted by her. Meanwhile word of the cure is circulated and the king offers Diarmaid payment in silver and his daughter's hand in marriage, but he refuses these, requesting only a ship to take him back to Ireland and the Féinn. The story ends with his return to a hearty welcome by his comrades.

In his accompanying notes Campbell tells us that the story was written down in 1860 by his chief assistant Hector MacLean from 'Roderick MacLean (tailor), Ken Tangval, Barra, who heard it frequently recited by old men in South Uist, about fifteen years ago. One of them was Angus MacIntyre, Bornish, who was about eighty years old at the time'. Campbell adds, 'I omit the Gaelic for want of room,[3] and translate closely but more freely'. Unfortunately only the English translation of the story, written in his own hand, survives among his papers. Scattered throughout the translation, however, are Campbell's notes on Gaelic expressions such as *saighead mialchoin* ('greyhound'),[4] *flath a's failt* ('a chief's honour and welcome') and *a falt 's a fionna*[5] (referring to the hideous woman's hair) which indicate that he was working directly from Hector MacLean's transcription.[6] Campbell makes it clear that he regards the above as a 'curious story', and 'manifestly imperfect', drawing attention to loose ends in the story such as the greyhound. He is clearly puzzled by the story's meaning, remarking that 'unless it is mythological it cannot be explained'. He then devotes the remainder of his notes to discussing similar or related motifs that he had encountered from oral and written sources.

In 1986 I recorded a version of the same tale in Nova Scotia from Peter MacEachern (*Pàdraig Aonghuis Iain 'ic Dhòmhnaill 'ic 'Phàdraig Bhàin 'ic Raghnaill*) of Glendale, Inverness County, Cape Breton.[7] The reciter learned it from his paternal

---

3 Campbell was coming under increasing pressure from his publishers to reduce the size of the MS.
4 More likely connected with the word *saigh* 'bitch' in an expression such as *saigh do mhialchoin* 'a greyhound bitch'. *Saigh* occurs elsewhere in Fenian lore cf. Carmichael (1928-1971), 2, 24 in Oisean's warning to his mother.
5 Details of this kind are popular in Gaelic descriptions of hideous women where *falt* and *fionna* refer to head and body hair respectively. For a parallel see the description of the grotesque woman seeking entrance to the hostel in Knott (1936), 16 – *tacmaicead a fés in t-ichtarach co rrici a glúin*.
6 Hector MacLean's Gaelic transcription is printed in MacKay (1917).

grandmother Isabel, née O Handley (*Iseabal nighean Aonghuis ic Ruairidh Mhóir*) who was born in neighboring Judique and was of South Uist descent. Pàdraig's is the only instance of the tale known to me among a good number of Fenian tales and ballads, complete and fragmentary, recorded or known to have existed on Cape Breton Island and the adjacent mainland. Since the item is something of a rarity Pàdraig has been encouraged to tell it on various occasions and a number of recordings and transcriptions exist from 1986 to 1995 which show great consistency, although he has clearly recalled more details since the first recording. A comparison shows that the tale is closely related to that noted down over a century earlier in Campbell's collection, but by no means so detailed, and differs from it in a number of minor particulars which are worth noting. Here the warriors named are Oscar, Oisean and Fionn, and they are approached by a dreadful apparition with a body half woman and half fish,[8] who is turned away by Oisean and Fionn but taken in by Oscar instead of Diarmaid. Immediately after her transformation she makes it clear to Oscar that he has released her from spells by enchantment (*fo gheasaibh le buidseachd*), and she lays down the same condition that he must never mention by way of reproach how she came to him. In addition to a bitch (*galla*) Oscar has a palfrey (*fàlaire*) and there is no mention of a magically appearing castle. They are married, to the great envy of Oscar's comrades, and when Oscar violates the prohibition the princess takes to her bed and expels three gulps of blood before she apparently disappears and the bitch and the palfrey die. He carefully gathers the blood into a napkin and makes his way to the shore, intending to drown himself, but instead falls asleep in a boat which transports him to a strange land. There he encounters a large woman gathering rushes for the princess, his wife, who is on her death bed. He carries the rushes to the princess and she asks for the three gulps of blood. He produces these and is told that she can be cured by a drink from the Brown Cup (*an Cupa Donn*) belonging to *Rìgh Bhan-rìghinn Fhionn*, likely a substitution for *Rìgh Magh an Ioghnaidh* in the Barra version. Guided by a deer in place of the russet man he reaches the palace, and after gathering a basketful of brambleberries in January[9] he wrestles with and puts down the cup's keeper, *An Gille Glas* 'the Grey Lad', who recognises him. The Grey Lad tells him that both he and his sister, Oscar's wife, were placed under spells by a witch, but that these have now been lifted. After vanquishing a regiment they return together to the palace of the Grey Lad's father, and Oscar's wife takes a drink from the cup and is cured. They return to Ireland together and Oscar is given land and the kingdom.

Peter MacEachern's version, particularly in the second half, is considerably shorter than that published in Campbell's *West Highland Tales*, and he remarks at the end of the first (1986) recording that he has 'forgotten the rest of it'. It is the

---

7 354A2: 1/12/86, Gaelic folklore project collection, St Francis Xavier University, Antigonish, Nova Scotia.
8 The 1986 version has *co-dhiubh 's e coltas boireannach na coltas iasg na gu dé a bh'ann* 'whether it was the appearance of a woman, or a fish, or whatever it was'; in later (1988, 1995) recordings she is half woman and half fish.
9 A difficult or impossible task widely featured in tales and proverbs.

only tale from the Fenian cycle in his repertoire and one of the very few to be recorded in western Cape Breton.

A third Scottish variant, titled *Stòiridh Oisein* ('The Story of Ossian'), was published in 1978[10] from the recitation of Alasdair 'Brian' Stewart, a Gaelic-speaking traveller in Sutherland who learned it from his grandmother Siusaidh Stewart, a native of Argyle. Here Oisean and his two younger brothers are living in three shieling bothies when the loathsome female arrives one stormy night in the form of a black crow (*feannag dhubh*). Significantly, in a variant recorded earlier from Mary Stewart of the same family she appears in the familiar form of 'the ugliest woman you ever saw' (*thànaig boireannach ann a' sin bu ghrànnd' a chunna sibh riamh*).[11] After being turned away by the brothers she is finally given shelter by Oisean, who also shares his supper. In the morning when he arises he beholds 'a woman there as beautiful as he had ever seen'(*boireannach ann a shin cho brèagh 'sa chunnaig e riamh*) who explains that she was under enchantments to remain in the form of a crow until someone provided her with bed and food, and that she will now be Oisean's wife so long as he does not throw up to her in a quarrel the shape in which she arrived, for if he does she will depart, becoming a crow again. Oisean agrees to her conditions. The two brothers – as in the Barra/Uist version – are envious, but many years pass and as the three of them are preparing to hunt deer with the stag-hounds (*mial-choin*), Oisean notes that the bitch is about to have pups and instructs his wife to put a string around the neck of the first born. Shortly after they depart the pups are born and a man arrives, demanding the first of them. Oisean's wife attempts to trick him, but he threatens her and takes the pup away under his arm. When Oisean returns and asks after the pups she tries to deceive him by putting a string around the neck of one of the other pups, again without success. When she relates what has occurred Oisean loses his head and breaks the injunction by calling her a black crow, and she returns to her former shape and goes out, saying that she cannot return. As she departs, however, she gives him a ring, saying that as long as he possesses it he will live and instructing him to keep it on his finger and never to give it away.

Oisean returns to his shieling where, now an old man unable to do much, he is sought out by Saint Patrick who is writing books about the story of Oisean and the places he knew. Eventually, after a number of adventures belonging properly to the story *Oisean an dèidh na Fèinneadh* ('Oisean after the Fèinn'), Oisean, now blind and failing, asks the young lad who has accompanied him to take him to the burn to bathe him. As he washes Oisean in the burn the lad takes the ring off his finger and lays it on a stone, and a crow makes off with it. Oisean immediately feels death coming on, and upon asking is told of the loss of the ring. As the lad washes him Oisean places his hand on the back of the lad's neck and breaks it, killing him so that

10 *Tocher* 29 (1978), 292-301. Recorded by David Clement: Linguistic Survey of Scotland, Tape 965.
11 *SA* 1957/48 B2. Mary gave her source as her father (Brian's uncle) Alec 'Aili Dall' Stewart who recorded the same variant (*SA* 1958/73 A11) which he learned from his maternal uncle. Cf. Bruford (1987), 52.

he will not recount what he has seen. He then returns to his shieling, never to rise again.

D. A. MacDonald and the late Alan Bruford in their remarks on the traveller variant observe that the proscription common to all Scottish variants against referring to the lady's origins (C31.9. in Thompson's *Motif Index*) is paralleled in oral Scottish versions of *Leigheas Coise Céin* ('The Healing of Cian's Leg'), a famous tale apparently consisting of twenty-four parts which survives in nineteenth-century recitations from Argyll, a brief summary from Gairloch and in a twentieth-century fragment from Cape Breton.[12] O'Croiniceard while hunting comes across a hare which transforms itself into a beautiful woman. He asks to marry her and she consents, usually under three conditions. The one which occurs consistently is that he not cast up to her the circumstances and form in which he found her. They arrive at O'Croiniceard's rudimentary dwelling which he finds transformed into a beautiful room when he awakens the next morning. He soon breaks the *geasa* or prohibitions, his wife departs in the form of a filly, and he finds himself in his former hut and the accompanying wealth nowhere to be seen. Interestingly, as in the Cape Breton version above, the woman's brother appears in the tale, though here it is in order to warn him after the tabu is broken for the second time. The violating of the *geasa* precipitates the catastrophe in the Scottish oral versions, which is echoed in the one known Irish oral version from Carna, county Galway. This feature, however, is not present in the MS tradition (the earliest MS, from county Cavan, is from the late fifteenth century), which leads Bruford to posit 'a common oral tradition whose basis may be even older than the surviving fifteenth-century MS'.[13] It also suggests that oral versions of the tale were widespread and robust among Scottish reciters.

In addition to incorporating the appearance of the crow in the role of the loathsome female apparition, along with the life-maintaining ring, *Stòiridh Oisein* is set apart from its Hebridean counterparts by a feature containing wider significance. In the travellers' tradition it not only precedes, but serves as a sort of introduction to, the tale of *Oisean an déidh na Féinne* ('Oisean after the Féinn'), placing it with some precision in the larger Fenian tradition. That such associated traditions have had oral currency in Scotland for some time is confirmed by the earliest version of the story[14] summarised in the Staffa Collection, a MS prepared for MacDonald of Staffa and now among the Campbell of Islay MSS.[15] According to the compiler's introduction the summary[16] is based on an oral version from Torosay, Mull going

---

12 Bruford (1969), 262; MacNeil (1987), 56-60, 454-5.
13 Bruford (1969), 136.
14 Bruford (1987), 53 ff.
15 National Library of Scotland Adv. MS. 73.2.1.
16 MS. p. 1.

Roimh-raite

An beagan sa leanas do Spruid-hleach Eachdruidh na Feinne: Ata nois air a ghabhail ann an Sgriobhadh, o *bheuladas, Dhomhnaill-mhic-an-Leathain, a rugadh Bliadhna cuig deug. Thuair an duinesa chuid as mo da t'seanachas O chalum mac phail a th'sean-athir Sa rinn tri-fichid Nolluig mhor sa dha Ann am Baile gan Ainm Rothill ann an Sgiothreachd Thorasay.

back at least to the late seventeenth century. In a section of the MS with its own heading, immediately following upon the summary of *Oisean an déidh na Féinne*, we find an account of the loss of Oisean's ring.[17]

Mar a chaill Oisin a fàinne

Bha Oisin na bhuachille re cuallach na meann, aig Padruig agus aig a nighin. Bha e sin la ga ascich fein agus agus thug e mach an sporan anns an rabh am fainne, agus chuir e air lar lamh ris e. agus na dheidh sin chadil e. Thanig am biatach air Iteaig anuas as na Speuribh, us e air Faicsin Taip mhor dhearg, thsaoil leis gum b'fheoil a bha ann agus sgob e leis e dhionnsuidh aneid far am rabh sia heoin aig an uairsin. Agus thuair e rithist e, n'air a chuir an Gille Blar odhar[18] leis a chraig e

[How Oisean Lost the Ring

Oisean was a herd tending the young goats belonging to Patrick and his daughter. One day he as he was bathing he brought out the purse containing the ring, placed it on the ground beside him, and went to sleep. The raven flew down out of the sky, seeing a large, red object and thinking it was meat spirited it off to its nest where it had six young birds. And he [Oisean] came into possession of it again when the pale, sallow lad directed him over the cliff]

Incorporated toward the end of the summary of *Oisean an déidh na Féinne* itself is the account alluded to here concerning the ring and its recovery by Oisean, unintentionally aided by his grandson:[19]

Le Iain Mac Mhuirich, Maighistir Sgoil san Eilein Mhuileach; aon do th'seirbhisich na cuideachd Urramaich' ta chum eolas Chriosd a Sgaolidh, feadth Gadhealteachd agus Eileana na h'Albann

April 1803

[Introduction

The little that follows of fragments of the history of the Feinn: now committed to writing from the [oral] tradition of Donald MacLean, born in the year [17]15. He received most of his tradition from his grandfather Malcolm MacPhail and spent sixty-two Christmases in the steading called Rothill in the parish of Thorasay.

By Iain MacMhuirich, schoolmaster in the Isle of Mull; one of the servants of the venerable congregation charged with spreading the knowledge of Christ throughout the Highlands and Islands of Scotland].

17 MS p. 35 = J. F. Campbell (1872), 38.
18 Oisean's grandson *An Gille Blàr Odhar* 'The Pale, Sallow Lad' is also thus named in a Cape Breton version of the story recorded from Joe Neil MacNeil (334A6-335A1, 18/1/82) Gaelic Folklore Project Collection, St Francis Xavier University, Antigonish, Nova Scotia.
19 MS pp. 34-35 = J. F. Campbell (1872), 39.

Ghluais e fein us odha chum pillidh do Ghleann caoin fheoir, Ach se 'chomhairl'
chinn an ceann odha Oisin gu feuchadh e fhuidhidh e Oisin a th'shean-athir a
chuir le craig. Chomhairlich a mhathir dha ro laimh sin a dheanamh.
Threoruich se e gu bruaich Uiridh-Bhiataich ris an gaorir gu cummanda nois
Uiridh 'n fhithich, agus dh'fag e sud e. Thuit e leis a chraig agus stad e meadhoin
na h-uiridh. Bha e car uine mam buirinn dha gluasad, ach cho luath sa chuir e
m preathal sin seachad, thoisich e air meurachadh man cuairt dha, gus an
d'fhuair e fainne, dhealluich ris uine roimhe so. Nois sann a Leannan sith a
thuair e n toisich e. Bha do bhuaidh air nach cailidh e radharc agus nach fhuid-
hidh e bas. Thainic e nsin dhathich, le 'fh'ainne agus le calpa 'n Luin, agus mar
a thubhairt e riu man d'fhalbh e, us amhluidh b'fior, be calpa 'n Luin moran bu
mho.

[He (Oisean) and his grandson set out to return to Gleann-caoin-fheoir, but
the advice arising in the mind of Oisean's grandson was for him to attempt
to throw his grandfather over a cliff. His mother had advised him beforehand
to do this. So he guided him [Oisean] to the precipice of Uiridh-Bhiataich,
commonly called Uiridh 'n Fhithich [The Raven's Shelf] and abandoned him
there. He [Oisean] fell over the cliff and landed on the middle of the shelf. It
was some time before he could move, but as soon as he recovered from his
dizziness he started feeling around him until he found the ring from which he
was parted earlier. Now he had originally obtained it from a fairy lover, and
it had properties that would prevent him from losing his sight or dying. He
returned home then with his ring and the blackbird's shank, and it was just
as he told them before he had set out: the blackbird's shank was much the larger.]

Most Scottish versions of *Oisean an déidh na Féinne* do not include Oisean's
killing his grandson at the end; however the episode does appear in a variant from
the Argyll mainland and in one of the summaries noted down by J. F. Campbell in
Mull in 1870.[20]

The travellers' accounts and the Mull traditions are closely associated with the
surviving story and ballad materials, mainly Irish, concerning Oisean's visit to the
Otherworld. In Ireland the themes of the hideous female visitor, the otherworld
journey and Oisín's last hunt appear in a small number of oral versions recorded this
century, and in metrical versions mainly from nineteenth-century MSS. Recently
Máirtín Ó Briain in his informative study of *Laoi Cholainn gan Cheann* ('The Lay
of the Headless Body'), a poem surviving in a small number of nineteenth-century
MSS, has brought to light much of the background to the oral narrative and metrical
versions of the tale.[21] The tale versions occur in some variety and deal mainly with

---

20 J. F. Campbell (1890-93), 3, 120; Adv. MS 50.2.2: 147.
21 Ó Briain (1997). I wish to thank Máirtín Ó Briain for making successive drafts of his work
    available to me.

Oisín's journey to *Tír na hÓige* ('The Land of Youth'). Ó Briain draws attention the wide distribution of the tale, taking in Galway, south Donegal, and Armagh, noting that the Irish prose narratives can be classed as either 'derivative', being prose retellings of *Laoi Cholainn gan Cheann* and limited to an area of Galway around Loch Corrib; or 'cognate' versions reflecting the lay's earlier oral source.[22] Among those classed as cognate versions the closest known parallel to the Sutherland travellers' version was taken down in Sligo at the beginning of this century.[23] Oisín's mother is placed under enchantments by her father, sent from *Tír na hÓige* and in the form of a deer is rescued by Oisín. She is transformed into a beautiful princess, gives him a magic ring and returns to her country. She sends a bird who steals the ring while Oisín is bathing, and he pursues the bird to his mother's land. After what seems a short time but is in fact 300 years, Oisín desires to return. His mother provides him with a cloak and a horse, saying that he must dismount onto the cloak lest he be overtaken by old age. When he meets Patrick Oisín forgets the advice and becomes a withered old man. Following upon this is the tale of 'Oisín and Patrick's Housekeeper', the Irish counterpart of *Oisean an déidh na Féinne*, which in its details closely corresponds to that given in the Scottish *Stòiridh Oisein* above.[24] Pointing to its wide distribution throughout Gaeldom, Murphy[25] regards the last story as a significant, fully evolved tale; and one, we may add, that presupposes oral transmission over some length of time. The remaining narratives dealing with our theme concentrate on Oisín's otherworld journey, a theme which itself is linked with the international type AT 470* '*The Hero Visits the Land of the Immortals*'.[26] The woman appears in a variety or forms including a headless body, a body with a cow's or pig's head, or simply a hideous woman,[27] and when she departs it is often in the form of a hare.

Laoi Cholainn gan Cheann, the most complete of the metrical versions of the story, has come down in 'a handful of nineteenth century manuscripts' from the vicinity of Lough Corrib, county Galway.[28] To summarise –

> One day the Fianna are approached by *Colainn gun Cheann*, a female of grotesque appearance. They are revolted by her looks and Conán Maol proposes killing her, but she places herself under Fionn's protection. Fionn then tries to bribe her to leave, but she rejects the bribe and offers herself to him. When he declines she tells them that she is the daughter of the King of *Tír na hÓige* ('The Land of Youth') under *geasa*, and that she will recover her head only when one of the Fianna sleeps with her. She accomplishes this

---

22 *Op. cit.*, 12-3.
23 Hyde (1930).
24 The two tales are also linked in a further county Galway variant kindly forwarded to me by Máirtín Ó Briain (*IFC* 181:17-45).
25 (1953), xix-xx with bibliography.
26 The nature of the relationship is not entirely clear – Bruford (1987), 50. Ó hÓgáin (1987), 234 points to possible medieval continental sources, which if valid would mean that the story of Oisín's otherworld journey 'can hardly be older than about the fourteenth century'.
27 Ó Briain (1997), 13.
28 *Op. cit.*, 4-11.

by placing Oisín under *geasa*, and when he awakens the following morning he finds her changed into a beautiful woman. The Fianna are envious – Diarmaid goes as far as to expose the love-spot (*ball searc*[29]) on his forehead that women find irresistible – to no avail. She elects to remain with Oisín under two conditions: that he not beat her with a hound's leash nor reproach her for her earlier physical appearance (*an cruth ina raibh mé*). After they have lived together and produced three sons Fionn comes to her one day and takes away one of Oisín's pups, taking care to select the one descended from Bran. Oisín questions her and, on being informed of the truth, violates the two conditions and his wife departs with her three sons. Oisín's search for his wife takes him by boat from Ireland to *Tír na hÓige*, a place of such beauty that his perceived year and a half stay is actually several hundred years. Eventually he has a vision that none of the Fianna remain alive, having been superseded by 'short men and clerics'. His wife discounts the vision, but gives him a cloak, a horse and a gold ring.[30] She instructs him that he must always wear the ring on his finger, and the cloak must always be placed between him and the ground should he dismount. On returning to Ireland Oisín confronts the fact that his comrades are long gone. As he dismounts to gather a bunch of watercress from Diarmaid's house as a keepsake he forgets to use the cloak, a bird steals the ring off his finger and he thus loses his protection from the passage of time, immediately turning into a wizened old man.

A less complete but closely related account of the Fianna's encounter with *Colann gan Cheann*, consisting of 15 quatrains, appears among the adventures recounted by Oisín to Patrick in the metrical composition *Agallamh Oisín agus Phádraig* ('The Dialogue of Oisin and Patrick'), based on a MS from Waterford written in 1780.[31] The episode is found in at least one other version of the poem,[32] which itself exists in numerous MSS and was composed not before the sixteenth century.[33] It has come down in a number of Scottish versions and the episode survives in a single fragment of 22 lines noted down in 1866 from a Ness, Isle of Lewis, reciter by a Rev. MacPhail, preserved in J. F. Campbell's papers and later published by him[34] under the title *Collun gun Cheann*. Campbell notes that the fragment is unique (MacPhail wrote 'No title' at the top of the MS) but draws attention to the parallel with the Barra/Uist version of the tale, and suggests that 'all these strange mythical legends were told in alternate prose and verse', presumably alluding to the practice associated with the recitation of Fenian tales that continued into modern times.[35]

---

29 The *ball searc* appears frequently as an attribute of Diarmaid in oral tradition cf. Ó hÓgáin (1987), 228 and Ó Briain (1997), 6.
30 Evidently the same rejuvenating ring alluded to in an earlier verse as being in the possession of his son Óscar.
31 *Transactions of the Ossianic Society* 4 (1856), xxxi, 24-9.
32 Ó Briain (1997), 12.
33 Murphy (1953), 124-6.
34 Adv. MS. 50.2.7: 362-3 = J. F. Campbell (1872), 212.
35 Cf. MacNeil (1987), 29.

A further metrical composition on the same theme titled *Laoi Oisín ar Thír na n-Óg* ('Lay of Oisin on the Land of Youths')[36] composed around 1750 by Micheál Cuimín is likewise attested in MSS no older than the nineteenth century. The episode of Oisín's otherworld sojourn is used to provide a plausible explanation for his outliving his comrades; although the date of composition is late the idea likely originates with older oral and possibly written sources.[37] Oisín's otherworld wife Niamh is represented as being of comely appearance, and his old age and blindness upon his return are brought about by violating a prohibition against touching the ground.

In spite of their being attested only in recent MS tradition, the distribution of the prose and metrical versions points to an earlier oral account of Oisín in the otherworld which bears all the hallmarks of being considerably older than Cuimín's poem.[38] There is, however, the matter of the notable absence of any mention of Oisean's otherworld journey in the Scottish traveller version, which in many of its other details agrees so closely with the Irish prose and metrical versions that we have examined. Unlike Ireland, the tale-type 470* in Scotland, though very similar to its Irish counterparts in other respects,[39] is not strongly associated with Oisean. A trace of the story has been retained, nevertheless, in a tale apparently from Skye which relates how Oisean was nursed by a deer who was not his mother, and was sent to *Tír na h- hÓige* to prevent any resulting talk.[40] Eventually he made his way to Ireland and found his daughter who was married to Patrick of the Psalms, setting the scene once again for the tale *Oisean an déidh na Féinne*. A similar tale (again in English) also recounts Oisean's meeting his mother in cervine form. She leads him into a hill where she is transformed into a beautiful woman and entertains him with food, drink and music. After three days Oisean determines to see the Féinn again and leaves the bower, only to find that he has been absent for three years.[41]

Our examination of the story of Oisean, his visit to the otherworld and his encounter with the Loathly Lady in the available variants shows us that the story, though often only recently attested, must be regarded as Pan-Gaelic and well established in oral tradition for a number of centuries. Whether its more recent history is to be found in Sutherland or Argyll, *Stòiridh Oisein*, the Scottish travellers' version, shares many more features with its Irish counterparts – Oisean as the main character, the appearance in the form of a crow, the age-defying ring and otherworld time-suspension – than it does with the Scottish Hebridean prose versions. These last, though clearly the same story, diverge from all other variants in Gaeldom known to me by incorporating details such as the princess' sickness, the three gulps of blood, the quest after the healing cup, the magic helper and the meeting with the brother-in-law. The substitution of the names Diarmaid and Oscar in a story elsewhere firmly

---

36 *Transactions of the Ossianic Society* 4 (1856), 234-79.
37 Ó hÓgáin (1987), 233-4; Bruford (1987), 49-50; Ó Briain (1997), 1.
38 Murphy (1953), xxiii.
39 Bruford (1987), 49-50.
40 J. G. Campbell (1891), 80.
41 Carmichael (1928-1971), 2, 22-3.

linked to Oisean indicates that the Outer Hebridean variants of our story, however conservative in some of their contents, had come to be regarded as less securely bound to the Fenian world than those we have seen elsewhere. Such a relative degree of independence would in turn explain the ease with which motifs could be attracted and borrowed from other tales. It is therefore likely that the disappearing castle and other incidents were drawn from oral versions of *Leigheas Coise Céin*, attracted by the common feature of *geasa* associated with marriage to an otherworldly woman. Surviving versions of *Leigheas Coise Céin* are not plentiful, but in their case as well a wide geographical distribution attested throughout Gaeldom suggests that a common oral source was in circulation, probably for a matter of centuries, before being written down. Interestingly, *Leigheas Coise Céin* by and large shares with *Oisean an déidh na Féinne* ('Oisín and Patrick's Housekeeper') a long history in oral tradition and a relatively recent appearance in MSS or field recordings.[42] In the range of tales and metrical versions the conditions relating to marriage to the supernatural bride show a remarkable uniformity,[43] suggesting that a number of widespread oral tales became associated through borrowings in Fenian tradition.

The motif of the Loathsome Lady is well known from early Irish literature, and the entries in Cross (1952) indicate that it is most frequently attached to the concept the Sovereignty of Ireland. The story is given in the *Cóir Anmann* ('The Fitness of Names'), dating in its edited version from around 1300, where one of Dáire Doimthech's sons, Lugaid Laígde (his four accompanying brothers are named Lugaid as well) allows a hag into his bed who once transformed identifies herself as the Lady Ériu, saying that this Lugaid will have the kingship.[44] An older and more complete account of the sovereignty story, *Carn Máil*, is found in the metrical version of the *Dindshenchus*, a medieval compilation of placename lore. It was written into the Book of Leinster between 1156 and 1166 but is believed to go back to at least the first quarter of the eleventh century.[45] The oldest account of the dual form of the goddess Sovereignty titled *Echtra mac n-Echdach Mugmedoin* is in the cycle of Niall of the Nine Hostages and cannot be older than the eleventh century.[46] We are told that the five sons of Eochaidh, while hunting, seek water from a well guarded by a hideous old woman – here as in the rest of Gaelic literature enthusiastically and graphically described – who demands a kiss in exchange. Niall, the last of the sons, not only complies but lies with her into the bargain, transforming her into a striking damsel. She informs him that the kingship of Ireland will be his, for she is the Sovereignty of Ireland, and that her transformation from repulsiveness to beauty is merely an allegory for the dual aspect of achieving same. She advises Niall to withhold the water from his brothers until they have granted him seniority.

---

42 The exceptions are the two Irish MS versions of *Leigheas Coise Céin* from the late fifteenth and seventeenth centuries which do not include the fairy wife's conditions (cf p. 305 above); Bruford (1969), 134-5, 262. The romance *Eachtra Chéadaigh Mhóir* also predates its nineteenth-century MSS and may be included in this category (*Op. cit.*, 126-7).
43 Ó Briain (1997), 13.
44 Stokes (1897), 317-23.
45 Gwynn (1924), 4, 134-43; Reinhard (1933), 352.
46 Dillon (1946), 38-41.

In the early Irish accounts given here the transformation is brought about by a youth of noble lineage. It is in the form of *Ériu* the Sovereignty Goddess that the motif travelled abroad from Ireland, attaching itself to the Arthurian Cycle and becoming the prototype of the Grail Bearer and the Loathly Damsel.[47] By the latter part of the twelfth century it had appeared in France in Crétien de Troyes' *Percival*, the portrayal of the damsel in her hideous aspect in the Welsh Arthurian romance *Peredur* echoes those that we have seen in the Irish stories above and derives from the same tradition. As for England, a version of the combined Sovereignty-Transformed Hag story appears in *The Weddynge of Syr Gawen and Dame Ragnell*, and subsequently in Chaucer's the *Wife of Bath's Tale*.

Productive and widespread as the form of the motif was, appearing in the tradition of at least four countries on the edge of the North Atlantic in medieval times, there is reason to question whether the Sovereignty form of the motif in Ireland is the oldest that can be traced. In his work on medieval romance and Celtic prohibition (*geis*) motifs Reinhard[48] considers the *Cóir Anmann* version to be not a single story but a combining of two originally separate traditions. He observes that in *Baile in Scáil* ('The Phantom's Ecstasy'), attested in sixteenth-seventeenth century MSS but mentioned by Flann Mainistreach who died in 1056, 'Sovereignty' is portrayed as a young woman in a splendid house with a golden crown upon her head distributing bowls of red ale, free of any hideous aspect and harbouring no apparent amorous intentions.[49] Likewise the theme of the Loathly Lady appears separately in the Fenian poem *Seilg Ghleanna an Smóil* ('The Chase of Thrush Glen') describing an encounter with a hag, once the daughter of the King of Greece, who must marry Fionn in order to lift the *geasa* laid on her by her father. In this case she fails in her quest and is not transformed. On the basis of these and later oral prose accounts (including Campbell's *Nighean Rìgh fo Thuinn*), he suggests two originally separate themes: that of sovereignty, probably a minor divinity, who magically bestows her qualities on deserving aristocrats; and that of a 'lady transformed out of her own shape by a spell or curse' and into that of a hag, or an animal.[50] Often the spell could be removed by 'physical contact, more or less intimate with a champion or king's son'.[51] Reinhard concludes that 'a simple story of a lady so cursed' antedated the combined forms of the story (e.g *Carn Máil*), and that the Barra/South Uist *Nighean Rìgh fo Thuinn*, in spite of its being an oral version attested only in recent times shows characteristics that place its origins well back in medieval times, if not before.[52] In his view the themes would have then been combined by an unknown

---

47 Loomis (1963), 51, 273.
48 Reinhard (1933), 351-2.
49 *Op. cit.*, 357.
50 *Op. cit.*, 356-70.
51 Cf. D565.5.1* Transformation by sexual intercourse.
52 *Op. cit.*, 366-7. The uncombined story, that of the hag's transformation, survived in Scottish ballad literature, notably in *Kemp Owyne* where the damsel gives her rescuer 'a royal ring ... /that I have found in the green sea;/ And while your finger it is on,/ Drawn shall your blood never be' - Child (1956), 309; Reinhard (1933), 344, 365-6 – suggesting a close affinity to the basis of what appears in oral Fenian tradition.

author to create a better dynastic story for political purposes sometime before the eleventh century, giving rise to stories such as *Echtra mac n-Echdach Mugmedóin* and *Carn Máil*. Such an hypothesis would account for the MS versions, and would require at least some oral versions of the second theme to be in circulation before the beginning of the eleventh century. While it is true that most versions of the bewitched princess turned hag story are not attested until the nineteenth century, the possibility of an oral tradition existing side by side with MSS versions over centuries would go far in explaining the geographical distribution (and variation) of the cognate oral versions.

A comparative look over a wider geographical area provides a further useful perspective to the background of our story. In a wide-ranging article on some hitherto overlooked aspects of the Loathly Lady motif in a range of cultures, Coomaraswamy draws attention to a number of suggestive oriental parallels, at the same time taking care to observe that these may represent 'universal mythical patterns'.[53] The Loathly Lady's ophidian nature is explicit in the *Brahmanas*; in the oldest Indic source, the *Rig Veda*, she is referred to as *apadí* ('footless'), a word which elsewhere characterises the serpent *Ahi-Vritra* in the Indra legend. It is as Apálá, Indra's bride, that she first appears in the same text, and later sources provide the story of her transformation into a fairer form. As the personification of Sovereignty in Indian tradition she is fickle in nature, as well as being closely associated with the Waters. Finally Coomaraswamy remarks that 'more than one Indian dynasty traces its descent from the union of a human prince with such an Undine'.[54] Whether these and the further motifs of the Fier Baiser – typically occurring in an Otherworld or under wave – or the bride's cup, can be rigorously traced and dated is only part of the question. Their co-occurrence elsewhere lends support to the early presence of oral variants of the motif in Gaelic tradition that we have examined above, and cautions us against too strict an adherence to Reinhard's suggestion that the sovereignty and Loathly Lady themes were originally separate.

Although it is true that any attempt to unravel the regional history of our motif and the attached stories inevitably will be plagued by questions associated with *Allerweltsmotive* and surface similarities, there is a parallel to the Fenian accounts found in the Icelandic story *Hrólfs saga kraka* which is striking enough to deserve a closer look:

> One stormy Yule-eve Helgi, the warrior-king of Denmark and the father of Hrólfr Kraki, is raised from his bed by a faint knocking and admits a tattered creature who pleads to share his bed. He is revolted but allows her to cover herself with straw and a bearskin, and keeps his distance by making her lie in her clothes at the edge of the bed. Later that night Helgi glances over to see the creature transformed into 'a woman lying there, so lovely that he thought

---

53 Coomaraswamy (1945), 399.
54 *Op. cit.*, 394-6.

that he had never before beheld woman more fair' (*at eigi þykkist hann aðra konu fríðari sét hafa*). She explains that Helgi has released her from spells cast on her by a wicked stepmother, and that she 'has visited many kings in their homes' seeking deliverance. She then asks to leave but is urged to remain by Helgi, who wants to marry her. They sleep together that night, and the following morning the woman announces that they will have a child and gives him instructions which it will cost him dearly to ignore: he must come and retrieve the child at the same time the following winter at his boat-house. Helgi disregards the instructions, but is visited at midnight three years later at the same house by the woman with three men bringing a girl child. The woman reproaches him for not complying with the conditions, saying that his kinsfolk must pay, adding that he shall 'reap the benefits' of releasing her from the spell and that the daughter's name is Skuld, meaning literally 'debt' or 'obligation'. They then ride away. Helgi hears no more of the woman and we are told that she is an elf-woman (*álf-kona*).[55]

Almost immediately preceding the elf-woman's appearance in the saga is the episode of the loss and recovery of Helgi's famous ring by his nephew Agnar. Helgi presents his brother Hroar, who lives in Northumberland, with the ring, which is his greatest treasure. It is also coveted by his cousin Hrókr, however, who at his mother's instigation approaches Helgi for a share of his kingdom or the ring, but to no avail. Hrókr then goes to visit its present owner Hroar. One day as he and Hroar have been sailing off the coast and are lying at anchor in a firth Hrókr asks him for the ring and, upon being refused, requests to examine it to see if it is indeed the precious jewel it is reputed to be. After inspecting it at his leisure he declares it best for no one to enjoy it and hurls it into the sea. Hroar punishes him by chopping off his feet, but is slain later by Hrókr in Northumberland. Meanwhile a son, Agnar, is born to Hroar. By the age of twelve he demonstrates unusual promise as a warrior and expresses an interest in the ring. He is directed to the firth and, to his enduring fame, dives in and recovers the ring on his third attempt. Such a parallel to the Fenian anecdotes of the loss and recovery of Oisean's ring by itself might appear too far-fetched or coincidental to deserve serious consideration, were it not for the fact that the word *hrókr* in Old Norse refers to a 'rook' i.e. a crow-like bird.

Over the last century or so the problem of Gaelic and Continental story-contacts with Iceland has produced a considerable literature.[56] It is known that 'a reasonable proportion of the population was Gaelic, coming from a cultural area where oral prose narrative was already well established'.[57] Gaels, being for the most part slaves, did not leave behind a substantial legacy of personal names, either in the population or in the saga literature. However, such imported, presumably orally

---

55 Summary based on translation by Jones (1961), 246-8.
56 See Sigurðsson (1988), *bibl.*
57 *Op. cit.*, 118.

transmitted, Celtic or Celtic-Norse motifs are particularly plentiful once the *fornaldarsögur* (sagas 'dealing with the legendary past' which appear between 1250 and around 1400) and the later *lygisögur* ('lying sagas') were committed to writing.[58]

Hrólfs saga kraka, which belongs to the older *fornaldarsögur* category, recounts the exploits of a Danish king from the fifth century. In the existing version the style and language indicate a relatively late date,[59] perhaps 1400. Nevertheless the saga incorporates many early motifs, and judging from the number of surviving MSS it enjoyed some popularity in Iceland.[60] Hrólfr Kraki's exploits are also recounted in the *Gesta Danorum*, written in Latin by the Danish historian Saxo Grammaticus and compiled around 1200; untypically for the genre it generally agrees with the Icelandic accounts[61] and Saxo's probable main source is the largely lost *Skjöldunga saga*. Of great interest to us is the fact that Skuld appears in Saxo's work, but there is no account of Helgi's encounter with the elf-woman, nor of the loss and recovery of his ring. Furthermore it has been observed that the Loathly Lady motif is virtually absent from the rest of Scandinavian tradition, leading to the suggestion that it originated in Britain or Ireland and arrived in Iceland quite early.[62]

Comparison with the Gaelic variants can provide some useful hints as to the probable origins of the episode in Icelandic, though the evidence is admittedly fragmentary. The parallel was first pointed out in 1882 by Francis James Child in his notes to the ballad *King Henry* where he observes that 'every point of the Norse saga, except the stepmother's wierd, is found in the Gaelic tale "Nighean Rìgh fo Thuinn"'.[63] Sovereignty is not an issue in the Hebridean story (or in the other Fenian tales) nor in this particular episode of *Hrólfs saga kraka*, making it likely that the version that reached Iceland did not incorporate the representations of Sovereignty that appear in the medieval Irish versions so widely exported into the Arthurian cycle by the twelfth century. In this respect the saga episode more closely resembles the Pan-Gaelic orally based prose versions proposed by Ó Briain and associated with the Fenian cycle, and may reflect an early 'uncombined' version of the story in Ireland. The absence of the otherworld-journey theme in the saga, however, contrasts significantly with the Gaelic Fenian tales. The theme of the

---

58 Sveinsson (1959), 16.
59 Einarsson (1957), 160.
60 Davidson & Fisher (1980), 39.
61 Einarsson (1957), 158; Davidson & Fisher (1980), 38.
62 Sveinsson (1959), 19. England or the Continent are possible but less likely sources for the elf-woman episode, though one survey of *lygisögur* – Einarsson (1957), 165 – produced 'more than 150 romances professing to be records of chivalry in foreign lands' including a translation of Crétien de Troyes *Percival* from the Arthurian Cycle. The motif's occurrence in Icelandic sagas and modern folktales is generally associated with transformations performed by wicked step-mothers (Sigurĺsson 1988, 101) although there is one modern folktale – Reinhard (1933), 394-5 – which shows the close parallels to Gaelic tradition that are found in *Hrólfs saga kraka*.
63 Child (1956), 297-8. See also Miss A. G. Gilchrist's notes to Frances Tolmie's collection of tra-ditional Scottish Gaelic songs – Tolmie (1911), 187. For other occurrences of D732 in Icelandic stories see Boberg (1966), 60.

otherworld journey is found elsewhere in the *fornaldarsögur* where it is apparently derived from a body of oral tales incorporating elements from Norse mythological tales and Celtic elements, most notably Gaelic tales dating from the early Viking period or before which were likely to have entered Iceland 'in oral form during the period of settlement in the late eighth and ninth centuries'.[64]

In the light of other borrowings we may therefore regard it as unlikely that the otherworld-journey theme was originally present in the Gaelic version which lay behind the episode of Helgi's encounter with the elf-woman and was subsequently dropped for some reason. We have already seen that the theme is not present in medieval Irish MS versions of the appearance of the Loathly Lady motif, which raises the possibility that the story entered Iceland before the international type AT 470* was borrowed into Ireland from the European continent from the fourteenth century.[65] If such is indeed the history of the tale-type in Ireland it fits well with the date of composition for *Hrólfs Saga Kraka*. If we attach any importance to the story of Helgi's ring, the likelihood increases that the Gaelic source was an oral one close to that shared by the Scottish travellers' *Stòiridh Oisein*, the recently attested Irish tales, metrical versions such as *Laoi Cholainn gan Cheann*, and the passage attached in some MSS to *Agallamh Oisín agus Phádraig*. The Mull story of the recovery of the ring with the involvement of Oisean's grandson may lead us to favour a Hebridean source, which is supported by the view that the Icelanders' contacts with the Hebrides and the Isle of Man may well have been closer than those they established with Irish Gaels.[66] Among the oral versions, *Nighean Rìgh fo Thuinn* from Barra/Uist contains the most striking parallels to the Helgi episode and at the same time displays the greatest anomalies within the Gaelic tradition. Firstly, it retains features such as the Undine appearance and 'underwave' origins,[67] reflecting a very early stage of the story, along with the healing/bridal cup which is present in *Echtra mac n-Echdach Mugmedoin* and Arthurian romance but absent from the other Gaelic oral versions. It is nominally associated with the body of Fenian tales; yet its associations with the metrical versions of the story are tenuous, and it has apparently attracted motifs from *Leigheas Coise Céin* rather than itself being drawn into the popular *Agallamh Oisín agus Phádraig/Oisean an déidh na Féinne* complex.[68]

The considerable antiquity and wide geographic range from southern Asia to western Europe of the Loathly Lady motif would seem to make it an excellent

---

64 Power (1985), 156, 167.
65 See n. 26 *supra*.
66 Almqvist (1996), 142. The association with our main story, however, is through *Oisean an déidh na Féinne*, and is at best tenuous.
67 Cf. Helgi's promise to collect his child by the elf-woman at the boathouse (*naust*) the next winter - Jones (1961), 247.
68 The princess's illness and the three gulps of blood, as noted *supra* p. 20, are unique to the Outer Hebridean versions. A reference to *Inghean Rìogh Thír fa Thuinn* ('Daughter of the King of Land Under Wave') who approaches the Féinn for protection, this time in her more presentable form, survives from the early sixteenth century in the Scottish Book of the Dean of Lismore – Ross (1939), 136-47.

candidate for a universal motif. Yet the information contained in Stith Thompson's *Motif Index* and Coomaraswamy's comparative work also reveals that it appears in a cluster on the North Atlantic seaboard from France to Iceland. Written and oral varieties of the motif developed in Ireland during the Middle Ages existed alongside each other, and were subsequently successfully exported, gaining considerable currency and popularity over a large geographic area. While the medieval written versions of the associated stories in Ireland have attracted the most attention, it is evident that a parallel and equally important oral tradition has existed from early medieval times[69] and has continued on to the time of the field collectors in the second half of the nineteenth century, and indeed into our own lifetimes.

---

69 Compare Calum Maclean's views concerning the primacy of oral tradition and the continuous oral transmission of traditions (e.g. the folk versions of the *Táin*) on which literary versions were based – Maclean (1959), 177 and *Tocher* 39 (1985), 85.

At the Bottom of Bottomless Pools

JACQUELINE SIMPSON

It may well seem strange to include a paper on a topic drawn from the corpus of English local legends in a collection devoted to Celtic, Nordic and Baltic material, for I am well aware that this corpus, viewed from an international perspective, is almost invisible. Where, one could well ask, are the English archives? Where are the printed collections of English legend texts, past and present? Where are there comparative studies, thematic studies, studies of narrators or of performances?

English scholars themselves have rarely grasped the subject of local legends as a unity, preferring to organise their work by region rather than by genre, so that legend texts are only found scattered about in general works on the folklore of such-and-such county, where they are presented with little if any discussion. The only attempts to gather a large and representative sample of them can be seen in Part B of Katharine Briggs's *Dictionary of British Folk-Tales*, and in Jennifer Westwood's *Albion*; there are also a few studies of legends on a specific theme, such as Katharine Briggs's *The Vanishing People* and my own *British Dragons*, but they are rare.[1]

This neglect probably springs from the attitude, rooted in nineteenth-century scholarship, that the only important genres were ancient and complex ones such as the Wonder Tale or the ballad; since England could offer only a meagre crop of Wonder Tales, it was apparently assumed that it had no oral narratives worth studying. It seems also to have been fairly widely believed that any supernatural legend (apart from tales about ghosts or witches) was a characteristically Celtic phenomenon; if there were kelpies and the 'Little People' in Scotland, pixies and giants in Cornwall, lake fairies in Wales, boggarts on the Isle of Man, this was simply because these are or were Celtic areas, and so, it was implied, there was little point looking for such things in purely English counties. Occasionally, some Scandinavian influence might also be suggested for beliefs and legends in what were once Danelaw areas. Such assumptions are still common among the general public in Britain.

Nevertheless, English local legends do exist, and offer interesting material for comparison with those from other countries. How far regional differences occur within the English corpus is a matter that has not yet been researched: certainly one can sometimes see clusters of similar stories grouped fairly closely (presumably as a result of imitative rivalry), but there is some risk that in trying to make a geographical analysis one is actually plotting the distribution not of folklore but of folklorists. The legends I will be discussing here are mostly from southern England, the area least

---

1 Briggs (1970-1); Westwood (1985); Briggs (1978); Simpson (1980).

likely to have had Celtic or Scandinavian contacts; many will be from Sussex, my own county. They are told in connection with certain unusually deep pools, and with deep places in river-beds and harbours.

Along the coastal plain of Sussex there are (or were, until recent times) certain deep, round pools fed by strong underground springs, locally called Nucker/Knucker Holes, or occasionally Nickeny Holes. The earliest writer to mention them, in 1855, says they 'are considered bottomless', and 'a mystery attaches to them among the common people, who seem to have a vague notion of their connection with another bottomless pit, and with the agency supposed to prevail there' (i.e. Hell and the Devil).[2] Another, in 1932, points out how dangerous they are: 'There is no bank, no edge to check you: if you make a step too far you will go in, "down. down, till you come out at Australia," the children say, for the pool has no bottom.'[3]

Tales have evolved to stress this alleged bottomlessness. Of one such pool, the Knucker Hole at Lyminster, it was said in 1866 that 'many years ago the six bell ropes of Lyminster Church were joined together and let down, without fathoming its dreadful depths';[4] while a journalist in 1937 improved on the story by claiming that a bell was attached to the end of the linked ropes and lowered into the pool, but never came up again, remaining fixed in an underground tunnel which many believed existed beneath the water.[5] (This motif brings the legend into the category of Tales of Lost Bells, which will be discussed below). Similar picturesque ways of expressing unfathomable depths are found in other parts of England too. Thus a pool at Albury, on the border of Hertfordshire and Essex, was said to be as deep as the nearby church tower was high, or, alternatively, to have no bottom at all and to belong to the Devil;[6] and there are various places where it is said that the local pool once swallowed up a fully loaded farm waggon, horses and all.

Such stories naturally could serve the practical purpose of warning little children to keep well away from a dangerous spot, and it would be even more effective to claim that some kind of ogre or monster was lurking in the pool. And so indeed we find, at any rate at Lyminster, where tradition says that at the bottom of the bottomless Knucker Hole there once lived The Knucker. This word is the direct descendant of the Anglo-Saxon *nicor*, meaning 'water monster', which survived till the fifteenth century in Standard English, but after that can only be found occasionally in some dialects, or as a meaningless element in minor place-names.[7] Originally, of course, it came from the same root as the Scandinavian *nykur, näkk, nøkke*, or *nykk*, and the German *Nix*, all of them water-dwellers, though some are in

---

2 *Notes and Queries* 1st Series 12 (1855), 501.
3 Stuart (1932), 154.
4 Evershed (1866), 180.
5 *The Worthing Gazette*, 2/6/1937.
6 Jones-Baker (1977), 28.
7 See the *OED* under *nicker*, Wright (1898-1905) under *nicker, nicker-pit* and *nuckar-hole*, and Smith (1950), II 50, under *nicor*. The connection has been noticed by several Sussex writers.

the form of horses and others in human form.

The Lyminster Knucker, however, is neither horse nor human. He is a dragon. This is particularly interesting because in the Anglo-Saxon epic *Beowulf* the mysterious pool where Grendel lives has *niceras* basking on its banks and 'the serpent-brood and strange water-dragons' swimming in it, so it may be that in England water-monsters were primarily thought of as reptilian. Lake monsters of snake-like form are a common motif, whether in Ireland, Scandinavia or Scotland, but as far as I know it is only in *Beowulf* and at Lyminster in Sussex that a word derived from the *nik-* root is applied to one.

One writer in the 1930s described The Knucker in a way which implies that he was seen as a threatening figure, a personification of the dangers of the pool. He calls him 'a dragon or a water demon who had a nasty way of grasping people and plunging into the water with them'[8] – a behaviour which recalls various stories about water-horses in Scotland or Scandinavia. This stress on the water is, however, unusual for a Lyminster story; in most accounts current there, whether written or oral, the concept of 'dragon' has become dominant and the pool merely incidental.

For at least 150 years, there have been stories explaining who killed the Lyminster dragon, how he did it, and what then became of him – a common pattern of migratory legend in Britain (I know about 75 variants, attached to 63 sites). The Lyminster tales fall into two groups. The first group is heroic and literary in tone, with a noble knight slaying the dragon in combat, and (sometimes) receiving the daughter of the King of Sussex as his reward; the legend of St George is a probable influence here. Versions of this type, first recorded in 1866, are popular with writers of guide-books.[9] But in the second group of versions the hero is some local lad, there is no maiden to be won, and the killing is brought about by some ingenious but rather underhand trick: by giving the dragon a poisoned pie, for instance, or one so indigestible that he gets the 'collywobbles', so that the farm-lad can easily chop his head off while pretending to give him a pill. Such stories are lively and humorous in tone; they may have been orally current for many generations, and have occasionally turned up in print in the present century; the earliest reference to a version of this type, a fragmentary one, was in 1911, and the fullest in 1929.[10]

---

8 Hopkins (1938), 45.
9 Evershed (1866), 180-3.
10 The poison version is briefly given in Lyminster church guide, written by Rosemary Sissons, who gave me a fuller account in correspondence (31/12/1971), having heard it in her childhood in the 1930s from a gardener and a farmer. The indigestion version is by Joiner (1929), 845-6, based on what he was told by a hedger. Arthur Beckett's version in Beckett (1911), 395-402, chiefly follows the romantic-heroic pattern, with a knight as hero, but inset in it is a brief reference to a miller who hoped to blind the dragon by throwing flour in its eyes and then chopping its head off with a butcher's cleaver.

Interestingly, the Lyminster pool still keeps a certain aura of sinister mystery, at any rate for some people, even though nobody now presents the dragon as a serious threat. Instead, there is a vague idea of some haunting or some curse – matters which are well within the bounds of possible belief in our own times. One informant told me, in 1977:

> It's a haunted pool. It's bottomless, and there are things that come up out of it at night.[11]

Another, in 1973, said:

> When we were children we were never allowed to go near the watercress beds which took their water from the Knucker Hole. There is some sort of curse on that water, and the cress is bad for you.[12]

Such stories can be updated remarkably fast. In 1974 a group of business men bought the field where the pool is, fenced it off, and drew water from it to supply a chain of shallow artificial ponds for trout farming, replacing the watercress beds. Hardly more than a year later, in December 1975, I was told:

> It's extremely unlucky to take fish from the Lyminster ponds, and there's a man on guard in a hut to stop people taking home any fish they catch there.[13]

There is indeed a hut, and occasionally a man on duty in it, presumably to ensure that only those who have bought fishing rights are using the ponds. Yet this unremarkable little fact has been linked, in the minds of at any rate some of the local people, with the former taboos surrounding the Knucker Hole. It was 'extremely unlucky' to take fish there, my informant had said; when I asked her why, she added 'It's because of a curse', and then, more hesitantly, that 'perhaps it was something to do with the dragon or the ghost.' This refers to a local story of a female ghost alleged to run screaming up the path to Lyminster Church, passing the pool on the way.

So much for the Lyminster Knucker Hole. Other Knucker Holes may once have had legends too, to match the implications of the name, but if so they are lost. There is, however, a curious allusion to a monster at a pool near Rye, which is another town on the coastal plain of Sussex; the name of the pool itself is unfortunately not given. The story was told as true, as part of their family tradition, by two elderly sisters living at Rye in the 1920s. They said that many years previously their father and mother, when courting, were once out walking one evening, with a dog:

---

11 An informant at Durrington to J. S., 10/2/1977.
12 An informant at Lyminster to J. S., 6/8/1973.
13 An informant at West Tarring to J. S., 8/12/1975; this informant's sister lives at Lyminster.
14 Grant (1927), 154; he comments on its similarity to kelpie tales.

They were in a field when a strange creature like a horse came galloping past them. It had the face of a man, and great eyes like saucers. The thunder of the galloping sound seemed to shake the earth. The young man tried to send the dog after it, but he was terrified and would not go. Nothing would induce him to stir. So the young man, leaving the girl, himself followed the creature, when it jumped a high fence and went padding down into a large deep pool just below Mountsfield.[14]

This appears to be akin to the widespread demonic water-horses – the Scottish *kelpie*, Irish *púca*, Icelandic *nykur*, and the rest. To find the creature so far from its usual habitats is perhaps a sign that the repertoire of English legend was once much richer than it now appears.

One particularly well attested Migratory Legend concerns the loss of a church bell in deep water, and the vain attempts to recover it (ML 7070, Motif V115.1). Examples are to be found in many parts of England, associated with lakes, deep river pools, or the sea; sometimes, too, the story is told about a site which had once been swampy, though now dry. Sussex has examples of all these types. One group concerns churches which have been covered by the sea as a result of coastal erosion, as at Bulverhythe, Selsea, and three or four other coastal villages; it is often said that one can at times hear the bells of the drowned church, and that this is a sign of bad weather. The alleged sound of the lost bells is in some cases identified as a particularly loud noise of waves raking the shingle, as in a fishermen's saying recorded at Bulverhythe in 1884.[15]

More fully developed legends are told of certain river sites. Near Isfield there is a section of the River Ouse locally called Bell Hole Brook, and near Arlington there is another Bell Hole, a deep pool in the bed of the Cuckmere River. In both cases it is said that a bell was hurled into the river by Puritans busily stripping the churches of 'popish' objects, and that it still lies hidden there, since only a team of pure white oxen would be able to raise it.[16] Two or three other similar examples were briefly noted by Sussex local historians in the nineteenth and early twentieth centuries;[17] it is a common legend pattern throughout England, though the identity of the wicked vandals varies from place to place. At Slinfold there is a more elaborated tale, which I have discussed elsewhere, about a bell which fell from a waggon and sank in a swamp, from which people tried to recover it, but in vain, as they broke the rule of silence imposed in such attempts.[18] However, the scene of the alleged event is not watery now, so it has no place in the present discussion.

---

15 For Bulverhythe, see Sawyer (1884), no. 24; for Selsea, Harrison (1935), 265. Similar tales were told me about Pett Level and Kingston Gorse in 1971.
16 Lower (1861), 227-8; Allcroft (1924), 62-3.
17 Lower (1861), 227-8.
18 Simpson (1985), 57-67.

The best known and fullest Sussex example of this type of tale is set in the small harbour at Bosham, where a particularly deep area of the main channel was formerly known as Bell Hole. Here, the villains of the story are Vikings, who supposedly raided Bosham and stole its biggest church bell, which they lashed to their ship. As they sailed away, the villagers rang the remaining bells, at the sound of which the stolen bell broke loose from its ropes and crashed through the bottom of the Viking ship, drowning everyone, and sinking into the depths. Many generations later, the men of Bosham were told that they could haul it back if they could get a team of pure white oxen (or white horses); after much searching they assembled such a team, and a diver fixed a rope to the bell. At the very moment when success seemed certain, when the bell had been dragged almost to the shore, the rope broke; on the tail of one ox (or one of the horses) there was a single black hair.[19] Alternatively, according to some tellers, the failure was due to a woman's tongue; the rescue was supposed to be done by men only, in silence, but a woman had hidden nearby to watch, and at the critical moment she cried out excitedly 'Up she comes!' – so down it went, and down it stayed.[20] Most versions conclude with the comment that when bells are rung in Bosham Church, the lost bell answers from beneath the waves. The story is locally popular, and a pub and a yachting club are both named after the bell.

Such stories often attract the attention of local historians by their apparent link with genuine history; guide-books and county magazines periodically raise the question of whether Vikings really did attack Bosham, or, similarly, whether the dragon at Lyminster should be 'decoded' as an allusion to dragon-headed Viking boats sailing up the Arun river, or to cruel medieval barons in Arundel Castle. In other parts of England, Cromwell's Puritan armies are often cast as the villains in 'stolen church bell' stories. However, there is no shred of evidence for such historical events at these places, outside the text of the actual legends which they are supposed to be explaining, and the frequency of parallels elsewhere counts heavily against a 'historical' basis for any individual instance. These are primarily tales about bells (or dragons) in the watery depths, and any historical setting they may be given is merely a device to increase their interest and plausibility.

A third theme commonly associated with watery sites is their use as a place of banishment for ghosts. Examples from counties in the south-west are Cranmere Pool on Dartmoor, Dozmary Pool on Bodmin Moor, and the Hound's Pool in a river near Buckfastleigh (Devon), each of them the haunt of a malevolent ghost bound there by the power of an exorcist, and condemned to try to empty the pool with a perforated shell.[21] At Cranmere there is the additional complication that the ghost was made to enter the body of a colt before being forced into the pool; at Hound's Pool, he is of course in the form of a black hound. In Somerset, there is the Witch's

---

19 The earliest reference I have found is Hare (1894), 190. It is also given by Beckett (1911), 228-
    9; by Cooke (1911), 168-70; and by many others since.
20 Chandler (c. 1980 ?), 40.
21 Brown (1979), 27-31, 71-2; Tongue (1965), 101.

Pool at Withycombe, to which the ghost of the wicked Madam Joan Carne was banished, but she is creeping homewards at the rate of one cockstride per year.[22] Also from Somerset is the tale of Sir John Popham's ghost; he is said to have died by drowning in an allegedly bottomless pool in Wilscombe Bottom, and to have gone straight down from there into Hell, but thanks to his wife's prayers his ghost re-emerged at midnight on the following New Year's Eve, and is now crawling towards the church by one cockstride a year, to join her in the tomb.[23] Sometimes ghosts are said to have been forced by the exorcist to enter a bottle or snuff-box, which is then thrown into a pool or a well, or into the sea; famous stories of this type include the laying of Madam Pigott's ghost (at Chetwynd, Shropshire)[24] and Black Vaughan's ghost at Kington (Herefordshire).[25] There are also many tales where the ghost, whether inside a bottle or not, is banished to the Red Sea, popularly believed to be immensely deep, and an entrance to Hell.

Yet another theme, particularly common in the counties next to the Welsh Border (Cheshire, Shropshire, Herefordshire), is that of a village suddenly swallowed up by a swamp or a lake on account of its wickedness.[26] Often it is said that its church bells can be heard ringing in the depths, or that if one drops a pebble down a well, it will strike the steeple of the sunken church. Various causes are given for these disasters; maybe some farmers were reaping on a Sunday, or the villagers danced instead of going to church on Christmas Eve, or a miser tried to charge people for drinking water from his well. There are of course some famous Welsh examples of this story-pattern,[27] so its popularity on the English side of the Border might be influenced by them.

Such tales have an obvious moral purpose, and they too, like the ghost-layings, imply that there is an affinity between deep water and the depths of Hell, so that sinners can be appropriately engulfed in water. Various Biblical models are probably operative here: Pharaoh's army overwhelmed by the Red Sea, Sodom and Gomorrah destroyed by fire and (allegedly) then covered by the newly formed Dead Sea, the Psalmists' frequent use of waves or deep waters as a metaphor for deadly danger, the possessed Gadarene swine plunging into the Sea of Galilee. Of course there are non-Scriptural parallels too, notably the Greek legend of Philemon and Baucis, but these would not have been widely known, whereas the influence of Bible stories was felt at all levels of society.

Finally, it may be worth noting themes that are not to be found here – though an argument from silence is notoriously risky, and all the more so when the material is as scanty and erratically distributed as these English legends are. For example,

---

22 Tongue (1965), 82-3; Palmer (1976), 67.
23 Tongue (1965), 103.24 Burne and Jackson (1883-6), 124-7.
25 Leather (1912), 29-30.
26 Leigh (1866), 233-5, 278-9; Burne and Jackson (1883-6), 64-6, 69-73; Leather (1912), 11.
27 Rhys (1901), 403-5, 408-16.

there are no benevolent or romantic water-fairies in England to set alongside the well-known Welsh ones; there are no treasures to be won from the water; water is not envisaged as an entrance to fairyland or an enticing Otherworld; no wondrous cattle emerge from it; heroes do not plunge into it in search of adventure. Occasional allusions to Arthurian literary motifs, as when it is claimed that Excalibur was cast into Dozmary Pool, do not really counteract the prevailing gloom. In these English local legends, deep water is consistently associated with danger, loss, destruction, banishment, confinement, and Hell.

Songs of Boats and Boatmen

Ríonach uí Ógáin

There are numerous songs in Irish tradition which are associated with the sea. These are found in English and in Irish and include a number of more specific song-types such as laments about shipwrecks or songs describing adventures at sea. Inevitably, some songs are capable of classification under a number of different types. I have chosen to concentrate here upon songs in praise of boats. I have further confined the range of the source material to songs in the Irish language and to songs from a particular region of the west coast of Ireland, that is parts of the baronies of Maigh Cuilinn and Baile na hInse, in the west and north-west of county Galway.

The source material is drawn from the collections of the Department of Irish Folklore and was brought together, for the most part, between 1935 and the present day. However, a number of the songs are probably a good deal older than 1935, as tradition holds that they were composed in the last hundred to one hundred and fifty years, in the dialect peculiar to this area. From the point of view of language, the songs are very rich and vivid and they document in a vibrant way part of the sea-faring traditions of Ireland.

Songs associated with the sea from the area in question may be divided into the following categories:

- songs about drownings
- shipwrecks
- songs in praise of boats
- some general songs of the sea (including accounts of smuggling, adventures at sea because of bad weather or other circumstances).

I have included, in addition, a song about an overloaded boat (which was rescued) and a song about a whale which was washed ashore on the island of Maínis.

Before embarking on a discussion about songs which fall into the first of these categories – songs in praise of boats – two issues may be accorded special mention. The first concerns the basic importance of boats in the economic and social life of Conamara at the time the majority of these songs were composed. The land in this part of the country is poor by any standards and so, in order to survive, farmers were obliged to fish also and, to a certain degree, this is still the situation to-day. Boats were essential until comparatively recent times, not only for fishing, but also for fetching, carrying and delivering indispensable items such as turf and food and for travelling from one island to another. Sea routes were and, some would argue, still are more conveniently traversed than the rather poor road-system serving much of Conamara. Sailing boats carried turf from Conamara to Galway city, to the Aran Islands, to Ballyvaughan in county Clare and to nearby Kinvara in county Galway. General supplies were shipped back for the local providers from Galway city and Kinvara. Turf-trading to the Aran islands came to an end only in the late 1960s. Boats were also used a great deal for carrying seaweed; other cargoes included wheat, beer and tea. One song composer described the passing of the era of the hooker as a working boat in the following terms:

> Ó, is minic a bhí na báid siúd, bhí siad ag seasamh i ngach uile áit,
> Bhí siad ag seasamh i ngach uile chaladh, ó, go Gaillimh is i gcontae an Chláir,
> Ag tarraingt chruithneacht as tí Tommy, ó, tae agus a togha leann,
> Dhá thabhairt anonn Cinn Mhara, Baile uí Bheacháin agus gach uile áit. [1]
> [Oh, those boats they often stopped in every place,
> They stopped in every harbour, Galway and in county Clare,
> Bringing wheat from Tommy's shop, tea and the best of ale,
> Bringing it across Kinvara Bay, Ballyvaughan and everywhere.]

On occasion, as well, songs refer to a keg of *poitín*, or home-distilled whiskey, hidden in the turf, carried on the journey across Galway Bay to Kinvara. A line from the above-mentioned song says: *Bhíodh an ceaig thíos sa móin acu le díol thoir i gcontae an Chláir* [They had the keg down in the turf to sell it over in county Clare].

A second point worthy of note is that the type of boat featured in these songs is very different from the large fishing trawlers of to-day. Most of the local sailing craft belong to one of four types, classified locally as follows: *bád mór, leathbhád, gleoiteog,* and *púcán.* The first two types – the *bád mór* and *leathbhád* – are also referred to as hookers or *húicéirí*. The *bád mór,* meaning 'large boat' measures 35-44 feet/*c.* 10.6-13.5 metres overall and the *leathbhád,* meaning 'medium-sized boat', about 32 feet/*c.* 9.7 metres. These two types of boat were costly and, generally speaking, fishermen would have tended to own one or other of the next two types, the *gleoiteog* or *púcán.* The *gleoiteog* is similar to the *bád mór* and *leathbhád* except with regard to size, being only 24-28 feet/ *c.* 7.3-8.5 metres long. The name may be derived from the Irish word *gleoite,* meaning 'pretty'; according to another theory, *gleoiteog* may be related to the word *geolta,* the Irish word for 'yawl'. The *púcán,* which is said to be the finest sailing craft on the Conamara coast, is the same size as the *gleoiteog,* but has a different rig. The word *púcán* is used to describe a wrapping

---

1 *IFC* 1774:23, where *IFC* = Irish Folklore Collection, being the Main Manuscripts Collection of the Department of Irish Folklore, University College Dublin; the numerals on either side of the colon represent the volume number and page number respectively. From a song called 'Amhrán na Seanbháid a Bhí i gConamara' collected by Ciarán Bairéad from Máirtín Mac Conaola, Cladhnach, An Cheathrú Rua, 9.12.1964.

or wrap-around, such as one might use to protect a sore finger. The connection here may be that one of the sails has to be swung or wrapped around the mast. The *púcán* is more of an inshore craft than the *gleoiteog*. The 'nobby' or the 'zulu' was another type of sailing craft, bearing little resemblance to the heavy-bellied hookers. These were built in Conamara from the late 1890s and were Manx and Scottish in origin. They were introduced by the Congested Districts Board and reached a total production of twenty nobbies and ten zulus. Nobbies were the type most used in Conamara and mention of these occurs in the song tradition as well. According to Richard Scott in his book *The Galway Hooker*,[2] a nobby called the 'Faugh a Ballagh' may have been one of those nobbies actually built in Peel in the Isle of Man to supplement the needs of Conamara fishermen. The 'Faugh a Ballagh' survived until the end of the thirties. This may be the same boat as the '*Fág an Bealach*' which is mentioned in the song tradition.

It is not always stated in the songs precisely which type of boat is the subject of the song. Sometimes, however, the type in question is obvious from the title, as in the case of the song '*Púcán Mhicil Pháidín*', or, alternatively, the words of the song may contain some indication as to the particular kind of boat. However, more often than not, words associated with sailing or rowing are the only indication given as to the general boat-type. For example in the song '*An Chláróg*' it is said:

> *Is éard a dúirt Tún is bád maith í ar iomramh,*
> *Is tá sí thar cinn ag gabháil trasna.*[3]
> [*Tún* said she is a good boat when she is rowed,
> And is powerful crossing the water.]

In the songs I have encountered it would appear that about half of the boats were given names in English – names such as '*An* Clear the Way', '*An* Cutlash' (the latter deriving, perhaps from the word 'Cutlass', a small sword used by sailors), '*An* Dingle', '*An* Mary Anne'. This last boat is said to have been called after the wife of the owner Colm P. Ó hUaithnín. Typically, song titles in Irish only, include the word *púcán* or simply *bád* meaning boat, followed by the owner's name, as in songs such as '*Púcán Mhicil Pháidín*', '*Bád Pheige Seoighe*', '*Báidín Sheáin Uí Niá*', '*Bád Chlann Dhonnchá*', '*Púcán Mór Sheáin Ántaine*', or simply a name such as '*An tSailchuach*' which means 'The Violet', or '*An Fág an Bealach*' (meaning 'The Clear the Way'). Incidentally, one of the first public transport buses to serve Conamara, was nicknamed the '*Fág an Bealach*'.[4] Most of these titles indicate that the composer of the song treated the boat with a certain intimacy, based on personal acquaintance with the vessel and its owner, sailor, and/or builder. In one instance, there is a

---

2 Scott (1983), 75.
3 *IFC* 969:285. Collected by Calum Mac Ghille Eathain from Seosamh Mac Liam (?), (31), Cora na Rón, Cill Aithneann, 13.12.1944. The song is said to have been composed by Pádraig Seoighe.
4 *IFC* 1770:361. Account collected by Ciarán Bairéad from Máire Ní Chonaola (58), An Baile Láir, Cora na Rón, Cill Aithneann, 22.7.1968.

further personalisation of the boat's name, in the case of the song 'An Cutlash' where the boat is called 'cutlasheen' in the body of the song, the suffix -*ín* being a diminutive form, frequently used in words of endearment. At the time these songs were composed, it was the custom in many Irish-speaking districts for people to use the anglicised form of their own names in formal situations and, although this practice has altered somewhat, it continues to the present day. It would appear that comparatively few boats carried the names of Irish or other saints, although the 'St Jude' certainly occurs, and a boat called the 'Ave Maria' is also mentioned. Belief in the protection of the Church is rarely expressed, although in one song – '*Báidín Sheáin Uí Néidh*' – we are told: *Is níor fhan aon choiscéim siúil aici gur bheannaigh an sagart í* [5] [And she was left with no movement until the priest blessed her]. Sometimes a boat, boatman or boat builder is placed in God's care, as is expressed in the song, '*Bád an Chaisil* (1)[6]': *Cuirimid rí an Domhnaigh dhá sábháilt* [7] [We ask the King of Sunday to save her.]

Boats were traditionally looked upon as female and are still so regarded to-day. *Sí*, the third person singular feminine pronoun, is used to describe a boat, and sometimes the language and emotion are so vivid that the boat almost seems to take on a personality of her own. In the case of the song '*An* Mary Anne', the boat is addressed directly: *A Mhary Anne bhocht nach tú bhí aonraic, is tú leat féin ag Ceann Léime ó dheas*[8] [Poor Mary Anne, you were so lonely, when you were alone south at Loop Head]. In one song, it is said that when the boat is forced into the wind she becomes stubborn and pulls to one side, and, in the same song, the boat's diligence as a worker is praised. Terms of endearment, frequently used by people in relation to one another, are often pressed into service in the songs. This is the first line of the song '*Amhrán na Curaí*'[9] (The Currach Song): *Grá mo chroí mo churaichín mar is aici a bheidheas an geall* [My currach is my love because she will win the race].

The principal aspects of the boats which are praised are exactly those one might expect. The beautiful appearance of the boats is mentioned, *Nár sheol sí isteach go Gaillimh mar d'éireodh sí ó dhraíocht* [10] [Didn't she sail into Galway as if she were rising out of a magical spell] or *Mar nuair a sheolaidís cois gaoithe ní raibh radharc ar bith ní b'fhearr* [11] [For when they sailed with the wind there was not a finer sight], and even the sound of a boat may be praised: *agus fuaim a cuid crannaíl go dtóigfeadh*

5 Cf. '*An Gruagach Bán*', *An Fíbín*, 1905,13.

6 This is the first of two songs which were composed in praise of this particular boat.

7 *IFC* 1280:735. Collected by Séamus Mac Aonghusa from Colm Ó Caodháin (49), Glinsce, Maíros, 1943. The song is said to have been composed by Nóra Ní Uaithnín.

8 *IFC* 1280:292. Collected by Séamus Mac Aonghusa from Seáinín Choilmín Mac Donncha, Fínis, Maíros, 1943.

9 *IFC* 607:557. Collected by Brian Mac Lochlainn in Ros an Mhíl, Cill Cuimín, 1938-39.

10 *IFC* 1311:466. Collected by Éamonn Ó Conghaile from Beairtle Ó Conghaile (50), An Aird Thiar, Maíros, 11.12.1952.

11 *IFC* 1311:465. Collected by Éamonn Ó Conghaile from Beairtle Ó Conghaile (50), An Aird Thiar, Maíros, 11.12.1952.

sé an ceo de mo chroí[12] [and the sound of her masts would lift the cloud from my heart]. Speed is, of course, very important and particular comparisons are made. For example, the 'Clear the Way' is said to be swifter than the foxes fleeing from their enemies, and it is said she would travel twice the speed of the hare if the force of the wind were strong enough.[13] In the song, '*Bád Chlann Dhonnchá*', the fact that the boat in question is faster than all of the other boats, even when carrying a load of seaweed, gives the composer great satisfaction.[14] A boat of exceptional speed is sufficient reason for composing a song. In connection with '*Amhrán na Curaí*' sic we are told that there was a boat-maker called Tomás Ó Ceallaigh in Trá Bhán, in Cillín parish, in the barony of Maigh Cuilinn, and he made a currach, and the currach was so swift on the water that he started to make a song about her, praising her.[15] Another example of a particularly speedy boat is '*An* Cashel Star', also known as '*An* Castle Star' and it is said in this song that it took her only nine minutes from the time she left Cill Rónáin until she passed beyond the harbours to the west and Ceann Mása.[16]

Many of the earlier songs appear to be anonymous compositions. However, in some instances, we are told the name of the composer. In the case of the song called '*An* Cutlash', a poet called Seán Ó Guairim is said to have been the composer.[17] Somewhat unexpectedly, perhaps, at least three of the songs are said to have been composed by a woman called Nuala Ní Uaithnín ('Nuala an Chnoic' or 'Nuala Thomáis Thuathail'). These songs include '*An* Dingle' and '*Bád an Chaisil*'[18] – the latter probably better known than the former. She is also said to have composed the song known as '*Réalt an Chaisil*' (The Cashel Star). Nuala Ní Uaithnín was originally from an island called Inis Ní and was said to have been living in an tOileán Gorm for a certain period at the time she composed one of the songs – '*Bád an Chaisil*' – in praise of the boat and its master – in the hope, it is said, of receiving a *síneadh láimhe* (gratuity) from him.[19] However, another account says that the owner of the boat, Seán Ó Lochlainn, who was a District Justice, helped many a person. He was a hotelier and used the boat, for the most part, to carry goods from Galway to his

12 *IFC* 1280:738. Collected by Séamus Mac Aonghusa from Colm Ó Caodháin (49) Glinsce, Maíros, 1943. The song is said to have been composed by Nóra Ní Uaithnín.

13 *IFC* 1280:281. Collected by Séamus Mac Aonghusa from Cóilín Mac Donncha (*c*.42), Fínis, Maíros, 1943.

14 *IFC* 525:459. Collected by Proinnsias de Búrca from Eoghan Ó Flatharta (50), Na Foraí Maola, Maigh Cuilinn, 13.4.1938.

15 *IFC* 607:557. Collected by Brian Mac Lochlainn in Ros an Mhíl, Cill Cuimín, 1938-1939.

16 *IFC* 1280:735. Collected by Séamus Mac Aonghusa from Colm Ó Caodháin (49) Glinsce, Maíros, 1943. The song is said to have been composed by Nóra Ní Uaithnín.

17 *IFC* 1281:370. Collected by Séamus Mac Aonghusa from Colm Ó Caodháin (49), Glinsce, Maíros, 1944-45.

18 *IFC* 1281:105-6. Collected by Séamus Mac Aonghusa from Colm Ó Caodháin (49) Glinsce, Maíros, 1944-45. *IFC* 1280:735. Collected by Séamus Mac Aonghusa from Colm Ó Caodháin (49), Glinsce, Maíros, 1943.

19 *IFC* 1280:735. Collected by Séamus Mac Aonghusa from Colm Ó Caodháin (49), Glinsce, Maíros, 1943.

own shop in Cashel; the boat was also well-known for winning races. This account says that Nuala Thomáis Thuathail composed this and many other songs. When Seán Ó Lochlainn heard that Nuala had composed the song he invited her to his house and rewarded her with a fine present.[20] This trading craft is said to have been made by a boat-builder whose surname was Gorham.

One of the most striking songs of all of this type is *'Púcán Mhicil Pháidín'*. A version of it was given to collector Proinnsias de Búrca by Beairtle Ó Conghaile, from An Aird Thoir, Carna in 1958. Beairtle told the collector that the song was composed by Seán Ó Guairim from Leitir Ard, west of Carna, about a *púcán* owned by a relation of the poet, whose name was Micil Ó Fatharta. Micil Ó Fatharta was a good helmsman and a gifted sailor.[21] In relation to this song, it was said of one version of it, that a man called Maidhc Ó Conaola from Caladh Mháínse, Carna, changed some of the words and verses so as to give the song greater local appeal. The folk-song collector, Séamus Ennis (Séamus Mac Aonghusa), noted that the version he collected from Maidhc Ó Conaola was said by Maidhc himself to be his own version which had more appeal for local people.[22]

The boat known as *'An* Cutlash' is praised because it is fitted out so well. The *'An* Mary Anne' is also praised for its fittings. Sometimes, as in the song, *'Bád Sheáin Uí Nia'*, boat, owner, and boatman are all praised together. The composer says that he spent a year and a half in Seán Ó Nia's boat and that he has never seen a man as generous as he. There was whiskey and wine, tobacco and good food. The composer has seen many places but has never seen such a fine boat. Seán Ó Nia is also praised for his fine performance as a boatman.[23] One boat, *'An Chláróg'*, is even said to have been able to smell the fish: *Níl ronnach, ná cnúdán aniar ó Cheann Gólaim, nach bhfaighfeadh sí ar an nóiméad a mboladh*[24] [There isn't a mackerel, or gurnard east of Gólaim Head, that she wouldn't get the smell of them immediately].

One of the best-known songs of praise composed by Feidhlim Mac Cumhaill (Féilim Mac Dúill) *'An tSailchuach'* (about a boat which was made by Máirtín Breathnach from Casla) is more subtle than one might think on first hearing it sung. Apparently, it was one of the worst boats ever to be built, but, nevertheless, the poet composed a song in praise of her. It is only through familiarity with the folklore of this particular sailing boat that one can appreciate the irony of the song. The song contains all of the standard characteristics of songs of praise; for example, speed is mentioned: *sháraigh sí ar luas an ghaoth Mhárta* [she was faster than the March wind], as well as appearance: *a bratacha breá uasal léi in airde* [her fine noble sails

20 *IFC* 1311:460. Collected by Éamonn Ó Conghaile from Beairtle Ó Conghaile (50), An Aird Thiar, Maíros, 11.12.1952.
21 *IFC* 1552:144-7.
22 *IFC* 1280:533-4.
23 See 'An Gruagach Bán', *An Fíbín*, 1905, 13-14.
24 *IFC* 969:285. Collected by Calum Mac Ghille-Eathain from Seosamh Mac Liam (*c*.31), Inis Bearachain, 4.12.1944.

hoisted], *is í an bád is deise múnla dár dearnadh* [she is the most finely designed boat ever built], and the builder is praised: *Pádraig Seoighe an ceardaí bheirim féin an barr dó*[25] [Páidín Seoighe is some craftsman and I praise him to the sky]. Obviously, if the lore of this song – '*An tSailchuach*' – or the original reason for its composition were to fade from memory, then it might easily be regarded as a song of praise with the loss of the satirical element, or, alternatively, the song might lose its function altogether and simply disappear from the tradition.

Praise of the boat, '*An Chríonach*', is very much to the fore in the lament for the demise of that particular vessel. The combination of speed and beauty is highlighted in the song, '*Bád Pheige Seoighe*', which praises a boat which has fallen into decay: *Go deimhin, a Pheige Seoighe, is breá í do bhád seoil, mar ghabhadh sí ar an ngaoithe go tréan is leis an scód*[26] [Indeed Peige Seoighe, your sailing boat is a fine one, because she would travel with strength on the wind when sailing free].

For a number of reasons, many of the airs to which these songs were sung have not been documented. The songs were collected for the most part in manuscript form only and few collectors in the 1930s and 1940s were skilled in music notation, and fewer still had sound recording equipment available to them. In most instances, no mention is made of an air. In some cases, however, it is stated that the song is sung to a particular air, usually a very well-known air, or the structure of the song itself gives an inkling as to the air to which it may have been sung. This is the case with '*An* Clear the Way' where each of the eleven five-line stanzas includes a one line chorus: *Is ólfaidh muid an crúiscín is tá sé lán* [Let us drink the jug and it is full], thus suggesting that the air was that of the well-known song, '*An Crúiscín Lán*'. Other songs are sometimes said to be sung to the air of some other well-known song. This is so in relation to '*Bád Pheige Seoighe*', said to be sung to the well-known air, '*Contae Mhaigh Eo*'.

Just as he is cursed in the songs of drowning, in these songs of praise, the boat-maker is praised. In relation to one song, '*An Púcán*', the collector obtained a three-page account about a boat-builder called Branley who lived in Kinvara, in county Galway. This song is about a particularly fast *púcán* which he built and it tells us:

> *Ba é Mister Branley rinne í le obair stuama lámh,*
> *Níor bhain sé mórán leas aisti, mar faraor fuair sé bás.*[27]
> [It was Mister Branley who made her, with his steady hand,
> He did not use her a great deal because, sadly, he died.]

---

25 See Ó Máille, T. & M. (1905), 20-1, 171.
26 *IFC* 1281:308. Collected by Séamus Mac Aonghusa from Colm Ó Caodháin (50), Glinsce, Maíros, 1944.
27 *IFC* 1281:332-5. Collected by Séamus Mac Aonghusa from Colm Ó Caodháin (50), Glinsce, Maíros, 1944.

The surname Ó Cathasaigh is closely associated with boat-building and a boat called '*An* Mary Anne', dating from 1885, was made by members of this family in Maínis, near Carna. The same family is mentioned in a number of songs. For example in '*Amhrán na Seanbháid a Bhí i gConamará* [The Song of the Old Boats in Conamara], it is said:

> *Na fir a rinne an t-am sin iad, ní fhéadfaí a leithéid a fháil ,*
> *Is iad na Cathasaigh tá i gCarna iad, togha na saora ab fhearr le fáil.*[28]
> [The likes of the men who built them at that time couldn't be found,
> The best of boat-builders, the Cathasaigh from Carna.]

In '*Amhrán na Curaí*' (sic) the boat-maker is told with approval: *Mo ghrá thú a Thomáis Shabha, is tú an máistir ar na saoir* [29] [You are my darling, *Tomás Shabha*, the master of craftsmen, you made the finest curach for me that was ever in the land.]

Many of the songs relate to a way of life which has changed greatly – for example, between the years 1890 and 1920 there were at least three boat-makers, three carpenters and one blacksmith working in the area of An Cheathrú Rua and, for the most part, these sported well-known local surnames such as Mac Donncha, Breathnach, Ó Conaola, Ó Cadhain, and Ó Cualáin. These surnames occur again and again in the songs, not only as builders or carpenters but also as boatmen and fishermen.

It would appear that the people who sang these songs as part of the routine of their daily lives – and who sang them as well for the collectors, of course – were men, and fishermen at that. But the songs indicate that although the boats were built by men, and sailed or rowed by men, there are also instances of boats being owned by women. One line in a song refers to '*bád mór Mhonica a ndeachaigh a cáil ar fud na tíre*[30] [Monica's big boat whose fame spread throughout the land]. This is probably a reference to a craft called 'Erin's Hope'. It was owned by Monica MacDonagh of Galway and was engaged in general trade to Conamara during the late 1930s. According to Richard Scott, it was probably one of the largest hookers ever built. It was used a great deal to carry turf. Peige Seoighe was another female owner, and a song – '*Bád Bhaibín* Reilly' – was made about her boat. The song tells of Baibín Reilly's boat – apparently a *gleoiteog* – whose working years ranged approximately from 1950 to 1960.

---

28 *IFC* 1774:21-5. Collected by Ciarán Bairéad from Máirtín Mac Conaola (Máirtín Mhurcha Pháidín), Cladhnach, An Cheathrú Rua, 9.12.1964.
29 *IFC* 607:557. Collected by Brian Mac Lochlainn in Ros an Mhíl, Cill Cuimín, 1938-1939.
30 *IFC* 1281:335. Collected by Séamus Mac Aonghusa from Colm Ó Caodháin (50), Glinsce, Maíros, 1944.

Possibly more than any other song-type, these songs show an intimate knowledge of coastal areas and islands and a familiarity with them. In order to appreciate the songs in every respect, one would need to be acquainted with the rocks, coves and inlets of the area in question and to be familiar with their lore. Another essential part of the songs about the journeys made by boats are the descriptions of the regular sea routes travelled by them, and the familiar landmarks they passed along the way. In this respect, the emphasis in more recent songs can be seen to be different to that of the earlier songs. Not only fishermen and boat-builders, but also the community in general, were to experience a great change in the sea traffic around them as the building of roads gradually made remote villages more accessible and the harsh reality of shifting cargo by sea no longer remained a pressing necessity.

This also signalled the passing of an indigenous part of the Conamara tradition. Since the 1970s, there has been a considerable revival of interest in the Conamara sailing craft and an integral element of this revival is the custom of composing songs about the hookers. Interestingly, these new compositions have elements in common with the earlier singing tradition. These new songs are often sung in so-called Country and Western style, but contain many features associated with the older unaccompanied traditional songs. Boat-makers and their creations are praised, and also the speed of the boat and skill of the crew, and the songs convey a great sense of adventure and the joy of the sea. For example, the song, '*An* Merican *Mór*', was composed by Tomás Seoighe about a hooker, which was restored as recently as 1967. The song is very popular and heard frequently. This boat was built by a Gorham of Inis Ní, a member of a family of boat-builders still remembered in the Roundstone-Cashel area. Two other recent songs which celebrate hookers are '*An* Hunter' and '*An Capall*', both composed by a well-known sailor, Seán Ó Ceoinín, from Leitir Ard near Carna, who died a few years ago. Seán was not a singer, although he could recite numerous songs and, today, his compositions about the hookers are sung in a Country and Western style for the most part. 'The Hunter' is a 32-foot/*c.* 9.7 metres *leathbhád*, and a regular competitor in races in Conamara. The first verse of the song in praise of her goes as follows :

Is bhí draíocht insan Hunter go cinnte, ó déanadh í i Leitir Mealláin,
Bhí sí déanta ó thogha na saortha, ab fhearr a bhí ann ag an am,
Mar rinne siad soitheach trí crainnte, agus sheol siad ó thuaidh is ó dheas ,
Is nach mba onóir do chlainne Chonfhaola, is don chontae dhá dtáinig siad as. [31]
[There was magic in the hunter certainly, since she was built in Leitir Mealláin,
She was made by the best of craftsmen at the time,
They made a vessel with three masts and sailed north and south,
And was it not an honour for the Confhaola family, for their native county.]

---

31 Ó Conghaile (1986), 66.

The hooker 'An Capall', [The Horse], was built near Leitir Móir in the 1860s by Michael Rainey and, after lying for many years in disrepair and following an extensive refit, made its re-appearance in 1980. The song 'An Capall', the song in praise of her, lauds the many feats of this large boat. Another song, 'Gleoiteog John Dairbe', was composed by Tomás Mac an Iomaire within the last twenty years. It contains the same kind of language and images as are met with in all the other songs of praise. Here, once again, the boat-making Ó Cathasaigh family of Maínis features and one member of this family in particular is singled out for special mention.

The boat-song tradition to-day is directly related to the revival of interest in the boats themselves where the emphasis is on *geallta* or boat races. Hardly a weekend passes by, during the summer months, without some kind of boat festival taking place along the Galway coast. The largest of these is at Kinvara, where the festival called *Cruinniú na mBád* (The Gathering of the Boats) takes place in August. Sometimes, the occasion may be associated with a religious festival, pilgrimage or pattern as in the case of *Féile Mhic Dara* ([St] MacDara's Festival) on the 16th of July each year, when local people, summer visitors and the boats foregather and songs are sung, and the sea-journey to Cruach na Cara, or St MacDara's Island, takes place.

It is in the songs about boat-racing that the unbroken tradition of boat-songs is most clearly depicted. Boat-racing is mentioned in a number of the older songs; the custom of celebrating a victory is mentioned in a song collected in the early 1940s, but undoubtedly the practice is much older. Other festive events and occasions may have lapsed and disappeared, but the boat-races still take place on a very regular basis. Some of the imagery of the songs connected with them is very vivid, as can be seen, for example, in the following lines:

> *Cháithfeadh sí chomh hard in aghaidh farraigí agus gála*
> *Is gan amhras go bhfliuchfadh sí na réalta.*[32]
> [She would throw the spray so high against sea and gale
> And without doubt she would wet the stars.]

In conclusion, we may observe that these songs provide an insight into many aspects of traditional life in the area in question. This particular singing tradition represents part of an unbroken chain in the heritage of song composition today. The boat-songs have their own particular local flavour. In this region, none were composed about boats from other districts and, in a sense, none of the songs mentioned here has acquired a relevance beyond the district in which it was composed. Within the region itself, some of the songs have lost their currency, but others have survived. Some of the older boats and associated songs have been replaced by both new boats

---

32 *IFC* 1701:242. Collected by Proinsias de Búrca from Pádraig Ó Loideáin (70) and Colm Ó Cualáin (50), Maínis, Carna, 6.07.1965.

and new songs. One way or another, the songs have served to retain folk memories of particular boats and their associated lore, including traditions about their builders, their owners and the races in which they once participated. The history of ownership is sometimes traced in the song, sometimes in the accompanying lore, or sometimes in both. The songs clearly describe the close association between man and the sea, demonstrate a healthy respect for the sea, and also show a certain fear of it.

It is probably true to say that many earlier compilers, publishers and editors of song in Irish have paid scant attention to lesser known songs such as songs about boats, as may be deduced from the relatively poor representation of such songs in the larger published collections. But the work of song-collecting in Ireland, and the efforts of folklore collectors, counterbalance this neglect to a large extent, as songs in praise of boats frequently attracted the attention of collectors of folklore during the 1930s and 1940s; many of the boat-songs which were documented then relate to boats which were at the height of their renown at that very time. In this way, the songs may be said to give a factual contemporary account of certain aspects of people's lives at that particular period in time. The more recent songs about local boats focus on aspects of community life and social history, while the older songs tend to concentrate on the merits of a craft which was once an essential part of the traditional economy of the area. As Richard Scott notes :

> Probably the last World War saw the final years when such craft were a community need, albeit a much diminished one. But it is very desirable, as part of Gaelic social history and of the history of the sea, that these boats should be preserved in living form, in numbers representative of the areas they once served.[33]

A number of the larger boats have been restored to their original state, keeping faith with traditional style in the process rather than modernising them. It is, of course, impossible to make any prediction regarding the future survival of these songs as part of a living tradition or to surmise that similar songs will be composed in years to come, but the hope may be expressed in relation to the songs, as does Richard Scott in relation to the vessels themselves, that old and new boat-songs will be sung, as long as the Irish-language singing tradition continues to thrive.

---

33 Scott (1983), 11.

The Guises of Estonian Water-Spirits in Relation to the Plot and Function of Legend

ÜLO VALK

The problem which arises in approaching folk religion as a field of study is that belief cannot be analysed directly since it is a mental reality, representing a complicated system of ideas, emotions and attitudes, related to the outer world. Belief can become the target of research only if it becomes actualized in human behaviour, ritual, art or verbal texts. The present paper aims at highlighting the connection between folk belief and folk legend which is one of the main sources for a study of popular religion. I wish to show how the descriptions of water-spirits in Estonian tradition depend on the narrative plot and situation described. I will also discuss possible conclusions that can be drawn with regard to the function of the legend on the basis of the visual guises of the supernatural being. In order to point out some common characteristics of water-spirits and other supernatural beings in Estonian tradition, I will compare the guises of the water-spirit with those of the devil. Finally, I will touch on the connection between legends and reality, which can be one way of explaining their popularity.

Water Spirits in Estonian Folklore

The following legend is fairly typical and thus serves as an introduction to the world of traditional Estonian folk belief about water-spirits. It was recorded in 1929 by a reliable collector, Rudolf Põldmäe, in Harju-Jaani parish, North Estonia. The informant was Emilie Kruuspak, a forty-two-year-old woman.[1]

> My great grandmother was on her way to the town. Near the bridge of Saula she saw the following: there was a woman in the river who was washing her breasts and was standing with her back towards her. She had yellow hair and broad hips. Great grandmother shouted: 'Good morning, mistress of water (*vee-emand*)!' The woman whom she had not seen before answered through her nose: 'Good day to you. Let your grandchildren live a happy life until the fourth and fifth generation; they will not die a watery death!' This happened in summer-time at sunrise. In the evening the great grandmother returned from the town and heard that in the same place where the water-spirit (*vee-vaim*) had sat a girl had drowned while washing the sheep. This unlucky girl had also had long yellow hair.

---

1 I *ERA* 18, 481/2 (1) (1929). The narrative might be called a memorate but it seems to include too many traditional motifs to reflect a genuine experience. Probably, it has been elaborated on by the tradition bearers. It is also plausible that the great grandmother has once told a traditional legend in the first person to reinforce its credibility. Note: all parish names are henceforth given in abbreviated form in the text (see Fig. 3).

This is one of thousands of examples of Estonian folk legends that tell about water-spirits. Such legends have mainly been recorded since the last quarter of the nineteenth century; they were still popular and widespread a hundred years ago, and even later, although changes in the traditional peasant culture and the process of urbanization slowly led to their decline. The legend told by E. Kruuspak contains some typical features that characterize the development of Estonian folk religion. The protagonist of the story uses the old respectful appellation – mistress of water – while addressing the spirit, who answers in a benevolent manner and endows her and her children with a happy life. Water would not be a peril for them. A later popular appellation of the water-spirit *näkk* has a perjorative connotation. Christian influences have brought about the demonization of various nature spirits. However, it seems that Estonian water spirits have an inherent inclination towards evil. Even the legend quoted above telling about the blessing of the water spirit has a sinister content. The woman described in the story is an evil omen which predicts the drowning of the girl.

In Estonian folk religion, it is possible to make a broad distinction between two classes of water-spirits. The guardians of fish and bodies of water had lost their former significance by the time Estonian folklore began to be recorded. There are relatively few legends about them. These guardians were called fish-fathers and fish-mothers (*kalajezä, kala-ima*, Lutsi), fish-masters (*kala-peremees*, Setu), fish-kings (*kalakuningas*, Räpina), and so on. Following his special study of them, Ivar Paulson has concluded that 'they belong to very ancient and archaic strata of religion. Many primitive peoples who were fishermen have images which correspond to these beliefs in content and form. They had been well preserved until recently in the folk religion practised by some Finno-Ugric peoples, such as the Lapps and Ob-Ugrians. As with these peoples, so also in Estonian folklore, fish-spirits can appear before man not only in anthropomorphic form, but also in the shape of fish,[2] or as a real fish.' Usually, this fish is an extraordinarily large pike with some anomalous traits, e.g. having one eye or three eyes, having a stubby tail as if it had been chopped off (*tölpsaba*), or with its back covered with moss.

It is not my intention, however, to concentrate on the guardian spirits of water. In a way, they represent a 'minority group' among the countless number of other water spirits that differ from them. My aim rather is to elucidate that part of folk belief connected with the demonic *näkk* who, Ivar Paulson asserts with justification, was 'known and feared everywhere in Estonia'. The name *näkk* is borrowed from a Germanic language: either from Scandinavia (the Swedish *näcken*) or from Germany (the south-eastern Estonian *näks, naks* are related to the German word *Nix, Nixe*).[3] These Germanic names are probably derived from the demonized image of St Nicholas. Felix Oinas has suggested that the purpose of giving the saint's name to

---

2 Paulson (1971), 84; see also Paulson (1963) and (1964a).
3 Paulson (1971), 93.

the dangerous spirit arises from the wish to secure its benevolence toward people.[4] (Cf. the respectful address to the water-spirit in the legend recorded by Põldmäe above.)

The *Näkk* and its Guises

There are several popular explanations of the origin of the *näkk*. Most often, drowned people were believed to become a *näkk*. Also, babies who were abandoned or drowned by their mothers were supposed to turn into these hostile creatures. In many coastal parishes, the soldiers of the Pharaoh's army who drowned in the Red Sea according to the Old Testament (*Exodus* 14) were believed to have turned into mythical water beings. The seals in the Baltic Sea have influenced the beliefs about the Pharaoh's people; they were often described as being half-human, half-theriomorphic – fish-like.[5] According to some folk interpretations, the *näkk* did not originate with drowned people, i.e. the demonized dead. They were also explained on the basis of the legend of the fallen angels who were cast down from heaven: those who dropped into water turned into evil spirits *näkk*s. There is another, lesser known belief according to which they were created by God.[6]

Many Estonian folk legends and memorates describe typical activities of the *näkk* who most often appears as a woman. Frequently the *näkk* is seen washing herself (sometimes going to the sauna); some legends mention soap, others describe a *näkk* who is drying herself with a piece of cloth. The *näkk* is often seen combing her hair (sometimes with a golden comb), singing, crying, or just sitting on the water, or on a stone near the shore. There are a few descriptions of *näkk*s doing handicraft (knitting a stocking), or washing clothes (e.g. kerchiefs). When the *näkk* realizes that somebody is observing her, she usually jumps into the water or disappears. In many legends the *näkk* is depicted as attacking people near the water in order to drown them. She seizes bathers and pulls them under the water, or lures men, women and especially children into the water.

The Estonian *näkk* is a demonic shape-shifter. Although the supernatural beings of folk religion do not have fixed forms, they tend to have certain heavily emphasized features. For example, the devil in Estonian folk legends and belief most often appears as a human being (a man, black man, landlord, and less frequently, as a woman or maiden). Zoomorphic guises are also frequent (e.g. a dog, cat, goat, horse, hare), while fantastic satyr-like guises, usually regarded as being typical of the devil, are actually relatively rare. To some extent, the *näkk* shares the same guises as the devil, but the frequency of occurrence of the various forms differs.

Usually the *näkk* appears in an *anthropomorphic* form: as a human being in green clothes (Iis), wearing a green jacket with glowing buttons (Trm), as a stranger in a boat (Rei). It appears most frequently in *female* guise as: a young maiden with

---

4 Oinas (1995), 250. See also Strakhov (1994).
5 See Loorits (1935).
6 E 26357 from Kroonlinn.

green hair, blue jacket and red stockings (Saa); a young woman (Rei); a maiden in white clothes (Võn); a woman with long light hair (Iis); a beautiful woman with golden hair (Pal); a naked woman with long hair/ long light-coloured hair/ yellow hair (Iis, Jür, Kei); a large maiden with a beautiful white body (Hag); a woman with big breasts which she throws over her shoulders while washing herself (Jõh); a woman with big breasts and long yellow hair (Tür); a naked woman, washing her big breasts (Kos); or a girl with beautiful hair and breasts (Khk).

In these descriptions we can see a clear tendency towards emphasizing the erotic aspects of the *näkk*. She is displaying her beauty by exposing her naked body, and combing her long hair which is the token of an unmarried female, i.e. 'free women' in traditional rural society. These traits are typical of narratives about supernatural beings in different North-European traditions appearing as women and seducing men in erotic encounters involving fairies, witches, revenants, forest- and water-spirits, and also the devil.[7] The female guise of the Estonian *näkk* corresponds to the ideas of medieval and early modern Christian demonology. In 1608, the learned Ambrosian monk Francesco Maria Guazzo wrote as follows about water-spirits:

> They dwell under water in rivers and lakes; and are full of wrath, they are turbulent, unquiet and fraudulent. They raise up storms at sea, sink ships in the deep, and destroy life in the waters. When such demons appear, they are more often women than men; for they live in humid places and lead a softer manner of life. But those which live in drier and harder places usually appear as men.[8]

Descriptions of *male* water-spirits of this kind are less frequent in Estonia. Such a water-spirit is sometimes described as: a black man with long black hair (Kei); black man (Kad); or a very old man (Pöi). At the same time, the male appearance has featured in personal-experience stories, such as the following:

> My uncle went fishing on a Sunday morning on the lake of Niinsaare. They saw the spirit then. He had long hair and a long beard and was combing his hair. This lake-spirit (*järvealdjas*) was a man.[9]

The *näkk* can also appear as a *child*: a red child who is walking on the water (VJg); a naked child (Mar); a small child (LNg); a small boy in a water-grey robe (Amb); a

---

7 Löfstedt (1993), 247-8. Cf. F420.5.3.1. 'Water-spirits sit on beach combing their long hair' (France, Austria); *F420.5.3.1.1. 'Mermaid Udenite sits on beach and combs her hair with golden comb' (Latvia); F265. 'Fairy bathes' (India, England, Irish myth); F420.1.2.1. 'Water-maidens are of unusual beauty' (Germany, France, Iceland, Latvia).
8 Guazzo (1988), 73.
9 *ERA* 125, 163 (18), (1936). This is a relatively rare case where the water spirit appears as a moralist, supporting Christian rules of conduct. He appears to the fishermen who have broken the prohibition on working on Sunday.

four- or five-year-old boy scabby as a toad (Kuu); a naked boy (Har). Sometimes, the legends lay emphasis on the *aristocratic traits* in the appearance of the *näkk*: she appears as a young aristocratic lady (*preili*) (Rid); a dark young lady with long black hair (Trm); or a German lady with a hooked nose and long teeth, holding a child in her lap and whisking it with a branch (Hls).

There are also several *zoomorphic* forms of the *näkk*, such as a red and white ox (Nis); a black ox; a black dog with a crooked tail (Rei); a red dog (Joh); a goat (Phl); a white foal (JMd); a white calf or foal (Vig); a white horse (Kos) or a hare (Amb). The *ornithomorphic* guises are relatively rare: a duck, as black as coal (Kos), and a black cock in one memorate (Jür). So also are the *fantastic* guises: a human being with big breasts and long hair or with a backside like a fish (Khn), or a calf with a man's head (Pöi). In one memorate the river-spirit (*jõealdjas*) appears as a grey hairy animal with the head of a human being and with a tail and hoofs (VNg). Sometimes the *näkk* is described as a *physical object*: a floating boat (Rid); a tin plate (Kos), or a golden ring (Kuu). In one legend the water-spirit (*vesihaldjas*) comes out of the river as a big hay-rick to follow the cart of the thief who has stolen firewood from the state forest (Trm).

There are legends which depict the *näkk* as a *shape-shifter*, e.g. as a small boy who grows bigger and bigger (Trm). In one narrative, the water fairy (*vesihaldjas*) appears in the sauna as a beautiful woman dressed in a long white robe. Later on, it is seen as a bird flying into the lake (Nrv). The ability to shift shapes, however, is more frequently referred to in belief accounts than in legends: it is said that the *näkk* used to appear as a maiden, combing her light brown hair with a golden comb and singing, or else she was sitting on a stone, nursing a child. Sometimes, it appeared as a horse or a cow (Tos). Occasionally, the *näkk* was seen as a human being, sometimes as a dog (Noa), or as a white horse, or as a grey man on a stone (Phl).

The two most popular types of legends about the *näkk* in Estonian folklore will now be analysed with the focus being placed on its physical appearance.

Connection of Guises with Legend Plots

Antti Aarne established only one Estonian *näkk* legend-type when he compiled his catalogue of Estonian fairy-tales and legends on the basis of the folklore collections of Jakob Hurt preserved in Helsinki.[10] According to Aarne, the *näkk* in the form of a horse lures children on its back and takes them into the sea (Fig. 1).

The following short example of a legend of this sort was recorded in Ridala parish, west Estonia:[11]

---

10 Aarne (1918), Sagen no. 58.
11 *ERA* 55, 31/2 (4), (1932).

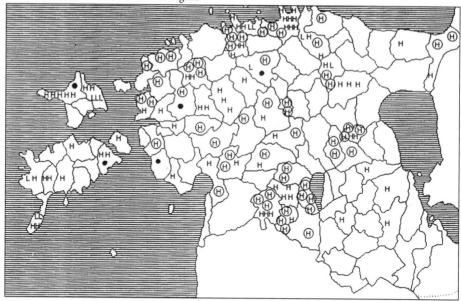

Fig. 1 : Water-spirit lures children onto his back and takes them into the water. (Aarne 1918, Sagen No. 58; MacDonald 1996, F 68). Guises of the *näkk* in Estonian variants:
H: horse; L: log; : others; O: white/grey

A white horse came out of the sea. The children climbed on its back and one of them said: 'I'll sit on top of the *näkk*.' Just as he said it, the *näkk* disappeared from under them.

There is a number of legends where one of the children mentions the name of the *näkk* or says something similar; on hearing its name the demonic being disappears, and the children make their escape. However, there are also many stories which end tragically: sometimes everybody is drowned and occasionally only one child out of the whole company is saved. In similar legends throughout Scandinavia, the *nøkk* is described as taking the shape of a horse in order to lure people, especially children, into the water. Often the intended victims are saved by saying '*nøkk*' or something similar.[12] The waterhorse of the Estonian legends is undoubtedly related to similar mythical beings in Scandinavia, Ireland and Scotland;[13] for example, a Scottish legend tells about children who are carried off into the lake when they are riding on an 'extensible' waterhorse.[14]

In Estonian tradition, the horse's colour is white or grey (no other colours have been mentioned); it is beautiful, small, young (a foal) – in one text it is

12 Kvideland & Sehmsdorf (1991), 257.
13 See Almqvist (1991a). Cf. *MLSIT*, 4086 'The Waterhorse As Work-Horse' and *MLSIT* 4087, The Waterhorse As Race-Horse' (Almqvist 1991b, 236-9)
14 MacDonald (1996), F68. The latter motif occurs in Estonia as well.

described as a foal with three legs. However, the horse-form is not the only guise of the *näkk* in this legend-type. A floating log is another traditional shape found in many parishes, often parallel to the legends about the horse.[15] Other forms, such as gates, a dining-table, a grey cow and white-girl figure, are extremely rare in the variants of this legend-type. In one text, a green duck is seen transforming itself into a horse (Pöi). The description of children sitting on the back of a water-horse which vanishes from under them might be regarded as the tableau scene (of the story) on the basis of Olrik's epic laws.[16] Horse-form as a guise of the *näkk* is a feature of this popular legend-type in particular, although it can be found in other legends also.

Let us now take a look at another, more amorphous, group of folk legends.

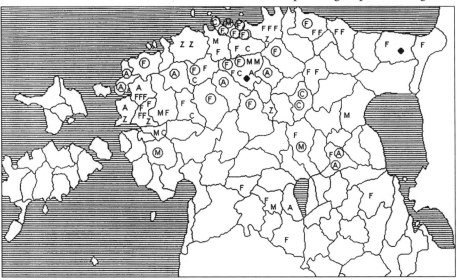

Fig. 2: *Näkk* as omen of drowning: A: anthropomorphic (gender unspecified); C: Child/boy; F: Female; M: Male; O: Naked; Z: zoomorphic/orinthomorphic;   other guises.

These are stories that speak of the *näkk* as a drowning omen (Fig. 2).

Somebody sees the *näkk* and later on it transpires that the vision had predicted someone's watery death. The following short example was recorded by Põldmäe in Viru-Nigula:[17]

Näkk is the water-spirit (*veealdjas*). If it was seen near the river, somebody was to get drowned. There was a person who drowned. Before it happened, this young lady (*preili*) was seen, she was dancing near the river. A woman got drowned there. These young ladies were said to be those spirits.

---

15 See Distribution Map (Fig. 1).
16 Olrik (1965), 138.
17 *ERA* 28, 622 (73), (1930).

In fact, there should be no close connection between the guise of the *näkk* and the tragic event which follows. One might think that any form of appearance of the *näkk* could occur here. However, as a drowning omen the *näkk* also has its preferences in terms of its guises. Most often it takes an *anthropomorphic* shape: it appears as a naked human being (Juu-2, JMd, Noa-2, Äks-2); a naked white human being (Nis); a human being (Kos, LNg, Rid); or a rider on a black horse (Trv). *Female* guises dominate: a white woman (Hlj); a young lady (VNg); two young ladies (Mar); two beautiful women (VNg); two women (VMr); a young maiden with golden hair (Kul); a maiden (Hag, Mar, Mär, Plt, Vai, Vig, Võn); a white maiden (Kuu); a maiden with red hair (Mar); a beautiful maiden (Mar); a girl with a red scarf (LNg); a naked woman (Amb, Hag, Hlj, Jõe-2, Kos, Ris, Tallinn, Tür); a naked woman with brown hair (Jõe); a naked woman with very big breasts (Kos); a fat naked woman with big breasts and long hair (Rap); a big fat woman (Jür); a woman (Jõh, HJn, Hlj, Kos, Kuu-2, LNg, VMr, Äks); a spinning woman (LNg); a woman with a kerchief, blue jacket and many-coloured skirt (Jõe). *Male* appearances of the *näkk* as a drowning omen are also traditional: a grey old man who is making a net (Kul); a gentleman in a green coat (Kir); a man (Jür, Kos); a naked man (Mih, Plt, Tln); a grey old man (Trm); an old man with a hat (Kos). Appearing as a *child* is another guise having a relatively high frequency: a naked three-year old child (Koe); a small naked child (Koe); a child (Hlj, Mär); a girl (HJn); a little boy with white hair (Kir); a naked boy with white curly hair (Jõe); or a small child (Hag).

Other guises are rare. There are only five cases when the *näkk* in a *zoomorphic* guise forebodes drowning, appearing as an animal (Kei); a goat (Kei, Rid); a dog (Jõe); a small piebald dog (Kuu). Twice it appears in an *ornithomorphic* form: as a white dove (Kos), and as a white goose (Mar). As a *fantastic* being, the 'classical' mermaid, is described once as follows: a white woman, her lower parts like the tail of a fish (Jõh). In two legend-texts recorded in the same parish, the *näkk* is seen as a *physical object* which forebodes someone's watery demise. This sinister thing is a long (tobacco) pipe (Kos-2).

The *näkk* can be regarded as one of the most evil demonic beings in Estonian folk religion. While the Devil as a protagonist of folk narratives can be neutral or even friendly, the main aim of the *näkk* in folk legends is to take life. What is striking about the guises of the *näkk* is the almost total absence of its fantastic demonic guises. This water-spirit usually appears as an ordinary human being, a nice horse, a dog, etc. There are not many traits in the descriptions which indicate its demonic supernatural nature (nudity is the most common one). How can this situation be explained?

The Meaning and Functions of the Legends

Ulrika Wolf-Knuts has written about the devil in folklore as a figure representing both nature and culture. As a fear-inducing being, the devil bears characteristics indicative of culture, but as a tempter he lures people into living a natural, unrestrained life.[18] Wild nature that is full of dangers is opposed to the world of peasants: the cultivated landscape, farms and villages. The perils of water acquire a symbolic expression in the descriptions of wild beings who have an anthropomorphic appearance but do not wear clothes – the sign of civilization. Nudity is one of the traditional features of anthropomorphic supernatural beings in Estonian folk religion. This is especially typical in the descriptions of the *näkk* who represents 'wilderness' and nature as opposed to culture. At the same time, being naked expresses the sex appeal of the spirit in female guise, displaying her feminine beauty in order to lure men into the water. The connection between female sexuality and demonism is a characteristic feature of medieval and early-modern Christian demonology and theory of witchcraft, most vividly expressed in treatises such as *Malleus maleficarum* (1487).[19] A similar mentality underpinned the popular Lutheran attitude which is expressed in Estonian belief legends about the female *näkk*, recorded in the nineteenth and twentieth centuries.[20]

There are also plenty of descriptions of the *näkk* as a young lady wearing stylish and expensive clothes, typical of the culture of country manors and towns but alien to rural society. Similar aristocratic traits are characteristic of the devil in Estonian folklore. The Evil One as a landlord can be interpreted as a clear sign of social antagonism between the local peasants and their foreign (German) masters.[21]

Let us now briefly compare the descriptions of the *näkk* with those of the devil in Estonian folk religion. The statistical breakdown of the manifestations of the devil in Estonian belief accounts, legends and memorates is as follows: 1) anthropomorphic (58.9%); 2) zoomorphic (20.8%); 3) satyr-like and other fantastic forms (15.2%); 4) natural phenomena, material objects (4.4%); 5) undetermined forms (0.7%).[22] These figures are based on the analysis of 1,723 texts from the Estonian Folklore Archives which contain evidence of the appearance of the devil.

These statistical data probably reflect the warning function of the legends about the devil. Attention has mostly been paid to his 'innocent' (mainly anthropomorphic and zoomorphic) manifestations, since one must be able to recognize him if he appears in reality. That seems to hold true also for the legends about the *näkk* as a

---

18 Wolf-Knuts (1992), 109.

19 Sprenger & Institoris (1991), I: 6. On the masculine ideals of early Christianity see Aspegren (1990).

20 One informant from Kuusalu, North Estonia has stressed that a male water spirit (*miesterahva altjas*) does not kill people. But rivers and lakes inhabited by female spirits (*naisterahva altjas*) are dangerous because such beings do kill (*ERA* 161, 393/395 (8-9).

21 Valk (1994a), 325-7.

22 Valk (1994b), 24.

demonic being, where it is seen to prefer natural guises. The statistical breakdown of the manifestations of the *näkk* is comparable to that of the devil, the main difference being that female guise dominates over male appearance while fantastic manifestations are rarer still. While the emphasis in the devil legends is mainly didactic the legends about the *näkk* convey a warning message, and there is a tendency towards eroticism which is untypical of Estonian folk belief about the Evil One. While the devil is most often associated with the colour black, the *näkk* seems to prefer white garments and guises (white horse, woman, etc.) Both black and white are the most frequently occurring colours in the descriptions of supernatural beings in Estonian folk religion.

The pragmatics of the folk legends about the devil centre around three basic points: how to avoid him; how to recognize him; and how to ward him off. The devil can be avoided by living a virtuous Christian life. It can be shown that his fantastic satyr-like descriptions in legends are related to his role as a moralist who upholds Christian values. The devil is the seducer into sin and the punisher, but the *näkk* does not have the function of supporting morals. The few legend variants of this kind can be interpreted as reflecting late Lutheran influences. The *näkk* is an evil demonic being *par excellence* – a killer. It cannot be avoided by following the Ten Commandments and Christian rules of behaviour; the only solution is to exercise extreme caution near bodies of water. Numerous legends about the *näkk* relate that children as a group are especially endangered. It is obvious that these narratives were to a great extent addressed to them and probably also to the parents who shared the belief in the *näkk*.

Ivar Paulson has written: 'As changeable as the mermaid's external manifestation was, this spirit did not have an especially outstanding or productive function in people's lives.'[23] This statement is open to contradiction. The changeable but, as a rule, 'innocent' manifestations of the *näkk* express the warning function of legends. The demonic water spirit symbolizes the dangers of water.

The Connection of the Legends with Reality
There are about 1,200 lakes and more than 7,000 rivers and brooks in Estonia. In the North, West and South, the country is surrounded by the Baltic sea with more than 1,500 islands dotting the shoreline. The eastern border faces Lake Peipsi which is the fourth largest lake in Europe. The present population of Estonia is about 1.5 million people. In the course of the last two years (1994-5), 235 Estonians drowned, most of them while swimming or boating in the sea, rivers and lakes.[24]

---

23 Paulson (1971), 93.
24 Aotäht (1996), 4. The victims of the catastrophic shipwreck of the boat 'Estonia' on the Baltic Sea (28 September 1994) are not included in this statistics. It is remarkable that out of those who were drowned, only sixteen were women. It remains open to debate, however, whether the male dominance of the victims nowadays can be connected with the female dominance of water-spirits in traditional Estonian legends. (e.g. the Scandinavian *näck* prefers male guises.)

In folk legends, the demonic *näkk* is responsible for the incidents of drowning which have been explained as violent death caused by the interference of demonic powers in human affairs. Water has proved an alien environment to the Estonian peasants, who have never been good swimmers. Tragic cases of death by drowning have occurred every so often. There are even some fatalistic traits in the legends about the *näkk* (e.g. ML 4050. *River Claiming its Due.* 'The hour has come but not the man', a legend-type well known in Estonia). They tell of the sudden and incomprehensible disruption of life which seems especially dreadful in the context of a senseless and unnatural death. The *näkk* is a mythical culprit in folk belief who has a double function: to explain cases of drowning, and to be an agent in avoiding such tragedies as a protagonist in warning legends.

Ilana Harlow has studied the connection between local tragedies and ghost stories. She shows that the local tragedy is assimilated to the traditional world view through affiliation with the legend.[25] The natural guises of the *näkk* in drowning omens, especially in the case of memorates, may have one more explanation. *Post factum*, after the tragic event, it is not difficult to remember a suspicious-looking human being or animal who was spotted near the same place where someone was subsequently drowned. In this manner, a natural situation may be interpreted later as a supernatural event, a manifestation of the numinous powers that ordain human fate. It may be said in conclusion that legends and beliefs about the *näkk* serve to relate cases of drowning to the traditional world view and provide religious connotations for them.

---

25 Harlow 1993.

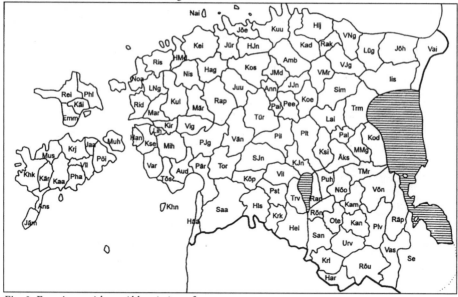

Fig. 3: Estonian parishes - Abbreviation of names

Estonian parishes

Vi - Virumaa
Hlj - Haljala
Iis - Iisaku
Jõh - Jõhvi
Kad - Kadrina
Lüg - Lüganuse
Nrv - Narva
Rak - Rakvere
Rkv - Rakvere
Sim - Simuna
Vai - Vaivara
VJg - Viru-Jaagupi
VNg - Viru-Nigula
VMr - Väike-Maarja

Jä - Järvamaa
Amb - Ambla
Ann - Anna
JJn - Järva-Jaani
JMd - Järva-Madise
Koe - Koeru
Pai - Paide
 Pee - Peetri
Tür - Türi

Ha - Harjumaa
Hag - Hageri
HJn - Harju-Jaani
HMd - Harju-Madise
Jõe - Jõelähtme
Jür - Jüri
Juu - Juuru
Kei - Keila
Kos - Kose
Kuu - Kuusalu
Nis - Nissi

Rap - Rapla
Ris - Risti
Tln - Tallinn

Lä - Läänemaa
Han - Hanila
Hps -
Haapsalu
Kir - Kirbla
Kse - Karuse
Kul -
Kullamaa
Lih - Lihula
LNg -
Lääne-Nigula
Mar - Martna
Mär -
Märjamaa
Noa -
Noarootsi
Rid - Ridala
Var - Varbla
Vig - Vigala

Hii - Hiiumaa
Emm - Emmaste
Käi - Käina
Phl - Pühalepa
Rei - Reigi

Sa - Saaremaa
Ans - Anseküla
Jaa - Jaani
Jäm - Jämaja
Kaa - Kaarma
Kär - Kärla
Khk - Kihelkonna
Kre - Kuressaare

Krj - Karja
Muh - Muhu
Mus - Mustjala
Pha - Püha
Pöi - Pöide
Vll - Valjala

Pä - Pärnumaa
Aud - Audru
Hää - Häädemeeste
Hls - Halliste
Khn - Kihnu
Krk - Karksi
Mih - Mihkli
Pär - Pärnu
PJg - Pärnu-Jaagupi
Prn - Pärnu
Saa - Saarde
Tor - Tori
Tõs - Tõstamaa
Vän - Vändra

Vl -Viljandimaa
Hel - Helme
KJa - Kolga-Jaani
Kõp - Kõpu
Pil - Pilistvere
Plt - Põltsamaa
Pst - Paistu
SJn - Suure-Jaani
Trv - Tarvastu
Vil - Viljandi
Vln - Viljandi

Ta - Tartumaa
Äks - Äksi
Kam - Kambja
Kod - Kodavere

Ksi - Kursi
Lai - Laiuse
MMg - Maarja-Magdaleena
Nõo - Nõo
Ote - Otepää
Pal - Palamuse
Puh - Puhja
Ran - Rannu
Rõn - Rõngu
San - Sangaste
TMr - Tartu-Maarja
Trm - Torma
Trt - Tartu
Võn - Võnnu

Võ - Võrumaa
Har - Hargla
Kan - Kanepi
Krl - Karula
Plv - Põlva
Räp - Räpina
Rõu - Rõuge
Urv - Urvaste
Vas - Vastseliina
Vru - Võru

Se - Setmaa

Kra - Kraasna (asundus
Venemaal)
Lut - Lutsi (asundus Lätis)

The Wizard from over the Sea:
Legend and Reality in the Seventeenth Century

BODIL NILDIN-WALL & JAN WALL

I

In the third book of his *Historia de gentibus septentrionalibus,* from the middle of the sixteenth century, Olaus Magnus treats the subject of magic and superstition. Among other things he writes about wizards and their travels across water without help of boats or other vessels. He retails one story of a man who carved charms on the bone of an animal and sailed forth as if he had the help of strong winds and perfect sails. We are also told, however, that one of these clever seafarers was finally drowned by a colleague, although he had wandered the depths of the sea. From a somewhat later period, witch trial testimonies reveal witches to have been observed sailing in small and fragile vessels such as eggshells.

Wizards had the power to render weapons useless and make themselves immune to cuts and blows. They ruled the weather and, according to Olaus Magnus, there were witches who sold wind to sailors. Three knots on a piece of string was all that was needed to work the magic: if one knot is undone a soft breeze would arise, if two a fair wind; slipping the third knot would unleash a storm that might easily sink ships.[1] Treatises on witchcraft, dating from the sixteenth and seventeenth centuries, stress the importance of wind magic on islands and in coastal areas.[2] Seas, lakes and rivers were of the utmost importance for communications. Transport for people as well as goods depended upon the strength and direction of the wind.

Winds could be bound by knots or kept in bags. A witch could let them loose to sink ships and vessels and to drown sailors and fishermen. In seventeenth-century witch trials such magic was regarded as real. There are reports of such things as favourable winds being summoned and of a cloth with three knots being cast into the sea in order to raise a storm. Were a bag of wind to be opened the water would seem to boil from the effects of gusts of wind. Certainly, it is no coincidence that, towards the end of the seventeenth century, a skipper from Gotland wrote in his log-book that a series of groundings at Easter were due to sudden, heavy squalls from all sides – as if emanating from an opened bag.[3]

---

1 Olaus Magnus ed., 1976, p. 163.
2 Nildin-Wall & Wall (1996), 212-3 and literature cited there. For Scotland, see Bruford (1967), 31-3; Bruford & MacDonald (1994), 391-4, 480. For Ireland, see Foran (1995).
3 *Ibid.,* 206.

In his third book, Olaus Magnus also tells of Kettil the wizard and his apprentice Gilbert. Both names appear in later tradition where, sometimes, Kettil is stated to be the apprentice who binds his master Gilbert. According to Olaus Magnus, Gilbert is confined in a cave under a church on the island of Visingsö in Lake Vättern. Gilbert was defeated by Kettil who owned a staff inscribed with runes. With the help of this staff, Gilbert was bound hand and foot, because anyone who touched the rune-staff got stuck to it. Kettil threw the staff to Gilbert and tricked him into trying to bite and kick himself free of it.[4] The name Gilbert for Kettil's opponent is found only in the vicinity of Lake Vättern – it is supposed to go back to Gerbert of Auvergne or Sylvester II who was Pope from approximately 940 – 1003. He suffered defamation through the slander and propaganda of his opponents and, as a result, is traditionally portrayed as a dangerous wizard collaborating with the devil. With the help of the devil he was said, *inter alia*, to have uncovered the hidden treasure of Octavian. The legend of Gilbert and Kettil was told to German visitors towards the end of the sixteenth century with the added comment that, on the island, there was still 'gewaltig viel Zaubere'. No one doubted the existence of sorcerers.[5]

In popular tradition, Kettil has been endowed with the additional name Runske, alluding to his rune-staff, i.e. a staff with runes carved on it. He is the hero of many legends, some of these legends seem to be of a literary character. Numerous, different versions of which were written down in the course of the seventeenth century. They show traits from folktales as well as picaresque novels. Kettil is the shrewd peasant boy who accidentally gets hold of a magic object – the rune-staff. With the staff in his hand he sets forth seeking adventures and fighting trolls and wizards. In some versions he is said to be almost a giant. His opponent is mostly reported to have a stronghold on an island, and is often said to be digging in order to undermine the island so as to make it sink; sometimes, it is already supposed to lie at the bottom of the sea.[6]

A recurring motif in the legends is that Kettil is said to travel over, through or under the water at the bottom of the sea – either using his own powers or in a home-made submarine. Another recurring motif is that, during his journey, he is supposed to come into contact with a very large fish. He defeats trolls and wizards on islands in different places all over the country through trickery and with the help of rune-staffs. The defeated opponents are then laid on hides and lime-wood charcoal to be held there for all eternity. In one variant from the beginning of the seventeenth century Kettil is said to have created a large glass-bottle to use as a submarine when travelling to the sunken island. Kettil was forced to contend with only one danger during the trip, namely huge snakes lying at the bottom of the sea, which could very easily have crushed his vessel.[7]

---

4 Olaus Magnus ed. 1976, pp. 165-6.
5 Ahnlund (1945), 37, 40 ff.
6 Hyltén-Cavallius (1863), 169-90; Svennung (1943), 281–305.
7 Tuneld (1934), 152.

During the sixteenth century open diving-bells began to be used in order to facilitate underwater work. Open bells of this sort were mainly shaped like church-bells and were submerged with a diver inside. The air inside was compressed and the water inside rose only to a certain level, depending on the depth. The first diving-bell in Sweden was constructed in the seventeenth century and was used *inter alia* in the period 1663-65 to salvage cannons from the Wasa – a disastrously designed flagship that was incapable of sailing and sank on her maiden voyage and which, nowadays, is housed in a purpose-built museum in Stockholm.

Kettil Runske also used a diving-bell, and a mobile one to boot. In a legend written down in Gotland – a large island in the Baltic Sea – in 1696, it is told how a young wizard living on Öland – the other sizeable Swedish island in the Baltic – is sent for. His instructions are to confine to his grave the ghost of one who had murdered a priest. No name is given to the wizard in question, but there is no doubt that Kettil Runske is the one intended. To get from Öland to Gotland, he walked the bottom of the sea inside a glass. The only danger he encountered was a large fish – the mother of eels – which swallowed him. For three days he was inside the eel, but eventually he got out and succeeded in completing an otherwise uneventful trip. It may be asked why he did not choose to sail, a method of transport which would certainly have been both safer and more comfortable than travelling underwater. The answer is simple – in earlier versions he was supposed to make for a sunken island controlled by a troll and bride-ravisher.

In Gotland the wizard outwits the ghost and defeats him with the help of his rune-staff. The murderer of the priest is at first confined to his grave with lead, with the wizard declaring: 'Lie till it rots!' The ghost answers: 'So be it, I'll outlive that.' The hide of a bear is then thrown over him and the wizard says: 'Lie there one year for each hair!' The ghost answers: 'I'll live that long, it will end sometime.' Then the wizard threw coals of lime-wood charcoal over him and said: 'Lie there till they rot!' The ghost answered: 'They never will!' Thus he was rendered harmless.[8]

The legendary wizard was fetched from Öland to Gotland to intervene in a difficult situation and avert a crisis. The dead priest-murderer and ghost constituted a plague to the neighbourhood by not keeping to his grave. The ghost was a danger to each and every one, and its existence was regarded as a shameful thing. The wizard outwitted the ghost and everything was put to rights. This is the sort of narrative that was current in Gotland and other places during the seventeenth century, alongside stories of contemporary living wizards.

---

8 Register to the manuscripts of O. V. Wennersten, no IX: 117, Visby Landsarkiv, Gotland. Printed in extenso by Läffler (1903-8), 38 ff. In Gotland, the legend of Kettil Runske has merged with legends of priest murders and hauntings (Läffler 1903-8).

II

In the middle of the seventeenth century there lived a man called Christian Snipp in Öland. He was a ropemaker and manufactured his products from pine-wood. He travelled about selling his wares, which were greatly valued by men who won their living from the sea. He often went to Gotland and even lived there for longer or shorter periods. Christian Snipp had been a soldier during the Thirty Years' War and had taken part in the battle of Lützen where the Swedish king, Gustavus Adolphus II, was killed.

Decades after that event, he was to tell a court of law in Öland that he had been very frightened during the battle. It seems, however, that he had been wiser than the king, since, with the help of a friend who owned a Black Book, he had rendered himself immune to bullet and sword. Snipp and his friend had called forth Satan – who had showed himself as a man or a bird – several times during the campaign. To be on the safe side Snipp had borrowed the book before the battle, but lost it in the heat of the fight. His friend had become angry and had demanded compensation for his missing property. In court, Snipp said he could not remember what the book had looked like. No one believed him, because it was well known that he was versed in magic and that he himself by all accounts was the owner of a Black Book.

Christian Snipp had sailed from his native island of Öland to Gotland during the spring of 1651 and had immediately come into conflict with the law. He had business to transact in a certain place on the island. District court documents show that he had arrived there together with his wife, another elderly woman, and a young boy. They had encountered bad weather and had been driven off course, and so had had to put in at one of the two islands called Karlsöar, west of Gotland, and stay there for a couple of days. These islands were normally used by inhabitants of the main island (Gotland) as pasture for sheep. When Snipp and his company left their port of refuge, some sheep were found to be missing. Salted herring and a kettle had also disappeared from a shed on the island. A search had been instigated for the stolen goods, which were subsequently found in Snipp's possession.

In court, Snipp explained that the elderly woman and the boy who had accompanied him from Öland had had no food for the crossing. When they found themselves storm-bound on one of the islands, the woman had slaughtered a young lamb and the boy a slightly older animal in order to get food. The woman confirmed that in her hour of need she had committed this crime, but the boy swore that it was Christian Snipp who had slaughtered the sheep. He also declared that Snipp had promised his parents in Öland to provide for him during the journey and that he would find him a master in Gotland.

Snipp denied everything for as long as he could, but in the end he was forced to confess to the thefts. He was sentenced to be hanged, according to the law. He stood in little danger of suffering the supreme penalty, however, as the sentence had to be submitted to the Court of Appeal and, as a rule, death penalties for theft were commuted by the higher court to a short prison term. The old woman who had confessed also received a death sentence, while the court – taking into account his age and considering how easy it was to lure a child into sin – acquitted the boy. It is not certain whether Snipp stayed in Gotland for a time after his term in prison or immediately returned to his native island, but we do know that he kept up his contacts with Gotland for, about twenty years later, he is once again mentioned in legal documents from the island – being at that point reported for the use of magic and ownership of a Black Book. Clearly, the man from Öland was a notorious wizard.

In 1670, an old man called Per Oförstånd – 'Peter the Fool' – was imprisoned in Gotland. The case against him for being a wizard was clear-cut and it was thought that he would be sentenced to death. It was said to be common knowledge that he was the owner of a Black Book. Oförstånd denied the accusation concerning the book, but confessed to having received copies of some charms from the wizard from Öland – Christian Snipp. The two of them had met at a farm, Hallinge, in Grötlingbo in southern Gotland, where Snipp had been a frequent guest.

Christian Snipp was sent for from Öland to be brought to trial in Gotland in company with his apprentice Per Oförstånd. As in the legends of Kettil and Gilbert, it is uncertain who may have been the teacher and who was the pupil. It looks as if both of them had been dabbling in magic before they met. The wizard Christian Snipp arrived by mail-boat from Öland. The farmer who rowed the boat brought a letter from the constable there which stated that, in his native island, Snipp had a reputation for magic. Farmers from the Swedish mainland sought his help in retrieving goods stolen by magical means. The constable urged that, when Snipp was being sent back to Öland, he should not be released till the constable was actually on the beach.

In the autumn of 1670, the two accused were brought to trial in southern Gotland and, afterwards, Christian Snipp was sent home. Early in 1671, he was again brought before a judge in Öland. The record of that interrogation shows that the court had access to notes made in Gotland the previous year. According to this information, Per Oförstånd had testified that Christian Snipp had written down three charms for his use when they were staying together at Hallinge, in the parish of Grötlingbo. Snipp was questioned about it and declared that he had written down only one formula, which had been dictated to him by the court. It seems clear that he had had to leave a sample of his handwriting, probably for comparison with the notes found in Oförstånd's possession. Unfortunately, as the charms were not taken down we have no means of knowing what they were.

When questioned about the meaning of the formulas, Snipp denied that he understood them. The subsequent question, namely whether he also denied having associated with Oförstånd at Hallinge, was answered by him in two different ways. First, he declared that he could not deny having known Oförstånd at Hallinge, as he had lived there for ten years. Then, he immediately contradicted this reply by saying that he had only visited the place for a couple of days three years previously. That was before Oförstånd, whom he considered to be half mad and of no fixed abode, had ever got there; he had met him and spoken to him, but only on his way between two farms in that parish.

Christian Snipp was then examined on another charge. He was accused of having borrowed gunpowder in order to make calm weather (*blek*), down by the sea. He answered that he had borrowed powder in order to make a fire at his boat and that he had not used it for any other purpose. The court suspected Snipp of having been engaged in working magic on the shore – of having tried to still the wind. As Snipp well knew, for a wizard who often crossed the sea in a small open boat, weather magic was a matter of the utmost importance.

Snipp was ordered to confess the truth with the threat that, sooner or later, he would be forced to do so; if not in court, the truth would emerge elsewhere. The accused answered with an oath and declared that he would never admit to such things. Even if they were to persist forever and a day, the devil could take him before he would confess anything. Needless to say, this somewhat undiplomatic response did nothing to improve Christian Snipp's situation.

The interrogation resumed. When questioned about some money he owned, Snipp declared that his son Olof had exchanged it with Oförstånd. Snipp had earned the money through selling pine-wood ropes. He was told that, when examined in Gotland, he had said that he could have earned a lot of money had he owned a Black Book. The court proved to him that he had made such a statement and declared as its opinion that the existence of the money indicated he still possessed such a book.

Christian Snipp had been examined several times during his imprisonment in Gotland. He now stated that Oförstånd, when they were both questioned by the governor in Visby (Gotland), had confessed to knowledge of more than the three charms the present court knew about. Proceedings from that hearing were apparently not available, so Snipp's statement was disregarded. The draft of a letter still extant proves, however, that he was telling the truth, at least in part. This letter demands that a judge in the southern part of Gotland should see to it that some people from that part of the island made their way to Visby in order to testify concerning the magic book Oförstånd was supposed to have got from Christian Snipp. Meanwhile, in Öland, the latter once more stated that he was not in possession of a Black Book. The examination was abandoned at that point. The court declared that Christian Snipp no longer belonged to the communion of the faithful and he was then locked up.

As he is referred to in a subsequent Öland trial in which his son Olof was prosecuted, Snipp was probably sentenced to a short term in prison and released after a time. About a year after his father's trial, Olof was caught by some farmers and hauled off to the castle of Borgholm. There he was imprisoned, and a long and complicated trial followed. Finally, he was sentenced to run the gauntlet. This punishment involved having to run between two long rows of men armed with sticks and cudgels. Each individual was to hit the condemned man as hard as he could, otherwise he himself was liable to be forced to run the gauntlet too. To avoid the gauntlet, and certainly with devious ulterior motives, Olof Christiansson Snipp confessed to a whole string of crimes in order to be condemned to death. Such a sentence would buy him time as it would have to come before the Court of Appeal.

While awaiting the judgement from the higher court Olof was imprisoned in the castle of Borgholm. Although he had been clapped in irons, he succeeded in escaping after a couple of months. The men responsible for the prisoner the evening he disappeared were later questioned. A guard had stayed in an outer room where there was a lighted fire and a candle on the table. In spite of that, suddenly Olof Snipp was found to have vanished from the prison cell and was nowhere to be seen. According to the guard, it was utterly impossible for the prisoner to have passed him in any natural way without being spotted. In his opinion, Olof Snipp had been aided by the devil, or, as he put it: 'Nothing good brought him out of the cell where the stocks are, and out of the castle, that time.'

We do not know what happened to the runaway after that, or to his father, Christian Snipp the wizard, but in Gotland there was still talk of the Black Book. At a district-court session in 1673, a church-warden from a parish in southern Gotland had to clear himself and his family of a rumour that had been circulating for a couple of years – namely that he, the warden, was guilty of witchcraft. The story was that he had taken over the Black Book from Per Oförstånd.[9]

When a crisis threatens an individual or a community, popular tradition recommends that help be sought from a man or a woman with knowledge of the supernatural world that exists parallel to the human world. Such a person was often

---

9 Nildin-Wall & Wall (1996), 106–15.

called a witch or a wizard. It is also well known that a person living far away was considered to be more powerful than an individual who lived in the immediate neighbourhood: no one is a prophet in his own country. Here, legend and reality follow the same pattern. The wizard from Öland existed in both worlds. The legend about him was told in Gotland during the same period as the wizard in reality from Öland was caught and examined. It is quite possible that the latter had also been called to Gotland on an errand involving magic, as implied by the court in Öland.

The legend of the priest-murderer was documented at an early period in six parishes in Gotland – one of which is Grötlingbo, the parish Christian Snipp was bound for and the parish where he resided for longer stretches of time. Only marginal reference is made to the magical knowledge and actions of the two wizards in extant documents. Christian Snipp had partaken in rites meant to call up the devil; he had rendered himself immune to bullet and sword; he had been consulted in the matter of retrieving stolen goods and exposing thieves; he had probably practised some kind of weather magic; and he owned a Black Book. People from the Swedish mainland sought help from him at his Öland home, an indication that his reputation had spread far beyond his native place. He was a much sought after and quite notorious wizard.

III

It is hazardous to compare a legendary figure to a man from real life, but, nevertheless, there are some interesting points of connection between the wizard of legend and the wizard of reality. They both brought their magic tools on their journeys. Even were we not to have Christian Snipp's confession, it would be safe to assume that he had owned some written formulas and that he had used them to gather riches during his sojourns in Gotland. We might ask whether or not these formulas contained runes, and further speculate if he was called upon to bind ghosts and spectres. Apparently, the detailed minutes that were taken during the initial trial which might provide answers to these questions have been lost and, while it is entirely possible that such was the case, we have no proof of it. We may observe, however, that formulas used to call forth, to bind and to dominate good as well as evil forces are common in the so-called Black Books. Reference is made to such charms in connection with other individuals searching for buried treasures in Gotland in or around the same time.[10]

Formerly, Gotland had been a very wealthy place, a circumstance demonstrated, *inter alia,* by treasure consisting of pieces of silver and coins found buried in the ground. That the earth contained silver was no secret, but to be able to abstract it therefrom one had to resort to magic. Supernatural guardians of the treasures had to

10 *Ibid.,* 90, 102 ff.

be mastered. When excavating mounds the dead had to be bound to their graves for the attempts to succeed. The services of a man with a reputation for magic would have been in great demand in connection with such enterprises. We may speculate that Christian Snipp was made welcome in Grötlingbo and not only as a ready supplier of pine-wood ropes. That area had long boasted large fertile farms owned by rich and powerful men, men with interests in fishing, trading and shipping. Riches lay buried there. We may conclude that it is quite possible that Christian Snipp was engaged to help in unearthing such treasures.

Be that as it may, at some point during the process of narration, the legendary wizard and the real one have merged into one character. We are fortunate to possess an interview from the 1950s that helps to prove this. A man from the parish of Lärbro, in northern Gotland, whose mother had been born and bred in Grötlingbo, but had moved to Lärbro, knew the legends of the priest-murderer – the tradition still has a very strong hold in Lärbro. When this informant described how people exposed to the haunting of the ghost finally had to send for the wizard from Öland, he also gave him a name. The wizard, he said, was called Snippen – the colloquial seventeenth-century name borne by Christian Snipp.

Although the linkage between legend and reality is recent and inconclusive, the two stories we are dealing with are products of the same century and the same environment. It is true that the seventeenth-century legend seems to be literary rather than oral, and it is doubtful if it was well known in Gotland, in the recorded form, during the seventeenth century. The live wizard's story – as we know it – has been pieced together from different sources and comes to us unfolding in the wrong order and full of gaps and omissions. His real business or his insights into magic are matters of conjecture and impossible to prove. Still, in both cases the order of events is highly similar and shows a common structure.

Kettil Runske	Christian Snipp
famous wizard	notorious wizard
owner of magic object (rune-staff)	owner of magic object (Black Book)
fetched from Öland to avert crises	travels from Öland on business
hazardous journey achieved by magical means	hazardous journey
crises averted	business accomplished (?)
(reward)	brought to trial
	(son later freed from prison by supposedly magical means)

357

The wizard in reality is punished for his magic, while the legendary one is, supposedly, rewarded. Kettil is sought after because his knowledge and competence are necessary for the whole community, which is under threat because a ghost will not stay in its grave. Snipp, on the other hand, was sought out by private citizens. His accomplishments might have been considered the same as Kettil's, but the documented tasks he undertook are less spectacular – wind-magic and the retrieval of stolen goods. In all probability, other kinds of magic that included charms were also known to him.

In the legendary form, society condoned acts and behaviour that served the good of the community by preserving values to which everyone could ascribe. In the real world, Christian Snipp was a convicted thief and the authorities apparently kept a close eye on his activities. But the acts he was supposed to be capable of performing were also of great importance to the whole community. For communities where fishing and trade held considerable economic value, an ability to control winds and weather must have been seen as a desirable accomplishment. The possession of a Black Book undoubtedly signified a Satanic pact, but so also, according to ecclesiastical reasoning, would the possession of rune-staffs or other magical objects.

Thus there is a discrepancy between the official attitude and official sanctions and the attitude and sanctions inherent in the legend. The events of the legend seem to have taken place in the dim and distant past. Nevertheless, seventeenth-century people apparently still found themselves in need of services and rituals of the very same kind. It seems safe, therefore, to conclude that – so long as the wizard was on their side – individual members of society, in spite of the various legal and ecclesiastical sanctions, condoned these acts, both in fiction and reality.

Maritime Referents in Irish Proverbs

Fionnuala Williams

Like the sea, the proverb repertoire is ever changing. Thus the current expression, *as useless as rearranging deckchairs on 'The Titanic'* would have been as meaningless to people before that ill-fated vessel's collision with an iceberg in 1912, as many a more ancient saw is now to us. In this spirit, the present paper offers a survey of those proverbs which are obviously concerned with the sea from the oral tradition past and present. Since the vast majority has been preserved out of context, like fish out of water, the focus must needs be on those proverbs which actually contain maritime referents, although it should be borne in mind that, when talking about the sea, many different kinds of proverb were and are used. I have included here proverbs drawn from both the Irish and English languages in Ireland. Where they exist, English-language counterparts – rather than literal translations – of proverbs in the Irish language are supplied. For proverbs quoted only in English, Irish-language versions are usually to be found.[1]

Proportion of Sea Proverbs

One is struck immediately by the fact that, with the exception of a few well-known proverbs, such as *Bíonn súil le muir, ach cha bhíonn súil le cill*[2] —*There is hope from the sea but no hope from the cemetery*[3] and *'Sin méadú ort!' arsa an dreoilín nuair a rinne sé a mhún san fharraige*[4]—'*Every little helps,' as the jinny-wren said when she pissed in the ocean,*[5] only a few common proverbs draw on the sea to illustrate their traditional wisdom.

A case in point is the Schools' Manuscripts Collection in the Department of Irish Folklore at University College Dublin, which dates from 1937-8 and which includes thousands of proverbs from oral tradition. Fifteen per cent of the proverbs from one of the counties included in this survey (the inland county of Monaghan) contain animal referents, whereas only about two per cent refer to bodies of water and associated phenomena. Interestingly, in the case of an equivalent corpus from

---

1 Author's editorial method: The sign — is used to separate variants in different languages; the sign / is used to separate translations of proverbs by editors of proverb collections etc. from the original, while square brackets denote author's translations.

2 Ó Muirgheasa (1976), No. 570(d). Here, and throughout, I supply specific referenced examples.

3 *IFC S* 219:15 (Leitrim); *IFC S* refers to the Schools' Manuscripts Collection in the Department of Irish Folklore, University College Dublin. The first figure is the volume number and the second the page number.

4 Literally: '*That will add to you!' as the wren said when he urinated in the sea*, Rosenstock (1993), 14.

5 Murphy (1990), 118. Slieve Gullion refers to the Slieve Gullion mountain area in the south of county Armagh. For comments on this proverb and citations in English from Great Britain and North America see Mieder & Kingsbury (1994), Introduction xvi and entry No. 730, etc.

Wexford in the extreme south-east, a maritime county which is bounded on two sides by the sea, no significant shift in these proportions is observed. Here, the small total of approximately two per cent not only includes all proverbs with particular aquatic reference, whether salt or fresh, but also several which could be applied to *any* body of water, for example, *Still waters run deep*, and oblique references such as *When you're not fishing be mending the nets.*[6]

It is evident from the Schools' Manuscripts Collection that proverbs ostensibly featuring sea referents are to be found even in inland counties; for example, *Any port in a storm* and *There is many a kind of a pebble on the beach*,[7] have both been recorded in the land-locked county of Monaghan. One possible difference, however, in the proverbs belonging to inland rather than coastal counties is that the coastal environment offers an enhanced potential for maritime variants. *Do not loose* [lose] *the ship for a halfporth of tar*,[8] for instance, may occur more frequently near the coast than *Don't loose* [lose] *your sheep for a halfpenny worth of tar;*[9] while the weather saying (a genre closely connected with proverbs) *A red sky* [or *rainbow*] *in the morning is the shepherd's warning* may sport more variants with *sailor* rather than *shepherd.*

This last saying is based on Biblical sources which, for most European languages, have proved to be a rich source of proverbs. How many biblical proverbs, we might ask, actually mention the sea? Wolfgang Mieder has listed over four hundred proverbs found in modern English which are derived from the Bible,[10] but most people would probably be greatly surprised to learn that only one of these mentions the sea – namely, *All rivers flow into the sea* – a proverb which has been duly recorded in Ireland in both English and Irish. It is also noteworthy that, of the one hundred and six pan-European proverbs in a comparative collection by Gyula Paczolay,[11] not a single one in any common version mentions the sea directly although six could possibly be said to indicate some degree of relationship to it: *A man drowning will catch at a straw; It is good fishing in troubled waters; The cat would eat fish but would not wet her feet; Big fish eat little fish; Fish and guests smell in three*

---

6 *IFC S* 929:139 and *IFC S* 936:227 respectively; both from county Monaghan. For an example in Irish of the former see Ó Muirgheasa (1976), No. 100(b); the latter proverb has not as yet been noted in the Irish language.

7 *IFC S* 945:46 and *IFC S* 942:73 respectively; neither has as yet been noted in Irish.

8 *IFC S* 202:21 (Leitrim). 'Halfporth' is a contracted form of 'halfpennyworth' meaning 'a very small quantity' (*OED*).

9 *IFC S* 200:170 (Leitrim). Irish-language examples noted in Ó Muirgheasa (1976), No. 968(b), for example, refer solely to sheep. Irish *caora* (sheep) and *long* (ship) or *bád* (boat) are not homophonous. However, clearly, other factors exist in the establishment of variants and the coastal connection is obviously paramount in the inclusion of ship in the Manx version of the proverbial expression: *milley yn lhong son feeagh-lherg dy herr/to spoil the ship for a ha'porth of tar.* See Kneen (1978), 76.

10 Mieder (1990).

11 Paczolay (1997). By 'pan-European proverbs' is meant proverbs common to at least twenty-eight (in other words, more than half) of fifty-five living languages of Europe (and thereby represented in various language groups). I am most grateful to Dr Paczolay for supplying this information prior to the publication of his work – see Paczopay (1997).

days, and *Fish always begin to stink at the head.*[12] The small amount of maritime proverbs evident in Ireland takes on an additional significance in the light of what appears to be a general dearth of such material elsewhere.

In his masterly survey of European proverbs,[13] Archer Taylor says 'Proverbs which show themselves to be the invention of sailors are not abundant'.[14] He goes on to list the few printed collections of sea proverbs which exist: these include sea proverbs in Dutch, Frisian, German, English and French. As far as I am aware, no special collections of Irish maritime proverbs have been published, nor have maritime proverbs ever been presented as a group within any published work. A collection of sayings from a coastal *Gaeltacht* [Irish-speaking area] in south Donegal known as *Teilionn na nEasg* ['Teelin of the fish'] made prior to 1947 by Seán Ó hEochaidh,[15] a full-time collector with the Irish Folklore Commission, does not appear to have a higher proportion of sea proverbs than any other general collection.

The works of regional writers might also constitute another potential source of sea proverbs, as the concordance of idiomatic expressions in Séamus Ó Grianna's writings compiled during the last decade by Ailbhe Ó Corráin indicates.[16] Ó Grianna's short stories and novels describe the Donegal coastal communitiy where he was born in 1889, and Ó Corráin's concordance notes just over two hundred proverbs – three per cent of which are maritime. This represents a slight, though not marked, increase on the proportion in the general collections.

Common Themes in Irish Maritime Proverbs

There are, roughly, three common themes discernible in Irish maritime proverbs, namely, the sea itself, sea-faring craft and, lastly, sea creatures and produce. There are, indeed, several proverbs which mention the sea directly, in addition to those which, like the above pan-European examples, could be taken as referring to any body of water. Several proverbs also contain references to vessels and fishermen, and others mention particular sea species, not only fish, but also some other sea creatures and products such as salt and seaweed. The important part that seaweed played as a fertilizer on island and coastal farms is highlighted by its being afforded a place in

---

12 *Ibid.*, Nos. 81, 83, 70, 91, 58 and 97 respectively. Only No. 81 and three others have any (and this is a very small number – three or four) versions or synonyms which mention the sea. An intriguing discovery made while annotating this paper is an Irish-language synonym for Paczolay, *op. cit.*, No. 38: *Do not sell the bear's skin before the bear is caught* etc. – *Cuir an breac san eangach sula gcuire tú sa phota é* [put the trout (small fish) in the net before you put it in the pot]. Only four other similar versions – in Albanian, Bulgarian, Estonian and Livonian have been noted by Paczolay; the Irish version appears in Rosenstock (1993), 62, a work published after material was already submitted for inclusion in Paczolay's work.
13 Taylor (1962).
14 *Ibid.*, 14.
15 Ó hEochaidh (1955).
16 Ó Corráin (1989).

the proverb record as the culminating best old thing: The three best old things – an old lamb, an old piglet, and old seaweed.[17]

The first of these categories, proverbs which refer to the sea itself, is undoubtedly the smallest. Here a unique characteristic of the sea, that is, the tide, often features. For example:
Trí nithe a chuaigh d'Arastatail a thuiscint: intinn na mban, obair na mbeach, agus teacht agus imeacht na taoide.[18] —
Three things you cannot comprehend: the mind of a woman, the working of the bees and the ebb and flow of the tide.[19]

In enumerative proverbs such as the above, the oral tradition in both languages of Ireland generally follows the epic law of the weight of the stern, where the most significant item is the last one. In triads, if there are two non-human items and one human, almost invariably the human item is the culminating one; however, in the variants known to me of this particular triad, the sea is placed last, making it the ultimate inscrutable thing. It would be worthwhile to examine further variants to see if this order is consolidated.[20] The order is also significant in that the opportunity to be more chauvinistic, an opportunity not often missed, is deferred.

Once more addressing the tide, a metaphorical proverb, *A rising tide lifts all boats*, has gone down in history linked to Seán Lemass (who was Taoiseach [Prime Minister] from 1959 to 1966) because of his use of it in characterising a phase of rapid economic development.[21] I have also noted its contemporary use by a prominent county Antrim farmer working under the shadow of BSE (*Bovine spongiform encephalopathy*) who was quoted in a daily newspaper as saying: 'We just keep on doing as good a job as we can but *when the tide comes in it takes all the boats* – if beef gets a bad name we all go down whether we're in quality assurance schemes or not.'[22]

This category, although limited in extent, contains one of the commonest proverbs in the English language in Ireland, viz. *Time and tide wait for no man.* This proverb is also known in Irish, but with a noteworthy difference – the English-language versions almost invariably mention *time* as well as *tide* but the Irish-language versions often include variants which mention only the tide, as in the following instance: *Ní fhanann tráigh le fear mall.*[23] This exemplifies a rather rare disparity between the English- and Irish-language versions and warrants a deeper investigation of the

---

17 Champion (1938), 57, No. 508. This is a translation from the original Irish; I have yet to find an English-language version of this proverb.
18 Literally: *Three things which Aristotle failed to understand: the minds of women, bees' work and the coming and going of the tide*, 'An Seabhac' [otherwise P. Ó Siochfhradha] (1984), No. 2322.
19 *IFC S* 958:177 (Monaghan).
20 All three versions under No. 4080 in Ó Máille (1952), also follow this order.
21 Coakley & Gallagher (1993), 97.
22 *The Belfast Telegraph*, 22/3/1996, 7: 'Beef Crisis: is it safe?'
23 Ó Máille, *op. cit.*, lists versions under No. 2953 – six with *time and tide* and four with *tide* only. Both variants are recorded in English literature – see Wilson (1970), 821, 822.

development of this particular proverb in Ireland. Also to be considered in this category is proverbial material about the sea as the epitome of the endless quantity of water which can never be emptied, as in the above-metioned proverb juxtaposing the tiny wren's contribution to its vastness. Finally, the sea's quality of fluidity is sometimes utilised, for example, in the following proverb:

Trí nithe is giorra 'na bhfanann a rian, .i. rian éin ar chraoibh, rian luinge ar linn agus rian fir ar mhnaoi. —

Three things which leave the shortest traces, bird on the tree, ship on the sea, man's company on woman.[24]

Here, in this intriguing triad, the contrasting elements of air, water and earth are combined, using the sea to symbolise one of them. This version is found in the Ó Longáin collection published by T. F. O'Rahilly in his *A Miscellany of Irish Proverbs*, a collection made up of a mixture of oral and literary proverbs in which O'Rahilly distinguishes this particular proverb as being 'popular' or oral, rather than literary at the time in question viz, the early nineteenth century.[25]

The next category of maritime proverbs which occurs in Ireland is that concerning sea vessels. In the Irish language there are many examples of proverbs containing the word *bád* ['boat'], a word which can mean either a small inshore craft or a ship, and there is also a significant number which use the word *long*, which can only be a ship or large, ocean-going vessel. We observe that while, in all likelihood, the smaller craft would have been of more immediate relevance to people in their day-to-day existence, the impact and strong visual image of the larger vessels is not ignored in the Irish proverb record.

Allied to boats are the fishermen themselves, and the life of the fisherman is depicted as hard and precarious as in the following proverb: *Deireadh iascaire an mála/the fisherman ends in taking the bag (to beg)*. This proverb, so far only noted in Irish, is quoted in Dinneen's Irish/English Dictionary.[26] This well-known work includes approximately seven hundred proverbs, mainly drawn from Irish oral tradition. As most *Gaeltacht* areas are located in coastal regions of Ireland it is likely that the vast majority of the proverbs in Dinneen's work is drawn from areas near the sea and one might, therefore, expect a higher proportion of them to contain sea referents. However, only three per cent of them do so, and this situation is also reflected in Scottish Gaelic proverb collections which, to a considerable extent, were gathered in island communities. Here, the proportion of proverbs with maritime

---

24 O'Rahilly (1922), No. 233. An English-language version has yet to be found. Similar versions were popular in sixteenth-century English literature – see Wilson (1970), 817-8.

25 I would like to take this opportunity to highlight the enormous contribution to proverb scholarship which Professor O'Rahilly made. In the *Miscellany*, for example, he identifies early Irish literary versions as well as contemporary oral versions in Irish, Scottish and Manx Gaelic, and in Welsh, and also in Scots and English, of the proverbs he lists. As a result the lengthy Irish pedigree of several aquatic proverbs can be traced.

26 Dinneen (1927), 703 under *mála*.

referents is similar to the Irish experience. In T. D. Macdonald's collection,[27] for example, sea proverbs represent less than two per cent of the total.

In the last of the common themes occuring in Irish maritime proverbs – sea creatures – it is immediately obvious that the creatures referred to in the proverbs are mentioned for one of three main reasons (or, frequently, for any combination of these): they refer to an aspect of the economy, usually food; they possess a unique characteristic; or they represent certain human traits metaphorically. While Irish waters abound in a variety of fish few are harvested, and even fewer species are eaten locally. Two named species stand out in the proverb record beyond all others, namely, *bradán* ['salmon'] and *breac* ['trout'], species which are referred to again and again in various other genres of narrative, and also in the older literature and placenames. Salmon and trout are, therefore, more than simply part of the diet but can be regarded as being present in the proverbs as cultural 'markers' with deeper significance. On a prosaic level, neither species is confined to the sea but also occurs in fresh-water habitats; thus their physical presence is widespread. They have even given rise to a parallel version, in both Irish and English, of the common proverb *A bird in the hand is worth two in the bush,* namely, *A trout in the ashes is better than a salmon in the water.*[28] The word *breac,* however, can also be used as a general term for any small fish caught by hook, and here, therefore, we find one of the many instances where knowledge of English-language versions of proverbs in Ireland could profitably assist the study of proverbs in Irish.

As well as salmon and trout a few other named species of fish, such as herring and mackerel, hake and sprat, have achieved a place in the proverb repertoire. The herring is often unfavourably compared with the salmon in the same proverb, although this fish would have been much more of a mainstay of the ordinary diet than salmon, and the ocean itself at one time was colloquially called the 'Herring-pond'.[29] Before the Great Famine years, herring was eaten in every single county in Ireland, not only fresh when in season, but also salted as a foodstuff throughout the year.[30] Herring was even more important in the Manx diet and economy, as the proverb *No herring, no wedding*[31] indicates. In fact, research into Manx marriage-records has shown that there were fewer weddings in years in which herring catches were low.[32]

---

27 Macdonald (1926).
28 *IFC S* 950:419 (Monaghan); for an example in Irish see Ó Muirgheasa (1976), No. 906(c).
29 Traynor (1953). Under *herring* three sources refer to the Irish [North?] Channel and one to the Atlantic Ocean as the 'Herring pond'; all date to approximately the first half of the twentieth century.
30 Clarkson & Crawford (1988), 171-92, especially 175 and Map 3.
31 Wood (1894), 229-74, No. 135a. A version in Manx is recorded in Kneen (1978), 5: *Gyn skeddan, gyn bannish* , [literally: *without herring, without wedding*].
32 Killip (1975), 79: 'For many people there was almost complete dependence on the herring fishing, and it has been noted that in the parish registers there was direct correspondence each year between the number of marriages recorded and the success or failure of the herring season.'

In addition to named species, the general term *fish* often occurs. These occurrences may be either in proverbs which are metaphors for human life, for example, *There's just as good fish in the sea as ever came out of it*,[33] meaning that there are plenty more potential partners; or in medical proverbs. The latter kind of proverb often employs the generic term *fish* to advise on its use in the diet, for instance, *Uisce i ndiaidh éisg agus bainne i ndiaidh feola,* meaning water is the best drink after fish and milk after meat, and *Snámhann an t-iasg beo agus marbh* [34] meaning, literally, that *the fish swims alive and dead.* While such proverbs provide an insight into the nature of Irish diet and attitudes to it, their international distribution should not be overlooked. Archer Taylor has identified French and English versions of the latter proverb, for instance, and pointed out that the belief that fish should be accompanied by liquid can be traced right back to classical Rome.[35]

Some other sea creatures such as the seal and whale, and shellfish, are also represented. Here, the proverb repertoire is related closely to other types of lore and also provides a good insight into aspects of folklife. As well as scale-fish, Ireland abounds in shellfish, but few species are locally utilised in any way. Top quality oysters and periwinkles are exported, while only cockles and limpets have played any significant part in the traditional diet of the recent past. Limpets, in the proverb record, reflect the general attitude to them – that they were but poor fare. While the humble limpet may not be celebrated as tasty food, the proverbs portray this simple creature as a force to be reckoned with, as the following example demonstrates: *An báirneach, an breac, is contabhairtighe sa bhfairrge,*[36] which translates as *the limpet is the most dangerous fish in the sea.* One explanation put forward for this reputation of the limpet is that it lives on rocks concealed at high tide and could, therefore, be a hazard to some types of craft. Another reason given in popular tradition is the limpet's supposed ability to hold fast a human being who tries to remove it until the tide comes in and drowns him. This alludes to the folktale AT105 *The Cat's Only Trick.*[37] In its standard form the protagonists in this tale-type are a cat and a fox, and it has been collected in Ireland in this form. However, there is also a succinct by-form where the protagonists are almost always a limpet and a fox, sometimes said to be the last fox in a certain area – Rathlin Island off the Antrim coast in the extreme north,[38]

33 *IFC S* 949:488 (Monaghan); for an Irish-language version see Ó Muirgheasa (1976), No. 382(c).
34 Ó Máille (1948), Nos. 1731 and 1727 respectively; for an English-language version of the latter see O'Farrell (1980), 62.
35 Taylor (1962), 125.
36 Ó Máille (1948), No. 2281; an English-language version of this has yet to be found.
37 Aarne & Thompson 1961, Tale-type 105.
38 Murphy (1975), 140, entry No. 117: 'I heard it told on the Island that the last fox in Ireland - or the [last] one on Rathlin – was drowned by a limpet on the shore. The fox came along and went to lick the limpet and it closed its shell on him and held him by the tongue till the tide came in and drowned him.' Michael Murphy, with whom I had the pleasure of doing fieldwork as a student, worked for many years as a full-time collector for the Irish Folklore Commission and later for the Department of Irish Folklore. He collected on Rathlin in 1954 and 1955 and this version is as he remembers hearing it there. With it I pay my respects to a gifted collector who died in May 1996, just before the Symposium.

or Corca Dhuibhne (the Dingle Peninsula), county Kerry in the south-west.[39] The by-form has also been collected in Scotland where two Scottish Gaelic metrical versions were noted by Alexander Carmichael.[40] As well as the Connacht proverb which reflects this folktale it is also represented in a wellerism, or quotation proverb, two variants of which were collected in Munster, probably in the Dingle Peninsula. One of these goes as follows:

> '*Airiú, nach é an fear é an bairneach,*' *mar a dúirt an mada rua.*[41]
> [Indeed, isn't the limpet some man!' as the fox said].

So much is conveyed in this ostensibly simple allusion – land meets sea, and the sea triumphs. The renowned tenacity of the limpet is referred to in the common current expression *to cling like a limpet*. No doubt the relationship between the different genres would prove difficult to unravel, but that it would be a task offering great potential for research is exemplified by Bo Almqvist (1982-83) in his exposition of the connection between another quotation proverb and a fable in *Siúl an Phortáin*[42] ['The Crab's Walk'].[43]

Sea Proverbs and Other Genres

In detailing proverbs about shellfish I have already embarked on the third aspect of this short paper – the relationship between maritime proverbs and other genres of folklore. The proverbs about limpets are connected to a folktale and the nature of this relationship has not yet been fully explored. One sea proverb often forms an integral part of another narrative. This concerns a hero who, unwittingly, is dining with an enemy. A servant, sympathetic to the hero, warns him by using the proverb 'A herring was never caught by its belly'.[44] This is a reference to the fact that a herring cannot be caught by a baited hook, and it conveys to the hero the message that he has been compromised. The hero understands the metaphor while his enemies are oblivious to its meaning. Ríonach uí Ógáin has studied versions of this anecdote in which the nineteenth-century politician Daniel O'Connell is the hero.[45] In many of the versions, the Irish language, known to the servant and O'Connell but not to the others, is used to convey the warning but it is noteworthy that, in some versions, a

---

39 *IFC* 702: 207; collected in 1940 in county Kerry; *IFC* refers to the Main Manuscripts Collection in the Department of Irish Folklore, University College Dublin.
40 Carmichael (1928-71), Vol. 4, 10/11; the material in this collection dates largely to the second half of the nineteenth century. In one version the protagonists are a limpet and an oyster-catcher (*Haematopus ostralegus*) while in the other they are a limpet and a rat.
41 'An Seabhac' (1984), No. 1001, see also No. 1002; English-language versions have yet to be found. The version and explanation in Rosenstock (1993), 54/55, are most likely derived from 'An Seabhac' – personal communication from the author, January 1996.
42 Almqvist (1982-83); in his summary he notes that the folktale has only previously been recorded in Latvia and Poland.
43 Aarne & Thompson (1961), Tale-type 276 *Crab Walks Backward: Learned from his Parents.*
44 *IFC* 1569:162 (Louth); recorded by M. J. Murphy in 1962.
45 uí Ógáin (1995), 119-75, especially 150-6. In the O'Connell versions, his drink or food is poisoned.

proverb metaphor – The herring isn't caught with bait – replaces the use of a language not intelligible to the enemy. This provides an indication as to how much proverbs were considered to belong to the group sharing the lore. In this case the narrative clearly hinges on the inclusion of the proverb (or similar code). A similar anecdote in which this proverb performs the same function is told of other hero figures in Ireland.[46] When this proverb forms part of a toast such as 'Here's to the herring that never took a bait!' the allusion may yet be to a narrative of this kind, particularly in view of the fact that the hero is often offered a poisoned drink.[47] Examples of such proverbs detached from the narrative can be found in Ó Máille's finely-detailed collection of Connacht proverbs.[48]

So far I have exemplified a maritime proverb which is probably in itself a condensed folktale, and also a proverb which fulfills a role in another narrative context. The latter has also been recorded as a toast and as a blessing and, we might add – like proverbs in general – maritime proverbs, particularly enumerative ones, can shapeshift into yet another genre, namely, the riddle. As we have already seen, O'Rahilly has identified a riddle version of the three things which leave the least trace.[49] This particular proverb/riddle is deeply embedded in the Irish tradition and its international occurrence should also be noted; I have heard a current Middle-Eastern proverb version which is perhaps not altogether surprizing, as its origin is most likely to be found in the Old Testament *Book of Proverbs*, chapter 30, verses 18-19.[50]

The final genre which I would like to consider here, in this section on sea proverbs and other genres, is folk belief. Several of these beliefs were referred to in the course of the symposium, mainly in connection with legends. A fair number occurs in proverb form, for example, *Caithfidh an fhairrge a cuid fhéin a fhagháil* [51] — *The sea must have its own* and *Ní dhéanfadh an grán aon talamh ar rón/Shot will*

---

46 For example, see Shaw (1930), 71-2. Sean McPherson, nicknamed *Seán Bearnach*, a county Tyrone outlaw, possibly of the eighteenth century, was invited to dine with the Brown family who had secretly notified the authorities that he would be there: 'The sarvint-girl [servant girl] that was hired at Brown's looked out over the half-door and lo and behowld ye there was the Yeomen from Clogher marchin' up the street. She was afeard [afraid] the Browns would kill her if she gave a sign to the Tories [outlaws] so she snapped [snatched] up the can like as if she was goin' to the well and jooked [darted] out of the house. As she went past the window she looked in at the Tories and she riz [raised] the chime of a song in Irish: "God love the herring that never was catched on a bait".' Collected by Shaw on the Monaghan/Tyrone border.
47 Joyce (1979), 111. This example is from Carlow and dates to the mid-nineteenth century.
48 Ó Máille (1948), No. 2349.
49 O'Rahilly (1922), No. 233; see p. 363 above for the proverb version: The riddle which was not fully quoted by O'Rahilly, but kindly supplied by Stuart Ó Seanóir, Manuscripts Department, Trinity College Dublin Library, runs as follows: *Cia híad na trí luirg nach bhfaghtar? Lorg luinge ar uisge, lorg éin air eiteóig, agus lorg mná tar éis coimhriachtain ria* [*What are the three traces which are not found? The trace of a ship on water, the trace of a bird flying and the trace of a woman after union with her*].The manuscript is now catalogued TCD MS 1381; the riddle begins at line 10 on p. 183.
50 *Idem.*
51 Ó hEochaidh (1955), 67, No. 305.

not kill a seal.[52] In their relationship with most genres maritime proverbs follow the pattern of non-maritime proverbs. However, there would appear to be a large number of beliefs about the sea in proverb form, no doubt reflecting the awe in which the sea is held. Expressing a belief in a set proverb form gives it an added potency.

Current Sea Proverbs

Finally, I would like to focus briefly on current proverbial lore. Some of the best-known proverbs today are of the maritime variety: *Ní shéideann gaoth nach seolann duine éicin* — *It is an ill wind that blows nobody good,*[53] *Is mairg a báidhtear i n-am an anaithe,*[54] often rendered in English-language versions simply as *After a storm comes a calm*[55] and, of course, *Time and tide* ... In addition to full-blown proverbs many proverbial phrases retain a currency. In a single issue of the *Business Telegraph,* a slim weekly supplement to the *The Belfast Telegraph,* I noted the following, all of which are also common in everyday speech: 'Tourism specialist, ICC, may well be the first *to dip a toe in the water* here,' '*Don't miss the boat,*' 'The company *landed the trophy,*' '... the IDB *runs a very tightly managed and well run operation*' and '*in a dramatic change of tack*'.[56]

Conclusion

Both historically speaking and in terms of current tradition it would seem that throughout Ireland there is a rich variety of maritime referents in proverbs. Although the proportion of sea proverbs is small compared with the overall total, nevertheless, there are indications that it may be higher than in other places. Some of the most widely and frequently used proverbs are maritime proverbs, while maritime proverbial

---

52 Dinneen (1927), 1166 under *talamh* ; this proverb has not yet been noted in English.

53 Literally: *A wind does not blow in which somebody is not sailing,* Ó Máille (1948), No. 1896, and *IFC S 934:41* (Monaghan).

54 Literally: *Woe to the person who is drowned in the storm,* Dinneen (1927), 43 under *anaithe.* A commonly-found Irish-language version of this proverb is exemplified by the English translation in Champion (1938), 50, No. 176: *Alas for him who is drowned in the storm which soon gives place to sunshine.* The proverb is based on the Old Testament Psalm 107 verse 29: *He* [the Lord] *maketh the storm a calm, so that the waves thereof are still.*

55 *IFC S 929:135* (Monaghan). Variations on this form of the proverb are currently very popular as newspaper captions; see, for example, *The Belfast Telegraph* 29/8/1996, 8: 'Playing calm with stormy music, the title for a recital review by 'Rathcol' who goes on to say 'The Rachmaninov, as one might expect from this composer, is tremendously difficult, but [the young pianist Finghin] Collins was completely in his element in this often storm-tossed music'. It is also being used currently to advertise beer on roadside billboards, for example, between Belfast and Dublin (see p. 370). One such billboard portrays two immense glasses of beer and carries the heading 'The storm before the calm' above the brand name and its catchphrase 'Kilkenny the Cream of Irish Beer'. The proverb was selected to emphasize the difference between Kilkenny and other beers, that is, that it needs some time to settle in the glass in the same way as stout; the campaign, consisting in total of ten billboards, began 9/9/1996 and was devised by Irish International (Details kindly supplied by Kilkenny Marketing).

56 'Business Telegraph' *The Belfast Telegraph* 16/1/1996, 1, 3, 16; ICC (Industrial Credit Corporation), a Dublin-based bank and IDB (the Industrial Development Board of Northern Ireland).

phrases abound. Alongside old referents, which maintain a stubborn existence, new referents, such as the twentieth-century Belfast-built *Titanic*, can be observed entering the repertory, whether locally or from abroad.

Acknowledgements

I would like to thank Bairbre Ní Fhloinn MA (Archivist/Collector Department of Irish Folklore) for her help in the preparation of this paper and my erstwhile professor, Bo Almqvist, for inspiring me to tackle this subject. Unpublished material from the archive of the Department of Irish Folklore, University College Dublin, is presented here by kind permission of the Acting Head of the Department of Irish Folklore.

THE STORM BEFORE THE CALM

The Cream of Irish Beer

Fig. 1. : Miniprint of billboard advertisement for Kilkenny beer designed by Dave McLoughlin of Irish International. Original in colour. Reproduced by courtesy of Guinness Ireland Ltd.

Implicit Context and Folk-Belief Records

Ulrika Wolf-Knuts

Folklore material, as collected at the turn of the century, has been criticised for its lack of context. We seldom know anything of the situation in which a folklore text was recorded, and we can only imagine that it fulfilled some kind of need for the interviewer. Probably he asked for it and the answer – that is, the text – satisfied his curiosity. We know even less what the authentic situation was like when somebody told the story with no collector present.

For some time this deficiency has been regarded by some scholars as very serious, as if the collections from olden times had no value at all. What kind of context are these scholars demanding, and is the lack of it really so serious that archive material is incomprehensible without it? We have to admit that in folklore texts from this period the situational context is usually completely lacking. This has consequences for scholars whose main interest lies in performance and field work i.e. in function. But is it also serious for researchers interested in other questions concerning folklore? To me it seems tempting to consider the demand for detailed knowledge of the situational context as yet another expression of the well-known folkloristic weakness, namely, the search for authenticity and genuineness. In this paper it is my intention to present some critical reflections on the missing context in a corpus of empirical material concerning water-spirits, which was collected among Finland-Swedes around the year 1900.

It is methodologically incorrect and unjust to accuse a folklore text of weaknesses which are due to the cultural prerequisites prevailing when the material was collected. If we, a century later, condemn it as unusable we fall into a methodological trap, because our predecessors cannot possibly have been aware of what coming generations would demand from folklore records. Second sight is a topic worth studying by folklorists, but it should not be a quality demanded of them!

In reality, archive material is surrounded by a lot of context. A century ago, the Finland-Swedish material was collected in order to show that this group of people had its own folklore different from Finnish folklore. In the type of research employed at that time, diffusionism was one of the most important interpretive methods. History was in effect the background for most kinds of humanistic research: where, when and how had a cultural phenomenon arisen and how did it change? This also means that the motifs occurring within recorded folklore records were central. When we, today, evaluate our archive material, however, the context of the folklore student – his scholarly milieu – is considered to be of the greatest importance. Consequently, our present critique should not be concerned with the lack of knowledge of context and function, but with scrutinizing the opportunities which we have to use the material for the analysis of motifs. If, in some cases, more use can be made of the old material it is a stroke of luck, an additional asset.

Bengt Holbek said that the archive material lacks context, but also that it is still possible to read and understand it because we know a lot about life in the society from which it was collected.[1] So, when I examine the traditional material on lake - and sea-dwellers in the Swedish parts of Finland around the turn of the century, I will consider it against the background of what we know about society at that time thanks to other disciplines like history, economics or geography. This means that the archive material does not lack context altogether – it just lacks some kinds of context that are in fashion today, but it does have the cultural context which we need in order to begin to understand it. Furthermore, the text itself, without context, is itself quite understandable as an aesthetic piece of reading material. Like any written text, it is capable of being understood and of being interpreted according to the needs, attitudes and associative skills of the reader. In this sense, every reader creates his own context at the very moment that he reads a folklore record.

Water-spirits appear in different genres in Finland-Swedish folklore. Memorates, legends, statements and fictions are, besides fairy tales and ballads, the usual kinds of folklore which people have concerning water-dwellers. Many such dwellers are female, such as mermaids and maids of the rapids, of the marsh or the lake. The female water-spirit is often described as naked, being beautiful from the front whereas her back is ugly – for instance hollow-shaped. Her hair is dark or fair, or she may wear a blue dress.

Water-spirits can also be male, like the old man of the sea or lake or the *näck*, the fiddler in the stream, similar to the Scottish kelpie. He is a distinguished gentleman or a bearded old man. The spirit can be a small new-born child, or, on the contrary, be of tremendous size. As an animal the spirit can appear as a horse, a pike, a bird, a sheep, a dog or a billy-goat. It can, indeed, also appear as a fish-trap, a steamship or a dark boat. Folklore itself does not presuppose any exclusive sex or special visual traits in the spirits. It most often tells just of a woman or a man or an old man, and only the fact that the editor of the text has categorized it as a spirit gives a hint that the woman or man is not human. In this way the editor has created his own kind of context.

Encounters of humans with water-spirits are often described. The effect of the meeting can be positive for man, who may indeed receive help from the spirit. For

1 Holbek (1981), 138.

instance, the spirit may tell when a storm is coming and prevent a man from going out in his boat. The spirit may feel gratitude towards a man and thus reward him with fish or favourable winds, or save him from being shipwrecked. The effect of the encounter can also be negative. The spirit may pull a bathing person under water till he drowns, or a man may be tempted to have sexual intercourse with a mermaid – which would lead to dangerous consequences. Another spirit may abduct the hostess on a farm; or the *näck* may teach a young man to play music, at the cost of his soul. A spirit may also frighten children or deprive the fishermen of fish. The functions of these kinds of texts can vary widely – they might have a didactic purpose, or they might express a belief, or they might merely constitute a good story.

Rather more often, however, the water-spirit and the human being have no real contact at all – a man only sees the spirit and nothing more happens. Most of such texts are local but neutral in purpose, being generalized belief-statements lacking a point. There is, for instance, a group of texts from Swedish Finland which tell of a water-spirit with long dark or fair hair and breasts that are so big or long that she throws one of them over her shoulder when she washes the other one. A human being – mostly a man or boy, but also possibly another woman – observes her. This is the point of most of the texts.[2] One text tells of how the spirit provides the fisherman with great catches;[3] one describes how the man, due to a curse by the spirit, starts to long for her till he dies;[4] two of them mention how the silence is interrupted by the man, with the consequence that the spirit vanishes;[5] and another two of them say that the man flees because of fear.[6] The following is from Storpellinge:

> In the Glosträsket, a small fen at Ölandet (Emsalö), in ancient times lived a mermaid. Once an old man from Mattas came to the fen, as she sat on the opposite shore washing herself. She had such big breasts that she threw them over her shoulders washing now one, now the other.[7]

The economic system of a society has been used as a means by which to understand folklore texts. For instance, Gunnar Granberg (1935) considered the tradition of the forest-spirits against the background of economic systems in Sweden, in order to explain why attitudes towards the spirits varied between the northern and the southern parts of the country. The idea of limited good (Foster 1965) can also be illustrated by accounts of water-spirits. Ecological aspects, too, have been observed, because of the prerequisites which such aspects entail for folklore (Löfgren 1981). These texts could probably also be studied as indications of belief.

---

2 Wessman (1931), no. 439:1-5, 7, 9-10, 12-15; 483:1.
3 *Ibid.*, 491:1.
4 *Ibid.*, 478:3.
5 *Ibid.*, 439:8, 11.
6 *Ibid.*, 439:6, 16.
7 *Ibid.*, 439:2.

After all we have a varied genre-distribution: one fairy tale,[8] one memorate,[9] three legends,[10] but mostly belief statements.[11] The question is, however, do they tell anything more than that in the Swedish parts of Finland there has been a conception of some kind of figure connected with water? Most of them do not explain anything of what people really believed in. We do not even know whether the informant himself believed in a water-spirit when he told the story. Belief has been a topic often discussed by students of folklore, and the old material has been seen as illustrative of belief, at least when the genre involved is counted as a genre of belief. So scholars have maintained that people tended to believe more in legends than in fairy tales, and it is accepted that the tellers of legends and memorates seldom make up a text intentionally. Normally, it is presumed that the informants are honest and that they do not invent their stories simply to please the collector. Knowing tradition and how it works, however, makes it possible for anybody who takes part in it to use its ingredients, and also to consciously create a memorate without having had the supernatural experience that folklorists often expect and see as a necessary condition for the trustworthiness of the text. Besides that, belief can vary greatly. What a person believes in as a young man or woman need not remain unchanged during all his or her life, nor even during part of it. When context is lacking we cannot say anything of the function of a text or of its potential for belief. We cannot give any qualitative statements, but we can – with the motif as a basis – say something about the contents and ideas found in the texts.

Another angle of analysis could be that the texts indicate conflict settlement. The texts, however, do not explicitly mention any conflict at all. Everything is complete harmony; but, if one takes into consideration the role sexuality played in rural Finland-Swedish society, the texts start to make sense. In this society extra-marital sexual relations were not approved of, and nakedness was considered shameful except for visiting the sauna. When a man without shame stares at a naked woman with extraordinarily big breasts, he is very close to the limit of what is considered appropriate.

As a corollary, one can ask whether the texts describe a beautiful woman, an erotically exciting woman, a mother figure or an old woman beyond sexual attraction (Schenda 1978). Beauty varies over time and in social class, and is very much a cultural construct (Krammer 1969). This means that it is impossible to tell if these texts express aesthetic values except where it is expressly stated that the woman was beautiful. Some texts say that she was good-looking only from the front, while her back was ugly in some way or other. Two exceptions, a tale,[12] and a belief statement,[13] describe her literally as handsome or as having a pretty face. Most of the

---

8 *Ibid.,* 478:3.
9 *Ibid.,* 439:6.
10 *Ibid.,* 466:1; 491:1; 500:7.
11 *Ibid.,* 439:1-5, 7-12, 14-6; 456:1; 483:1.
12 *Ibid.,* 478:3.
13 *Ibid.,* 491:1.

texts do not tell whether or not the woman herself was considered beautiful, neither do they value big breasts as a sign of beauty. Only one of them, a legend, tells that the water-spirit gave milk to a child, that is, that the breasts were used in a biological way. It might be possible to look upon these texts from the angle of the classic pair of concepts of madonna versus whore. If the big or long breasts are seen as a means of nursing – in other words, if it is possible by comparison to draw wider conclusions from the only text that we have telling about this – the madonna part of the pair is consolidated. On the other hand, if we want to see a whore in the female water-spirit, this is possible if we remember the role of sexuality in the society of that time and take into consideration folk tradition on female spirits in general, where erotic traits are central.[14]

Jochum Stattin has shown that the Swedish water-beings can be seen as guardians of boundaries in time, space and social aspects, turning up when man transgresses some kind of norm. It is possible to regard, at least the accounts of when man and spirit meet in the morning, as records of passing a boundary between night and day or darkness and light. The majority of these Finland-Swedish texts, however, cannot be understood as accounts concerning the passing of a time limit, and therefore cannot be taken as explanations of norm-transgression.

Is it then possible to apply Stattin's view of space circumstances to the Finland-Swedish material? Where does the man look at the spirit? Both can be on the same shore;[15] or the spirit can be sitting on the opposite shore,[16] on a rock,[17] on the path to the shore,[18] on the water,[19] on a stone in the water;[20] or she may be moving from water to land.[21] A special place-name is usually mentioned,[22] but in no case is this place said to be dangerous or otherwise forbidden to visit. Neither time nor place are thus connected with limits in this small body of material. The knowledge gained from related studies has not so far helped in understanding these texts.

Seen as a guardian of borders, the water-spirit prevents man from crossing them. Hence it might be expected not to find any contact between spirit and man, and so indeed is the situation. There is no mention of transgressed norms, such as hunting on Sundays, drinking too much, playing cards, or swearing. Neither is there very often any well-known border in time or in space. The limits referred to by Stattin are not very clear, nor are they consistent in this material.

---

14 Holbek & Piø (1967), 58, 72; Granberg (1935); cf. Schenda (1979), 959.
15 Wessman (1931), no. 439:4, 12; 478:3.
16 *Ibid.*, 439:16.
17 *Ibid.*, 456:1.
18 *Ibid.*, 478:3.
19 *Ibid.*, 439:1, 6, 10.
20 *Ibid.*, 439:7; 500:7.
21 *Ibid.*, 466:1.
22 *Ibid.*, 439:1-3, 5, 7, 8, 10, 11, 12, 14, 15; 483:1; 491:1.

Nevertheless the accounts seem to entail some kind of limit which man is not allowed to cross. If the spirit is an erotic one, the male viewers might be expected to try to get into contact with her. This usually does not happen in the belief-statements, nor in the legend, but a better case could be made for the fairy tale. This latter tells of a young fisherman who had intercourse with a female spirit and, shortly afterwards, when on the recommendation of the priest he tries to shoot her with a silver bullet, he dies. The question may be asked, why does this kind of text not take advantage of the situation and tell of a man seducing an erotically stimulating woman?

Extra-marital sex was not the only practice to be rejected in this society. Sexual intercourse with animals was considered to be much worse. This is clear from several Swedish court records from the seventeenth and eighteenth centuries. No such contact should take place between man and animal. If it did take place, it was a clear sign of the interference of the devil, a tradition known from the Middle Ages in the case of demons called either *succubi* or *incubi*. The devil often appeared as an animal and the witch had intercourse with him at Blåkulla, which earned the witch capital punishment. The punishment for bestiality was the same. Interestingly enough, these kinds of abnormal sexual behaviour are connected: a person in Swedish Hälsingland accused of intercourse with animals admitted that he also had sexual intercourse with the female water-spirit.[23] So we can possibly look upon these texts as stories telling about men who felt tempted by water-spirits resembling beautiful women from the front, but who did not yield to the temptation.

Gunnar Granberg (1935), in his psychological analysis of the forest-spirit tradition, discusses this idea – the female spirit tries hard to entice the masculine human into sleeping with her, but very seldom succeeds. Granberg explains the tradition by the practical fact that the man has been isolated from his wife or other women for a long time and therefore has sexual dreams. In legends Granberg finds that the human often triumphs over the supernatural spirit. The fact that the Finland-Swedish texts do not go into details, but only tell that a man has seen a beautiful water-spirit and has not touched her, can be explained by the circumstance that this tradition is mostly from a lake district, where the man is not out fishing for weeks or months, but is able to satisfy his sexual needs at home with his wife. Accordingly, it is possible to regard these as erotic texts describing a temptation to which the man does not yield. They may be regarded, moreover, as texts describing the borderline for what was not an appropriate folklore tradition – at least for printing in a scholarly book. The more or less national romantic aims of the collector and editor are relevant to all of this.

---

23 Liliequist (1992), 152.

To sum up, it is clear that we have to qualify the claim that archive material lacks context. It is true that some kinds of context are not available, but much more can be provided. Relevant to the general context are the more or less conscious aims and intentions of collectors, editors and readers, combined with scholarly facts from related disciplines. These remain important for the understanding of the folklore record, because folklore is always part of the surrounding culture.

Bibliography

AARNE, A., (1913), *Leitfaden der vergleichenden Märchenforschung, FFC* 13, Hamina.

– (1914), *Der tiersprachenkundige Mann und seine neugierige Frau: eine vergleichende Märchenstudie, FFC* 15, Hamina.

– (1918), *Estnische Märchen- und Sagenvarianten, FFC* 25, Hamina.

AARNE, A., & THOMPSON, S., (1961), *The Types of the Folktale, FFC* 184, Helsinki.

AHNLUND, N., (1945), 'Kettil Runske och Gilbert', *Saga och sed,* 37-42.

ALEXANDER, M., (1980), trans., *Old English riddles from the Exeter Book,* London.

ALLCROFT, A.H.A. , (1924), *Downland Pathways,* London.

ALMQUIST, SOLVEIG, (1984), *Gengångarföreställningar i svensk folktro ur genreanalytisk synpunkt,* Stockholm.

ALMQVIST, B., (1971), 'Niða(n)agrísur', *Arv. Tidskrift för nordisk folkminnesforskning* 27, 97-120.

– (1978-81), 'Scandinavian and Celtic Folklore Contacts in the Earldom of Orkney', *Saga-Book of the Viking Society* 20, 80-105.

– (1982-83), 'Siúl an Phortáin. Friotalfhocal agus Fabhalscéal (AT 276)'. *Sinsear, The Folklore Journal* 4, 35-62.

– (1990a), 'Upp flöt lever och lunga. En preliminär omtuggning av problemen rörande de nordiska vattenhästsägnernas ursprung', *Inte bara visor. Studier kring folklig diktning och musik tillägnade Bengt R. Jonsson den 19 mars 1990 (Skrifter utgivna av svenskt visarkiv* 11), 15-42, Stockholm.

– (1990b), 'Of Mermaids and Marriages', *Béaloideas* 58, 1-74.

– (1991a), 'Waterhorse Legends (MLSIT 4086 & 4086B). The case for and against a connection between Irish and Nordic tradition', *The Fairy Hill is on Fire! Proceedings of the Symposium on the Supernatural in Irish and Scottish Migratory Legends, Dublin 7 - 8 October 1988, Béaloideas* 59, 107-120.

– (1991b), 'Crossing the border. A sampler of Irish Migratory Legends about the supernatural', *The Fairy Hill is on Fire! Proceedings of the Symposium on the Supernatural in Irish and Scottish Migratory Legends, Dublin 7 - 8 October 1988, Béaloideas* 59, 209-78.

– (1992a), trans., *Färingasagan,* Södertälje.

– (1992b), 'En norsk sjødraug i fornisländsk litteratur', *Sólhvarfasumbl saman borið handa Þorleifi Haukssyni ...,* Reykjavík.

– (1996), 'Gaelic/Norse Folklore Contacts', *Irland und Europa im früheren Mittelalter*, edited by Próinséas Ní Chatháin & Michael Richter, Stuttgart, 139-72.

– (1997), 'Before Columbus. Some Irish Folklore Motifs in the Old Icelandic Traditions about Wineland', in Josephson (ed.), 225-52.

ALMQVIST, B., Ó CATHÁIN, S. & Ó HÉALAÍ, P. (1987), eds., *The Heroic Process. Form, Fiction and Fantasy in Folk Epic*, Dublin.

ANDERSEN, N., (1895), *Færøerne 1600-1709*, København.

ANDERSON, A.O. & ANDERSON, M.O. , (1961), *Adomnan's Life of St. Columba*, London (revised by M.O. Anderson, *Oxford Medieval Texts*, Oxford, Clarendon Press, 1991).

ANDREASSEN, E., (1976), '"Ófrættatíðindi". Om varsel i færøysk folketradition'. Magistergradsoppgave ved Institut for folkeminnevitskap. Universitetet i Oslo (Unpublished).

ANDREWS, A.L., (1909), ed., *Hálfs saga ok Hálfsrekka*, (*Altnordische Saga- Bibliothek* 14), Halle.

ANDREWS, ELIZABETH, (1913), *Ulster Folklore*, London.

AN SEABHAC – see Ó SIOCHFHRADHA.

AOTÄHT, A., (1996), 'Tänavu suvel uppus Eesti veekogudes 43 inimest', *Postimees*, 9 September 1996, 4.

ARNARSON, Örn, (1949), *Illgresi*, Reykjavík.

ÁRNASSON, Jón, (1961), *Íslenzkar þjóðsögur og ævintyri*, ný útgáfa (Árni Böðvarsson og Bjarni Vilhjálmsson önnuðust útgáfuna), 1-6, Reykjavík.

ARENSBERG, C. M., (1950 [1937]), *The Irish Countryman*, New York [London].

ARENSBERG, C.M., & KIMBALL, S.T., (1940), *Family and Community in Ireland*, Cambridge, Mass.

ARVIDSSON, A., (1993), ed. *Muntligt berättande.Verklighetskonstruktion och samhällsspegel*, Umeå.

ASBJØRNSEN, P.C. & MOE, J., (1960), *Norwegian Folk Tales from the Collection of Peter Christen Asbjørnsen and Jørgen Moe*, Oslo.

ASPEGREN, KERSTIN, (1990), *The Male Woman. A Feminine Ideal in the Early Church. Acta Universitatis Upsaliensis (Uppsala Women's Studies. Women in Religion* 4), Uppsala.

ATLANTIC EUROPEAN RESEARCH (1990) 'The Blaskets: a Heritage Report', Part 1 (unpublished).

AUDEN, W.H., (1968), *Secondary Worlds*, London.

BALLARD, LINDA-MAY, (1983), 'Seal stories and belief on Rathlin Island', *Ulster Folklife* 29, 33-42.

BASCOM, W.R., (1954), 'Four Functions of Folklore', *Journal of American Folklore* 67, 333-49.

BATTAGLIA, F., (1991), 'The Germanic Earth Goddess in *Beowulf*', *Mankind Quarterly* 31, 415-6.

BECKETT, A., (1911), *The Wonderful Weald and the Quest of the Crock of Gold*, London.

BÉASLAÍ, P., (n.d.), ed., *Songs, Ballads and Recitations by Famous Irishmen: Arthur Griffith*, Dublin.

BENEDIKTSSON, Jakob, (1950), ed., Arngrimi Jonae, *Opera latine conscripta, in Bibliotheca Arnamagnaeana* IX, Copenhagen.

– (1986), *Íslendingabók-Landnámabók, ÍF* 1, Hið íslenzka fornritafélag, Reykjavík.

BERGIN, O., BEST, R.I., MEYER, K., O'KEEFFE, J.G., (1910), eds. *Anecdota from Irish Manuscripts*, Halle A. S.

BEST, R.I., BERGIN, O., O'BRIEN, M. A., (1954-67), *The Book of Leinster*, Vols. 1-5, Dublin.

BERRY, P., (1987), *More Wexford Ballads*, Wexford.

BIELER, L., (1953), *The Works of St. Patrick*, London.

BJERSBY, R., (1964), *Traditionsbärare på Gotland vid 1800-talets mitt. En under sökning rörande P. A. Säves sagesmän*, Uppsala.

BOBERG, INGER M., (1966), *Motif-Index of Early Icelandic Literature* (Bibliotheca Arnamagnæana), *Vol. XXVII* Copenhagen.

BÖÐVARSSON, Árni & VILHJÁLMSSON, Bjarni, (1954-5), eds., *Íslenzkar þjóðsögur og ævintyri, safnað hefur Jón Árnason*, Vol. 1, Ný útgáfa, Vol. 3 Nýtt safn, Reykjavík.

BOER, R. C., (1924): 'Gylfes Mellemværende med Aserne', *Festschrift til Hugo Pipping* (Svenska Litteratursällskapet i Finland 175), 17-24, Helsingsfors.

BOURKE, ANGELA, (1993), 'Fairies and Anorexia: Nuala Ní Dhomhnaill's "Amazing Grass"', *Proceedings of the Harvard Celtic Colloquium* XIII, 25-38.

– (1996), 'The Virtual Reality of Irish Fairy Legend', *Éire-Ireland* 31, 1 & 2, 7-25.

BREEN, R., (1984), 'Dowry Payments and the Irish Case', *Comparative Studies in Society and History* 26, No. 2, 280-96.

BRIEM, Ólafur, (1945), *Heiðinn siður á Íslandi*, Reykjavík.

BRIGGS, KATHARINE M., (1970-1), *A Dictionary of British Folk-Tales in the English Language*, Vols. 1-4, London.

– (1978), *The Vanishing People: A Study of Traditional Fairy Beliefs*, London.

BRIMNES, ANNA, (1992), 'En beskrivelse af huldrenes betydning i den færøske forestillingsverde'. Speciale til magisterkonferens. Københavns Universitet. Institut for folkloristik. (Unpublished).

– (1993), 'Forestillingen alom sækvinden i vestnordisk tradition', in Chesnutt & Larsen (eds.).

BROMWICH, RACHEL, (1961), *Trioedd Ynys Prydein,* Cardiff.

BROWN, A.C. L., (1943), *The Origin of the Grail Legend,* Cambridge.

BROWN, T.T., (1979), *The Fate of the Dead: Studies in Folk Eschatology in the West Country after the Reformation* (*Mistletoe Series* 12, Folklore Society), Ipswich & Totowa.

BRUEN, MÁIRE COMER & Ó hÓGÁIN, D., (1996), *An Mangaire Súgach,* Dublin.

BRUFORD, A. J., (1967), 'Scottish Gaelic Witch Studies', *Scottish Sudies* 11, 13-47.

– *(1969), Gaelic Folk-Tales and Mediaeval Romances,* Dublin.

– (1987), 'Oral and Literary Fenian Tales' in *Fiannaíocht. Essays on the Fenian Tradition of Ireland and Scotland,* in Almqvist, Ó Catháin & Ó Héalaí, 25-56.

BRUFORD, A.J. & MacDONALD, D.A., (1994), eds., *Scottish Traditional Tales,* Edinburgh.

De BURGH DALY, MRS. (1980), ed., *Percy French, Prose & Parodies,* Dublin. Reprint.

BURNE, C.S. & JACKSON, G.F., (1833-6), *Shropshire Folk-Lore,* London.

BUSS, R.J., (1973), *The Klabautermann of the Northern Seas. An Analysis of the Protective Spirit of Ships and Sailors in the Context of Popular Belief, Christian Legend, and Indo-European Mythology* (*Folklore Studies* 25), Berkeley, Los Angeles & London.

BYRNE, F.J., (1973), *Irish Kings and High-Kings,* London.

CAMPBELL, J.F., (1969), *Popular Tales of the West Highlands.,* second ed., 4 vols. 1890-93, Detroit. Reprint.

– (1972), *Leabhar na Féinne,* 1872. Shannon, Reprint.

CAMPBELL, J.G., (1908), 'The Green Island', *Scottish Historical Review* 5, 191- 202.

– (1973), *The Fians. Waifs and Strays of Celtic Tradition,* Vol. 4, 1891. Reprint.

CARMICHAEL, A., (1928-71), *Carmina Gadelica,* 6 vols., Edinburgh.

CARNEY, MAURA, (1957), '*Fót báis/banapúfa*', *Arv. Tidskrift för Nordisk Folkminnesforskning* 13, 172-9.

CELANDER, H., (1943), 'Oskorien och besläktade föreställningar i äldre och nyare nordisk tradition', *Saga och Sed* 2, 71-175.

CHADWICK, H.M., (1924), *The Origin of the English Nation,* Cambridge.

CHADWICK, NORA K., (1947), 'Norse Ghosts II', *Folklore* 58, 50-65,106-27.

CHAMPION, S., (1938), *Racial Proverbs*, London.

CHANDLER, A., (c.1980 ?), *Chichester Harbour*, Chichester.

CHESNUTT, M., (1968), 'An unsolved problem in Old Norse-Icelandic literary history', *Mediaeval Scandinavia* 1, 122-37.

– (1970), 'Norse-Celtic Bibliographical Survey: first report', *Mediaeval Scandinavia* 3, 109-37.

– (1993), ed., *Telling Reality. Folklore Studies in Memory of Bengt Holbek*, Turku.

– (1989), 'The Beguiling of Þórr', in McTurk & Wawn, 35-63.

CHESNUTT, M. & LARSEN, K., (1993), eds., *Unifol. Årsberetning 1991-1992. Folklore på Færøerne*, Copenhagen.

CHILD, F. J., (1882 [1956]), *The English and Scottish Popular Ballads*, New York.

CHILDS, R. de S., (1949), 'Phantom Ships of the Northeast Coast of North America', *New York Folklore Quarterly* 5, 146-65.

CHRISTIANSEN, R.Th., (1935), 'Til de norske sjøvetters historie: vandring of stedegent', *Maal og minne*, 1-25.

– (1959), *Studies in Irish and Scandinavian Folktales*, Copenhagen.

– (1971-73), 'Some Notes on the Fairies and the Fairy Faith', *Béaloideas* 39-41, 95-112.

CIRLOT, J.E., (1981), *A Dictionary of Symbols*, London. Reprint of second edition 1971.

CLARKE, B., (1973), ed., *Life of Merlin. Geoffrey of Monmouth*, Vita Merlini, Cardiff.

CLARKSON, L.A. & CRAWFORD, E.M., (1988), 'Dietary Directions: A Topographical Survey of Irish Diet, 1836' in Mitchison & Roebuck, 171-92.

COAKLEY, J. & GALLAGHER, M., (1993), *Politics in the Republic of Ireland*, Tallaght.

COOMARASWAMY, A.K., (1945), 'On the Loathly Bride', *Speculum* 20, no 4, 391-404.

COOKE, A.S. , (1911), *Off the Beaten Track in Sussex*, Hove, 168-70.

CROFTS, J.M., (1966),*Walton's New Treasury of Irish Ballads and Songs*, Part 2, Dublin.

CROKER, T.C., (1825-8), *Fairy Legends and Traditions of the South of Ireland* II, London.

– (1834), *Fairy Legends and Traditions of the South of Ireland*, London.

– (1839), *The Popular Songs of Ireland*, London.

Bibliography

CROSS, T. P., (1952), *Motif-Index of Early Irish Literature*, Bloomington.

CROSS, T..P. & SLOVER, C.H., (1969), *Ancient Irish Tales*, Dublin.

CULLMANN, O., (1966), (abridged ed.), *The Early Church*, London.

CURTIN, J., (1911), *Hero-Tales of Ireland*, Boston.

DANAHER, K., (1972), *The Year in Ireland*, Dublin & Cork.

DAVIDSON, HILDA ELLIS, (1998), *Roles of the Northern Goddess*, London & New York.

DAVIDSON, HILDA ELLIS, & FISHER, P., (1980), eds., *Saxo Grammaticus. The History of the Danes*. 2 Vols., Cambridge.

DAVÍÐSSON, Ólafur, (1935-9), *Íslenzkar þjóðsögur* (ed. Þorsteinn M. Jónsson), I, 1-2, Akureyri.

DEBES, L. JACOBSØN, (1673), *Færoæ et Færoa reserata. Det er Færøernis de Færøeske Indbyggeris Beskrivelse...* København. Facsimile edition: Lucas Debes 1963: Færøernes Beskrivelse. Udgivet for selskabet til Udgivelse af færøske Kildeskrifter og Studier af Jørgen Rischel, København.

DELARGY, J.H., (1945), 'The Gaelic Storyteller', *Proceedings of the British Academy* 31, 177-221; also published as Reprint in *Irish Studies* 6, Chicago 1969.

DILLON, M., (1946), *The Cycles of the Kings*, London.

DINNEEN, P., (1927), *Foclóir Gaedhilge agus Béarla/An Irish-English Dictionary*, Dublin.

DOUGLAS, MARY, (1989), *Purity and Danger*, London.

DUMÉZIL. G., (1968), *Mythe et épopée* I, Paris.

– (1973), 'Comparative Remarks on the Scandinavian God Heimdall', in *Gods of the Ancient Northmen* (ed. and trans. E. Haugen), Berkeley.

DUNDES, A., (1965), ed., *The Study of Folklore*, Englewood Cliffs, N.J.

EARLS, B., (1992-1993), 'Supernatural legends in nineteenth-century Irish writing', *Béaloideas* 60-1, 93-144.

EGARDT, BRITA, (1944), 'De svenska vattenhästsägnerna och deras ursprung', *Folkkultur* 4, 119-66.

EIKE, CHRISTINE N.F., 'Oskoreia og ekstaseriter', *Norveg* 23, 229-309.

EINARSSON, Stephan, (1957), *A History of Icelandic Literature*, New York.

EISEN, M.J., (1995), *Eesti Mütoloogia*, Tallinn.

ELIADE, M., (1959), *The Sacred and the Profane*, New York.

EMAKEELE SELTSI TOIMETISED 21. Tallinn, 13-29, ill. [Zusammenfassung:Fremdsprachige adaptierte Elemente in der estnischen Folklore].

ERLINGSSON, Davíð, (1980), 'Hjörleifur kvensami og Fergus Mac Léite', *Gripla, The Journal of the Arnamagnean Institute* 4, 198-205.

ERNITS, E., (1987), Muukeelsetest mugandustest eesti folklooris. Rahvaluulest.

EVERSHED, S., (1866), 'The Legend of the Dragon-Slayer of Lyminster', *Sussex Archaeological Collections* 18.

EVELYN-WHITE, H.G., (1959), *Hesiod, the Homeric Hymns, and Homerica*, London.

EWING, T., (1995), 'The Birth of Lugh - Odinn and Loki among the Celts', *Sinsear. The Folklore Journal* 8, 119-31.

FEILBERG, H. F., (1910), *Bjærgtagen. Studier over en gruppe træk fra nordisk alfetro* (*Danmarks Folkeminder* 5).

FOOTE, P., (1984), 'Færeyinga saga, chapter 40', *Aurvandilstá,* Odense, 209-21 – originally published in *Fróðskaparrit* 13.

FORAN, D., (1995), 'The Three Wind Knots', *Sinsear. The Folklore Journal* 8, 55-70.

FOSTER, G.M., (1965), 'Peasant society and the image of limited good', *American Anthropologist* 67, 293-315.

FRANK, ROBERTA, (1978), *Old Norse Court Poetry* (*Islandica* 42), Ithaca/London.

FROST, J., (1893), *The History and Topography of the County of Clare*, Dublin.

GALBRAITH, V.H., (1944), *Roger Wendover and Matthew Paris*, Glasgow.

GANANDER, Kristfried, (1960), *Mythologia Fennica*, Turku 1789, reprint Helsinki.

GASTER, M., (1905), 'The Legend of Merlin', *Folklore* 16, 407-27.

GENNEP van, A., (1960), *The Rites of Passage*, London.

GERNDT, H., (1971), *Fliegender Holländer und Klabautermann* (*Schriften zur Niederdeutschen Volkskunde*), Göttingen.

GILL, W.W., (1929), *A Manx Scrapbook*, London & Bristol.

GRANBERG, G., (1935), *Skogsrået i yngre nordisk folktradition* (*Skrifter utgivna av Gustav Adolfs Akademien för folklivsforskning* 3), Uppsala.

GRANLUND, J., (1951), trans., *Olaus Magnus, Historia de gentibus septentrion alibus – Historia om de nordiska folken*, Stockholm.

Bibliography

GRANT, L., (1927), *A Chronicle of Rye*, London.

GRAVES, R., (1960), *The Greek Myths*, Vols. 1-2, Middlesex.

GRAY, ELIZABETH A., (1982), *Cath Muige Tuired*, Dublin.

GREEN, M., (1967), *Why Was He Born So Beautiful and Other Rugby Songs*, London.

GREGORY, LADY AUGUSTA, (1920), *Visions and Beliefs in the West of Ireland*, London.

GRIMM, J., (1883/1966), *Teutonic Mythology* (4 Vols.), trans. J. Stallybrass from 4th. ed. London / New York.

GUAZZO, F., (1988), *Compendium Maleficarum* (The Montague Summers Edition. Translated by E.A. Ashwin), New York.

GUÐMUNDSSON, Einar, (1932), *Íslenzkar þjóðsögur* 1, Reykjavik.

GUÐMUNDSSON, Gils, (1949), *Þjóðlífsmyndir*, Reykjavík.

GUÐMUNDSSON, Helgi, (1997), *Um haf innan vestrænir menn og íslenzk menning á miðöldum*, Reykjavík.

GUSTAVSON, H. and NYMAN, ÅSA, (1959), *Gotländska sägner upptecknade av P. A. Säve*, Vol. 1, part 1, Uppsala.

GUTHRIE, W. K. C., (1950), *The Greeks and their Gods*, London.

GWYNDAF, R., (1992-1993), 'A Welsh lake legend and the famous physicians of Myddfai', *Béaloideas* 60-l, 241-66.

GWYNN, E. J., (1913, 1924), ed., trans., *The Metrical Dindshenchas*, Vols. 3-4, RIA Todd Lecture Series X, XI, Dublin.

HAAVIO, M., (1948), 'Ne jäävät virran vuolaan taa', *Virittäjä*, 28-46.

– (1959), *Essais folkloriques. Studia Fennica* 8, Porvoo.

– (1967), *Suomalainen mytologia*, Porvoo.

HAGBERG, LOUISE, (1937), *När döden gästar*, Stockholm.

HALDANE, S., (1996), *John Donne*, London.

HALL, Mr & MRS S.C., (1842), *Ireland, Its Scenery, Character, etc.*, 3 vols., London.

HALLDÓRSSON, Ólafur, (1969), ed., *Jómsvíkinga saga*, Reykjavík.

– (1978), *Grænland í miðaldaritum*, Reykjavík.

– (1985), ed., *Eiríks saga rauða. Texti Skáltholtsbókar . . .*, *ÍF* 4, Reykjavík.

– (1987), ed., *Færeyinga saga*. Reykjavík.

– (1991 [1992]), 'Af blendingum drauga og dyra', *Sólhvarfasumbl, saman borið handa Þorleifi Haukssyni* ... Reykjavík.

HAMEL van, A. G., (1932), *Lebor Bretnach*, Dublin.

– (1941), *Immrama*, Dublin.

HAMMERSHAIMB, V.U., (1851-55), *Færøske Kvæder samlede og besørgede ved V. U. Hammershaimb.* Udgivet af det Nordiske Literatur-Samfund I-II. København (Fotografisk genoptrykt [Faximile-edition]), Tórshavn 1969).

– (1891), *Færøsk Anthologi*, København.

HAMMOND, D., (1978), ed., *Songs of Belfast*, Dublin.

HARÐARSON, Gunnar & KARLSSON, Stefán, (1993), 'Hauksbók', in Phillip Pulsiano *et al.*, eds., *Medieval Scandinavia: an encyclopedia*, New York.

HARE, A.J.C., (1894), *Sussex*, London.

HARLOW, ILANA, (1993), 'Unravelling Stories: Exploring the Juncture of Ghost Story and Local Tragedy', *Journal of Folklore Research* 30, No. 2/3, Bloomington, Indiana.

HARRISON, E.F., (1935), 'Selsey's Submerged Bells', *Sussex County Magazine* 9.

HEALY, J.N., (1962), ed., *The Second Book of Irish Ballads*, Cork.

– (1967), *Irish Ballads and Songs of the Sea*, Cork.

HEDDERMAN, B. N., (1917), *Glimpses of my life in Aran: Experiences of a District Nurse*, Bristol.

HELLAND, A., (1906), ed., *Norges Land og Folk* 20:2.

HENNESSY, W.M., (1866), *Chronicon Scotorum*, London.

– (1887), *Annals of Ulster*, Vol. 1, London.

HERMANNSSON, Halldór, (1912), *Bibliography of the mythical-heroic sagas*, Ithaca, N.Y.

– (1937), *The sagas of the kings and the mythical-heroic sagas : two bibliographical supplements*, Ithaca, N.Y.

HERVEY, F., (1907), ed., *Corolla Sancti Eadmundi. The garland of Saint Edmund, king and martyr*, London.

HÖFFLER, O., (1934), *Kultische Geheimbunde der Germanen* I, Frankfurt.

– (1936), 'Der germanischer Totenkult und die Sagen vom Wilden Heer', *Oberdeutsche Zeitschrift für Volkskunde* 1, 33-49.

– (1973), *Verwandlungskulte Volksagen und Mythen*, Vienna.

HOGAN, E., (1910), *Onomasticon Goedelicum*, Dublin.

HØJ, C., (1979), *Til fjalls og fjøru*, Tórshavn.

HOLBEK, B., (1981), *Moderne folkloristik og historisk materiale, Folkloristikens aktuella paradigm* (ed. Gun Herranen), Åbo.

HOLBEK, B. & PIØ, I., (1967), *Fabeldyr og sagnfolk*, København.

HOLE, CHRISTINA, (1976), *A Dictionary of British Folk Customs*, London.

HOLLOWAY, J. & BLACK, JOAN, (1979), *Later English Broadside Ballads*, Vol. 2, London.

HOLTSMARK, ANNE, (1944), 'Gevjons Plog', *Maal og minne*, 169-79.

HONKO, L., (1962), *Geisterglaube in Ingermanland, FFC* 185, Helsinki.

– (1973), 'Metodiska och terminologiska betraktelser', in Klintberg af, (1973).

– (1996), *Oral Epics. Oral Epics Conference*, Turku.

HONKO, L. & LÖFGREN, O., (1981), eds., *Tradition och miljö. Ett kulturekologisk perspektiv*, Lund (*Skrifter utgivna av Etnologiska sällskapet i Lund* 13 [NIF Publications 11]).

HOPKINS, R. THURSTON [1938], *Sussex Rendezvous*, London

HUGHES, KATHLEEN, (1959), 'On an Irish Litany of Pilgrim Saints Compiled c. 800', *Analecta Bollandiana* 77, 305-31.

– (1960), 'The changing theory and practice of Irish pilgrimage', in *The Journal of Ecclesiastical History* 9, 143-51.

HUGILL, S., (1961), *Shanties from the Seven Seas*, London.

– (1969), *Shanties and Sailor's Songs*, London.

– (1977), *Songs of the Sea*, New York.

HULL, ELEANOR, (1928), *Folklore of the British Isles*, London.

HUNTINGDON, G., HERRMANN, L., MOULDEN, J., (1990), eds., *Sam Henry's Songs of the People*, Athens and London.

HÜSING, G., (1903-6), *Beiträge sur Kyros-Sage ...Verbesserte und vermehrte Sonderabzüge aus der orientalischen Litteratur-Zeitung*, Berlin, 143-4.

HYDE, D., (1930), 'Sgéalta ar Oisín', *Béaloideas* 2, 252-60.

HYLTÉN-CAVALLIUS, G.O., (1863), 'Sägner om Kettil Runske', *Läsning för folket* 8, h 2, Stockholm, 169–90.

JACKSON, K., (1938), *Scéalta ón mBlascaod*, Baile Átha Cliath.

– (1961), *The International Popular Tale and Early Welsh Tradition*, Cardiff.

JACOBSEN, M.A. & MATRAS, Chr., (1961), *Føroysk-donsk orðabók. Færøsk-dansk ordbog*, Tórshavn.

JACOBY, A., (1913), 'Zum Prozessverfahren gegen die bösen Geister', *Zeitschrift des Vereins für Volkskunde* 23, 184-7.

JAKOBSEN, J., (1898-1902), *Færøske folkesagn og æventyr*, København, (New edition Tórshavn 1961-64).

JAMES, M.R., (1983), ed. and trans.,*Walter Map, De Nugis Curialium: Courtiers' Trifles* (revised C.N.L. Brooke and R.A.B. Mynors), Oxford.

JOENSEN, J.P., (1975a), *Færøske sluppfiskere. Etnologisk undersøgelse af en erhvervsgruppes liv*, Lund.

– (1975b), '"Lemperen" eller "Manden ombord"', *Arv. Journal of Scandinavian Folklore* 31, 74-108.

– (1978), 'Niðagrísur', *Mondul* 2, 3-8.

– (1981), 'Tradition och miljö i färöiskt fiske', in Honko & Löfgren (eds.), 95-134.

– (1985), 'Hammershaimb sum heimildarmaður', *Fróðskaparrit* 32, 99-102.

– (1987), *Fra bonde til fisker. Studier i overgangen fra bondesamfund til fiskersamfund på Færøerne*, Tórshavn.

– (1990), *Fróðskaparsetur Føroya 1965-90*, Tórshavn.

JOINER, C.G., (1929), 'The Knucker of Lyminster', *Sussex County Magazine* 3, 845-6.

JONES, G., (1961), trans., *Erik the Red and other Icelandic Sagas*, London.

JONES-BAKER, DORIS, (1977), *The Folklore of Hertfordshire*, London.

JÓNSSON, Guðni, (1981), *Fornaldar Sögur Norðurlanda*. 4 vols. Íslendingasagnaútgáfan, Reykjavík.

JÓNSSON, Finnur & JÓNSSON, Eiríkur, (1892-96), *Hauksbók, udgiven after de arnamagnæanske håndskrifter no. 371, 544 og 675, 4to samt forskellige papirshåndskrifter*, København.

JÓNSSON, Joh. Örn., (1956), *Sagnablöð hin nýju*, Reykjavík, 269-70.

JOSEPHSON, F., (1997), ed., *Celts and Vikings, Proceedings of the Fourth Symposium of Societas Celtologica Nordica, Meijerbergs Archiv för Svensk Ordforskning* 20, Göteborg.

JOYCE, P.W., (1879), *Old Celtic Romances*, London.

– (1879), *English as we speak it in Ireland*, Dublin (Reprint 1991).

KAHIL, L., (1977), 'L'Artemis de Brauron: rites et mystère', *Antike Kunst* 20, 86-98.

KAVANAGH, JEAN, (1995), 'The Mélusine legend in Irish folk tradition', *Sinsear, The Folklore Journal* 8, 71-82.

KEATING, G., (1908), *Foras Feasa ar Eirinn: The History of Ireland*, I, ed. Patrick S. Dinneen, London.

KEATING, G. (1902-14) *History of Ireland*, Irish Texts Society, Vols. IV, VIII, IX, XV, London.

KIIL, L., (1965), 'Gevjonmyten og Ragnarsdråpa', *Maal og minne* 63-70.

KILLIP, G.M., (1975), *The Folklore of the Isle of Man* (The Folklore of the British Isles 3, ed. V.J. Newall), London & Sydney.

KLARE, H.-J., (1933-4), 'Die Toten in der altnordischen Literatur', *Acta Philologica Scandinavica* 8, 1-56.

KLINTBERG af, B., (1973), ed., *Tro, sanning, sägen. Tre bidrag till en folkloristisk metodik*, Stockholm.

KNEEN, J.J., (1925), *The Place-Names of the Isle of Man*, Douglas.

– (1978), *Manx Idioms and Phrases/Idiomyn as Raaghyn Gaelgach*, Castletown, Isle of Man. Reprint of original instalments (commencing March 1938) in *Mona's Herald*.

KNOTT, ELEANOR, (1936), ed., *Togail Bruidne Da Derga*, Dublin.

KÕIVA, MARE, (1990), *Estonskije zagovorõ. Klassifikatsija i zhanrovõje osobennosti*, Tallinn.

KRAMMER, H., (1969), *Das entblößte Frauenzimmer*, München.

KRAPPE, A., (1929), 'Le Rire du Prophète', in *Studies in English Philology. A miscellany in honour of Frederick Klaeber*, Minneapolis.

KRISTJÁNSSON, Vigfús frá Hafnarnesi, (1945), *Sagnþættir* 1, Reykjavík.

KVIDELAND, R. & SEHMSDORF, H. K., (1991), *Scandinavian Folk Belief and Legend*, Minneapolis.

LÄFFLER, L.F., (1903-8), 'Den gotländska Taksteinar-sägnen', *Svenska landsmål och svenskt folkliv*, 1906, 37-60.

– (1916), 'Den gotländska Taksteinar-sägnen en vandringssaga?', *Svenska landsmål och svenskt folkliv*, 23.

LANDT, J., (1800), *Forsøg til en Beskrivelse over Færøerne*, København (New edition Tórshavn 1965).

LANDTMAN, G., (1919), *Övernaturliga väsen, FSF* VII:1.

LAOIDE, S., (1913), *Cruach Chonaill,* Baile Átha Cliath.

LARMINIE, W., (1893), *West Irish Folk-Tales and Romances,* London.

LAWS Jr., G.M., (1957), *American balladry from British Broadsides.* Philadelphia, (American Folklore Society Publication).

LEATHER, E.M., (1912), *The Folk-Lore of Herefordshire,* Hereford & London.

LECOUTEUX, C., (1982), *Mélusine et le Chevalier au Cygne,* Paris.

LEIGH, E., (1866), *Ballads and Legends of Cheshire,* London.

LÉVI-STRAUSS, C., (1987), *Anthropology and Myth,* Oxford & New York.

LIDÉN, E., (1928), 'Gullvarta-Síbilia', *Festskrift til Finnur Jónsson 29. maj 1928* (eds. Johs. Bröndum-Nielsen *et al.*), Copenhagen, 358-64.

LILIEQUIST, J., (1992), *Brott, synd och straff,* Umeå.

LIESTØL, K., (1926), ed., *Moltke Moes samlede skrifter,* Vol. 2, Instituttet for sammenlignende kulturforskning B 6, Oslo.

LÖFGREN, O., (1981), 'De vidskepliga fångstmännen - magi, ekologi och ekonomi i svenska fiskarmiljöer', in Honko & Löfgren, 64-86.

LÖFSTEDT, T.M.G., (1993), 'Russian Legends about Forest Spirits in the Context of Northern European Mythology'. A Dissertation submitted in partial satisfaction of the requirements for the degree of Doctor of Philosophy in Slavic Languages and Literatures in the Graduate Division of the University of California at Berkeley. Manuscript.

LOOMIS, G., (1932), 'The growth of the Saint Edmund legend', *Harvard studies and notes in philology and literature* 14, 83-113.

LOOMIS, R.S., (1963), *The Grail from Celtic Myth to Christian Symbol,* Cardiff.

LOORITS, O., (1926), *Liivi rahva usund,* Tartu.

– (1929), *Livische Märchen- und Sagenvarianten, FFC* 66, Helsinki.

– (1931), 'Der norddeutsche Klabautermann im Ostbaltikum', *Sitzungsberichte der Gelehrten Estnischen Gesellschaft,* Tartu, 76-125 (*Õpetatud Eesti Seltsi Aastaraamat),* Tartu, 76-125.

– (1932), *Volksdichtung und Mythologie,* Tartu.

– (1935), *Pharaos Heer in der Volksuberlieferung* (*Eesti Rahvaluule Arhiivi toimetused* 3. *Acta et Commentationes Universitatis Tartuensis* [Dorpatensis] B XXXIII 40), Tartu.

– (1951), *Grundzüge des Estnischen Volksglaubens*, Lund.

LOWER, M.A., (1861), 'Old Speech and Old Manners in Sussex', *Sussex Archaeological Collections* 13, 227-8.

LYSAGHT, PATRICIA, (1996), *The Banshee. The Irish supernatural death-messenger*, second edition, Dublin.

MACALISTER, R.A.S., (1939-40), *Lebor Gabála Érenn*, Vols. 2-3, Dublin.

MAC AN BHAIRD, A., (1980), 'Tadhg mac Céin and the Badgers', *Ériu* 31, 150-5.

MAC CANA, P., (1970), *Celtic Mythology*, London.

MAC CÁRTHAIGH, C., (1991), 'Midwife to the Fairies (ML 5070)' in *The Fairy Hill is on Fire! Proceedings of the Symposium on the Supernatural in Irish and Scottish Migratory Legends, Dublin 7 - 8 October 1988 = Béaloideas* 59, 133-43.

MAC CÁRTHAIGH, M., (1966), 'Dursey Island and Some Placenames', *Dinnseanchas* 2, 51-5.

McCARTHY, W.B., OXFORD, CHERYL & SOBOL, J.D., (1994), ed., *Jack in Two Worlds. Contemporary North American Tales and their Tellers*, University of North Carolina.

MAC COISDEALA, L., (1942), 'In Memoriam, Éamonn (Liam) a Búrc (Aill na Brón, Carna, Co. na Gaillimhe)', *Béaloideas* 12, 210-4.

– (1946), 'Im' Bhailitheoir Béaloideasa', *Béaloideas* 16, 141-71.

– (1983), 'Fear Inste an Scéil', in Ó Ceannabháin (ed.).

MacDONALD, A., (1894), *The Uist Collection. The Poems and Songs of John MacCodrum*, Glasgow.

MacDONALD, D.A., (1994-5), 'Migratory Legends of the Supernatural in Scotland: A General Survey', *Béaloideas* 62-3, 29-78.

MacDONALD, T.D., (1926), *Gaelic Proverbs and Proverbial Sayings*, Stirling.

MAC GIOLLARNÁTH, S., (1936), *Loinnir Mac Leabhair agus Sgéalta Gaisgidh Eile*, Baile Átha Cliath.

MacKAY, J.G., (1917), ed., 'Nighean Rìgh-fo-Thuinn' in *An Ròsarnach* 1, 211-27, Glasgow.

MacLEAN, C., (1959), 'A Folk Variant of the Táin Bó Cúailnge from Uist', *Arv. Tidskrift för nordisk folkminnesforskning* 15, 160-81.

MacLYSAGHT, E., (1957), *Irish Families*, Dublin.

MAC MATHÚNA, S., (1985), *Immram Brain*, Tübingen.

– (1994), 'The structure and transmission of early Irish voyage literature', in *Text und Zeittiefe* (ed. Hildegard L.C. Tristram), *ScriptOralia* 58, 313-57.

– (1996), 'Motif and episodic clustering in early Irish voyage literature', in *Reoralisierung* (ed. Hildegard L.C. Tristram), *ScriptOralia*, Tübingen, 247-62.

– (1997), 'Hvítramannaland', in Josephson (ed.), 211-24.

MacNEIL, J.N., (1987), *Tales until Dawn/Sgeul gu Latha: The World of a Cape Breton Gaelic Story-Teller*, edited and translated by John Shaw, Edinburgh.

MAC NEILL, MÁIRE, (1962 [1982]), *Festival of Lughnasa*, Oxford (Dublin).

MAC SUIBHNE, S., (1961), *Tótamas in Éirinn*, Baile Átha Cliath.

McTURK, R., (1991a), *Studies in Ragnars saga loðbrókar and its major Scandinavian analogues*, Oxford.

– (1991b), 'Loðbróka og Gunnlöð', *Skírnir. Tímarit Hins íslenska bókmenntafélags* 165, 343-59.

– (1994), 'Blóðöm eða blóðömur ?', in Sigurðsson *et al.* (1994).

– (1997), 'No man is an island: Matthew Paris on Munkholmen'. *Sagas and the Norwegian experience'. Sagaene og Noreg 10. Internasjonale Sagakonferanse:10th International Saga Conference. Trondheim, 3.-9. August 1997, Preprints: ortrykk.* 445-52. Trondheim.

McTURK, R. & WAWN, A.,(1989) , ed., *Úr Dölum til Dala: Guðbrandur Vigfússon Centenary Essays* (*Leeds Texts and Monographs* n.s. 11), Leeds.

MAGNÚSSON, Ásgeir Blöndal, (1989), *Íslensk orðsifjabók*, [Reykjavík].

MAGNUSSON, Magnus & PÁLSSON, Hermann, (1965), trans. *The Vinland Sagas. The Norse Discovery of America*, Penguin Classics, Harmondsworth.

– (1969), trans., *Laxdæla saga*, in Penguin Classics, Harmondsworth.

MANNING, W.H., (1971): 'The Piercebridge Plough Group', *British Museum Quarterly* 35, 125-36.

MARCUS, G.J., (1952-4), 'Factors in Early Celtic Navigation', *Études Celtiques* 6, 312-27.

MASING, U. (1995), *Eesti usund*, Tartu.

MEISEN, K., (1935), *Die Sagen vom wütenden Heer und wilden Jäger*, Münster.

MIEDER, W., (1990), *Not by Bread Alone. Proverbs of the Bible*, Vermont, U.S.A.

MIEDER, W. & KINGSBURY, S.A., (1994), eds., *A Dictionary of Wellerisms*, New York & Oxford.

MITCHISON, R. & ROEBUCK, P., (1988), eds., *Economy and Society in Scotland and Ireland*, Edinburgh.

MOE, M., (1906), 'Eventyrlige sagn i den ældre historie', in Helland (1906); also in Liestøl (1926), 85-210.

MOGK, E., (1919),'Altgermanische Spukgeschichten', *Neue Jahrbücher für klassische Altertum Geschichte und deutsche Literatur* 22, hrsg. von J. Ilberg.

MOORE, A.W., (1890), *The Surnames and Place-Names of the Isle of Man*, London.

MORAN, G., (1996), '"In Search of the Promised Land": The Connemara Colonization Scheme to Minnesota, 1880', *Eire-Ireland* XXXI, 3 & 4, 130-49.

MOULDEN, J., (1990), *Sam Henry's Songs of the People*, Athens & London.

MÜLLENHOFF, K., (1892), *Deutsche Altertumskunde*, Vol. 5, Berlin.

MÜLLER-LISOWSKI, KATE, (1948), 'Contributions to a Study in Irish Folklore: Traditions about Donn', *Béaloideas* 8, 143-99.

MUNNELLY, T., (1980-81), 'Songs of the Sea: A general description with special reference to recent oral tradition in Ireland', *Béaloideas* 48-49, 30-58.

   – (1994), *The Mount Callan Garland: Songs from the Repertoire of Tom Lenihan, Knockbrack, Miltown Malbay, County Clare*, Dublin.

MURPHY, D., (1896), *The Annals of Clonmacnoise*, Dublin.

MURPHY, G., (1953-5), 'Notes on Cath Maige Tuired', *Éigse* 7, 191-8.

   – (1953), *Duanaire Finn*, Part 3, Dublin: The Irish Texts Society.

   – (1956-7), 'Duanaire Finn', *Éigse* 8, 168-71.

MURPHY, M.J., (1975), *Now You're Talking . . .* Belfast.

   – (1987), *Rathlin: Island of Blood and Enchantment*, Dundalk.

   – (1990), *Sayings and Stories from Slieve Gullion*, Dundalk.

NABER, REET; (1995), 'Lucky voyage!', *Folk Belief Today*, Tartu, 334-45.

NANSEN, F., (1911), *In Northern Mists*, II, London, 42-56.

NÄSSTRÖM, B., (1995), *Freya - the Great Goddess of the North* (*Lund Studies in History of Religions* 5) Lund.

NEULAND, LENA, (1981), *Motif-Index of Latvian Folktales and Legends*, FFC 229, Helsinki.

NÍ DHUIBHNE, ÉILÍS, (1993), '"The Old Woman as Hare", Structure and meaning in an Irish Legend', *Folklore* 104, i & ii, 77-85.

NÍ LOCHLAINN, NIAMH, (1993), 'Tadhg agus Donnchadh. A Story about Seals', unpublished essay in Department of Irish Folklore, University College Dublin.

NILDIN-WALL, BODIL & WALL, J.-I., (1996), *Det ropades i skymningen …Vidskepelse och trolldomstro på Gotland* (*Skr. utg. av Språk- och folkminnesinstitutet. Dialekt-, ortnamns- och folkminnesarkivet i Göteborg* 3), Uppsala.

Ó BRIAIN, M., (1997), *Laoi Cholainn gan Cheann: Oisín's headless bride in Gaelic Tradition*, in *Proceedings of the 10th International Congress of Celtic Studies*, ed. R. Black, W. Gillies and R. Ó Maolalaigh, East Linton, East Lothian.

O'BRIEN, M.A., (1962), *Corpus Genealogiarum Hiberniae*, Vol. 1, Dublin.

Ó CADHAIN, M., (1934), 'Sgéaluigheacht Chois-Fhairrge, *Béaloideas* 4, 62-63, 78.

Ó CATHÁIN, S., (1980), *The Bedside Book of Irish Folklore*, Cork & Dublin.

– (1983), *Scéalta Chois Cladaigh / Stories of Sea and Shore, told by John Henry*, Dublin 1983.

– (1988), 'Súil Siar ar Scéim na Scol 1937-1938', *Sinsear. The Folklore Journal* 5, 19-30.

Ó CEANNABHÁIN, P., (1983), ed., *Éamon a Búrc: Scéalta*, Dublin.

Ó CONGHAILE, M., (1986), *Croch Suas É!*, Galway.

Ó CORRÁIN, A., (1989), *A Concordance of Idiomatic Expressions in the Writings of Séamus Ó Grianna*, Belfast.

Ó CRIOMHTHAIN, T., (1928), *Allagar na hInise*, Baile Átha Cliath.

– (1929), *An t-Oileánach*, Baile Átha Cliath.

Ó CRÓINÍN, D., (1985), ed., *Seanchas ó Chairbre* 1, collected by Seán Ó Cróinín, Baile Átha Cliath.

Ó CUINN, C., (1990), *Scian a Caitheadh le Toinn* (eds. A. Ó Canainn and S. Watson), Dublin.

Ó CUÍV, B., (1945), *Cath Muighe Tuireadh*, Dublin.

– (1954), 'Lugh Lámhfhada and the death of Balar Ua Néid', *Celtica* 2, 64-5.

Ó DANACHAIR, C. (1974-6), 'Some Marriage Customs and their Regional Distribution', *Béaloideas* 42-4, 136-75.

Ó DIREÁIN, P., (1926), *Sgéalaidhe Leitir Mealláin*, Baile Átha Cliath.

ODDSSON, Bishop Gísli, (1942), *Undur Íslands* [*De mirabilibus Islandiæ*], Annalium in Islandia farrago, trans., Jónas Rafnar, Akureyri.

O'DONAGHUE, D., (1994), *Lives and Legends of Saint Brendan the Voyager*, Felinfach. Facsimile reprint (originally published as Brendaniana, Dublin 1893).

Ó DOMHNAILL, E., (1940), *Scéal Hiúdaí Sheáinín*, Baile Átha Cliath.

Bibliography

Ó DÓNAILL, N., (1948), *Scéalta Johnny Shéimisín*, Béal Feirste.

O'DONOVAN, J., (1835), Ordnance Survey Letters for Co. Donegal, Typescript.

– (1851) *Annals of the Kingdom of Ireland*, Vol. 1, Dublin.

Ó DUILEARGA, S., (1948), *Leabhar Sheáin Í Chonaill*, Dublin.

– & Ó hÓGÁIN, D., (1981), *Leabhar Stiofáin Uí Ealaoire*, Dublin.

– (1981), *Seán Ó Conaill's Book* (translated by Máire MacNeill), Dublin.

O'FARRELL, P., (1983), *How the Irish speak English*, Dublin & Cork.

O'FLAHERTY, R., (1846), *Chorographical Description of West or H-Iar Connaught*, ed. James Hardiman, Dublin.

Ó GIOLLÁIN, D., (1984), 'The *Leipreachán* and Fairies, Dwarfs and the Household Familiar: a Comparative Study', *Béaloideas* 52, 75-150.

O'GRADY, S.H., (1892) *Silva Gadelica*, Vol. 2, London.

O'GRADY, S.H., (1892), *Silva Gadelica*, Irish Text , London.

O'HANLON, J., (1875), *Lives of the Irish Saints*, Vol. 1, Dublin.

Ó hEOCHAIDH, S., (1955), *Sean-Chainnt Theilinn*, Baile Átha Cliath.

Ó hEOCHAIDH, S., Ní Néill, Máire, Ó Catháin, S., (1977), *Síscéalta ó Thír Chonaill / Fairy Legends from Donegal*, Dublin.

Ó hÓGÁIN, D., (1974-6), '"An É an tAm Fós É ?" Staidéar ar fhinscéal Barbarossa (Móitíf S1960.2) in Éirinn', *Béaloideas* 42-4, 213-308.

– (1982), *An File*, Dublin.

– (1987), 'Magic Attributes of the Hero in Fenian Lore' in Almqvist, Ó Catháin & Ó Héalaí, 207-42.

– (1990), *Myth, Legend and Romance: an Encyclopædia of the Irish Folk Tradition*, London.

– (1991), '"Has the Time Come ?" (MLSIT 8009). The Barbarossa Legend in Ireland and its Historical Background', *Béaloideas* 59, 197-207.

– (1999), *The Sacred Isle. Belief and Religion in pre-Christian Ireland*, Cork.

OINAS, F.J., (1979), *Kalevipoeg kütkeis ... Kalevipoeg in Fetters and Other Essays on Folklore, Mythology and Literature* (*Studia Estonica, Fennica, Baltica* 1), Toronto.

– (1995), 'Remarks on St. Nicolas', *Palaeoslavica* III, 249-51.

OLAUS MAGNUS, *Historia de gentibus septentrionalibus*, translated into Swedish by R. Geete, G. Thörnell, C. Cavallin & A. Almqvist, 2nd rev. ed., Stockholm 1976.

O LOCHLAINN, C. (1939), *Irish Street Ballads*, Dublin London.

– (1965), *More Irish Ballads*, Dublin.

O'LOONEY, B., (1859), *Laoidh Oisín ar Thír na nÓg*, Dublin.

OLRIK, A. (1901), 'Odinsjægern i Jylland', *Dania* 8, 139-73.

– (1910), 'Gefion', *Danske Studier*, 1-31.

– (1965), 'Epic Laws of Folk Narrative' in Dundes (1965), 129-41.

– (1992), *Principles for oral narrative research*, trans. Kirsten Wolf & Jody Jensen, Bloomington, Indiana.

OLSEN, M., (1906-08), ed., *Völsunga saga ok Ragnars saga loðbrókar*, Copenhagen.

Ó MÁILLE, T.S., (1948), *Sean-fhocla Chonnacht* 1, Baile Átha Cliath.

– (1952), *Sean-fhocla Chonnacht* 2, Baile Átha Cliath.

Ó MÁILLE, T. & M., (1905), *Amhráin Chlainne Gaedheal*, Baile Átha Cliath.

O'MEARA, J. J., (1981), *The Voyage of Saint Brendan*, Dublin.

Ó MUIRGHEASA, É., (1976), *Seanfhocla Uladh*, new edition, Baile Átha Cliath.

Ó MURCHADHA, G. & Ó SÚILLEABHÁIN, S., (1939), review of W. Matheson, *The Songs of John MacCodrum, Bard to Sir James MacDonald of Sleat* (Edinburgh 1938), *Béaloideas* 9, 135-8.

Ó NEACHTAIN, E., (1922), *Torolbh Mac Stáirn*, Dublin.

Ó NÉILL, E.R., (1991), 'The King of the Cats (ML 6070B). The Revenge and the Non-Revenge Redactions in Ireland', *Béaloideas* 59, 167-88.

Ó NUALLÁIN/O'NOLAN, C./K., (1982), *Eochair, Mac Rí in Éirinn/Eochair, a King's Son in Ireland*, Dublin.

ONG, W., (1982), *Orality and Literacy: the Technologizing of the Word*, London.

O'RAHILLY, T.F., (1922), *A Miscellany of Irish Proverbs*, Dublin.

O'RAHILLY, T.F., (1927), ed., *Measgra Dánta*, 2 vols, Cork.

O'ROURKE, F.J., (1945), 'A kitchen-midden at Dog's Bay, Roundstone, Co. Galway', *The Journal of the Royal Society of Antiquaries of Ireland*, 75 (2), 115-8.

    – (1970), *The Fauna of Ireland*, Cork.

Ó SIOCFHRADHA, P., (1941), *Laoithe na Féinne*, Dublin.

    – (1984), ('An Seabhac'), *Seanfhocail na Mumhan*, new edition, Baile Átha Cliath.

OSKAMP, H.P.A., (1970), *The Voyage of Máel Dúin*, Groningen.

Ó SÚILLEABHÁIN, S., (1937), *Diarmuid na Bolgaighe agus a chómhursain*, Baile Átha Cliath.

    – (1942), *A Handbook of Irish Folklore*, Dublin, reprint Detroit 1970.

    – (1952), *Scéalta Cráibhtheacha*, Dublin (*Béaloideas* 21 [1951]).

    – (1967), *Irish Folk Custom and Belief*, Dublin.

    – (1973), *Storytelling in Irish Tradition*, Cork.

Ó SÚILLEABHÁIN, S. & CHRISTIANSEN, R.Th., (1967), *The Types of the Irish Folktale*, FFC 188, Helsinki 1963. Second printing 1967.

O'SULLIVAN, S., (1966), ed., *Folktales of Ireland*, Chicago & London.

    – (1977), *Legends from Ireland*, London.

OTTÓSSON, Kjartan G., (1983), *Fróðárundur í Eyrbyggju* (*Studia Islandica* 42), Reykjavik.

PACZOLAY, G., (1997), *European Proverbs in 55 languages ... Európai köz mondások 55 nyelven*, Veszprém.

PALMENFELT, U., (1993a), 'On the Understanding of Folk Legends' in Chesnutt (ed), 143-67.

    – (1993b), *Per Arvid Säves möten med sägner och människor. Folkloristiska aspekter på ett gotländskt arkivmaterial*, Stockholm.

    – (1993c), 'Retorikens grammatik, mekanik och teknik: hemma hos fyra berättare', in *Arvidsson*, 68-81.

    – (1994), 'The Tug of War of Talking. Folklore as a Cultural Weapon in Conversations', *Arv. Nordic Yearbook of Folklore*, 71-9.

PALMER, R., (1976), *The Folklore of Somerset*, London .

    – (1980), ed., *Everyman's Book of British Ballads*, London.

PÁLSSON, Hermann, (1960), 'Hvítramannaland', *Tímarit Máls og Menningar*, 48-54.

    – (1992), 'Um Glám í Grettlu; Drög að íslenskri draugafræði', *The International Saga Society Newsletter* 6.

– (1997), *Keltar á Íslandi*, [Reykjavík].

PATON, LUCY A., (1903), *Studies in the Fairy Mythology of Arthurian Romance*, Boston.

PAULSON, I., (1963), 'Wildgeistvorstellungen in Nordeurasien', *Paideuma. Mitteilungen zur Kulturkunde*. Band 8, Heft 2, Frankfurt a/M, 70-84.

– (1964a), *Eesti rahva usund*, Stockholm.

– (1964b), 'The Animal Guardian: a Critical and Synthetic Review', *History of Religions*, Vol. 3, No. 2, 202-19.

– (1971), *The Old Estonian Folk Religion (Indiana University, Bloomington. Uralic and Altaic Series*, Vol. 108), The Hague.

PEEGEL, J.,(1968), 'Pisut koerakoonlastest', *Keel ja Kirjandus* 1968:8, 480-2.

PENTIKÄINEN, J., (1968), *The Nordic Dead-Child Tradition. Nordic Dead-Child Beings. A Study in Comparative Religion, FFC* 202, Helsinki.

– (1969), 'The Dead without Status', *Temenos* 4, republished (1978) *Folkloristics and Comparative Religion* 10.

– (1978), *Oral Repertoire and World View, FFC* 219, Helsinki.

– (1983), 'Voluntary Death and Single Battle: Suicidal Behavior and Arctic World Views', *Suicide Research II. Proceedings of the Symposium on Suicide Research by the Yrjö Jahnsson Foundation* (ed. K. Achté, K. Nieminen and J. Vikkula), *Psychiatria Fennica Supplementum*, Helsinki, 123-36.

– (1986), 'Transition Rites. Cosmic, Social and Individual Order', *Proceedings of the Finnish-Swedish-Italian Seminar held at the University of Rome 'La Sapienzia, 24th-28th March 1984* (ed. U. Bianchi), Estratto da *'Storia delle religioni'* 2, 1-27.

– (1989), *Kalevala Mythology*, trans. and ed. Ritva Poom (Folklore Studies in Translation), Bloomington &Indianapolis.

– (1993), *The Grammar of Mind and Body. On the Fringes of Sport*, ed. Leena Laire. *The Finnish Society for Research in Sport and Physical Education, Publication* 134, Sankt Augustin, 100-1.

– (1994), 'Shamanism as the Expression of Northern Identity', *Circumpolar Religion and Ecology. An Anthropology of the North* (ed. T. Irimoto & T. Yamada), Tokyo, 375-403.

– (1996), 'Khanty shamanism today: Reindeer sacrifice and its mythological background', *Shamanism and Northern Ecology*, Berlin & New York, 153-81.

PETERSEN, SOFÍA, (1988), 'Í skýmingini', *Skjaldur og Ævintyr* 3rd edition, Tórshavn.

PHILIP, N., (1991), ed., *The Penguin Book of Scottish Folktales*, London.

PLISCHKE, H., (1914), *Die Sage vom Wilden Heere im deutschen Volke*, Leipzig.

PLUMMER, C., (1910), *Vitae Sanctorum Hiberniae*, Vols. 1-2, Oxford.

– (1922), *Bethada Náem nÉrenn /Lives of Irish Saints*, Vols. 1-2, Oxford.

POWER, ROSEMARY, (1985), 'Journeys to the Otherworld in the Icelandic *Fornaldarsögur*', *Folklore* 96, 156-75.

PRESS, MURIEL A.C., (1934), trans., *The Saga of the Faroe Islanders*, London.

QVIGSTAD J.K., (1928), *Lappiske eventyr og sagn*, 4 Vols., Oslo.

RALSTON, W.R.S., (1872): *The Songs of the Russian People*, second ed., London.

RANSON, J. , (1948), *Songs of the Wexford Coast*, Enniscorthy.

REES, A. & B., (1961), *Celtic Heritage*, London.

REINHARD, J.R., (1933), *The Survival of Geis in Medieval Romance*, Halle.

RHYS, J., (1901), *Celtic Folklore, Welsh and Manx* (2 vols.), London.

RIETI, BARBARA, (1991), *Strange Terrain: the Fairy World in Newfoundland*, St. John's, Newfoundland.

RIEU, E.V., (1946), Homer: *The Odyssey*, Middlesex.

RIA DICTIONARY = Royal Irish Academy, *Contributions to a Dictionary of the Irish Language*, Dublin, 1913-1975.

RIMMON-KENAN, S., (1983), *Narrative Fiction: Contemporary Poetics*, London etc.

RIVET, A.L.F., & SMITH, C., (1979), *The Place-Names of Roman Britain*, London.

ROBERTS, B., (1999), 'Melusina: medieval Welsh and English analogues', in *Melusines continentales et insulaires*, eds. Jeanne-Marie Boivin and P. Mac Cana, Paris, 287-302.

ROBINSON, T., (1990), *Connemara: a Gazetteer and Map*, Roundstone.

ROIDER, ULRIKE, (1979), *De Chophur in Da Muccida*, Innsbruck.

ROINN OIDEACHAIS, AN (1937), *Irish Folklore and Tradition. Béaloideas Éireann*, Dublin.

– (1978), *Ainmneacha Plandaí agus Ainmhithe*, I, Baile Átha Cliath.

ROLLESTON, T.W., (1949), *Myths and Legends of The Celtic Race*, London, second edition.

ROSENSTOCK, G., (1993), *The Wasp in the Mug. Unforgettable Irish Proverbs*, Cork & Dublin.

ROSS, M., (1994), 'The Knife against the Wave: A Uniquely Irish Legend of the Supernatural?', *Folklore* 105, 83-8.

ROSS, M.C., (1978), 'The Myth of Gefjon and Gylfi and its function in *Snorra Edda* and *Heimskringla*', *Arkiv för nordisk filologi* 93, 149-65.

ROSS, N., (1939), ed., *Heroic Poetry from the Book of the Dean of Lismore*, Scottish Gaelic Texts Society, Edinburgh.

SANDERLIN, S., (1975), 'The Date and Provenance of the "Litany of Irish Saints - II" (The Irish Litany of Pilgrim Saints)', *PRIA*, 75C, 251-62.

SANDARS, N.K, (1972), *The Epic of Gilgamesh*, Middlesex.

SAWYER, F.E., (1884), *Sussex Place-Rhymes and Local Proverbs*, Brighton.

SCHENDA, R., (1978), 'Witze, die selten zum Lachen sind', *Zeitschrift für Volkskunde* 74.

– (1979), ' Brust, Brüste', *Enzyklopädie des Märchens*, Berlin & New York.

SCHLAUCH, MARGARET, (1930), *The saga of the Volsungs, the saga of Ragnar Lodbrok together with the lay of Kraka translated from the Old Norse*, New York.

– (1934), *Romance in Iceland*, London.

SCHLUITJER, PAULA C., (1936), *Ijslands volksgeloof*, Harlem.

SCHONELL, F.J. & FLOWERDEN, PHYLLIS, (1976), *Wide Range Readers*, Blue Book 4, Edinburgh.

SCHREUER, H., (1915 & 1916), 'Das Recht der Toten: Eine germanische Untersuchung', *Zeitschrift für vergleichende Rechtswissenschaft* 33, 333-423 and 34, 1-208.

SCOTT, H. Von E. & SWINTON BLAND, C. C., (1929), *The Dialogue on Miracles: Caesarius of Heisterbach*, 2 vols., London.

SCOTT, R.J., (1983), *The Galway Hookers*, Dublin.

SEELOW, H., (1981), ed., *Hálfs saga ok Hálfskrekka*, Stofnun Árna Magnússonar á Íslandi, Reykjavík.

SELMER, C., (1956), 'The Vernacular Translations of the *Navigatio Sancti Brendani*: A Bibliographical Study', *Medieval Studies* 18, 145-57.

– (1959), ed., *Navigatio Sancti Brendani Abbatis*, Notre Dame, Indiana.

SHAW, R., (1930), *Carleton's Country*, Dublin & Cork.

SHULDAM-SHAW, P., LYLE, EMILY B., & PETRIE, ELAINE, (1995), eds., *The Greig-Duncan Folk Song Collection*, Vol. 6, Aberdeen.

SIGFÚSSON, Sigfús, (1982-93), *Íslenzkar þjóðsögur og sagnir*, ný útgáfa (Óskar Halldórsson bjó til prentunar), 1-11, Reykjavík.

SIGURÐSSON, Gísli, (1988a), *Gaelic Influence in Iceland*, Reykjavík.

    – (1988b), 'Gaelic Influence in Iceland. Historical and literary contacts. A survey of research, *Studia Islandica* 46.

    – et al., (1994), eds., *Sagnaþing helgað Jónasi Kristjánssyni sjötugum 10. apríl*, 2 vols., Reykjavík.

SIIKALA, ANNA-LEENA, (1978), *The Rite Technique of the Siberian Shaman*, FFC 220, Helsinki.

SIMONSUURI, L., (1961), *Typen- und Motivverzeichnis der finnischen mythischen Sagen*, FFC 183, Helsinki.

SIMPSON, Jacqueline, (1980), *British Dragons*, London.

    – (1985), 'The Lost Slinfold Bell: Some Functions of a Local Legend', *Lore and Language* 4:1, 57-67.

SMITH, A.H., (1950), *English Place-Name Elements*, II, Cambridge.

SMYTH, A.P., (1975-9), *Scandinavian York and Dublin: the history and archaeology of two related Viking kingdoms*, 2 vols., Dublin.

SOLHEIM, S., (1940), *Nemningsfordomar ved fiske*, Oslo.

    – (1952), *Norsk sætertradisjon*, Oslo.

    – (1958), 'Draug', *KL* 3, 297-9.

SPRENGER, J. & INSTITORIS, H., (1991), *Molot ved 'm*, Saransk.

STATTIN, J. (1984), *Näcken. Spelman eller gränsvakt (Skrifter utgivna av Etnologiska sällskapet i Lund)*, Lund.

STERCKX, C. (1986), *Elements de cosmogonie celtique*, Bruxelles.

STEWART, J., (1967), 'The Burial of the Priest's Concubine', *Arv. The Journal of Scandinavian Folklore* 23, 137-42.

STOKES, W., (1888), ed., 'The Voyage of Máel Dúin', *Revue Celtique* 9, 447-95.

    – (1893), ed., 'The Voyage of the Húi Corra', *Revue Celtique* 14, 1, 22-69.

    – (1897), trans, ed., *Cóir Anmann* in W. Stokes & E. Windisch, *Irische Texte*, III, 2, Leipzig.

    – (1905), ed., *Félire Óengusso Céli Dé*, London.

STRAKHOV, A.B., (1994), 'Na svjatogo Nikolu', *Palaeoslavica* II, 49 - 83.

STRÖM, F., (1958), 'Döden och de döda' in *KL* 3, 432-38.

– (1960), 'Gengångare', *KL* 5, 252-3.

STRÖMBÄCK, D., (1935), 'Kungshatt. Sägen och dikt omkring ett ortnamn', *Namn och bygd* 23, 135-44.

– (1955), 'Draken i Hjörungavåg' in *Scandinavica Fenno-Ugrica. Studier tillägnade Björn Collinder*, Uppsala, 383-9.

– (1967), 'Näcken', *KL* 12, 432-8.

STUART, G.B., (1932), 'The Dragon's Pool', *Sussex County Magazine* 6, 154.

SVEINSSON, Einar Ólafur, (1929), *Verzeichnis isländischer Märchenvarianten* , *FFC* 83, Helsinki.

– (1934), ed., *Laxdæla saga* (= *ÍF* 5), Reykjavík.

– (1954), ed., *Brennu-Njáls saga* (= *ÍF* 12), Reykjavík.

– (1959), 'Celtic elements in Icelandic Tradition', *Béaloideas* 25, 3-24.

SVEINSSON, Einar Ólafur & ÞÓRÐARSON, Matthías, (1935), eds., *Eyrbyggja Saga*, *ÍF* 4.

SVENNUNG, J., (1943), 'Sägnen om Kettil Runske', *En bok om Småland*, Stockholm, 281–305.

SYDOW von, C.–W., (1935), 'Övernaturliga väsen', *Nordisk Kultur* 19 (Folktro), 91-159.

– (1948), *Selected Papers on Folklore*, Copenhagen.

TANGHERLINI, T. R., (1994), *Interpreting Legend. Danish Storytellers and Their Repertoires*, New York & London.

TARNOVIUS, T., (1950), *Færøers Beskrifvelser*. Utgitt av Håkon Hamre. Færoensia Textus & Investigationes, København.

TAYLOR, A., (1962), *The Proverb and An Index to 'The Proverb'*, Hatboro.

THOMSON, D., (1965 and 1980), *The People of the Sea*, London.

THOMPSON, R.L., (1960-3), The Manx traditionary ballad', *Études Celtiques* 9-10, 521-48, 60-87.

THOMPSON, S., (1955-8), *Motif-Index of Folk Literature*, 6 Vols., Copenhagen & Bloomington. Revised and enlarged edition.

THORSSON, Örnólfur, (1985),*Völsunga og Ragnars saga loðbrókar*, Örnólfur Thorsson bjó til prentunar, Reykjavík.

Bibliography

TIERNEY, J.J. , (1967), trans., ed., *Dicuili liber de Mensura Orbis Terrae. Scriptores Latini Hiberniae*, VII.3, 6, Dublin.

TIMONY, M. [Ó TIOMÁNAIDHE, M.], (1906), *Scéalta Gearra So-léighte an Iarthair II*, Dublin.

TODD, J.H., (1848), ed., *The Irish Version of the Historia Britonum of Nennius*, Dublin.

TOLMIE, FRANCES, (1911), '105 Songs of Occupation from the Western Isles of Scotland with Notes and Reminiscences', *Journal of the Folk Song Society* 16, 143-270.

TOLLEY, C., (1995), 'The Mill in Norse and Finnish Mythology', *Saga-Book* 25, parts 2-3, 63-82.

TONGUE, RUTH, (1965), *Somerset Folklore*, London.

TRAYNOR, M., (1953), *The English Dialect of Donegal*, Dublin.

TUNELD, J., (1934), ed., *Prästrelationerna från Skåne och Blekinge av år 1624*, Lund.

TURNER, V.W., (1969), *The Ritual Process*, Chicago.

– (1974), *Dramas, Fields and Metaphors*, Ithaca.

TURVILLE-PETRE, E.O.G., (1976), *Scaldic Poetry*, Oxford.

UÍ ÓGÁIN, RÍONACH, (1995), *Immortal Dan. Daniel O'Connell in Irish Folk Tradition*, Dublin.

UNGER, C.R., (1868), ed., *Maríu saga* 1, Christiania.

– (1877), *Heilagra Manna Søgor*. Christiana; translated into German by Carl Wahlund, 'Ein norweg.-isl. Brendan-Fragment,' *Die altfranzösische Prosaübersetzung von Brendans Meerfahrt*, Uppsala, 1900, xliv-xlviii.

VALK, Ü., (1994a), 'On the Descent of Demonic Beings. Fallen Angels, Degraded Deities and Demonized Men', *Mitteilungen für Anthropologie und Religionsgeschichte*, Band 9, 311-32 (in Memoriam Alfred Rupp).

– (1994b), 'Eesti rahvausu kuradi-kujutelm kristliku demonoloogia ja rahvusvahelise folk-loori kontekstis: ilmumiskujud.' Dissertationes Philologiae Estonicae Universitatis Tartuensis 3, Tartu (Summary of the dissertation).

VAUGHAN, R., (1958 [1979]), *Matthew Paris*, Cambridge. Reprinted 1979.

VENDRYES, J., (1981), *Lexique etymologique de l'lrlandais ancien*, Dublin.

VILDALEPP, R., (1938),' Ühest suurjutustajast ja tema toodangust', *Litterarum Sozietas Esthonica 1838-1938. Liber Sæeularis. Õpetatud Eesti Seltsi Toimetused* 30:2, 830-45.

VILHJÁLMSSON, Bjarni & HALLDÓRSSON, Óskar, (1979), *Íslenzkir málshættir*, 2. útg., Reykjavík.

VRIES de, J., (1922) , 'Oudnoorsche sagen op de Færöer', *Neophilologus* 7, 23-35.

– (1927a), 'Die ostnordische Überlieferung der Sage von Ragnar Lodbrók', *Acta philologica Scandinavica* 2, 115-49

– (1927b), 'Die Wikingersaga', *Germanisch-romanische monatsschrift* 15, 81-100.

– (1928a), 'Die westnordische Tradition der Sage von Ragnar Lodbrok', *Zeitschrift für deutsche Philologie* 53, 257-302.

– (1928b), 'Die Entwicklung der Sage von den Lodbrokssöhnen in den historischen Quellen', *Arkiv för nordisk filologi* 44, 117-63.

– (1957), *Altgermanische Religiongeschichte*, 2 vols., second. ed., Berlin.

– (1961), *Keltische Religion*, Stuttgart.

WAGNER, H., (1981), 'Origins of Pagan Irish Religion', *Zeitschrift für celtische Philologie* 38, 1-28.

WALSH, P., (1920), ed., *Leabhar Chlainne Suibhne: The Book of the MacSweeney*, Dublin.

WARD, H.L.D., (1893), 'Lailoken (or Merlin Silvester)', *Romania* 22, 504-26.

WARRACK, J., (1973), 'Synopsis', Carl Maria von Weber (1789-1826), *Der Freischütz. Romantische Oper in drei Aufzügen*, explanatory booklet with compact disk, Polydor International, Hamburg.

WASCHNITIUS, V., (1913), *Perht, Holda und verwandte Gestalten*, Sitzungsberichte Kais. Akad. d. Wissenschaften (Philos-Hist.) 174 (2), Vienna.

WEBER, von, C.M., (1786-1826), (1973), *Der Freischütz. Romantische Oper in drei Aufzügen*, compact disk, Polydor International, Hamburg.

WEIHE, A., (1933), *Søga og søgn*, Tórshavn (2nd. edition 1988).

WEISER, LILY, (1927), *Altgermanische Jünglingsweihen und Männerbünde* (= Bausteine zur Volkskunde und Religionswissenschaft, hhg. vom E. Fehrle, Vol. 1).

WESSELSKI, A., (1909), *Mönchslatein: Erzählungen aus geistlichen Schriften des XIII. Jahrhunderts*, Leipzig.

WESSMAN, V.E.V., (1931), *FSF II, Sägner, 3 Mytiska sägner*. Skrifter utgivna av svenska litteratursällskapet i Finland CCXXVI, Helsingfors.

WESTROPP, T.J., (1911-5) 'A Biological Survey of Clare Island in the County Mayo', *PRIA* 3, part 2, 1-78.

– (1912), 'Brasil and the Legendary Islands of the North Atlantic', *PRIA* 30 C, 223-60.

– (1913), 'County Clare folk-tales and myths, III', *Folk-Lore* 24, 378-80.

WESTWOOD, JENNIFER, (1985), *Albion: A Guide to Legendary Britain*, London.

Bibliography

WILLIAMS, J., (1861), ed., *The Physicians of Myddvai*, Llandovery & London.

WILLIAMSON, C., (1977), ed., *The Old English riddles of the Exeter Book*, Chapel Hill, N. C.

WILSON, F.P., (1970 & 1975), *The Oxford Dictionary of English Proverbs*, Oxford.

WINDISCH, E., (1880-1909), *Irische Texte: mit Worterbuch*, Serie 1-4, Leipzig.

WINTHER, N., (1875), *Færøernes Oldtidshistorie*, København, second ed.,Torshavn 1985.

WOLF-KNUTS, ULRIKA, (1992), 'The Devil between Nature and Culture', *Ethnologia Europaea* 22: 2, 109-14.

WOLF, KIRSTEN & JENSEN, JODY, (1992), trans. Axel Olrik, *Principles for oral narrative research*, Bloomington, Indiana.

WOOD, JULIETTE, (1992), 'The Fairy bride legend in Wales', *Folklore* 103, i, 56-72.

WOOD, G.W., (1894), 'On the Classification of Proverbs and Sayings of the Isle of Man', *Folk-Lore* 5, 229-74.

WOULFE, P., (1923), *Irish names and surnames*, Dublin.

WRIGHT, R.L., (1975), ed., *Irish Emigrant Ballads and Songs*, Bowling Green.

YOUNG, JEAN, (1937), 'Some Icelandic Traditions showing traces of Irish Influence', *Études Celtiques* 2, 118-26.

ZWICKER, J., (1934), *Fontes Historiae Religionis Celticae*, Berlin.

Discography

THE DUBLINERS, (1968), *Seven Deadly Sins*. EMI/Starline, SRS 5101, London.

HARTE, F., (1973), *Through Dublin City*, Topic Records, London.

TOPIC RECORDS 12T194, (1969), *Sailormen and Serving Maids: The Folksongs of Britain*, Vol. 6, London.

TUNNEY, P., (1976), *The Flowery Vale*, Topic Records, London.

Abbreviations

ERA = The manuscript collections of the Estonian Folklore Archive (Tartu)

FFC = Folklore Fellows Communications (1910-), Helsinki.

FKA = Recordings in *Svenska Litteratursällskapets folkkultursarkiv*, Helsingfors.

FMD = Føroyamálsdeildin (Department of Faroese, University of the Faroese).

FSF = Finlands svenska folkdiktning. Skrifter utgivna av Svenska litteratursällskapet i Finland, Helsingfors.

FW = Funk & Wagnalls *Standard dictionary of Folklore Mythology and Legend*, ed. Maria Leach, 2 vols., New York 1950.

HDA = *Handwörterbuch des deutschen Aberglaubens*, eds. H. Hoffmann-Krayer & H. Bächtold-Stäubli, Berlin und Leipzig 1927-42.

ÍF = Íslensk Fornrít (1933 –), Reykjavík.

IFC = Irish Folklore Collection, the Main Manuscripts Collection of the Department of Irish Folklore, University College Dublin, National University of Ireland, Dublin.

IFC S = Irish Folklore Collection, the Schools' Manuscripts Collection of the Department of Irish Folklore, University College Dublin, National University of Ireland, Dublin.

KL = Kulturhistoriskt lexikon för nordisk medeltid (1956-78).

ML = Migratory Legend.

MLSIT = Migratory Legend Suggested Irish Type.

OED = Oxford English Dictionary.

RIA = Traditional Irish Mss in the Royal Irish Academy, Dublin.

Bibliography

PRIA = Proceedings of the Royal Irish Academy, Dublin.

SA = Sound Archive, School of Scottish Studies, University of Edinburgh.

YLE = Oy Yleisradio Ab (The Finnish Broadcasting Company).

Illustrations

EDITORS

Patricia Lysaght, PhD, is an Associate Professor in the Department of Irish Folklore, University College Dublin. Initially she studied law and was called to the Irish Bar. As an Alexander von Humboldt Scholar she studied at Westfälische Wilhelms-Universität Münster, Germany, 1997-8, and carried out extensive fieldwork in Rhineland-Westfalia. She was Guest Professor of Folklore at Georg-August-Universität, Göttingen, 1996-7 and at Westfälische Wilhelms-Universität Münster, 1998-9. She has lectured extensively in Europe and North America and her published work on folklore and ethnology has appeared in a wide range of international publications. She is President of the International Commission for Ethnological Food Research and has edited three volumes of the Commission's proceedings. She is a review editor for *Béaloideas*, the Journal of the Folklore of Ireland Society, and associate editor of *Folklore*, the journal of the British Folklore Society. She is also a contributor to this volume.

Séamas Ó Catháin is an Associate Professor and Acting Head of the Department of Irish Folklore at University College Dublin where he served two terms as Dean of the Faculty of Celtic Studies (1990-1996). He received his MA and PhD from Queen's University Belfast. Before joining University College Dublin, he taught at University College Galway and at the University of Uppsala. Apart from extensive fieldwork in Ireland he has collected folklore in Scotland, Lapland and the USA. Together with radio producer Harry Bradshaw he initiated the popular programme Folkland. His numerous publications include several books based on his fieldwork in Mayo and Donegal, onomastical and topographical works and calendar customs, as well as papers on folk legends and beliefs. He is editor of *Béaloideas*, the Journal of the Folklore of Ireland Society.

Dáithí Ó hÓgáin, MA (University College Dublin), PhD (National University of Ireland). Associate Professor in the Department of Irish Folklore, University College Dublin. He is a frequent contributor to *Béaloideas*, the Journal of the Folklore of Ireland Society; and served as Rapporteur-General at the Conference in 1987 at which the Unesco Recommendation on the Safeguarding of Folklore was drafted. He is also well known as a poet and short story writer. He has lectured and given poetry-readings in many countries, and has taken part in a large number of radio and television programmes. His most recent books include *Fionn mac Cumhaill: Images of the Gaelic Hero* (Dublin 1988); *Myth, Legend and Romance: An Encyclopaedia of the Irish Folk Tradition* (London 1990); *Gadaí an Cheoil* (1994); *An Mangaire Súgach* (1996); *Celtic Warriors* (1999) and *The Sacred Isle* (1999). He is also a contributor to this volume.

CONTRIBUTORS

Bo Almqvist, Emeritus Professor, Head of the Department of Irish Folklore, University College Dublin 1972-96. He studied at Uppsala University, where he received his fil. dr. for his thesis on Old Icelandic magic satire, and at the University of Iceland in Reykjavík, where he also taught for several years. From 1966 on he has carried out extensive field collecting in Ireland, particularly in the Dingle Peninsula. Apart from Irish folk narrative, he has specialized in the study of west-Nordic tradition, especially Icelandic and Faroese folklore and philology, translating Old Icelandic sagas into Swedish and studying culture contact between the Northern and Western European worlds. A selection of his articles on such topics was published in 1991 under the title *Viking Ale.* Among the works that he is engaged in at present is a Type List of Icelandic migratory legends and an edition of the stories collected from the well-known storyteller Peig Sayers.

Angela Bourke, Statutory Lecturer in Irish at University College Dublin, is author of *Caoineadh na dTrí Muire: Téama na Páise i bhFilíocht Bhéil na Gaeilge,* (Dublin: An Clóchomhar, 1983), a study of religious oral poetry in Irish, and of a collection of short fiction, *By Salt Water* (Dublin: New Island, 1996), as well as numerous essays and reviews. She has been a visiting professor at Harvard and at the University of Minnesota, has lectured widely in Europe and North America, and contributes regularly to radio and television programmes.

Michael Chesnutt, MA (University of Oxford), Chairman of the Department of Folklore, University of Copenhagen, formerly a lecturer at the Department of Old and Middle English Language, University College Dublin. He has published extensively on folklore and medieval literature; the focus of his most recent work has been on Faroese and Anglo-Scottish balladry and the history of folkloristics.

Hilda Ellis Davidson is a former lecturer in early literature at Royal Holloway College and Birkbeck College, University of London, and Lucy Cavendish College, Cambridge, where she was Fellow and Vice-Principal. She was President of the Folklore Society (London), 1973-6. She is the author and editor of many books, including *Gods and Myths of Northern Europe* (1964), *Lost Beliefs of Northern Europe* (1993) and *Roles of the Northern Goddess* (1998).

Davíð Erlingsson teaches Icelandic literature and folklore in Háskóli Íslands, Reykjavík. He studied at the Dublin Institute of Advanced Studies, and has taught Icelandic and Icelandic literature and philology at University College Dublin, and at the universities of Uppsala, Frankfurt-am-Main and Copenhagen. For a time he represented Iceland on the governing board of the former Nordic Institute of Folklore.

Ann-Mari Häggman took her doctorate in folklore at the University of Helsinki in 1992, her topic being *Visan om Maria Magdalena* ('The Ballad of Mary Magdalene's Conversion'). She has served as an archivist in the Folklore Archive of the Swedish Literature Society from 1969-85, as Head of the Archive from 1992-93, and as Assistant Professor of Folklore at Helsinki University from 1993-95. She is currently Head of the Institute of Finland-Swedish Traditional Music in Vasa. She has published many books and articles about the folklore and folk music of the Swedish-speaking community in Finland and has continued to popularise the subject in radio and television programmes.

Jóan Pauli Joensen obtained his PhD in ethnology at the University of Lund, Sweden in 1975, and his DPhil in cultural history at the University of Aarhus, Denmark in 1987. He has been curator and head of the Folklife Department at the Faroese National Museum, and since 1989 professor of ethnology and cultural history at the University of the Faroe Islands. He has published articles on Faroese folklore and has written several books and articles on Faroese culture, mostly on the transition from a peasant society to a fishing society. In 1968 he was, as a young student, invited by Séamus Ó Duilearga to Ireland to work with professional Irish folklore collectors in Donegal and Conamara.

Kõiva, Mare, PhD, folklorist, head of the Department of Folk Belief and Folk Narrative, in the Institute of Estonian languages. She has studied Estonian incantations, changes in the role of folk healers, and contemporary children's lore, especially horror stories. She has recently become editor of e-journals *Mäetagused, Folklore*, and the *Journal of Baltic Folklore*, and compiler and editor of a volume of Estonian mythology.

Geraldine Lynch obtained her MA at University College Dublin for her thesis on riddles from Co. Wicklow in 1979, and qualified as a primary school teacher in the following year. She received her PhD from the National University of Ireland in 1995 for her dissertation on skipping games in Ireland. Her publications include articles on children's folklore. She is currently principal teacher of Gaelscoil Chill Mhantáin (an Irish-language primary school) in her native Wicklow.

Proinsias Mac Cana is senior professor emeritus at the School of Celtic Studies of the Dublin Institute for Advanced Studies. He was a professor at that Institute from 1961 to 1963, professor of Welsh at University College Dublin from 1963 to 1971, professor of Old (including Medieval) Irish at University College Dublin from 1971 to 1985, senior professor at the Dublin Institute for Advanced Studies from 1985 to 1996, and annual visiting professor at Harvard University from 1987 to 1992. He is a former president of the Royal Irish Academy and a member of the Royal Gustavus Adolphus Academy (Uppsala).

Críostóir Mac Cárthaigh is a graduate of the National University of Ireland (University College Dublin). He received his MA in 1988 for his study of the migratory legend ML 5080 'Midwife to the Fairies'. He is presently employed as archivist-collector in the Department of Irish Folklore, University College Dublin, and has previously worked in the Folklife Division of the National Museum of Ireland. His published work includes articles on various aspects of the oral narrative tradition in Ireland. He is at present engaged in a study of Irish traditional boat types and fishing methods, and local studies of vernacular architecture.

Séamus Mac Mathúna is Professor of Irish and Director of the Centre for Irish and Celtic Studies at the University of Ulster, Coleraine, and has held lectureships at the University of Uppsala and University College, Galway. He studied at Queen's University, Belfast, at the University of Zürich and at the University of Iceland. His publications include numerous works on medieval voyage literature and on various aspects of Irish language and literature.

Rory McTurk, MA (Oxford), B Philol (Iceland), PhD (National University of Ireland), has taught at the Universities of Lund and Copenhagen, at University College Dublin, and at the University of Leeds, where, since 1994, he has been a Reader in Icelandic Studies. He is the author of Studies in *Ragnars saga loðbrókar and its major Scandinavian analogues* (Oxford, 1991) and of numerous articles on the inter-relationship of the Icelandic, Irish, Anglo-Irish and Old and Middle English literary and folk traditions. Since 1991 he has been an editor of the *Saga-Book* of the Viking Society for Northern Research, of which he was President in 1994-96, and in 1997 he was appointed Visiting Professor of English at Vanderbilt University, Nashville, Tennessee, for the academic year 1998-99.

Tom Munnelly is a Dubliner who has been living and working in West Clare for more than twenty years. Employed as a field collector for the Department of Irish Folklore, University College Dublin, he has recorded some 1,500 tapes for the archive of that Department. While this collection contains a very broad range of folklore, including folktales and legends, the majority of the tapes consist of traditional songs in the English language tradition of Ireland. This is the largest known collection of traditional song, in English or Irish, recorded by any individual in Ireland. Among his principal publications is *The Mount Callan Garland. Songs from the repertoire of Tom Lenihan* (1994).

Bairbre Ní Fhloinn, MA, works as an archivist/collector in the Department of Irish Folklore in University College Dublin. Her published work includes articles on the subject of luck beliefs attached to fishing, and on related topics. Her study of contemporary Irish fishing beliefs is at present being prepared for publication in book form by Comhairle Bhéaloideas Éireann, and she is currently writing her doctorate on the lore of seals in Irish tradition.

Ulf Palmenfelt is assistant professor in Folklore at the University of Bergen. He holds a PhD in ethnology from Stockholm University (1994). His research interests include folk legend, contemporary folklore, children's folklore, and narration. He is currently involved in collecting cyberlore by electronic fieldwork.

Juha Yrjänä Pentikäinen, PhD (The University of Turku). Professor and Chair of the Department of Comparative Religion at the University of Helsinki. He has published 15 books, c. 300 articles, edited *Temenos* and *Ethnologica Uralica*, and produced several ethnographical film documentaries on his field work with Circumpolar, Nordic and Finnish peoples. Among his books are: *The Nordic Dead-Child Tradition* (FFC 202, 1968), *Oral Repertoire and World View* (FFC 219, 1978), *Kalevala Mythology* (1989), *Shamanism and Northern Ecology* (1995), *Cultural Minorities in Finland* (1995), *Die Mythologie der Saamen* (1997), *Shamanism and Culture* (1997), *Religion: Global and Arctic Perspectives* (1998), *Starovery –The Old Believers* (1998).

Miceál Ross initially studied economics, in which he holds a PhD. An early holder of a Norwegian State Scholarship, he has worked in Austria, Pakistan, the Philippines and Poland, and held professorships in Turkey and at Harvard. He chose early retirement from the Economic and Social Research Institute, Dublin, subsequently qualified in Irish Folklore at BA level in University College Dublin, and has for seven years taught that subject at Saor-Ollscoil na hÉireann (Free University of Ireland). He organises monthly storytelling sessions at the Dublin Yarnspinners.

John Shaw obtained his PhD from Harvard University in Celtic Languages & Literatures for his thesis on Gaelic storytelling in Cape Breton, Nova Scotia. He studied Celtic languages at the École Practique des Hautes Études, Paris, and the Dublin Institute for Advanced Studies. His publications deal with Gaelic oral narrative, song and instrumental music, based on extensive fieldwork carried out since the 1960s. He held a Lectureship in Celtic at the University of Aberdeen and is presently Senior Lecturer at the School of Scottish Studies at the University of Edinburgh.

Jacqueline Simpson studied English Literature at London University, and her liking for medieval poetry and Icelandic sagas later led her to an interest in folklore, both British and Scandinavian. Her chief books are *Icelandic Folktales and Legends* (1972), *The Folklore of Sussex* (1973), *The Folklore of the Welsh Border* (1976), *British Dragons* (1980), *European Mythology* (1987), and *Scandinavian Folktales* (1988), besides numerous articles; a book of translations from the Danish legends of E.T. Kristensen is in the press. She has served on the Committee of the Folklore Society since 1966; she was Editor of *Folklore* 1979-93, President of the Folklore Society 1993-6, and is currently Secretary of that Society.

Ríonach uí Ógáin, MA, PhD (National University of Ireland), is an archivist/collector with the Department of Irish Folklore, University College Dublin. She has published numerous articles on traditional song and music and has lectured widely on the subject. Among her publications is a compact disc/audio-cassette entitled *Beauty an Oileáin: Music and Song of the Blasket Islands* (Ceirníní Cladaigh), a book entitled *Immortal Dan: Daniel O'Connell in Irish Folk Tradition* (1995), and an article entitled 'Colm Ó Caodháin and Séamus Ennis: A Conamara Singer and his Collector' (*Béaloideas* 1996-97). She has edited *Faoi Rothaí na Gréine: Amhráin as Conamara a bhailigh Máirtín Ó Cadhain* (1999).

Ülo Valk graduated from the University of Tartu as a folklorist in 1986. He received his DPhil degree at the same university for a thesis on the image of the Devil in Estonian folk religion. Since 1995 he holds the Chair of Estonian and Comparative Folklore, University of Tartu. In 1997 he was elected the Professor Ordinarius of folklore. He has published articles on folk religion, belief legends and comparative mythology, and is the editor of *Studies in Folklore and Popular Religion* (Tartu, 1996).

Jan I. Wall, fil.dr of ethnology, University of Uppsala 1977; docent (Uppsala) 1979. Head of Folklore Research at Folkminnesenheten, The Swedish Institute of Dialectology, Onomastics and Folklore Research (SOFI), Uppsala. His main works deal with folklore aspects of witchcraft.

Bodil Nildin-Wall, fil. mag at Uppsala University 1971; researcher at Folkminnesenheten (Department of Folklore Research, SOFI), Uppsala.

Fionnuala Williams, MA (1978), is a graduate of the National University of Ireland (University College Dublin). She lectures in the Institute of Irish Studies, The Queen's University of Belfast. She has published various articles, mainly on proverbs, and she has also edited a collection of English-language proverbs in Ireland. She is the recipient of the John Campbell Fellowship of the Northern Ireland Community Relations Council with a brief to examine the folklore of 'The Troubles' in Northern Ireland (1968-98).

Ulrika Wolf-Knuts, fil. dr. Åbo Akademi University (1991), Docent, Department of Comparative Religion and Folkloristics, Åbo Akademi University, Finland. Her doctoral dissertation was entitled *Människan och Djavulen* ('Man and the Devil'). Her published work includes articles on Finland-Swedish folklore, folk belief, Finland-Swedish identity and history of research in folkoristics. She is currently editor of *Arv. Nordic Yearbook of Folklore,* and one of the two co-ordinators of Nordic Network of Folklore (successor of NIF). She is also Secretary-General of the 1999 Folklore Fellows' Summer School, Finland.